NEWCO
HANDBOOK

FOR MOVING TO AND LIVING IN

PORTLAND

Including Vancouver, Gresham,
Hillsboro, Beaverton, and Wilsonville

Bryan Geon

FIRST BOOKS

6750 SW Franklin
Portland, OR 97223
503-968-6777
www.firstbooks.com

Author: Bryan Geon
Editors: Emily Horowitz, Linda Weinerman
Series Editor: Linda Weinerman
Cover design: Masha Shubin and Nicholas Winchester
Interior design: Erin Johnson Design and Tricia Sgrignoli/Positive Images
Interior layout and composition: Tricia Sgrignoli/Positive Images
Maps provided by Jim Miller/fennana design
TriMet MAX Light Rail map provided courtesy of TriMet
Published by First Books®, 6750 SW Franklin Street, Portland, OR 97223-2542, 503-968-6777, www.firstbooks.com

ISBN-13: 978-0-912301-77-8
ISBN-10: 0-912301-77-5

Printed in the USA on recycled paper

What readers are saying about Newcomer's Handbooks:

I recently got a copy of your Newcomer's Handbook for Chicago, and wanted to let you know how invaluable it was for my move. I must have consulted it a dozen times a day preparing for my move. It helped me find my way around town, find a place to live, and so many other things. Thanks.

– Mike L.
Chicago, Illinois

Excellent reading (Newcomer's Handbook for San Francisco and the Bay Area) ... balanced and trustworthy. One of the very best guides if you are considering moving/relocation. Way above the usual tourist crap.

– Gunnar E.
Stockholm, Sweden

I was very impressed with the latest edition of the Newcomer's Handbook for Los Angeles. It is well organized, concise and up-to-date. I would recommend this book to anyone considering a move to Los Angeles.

– Jannette L.
Attorney Recruiting Administrator for a large Los Angeles law firm

I recently moved to Atlanta from San Francisco, and LOVE the Newcomer's Handbook for Atlanta. It has been an invaluable resource—it's helped me find everything from a neighborhood in which to live to the local hardware store. I look something up in it everyday, and know I will continue to use it to find things long after I'm no longer a newcomer. And if I ever decide to move again, your book will be the first thing I buy for my next destination.

– Courtney R.
Atlanta, Georgia

In looking to move to the Boston area, a potential employer in that area gave me a copy of the Newcomer's Handbook for Boston. It's a great book that's very comprehensive, outlining good and bad points about each neighborhood in the Boston area. Very helpful in helping me decide where to move.

– no name given (online submit form)

TABLE OF CONTENTS

CONTENTS

CONTENTS

WELCOME TO PORTLAND, ONE OF THE MOST LIVABLE URBAN AREAS in America! Call it Stumptown, Rose City, Beervana, Bridgetown, Puddletown, or PDX, it's your town now. (Just don't call it Portland, or-eh-GONE. The state name is pronounced OR-uh-gun. Practice before you arrive.) Portland is located at the northern end of the fertile Willamette Valley, roughly an hour east of the coast—it's called the coast here, not the shore or the beach—and an hour west of the crest of the Cascade Mountains. The high desert is a two-hour drive to the east, and world-class wineries are less than an hour south-west. Abundant recreational opportunities make the city a favorite of outdoor enthusiasts, and from the city's West Hills, and even from some downtown office buildings, it's possible to see the Columbia River Gorge and five snowcapped volcanoes: Mounts Hood, St. Helens, Adams, Rainier, and Jefferson. Top that, Topeka!

Of course, Portland's appeal transcends its spectacular setting. The city is known for its vibrant neighborhoods, progressive urban planning, environmental awareness, liberal politics, coffeehouse and brewpub culture, and, yes, for its rain. So what's it really like here? Well, though Portland enjoys more than its fair share of pleasant, well-preserved urban neighborhoods, connected to one another by bike lanes and transit—and state law limiting the extent of urban sprawl—it is also afflicted with strip malls, traffic congestion, ill-conceived development, and other assorted ills of the modern American metropolis. The key difference is that in Portland you can arrange your life so that you don't *have* to deal with those problems. If you want to live in a close-in neighborhood, within walking distance of cafés and food markets, and ride your bike to work every day, you can. (You won't necessarily be able to afford a house in such a neighborhood, however.) If you prefer to live in a suburban community, you can do that, too.

As for politics, Portlanders on average are more liberal than the citizens of the typical American burg—when *Money* magazine rated Portland the country's best place to live in 2000, it warned conservatives to stay away—but the city has a surprising diversity of political opinion, ranging from a strong libertarian contingent to a small community of Trotskyites. (The latter get nervous around ice picks.) Suburban communities are generally more conservative, and the region as a whole is probably no more liberal (or conservative) than any other large coastal metropolitan area.

If it's craft beer or coffee you're after, suffice it to say you won't be disappointed. There are 38 breweries in the Portland metro area, and locally produced craft beer makes up 11% of Oregon's beer consumption. (That figure may sound low, but it's by far the highest rate in the country.) And Portland's coffee scene is every bit the equal of Seattle's, with local roasters like Stumptown Coffee Roasters (www.stumptowncoffee.com) winning awards for both quality and sustainable business practices. Don't miss the burgeoning tea scene, either, based on well-established local tea manufacturers as well as an increasing number of unique tea houses. Many Portlanders consider coffee (or tea) essential for coping with the rain.

Ah, the rain. While it's true that Portland has its share of rainy days, much of the city's rainfall arrives in the form of a fine mist or drizzle. Often a day that starts out cloudy becomes bright and sunny by afternoon (or vice versa). Many locals will tell you that the rain is easier to cope with than the seemingly interminable parade of cloudy days we endure in late autumn and winter. Spring and fall have their share of bright days, however, and summers are reliably warm and sunny.

Whatever you think about the weather, it certainly isn't keeping anyone away. Lured by Portland's reputation, by job opportunities in certain industries, and even by the results of online relocation quiz sites like www.findyourspot. com and Find Your Own Best Place (www.bestplaces.net/fybp/), it seems like everyone knows someone who's moving to Portland (or thinking about it). Portland's regional government, Metro, estimates than a million newcomers will arrive in the area over the next twenty years.

Despite (and in some cases because of) the population influx, not everything is rosy in the Rose City. The region's economy is still recovering from a sharp recession in the early 2000s, and the unemployment rate is above the national average. At the same time, the median income is relatively low. Perhaps low incomes wouldn't be a problem if you could still buy a home for $100,000, but those days are gone. As of mid-2007, the median home price in the metropolitan area was about $300,000, and still rising, unlike in many parts of the country— and good luck finding a close-in house for anything close to that figure. (For the sake of comparison, the median price in 2002 was about $175,000.) The housing price boom produced a corresponding explosion in residential construction, with new condo towers and infill development changing the faces of many neighborhoods.

The faces of Oregon's residents are changing as well. Portland has had a vibrant African-American community since the First World War, and substantial Chinese and Japanese communities have been present since the nineteenth century, but the city is still, by some measures, the whitest major city in the country. Nonetheless, the metropolitan area is becoming more ethnically and racially diverse. The Hispanic population is fast-growing, and the area has also experienced substantial immigration from East and South Asia (especially Southeast Asia), Eastern Europe, and East and West Africa. Moreover, much of the growth in the nonwhite population has taken place in the suburbs, so the demographics of the entire region are changing. Still, while we are definitely becoming more diverse, the region has a long way to go before it mirrors the population in the United States as a whole.

LOCAL QUIRKS

The *Los Angeles Times* ran a story in May 2007 entitled, "Wired for Weird: Bohemian Street Life, Cutting-Edge Cafés and Wacky Public Art. Is Portland the Most Eccentric City in America?" Putting aside the pot-calling-the-kettle-black issue of a Los Angeles publication calling another city eccentric, the paper has a point. You'll see plenty of bumper stickers proclaiming a desire to "Keep Portland Weird!" Indeed, quirkiness (along with environmentalism) is the closest thing the city has to an official religion. The following are a few local quirks you should know about in advance:

• You can't pump your own gas in Oregon. It's against the law. (The only other state with this restriction is New Jersey.)
• There's a nickel deposit on soft drink and beer cans and bottles (and, beginning in 2009, on plastic water bottles). Oregon was the first state in the country to pass a bottle bill.
• Despite the damp winter climate, most Portlanders don't carry umbrellas, and some don't even own one.
• The Oregon Supreme Court has interpreted the Oregon Constitution to protect nude dancing as expressive speech. As a result, Portland supposedly has more strip clubs per capita than any other city in the country.
• Many intersections in Eastside residential neighborhoods lack stop signs, resulting in trepidation for motorists, bicyclists, and pedestrians alike.

LOCAL LINGO

Portland lacks a distinctive local dialect, and most Oregonians do not have a discernible regional accent (unless they've brought one from somewhere else). Most slang is age-based, rather than regional—who knows what teenagers are talking about half the time?—but some localisms can throw off the newcomer. Here's a handy guide to a few potentially confusing expressions and pronunciations:

Back East: Anywhere east of Denver.
Big Pink: The US Bancorp Tower at Southwest Oak Street and Fifth Avenue downtown; this decidedly pinkish 42-story skyscraper is the second tallest building in Oregon.

Car Prowl: Theft from an automobile.

Civil War: The annual football game between in-state rivals University of Oregon and Oregon State University.

Couch Street: It's pronounced "cooch," not like a sofa.

Doug Fir: The Douglas fir, Oregon's state tree. Also the name of a trendy bar on East Burnside.

Freddy's: The Fred Meyer one-stop-shopping chain, now owned by Ohio-based Kroger. Fred Meyer was an actual person, and long-time residents still refer to the market as "Freddy's."

"Free Is a Very Good Price": Long-time catchphrase used by local furniture and appliance dealer Tom Peterson. (Apparently free was not such a great deal for Mr. Peterson, whose company went out of business in the early 1990s.)

Front Avenue: The old name for Naito Parkway, which runs along the Willamette River downtown.

Glisan Street: Almost universally pronounced "GLEE-son," although a few purists insist that it should be pronounced "glisten."

The Gorge: The Columbia River Gorge east of the city, where the Columbia cuts through the Cascade Mountains.

Gorge Winds: The strong east winds that sometimes blow through the Gorge and into the metropolitan area.

The Kicker: The somewhat controversial tax refund that is distributed every two years when actual state revenues exceed projected revenues.

Macadam: The name for Highway 43 between downtown Portland and Lake Oswego. Pronounced "mac-AD-um."

MAX: Metropolitan Area Express, Portland's light rail system.

McLoughlin: The name of a major thoroughfare in Southeast Portland and the adjacent suburbs. Pronounced "McLofflin."

NoPo: Hipster name for North Portland.

The Pearl: The Pearl District, a hot neighborhood of high-end condos, restaurants, and boutiques, a few blocks northwest of downtown Portland.

Pill Hill: Marquam Hill, just south of downtown Portland, home to Oregon Health & Science University and its associated hospitals and clinics, along with the Portland Veterans Administration Hospital.

Spendy: Expensive.

Webfoot: A native or thoroughly naturalized Oregonian.

Willamette: The river that flows through the city, and everything named after it, should be pronounced "will-AM-it," *not* "will-um-ETTE." If you forget, locals will remind you that it rhymes with "dammit."

You might also glance through the **Transportation** chapter to get a feel for the nicknames of major highways.

LOCAL BLOGS AND NEIGHBORHOOD WEB SITES

It's easy to get the official line on Portland, but what do people who live here really think? Here are a few sites to get you started. Keep in mind that some bloggers are complete nutcases, so take what you read on the web with a grain of salt:

- **www.news4neighbors.net** lists local goings-on, with an emphasis on neighborhood events.
- **Metroblogging Portland**, portland.metblogs.com, is a single blog written by several different authors. It has no particular focus.
- **www.orblogs.com** provides links to several hundred local blogs.
- While not a blog, the **"For Portlanders Only"** site (www.platypuscomix. cartoonsdammit.com/fpo/) offers an interesting grab bag of Portland cultural history.

URBAN PLANNING

Entire books have been written, bureaucracies built, and legal careers made on interpreting Oregon's land use planning laws. Anything beyond a brief overview is way beyond the scope of this book, but as a newcomer you should have a general understanding of the region's urban planning arrangement.

Under the leadership of legendary governor Tom McCall, the Oregon legislature enacted a state land use planning system in 1973. The purpose was to curb urban sprawl and protect rich farmland, forestland, rangeland, and scenic vistas from development. The law required local governments to create a comprehensive land use plan for its region. In making planning decisions, local governments are required to adhere to a set of 19 statewide goals—energy conservation, preservation of farmland, discouraging development on land subject to natural disasters…. The law also requires every city or metropolitan area to establish an Urban Growth Boundary (UGB), outside of which large-scale residential development (among other things) is generally prohibited.

In the Portland area, the regional government, Metro, is responsible for maintaining the metropolitan area's UGB. (Its predecessor agency created the original boundary.) By law, the UGB must include enough land to meet the projected need for residential development for twenty years. Every few years, Metro expands the boundary accordingly. The last expansion, in 2005, added a large chunk of rural land in Clackamas County (the southeastern part of the metro area) to the urban growth area. Several outlying communities in the Portland area, such as Sandy, North Plains, and Estacada, are outside the main Portland UGB, and have established UGBs of their own.

It is important to understand what the land use laws generally, and the UGB in particular, do not do. For one thing, they do not prohibit all residential use of rural land. The so-called rural exception lands, already subdivided lands outside the UGBs, are available for rural, non-farm uses. (Areas such as Stafford fall within this category.) Furthermore, they do not directly mandate dense development inside the UGB, as a drive down one of the area's many suburban strip mall–lined highways will show you. The UGB may indirectly increase density, however, by artificially restricting the supply of buildable land in the metropolitan area. Local governments may also set density requirements, and generally permit or even encourage infill development, such as houses built on "flag lots" that have become common (and controversial) in outer Southeast Portland and some suburban communities. Perhaps most importantly, Oregon's land use laws have no effect in fast-growing Clark County, Washington, just across the Columbia River. (Washington state recently enacted its own urban growth management laws, and Clark County communities now have their own urban growth boundaries.)

In 2004, Oregon voters passed Measure 37, a sweeping property-rights measure that essentially says, when a land use or zoning rule prohibits a use that might have been permitted once upon a time, under certain circumstances the government agency responsible for the rule (generally city or county governments) must pay compensation to the landowner or permit the requested use. Since the law did not provide funds for compensation, in practice Measure 37 means the use must be allowed. The measure was poorly drafted, and it may take years to figure out exactly what it means, including whether rights granted under Measure 37 can be transferred to new property owners. More than 7,500 applications for compensation or to allow a prohibited use were submitted to local governments by the filing deadline, these claims covering three-quarters of a million acres. In the city of Portland alone, claims for compensation totaled more than $250 million. Many of the applications around the state were for massive proposed development projects (in contrast to the impression conveyed by poster-little-old-lady for Measure 37 during the election, nonagenarian Dorothy English, who just wanted to build a house for her children on the property behind her house). The state legislature has referred a clarification/limitation of Measure 37 to the voters for fall 2007.

WHAT TO BRING

- **A detailed map**; although most of Portland proper is on a straightforward grid, parts of western Portland and many of the suburbs don't follow the rules.
- **Rain gear**; unless you move during the summer, there's a good chance it will be raining when you arrive. A water-resistant coat and rain hat are the most common forms of rain gear. Bring an umbrella if you like, but be aware that you'll stick out like a sore thumb. (See "Local Quirks" above.) No adult wears galoshes in Portland.
- **A cell phone**; a cell phone is convenient for contacting potential landlords from the road, setting up utilities, and generally staying in touch during your transition.

- **A car or bike**; public transportation is perfectly adequate in many neighborhoods, but it can be difficult to househunt or otherwise explore the area quickly without your own transport. Once you settle down, unless you're in a close-in neighborhood, you'll need a bike or car; in the suburbs and in much of the Westside, a car is almost essential. If you want to blend in, consider a Subaru or a Toyota Prius. If you don't own a car yet but plan on buying one, wait until after you move; you won't pay any sales tax in Oregon.
- **Tolerance**; no matter how narrow- or broad-minded you are (or think you are), something or someone in Portland is bound to annoy you. Bring a good attitude and a smile, and you'll get along just fine.

ADDRESS LOCATOR

Since the city was founded, Portland's street layout has followed the so-called Philadelphia pattern, with a grid comprised of named east-west streets intersecting numbered avenues, which run north-south parallel to the riverfront. The grid pattern largely vanishes in the West Hills and other high-relief parts of the city, and all bets are off in the suburbs, but the basic framework remains.

The Willamette River naturally divides the city into east and west halves, while Burnside Street has been designated the north-south divider. The city is thus divided into quadrants: Northwest (west of the river and north of Burnside), Southwest (west of the river and south of Burnside), Northeast (east of the river and north of Burnside), and Southeast (east of the river and south of Burnside). The Columbia River forms the city's northern boundary. North of downtown, the Willamette flows northwest before joining the Columbia; the resulting peninsula, to the west of Northeast Portland, is designated as North Portland. North Williams Avenue is the divider between North and Northeast Portland.

The numbered avenues begin on each side of the river; the numbers increase with distance from it. Southwest 10th Avenue, for example, is roughly 10 blocks west of the Willamette, while Southeast 10th Avenue is ten blocks east of the river. Numbered avenues are used throughout the city, with a few exceptions. On the Eastside, Martin Luther King Jr. Boulevard (or MLK) takes the place of 4th Avenue and Grand Avenue takes the place of 5th, while on the Westside, Broadway substitutes for 7th Avenue and Park for 8th Avenue.

Named streets run from east to west. Except in the "Alphabet District" of Northwest Portland, where the street names are in alphabetical order from B (Burnside) through W (Wilson), there is no special system in place for street names.

There are 100 street numbers per block (although obviously few blocks contain 100 addresses). Thus, once you learn the system, it is fairly easy to find a specific address. For example, the 4300 block of Southeast Hawthorne Boulevard would begin at Southeast 43rd Avenue and Hawthorne; the 3000 block of Northeast 33rd Avenue would begin 30 blocks north of Burnside. (By the way, even numbers are on the south and east sides of the street, odd numbers on the north and west sides.) There are only two significant wrinkles to this pattern. In North Portland, east-west streets are numbered according to their distance from North Williams Avenue. In the Johns Landing area of South Portland, certain addresses, while west of the Willamette, are actually east of the downtown riverfront; these addresses are prefaced by a "0."

Some suburbs, like Beaverton and Tigard, number their streets and addresses according to the Portland street grid. Others, including Vancouver, Lake Oswego, West Linn, and Hillsboro, are laid out in their own grid, usually centered on their city hall or some other landmark. The bottom line: Don't expect addresses in Portland and the 'burbs to match up.

A (VERY) BRIEF PORTLAND HISTORY

The first Native American inhabitants of the Portland region arrived about 10,000 years ago. By the eighteenth century, various tribes and bands of the Chinook people occupied the land. The Chinook had a salmon-based economy, and the resource was sufficiently abundant to allow them to live settled lives in large plank houses, and to develop social classes and rules of property ownership and inheritance. Like indigenous people throughout North America, their lives would change radically following European contact.

While Spanish, English, and other European ships sailed along the Oregon coastline as early as the sixteenth century, the first European ships to sail upstream past the mouth of the Columbia River arrived in the 1790s. The Lewis and Clark expedition reached the area from the other direction, passing the current site of Portland on their outbound journey in 1805 and again upon their return in 1806. In 1811, the American Fur Company, owned by John Jacob Astor, founded Astoria as its Pacific headquarters. The following year Robert Stuart traveled overland from Astoria to St. Louis, marking the first traverse of the route that would ultimately become the Oregon Trail. Shortly after its founding, Astoria was abandoned to the British Hudson Bay Company, which rechristened it Fort George. In 1825, the Company founded Fort Vancouver, the first European settlement in what is now the Portland metropolitan area. Both the British and the Americans, who each claimed and jointly occupied what had become known as the Oregon Country, conducted official and unofficial explorations of the Pacific Northwest region.

A few early pioneers began to settle in the area around modern Portland in the 1830s. Beginning in 1840, an increasing flow of American emigrants began to make the trek from Missouri to Oregon (although the California gold rush interrupted the stream of migrants in 1848 and 1849.) Having crossed the Great Plains, the Rocky Mountains, and the arid inland Northwest, early emigrants had to float down the Columbia River from The Dalles to Fort Vancouver; the Barlow Road, an alternate toll route over the shoulder of Mount Hood, opened in 1843, and terminated at Oregon City. Also in 1843, a group of pioneers gathered at Champoeg, in the Willamette Valley between present-day Portland and Salem, to establish a provisional territorial government with its seat at Oregon City. (The Oregon Territory did not formally come into being until 1848, and originally included all land north of California and south of Canada between the Pacific Ocean and the Continental Divide.) The Oregon Treaty of 1846 set the 49th parallel as the boundary between British and American territory, and the Washington Territory was carved out of the northern half of the Oregon Territory in 1853. Oregon was granted statehood in 1859.

In the meantime, successive epidemics of smallpox, measles, and other infectious diseases in the first half of the nineteenth century, combined with the arrival of malaria in about 1830, took a devastating toll on the native population. Outright warfare, however, was mainly confined to eastern and southern Oregon. In the 1850s, ratified and unratified treaties dispossessed the tribes of their Willamette Valley lands, and the surviving Indians were removed to reservations.

Portland itself began as a river city, which of course it remains to this day. Downtown Portland lies at the effective head of navigation on the Willamette River for oceangoing ships, and in 1843 William Overton recognized the potential of the site and filed a land claim there. (The story goes that he could not afford the 25-cent filing fee, so he got a quarter from fellow pioneer Asa Lovejoy in exchange for half the 640-acre claim.) In 1845, Overton sold his half of the claim to Francis Pettygrove and moved on. Lovejoy and Pettygrove—who had perhaps the least rugged names of any pioneers in the history of the American West—could not agree on a name for their new settlement. Lovejoy, a Massachusetts native, wished to name the place Boston; Pettygrove was from Maine, and preferred the name Portland. They agreed to flip a coin—now known as the Portland penny—for the right to name the town. Pettygrove won best two out of three.

Having finished the hard work of choosing a name, Lovejoy and Pettygrove platted a 16-block grid the same year. The city grew rapidly, and at the time of its incorporation in 1851 covered just over two square miles. Portland had a series of early rivals, including Oregon City, Sellwood, and Linnton, but it eventually emerged as the center of trade for the Willamette Valley and the largest city in the Northwest. The first of three transcontinental railroads reached Portland in 1883, and this crucial connection cemented the city's status as a major trading center. The population of Portland and its surrounding areas nearly tripled during the 1880s, and the first streetcar lines reached the Eastside during that decade.

A series of annexations beginning in the 1880s extended the city's size and population dramatically. In 1891, Portland consolidated with the cities of East Portland (incorporated in 1870) and Albina (incorporated in 1887). Despite an economic slowdown in the 1890s, Portland remained the largest city in the Northwest until the early twentieth century, when Seattle (spurred by growth during the Klondike Gold Rush) surpassed it. By 1900, Portland had a population of nearly 100,000. The Lewis and Clark Centennial Exposition of 1905 had 1.5 million visitors and marked the beginning of Portland's greatest wave of growth and prosperity. In 1906, the Eastside population surpassed that of the Westside, and by 1910, the city's population had more than doubled, to 207,000. In 1915, Portland absorbed the cities of St. Johns (incorporated 1903) and Linnton (incorporated 1910), and the shipbuilding industry attracted more workers during the First World War. The twenties saw another wave of growth on the Eastside, and even the Depression, which spawned Hoovervilles in locations like Sullivan's Gulch and under the Ross Island Bridge, did not halt the city's expansion. By the eve of the Second World War, the city had a population of more than 300,000.

The war kicked Portland's growth into overdrive. The Kaiser shipyards built more than 1,000 ships during the war, and the demand for labor was intense, and not confined to Portland proper: 38,000 people worked at the Kaiser shipyard in Vancouver, Washington, and the population of the metropolitan area increased by one-third during the war years. Housing was in short supply; a few small houses were built on vacant lots in the old Eastside neighborhoods during the war, but most workers were placed in huge housing projects like Vanport, located in North Portland at the present site of Delta Park. Vanport was the largest public housing project ever built in the United States, with some 40,000 inhabitants. (A massive flood in 1948 destroyed Vanport, and its residents, many of whom were African-American, were relocated to other parts of the city.)

After the war, the pent-up demand for housing drove a wave of suburban expansion that has lasted for more than half a century. Portland's population actually declined slightly during the 1950s. The Interstate Highway System encouraged development in areas that were formerly well outside the metropolitan area. In 1950, the three largest suburbs on the Oregon side of the river, Gresham, Hillsboro, and Beaverton, had a combined population of less than 11,000; today, roughly a quarter-million people live in these three cities. Clark County also experienced rapid population growth in the postwar years. The population of the city of Portland has continued to grow since the 1960s, but much of this growth is due to annexation in eastern Multnomah County.

In the early 1970s, state land use laws mandated the creation of an urban growth boundary (see "Urban Planning," above), which helped channel and restrain suburban growth. At about the same time, a grassroots effort by local community activists killed the Mount Hood Freeway project, which would have bulldozed large sections of Southeast Portland to make way for a freeway to Gresham. The transportation dollars that had been earmarked for the freeway instead went to several smaller-scale road projects and to the development of Portland's first light-rail line. The decisions made in the 1970s and 1980s have literally shaped Portland and earned it a worldwide reputation as a leader in land use and transportation planning. It remains to be seen whether Portland can maintain that reputation in the face of continued growth.

For Portland continues to grow. New residents, often drawn by the region's vaunted high quality of life, continue to arrive. Presumably you are one of them. Welcome to Portland. Please help us keep the character and livability of this special part of the world intact.

THE NEIGHBORHOOD AND COMMUNITY PROFILES BELOW ARE IN-
tended to help you get a feel for the character of each Portland neighborhood or suburban community. There is no substitute for scouting out
a neighborhood in person or meeting face-to-face with a knowledgeable local
real estate agent, but these introductions will let you know what to expect.

CITY OF PORTLAND

Boundaries: North: Columbia River; **West**: Beaverton; Cedar Mill, West Haven,
West Slope, Raleigh Hills, Garden Home (unincorporated Washington County);
Tigard; **South**: Lake Oswego; Dunthorpe (unincorporated Multnomah and Clack-
amas counties); Milwaukie; Clackamas (unincorporated Clackamas County);
Happy Valley; Damascus; **East**: Gresham; Unincorporated Multnomah County;
Area: 134 square miles; **Population:** 535,000

Oregon's largest city is, above all, a city of neighborhoods. Portland's Office of
Neighborhood Involvement (http://www.portlandonline.com/oni/) officially
recognizes 95 neighborhood associations—although the names and boundaries of the "official" neighborhoods don't necessarily correspond to commonly
used neighborhood designations—and every neighborhood is unique. Many
Portland neighborhoods began as small communities located outside the city
limits, while others sprang into being along new electric streetcar lines in the
early twentieth century (just as new developments today sometimes follow
freeways), and these neighborhoods tend to have a distinct and cohesive feel.
Neighborhoods developed in the postwar, automobile-oriented era are generally more homogeneous, but they are not nearly as interchangeable as their
detractors would have you believe.

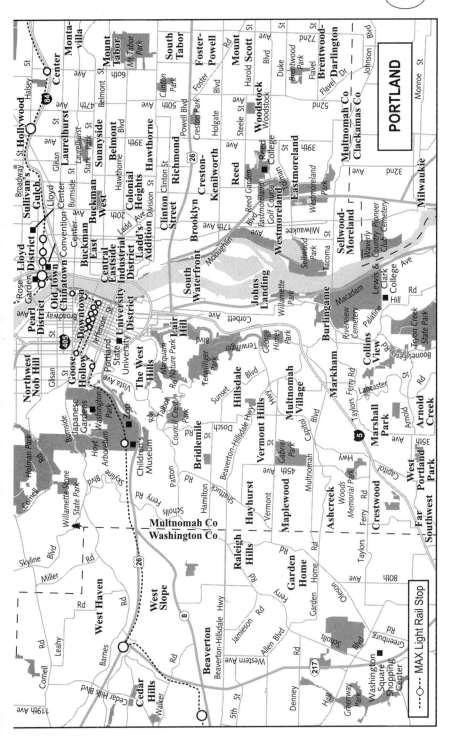

The Willamette River cleaves Portland into two very different realms, the Westside and the Eastside, and many Portlanders swear that never the twain shall meet. Some people consider it a minor sport to mock the denizens of the opposite side of the river with crude stereotypes—Westsiders are rich, conceited, materialistic, and car-bound, Eastsiders are methhead yokels or flag-burning communists—that in most cases are simply false. In fact, wealth and poverty, crime and security, liberals and conservatives, are found in every quadrant of the city (albeit in varying concentrations), and the two halves of Portland have much more in common with one another than either half does with, say, Houston. In short, don't let mean-spirited stereotypes cause you to write off entire sections of the city; make your own explorations, and see what neighborhood feels like the best fit.

A final note on Portland neighborhoods: East Burnside Street forms the official boundary between Northeast and Southeast Portland, but most people (including the Office of Neighborhood Involvement) consider the much-harder-to-cross Banfield Freeway (Interstate 84) to be the informal boundary between them. This chapter follows the unofficial convention.

THE WEST SIDE

DOWNTOWN PORTLAND AND ENVIRONS

Boundaries: North: Interstate 405; Burnside Street (west of 405); **West:** Interstate 405; Washington Park; **South:** Interstate 405, Sunset Highway (US 26); **East:** Willamette River

DOWNTOWN PORTLAND

Neighborhood Association: Downtown

Downtown Portland (www.downtownportland.org) is generally understood to encompass the city's central business district and the immediately surrounding area within the Interstate 405 loop and south of Burnside Street. Downtown occupies the west bank of the Willamette River, on the site where the city was founded in 1845. This former riverside clearcut—the original Stumptown—has been the commercial and cultural heart of the city and of Oregon as a whole for more than 150 years.

Today, downtown is a mix of new and old buildings on sites with evolving uses: Pioneer Courthouse Square, the city's innovative "living room," was by turns a school, the opulent Portland Hotel, and a parking lot. Most downtown structures are commercial or civic in nature—office buildings, retail stores, courthouses, etc.—and while the area remains reasonably vibrant even after business hours, not many people have chosen to live here. The few housing units in the heart of downtown tend to fall into the "transitional" or residential hotel category, with a few notable exceptions (such as the luxury condominiums on the upper floors of the Koin Tower). A few new market-rent apartment and condominium towers are planned or under construction in the core area, however, especially in or near the so-called **Cultural District** along Broadway and the South Park Blocks (home of the Portland Center for the Performing Arts, the Portland Art Museum, and the Oregon Historical Society).

Somewhat shabby subsidized housing has traditionally been the residential norm in the once-forlorn **West End**, an area located roughly between Park Avenue and Interstate 405, which also features several historic churches, some low-rent office and retail buildings, and various bars and parking lots. This area is undergoing rapid redevelopment, however, spurred in part by the dramatic evolution of the Pearl District just across Burnside. Apartments are being spiffed up, new condominiums are rising, and the edgy, quirky new Ace Hotel (www.ace hotel.com) has become an unexpected darling of the travel press. The Safeway on 10th Avenue, once known as the "scary Safeway" because of its many mentally ill or drug-addled customers, has been reconstructed as the centerpiece of the mixed-use Museum Place complex; the spiffy Eliot Tower condominium building is just across the street. The beautifully restored Central Library, unquestionably one of the finest historic library buildings on the West Coast, stands proudly on 10th Avenue. The Portland Streetcar, which trundles along 10th and 11th Avenues, has helped attract investment to the area. The northern portion of the West End includes the "Burnside Triangle," one of the less salacious names for the triangular wedge between West Burnside Street and Southwest Alder Street, which has long been a center of the Portland gay community. Despite the rise in the West End's fortunes, periodic proposals to cap Interstate 405 and cover it with apartments and office buildings have so far gone nowhere.

Portland State University dominates the south end of downtown, which has accordingly been dubbed the **University District**. Much of the housing in this end of downtown is intended for and occupied by students, with all that implies for the condition and noise level of buildings, but the area near Keller Auditorium features several upscale residential towers dating from the 1970s, with magnificent river and mountain views. The extension of the Portland Streetcar through the PSU campus to the South Waterfront district has encouraged the construction of new condominiums and apartment buildings in the area, and some of the more dilapidated housing will likely be demolished in the next few years.

Downtown Portland is possibly the only part of the city in which having a car is not merely optional but a positive liability. Ongoing construction of the new transit mall has wreaked havoc with automobile traffic; moreover, because downtown Portland was platted before the rest of the city, the streets are not oriented to true north, but instead to magnetic north. (The reason for this is unclear, although presumably early planners tried to plat numbered streets to run parallel to the waterfront along the Willamette.) The result is a series of difficult-to-navigate corners (and interesting architecture) where downtown streets hit

Burnside. Fortunately, downtown Portland is pedestrian-friendly (assuming you can endure the ubiquitous and often creative panhandlers), and new aluminum directional signs help orient foot travelers. Downtown is also the hub of the region's transit system, with frequent bus, light rail, and streetcar service within downtown and to other parts of the city.

No one moves to downtown Portland for its wide open spaces, but several parks nonetheless provide opportunities to stretch your legs, get some fresh air, and maybe witness a drug deal or two. Waterfront Park and the leafy South Park Blocks are downtown's prime parklands, but smaller parks like the Plaza Blocks, between 3rd and 4th avenues near the county and federal courthouses, also provide oases of green in the heart of the city. The parks also provide a home for the two farmers' markets: the Saturday PSU market on the South Park Blocks at Portland State University and the Wednesday Downtown market on the South Park Blocks at Salmon. (See www.portlandfarmersmarket.com for details.)

GOOSE HOLLOW

Neighborhood Association: Goose Hollow

Goose Hollow is a social and topographical transition zone between relatively flat downtown Portland and the loftier and more genteel precincts of the West Hills. The neighborhood was once dotted with grand Victorian- and Edwardian-era homes, many of which are still standing; some have been divided into condos or professional offices, while others remain in use as very expensive single-family homes. At the south end of the neighborhood, Gander Ridge and Vista Ridge, which form the rims of the "hollow" for which Goose Hollow is named, contain an abundance of older homes and winding streets that are more reminiscent of Portland Heights. A wave of building in the 1920s left a legacy of attractive old-fashioned apartments, especially near Southwest Vista Avenue, while later apartment construction resulted in a crop of high-rises, some with magnificent views.

Many of the neighborhood's historic buildings were lost to the wrecking ball in the 1960s, especially in the lower part of the neighborhood, which is now largely devoted to non-residential uses, including the PGE Park Stadium, Lincoln High School, a few manufacturing facilities and auto-related businesses, and the ultra-exclusive Multnomah Athletic Club. As proximity to the Pearl District and downtown has become more desirable in recent years, some new condominium projects have begun to spring up, especially in the vicinity of PGE Park.

With a few exceptions, most notably the Goose Hollow Inn (www.goosehol-lowinn.com) owned by former Portland mayor Bud Clark (mildly famous as the flasher in the popular "Expose Yourself to Art" poster), the neighborhood lacks much in the way of dining or shopping except along the fringes, close to Interstate 405 or along Burnside. Nonetheless, it is a quick stroll from any point in Goose Hollow to the tantalizing offerings of downtown Portland or Northwest

23rd Avenue. (Keep in mind that your walk home will be uphill.) Moreover, transit service is very good: several bus lines pass through or along the edges of the neighborhood, and the Westside MAX light rail line passes right through Goose Hollow, with stops at PGE Park, Kings Hill/SW Salmon, and Goose Hollow/SW Jefferson.

Goose Hollow's central location and semi-urban ambiance have made it popular with a diverse set of residents—PSU students, empty nesters, young professionals, and even some families who are happy to take advantage of the excellent public schools that serve the neighborhood (Chapman Elementary, West Sylvan Middle, and Lincoln High). At the same time, these characteristics have made it expensive; the average home price in 2006 was over half a million dollars (although condo prices were closer to $300,000). While Goose Hollow itself is densely populated, the upper end of the neighborhood lies on the door-step of 130-acre Washington Park. Note that, while on-street parking is generally free in the neighborhood (if not necessarily easy to find), a resident parking permit is required.

OLD TOWN AND THE PEARL DISTRICT

Neighborhood Associations: Old Town–Chinatown, Pearl

It was the best of times; it was the worst of times. These two adjacent neighborhoods that lie just north of West Burnside Street tell, if not a tale of two cities, at least a tale of two districts with very different fortunes. **Old Town** is indeed filled with many old brick and masonry buildings, some of which date back to the 1870s and 1880s, and which in many cases still retain their original cast iron facades. The neighborhood is honeycombed with underground tunnels—the so-called Shanghai tunnels in which hapless, drunken saloon patrons were purportedly carried off to ships that needed crew members in the nineteenth and early twentieth centuries. While many of the buildings in Old Town are undergoing renovation, and some new businesses have opened in the area, a reputation as a haven for drug-dealing and a high concentration of homeless shelters, soup kitchens, and other social service providers limits the area's appeal. Old Town has traditionally had few real apartments or condos—most residential units are either subsidized or of the short-stay, transitional variety, and in 2005, only 4% of the neighborhood's housing units were owner-occupied. The neighborhood also has a high concentration of paroled sex offenders, in part because few children live here (although, ironically, the area is served by some of the best public schools in the city).

Old Town has a couple of notable sub-neighborhoods. **Skidmore Historic District**, which extends south under the Burnside Bridge along the waterfront, is home to the long-running Portland Saturday Market (www.portlandsaturdaymarket.com), as well as a host of nightclubs. **Chinatown**, easily identified by the Chinatown Gate that looms over Fourth Avenue at West Burnside and by a cluster of Chinese restaurants, is a shadow of its former self: Most of the area's Chinese residents and some of its businesses have long since decamped to other neighborhoods, notably the area around 82nd Avenue in the outer Eastside. Nonetheless, Chinatown is home to the lovely new Portland Classical Chinese Garden (www.portlandchinesegarden.org).

Old Town's fortunes may slowly be changing, as a few market-rate apartment buildings and luxury loft-type condominiums have been built or are under construction along the river and near Union Station, Portland's quasi-Romanesque train station. Union Station, built in 1896, is recognizable by the neon "Go By Train" sign on the station's clock tower and is still an active passenger station, with trains heading north to Seattle and Vancouver, British Columbia, south to Eugene and California, and east to Minneapolis and Chicago.

In sharp contrast to Old Town, on the other side of the North Park Blocks and just to the northwest of the downtown skyscrapers lies Portland's urban Cinderella, the **Pearl District**. The Pearl is Portland's closest analogue to New York's SoHo. Like SoHo, it was once a warehouse district where real artists lived and worked; also like SoHo, it has been redeveloped and gentrified to such a degree that most artists have moved elsewhere. As for the name, the story goes that the neighborhood's old warehouses, like crusty oyster shells, contained hidden "pearls" in the form of galleries and lofts. Most of the warehouses have been wholly renovated (or just torn down) and while there are still plenty of galleries, the Pearl is now positively packed with trendy boutiques, creative workspaces, and some of the city's best restaurants. While most neighborhoods contain discrete commercial districts, the Pearl is unique in Portland in that the entire neighborhood is basically a commercial district. Thanks to its proximity to downtown and the laziness of some travel writers, the Pearl has been the focus of many recent articles, including features in the travel sections of the *Los Angeles Times* and *The New York Times*.

The modern furniture stores and fancy eateries coexist with, and often are actually part of, the neighborhood's residential buildings. The area is awash in a sea of mostly new, *very* high-end lofts and condominiums, with a smattering of urban rowhouses in the idealized Brooklyn mode. Per-square-foot prices for residential real estate are possibly the highest in the state. In part because of its high profile (and high prices), the Pearl District and its generally affluent inhabitants get hit with a lot of verbal vitriol. Part of this resentment is pure envy, but part of it is the perception that the Pearl is somehow antithetical to Portland values: unaffordable, unfriendly, increasingly dominated by out-of-state chains, and definitely not egalitarian. Residents who complain about the train whistles from railroad tracks that run along the edge of the neighborhood do not help to erase this perception. (The tax abatements that were given to condo developers and transferred to residents didn't do much to alleviate resentment, either.) Still, the Pearl is a great place to wander around, on foot or by streetcar, and it exerts a strong pull for both affluent young professionals and empty nesters.

A few businesses, like Powell's Books (www.powells.com) and the Pearl Bakery (www.pearlbakery.com), are holdovers from the days before the Pearl's virtually wholesale transformation into Trend Central. Another holdover is First Thursday—the first Thursday evening of each month—when gallery owners and other businesses throw open their doors to the public. (Of late, First Thursday is more about the scene—and being seen—than about art, but it can still be a lot of fun.) Some of the more architecturally interesting buildings in the Pearl are the mixed-use Brewery Blocks, on the site of the old Henry Weinhard brewery; the old Portland Armory, which has undergone a "green" makeover into the Gerding Theater, home of Portland Center Stage; and the Ecotrust building, a repurposed warehouse that is a model of sustainable design. (It even has an eco-roof.) The Ecotrust building hosts a farmers' market (www.portlandfarmersmarket.com) on Thursday afternoons from June through September. The only supermarket in the Pearl is a Whole Foods; this fact may tell you everything you need to know about the neighborhood's demographics.

Some families with small children live in the Pearl, in part because the area is so walkable and because the schools that serve it are excellent. Besides the high cost of even a two-bedroom pad, a possible drawback for families is the complete absence of yards and the relative dearth of parks. There are only three parks in the neighborhood—Jamison Square Park (famed for its fountains on summer days), Tanner Springs Park, and the North Park Blocks—and only the last of these is a "real" park with grass and a play structure.

Both Old Town and the Pearl District are unusually well served by transit. The downtown Portland transit mall extends north of Burnside to Union Station, and new MAX light rail trains will begin running along 5th and 6th avenues in 2009. MAX trains already run along 1st Avenue, with stops at Skidmore Fountain (under the Burnside Bridge) and Old Town/Chinatown. The Portland Streetcar route runs north-south along 10th and 11th avenues to Lovejoy and Northrup streets, at which point the line goes east-west. There is talk of yet another streetcar line along Burnside and Couch. All of Old Town and most of the Pearl District is within Fareless Square (see the **Transportation** chapter for more on Fareless Square).

Downtown and Environs Neighborhood Information

Zip Codes: 97201, 97204, 97205, 97209

Post Offices: Central Post Office, 204 SW 5th Ave; Portland Post Office, 715 NW Hoyt St; Solomon Courthouse Post Office, 620 SW Main St, Suite 101; University Post Office, 1505 SW 6th Ave

Police Station: Portland Police Bureau, Central Precinct, 1111 SW 2nd Ave, 503-823-0097 (non-emergency)

Emergency Hospitals: Legacy Emanuel Hospital and Health Center, 2801 N Gantenbein Ave, 503-413-2200, www.legacyhealth.org; Legacy Good Samaritan Hospital and Medical Center, 1015 NW 22nd Ave, 503-413-7711, www.legacy

health.org; OHSU Hospital, 3181 SW Sam Jackson Park Rd, 503-494-8311, www.ohsu.org/health/clinics-and-services/

Library: Central Library, 801 SW 10th Ave, 503-988-5123

Parks: Major parks include Washington Park, Waterfront Park, and the Park Blocks (north and south); www.portlandparks.org

Community Publication: *Northwest Examiner*, www.nwexaminer.com

Public Transportation: TriMet, 503-238-RIDE, www.trimet.org; comprehensive bus, light rail, and streetcar service. Travel within the Interstate 405 loop south of Northwest Irving Street is free.

WEST HILLS

Boundaries: North: Forest Park; Northwest Industrial District; **West:** Forest Heights; unincorporated Multnomah County; unincorporated Washington County; **South:** Hillsdale; Bridlemile; **East:** Downtown; Goose Hollow; Northwest Portland/Nob Hill; South Portland

Neighborhood Associations: Healy Heights, Hillside, Homestead, Northwest, South-west Hills, Sylvan-Highlands

When Art Alexakis, frontman of the Portland band Everclear, promises, "I will buy you a big house way up in the West Hills" (in the song "I Will Buy You a New Life"), he is channeling the aspirations of generations of Portlanders. Not every house in the West Hills is big—some are tiny, in fact—and not everyone who lives here is rich or even upper-middle class. But ever since the late nineteenth century, when timber barons, successful merchants, and other members of the city's incipient upper crust began to literally look down on the flatlands from their palaces in the hills, the West Hills have been the destination of choice for many socially and financially successful Portlanders.

It's not hard to see why. The West Hills is the colloquial name for the portion of the Tualatin Mountains that parallels the Willamette River to the west and forms the backdrop to downtown Portland. The hills rise to more than 1,000 feet above sea level in places, and the often fog-shrouded slopes and canyons are forested with mature conifers. Many homes here have incomparable views—a few choice homes offer expansive vistas of virtually the entire city, along with several snow-capped volcanoes—and others feel as if they are vacation homes in the woods. The icing on the West Hills cake is the incredible proximity of these woodsy neighborhoods to downtown Portland—some West Hills homes are a five-minute drive (and perhaps a 30-minute walk) from the center of the city.

Many less fortunate (or simply more hip) Portlanders mock denizens of the West Hills, sometimes out of envy, and sometimes—well, in any city (except perhaps Los Angeles), tanned, well-coifed people zipping to their botox appointments in luxury SUVs will be a target of derision. While the stereotype of the mansion-dwelling executive certainly applies to some residents, the reality is that the neighborhoods of the West Hills feature residents with a mix of ages, professions, educational backgrounds, and incomes, and many of these supposed snobs are actually quite unassuming people. West Hills houses are equally heterogeneous, and the area encompasses several distinct neighborhoods with different characteristics. Yes, there are ridiculously huge mansions that look as if they were brought over lock, stock, and barrel from Sussex, but there are also small, wisteria-shrouded cottages, charming bungalows, unrenovated 1950s ranches, and the city's highest concentration of custom-designed, often modernist homes. To cope with steep slopes, many houses are built on piers or stilts: the structures jut out over the hillside, with a gulf underneath. From the street, only a garage (or garages) and a front door are visible, and sometimes passers-by see only a wall with a gate. These houses usually have decks, but yards are clearly impossible.

Not every part of the West Hills is actually hilly, but the entire area is laced with narrow, winding, steep streets that utterly abandon the city's street grid and that make traveling through these neighborhoods a bit of an adventure (especially during rare snow or ice storms). Virtually the entire West Hills region is at risk from landslides, wildfire, and earthquake damage. An additional hazard is the acrimonious disputes that erupt when a tree in one person's yard grows tall enough to block his neighbor's mountain view. If you can live with these dangers, and have the money and desire to buy into the West Hills, read on.

Just southwest of (but high above) downtown Portland, **Portland Heights** is a relatively flat neighborhood with sidewalks and mature street trees. Unlike almost any other West Hills neighborhood, Portland Heights mostly adheres to downtown's grid pattern and street orientation, although steep slopes and winding streets separate the two areas. Also unlike most other parts of the West Hills, Portland Heights has a tiny commercial district, centered on Southwest Vista Avenue and Spring Street (home of the aptly named Vista Spring Café, which serves up great pizza). (Lamb's at Stroheckers—just Strohecker's to most people—an upscale supermarket, is just up the hill on Southwest Patton Road.) Ainsworth Elementary School, one of the top elementary schools in the city, is also at the intersection of Vista and Spring; the surrounding area has a strong attraction for affluent families with young children.

Portland Heights was largely developed in the 'teens and 1920s, and consequently the area feels more like an East Side neighborhood (albeit an exceptionally well-moneyed one) than any other neighborhood in the West Hills. Most homes here are in traditional styles—foursquares, bungalows, English Tudors, and colonials—and generally range in size from large to palatial. Some newer contemporary and custom homes perch on the hillsides. The sinuous streets leading up to Portland Heights feature an interesting cross-section of structures, from virtual mansions to condo complexes and even a few mossy, tumbledown shanties in the woods.

Uphill to the south, **Healy Heights** and **Council Crest** boast the loftiest real estate in Portland, and feature prices to match. These neighborhoods occupy a saddle on the very pinnacle of the West Hills, between Council Crest Park (the highest point in the city) and the giant red-and-white KGON radio tower (known as Stonehenge, to which it has no resemblance whatsoever). A streetcar line once served Council Crest, which was home to an amusement park, complete with roller coaster and, somewhat absurdly, a giant paddleboat. A few homes survive from this era—the park closed in 1929, just before the stock market crash of that year—but most houses date from the post–World War II period. The neighborhood includes some surprisingly modest 1950s ranch-style houses, as well as a large number of large, architect-designed dwellings; the latter are especially common on lots with prime views. Level Fairmount Boulevard, a favorite walking and biking loop, circles around these high points; the downhill side of the street is lined with architecturally interesting "stilt" homes and other structures built to cope with steep slopes. Council Crest's labyrinthine street layout and confusing access routes tend to discourage nonresidents from driving through, and this neighborhood often has the city's lowest crime rate. Despite its lofty perch, the neighborhood enjoys some sidewalks and even a bus line, the modern descendant of the old streetcar line. This area is also a center of the Southwest Trails system, which threads through the hills and fans out into surrounding residential neighborhoods.

On the eastern slope of Council Crest, Oregon Health and Science University is a sprawling complex of clinics, labs, classrooms, and hospitals that stands prominently atop Marquam Hill, a.k.a. "Pill Hill." The **Homestead** neighborhood is tucked into the hills around and just above OHSU. While there are plenty of interesting single-family homes here, this area also features a large crop of apartment and condominium buildings, which primarily serve the population of medical students and residents at the university and its hospitals; unusually for the West Hills, renters in the neighborhood outnumber owners. Many houses and apartments here have amazing Mount Hood views, while others back onto greenspaces like Marquam Nature Park. On-street parking is at a premium in and around OHSU, and resident parking permits are required for long-term parking.

Arlington Heights, a tiny neighborhood tucked in between Washington Park and Hoyt Arboretum, experienced a blistering 236% increase in home prices between 2001 and 2006. Residents enjoy practically backyard access to walking trails in the Arboretum and around Washington Park. Most of the homes here are of prewar vintage—English Tudor–style homes, small cottages, and the like—although some custom homes have been built in recent years. The neighborhood has few through streets, and is very quiet—except on Sunday nights, when the Zoobombers tear down Fairview Boulevard. The Zoobombing phenomenon involves a group of otherwise sensible grownups who modify kids' bikes and other small two-wheeled vehicles (often removing brakes and other critical components), take them on the MAX line to the Oregon Zoo, then blast downhill to

Goose Hollow, where they hop back on the MAX and repeat the process. The Zoobombers maintain a "pile" of minibikes across the street from Powell's Books. Some Arlington Heights residents are not enamored of this group.

Across Burnside Road to the north, **Kings Heights** spreads across the hillside just above the bustle of Northwest 23rd Avenue and below the grandest West Hills palace of them all, Pittock Mansion (www.pittockmansion.com). Most of the homes on the steep, winding streets are gracious older homes, generally without much of a yard but often with city and mountain views. Some condominium complexes have been built in the lower reaches of the neighborhood. Tiny Hillside Park, with its small community center, indeed perches on the hillside in the middle of the neighborhood.

A bit further north, across Cornell Road, **Willamette Heights** lies at the doorstep of the immense foggy vastness of Forest Park; some homes are literally a stone's throw from a trailhead, and the neighborhood's main thoroughfare, Northwest Thurman Street, dead ends at Leif Erikson Drive, the main mountain bike into the park. Willamette Heights is full of grand early twentieth-century homes, some of which stand high above the street with only a steep staircase for access. Most views here are northward, over the industrial district and Willamette River toward Mount St. Helens, although many homes are tucked down into woodsy ravines with no views at all. One of the neighborhood's significant advantages is its proximity not only to the Northwest 23rd district, but also to the commercial zone along Thurman Street itself west of 23rd; neighborhood gems include the St. Honoré Boulangerie (www.sthonorebakery.com) and Food Front Cooperative Grocery (www.foodfront.coop). The Northwest branch library is also located here. For a literary perspective on the thoroughfare, you might want to grab a copy of Thurman Street resident Ursula K. Le Guin's *Blue Moon Over Thurman Street*.

West of the main ridge of the West Hills—the neighborhoods along Skyline Boulevard near **Sylvan**, where the Sunset Highway crests the hills on its congested way to Beaverton—development is far less dense and generally newer, with homes dating anywhere from the 1950s to last week. Many homes are on large lots, giving parts of the neighborhood an almost rural feeling. The neighborhoods south of the Sunset Highway, off Humphrey Boulevard and Scholls Ferry Road, are similar. The area just north of the Sylvan exit has a concentration of small office buildings, restaurants, and apartment complexes. (For information about Forest Heights, Linnton, and other neighborhoods near Forest Park, see "Forest Park and Environs" below.)

Given the terrain and the low population density, the West Hills enjoy surprisingly good bus service. Bus lines serve Portland Heights, Council Crest and Healy Heights, Willamette Heights, Kings Heights, the Homestead/OHSU neighborhood, Sylvan, and the area around Washington Park. Of course, many residents who are more than a few blocks from a bus line may have difficulty safely reaching the nearest bus stop.

West Hills Neighborhood Information

Zip Codes: 97201, 97210, 97221, 97239

Post Office: Forest Park Post Office, 1706 NW 24th Ave; also see "Downtown and Environs"

Police Station: Portland Police Bureau, Central Precinct, 1111 SW 2nd Ave, 503-823-0097 (non-emergency)

Emergency Hospitals: Legacy Good Samaritan Hospital and Medical Center, 1015 NW 22nd Ave, 503-413-7711, www.legacyhealth.org; OHSU Hospital, 3181 SW Sam Jackson Park Rd, 503-494-8311, www.ohsu.org/health/clinics-and-services/; Providence St. Vincent Medical Center, 9205 SW Barnes Rd, 503-216-1234, www.providence.org/Oregon/

Libraries: Central Library, 801 SW 10th Ave, 503-988-5123; Northwest Library, 2300 NW Thurman St, 503-988-5560

Parks: Several major parks, including Washington Park, Hoyt Arboretum, Council Crest Park, Macleay Park, Marquam Nature Park, Forest Park, and Keller Woodland; www.portlandparks.org

Community Publications: *Multnomah Village Post*, www.multnomahvillagepost.com; *Northwest Examiner*, www.nwexaminer.com

Public Transportation: TriMet, 503-238-RIDE, www.trimet.org; bus service on several routes, MAX light rail service available at Washington Park

SOUTHWEST PORTLAND

Boundaries: North: Burnside Street (official); West Hills (unofficial); **West:** Beaverton; West Slope, Raleigh Hills, Garden Home (unincorporated Washington County); Tigard; **South:** Lake Oswego; **East:** Willamette River

With a couple of notable exceptions like the South Waterfront district, Southwest Portland as a whole feels more suburban than any other quadrant of the city. Many Portlanders from other parts of the city either dismiss the neighborhoods here as insufficiently interesting or too "white bread" or ignore them entirely. At the same time, many parts of Southwest Portland are closer to downtown, both in distance and in travel time, than some "urban" Eastside neighborhoods are, and no bridge crossing is required to get there. Southwest Portland is also one of the more family-friendly parts of the city, with generally good-to-excellent schools, relatively low crime rates, and plenty of open space; if you take the time to look, there are some decent restaurants and quirky shops, too.

That said, Southwest's nightlife and cultural scene is admittedly inferior to the hot spots of the Pearl and the Eastside, and the area also lacks some of the attributes that many newcomers to Portland seek. Most houses in this part of the city are postwar or newer structures, not the cute bungalows or English Tudor cottages of the older streetcar neighborhoods of the Eastside. The general lack of sidewalks discourages walking, and the hilly terrain makes cycling a challenge, although the Southwest Trails network offers off-street and low-traffic routes for hikers. Some parts of Southwest Portland feel almost rural, with rutted, unpaved streets (a characteristic that disconcerts some people). Keep in mind that Southwest Portland, like all parts of the city, is comprised of a diverse set of neighborhoods; chances are that *somewhere* in Southwest may have the specific attributes you're looking for.

SOUTH PORTLAND

Neighborhood Association: South Portland (formerly Corbett–Terwilliger–Lair Hill)

The neighborhoods that border the west bank of the Willamette River south of downtown are among the oldest residential areas in Portland, yet also include some of the most rapidly changing parts of the city. The area offers a diverse range of housing and a quick commute to OHSU or to downtown Portland via various transit options, bicycle path, and a network of major roads: Barbur Boulevard, Interstate 5, Macadam Avenue, and Corbett Avenue. This easy access to highways is also a curse, however; the roads chop up entire neighborhoods, and many parts of South Portland are never free of the roar of traffic.

The **Lair Hill** neighborhood occupies the lower slopes of Marquam Hill just south of Interstate 405 and downtown Portland. This compact area harbors the oldest largely intact residential development in the city, with a relative abundance of Victorian houses, including Queen Anne and Italianate styles, which are otherwise rare in Portland. These homes were built for workers, not captains of industry, so they are generally small. Many of these old homes have been beautifully renovated since the 1960s, when the then-blighted area was slated for demolition and "urban renewal." Some houses remain in poor condition, several major thoroughfares cut through the area, and various modern buildings—small commercial buildings, apartments, and townhouses—have mixed in with the old homes, so the neighborhood is by no means pristine. At the same time, the "bones" of the old neighborhood remain, and the close-in location is a significant draw for some newcomers.

The shiny metallic pods of the Portland Aerial Tram soar over the south end of the neighborhood as they shuttle between OHSU atop the hill and the **South Waterfront** district on the east side of Interstate 5. Major controversy erupted when the tram was first proposed; most Lair Hill residents opposed the project, pointing out quite reasonably that it would not directly serve the neighborhood and that tram riders would be able to peer down directly into residents' back yards. Despite these concerns, the tram was built and began operation in 2007. Local attitudes toward the tram are currently mixed; many residents still object to the invasion of privacy, but others embrace the tram as a new, distinctive neighborhood symbol.

Meanwhile, in the South Waterfront district (which the tram directly serves), the advent of this novel form of transportation has helped fuel a major boom. Once the province of shipbuilders and scrapyards, the district that syllable-challenged hipsters often ironically call SoWa now bristles with several new high-rises. OHSU's Wellness Center, one of the greenest buildings in the country (the toilets use harvested rainwater), stands just off the freeway at the lower terminus of the tram. OHSU, which has run out of space on Pill Hill, is planning a major expansion in this area. Two gleaming condo towers, the Meriwether and the John Ross, are already occupied, and a forest of cranes and skeletal structures promises more condos to come. The city estimates that the South Waterfront will have 5,000 residents by 2020, and planners and developers seem to be envisioning a sort of mini-Manhattan (or at least mini–Vancouver, BC) on the banks of the Willamette. For now, shops, restaurants, and other amenities that most people associate with dense urban living are still thin on the ground. The Portland Streetcar was extended to serve the South Waterfront in 2007, but the pace and extent of residential development in this area will likely depend on the demand for high-end condos.

The neighborhoods south of Lair Hill and the South Waterfront are a mix of commercial, residential, and light industrial uses. Terwilliger Boulevard was one of four city parkways that famed park planner John C. Olmsted envisioned for Portland at the beginning of the twentieth century; it was the only one actually built, and today it winds along the slopes of Marquam Hill high above the rest of the city, passing just below OHSU. (If the boulevard's name seems oddly familiar, it may be because Simpsons creator Matt Groening appropriated "Terwilliger" as the surname for the show's Sideshow Bob character.) A broad pedestrian path parallels the road, and the adjacent corridor is almost entirely semi-natural woodland. A small enclave of prewar single-family homes downhill from this parkway, between Terwilliger and Barbur Boulevard, is within strolling distance of OHSU, and offers a rare combination of expansive views and sidewalks. This small neighborhood is popular with doctors and others who work on Pill Hill.

East of Barbur Boulevard, newer offices, townhomes, and condos mix with bungalows and the occasional ranch-style home. The **Johns Landing** area is largely devoted to suburban-style office buildings, retail uses, and townhomes, condominium complexes, and apartment buildings. Many of the residences have views of the Willamette River and Mount Hood. Johns Landing is also home to a community of houseboats floating in the Willamette. Further south, single-family homes reappear, mixed with townhomes and apartments, in the blocks behind popular Willamette Park on the riverfront.

The neighborhoods of South Portland in general have a more transient population than some other parts of the city; more than half the residents are renters. Because of its abundant supply of rental housing and its close-in location, this area is a popular place for newcomers to settle, at least initially.

HILLSDALE AND MULTNOMAH VILLAGE

Neighborhood Associations: Hillsdale, Multnomah

Hillsdale (not to be confused with Hillsboro, a western suburb) combines a pleasant small-town/suburban ambiance with proximity and easy access to downtown Portland and OHSU. As its name suggests, the neighborhood straddles the lower slopes and dales of the West Hills, between Barbur Boulevard and Dosch Road/Bertha Boulevard. The heart of the neighborhood is Hillsdale Town Center, a 1950s-era business district along SW Capitol Highway that boasts boutiques, several popular restaurants and cafés such as Three Square Grill (www. threesquare.com) and Baker & Spice (www.bakerandspicebakery.com), a Wild Oats natural foods supermarket, and a new green-built branch library. The Hillsdale Town Center area also encompasses the full range of K–12 public schools: Wilson High School, Robert Gray Middle School, and the highly regarded Mary Rieke Elementary School.

Hillsdale's amenities and convenient location appeal to young families, although the dramatic rise in home prices over the last five years has made the area prohibitively expensive for some buyers. Housing here is largely a mix of postwar single-family styles—Cape Cods, ranches, split-levels, and contemporary homes, many of them extensively remodeled—although a few older bungalows, English-style cottages, and farmhouses survive. Some apartments and townhouses line the major thoroughfares. The Wilson Park neighborhood south of Wilson High School is a 1950s-era subdivision, with sidewalks; in the hilly terrain north of Capitol Highway, the sidewalks vanish, and many homes occupy steep, forested lots with expansive westward or southward views. Some of these homes are fairly ordinary daylight ranches, notable mainly for their hillside perches, but others are dramatic modern structures, custom-designed for their sites. These hillside neighborhoods share many of the wildfire and landslide hazards of the West Hills (which, geographically if not necessarily socially, they are part of). The popular open-air Hillsdale Farmers' Market (www.hillsdalefarmersmarket.com) takes place every Sunday during summer and every other Sunday in winter.

If you're in the vicinity of Seasons and Regions (www.seasonsandregions. com), a popular seafood restaurant, in the 6600 block of Capitol Highway, you may notice, especially on Friday through Saturday evenings, a large number of folks walking by in traditional Orthodox Jewish attire. This block is home to the synagogue, day school, and more run by the Chabad Lubavitch of Portland group, and consequently a large number of primarily Orthodox Jews live in the area. The Mittleman Jewish Community Center and attached Portland Jewish Academy, more or less across the street, serve a much more diverse group of both Jews and non-Jews.

Down Capitol Highway to the southwest, **Multnomah Village** bills itself as "the village in the heart of Portland." This moniker, while not strictly true—it lies a full five miles from downtown—effectively conveys the neighborhood's urban village vibe. (Built around an electric railway station, Multnomah *was* a village until Portland annexed it in the mid-twentieth century.) Like Hillsdale, Multnomah Village centers on a thriving business district (www.multnomahvillage.org), which encompasses several short blocks of antique stores, restaurants, bars, and quirky specialty shops; local favorites include Marco's Café (www.marcos cafe.com) and independent bookstore Annie Bloom's Books (www.annieblooms.com). The historic Multnomah Arts Center hosts music and theater classes, exercise programs, and community events.

Although there are plenty of mid-century ranches and funky contemporary homes in the neighborhood, Multnomah has a larger stock of prewar bungalows and cottages than most other parts of Southwest Portland; recent infill development has also brought an onslaught of rowhouses and even lofts. Some homes situated on the higher ridges have views of the Cascades or the Coast Range. Home prices here tend to be slightly lower than in Hillsdale, and there are a few truly dilapidated shacks on some streets. Thanks in part to its older urban fabric, Multnomah Village is relatively pedestrian-friendly, and the area accordingly attracts lots of families with small children. Thousands of residents and visitors turn out each August for Multnomah Days, a two-day community celebration complete with street fair and parade. Multnomah Village is popular enough, and unusual enough in the context of Southwest Portland, that some real estate listings describe homes that are actually one or two miles away as being in or "close to" Multnomah Village.

Busy Barbur Boulevard, which parallels Interstate 5 and borders both Hillsdale and Multnomah on the south and east, is lined with supermarkets, fast-food restaurants, auto repair stores, and other services (some of a less than savory nature). Multnomah Village and the southern half of Hillsdale, including the Town Center, have frequent bus service to downtown Portland, Beaverton, and Tigard.

BRIDLEMILE AND VERMONT HILLS

Neighborhood Associations: Bridlemile, Hayhurst, Maplewood

As its unimaginative name suggests, Beaverton-Hillsdale Highway runs from the edge of Hillsdale west to Beaverton. Lined for miles by apartment complexes, restaurants, small businesses, supermarkets and strip malls, this thoroughfare is not especially inviting, but the pleasant neighborhoods on either side of the highway are popular with families and with others who are looking for a quiet lifestyle. These areas have many happy long-time residents, however, and there is typically a low inventory of houses for sale.

To the north of the highway, **Bridlemile** is the sort of neighborhood that real estate agents describe as "coveted." Not quite in (or of) the West Hills, Bridlemile nonetheless shares some of the characteristics of that area (including hills). Indeed, the boundary between these regions is indistinct: the neighborhood's northeast corner is disputed territory claimed by both the Bridlemile Neighborhood Association and the Southwest Hills Residential League. Turf wars aside, Bridlemile is generally quiet and almost wholly residential. Lower Bridlemile, south of Hamilton Street, is largely comprised of relatively small, but by no means inexpensive, one-level ranch homes in tidy subdivisions like Brookford. North of Hamilton, houses are generally larger, and a few small gated communities wall themselves off from the essentially nonexistent crime of the surrounding neighborhood. Wilcox Manor, in the western part of Bridlemile, is a former mansion that has been turned into a condo complex. Bridlemile Elementary School, one of the best public elementary schools in the city, feeds into the city's most sought-after middle and high schools; school quality is one of the area's biggest draws. One of the neighborhood's drawbacks is the almost complete absence of sidewalks, or even reasonably wide shoulders, on the main thoroughfares; residents are dependent on vehicles to travel even a few blocks without great risk to their lives.

Vermont Hills is the generic name given to the Hayhurst and Maplewood neighborhoods south of Beaverton-Hillsdale Highway. The terrain is indeed somewhat hilly; the main east-west thoroughfare is Vermont Street, which passes along the northern edge of 90-acre **Gabriel Park**, one of the city's best neighborhood parks. (Some people colloquially apply the name Gabriel Park to the entire surrounding area.) Gabriel Park is home to the Southwest Community Center complex, which includes a popular set of indoor pools. Like Bridlemile, Vermont Hills is mostly residential, but a small shopping center across the street from the Southwest Community Center contains several businesses, including the child-oriented Peanut Butter & Ellie's (www.peanutbutterellies.com). These neighborhoods are also reasonably close to Multnomah Village: Maplewood homes are routinely identified in real estate listings as being "in" Multnomah Village despite being perhaps two miles away.

Vermont Hills was developed mostly in the decades after the Second World War, and daylight ranches and other styles of the 1950s and 1960s dominate here. However, since many homes originally had large lots, the neighborhood is experiencing substantial infill development, with many large new homes rising in former side yards. There are also pockets of contemporary homes scattered on culs-de-sac throughout the area. A unique feature of the Hayhurst neighborhood is Alpenrose Dairy on Southwest Shattuck Road (www.alpenrose.com), an actual working dairy with an attached little league stadium, velodrome, and child-sized replica of an old western town.

TriMet buses serve both Bridlemile and Vermont Hills along the main thoroughfares, with particularly frequent service along Beaverton-Hillsdale Highway, although some routes operate only at rush hour.

BURLINGAME AND THE TRYON CREEK AREA

Neighborhood Associations: Arnold Creek, Collins View, Marshall Park, South Burlingame

The neighborhoods south of Interstate 5's Terwilliger curves in Southwest Port-land are among the city's hidden delights. These leafy precincts offer generally good schools, low crime rates, and abundant recreational opportunities, but are just minutes away from downtown Portland and from the antique stores and restaurants of Sellwood. These neighborhoods lie between the West Hills to the north and Dunthorpe and Lake Oswego to the south, and some residents feel that the area offers many of the benefits of those areas without the stratospheric real estate prices or perceived snobbery. That's not to say these neighborhoods are cheap—the average home price is nudging $400,000, and many newer homes cost substantially more—but they are certainly less expensive than more "established" parts of the city.

The **Burlingame** neighborhood on either side of Southwest Terwilliger Boulevard was largely developed from the 1930s through the 1960s, although some houses in the area date to the 1920s or earlier. Home styles tend toward gracious Cape Cods and ranches, with quite a few English Tudor–style houses in the mix. Unfortunately, the construction of Interstate 5 in the 1960s split Burlingame in two; the northern half of the neighborhood became part of Hills-dale (including the "Burlingame" Fred Meyer on Barbur Boulevard), while the southern half became South Burlingame. The grandest houses stand high on a ridge above Terwilliger, often with excellent views of Mount Hood and Mount St. Helens; more modest homes are tucked into the valleys on either side or in the blocks adjacent to the freeway. (Traffic noise can be troublesome in the areas closest to Interstate 5.) A commercial district at Terwilliger and Southwest Taylors Ferry Road includes a high-end Market of Choice supermarket, a Eugene-based competitor of New Seasons and Whole Foods.

To the south, the **Collins View** neighborhood occupies the slopes above Riverview Cemetery near Lewis and Clark College. The area is popular with professors and others who enjoy living in close proximity to a collegiate envi-ronment; it also is popular with students, and some residents have complained about recurring, occasional problems with noise and litter from off-campus par-ties. At its southern end, Collins View borders, and merges rather seamlessly with, the unincorporated Dunthorpe neighborhood; Dunthorpe's high school, River-dale High, is actually in Collins View (although it does not serve students in the neighborhood).

Tryon Creek State Natural Area comprises nearly 650 acres of forested hills and canyons between Terwilliger Boulevard and Southwest Boones Ferry Road. The **Marshall Park** and **Arnold Creek** neighborhoods lie just to the west of this unique and eminently hikeable urban park. Both neighborhoods are character-ized mainly by homes built from the 1960s to the present, often on large wooded

lots. A few old homes from the early twentieth century stand moldering in the shade, while some brand-new small-scale developments (of large homes) are being built in the neighborhood's vacant parcels. A few large properties that have not been subdivided are still farmed or otherwise used for traditionally rural purposes. In addition to the State Natural Area, these neighborhoods include several other natural areas, including Marshall Park, which lies along Tryon Creek upstream of the state park.

OUTER SOUTHWEST NEIGHBORHOODS

Neighborhood Associations: Ashcreek, Crestwood, Far Southwest, Markham, West Portland Park

The neighborhoods in Portland's far southwest—including the neighborhood aptly named Far Southwest—are often overlooked by newcomers and long-time Portlanders alike. While they lack any real commercial districts (barring the strip mall of Barbur Boulevard), they offer relative convenience. The quiet **Ashcreek** neighborhood, between Multnomah Village and the Washington County border, had the lowest crime rate in the city in 2006. Most homes date from the 1950s to the 1980s, with some older homes along Garden Home Road. Infill development has resulted in a scattered crop of new homes mixed in with existing houses. Nearby, **Crestwood** is something of a southwestern extension of Multnomah Village (and is usually identified as Multnomah Village in real estate listings). The crime rate is nearly as low as Ashcreek's. Homes here are generally well-kept, and the neighborhood has excellent access to Interstate 5; it's also fairly close, via back routes, to the Washington Square mall area. In the heart of the neighborhood, the vegetation in 32-acre Woods Memorial Natural Area is almost entirely native, and the park occasionally attracts elk.

South of Interstate 5, the mostly residential **Markham** neighborhood has fairly large, fairly new homes on curving streets; 17-acre Maricara Natural Area provides the only significant open space. Freeway noise can be a problem in the northern part of the neighborhood. The hilly **Far Southwest** and **West Portland Park** neighborhoods border Portland Community College's Sylvania campus. The area around the campus features some apartment complexes, but most residential areas are comprised of fairly large, well-kept contemporary and ranch-style single-family homes. These neighborhoods border the Mountain Park neighborhood of Lake Oswego, and are very convenient to that city's Kruse Way business district. Some homes have good views south over the northern Willamette Valley and west to the Coast Range. Freeway noise is a potential problem near Interstate 5.

Bus service in most parts of outer Southwest Portland is adequate, with frequent service along Barbur Boulevard and to the Portland Community College campus.

Southwest Portland Neighborhood Information

Zip Codes: 97219, 97221, 97239

Post Office: Multnomah Post Office, 7805 SW 40th Ave

Police Station: Portland Police Bureau, Central Precinct, 1111 SW 2nd Ave, 503-823-0097 (non-emergency)

Emergency Hospitals: OHSU Hospital, 3181 SW Sam Jackson Park Rd, 503-494-8311, www.ohsu.org/health/clinics-and-services/; Providence St. Vincent Medical Center, 9205 SW Barnes Rd, 503-216-1234, www.providence.org/Oregon/

Libraries: Capitol Hill Library, 10723 SW Capitol Hwy, 503-988-5385; Hillsdale Library, 1525 SW Sunset Blvd, 503-988-5388

Parks: Parks throughout area; major parks include Gabriel Park, George Himes Park, and Woods Memorial Park, www.portlandparks.org, and Tryon Creek State Natural Area

Community Publications: *Multnomah Village Post*, www.multnomahvillage post.com; *Southwest Community Connection*, www.swcommconnection.com; *Southwest Neighborhood News*, 503-823-4592, www.swni.org

Public Transportation: TriMet, 503-238-RIDE, www.trimet.org; frequent bus service along Barbur Boulevard and Beaverton-Hillsdale Highway between downtown Portland, Beaverton, and Tigard. Additional bus lines with standard service serve most neighborhoods. No light rail service; Portland Streetcar and Portland Aerial Tram serve South Waterfront district.

NORTHWEST PORTLAND

Boundaries: North: Unincorporated Multnomah County; **West:** Unincorporated Multnomah County; Unincorporated Washington County; **South:** Burnside Street (official); West Hills (unofficial); **East:** Willamette River

It's a bit of an understatement to call Northwest Portland diverse. This part of the city includes the state's most densely populated residential neighborhood, a major industrial complex, and a 5,000-acre expanse of virtual wilderness—all within a few minutes of one another. The close-in Northwest neighborhoods are among the city's most desirable and dynamic areas; at the same time, much of Northwest Portland is effectively uninhabited, and large tracts of unincorporated rural land lie just to the west, while historic Linnton on the lower Willamette River was an early rival to Portland. On the west slope of the Tualatin Mountains, the new Forest Heights neighborhood attracts professionals to a slice of suburbia. Whatever you're looking for in a neighborhood, someplace in Northwest Portland is likely to have it.

NORTHWEST–NOB HILL

Neighborhood Association: Northwest

When Portlanders refer to "Northwest Portland" they generally mean the busy commercial and residential district centered on Northwest 21st and 23rd (or "trendy-third," in ironic hipster parlance) avenues, north of Burnside Street at the foot of the West Hills. The area is sometimes known as Nob Hill, after the San Francisco district, and rarely as the "Alphabet District," the semi-official name that appears on street signs. This neighborhood is one of the oldest in the city: Captain John Couch claimed the land just north of the incipient settlement of Portland in 1845, and platted the area in 1865, with the east-west streets designated by letters of the alphabet in ascending order (i.e., A Street, B Street, and so on) moving north from downtown; for this reason, the area came to be known as the Alphabet District. In 1891, the streets were given names—Captain Couch's name now graces his original C Street—but the alphabetical street order remained. ("Simpsons" fans may notice that Flanders, Lovejoy, and Quimby streets—formerly F, L, and Q streets—have lent their names to prominent characters on the show.)

Although it is small, the Northwest district is arguably the most architecturally diverse and interesting part of the city. The early industrialists' grand Victorian houses—some of which have been turned into offices, and some of which are still used for residential purposes—stand amid modernist residences and offices, uninspired 1960s commercial buildings, apartment buildings and condominiums that span a century of styles, nineteenth-century churches, and the imposing 1928 temple of the Beth Israel congregation. The neighborhood has a particular abundance of vintage apartment buildings, many of which are quite ornate and retain their period features; they are found throughout the district, and the concentration of apartments is such that Northwest Portland has long had the state's highest population density. Some of these apartments have been converted to condos in recent years, and rents have increased dramatically, but the area still exerts a powerful draw for newcomers, especially young singles and couples, both gay and straight.

A large part of the district's appeal is its stunning variety of shops, bars, and restaurants. For years, before the Eastside commercial districts became the hotspots they are today, and before the Pearl District was even a gleam in a condo developer's eye, Northwest Portland was *the* place to go for nontraditional shopping and dining. (The late lamented Zefiro, which opened on Northwest 21st Avenue and closed ten years later, is widely credited with starting Portland's foodie revolution.) Now that other parts of the city have found their commercial legs, Northwest Portland is still going strong. It would be pointless to try to pick out highlights—Northwest 23rd, and to a lesser extent 21st, are lined with temptations all the way from Burnside to Thurman Street. (Remember, that's B Street to T Street, or 18 blocks.) Just wander down the street and see what strikes your fancy. Some interesting places have cropped up away from these main thoroughfares; for example, Saint Cupcake (www.saintcupcake.com) at 17th and Flanders draws fans from across the city for its cupcakes and other baked goods. If you need some visual entertainment, Cinema 21 (www.cinema21.com) on 21st Avenue screens art house films, foreign films, classic films, edgy documentaries, and animation festivals, while the Mission Theatre on Glisan Street shows second-run Hollywood movies accompanied by pizza and beer; CoHo Productions (www.cohoproductions.org) puts on plays at its performance space on Raleigh Street.

It is possible—desirable, even—to live in Northwest without a car. Because so many old apartments lack off-street parking, on-street parking is hard to find. Even though resident parking permits are required, you might have to park several blocks away from your apartment, which is probably not a big deal if you've moved from New York City but may be a shock if you're coming from, say, Omaha. On the other hand, public transit is frequent and comprehensive; in addition to several bus routes, the Portland Streetcar serves the northern end of the neighborhood. It is also quite feasible to walk to downtown Portland. Moreover, unlike many neighborhoods, Northwest Portland has a full crop of markets within walking distance: Fred Meyer and Zupan's are on Burnside, the upscale City Market is on 21st (just down the street from Ken's Artisan Bakery, www.kensartisan.com), and a Trader Joe's occupies the site of the old Thriftway supermarket (known to many neighborhood residents as "Theftway" for its perceived high prices). If a craving for unusual organic fruit strikes you, the Whole Foods supermarket in the Pearl District is just a few blocks away. Need to get out of town? Flexcar stations several vehicles in the neighborhood. In short, if you want to live an urban, car-free lifestyle without paying Pearl District rents, Northwest Portland might be for you.

Northwest Portland seems about as developed as it can possibly be, but the district has a last frontier in charmingly named Slabtown, west of 20th Avenue and north of Lovejoy Street (or NoLo, as some would have it, tongue not entirely in cheek—see www.nolopdx.com). This zone of formerly (or currently) dilapidated warehouses and commercial structures is poised to undergo a Pearl-like transformation in the next few years.

Northwest is perhaps most attractive to the young and stylish, but it also appeals to families; Chapman Elementary School, on Northwest Pettygrove, is one of the best public elementary schools in the city, and Northwest feeds into equally high-quality middle and high schools. The entire area is walkable, although you'll have to dodge the occasional junkie or homeless person, especially in the eastern part of the neighborhood. A potential downside of the neighborhood for families, besides the traffic congestion, is the relative dearth of parks: the area's two city parks, Couch Park and Wallace Park (next to Chapman elementary), both have playgrounds, but they can seem painfully far away on a rainy day when junior is melting down in your third-floor, two-bedroom walkup apartment.

FOREST PARK AND ENVIRONS

Neighborhood Associations: Forest Park, Linnton, Northwest Heights, Northwest Industrial

Most of the land west of Forest Park, along Skyline Boulevard and Thompson Road, is steep, wooded terrain that is lightly populated and generally outside city limits; the homes that do exist here tend to be either mid-century outposts or large, custom-designed houses, often with spectacular views, but generally with a negligible or nonexistent yard. The exception to the area's sparse development is **Forest Heights**, a vast new neighborhood created from scratch in the 1990s. Forest Heights spreads across the western slopes of the West Hills, west of Skyline and north of Cornell Road. While Forest Heights could have become a standard suburban cookie-cutter development, an attempt was made to create a community with varied architectural styles and with such neighborhood amenities as walking paths, common areas, and open spaces. The result won't fool you into thinking you're in a traditional urban neighborhood, and the newness of it all creeps some people out, but Forest Heights is arguably one of the better-executed suburban developments in the Portland area.

Home styles in Forest Park range from townhomes and single-family structures built in a quasi-traditional "Craftsman" style to bold contemporary houses and custom-built luxury homes (with not a few McMansions thrown in). The entire neighborhood is part of one homeowners association, and an architectural review committee must approve all building plans and color schemes, so the neighborhood may not be the best place to try out that "pirate ship" addition you've always wanted; townhouse and condominium owners also belong to homeowners associations of their own. Home prices range from above average to *way* above average. While the neighborhood is almost entirely residential, there is a small commercial zone that features a gourmet grocery, a Starbucks, a day spa, and other essential community services. Forest Park Elementary School, a new school in the middle of the neighborhood, has an excellent academic reputation but suffers from enrollment levels that substantially exceed its design capacity: several classes camp out in portable classrooms.

Forest Heights is not especially close to anything, and it feels less like an integral part of Portland than perhaps any other neighborhood in the city. Still, it is a reasonable commute from downtown Portland via Cornell Road or to the employers of Washington County's Sunset Corridor. (The neighborhood seems to be a particular favorite of Intel employees, who can live here with a Portland address but can still avoid a grueling commute on the Sunset Highway.) There is no public transit, but the homeowners association operates a private shuttle between Forest Heights and the MAX stop at the Sunset Transit Center.

On the other side of Forest Park, and in sharp contrast to Forest Heights, **Linnton** is an old, mainly industrial neighborhood. Founded about the same time as Portland, Linnton and Portland were originally rivals; the larger city, having won the battle for pre-eminence, absorbed the smaller one in 1915. Most of the houses here perch on the hills or are tucked into wooded canyons west of Highway 30 on the edge of Forest Park, high above the tank farms and other industrial facilities that line the Willamette riverfront. Many homes overlook the river, which is a busy maritime thoroughfare at this point. Most Linnton houses are old, and many have been lovingly restored. A small commercial district along the highway has a few taverns, convenience stores, gas stations, and a community center. (The district used to be larger; the state bulldozed half of it to make way for extra highway lanes in the 1960s.)

Although Linnton no longer has the job base it once had, it is centrally located for commuting to downtown Portland, zipping across the St. Johns Bridge (which connects Linnton directly to North Portland), or even for winding over the hills to Washington County. Despite the industrial character of the lower parts of the neighborhood, Linnton has a strong community spirit. Linnton residents have proposed a rezoning and redevelopment plan that envisions a mixed-use development—shops, a park, offices, and rowhouse condos—in place of a derelict lumber mill on the waterfront. The City Council put the kibosh on that plan, citing multiple dangers from earthquakes, landslides, explosions, and other industrial accidents, and some community leaders, bitter over the rejection of their efforts, have called for Linnton to secede from the city.

South of Linnton, the **Northwest Industrial** neighborhood is, as the name indicates, a predominately industrial neighborhood. A few houses huddle under the eaves of the forest west of Highway 30, overlooking the area's industrial facilities, but these dwellings are really only appropriate for trainspotters and fans of industrial chic.

Northwest Portland Neighborhood Information

Zip Codes: 97210, 97229, 97231

Post Offices: Forest Park Post Office, 1706 NW 24th Ave; Portland Post Office, 715 NW Hoyt St

Police Stations: Portland Police Bureau, Central Precinct, 1111 SW 2nd Ave, 503-823-0097 (non-emergency); North Precinct (for Linnton), 7214 N Philadelphia St, 503-823-2120 (non-emergency)

Emergency Hospitals: Legacy Good Samaritan Hospital and Medical Center, 1015 NW 22nd Ave, 503-413-7711, www.legacyhealth.org; Providence St. Vincent Medical Center, 9205 SW Barnes Rd, 503-216-1234, www.providence.org/Oregon/

Library: Northwest Library, 2300 NW Thurman St, 503-988-5560

Parks: Major parks include 5,000-acre Forest Park and Linnton Park; see www.portlandparks.org

Community Publication: *Northwest Examiner*, www.nwexaminer.com

Public Transportation: TriMet, 503-238-RIDE, www.trimet.org; frequent bus and streetcar service to Northwest Portland–Nob Hill and vicinity; standard bus service along Burnside/Barnes Road to Beaverton and to Linnton, St. Johns, and Sauvie Island via the St. Helens Road. Forest Heights neighborhood has a private shuttle to Sunset Transit Center.

THE EAST SIDE

NORTHEAST PORTLAND

Boundaries: North: Columbia River; **West**: North Williams Avenue; **South**: East Burnside Street (official); Interstate 84 (unofficial); **East**: 82nd Avenue (unofficial)

Northeast Portland offers some of the city's most distinctive and desirable neighborhoods, ranging from the grand homes of Irvington and Alameda Ridge to the family-friendly Grant Park neighborhood and the self-consciously hip Alberta Arts District. Most neighborhoods in this part of the city have tree-lined, bikeable streets, attractive parks, and access to pleasant, walkable commercial districts. The southern half of Northeast Portland is only a few minutes away from downtown or the Pearl District. All these advantages come at a price—median home prices in some neighborhoods are over half a million dollars, although there are still a few pockets of (relatively) affordable houses—but many newcomers who can afford to buy here fall in love with this part of the city.

IRVINGTON, SABIN, AND THE LLOYD DISTRICT

Neighborhood Associations: Irvington, Lloyd, Sabin, Sullivan's Gulch

Stately **Irvington** (www.irvingtonpdx.com), a fashionable residential neighborhood in inner Northeast Portland, started its development in the late nineteenth century, when Portland's streetcar system expanded to the Eastside; the neighborhood was essentially completely built-up by the end of the 1930s. The neighborhood's first residents were generally middle-class tradespeople. (The city's upper classes mainly lived on the established Westside.) For many of these early residents, the house they built or bought in Irvington was the first home they had ever owned. Urban decay and rising crime in the 1960s and 1970s threatened the neighborhood's livability, but a renaissance that began in the 1980s and gathered steam in the 1990s is now essentially complete. Irvington is no longer a starter-home neighborhood by any stretch of the imagination. The average home is now worth close to half a million dollars, and some of the neighborhood's grander homes can easily sell for over a million dollars.

Along with the standard Eastside assortment of bungalows, "Old Portlands" (foursquares), barn-like Dutch colonials, and English cottages and Tudor-style homes, Irvington has fine examples of other early late nineteenth- and early twentieth-century styles: Spanish colonial pseudo-villas, Victorians, large arts-

and-crafts mansions, prairie style homes, and plantation-style colonial revival homes. The annual Irvington Home Tour (www.irvingtonhometour.com) held each May shows off a selection of the neighborhood's historic houses. Not surprisingly, given the area's high property values, most homes here have been renovated, and nearly all have been well-tended. The area between Northeast 7th and 15th avenues, which tends to have slightly more modest homes, was once considered a bit dicey, and revitalization has occurred more slowly there; it is perhaps the only part of Irvington with a more than negligible stock of fixers. (The area is rumored to have been "redlined" by real estate agents for years.) Many of Irvington's larger homes were turned into boarding houses for shipyard workers during the Second World War; most houses reverted to owner-occupied status after the way, but west of 15th Avenue many homes remain divided into two or three apartments to this day. In addition, a few apartment buildings, including some lovely prewar walkup buildings but also some unattractive concrete structures, occupy a few blocks just north of Northeast Broadway.

The reasons for Irvington's popularity are obvious. It is a neighborhood of sidewalks, well-kept yards, and attractive homes, yet it is remarkably close to downtown Portland—parts of the neighborhood are scarcely more a mile away from the central business district. Much of the neighborhood is reasonable walking distance from the MAX stop at Lloyd Center or from the Rose Garden arena. Few major streets run through the core of Irvington, and those that do, like Knott (which also boasts some of the neighborhood's grandest homes) mainly carry neighborhood traffic, not commuters. These characteristics appeal to a wide range of buyers, from affluent empty nesters to families with young children, who like the good-to-excellent set of public schools that serve Irvington. (There is, however, only one park in the neighborhood.) The Irvington area has also become a popular choice for gay and lesbian couples in recent years.

Although most of Irvington proper is residential—a few high-end retailers on 15th Avenue and a smattering of B & Bs notwithstanding—the neighborhood is within walking distance of at least two shopping districts. Northeast Broadway, which forms Irvington's southern boundary, offers a dazzling range of shops, restaurants, bars, and services, ranging from independent bookseller Broadway Books to old-timey Helen Bernhard Bakery (since 1924, www.helenbernhard bakery.com). Although the Northeast Broadway strip is not as trendy as certain other shopping districts—we're looking at you, Pearl District—it has a fair number of hip nightspots, such as the modernistic Pour Wine Bar & Bistro and the Thatch Tiki Bar (which is exactly what it sounds like). The area just south of Broadway also includes the Lloyd Center mall and surrounding stores (see below).

Northeast Fremont Street forms Irvington's northern boundary. This area was somewhat derelict a decade ago, but today a small commercial district has sprung up at 15th and Fremont. Here you'll find a Wild Oats supermarket and a host of small shops and restaurants, such as County Cork Public House (www.

countycorkpublichouse.com) and, a few blocks to the east, the specialty nurs-ery Garden Fever. The neighborhood north of Fremont, **Sabin**, is culturally and geographically a transition zone between Irvington and the funkier precincts of the Alberta Arts District. Homes in Sabin tend to be more modest than those in Irvington, with a higher concentration of bungalows, foursquares, and cottages, but average prices are not dramatically lower. "Upper" Sabin, the area where the Alameda Ridge begins to rise, is dominated by the city's enormous Vernon wa-ter tank; nonetheless, some homes in the tank neighborhood have good views of downtown Portland, and the area surrounding the tank is scheduled to be turned into a "hydropark." Sabin attracts some young families—Sabin School, the local elementary, is well-regarded—as well as straight and gay couples and some singles.

The **Lloyd District** is sort of an auxiliary downtown on the east bank, tucked between Northeast Broadway and Interstate 84. The center of the neighborhood is Lloyd Center, the city's oldest mall, which shelters the usual range of middle-brow stores. New mid-rise office buildings and hotels dominate the area to the west of the mall. Many of these hotels cater to attendees of events at the nearby Oregon Convention Center; the Rose Garden arena (home court for the NBA's Trail Blazers) and Memorial Coliseum are in the western portion of the Lloyd District, known as the Rose Quarter. Apart from a few condos and apartments and the odd stranded house, the Lloyd District does not offer many residential options.

To the east of Lloyd Center, the colorfully named **Sullivan's Gulch** neigh-borhood is squeezed between Northeast Broadway and the bluff overlooking Interstate 84 and the adjacent train tracks. (Interstate 84 was built in the actual gulch during the 1950s.) The neighborhood has a mix of old and new apartment buildings and a few old bungalows and other single-family homes; many of the apartments stand on the edge of the gulch with the freeway and train tracks essentially in the backyard. The buildings a bit further north tend to be quieter, and offer quick access to the shops and services along Broadway. Most residents here are renters.

The southern half of this swath of Northeast Portland is extremely well con-nected to the rest of the city, both by road and by transit. The Eastside MAX line runs through the Lloyd District, and connects with the Interstate MAX line at the Rose Quarter Transit Center. Bus lines run along Northeast Broadway, Fre-mont, 15th Avenue, and 24th Avenue. The Lloyd District is within TriMet's Fareless Square, so trips downtown by bus or light rail are free. A streetcar line along Northeast Broadway has also been proposed, although competing priorities may doom or delay the project. Access to downtown Portland by road is five to ten minutes via the Broadway Bridge or the Steel Bridge. These neighborhoods also have easy access to Interstate 5 and Interstate 84.

ALAMEDA, GRANT PARK, AND HOLLYWOOD

Neighborhood Associations: Alameda, Grant Park, Hollywood

Between 18,000 and 12,000 years ago, glacial Lake Missoula (in present-day Montana) formed behind a tongue of the ice sheet that covered much of the inland Northwest. The lake periodically broke through the ice dam, unleashing massive floods, each of which carried the volume of about 60 Amazon Rivers. These floods repeatedly scoured the Columbia Basin and flowed downstream to the sea past the site of Portland, carrying and depositing massive amounts of debris. (Eddies of the Missoula Floods reached all the way up the Willamette Valley, burying much of the land in hundreds of feet of silt.) One of the many effects of these floods was to create the rock-filled escarpment that is now known as Alameda Ridge.

The ridge begins to rise in the Sabin neighborhood, and the crest runs east, just north of Fremont Street, eventually turning southeast to cross Fremont; it finally peters out in the Rose City Park neighborhood. The ridge's southern slope is fairly steep—most streets wind up the ridge rather than tackling the grade head-on—while the more gentle northern slope descends gradually toward the Columbia River. The highest section of ridge, west of Northeast 33rd Avenue, is the heart of the **Alameda** neighborhood. The neighborhood features a mix of older houses—bungalows, English Tudors, colonial revival, and stucco-sided, tile-roofed mission revival homes—on tree-lined streets with sidewalks. The houses on the ridge itself or high up on the southern slopes tend to be grand, category-busting homes (what do you call an enormous arts-and-crafts home with half-timbered details and stucco siding?), often with rich architectural detailing, and most offer tremendous views over the city to the south and west; on the rare occasions these homes go on the market, they usually sell for well over a million dollars.

Off the ridge, most Alameda houses are more standard (if not necessarily modest) and less expensive, although they are by no means cheap. Some houses north of the ridge have views of Mount St. Helens. More than 90% of Alameda residents own their homes, and homes are generally well-maintained and yards well-tended. Moreover, Alameda was one of only ten Portland neighborhoods that experienced no reported violent crimes in 2006. The neighborhood is overwhelmingly residential, but most homes are within a reasonable walk of the shopping districts at Beaumont Village (further east on Fremont), or the Alberta Arts District, about a half-mile north of the ridge. While the area has many long-time and in many cases elderly residents, Alameda Elementary School, on Fremont Street, is one of the most sought-after grade schools in the city, and the area attracts young families who can afford to live here.

Adjacent **Grant Park,** at the southern foot of Alameda Ridge, is a similarly family-friendly neighborhood, also filled with bungalows, English Tudors, cottages, Dutch colonials, and the like (albeit generally smaller than those in Alameda).

The neighborhood takes its name from the large park at its center, which offers a playground, tennis courts, off-leash dog park, and picnic tables; thanks to the presence of Grant High School, there is also a quarter-mile running track, tennis courts, and a swimming pool. Children's author Beverly Cleary lived in the Grant Park neighborhood for much of her childhood, and several of her stories are set here. (Ramona "The Pest" Quimby lived on Klickitat Street.) Near the playground in Grant Park, a collection of bronze statues of several Cleary characters is set amid a children's play fountain (a popular gathering place for neighborhood families on hot summer days).

Grant Park has one of the highest concentrations of families on the Eastside, thanks not only to its quiet, walkable streets and the amenities of Grant Park, but also to the desirable cluster of schools that serve the neighborhood. Hollyrood Elementary, at the north end of the park, had the highest standardized test scores in the entire metropolitan area during the 2005–06 school year. Amid great controversy, however, Hollyrood is being merged with nearby Fernwood Middle School to create a new K–8 school. (Kids in grades K–2 will remain at Hollyrood for the 2007–08 school year.)

West of 33rd Avenue, the **Dolph Park** area, while nominally part of the Grant Park neighborhood, is essentially a transition zone between Irvington to the west and Grant Park proper to the east. Spiffy new street signs identify the neighborhood, although the term is not widely used or recognized outside (or necessarily inside) the Dolph Park area. Homes here are generally larger than those in Grant Park, but are in similar styles.

With the exception of a few small professional offices and the QFC supermarket on Northeast 33rd Avenue, Grant Park is primarily residential. The library, shops, and restaurants of nearby **Hollywood**, however, are a short walk away. Cinematic-sounding Hollywood was named after the Hollywood Theatre (www.hollywoodtheatre.org), a 1926 movie palace that still stands (and still screens films and hosts special events) on Northeast Sandy Boulevard, Hollywood's main drag. Sandy was once the haunt of streetwalkers; while that element has not entirely vanished from Hollywood, the street is rapidly improving here, and features a Trader Joe's market, several coffee shops, and various shops and small restaurants. The streets south of Sandy have an increasing number of retail stores and other businesses, too, and the Hollywood Farmers' Market (www.hollywoodfarmersmarket.org) is held in the Value Village parking lot on Saturday mornings from May through October.

A few businesses and other non-residential uses cluster within a block or so to the north of Sandy, including the new mixed-use Hollywood Library on Northeast Tillamook, which includes a Beverly Cleary–themed wall. Fleur de Lis Bakery, in the old library building at 40th and Hancock, is a favorite neighborhood gathering place. Otherwise, the blocks between Sandy Boulevard and the foot of Alameda Ridge are filled mainly with 1920s bungalows. The homes tucked under the brow of Alameda Ridge north of Sandy Boulevard can be dark during winter.

The neighborhoods of central Northeast Portland have generally good bus service along North Broadway, Fremont Street, 33rd Avenue, and Sandy Boulevard; eastbound and westbound MAX service is available from the Hollywood/Northeast 42nd Avenue Transit Center. By car, these neighborhoods are less than a 10-minute drive from downtown Portland, and the airport is only 15 to 20 minutes away.

BEAUMONT VILLAGE, WILSHIRE PARK, AND ROSE CITY PARK

Neighborhood Associations: Beaumont-Wilshire, Rose City Park

Although the name is often used for the surrounding neighborhood as well, **Beaumont Village** refers to the three-quarter-mile stretch of Northeast Fremont Street between 33rd and 50th avenues, on the plateau just north of Alameda Ridge. The street is lined with upscale (and a few downscale) boutiques, several restaurants, a brew pub, a hardware store, and Beaumont Market (www.beaumontmarket.com), a high-end but well-loved neighborhood grocery. While Beaumont Village lacks the high hipness quotient of some other eastside neighborhoods, it has variety enough to suit most non-hipster needs. (The area surrounding Beaumont Village has more families with young children than, say, the Alberta area, and neighborhood businesses in general tend to be less edgy and more family-friendly.) Traditional one-story storefronts mix with oddities like the so-called Swiss House—a Tudor-style half-timbered building from the 1920s—and dramatic architectural statements like the hulking rust-colored block of Fife (www.fiferestaurant.com), a restaurant known for its use of local and organic ingredients.

The walkable, tree-lined residential streets nearby boast a bumper crop of bungalows and English-style homes, along with some Cape Cods and ranches. The grandest homes in the neighborhood are concentrated along the section of Alameda Ridge that runs south of Fremont; many of these homes stand on curving streets and offer expansive southwest views. A few blocks to the north of Fremont, the **Wilshire Park** neighborhood surrounds the 14-acre park of the same name. Homes around Wilshire Park tend to be slightly more modest than those south of Fremont, with a higher concentration of ranches. Although recent real estate appreciation in the Beaumont-Wilshire neighborhood has not been as jaw-droppingly steep as in many other neighborhoods—the area has been a desirable one for a long time, so values were fairly high to begin with—the median home price as of early 2007 is well over $400,000.

To the east, the **Rose City Park** neighborhood is bungalow heaven (although other older house styles certainly exist). Until a few years ago, Rose City Park was full of long-term residents, the sort of deep-rooted neighborhood where most of the front steps are covered in Astroturf. Few people moved in, and few people moved out—except perhaps into the neighborhood's Rose City Cemetery—which may explain why the area is mysteriously off the radar screen for most Portlanders. The area is at last undergoing a change, however. A minor influx of Southeast Asians has helped diversify and energize the neighborhood. Prices have risen sharply, but not as sharply as in some other neighborhoods, and Rose City Park, while not cheap, is a relative bargain compared to the more sought-after neighborhoods a mile or two west. The Fremont Street commercial strip extends into Rose City Park; moreover, the once notoriously skanky section of Sandy Boulevard that bisects the neighborhood is being revitalized, and now features some decent restaurants and shops. Woodsy Normandale Park in the south part of the neighborhood has sports fields and a dog park. Homes in the southern part of the neighborhood endure noise from Interstate 84 and the adjacent railroad tracks.

While Beaumont-Wilshire and Rose City Park are farther (as the crow flies) from downtown Portland than some other Northeast neighborhoods, they're a relatively quick trip downtown by car—about 10 to 15 minutes on Broadway, Sandy, or (during non–rush hours) Interstate 84—or by bus. Beaumont Village is reasonably close to the Hollywood Transit Center light rail stop, and the 60th Avenue stop is on the southern border of Rose City Park. These neighborhoods are also a short journey from the airport, yet are out of the normal airport flight path and do not suffer from noise from low-flying planes.

THE ALBERTA ARTS DISTRICT AND CONCORDIA

Neighborhood Associations: Concordia, King, Vernon

Before a real estate agent with a flair for marketing coined the term "Alberta Arts District," there was simply Northeast Alberta Street, a minor east-west thoroughfare with some basic neighborhood shops and services and an abundance of boarded-up storefronts. The area experienced flare-ups of gang violence, which made the name of another neighborhood street, Killingsworth, a sort of grim joke. And then something happened. Through a mysterious and apparently uncoordinated process involving artists priced out of the Pearl District, couples (gay and straight) who saw potential in the neighborhood's inexpensive and often dilapidated old houses, entrepreneurs dealing in exotic niche goods, and other so-called urban pioneers, the neighborhoods north and south of Alberta became the Next Big Thing. In the last few years, the transformation—or gentrification, depending on your point of view—of the neighborhood has become largely complete, and Next-Big-Thing status has migrated westward to North Portland. Some edginess remains, and crime isn't exactly nonexistent, but to see how far the neighborhood has come you need only recall that this part of town couldn't even support a supermarket in the late 1990s. (There is now a popular New Seasons on Northeast 33rd, while the Alberta Cooperative Grocery, www.

albertagrocery.coop, is on Alberta proper. There is even a farmers' market at 15th and Alberta on Saturdays from May through September.)

This part of the city slopes gently northward from Alameda Ridge toward the Columbia River, and many residents opine that the area gets more light and has an airier feeling than neighborhoods like Hollywood that lie at the foot of the ridge's southern (steeper) slope. The modern heart of the neighborhood is the stretch of Northeast Alberta Street from Martin Luther King Jr. Boulevard east to 33rd Avenue. This newly christened "Alberta Arts District" (www.alberta-artsdistrict.com) is lined with funky and sometimes aggressively countercultural establishments—hair salons (and a dog salon), coffee houses, bars, restaurants, clothing and knick-knack boutiques, and a rain barrel store—mixed in with traditional businesses like Acme Glass. Most businesses are locally owned, although rising rents threaten the viability of some smaller merchants. There are also plenty of art galleries, although fewer than the "arts district" label would suggest; during the Last Thursday art walk, created in response to (or in mockery of) the Pearl's First Thursday and held on the last Thursday evening of each month, galleries and other businesses stay open late and the street becomes a freaky carnival of sorts. Last Thursday has become somewhat controversial, in part because it draws so many non-locals, who cause parking and traffic problems and who are not necessarily respectful of the neighborhood.

The blocks north and south of Alberta are filled with bungalows, foursquares, and homes in other early twentieth-century styles. Many of these houses have been lovingly restored, while others have been quickly remodeled and "flipped" for a quick profit as real estate prices in the neighborhood have continued to skyrocket. Still others are decidedly fixers. The neighborhood's transition started earlier in the zone south of Alberta Street (i.e., closer to the expensive homes on Alameda Ridge) than in the area to the north; the percentage of renovated homes is generally lower the further north you go, but don't expect a bargain even on a rundown house within walking distance of Alberta. Keep in mind, too, that gentrification has not brought an end to crime or to urban annoyances like graffiti, and spending half a million dollars for a bungalow does not guarantee that your neighbor won't be selling drugs out of his house.

The **Concordia** neighborhood, named for Concordia University, includes the eastern half of the Alberta district (which is not an official neighborhood), but also extends further north and east. The blocks beyond Alberta consist of quiet, generally well-kept single family houses, with a couple of exceptions: Killingsworth Street, which runs parallel to Alberta several blocks to the north, is undergoing a revitalization of its own, with new businesses opening on a regular basis; the intersection with 33rd Avenue is particularly hopping, thanks to the presence of the New Seasons market. Just to the north, McMenamins Kennedy School is an old elementary school that has been converted to a bar–hotel–movie theater complex; the clever remodel includes kid-height drinking fountains, blackboards in the guest rooms, and "Honors" and "Detention" bars. The tiled soaking pool, which is otherwise only open to overnight guests and paying members of the public, is available for neighborhood residents with picture ID to use for free. The mix of homes in Concordia is similar to the mix near Alberta, but with a few Cape Cods and ranches thrown in. Many of the old one-and-a-half-story bungalows have attic space that has been converted into office space, bedrooms, or luxurious (albeit low-headroom) master suites.

While the area around Alberta Street is definitely urban and relatively close-in, the city's grid layout means there is no direct route to downtown Portland, which lies due southwest of the neighborhood. Cars and buses alike either have to travel west to Interstate 5 or Martin Luther King Jr. Boulevard and head south, or travel down 33rd Avenue to Broadway or Interstate 84 and head west. (To put it in geometrical terms, to get to downtown Portland you have to travel down two sides of an isosceles triangle rather than along the hypotenuse.) As a result, travel times are longer than the relatively short distance would suggest: about 15 minutes by car, and at least 20 minutes by bus. Several bus routes serve the area, but many transit trips involve a transfer to light rail.

OTHER NORTHEAST NEIGHBORHOODS

Neighborhood Associations: Cully, East Columbia, Madison South, Roseway, Sunderland

The neighborhoods that lie in the triangle from the Portland Airport vicinity to Interstate 205 and south to Interstate 84 are often overlooked in home searches, although some homes here offer excellent value. **Sunderland** and **East Columbia**, near the airport, are mainly industrial, although East Columbia includes an enclave of single-family contemporary homes near the Columbia Edgewater Country Club. Sunderland is home to the city's recycling yard as well as to Dignity Village, a semi-permanent, self-governing tent camp for the city's homeless. The northern tip of Sunderland touches the Columbia River, where some houseboats are moored. The **Cully** neighborhood, however, has a substantial population—about 13,000 people—and is one of the most diverse areas of the city. The areas adjacent to the Rose City Park and Beaumont Village/Wilshire Park areas, north of Fremont and the Rose City Cemetery, offer some attractive small bungalows along with newer (but still small) ranch homes and some infill development. The northern part of the neighborhood is largely light industrial. This part of Cully sometimes suffers from airplane noise. Much of the neighborhood lacks sidewalks, and many of the streets are unpaved.

The **Roseway** neighborhood straddles a not very attractive, but slowly improving, section of Northeast Sandy Boulevard. The neighborhood has more than its share of "adult" shops on Sandy, but it also has some lovely bungalows, English-style cottages, Cape Cods, and ranches on quiet, walkable streets. Home prices here are a bit higher than in other outlying parts of Northeast Portland—the median price is about $300,000—but are substantially lower than in the more fashionable closer-in neighborhoods. Roseway has good bus service along

Sandy, Fremont, Prescott and 82nd, and the neighborhood is reasonably close to the airport and main Eastside MAX lines. The adjacent **Madison South** neighborhood has somewhat newer homes on average, although there are still plenty of prewar homes "with character" here. Homes on Rocky Butte, the hill abutting Interstate 205, tend to be custom-designed structures with excellent views toward downtown Portland, the Cascades, or less appealingly, over the airport; these homes are much pricier than homes closer to 82nd Avenue—some Rocky Butte homes are valued at more than a million dollars. Rocky Butte features a summit lookout and some popular hiking and rock climbing locations. Madison South is also home to the Grotto, a peaceful Catholic garden/retreat that is famed for its Christmas light show and musical performances. The small neighborhood of **Sumner** to the north has a few small cottages, but is dominated by light industrial facilities and various hotels, restaurants, and other uses associated with the nearby airport. Madison South and Sumner have excellent bus and MAX access.

Northeast Portland Neighborhood Information

Zip Codes: 97211, 97212, 97213, 97218, 97220, 97232,

Post Offices: Airport Mail Facility, 7460 NE Airport Way; Holladay Park Post Office, 815 NE Schuyler St; Piedmont Post Office, 630 NE Killingsworth St; Rose City Park Post Office, 2425 NE 50th Ave

Police Stations: Portland Police Bureau, Northeast Precinct, 449 N Emerson St, 503-823-5700 (non-emergency); East Precinct, 737 SE 106th Ave, 503-823-4800 (non-emergency)

Emergency Hospitals: Legacy Emanuel Hospital and Health Center, 2801 N Gantenbein Ave, 503-413-2200, www.legacyhealth.org; Providence Portland Medical Center, 4805 NE Glisan St, 503-215-1111, www.providence.org/Oregon/

Libraries: Albina Library, 3605 NE 15th Ave, 503-988-5362; Gregory Heights Library, 7921 NE Sandy Blvd, 503-988-5386; Hollywood Library, 4040 NE Tillamook St, 503-988-5391

Parks: Major parks include Irving Park, Grant Park, Wilshire Park, Normandale Park, and Rocky Butte; www.portlandparks.org

Community Publication: *Hollywood Star*, www.hollywoodstarnews.info

Public Transportation: TriMet, 503-238-RIDE, www.trimet.org; extensive bus network on main streets, especially in close-in neighborhoods; Eastside and Airport MAX lines serve southern and eastern neighborhoods.

SOUTHEAST PORTLAND

Southeast Portland is in many ways the epitome of the image some people conjure up when they think of Portland: funky cafés, second-hand boutiques, tree-lined streets lined with old houses, plenty of aging hippies and young greens, bike riders galore, and one of the most consistently liberal voting records of any neighborhood in the country. While the Legalize Pot and Free Mumia crowds are certainly a part of the neighborhood fabric, Southeast Portland is also the haunt of families, immigrants, students, professionals working for The Man, artisans, drug addicts, retirees, construction workers, and community and political activists of every stripe. Since not all of these types of people are usually found in the same place, it's safe to say that most people will feel at home somewhere in Southeast Portland—unless you're, like, too uptight, man.

INNER SOUTHEAST PORTLAND

Neighborhood Associations: Brooklyn, Buckman, Hosford-Abernathy, Kerns

The neighborhoods of inner Southeast Portland—the zone extending east of the Willamette River to roughly 28th Avenue—are a pastiche of tight-knit, generally laid-back urban environments where the neighborhood coffee shop is just around the block and there's always a new up-and-coming band at the bar down the street.

The blocks closest to the river make up the **Central Eastside Industrial District**, a district zoned for commercial, warehouse, and light industrial use. In many ways it is the city's workshop, with many "artisanal" industries—tile makers, lampwrights, specialty food companies, etc.—headquartered here, along with some less sexy but equally necessary businesses, like used office furniture stores. Some worthy bars and eateries appear among the warehouses; cheeky, popular Bistro Montage (www.montageportland.com) lurks, troll-like, under the Morrison Bridge approach ramps, while the Produce Row Café has a popular outdoor beer garden. A formerly sketchy stretch of East Burnside has garnered some trendy establishments, like the neo-mid-century Doug Fir Lounge (www.dougfirlounge.com) and celebrated restaurant Le Pigeon (www.lepigeon.com).

This area is also home to the Oregon Museum of Science and Industry (OMSI), which sits along the river almost underneath the clunky double deck of Interstate 5's Marquam Bridge. Unfortunately, Interstate 5 cuts off the rest of the Inner Eastside from its riverfront; the only river access between OMSI and the Steel Bridge is the Vera Katz Eastbank Esplanade. Opened in 2001, the Esplanade is a sometimes-fixed, sometimes- floating bike and pedestrian walkway that runs between the Hawthorne and Burnside bridges. Signs indicate where the main east-west streets would run (if they weren't on the other side of six lanes of roaring traffic).

The Industrial District is essentially an industrial reserve, intended to maintain space where high-wage businesses can start and grow close to the city center, and housing developments are not allowed. Still, a few old Victorian houses, many of them beautifully (and colorfully) restored, linger poignantly among the industrial facilities and warehouses. Ten blocks or so in from the river, apartment buildings and other residential buildings start to become more common.

In the Kerns and Buckman neighborhoods, to the north and south, respectively, of East Burnside Street, prewar walkup apartment buildings and duplexes mix with many old single-family homes, a crop of newer (i.e., 1960s-era) apartment complexes, and some seemingly randomly sited commercial establishments. The intersection of East Burnside and 28th Avenue draws visitors from around the city to its strip of businesses, including boutiques, wine bars, acclaimed restaurants like Ken's Artisan Pizza (www.kensartisan.com), cafés, and the second-run, multi-screen, deco-style Laurelhurst Theater. A smaller commercial zone at Glisan and 28th includes popular Cuban restaurant Pambiche (www.pambiche.com) and the funky Laurelthirst Public House. The Eastbank Portland Farmers' Market (www.portlandfarmersmarket.com) is held at Southeast Salmon Street and 20th Avenue on summer Thursday afternoons and evenings. The historic Lone Fir Cemetery, between Stark and Belmont streets, is the final resting place to many of Portland's early movers and shakers.

South of Hawthorne Boulevard, between 12th and 20th avenues, **Ladd's Addition** smashes the street grid of Southeast Portland with a series of diagonal streets and circles that slice the neighborhood into a group of circles, triangles, quadrilaterals, diamonds, and other shapes that would make any middle-school geometry teacher drool. The neighborhood has five rose gardens: a large one in the central circle, with four smaller, diamond-shaped gardens. Unfortunately, virtually no one from outside the neighborhood gets to see these gardens, because to the uninitiated they are impossible to find. On the plus side for residents, the confusing street layout ensures that few drivers try to take short cuts through the neighborhood (and those that do rarely attempt a second incursion). The story behind the neighborhood's unusual geometry is that the developer, William S. Ladd (who was posthumously responsible for Laurelhurst, Eastmoreland, and several other notable Portland neighborhoods), supposedly sought to emulate Pierre L'Enfant's design for Washington, D.C., on a small scale. Ladd's Addition was platted in 1891, but due to an economic downturn no homes were built until 1905.

The homes that were built in Ladd's range from petite bungalows to enormous Arts and Crafts homes, with a few postwar ranches and Cape Cods thrown into the mix. A few apartments crop up along the neighborhood's periphery. The neighborhood has become very expensive; its elm-shaded streets and grand old homes, combined with its location just over a mile from downtown Portland, make it one of the most-sought after places to live in Southeast Portland. Most residents are either retired or are high-income professionals, including professionals with children. (The neighborhood's Abernethy Elementary School has an innovative curriculum and is highly regarded.) While the heart of Ladd's Addition is residential (barring the Palio Dessert and Espresso house on Ladd Circle, at the very center of the neighborhood, if you can find it), the entire neighborhood is within walking distance of the shops, restaurants, and cafés on Hawthorne Boulevard and Division Street.

The gently rising area to the east of Ladd's Addition is known as **Colonial Heights**. The neighborhood's name does not refer to the houses themselves; while there are a few Dutch colonial houses in the neighborhood, the bulk of the housing stock is bungalows and other styles from the 1920s and 1930s, with a fair number of infill 1950s ranches mixed in. The neighborhood has a preponderance of churches, but is otherwise generally residential; as in Ladd's Addition, however, the shopping zones along Hawthorne Boulevard and Division Street are within a short walk of any point in the neighborhood. Colonial Heights does sit on a small hill, and some homes have peek-a-boo views of downtown Portland and the West Hills.

The **Clinton Street** neighborhood centers on the cluster of restaurants, bars, cafés, and the Clinton Street Theater (www.clintonsttheater.com) at Southeast 26th and Clinton, but the area popularly identified as Clinton Street reaches as far west as 12th Avenue. (Although Division Street is a main thoroughfare and carries substantially more traffic than Clinton Street, the prewar streetcars ran along Clinton, and locals continue to use the old name for the neighborhood.) The neighborhood housing stock consists mostly of small to mid-size bungalows with small but often lovingly landscaped yards, along with some 1960s apartment buildings and a smattering of warehouses and other commercial buildings, especially in the western end of the neighborhood. Many of the older homes have been renovated, while some haven't seen a paintbrush in decades, although the former are beginning to outnumber the latter. A few modern condos, townhomes, and commercial buildings have gone up in the neighborhood, and new businesses are opening up and down Clinton Street.

New businesses have cropped up on Division Street, too, most notably the New Seasons supermarket, which is credited with helping spark a neighborhood renaissance. The Seven Corners intersection at Division and 21st is sometimes called the Seven Corners Progressive Vortex because of its concentration of progressive businesses like the Red & Black Café (www.redandblackcafe.com). Just south on 21st, the venerable People's Food Co-op (www.peoples.coop) supplies the neighborhood with organic produce and bulk foods; the store also hosts one of the city's few year-round farmers' markets.

South of Powell Boulevard, historic **Brooklyn** began its existence in the nineteenth century as a working-class, largely Italian enclave centered on the neighborhood's extensive rail yards. The Italians are mostly gone, but the rail yards remain, and, between freight trains to the east and truck and commuter traffic on McLoughlin Boulevard to the west, this triangle-shaped neighborhood remains a transit hub. Brooklyn contains some warehouses and light industrial buildings, along with a few bars and restaurants and the Aladdin Theater, one of the best places in the city to see live music, on Milwaukie Avenue, but the bulk of the neighborhood is residential. Homes here range from grand Victorians and cute bungalows to a few postwar ranches. Despite the neighborhood's working-class roots, the houses for sale here don't boast working-class price tags: the average home price is more than $350,000. Many of the larger homes have been converted to multi-family use, and about two-thirds of Brooklyn residents are renters. The neighborhood is a demographic mixed bag, with a mingling of families, singles, childless couples, and long-time elderly residents of widely varying income levels.

All the Inner Southeast neighborhoods are within a five-minute drive or ten-minute bus trip or bike ride of downtown Portland. There is currently no non-bus transit service, although a planned light rail line to Milwaukie would pass through Brooklyn, and several Eastside streetcar lines have been proposed.

LAURELHURST

Neighborhood Association: Laurelhurst

The imposing sandstone arches that mark the main entrances to Laurelhurst suggest that the neighborhood is special—or "high-class," as the Laurelhurst Company promised in its circa 1910 promotional materials. From the beginning, Laurelhurst was intended to be a relatively exclusive district. The company, which purchased the property from William M. Ladd (son of William S. Ladd, whose estate was responsible for creating the Eastmoreland, Westmoreland, and eponymous Ladd's Addition neighborhoods in Southeast Portland), hired the Olmstead brothers to design the neighborhood's sinuous streets, and enforced a minimum home cost to keep the riff-raff out.

Nearly a century later, Laurelhurst is still one of the most sought-after (and thus expensive) neighborhoods on Portland's East Side. Prices here have risen dramatically in the last few years, and most family-size homes sell for a half-million dollars or more. Laurelhurst is entirely residential, and the overwhelming majority of homes are single-family detached houses built between 1910 and the Second World War. Architecture runs the gamut of pre-war styles, from foursquares to tile-roofed Spanish colonials, although bungalows of various sizes and configurations are the most common house types. Although many of these houses are quite grand, and some are bona fide mansions, lot sizes tend to be relatively small.

Demographically, the neighborhood is a mix of long-time residents and young families; many of the latter are attracted by the quality of the neighborhood's Laurelhurst Elementary School (www.laurelhurst.pps.k12.or.us). Another attraction is Laurelhurst Park, which is sometimes referred to as the Portland equivalent of New York's Central Park. That comparison overstates things, but the park is undoubtedly lovely, and features a spring-fed lake, mature trees, a playground, and tennis and basketball courts. (Like Central Park, however, Laurelhurst Park is not entirely safe at night, although the neighborhood itself has a relatively low crime rate.) Laurelhurst's other notable landmark, Coe Circle, at the intersection of Northeast Glisan Street and 39th Avenue, contains a gilded statue of Joan of Arc.

Laurelhurst's curving streets are generally quiet, but busy Burnside, Glisan, and Stark streets, and 39th Avenue all cut through or border the neighborhood, and Interstate 84 runs along the northern boundary. While these major thoroughfares bring traffic and noise concerns, they also ensure that the neighborhood is well-connected, with plenty of transit options. Several bus lines serve Laurelhurst, and the Hollywood/42nd Avenue MAX stop is a short walk away; downtown Portland is about a ten-minute drive down Burnside or on the freeway. There are no restaurants or other businesses within Laurelhurst proper, but most homes are within walking distance of at least one of the nearby business districts in Hollywood, the Belmont district, or along Northeast 28th Avenue.

THE HAWTHORNE AND BELMONT DISTRICTS

Neighborhood Associations: Richmond, Sunnyside

Hawthorne Boulevard was known as Asylum Avenue until the late 1880s. Although a few people still call it that, tongue-in-cheek, it is known today as the heart of the **Hawthorne District**, a strip of restaurants, bars, cafés, and many kinds of shops that stretches for nearly 30 blocks from the vicinity of Ladd's Addition toward the base of Mount Tabor. Sometimes described as Portland's "Bohemian" neighborhood, or the Portland equivalent of Haight-Ashbury, Hawthorne has nonetheless lost much of its countercultural vibe in recent years (and, for that matter, the neighborhood has few immigrants from the Czech region of Bohemia). Yes, there are head shops and Grateful Dead–themed pubs along Hawthorne, but they are overwhelmingly outnumbered by a diverse host of other businesses.

There are far too many interesting establishments along Hawthorne to flag just one or two examples, but the heart of the business district is at 37th and Hawthorne, a spot that used to be called karma corner because you would inevitably run into old acquaintances (or boy- or girlfriends) there. This is still a danger, thanks to attractions like the Bagdad Theater and Pub on the southeast corner, or the Powell's Books branch on the north side of the street, which pull visitors from all over the city. The business district continues east of 39th Avenue as far as 50th Avenue, although development is less dense here. The trendy bars at the upper end of Hawthorne are popular destinations for pub crawls.

Paralleling Hawthorne six blocks to the north, **Belmont Street** has a similar, but smaller, selection of businesses. The Belmont Dairy mixed-use complex houses apartments, townhomes, and an upscale Zupan's supermarket; to either side and across the street are restaurants, coffeehouses, an old movie theater-*cum*-video arcade (the Avalon), antique stores, and boutiques. The Theater! Theatre! space hosts live dramatic (and otherwise) presentations. A Walgreen's on the corner of Belmont and 39th does a brisk late-night trade. The Belmont business district continues east of 39th in an intermittent, desultory way; highlights include Movie Madness (possibly the best video rental store in the Northwest, www.moviemadnessvideo.com) and the British-style Horse Brass Pub (www.horsebrass.com).

The residential neighborhoods that flank Hawthorne and Belmont house a mix of twenty-something singles, original hippies and their latter-day wannabes, skate punks, professionals, blue-collar workers, and both bona fide and aspiring indie pop stars. Some families with children live in the area, particularly east of 39th Avenue. The neighborhood south of Hawthorne, officially known as Richmond, has a higher proportion of homeowners than the blocks north of Hawthorne (officially known as Sunnyside), but single-family and multi-family dwellings are found throughout the area.

Most homes in the Hawthorne and Belmont areas are bungalows, foursquares, or other prewar types, although some new townhomes and tall, skinny detached homes on narrow lots are being built as infill or as replacements for dilapidated older homes. The old streetcar line down Belmont, opened in the 1880s, was first the line on the Eastside and the blocks have a higher concentration of Victorians than most other parts of the city. (The Pied Cow coffeehouse on Belmont occupies one of these.) There are also plenty of 1920s garden apartments and brick walkups, along with hulking 1960s-era low-rise apartment complexes and some spanking new condos like the strikingly modern (and controversial) Belmont Street Lofts.

Thanks to the close-in location and the abundant local shopping and dining opportunities, the median price for a single-family home in this area is creeping toward the $400,000 mark. Homes tend to be a bit more expensive east of 39th Avenue, where there are fewer apartments. These streets also offer other varieties of old houses, including English Tudor-style cottages, Cape Cods, and even a few ranches. (Peacock Lane, which parallels 39th Avenue one block to the east just north of Belmont, is a street of 1920s-vintage English cottages known for its annual holiday light display.) Homes are generally less expensive south of Division Street, in an area that has not improved as rapidly as have the streets closer to Hawthorne Boulevard. The Waverly Heights neighborhood, west of 39th Avenue, is a good bet for more affordable older homes.

Throughout the area, home conditions and neighborhood "feel" can vary tremendously from one block to another: Some blocks are lined with restored Craftsman bungalows with mature shade trees and laughing children on tricycles, while others have ramshackle houses with overgrown yards next to grim, windowless mystery buildings. Unless you are a fan of loud, late-night drunken conversations, you should try to live at least a block or two from the main commercial zones. Also be aware that on-street parking can be in short supply near Hawthorne and Belmont. Many of the old houses in these neighborhoods maximize their small lot sizes by sharing a single driveway between two neighboring homes; often each house will have its own small garage at the rear of the lot.

The Hawthorne and Belmont districts enjoy frequent bus service down Hawthorne, Belmont, Division, and Powell to downtown Portland, and north along

39th Avenue to the Hollywood MAX stop. It is a quick bike ride down designated low-traffic "bike boulevards" to downtown Portland, and these neighborhoods have probably the city's highest percentage of bike commuters. If you must drive, it's a ten-minute shot west over the Hawthorne or Morrison bridges into downtown Portland.

MOUNT TABOR

Neighborhood Association: Mount Tabor

Mount Tabor, the tree-clad butte that dominates the landscape about three miles due east of downtown Portland, is home to one of the city's most diverse and popular parks. The park includes playgrounds, picnic areas, hiking trails, tennis courts, an off-leash dog park, and, famously, an extinct volcano. The park also has three open-air (but fenced-off) reservoirs, built in the late nineteenth and early twentieth centuries. (The city's effort to cap the reservoirs for security reasons after the September 11 attacks met with a firestorm of opposition, and the reservoirs will remain uncovered for now.) Mount Tabor offers fantastic, tree-framed views of Mount Hood, Mount St. Helens, and downtown Portland, too; the lawn on the west slope, just below the summit, is a favorite spot to watch the sun set over downtown and the West Hills, as the lights of Hawthorne Boulevard begin to twinkle on.

Forest (and later, fruit orchards) covered Mount Tabor and the surrounding area until the late nineteenth century, when the streetcar line up Belmont reached the neighborhood and significant residential development began. The western part of the neighborhood, especially the area between Hawthorne Boulevard and Stark Street just downhill from the park, contains some truly grand houses in a mix of styles ranging from Italianate and Queen Anne Victorian to Arts and Crafts and Colonial Revival. Many of these homes have views of the downtown skyline, and some have large yards with massive specimen trees— giant sequoias, monkey-puzzle trees, or European beeches, for example—that are now well over a century old. Interspersed with these elegant near-mansions are a host of more modest bungalows, foursquares, Dutch colonials, and English cottages; the first two styles are especially prevalent on the blocks south of Hawthorne, which are similar to the residential areas of the Hawthorne District proper and generally feature a younger mix of residents. The north side of Mount Tabor, which was developed much later, includes a large number of mid-century ranches, many with views north to Mount St. Helens. The slightly less fashionable blocks to the east and northeast of the park have a mix of prewar and mid-century homes, many of which have been restored in recent years, and some of which have views of Mount Hood and Interstate 205 (which, from a distance of about a mile, is actually not a bad prospect).

Warner Pacific College, a Christian liberal arts college, has a campus on Southeast Division Street, adjacent to the south end of the park. (A proposed college expansion onto city-owned land generated heated neighborhood opposition, and appears to be dead.) Apart from a few isolated businesses, there are essentially no commercial areas within the Mount Tabor neighborhood, but most homes are within walking distance of a shopping district: the Hawthorne and Belmont districts on the west side, the burgeoning commercial district along Southeast Stark Street in Montavilla on the east side, and, from the north side, the QFC supermarket on Burnside Street and the Fred Meyer on Northeast Glisan Street, along with some smaller associated businesses.

It's a 10- to 15-minute drive or 20- to 25-minute bike ride from Mount Tabor west to downtown Portland. Buses run east-west along Burnside, Belmont, and Division streets, and north-south along Southeast 60th Avenue; the northern part of the neighborhood is within walking distance of the MAX stop at Northeast 60th.

SELLWOOD, WOODSTOCK, & THE MORELANDS

Neighborhood Associations: Eastmoreland, Sellwood-Moreland, Woodstock

Eastmoreland lies south of (but technically includes) the classic campus of Reed College, with its old brick buildings and lawns filled with frisbee-throwing undergraduates. The neighborhood is worthy of its setting, with many truly grand homes on wide, tree-lined, curving streets that desultorily defy the city's grid. (Eastmoreland, like several other classic Eastside neighborhoods, was developed by the Ladd Estate Company, which seemed to disregard the grid almost as a point of pride.) Most of the homes predate the Second World War, although unlike other Southeast Portland neighborhoods, Eastmoreland has a dearth of bungalows: the area developed after the bungalow style had become passé. Instead, one finds an abundance of generally large, well-maintained Tudor, colonial revival, stone manors and other traditional styles, and also some nicely designed mid-century homes, mostly on corner lots that had remained vacant during the war.

Eastmoreland residents are generally affluent—most homes are well over $400,000, and some cost upwards of a million dollars—but are otherwise a mix of tenured professors, mid-career professionals, retirees, and young families. In addition to the lush grounds of many homes in the neighborhood, Eastmoreland offers the small, central Berkeley Park, the Crystal Springs Rhododendron Garden, the grounds of Reed College (including a small, surprisingly wild canyon), and the Eastmoreland Golf Course. There are no businesses within Eastmoreland, but the neighborhood is a relatively short walk or drive from either Woodstock or Westmoreland (see below). An unusual feature of the neighborhood is the Reed College nuclear reactor. The reactor produces very little heat, so despite the terrifying prospect of liberal arts students operating a nuclear reactor, a China Syndrome–style (or Modern Chinese Studies Syndrome–style) meltdown is not really a concern. A single bus line to downtown Portland serves the heart of Eastmoreland, although additional bus service is available on nearby streets.

Across the tracks, **Westmoreland** was another Ladd development that, amazingly, is laid out according to the city grid. Milwaukie Avenue (which, although a named thoroughfare, runs north-south) is the neighborhood's main drag, with restaurants, shops, banks, a hardware store, the 1920s-vintage Moreland Theatre, and other establishments that give the neighborhood a small-town feel. The densest concentration of businesses is at the intersection of Milwaukie and Bybee Boulevard, which features (among other worthy establishments) Caprial's Bistro, a familiar location for many public television viewers. The Moreland Farmers' Market (www.morelandfarmersmarket.com) takes place a block to the west on Wednesday afternoons from mid-May through September. On either side of Milwaukie, quiet, shady side streets are lined with Old Portlands, bungalows, Victorians, and other older homes, with the odd 1950s ranch for the sake of variety.

While it is connected both physically and in most Portlanders' minds to Westmoreland, Sellwood predates its neighbor to the north. The area was an independent city and early rival of Portland before it was annexed in 1893, and it has tried for more than a century to maintain its identity. Bustling commercial districts line Southeast Tacoma Street and 13th and 17th avenues, and most establishments are locally owned. Sellwood's best-known shopping experience is Antique Row, the parade of antique stores and malls along 13th Avenue, but the area offers everything from bakeries and children's clothing stores to paint stores and drive-through fast-food joints. Looking Glass Books (www.lookingglasbooks.com) recently relocated here from downtown Portland; look for the red caboose on 13th Avenue. New Seasons on Tacoma is the favorite local supermarket.

Sellwood, like Westmoreland, is filled with attractive Victorians, bungalows, and Old Portlands, along with some small-scale apartments. Homes at the top of the bluff offer views north to downtown Portland. A condo complex overlooks the Willamette River near the Sellwood Bridge; a community of houseboats provides an even more water-oriented living option. Just south of Sellwood, the small enclave of Garthwick lies within Clackamas County but is technically part of the city of Portland. This neighborhood is adjacent to Waverly Country Club and is full of formal, traditional-style homes. Apart from the wealthy anomaly of Garthwick, homes in Westmoreland and Sellwood have steadily increased in price for several years, and while the median home price is less than $350,000, you would be increasingly hard-pressed to find a family-sized home in decent condition for under $400,000.

Sellwood and Westmoreland are home to all sorts of people—young professional couples, singles, retirees, blue-collar workers, and 1960s dropouts—but both are becoming known as great family neighborhoods, with plenty of events like the Moreland Monster March around Halloween. The area has some excellent parks, such as Oaks Bottom Wildlife Refuge, a prime birdwatching spot along the Willamette River, and Westmoreland Park, which includes an artificial casting pond. The Springwater Corridor, a long-distance bike and pedestrian path, runs from OMSI south to Sellwood, loops around the neighborhood, then follows an old rail line to Boring in Clackamas County. Other family-friendly neighborhood features include the Sellwood-Moreland Library, which is walking distance from both Sellwood and Westmoreland, and century-old Oaks Amusement Park (www.oakspark.com), near the west end of the Sellwood Bridge.

Speaking of the Sellwood Bridge, the rickety, two-lane span is the weak link in the local transportation infrastructure; everyone acknowledges that it needs replacement, but there has not been agreement on the design, cost, or placement of the new bridge. Meanwhile, hold your breath while crossing. Other road connections north to downtown Portland or south to Clackamas County are reasonably efficient, but because railroad tracks and the high-speed thoroughfare of McLoughlin Boulevard cut off Westmoreland and Sellwood from the rest of the city, alternate routes are not plentiful. Bus service north to downtown Portland or south to the Milwaukie Transit Service is decent, although buses do not cross the weight-limited Sellwood Bridge. A planned light rail line to Milwaukie would run through (or along the edge of) the neighborhoods.

A mile or two to the northeast, across 39th Avenue, just east of Eastmoreland—you could call it the land more east of Eastmoreland, in semi-palindromic fashion, but you would probably be the only one who called it that—lies increasingly popular **Woodstock**. The neighborhood's "downtown" is an unpretentious old commercial strip along Southeast Woodstock Boulevard that contains about every kind of business you're liable to need on a daily basis: a gourmet coffee house, a hardware store, a supermarket, a pub, a wine store, and several restaurants, such as the popular Otto's Sausage Kitchen (www.ottossausagekitchen.com). The streets nearby are lined with the kinds of homes that make Southeast Portland a popular place to live, such as bungalows and cute cottages, but they are generally smaller and much less expensive here than in trendier neighborhoods; the median home price in Woodstock is less than $250,000. The outer edges of the neighborhood include many ranch-style homes. The Woodstock Festival and Parade brings the whole neighborhood out each July. Bus service on the major streets is adequate; it's about a half-hour ride to downtown Portland. By car, it takes about 15 to 20 minutes.

OTHER SOUTHEAST PORTLAND NEIGHBORHOODS

Neighborhood Associations: Brentwood-Darlington, Center, Creston-Kenilworth, Foster-Powell, Montavilla, Mount Scott, Reed, South Tabor

East of an imaginary line that follows 50th Avenue (with a large eastward bend around Mount Tabor), the neighborhoods of Southeast Portland become less fashionable. This fact also means they become less expensive. Some people who make it their business to claim to know such things predict that the Southeast neighborhoods just inside of 82nd Avenue are destined to become the city's next hotspot. The process has already started in some neighborhoods, so you might want to get in while the getting's good. At the same time, parts of Southeast Portland are not for everyone. Some areas have a high crime rate, and 82nd Avenue has a long way to go before it overcomes its totally justified reputation as an enormous seedy strip mall. (Even 82nd, however, is beginning to improve, as an influx of Asian businesses, including the enormous Fubonn Mall, www. fubonn.com, start to replace the "lingerie modeling" shacks and windowless taverns.)

The **Center** neighborhood, north of Mount Tabor, fancies itself an eastern extension of Laurelhurst. While that perception is not strictly true (and certainly Laurelhurst residents don't see it that way), the neighborhood contains some attractive bungalows that would not be totally out-of-place in its western neighbor. Both Burnside and Glisan streets have supermarkets and other businesses, and a small business node at 60th and Glisan has a few popular bars. Apartment buildings are scattered throughout the neighborhood, with a high concentration in the northwestern part, around Providence Portland Hospital. This area also has American Dream Pizza, home of the hand-twisted crust (when they're not too busy). The southeastern part of the neighborhood is within walking distance of Mount Tabor Park, and the 60th Avenue MAX stop offers a quick trip downtown or to the airport. While not literally the center of anything, the neighborhood has easy access to major highways and transit.

To the east, the large **Montavilla** neighborhood (a contraction of "Mount Tabor Villa") contains both quiet neighborhoods of modest, well-kept single-family houses and giant apartment complexes. Montavilla is one of the city's least expensive neighborhoods—the median home price in 2006 was just over $200,000—but it also has a rapidly gentrifying commercial district along Stark Street east of Mount Tabor. New businesses like the Bipartisan Café, spruced-up old businesses like the restored Academy Theater (www.academytheaterpdx. com), and a farmers' market held on Sundays from late July through September (www.montavillamarket.org) have helped bring new investment to the area. **South Tabor** is a small neighborhood that indeed lies just south of Mount Tabor. Most homes here are relatively modest, and the neighborhood is substantially less expensive than the Hawthorne-area neighborhoods just to the west. Clinton Park, in the western part of the neighborhood, contains various sports fields and is a popular gathering place on summer evenings.

The **Creston-Kenilworth** neighborhood, south of Powell Boulevard, is relatively close to the Division Street and Hawthorne Boulevard shopping districts, but is far enough south of them to be overlooked in home searches. The neighborhood is named for two city parks in the area; wooded Creston Park has an outdoor pool. The neighborhood is a mix of older homes, similar to that in the Hawthorne District, but with more apartment houses (and more homes in obvious need of maintenance). Some streets are lined with beautifully restored classic homes, while others could use many gallons of paint (and a lead remediation crew). The **Reed** neighborhoods, to the south of Holgate Boulevard and north of Reed College, are a mix of apartment complexes, some built in the 1960s, and small single-family homes (many rented by groups of students, wanna-be students, and others attracted by the proximity of Reed). While most of the neighborhood is residential, Southeast 39th Boulevard hosts a popular Trader Joe's and the neighboring produce store, Limbo. The Brooklyn rail yards border both Reed and Creston-Kenilworth to the west, and can cause sleepless nights for noise-sensitive people.

Foster-Powell is a triangular neighborhood between the major thoroughfares of Powell Boulevard and Foster Road. The neighborhood is home to both long-time residents and to recent immigrants with very different origins, as the business signs in Russian, Vietnamese, and Spanish attest. The **Mount Scott** neighborhood to the south centers on the tree island of Mount Scott Park, a shady park with a popular community center (which contains both a mini–roller rink and an awesome indoor pool complex, complete with an artificial "river"). The homes around the park are generally modest, but many have been fixed up nicely. (Note that not only is the Mount Scott neighborhood essentially flat, it is nowhere near Mount Scott itself. That prominent butte is in Clackamas County, near Clackamas Town Center.) Hard against the Clackamas County line, the Brentwood-Darlington neighborhood is one of the most affordable neighborhoods in the city, but has a relatively high rate of violent crime. Both the extreme western portion and extreme eastern portion of the neighborhood have access to the Springwater Trail Corridor, a multiuse bike path that runs from the Willamette River east to Gresham and Boring.

Bus service along the main east-west streets is good throughout these neighborhoods; the only north-south bus lines run along 82nd Avenue and 60th Avenue. The Montavilla and Center neighborhoods have direct access to light rail.

Southeast Portland Neighborhood Information

Zip Codes: 97202, 97206, 97213, 97214, 97215, 97232

Post Offices: Brooklyn Post Office, 1410 SE Powell Blvd; Creston Post Office, 5010 SE Foster Rd; East Portland Post Office, 1020 SE 7th Ave; Sellwood Post Office, 6723 SE 16th Ave

Police Station: Portland Police Bureau, Southeast Precinct, 4735 E Burnside St, 503-823-2143 (non-emergency)

Emergency Hospitals: Adventist Medical Center, 10123 SE Market St, 503-257-2500, www.adventistmedicalcenter.com; OHSU Hospital, 3181 SW Sam Jackson Park Rd, 503-494-8311, www.ohsu.org/health/clinics-and-services/; Providence Milwaukie Hospital, 10150 SE 32nd Ave, Milwaukie, 503-513-8300, www.providence.org/Oregon/; Providence Portland Medical Center, 4805 NE Glisan St, 503-215-1111, www.providence.org/Oregon/

Libraries: Belmont Library, 1038 SE 39th Ave, 503-988-5382; Holgate Library, 7905 SE Holgate Blvd, 503-988-5389; Sellwood-Moreland Library, 7860 SE 13th Ave,

503-988-5398; Woodstock Library, 6008 SE 49th Ave, 503-988-5399

Parks: Major parks include Mount Tabor Park, Laurelhurst Park, Westmoreland Park, Creston Park, Oaks Bottom Wildlife Refuge, Woodstock Park, and Crystal Springs Rhododendron Garden; www.portlandparks.org

Community Publications: *Southeast Examiner*, www.southeastexaminer.com; *The Bee*, www.thebeenews.com

Public Transportation: TriMet, 503-238-RIDE, www.trimet.org; comprehensive bus service, including frequent service routes, west of about 50th Avenue, with service in main routes east of 50th Avenue. Light rail stations are along Interstate 84 at the northern end of Southeast Portland.

NORTH PORTLAND

Boundaries: North: Columbia River; **West:** Willamette River; **South:** Willamette River; **East:** North Williams Avenue

Until relatively recently, Portland's "fifth quadrant"—the peninsula between the Willamette and Columbia rivers, where a wide deviation in the Willamette's course makes mincemeat of the city's Burnside-and-river-oriented directional system—was typically overlooked or avoided by outsiders and snobbish Portlanders alike. Crime rates in much of the area were sky-high, schools were perceived as appalling, and the urban fabric was in a general state of decay. While it's not exactly yuppie central—and most North Portlanders are fine with that—the district has undergone dramatic changes in the last five years. Buoyed in part by a new light rail line along Interstate Avenue, in part by increasingly unaffordable home prices in more traditionally fashionable parts of the city, and in part by urban renewal districts and investment incentives offered by the Portland Development Commission, North Portland has experienced the city's fastest real estate appreciation over the last few years. At the same time, many homes—and in some neighborhoods, entire blocks—await revitalization.

Of course, one person's revitalization is another person's gentrification, and not everyone in North Portland (or NoPo, as some young newcomers gratingly call it) welcomes the change. Rising housing prices have forced many long-time residents to move away, and many businesses are perceived as catering more to affluent newcomers and visitors from other parts of the city than to local needs. Moreover, many of the area's new residents are childless, and some of the area's public schools suffer from declining enrollments and a continuing need for improvement. Still, the influx of newcomers has also brought (or coincided with) some positive changes, like a declining crime rate. In sum, North Portland might be a great choice for people who are looking for relatively inexpensive housing in a transitioning or newly "hot" neighborhood, and who are willing to live with some grittiness in exchange.

BOISE-ELIOT, THE NORTH MISSISSIPPI DISTRICT, AND OVERLOOK

Neighborhood Associations: Boise, Eliot, Overlook

The **Boise** and **Eliot** neighborhoods, just east of Interstate 5 and the Willamette River in close-in North Portland, have undergone perhaps the swiftest and most dramatic renaissance of any neighborhood in the city. Once part of the independent city of Albina, these neighborhoods were originally built as middle-class housing for northern European immigrants. After the Vanport flood of 1948, which wiped out a World War II–era public housing project near the Columbia River, many former Vanport residents, mostly African-Americans, were relocated to Albina. (At that time, housing covenants and discriminatory real estate practices effectively barred African-Americans from most other parts of the city.) The neighborhood was almost entirely African-American by the 1960s.

Interstate 5 was plowed through the heart of Albina, and the community began a long decline.

Beginning in the 1990s, a few people from other parts of the city recognized the untapped potential of the then-blighted, high-crime Boise and Eliot neighborhoods—a close-in location, a stock of classic old homes, and a commercial district (albeit one that was largely boarded up). Some started to buy and renovate homes and businesses. This influx has continued and accelerated, and today these neighborhoods are very much desegregated. Indeed, Boise-Eliot (as the two neighborhoods are collectively called) is probably the most diverse neighborhood in the state.

North Mississippi Avenue is ground zero in the revitalization/gentrification of North Portland. This bustling part of the street is just a few blocks long, running roughly from Fremont Street to Skidmore Street. In less than a decade, and really only in the last five years, the street has gathered an assortment of eateries (and beverageries) and a collection of shops that is, to put it mildly, eclectic: establishments include a lightbulb store (Sunlan, www.sunlanlighting.com), a small nursery (Pistils, www.pistilsnursery.com), and The Meadow (503-288-4633, www.themeadowflowers.com), which purveys chocolate, wine, flowers, and, most notably, gourmet finishing salt varieties from around the world. The Rebuilding Center (www.rebuildingcenter.org), a popular source of recycled building materials and fixtures, dominates the south end of the strip.

North Mississippi's trendiness has spilled over onto other nearby streets—North Williams Avenue now boasts a Pix Patisserie café (www.pixpatisserie.com) and the popular Fifth Quadrant pub, and a Grand Central Bakery sits on Fremont—but not every commercial building is hipster central. The area is still full of old fixtures, like the Wonder Bread outlet at the end of the North Kerby offramp from the Fremont Bridge, as well as a preponderance of mysterious purple buildings with cracked, weedy parking lots. The Boise-Eliot neighborhood housing stock is similarly diverse, and includes everything from foursquares, Craftsman bungalows, tiny cottages, and a few old Victorians to converted churches, mixed-use buildings, and brand-new modernist lofts. Not every house has been redone, and there are still plenty of long-time residents living in well-kept but dated homes (along with some dilapidated and dated homes), but the gentrification juggernaut has resulted in a wave of renovation and new construction in the area. Many residents, both old and new, have already cashed out and moved on. The new denizens of the North Mississippi Avenue district fall predominantly into the "youthful hipster" demographic. The area has so far failed to attract many new families, in part because some people consider the schools to be less desirable than those in some other parts of the city.

On the west side of Interstate 5, the **Overlook** neighborhood owes its name to its position atop Swan Island Bluff "overlooking" the port and the Willamette River. This area of gracious Craftsman bungalows, English Tudors, and some ranches and Cape Cods has become a hot real estate market since Adidas America opened its headquarters, Adidas Village, here in 2002. The opening of the Interstate MAX line, which runs through Overlook's eastern end, further primed the pump, and home prices in the neighborhood have nearly doubled in the last five years. Overlook Park, at the edge of the bluff, is a 12-acre greenspace with a great view of the river and port, the Fremont Bridge, downtown Portland, and the West Hills. The park is also the site of the Interstate Farmers' Market (www.interstatefarmersmarket.com) on Wednesdays from mid-May through September. The nearby Tudor-style Overlook House, built in 1927, today serves as a community center. The huge Swan Island industrial and port complex lies within Overlook's boundaries; most of the remainder of the neighborhood is residential, with commercial zones along Killingsworth Street and North Interstate Avenue. Some trendy new businesses have opened their doors, but older establishments, like The Palms Motel and the tiki-from-before-tiki-became-cool-again Alibi Restaurant, are still going strong.

The true bargains in Overlook are gone, but the neighborhood still has some affordable fixers. About two-thirds of residents own their homes, but a fair number of rental properties are usually available if you're interested in metaphorically dipping your toes in the neighborhood water. The neighborhood attracts a mix of young singles, straight, gay, and lesbian couples, and professionals who work at Adidas.

Both Overlook and the Boise-Eliot neighborhood are extremely well-connected to the area's highway and transit system. Downtown Portland is only a short light-rail ride away on the Interstate MAX line; although the line does not run through Boise-Eliot, it is accessible from that neighborhood by a short walk over Interstate 5 on the Failing Pedestrian Bridge (which, despite the ominous name, is actually quite sturdy). The neighborhoods are very close to the Fremont Bridge on- and off-ramps and to Interstate 5, as well as to alternate north-south routes like Vancouver Avenue and North Interstate Avenue. The downside to this easy highway access is high levels of pollutants from auto exhaust; some studies have shown that residents of neighborhoods within a quarter-mile or so of Interstate 5, especially east (downwind) of the freeway, have higher rates of respiratory disease than people who live farther away from major highways.

ST. JOHNS AND UNIVERSITY PARK

Neighborhood Associations: Cathedral Park, St. Johns, University Park

St. Johns, the old neighborhood out near the end of the North Portland peninsula, has been the next big thing for years. In the meantime, other next big things—the Northeast Alberta and North Mississippi neighborhoods, for example—have taken off, while St. Johns has languished. But St. Johns—named after James John, a settler whose morals were reputedly above reproach (or who was a crazy hermit, depending on what story you believe)—may yet have its turn as Portland's hot new neighborhood. The area was a separately incorporated city from 1903 until 1915, when Portland annexed it, and the bones of its historic center remain, including the old City Hall, now used as a police station. Given its relative proximity to downtown Portland (about 15 to 20 minutes away), its old-fashioned, low-key "downtown," its relatively affordable housing stock, and a distinctive icon in the form of the St. Johns Bridge (which, suspended between two Gothic-style towers, soars across the Willamette River here), it's hard to imagine that St. Johns can remain "undiscovered" indefinitely.

In fact, people here will tell you that St. Johns is not undiscovered; the current residents "discovered" it a long time ago. They will likely extol the community spirit of this traditionally working-class neighborhood and its locally owned businesses, and you may come away with the feeling that, if becoming the next "in" neighborhood means undergoing an influx of wisecracking hipsters, locals want none of it. Not that long-time residents may have a choice: Portents of change are already clearly visible in the main business district, which centers on North Lombard Street at Philadelphia Avenue. Established hangouts like Tulip Donuts, with its six-decade-old recipes—the baked goods are considerably fresher—rub facades with such new businesses as vegan-focused Proper Eats Market and Café (www.propereats.org), which opened a couple blocks away in 2006. Across the street, the St. Johns Historic Twin Cinema and Pub (www.stjohnscinema.com) shows first-run movies at discount prices; the McMenamins St. Johns Theater and Pub shows second-run movies at even cheaper prices. Mixed in with the seedy bars and old-time diners is a Starbucks, the ultimate harbinger of shifts in neighborhood demographics.

Despite the ubiquitous signs of evolution, the neighborhood is still a bit rough around the edges, and the crime rate remains relatively high. Away from the St. Johns downtown area, Lombard Street is largely a grim thoroughfare lined with check cashing establishments, smoky bars, fast food restaurants, convenience stores, and a few coffee shops. The neighborhood is virtually surrounded by industrial facilities: this part of the lower Willamette has been a manufacturing and maritime center for close to a century, and St. Johns really boomed during the shipbuilding frenzy of the Second World War. At the same time, a fair number of natural areas are within or close to the neighborhood: woodsy Pier Park is on the northern fringes, Smith and Bybee lakes (and the Columbia Slough, which connects them) form an important wetland, and Forest Park lies just across the St. Johns Bridge. From Kelley Point Park, at the very tip of the peninsula, you can ponder the confluence of the Willamette and Columbia Rivers.

In keeping with the neighborhood's working class roots, most houses are fairly modest structures; ranches, Cape Cods, and small cottages predominate, with a few old bungalows or Victorians thrown into the mix. The Cathedral Park neighborhood, named for the city park on the river under the cathedral-like eastern pier of the St. Johns Bridge, is technically a separate neighborhood but is functionally part of St. Johns. The same cannot be said for **University Park**, a more genteel neighborhood that sits atop the bluff near the University of Portland. The neighborhood's name actually predates the current university—a Methodist institution called Portland University was established here in 1891, and the sale of neighborhood lots was intended to provide funds for the university's operation and endowment. Streets were platted and named after colleges and universities, famous educators, and various Methodist worthies. The promoters of the subdivision were overzealous in some respects, dubiously promising that the "proximity of a large student body has a tendency to elevate the tone of all things." In other respects, their claims were underwhelming: the formal prospectus contained the helpful factoid that "University Park is entirely free from malaria."

While University Park is still free of malaria, an economic panic caused the subdivision scheme to founder, and the university closed. In 1901, the abandoned university reopened as a Catholic institution, which it remains to this day, and with better economic times the area around the campus gradually developed. As in St. Johns, housing styles here are a mix of many styles: Cape Cods, bungalows, ranch houses, small cottages, and a few Victorians. The streets here run northeast-southwest and northwest-southeast, rather than north-south and east-west as in the rest of the city; this arrangement was supposed to ensure that houses catch the maximum amount of sunlight. Despite the proximity of the University of Portland, there are few apartments, and essentially no commercial district except for the relatively unappealing stretch of Lombard Street that forms the neighborhood's northern border. Columbia Park, on the neighborhood's eastern edge, is walking distance from most homes. Astor Elementary School, which serves University Park, is considered the best elementary school in North Portland, and one of the best in the city. The crime rate in University Park is lower than in other parts of North Portland.

Several TriMet bus lines serve St. Johns and University Park, but many trips involve long detours or transfers to the Yellow Line MAX, which does not serve the immediate area. The neighborhoods are a relatively short drive to downtown

Portland, and some residents commute to Washington County via the St. Johns Bridge and Germantown Road.

OUTER NORTH PORTLAND NEIGHBORHOODS

Neighborhood Associations: Arbor Lodge, Bridgeton, Hayden Island, Humboldt, Kenton, Piedmont, Portsmouth

The outer neighborhoods of North Portland are not as well known as close-in hotspots like North Mississippi, but many of them are changing just as rapidly. **Kenton** (www.historickenton.com), with its neighborhood pride kindled by a kitschy giant statue of Paul Bunyan, is poised to catch fire, at least figuratively. The Interstate MAX line brought new interest and new investment to the neighborhood, and many storefronts and houses are being spruced up. The neighborhood began as a company town for a meatpacking plant—cattle were once driven along North Denver Avenue—so most houses are not especially grand, but the area offers plenty of opportunity; some boosters predict Kenton will be "the next Mississippi." (That's a reference to the avenue, not the state.) Nearby **Arbor Lodge** is even closer in, and is correspondingly further along the renaissance trajectory, with MAX-driven development along North Interstate Avenue (including a giant new two-story Fred Meyer supermarket and a New Seasons natural foods supermarket). Further west, away from the MAX line, the working-class **Portsmouth** neighborhood includes New Columbia (www.newcolumbia.org), an 82-acre subsidized housing development that is a showcase of environmentally sustainable design (and which replaced a notoriously crime- and gang-ridden old-style housing project).

East of Interstate 5, the century-old foursquares and bungalows in the multicultural **Piedmont** and **Humboldt** neighborhoods are rapidly appreciating in value. These areas bask in the radiance of North Mississippi hipness (only a short walk or bike ride away), but are starting to develop some neighborhood cachet of their own. The neighborhood jewel is Peninsula Park, with a 95-year-old rose garden, a swimming pool, and a community center. North of the Columbia Slough, in the Delta Park area, most land is either commercial or parkland of some kind (if you define parkland broadly to include uses like golf courses, the Portland Meadows horse racing track, and Portland International Raceway). This area was the site of the community of Vanport, the largest public housing project in the United States, which was washed away in a devastating 1948 flood. Understandably, many people have since been reluctant to build here, but the **Bridgeton** neighborhood (www.bridgetonpdx.com) has housing right along the shore of the Columbia River, including some pricey new condominiums. Bridgeton also includes a large community of houseboats and live-aboard boats, a feature that **Hayden Island**—an actual island, in the Oregon portion of the Columbia River—shares. Hayden Island is best known as the site of the Jantzen Beach Center, a mall that attracts Washingtonians for tax-free shopping sprees, but east of Interstate 5 the island has a strong nautical character, with an abundance of docks and moorages, as well as some new, expensive condominiums, along Tomahawk Island Drive.

North Portland Neighborhood Information

Zip Codes: 97203, 97217, 97227

Post Offices: Kenton Post Office, 2130 N Kilpatrick St; St. Johns Post Office, 8420 N Ivanhoe St

Police Stations: Portland Police Bureau, North Precinct, 7214 N Philadelphia St, 503-823-2120 (non-emergency); Northeast Precinct (neighborhoods east of I-5), 449 N Emerson St, 503-823-5700 (non-emergency)

Emergency Hospital: Legacy Emanuel Hospital and Health Center, 2801 N Gantenbein Ave, 503-413-2200, www.legacyhealth.org

Libraries: North Portland Library, 512 N Killingsworth St, 503-988-5394; St. Johns Library, 7510 N Charleston Ave, 503-988-5397

Parks: Major parks include Pier Park, Cathedral Park, Columbia Park, Peninsula Park, and Overlook Park; www.portlandparks.org

Community Publications: *St. Johns Sentinel* (www.stjohnsentinel.com), *St. Johns Review*

Public Transportation: TriMet, 503-238-RIDE, www.trimet.org; bus service along major thoroughfares, and MAX service along Interstate Avenue line to downtown Portland

OUTER EAST PORTLAND

Neighborhood Associations: Argay, Centennial, Glenfair, Hazelwood, Lents, Mill Park, Parkrose, Parkrose Heights, Pleasant Valley, Powellhurst-Gilbert, Wilkes, Woodland Park, plus Maywood Park (independently incorporated)

Outer East Portland, or even just East Portland, is not an official designation. Still, the vast swath of the Portland grid that lies east of 82nd Avenue and especially east of Interstate 205 is palpably different from the rest of the city. It has its own school districts, its own neighborhood centers, its own concerns, and very different demographics. It is generally more socially and politically conservative than other parts of Portland. It offers some of the lowest housing prices in the city; at the same time, some neighborhoods have some of Portland's highest crime rates, while others are fairly peaceful, essentially suburban enclaves.

These neighborhoods were mostly rural until well into the twentieth century; after the Second World War, they slowly filled up with middle-class homes, usually on large lots. Even after the area was mostly built-up it remained unincorporated. Bit by bit, Portland has gradually annexed much of what used to be known as Mid-County (and Gresham annexed the rest from the opposite direction), but many residents feel neglected by the city. They point to the city's investment in places like the Pearl District and South Waterfront, and contrast those areas with the unpaved streets of their own neighborhoods.

Despite the area's underdeveloped infrastructure, much of the area is experiencing heavy infill development, in some cases on "flag lots"—lots behind an existing residence that are linked to the street by a skinny "panhandle" (or flagpole) of property, which usually has a driveway. In some areas, especially near the Eastside MAX line, large apartment buildings and some mixed-use developments are rising. This tide of development is dramatically changing the character and the face of East Portland. The human faces of East Portland are changing, too. Many neighborhoods have experienced an influx of recent immigrants from East Asia, Russia and the Ukraine, and Latin America.

The neighborhoods north of Halsey Street tend to feature ranch homes, split levels, contemporaries, and other standard postwar styles. Some neighborhoods, like **Argay** and **Wilkes**, have the sort of curving streets and culs-de-sac that are common in suburban communities but are rare on the Eastside. **Parkrose** and slightly more affluent **Parkrose Heights** and **Woodland Park** have some older homes—Cape Cods, bungalows, English-style cottages, and the like—in the mix. Some of the neighborhoods closest to the airport are plagued by aircraft noise. If the sound of jet engines bothers you, be sure to consult a map of flight paths (or just stand around outdoors and listen for airplanes) before committing to a house here. (On the plus side, Parkrose has a station on the Airport MAX line.)

Tucked in between Parkrose and Interstate 205, tiny **Maywood Park**, with only 750 residents, is an independent city. Completely surrounded by (and functionally a part of) Northeast Portland, Maywood Park was incorporated in 1967 in an ultimately futile attempt to prevent Interstate 205 from being routed through the community. Most of the homes date to the late 1930s, and two-story cottages predominate. The neighborhood has an unusual abundance of mature trees, and although there are few sidewalks the streets are wide and traffic is light. Potential annexation to Portland is a perennial political issue here.

The neighborhoods south of Halsey are generally, if unfairly, considered less desirable. The central neighborhoods—**Hazelwood**, **Glenfair**, **Centennial**, and **Mill Park**—have some of the city's highest rates of violent crime. They are by no means no-go areas, however, and random violence is uncommon. Many blocks are quiet, respectable streets lined with ordinary-looking houses. These neighborhoods also offer access to the Eastside MAX line between Portland and Gresham, and several transit-oriented developments have sprung up along Burnside Street (along which the light rail trains run). Further south, **Powellhurst-Gilbert** also has above-average crime rates, but is nonetheless experiencing plenty of development, both infill and subdivisions of undeveloped land. This neighborhood, along with Hazelwood, Glenfair, Centennial, and Lents (see below), has the lowest home prices in the city, averaging just over $200,000.

The **Lents** neighborhood was once notorious for poverty and high crime rates. While the neighborhood is not exactly thriving, it has been designated an urban renewal zone. More importantly, a new MAX line from Gateway Transit Center south to Clackamas Town Center (scheduled to open in 2009) will pass through Lents, and investment in the area is rising in anticipation of a real estate boom like the one that North Portland experienced when the Interstate MAX line opened. In a hopeful sign, Lents has a new "international" farmers market (Sundays, June through mid-October).

In Portland's southeasternmost corner, the **Pleasant Valley** neighborhood wraps around the base of Powell Butte, a prominent volcanic butte now protected as a nature park. Much of the neighborhood feels surprisingly rural, with horses grazing in pastures in some areas. This area also offers new homes in several developments. In addition to Powell Butte, the neighborhood is home to several other parks and natural areas, including Leach Botanical Garden (www. leachgarden.org). The Springwater Corridor, a bike and pedestrian trail that runs between downtown Portland and east Multnomah County, passes through both Lents and Pleasant Valley.

The existing and soon-to-be-existing MAX lines are significant boons to this area. Bus transit is only available on the main east-west streets, with the exception of a north-south line along busy 122nd Avenue. Several different school districts serve the area: rapidly growing David Douglas School District (www. ddouglas.k12.or.us) serves the largest portion of outer Southeast, while Parkrose School District (www.parkrose.k12.or.us) covers Parkrose and the adjacent neighborhoods, Reynolds School District (www.reynolds.k12.or.us) serves part of outer Northeast Portland, and Centennial and the surrounding neighborhoods are part of Centennial School District (www.centennial.k12.or.us).

Outer East Portland Neighborhood Information

Zip Codes: 97216, 97220, 97230, 97233, 97236, 97266

Post Offices: Lents Post Office, 3850 SE 82nd Ave; Midway Postal Store, 400 SE 103rd Ave; Parkrose Post Office, 4048 NE 122nd Ave

Police Station: Portland Police Bureau, East Precinct, 737 SE 106th Ave, 503-823-4800 (non-emergency)

Emergency Hospitals: Adventist Medical Center, 10123 SE Market St, 503-257-2500, www.adventistmedicalcenter.com; Kaiser Sunnyside Medical Center, 10180 SE Sunnyside Rd, Clackamas, 503-652-2880

Libraries: Midland Library, 805 SE 122nd Ave, 503-988-5392; Rockwood Library, 17917 SE Stark St, 503-988-5396

Parks: Major parks include Powell Butte Nature Park, Beggars Tick Wildlife Park, Leach Botanical Garden, and Springwater Corridor Trail; www.portlandparks. org

Community Publications: *East County News*, www.eastcountynews.com; *Mid-County Memo*, www.midcountymemo.com

Public Transportation: TriMet, 503-238-RIDE, www.trimet.org; bus lines on major east-west routes, and north-south on 122nd Ave. Eastside MAX on Burnside,

GREATER PORTLAND

Airport MAX service to Parkrose along Interstate 205; new MAX service from Gateway to Clackamas Town Center along Interstate 205 scheduled to begin 2009.

SURROUNDING COMMUNITIES

WASHINGTON COUNTY

Fast-growing Washington County is simultaneously the epicenter of the Portland area's high-tech boom, a region of working farms and timberland, and an important residential area with a population approaching half a million. The county is not without its problems; it has struggled to manage its growth so far and certain areas are notorious for traffic congestion, sprawl, and other ills. Still, the region's dynamic economy, natural beauty, and high level of amenities continue to attract newcomers who wish to settle in a suburban location with a relatively high quality of life.

BEAVERTON AND SURROUNDING AREAS

Portlanders have traditionally regarded Beaverton and the surrounding areas as the epitome of suburbia. While that stereotype has some merit—the area is decidedly suburban, with the good and bad aspects the term implies—it is becoming less accurate over time, and already by some measures is plain wrong. For example, Beaverton has a higher population density than Portland, and the Westside light rail line brings commuters from Beaverton to downtown Portland in less time than it takes some people to drive in from outlying Portland neighborhoods.

Beaverton is the center of gravity for eastern Washington County, but tens of thousands of people live in areas that are immediately adjacent to, but not formally a part of, the city. Washington County is encouraging an eventual consolidation of services, and Beaverton, which has been on an annexation binge in recent years, is likely to swallow up many of the remaining unincorporated areas around it in the next ten to twenty years. Beaverton's annexation plans are not without controversy—Nike, in particular, has fought the city's attempted annexation of its headquarters, in large part because the city's property taxes are higher than the county's—but there is an air of inevitability about them.

BEAVERTON

Boundaries: North: West Haven, Cedar Mill, Bethany, Oak Hills (unincorporated Washington County); **West**: Aloha (unincorporated Washington County); **South**: Tigard; unincorporated Washington County; **East**: Portland; West Slope, Raleigh

Hills, Garden Home (unincorporated Washington County); **Area**: 18.6 square miles; **Population**: 83,106

Well into the twentieth century, Beaverton was a small town that functioned primarily as a service center for the surrounding farms, which succeeded the rich beaverdam meadows that gave the city its name. The region's produce traveled to market in Portland, seven miles away, at first over a plank road through the West Hills where Canyon Road and the Sunset Highway now run, and later by train or truck. During the suburban boom following the Second World War, Beaverton became primarily a residential community, then further evolved into a center for new kinds of commerce, becoming the headquarters for multinational companies like Tektronix and Nike. (The latter company is actually located in unincorporated Washington County, literally across the street from Beaverton.) New residents and new companies continued to pour in during the 1980s and 1990s, and the city is essentially fully built-out. Nonetheless, the city has continued to increase in population through both growth and an aggressive annexation policy, and within a decade or so Beaverton is likely to be the second-largest city in the state.

Beaverton does not have a business district per se; rather the whole city is a business district, with strip malls and office parks lining most of the main roads. That said, the commercial center of gravity is the area around the tiny, hard-to-find historic downtown, near the intersection of Southwest Hall Boulevard and Highway 10 (Beaverton-Hillsdale Highway/Farmington Road). This area includes a beautiful new public library, a swim center, and a small park; on Wednesdays and Saturdays during the summer the neighborhood hosts a farmers market (www.beavertonfarmersmarket.com) that bills itself as the largest agricultural-only farmers market in the Northwest. Beyond this small node, central Beaverton is a zone of supermarkets, not-so-super markets, big box stores, and chain restaurants. To the north along Cedar Hills Boulevard, the once nearly moribund Beaverton Mall has become the upscale Cedar Hills Crossing. The city has tried, semi-successfully, to promote high-density, mixed-use developments near light rail stations; along with some old prewar homes that hang on in the area of the original town center, these transit-oriented developments are essentially the only residential options in the center of Beaverton.

Away from the sprawling center and the congested main roads, however, Beaverton wears a different face. The city is more ethnically and racially diverse than Portland, and has a higher population density but a much lower crime rate; with 13 different neighborhood associations, there is almost literally something here for everyone. Much of the city's housing is new, but the ages of individual developments vary widely. Notably, roughly half the city's housing units are detached single-family homes; the other half are townhomes, apartments, and condominiums, most of which are relatively new. Many Beaverton apartment complexes are massive mini-villages, with recreation centers, swimming pools, walking trails, and other amenities; these complexes almost always have vacancies, and are common places for newcomers to settle initially.

While every neighborhood in Beaverton has potential advantages, newcomers tend to land in one of a few areas. Hyland Hills, Ridgeview Heights, and other older subdivisions south of central Beaverton offer ranch, split-level, and other postwar-era single-family homes on reasonably large lots; most of these developments have homeowner associations, and some homes have distant views of Mount Hood. There are also a few mid-century modern "Rummer" homes in the neighborhood. The Greenway neighborhood west of Highway 217 is an established area of single-family homes and apartment complexes along the Fanno Creek Greenway; the neighborhood has a recreation center and offers quick access to the Washington Square area. Southwest Beaverton has a sea of cookie-cutter newer homes, mostly multi-story structures on small lots along with some townhomes. Sexton Mountain in western Beaverton is a vortex of culs-de-sac, with mostly newer (1980s–1990s) homes on large lots. The Five Oaks and Triple Creek neighborhoods of northwestern Beaverton are comprised of mostly newer homes on winding streets; this part of Beaverton is close to both the Sunset Highway and the Tanasbourne area of Hillsboro, and is popular with people who work at the region's high-tech employers.

Although not yet technically part of Beaverton, the unincorporated area of **Cedar Hills** (not to be confused with Cedar Mill, north of the Sunset Highway) is a neighborhood of single-family homes dating anywhere from about 1950 to 1980. Cedar Hills is close to the Sunset Highway and is a short drive or bus ride from the Sunset Transit Center MAX station.

Beaverton has a wealth of parks, community centers, aquatic centers, and recreation complexes, including natural areas like Tualatin Hills Nature Park. The city does not have a parks and recreation department; park facilities are managed by the Tualatin Hills Park and Recreation District, www.thprd.org. The Beaverton School District (www.beaverton.k12.or.us) is the third largest district in the state, and covers a large swath of unincorporated Washington County.

Beaverton traffic is legendarily congested. Both the Sunset Highway and Highway 217 can be horrible during rush hour, and 217 is often bumper-to-bumper even on Saturdays. Main through streets aren't always much faster. Fortunately, Beaverton has excellent transit connections for a suburban community; buses run along the major streets, and the MAX line whisks commuters to downtown Portland in a little over 20 minutes. Because many jobs in the area are in suburban office parks and industrial campuses, however, the majority of Beaverton commuters drive to work. A new commuter rail line to Wilsonville is scheduled to open in 2008.

Web Site: www.beavertonoregon.gov
Zip Codes: 97005, 97008, 97225
Post Office: Beaverton Post Office, 4550 SW Betts Ave

Police Station: Beaverton Police Department, 4755 SW Griffith Dr, 503-629-0111 (non-emergency), www.beavertonpolice.org

Emergency Hospital: Providence St. Vincent Medical Center, 9205 SW Barnes Rd, 503-216-1234, www.providence.org/Oregon/

Library: Beaverton City Library, 12375 SW 5th Ave, 503-644-2197, www.beavertonlibrary.org

Parks: More than 30 parks, open spaces, and recreational facilities, including Tualatin Hills Nature Park, Hyland Forest Park, Fanno Creek Park, and Greenway Park; Tualatin Hills Park and Recreation District, 503-645-6433, www.thprd.org

Community Publication: *Beaverton Valley Times*, www.beavertonvalleytimes.com

Public Transportation: TriMet, 503-238-RIDE, www.trimet.org; bus service on main routes to Hillsboro, downtown Portland, Tigard, and Southwest Portland. MAX light rail service to Hillsboro and downtown Portland; commuter train to Wilsonville scheduled to begin running in 2008.

WEST SLOPE, RALEIGH HILLS, AND GARDEN HOME

Boundaries: North: Unincorporated Washington County; **West:** Beaverton; **South:** Tigard; Metzger (unincorporated Washington County); **East:** Portland; unincorporated Multnomah County; **Area:** 5.1 square miles; **Population:** Approximately 19,500

The three communities of West Slope, Raleigh Hills, and Garden Home lie in a narrow band between Beaverton and Portland, just west of the Multnomah County line. Residents of this mostly unincorporated area have Portland mailing addresses but generally enjoy lower Washington County property taxes. This awkward (but advantageous) arrangement will change soon, as the city of Beaverton is poised to annex the entire area in the next few years.

West Slope is aptly named, as it sprawls across the west slope of the West Hills south of the Sunset Highway. The main drag here is Canyon Road, a rather unattractive strip mall that gathers car dealerships as it descends toward the flatlands of Beaverton proper. Some apartment complexes stand on or close to Canyon Road, but the neighborhoods on either side are largely comprised of single-family houses in styles ranging from modest ranches, split-levels, and Cape Cods to large contemporary and custom-designed homes. Beaverton has already annexed part of West Slope, which is connected to the rest of the city by a narrow tendril of land that in some places is less than a block wide. To complicate matters, much of the neighborhood is part of the Portland Public Schools district, and West Sylvan Middle School, which serves much of Portland's Westside, is technically in Beaverton.

Moving south, **Raleigh Hills** centers on the busy commercial area where Scholls Ferry Road intersects Beaverton-Hillsdale Highway. The neighborhood was originally named Raleigh; the authors of *Oregon Geographic Names* observe that Raleigh Hills "sounds like a name coined by real estate operators." (The neighborhood is rolling, but not especially hilly.) Traffic on the main roads can be painfully congested during rush hour, and the concentration of shops and services draws traffic from surrounding neighborhoods. (For example, there are at least four supermarkets—a Safeway, New Seasons, Fred Meyer, and Zupan's—along a short stretch of Beaverton-Hillsdale Highway.) Off the main roads, however, Raleigh Hills has some quiet and attractive neighborhoods, with many well-kept ranch homes and some newer contemporaries. In the Vista Brook area, near the Portland Golf Club, east of Scholls Ferry Road, there is a high concentration of modernist post-and-beam "Rummer" homes, built by the Rummer Company in the 1960s essentially as design knockoffs of California Eichler homes. As in West Slope, Beaverton has selectively annexed small portions of Raleigh Hills, although here only the width of a single street connects these areas to the rest of the city.

Still further south, almost to the Tigard border, **Garden Home** features homes that are similar to, although often more modest than, those in Raleigh Hills. Most houses here date from the 1950s through the 1970s; one-level or daylight ranches are the predominant, but not the only, style. Here, Portland has pulled a Beaverton, and extended a couple of annexation tentacles into Washington County. Garden Home has a large and popular recreation center.

With the exception of parts of West Slope, most of this area is part of the Beaverton School District (www.beavton.k12.or.us). The neighborhood is well connected by road to downtown Portland, Beaverton, and the Washington Square area, all of which are accessible if necessary without traveling on major highways. Bus service along the main east-west routes to Portland, Beaverton, or Tigard is adequate to good.

Web Sites: www.co.washington.or.us; www.beavertonoregon.gov

Zip Codes: 97223, 97225

Post Office: West Slope Post Office, 3225 SW 87th Ave

Police Station: Washington County Sheriff's Office, East Precinct, 3700 SW Murray Blvd, Beaverton, 503-629-0111 (non-emergency), www.co.washington.or.us/sheriff/; Beaverton Police Department, 4755 SW Griffith Dr, 503-629-0111 (non-emergency), www.beavertonpolice.org

Emergency Hospital: Providence St. Vincent Medical Center, 9205 SW Barnes Rd, 503-216-1234, www.providence.org/Oregon/

Libraries: Garden Home Community Library, 7475 SW Oleson Rd, 503-245-9932; West Slope Community Library, 3678 SW 78th Ave, 503-292-6416

Parks: Community parks include Raleigh Park, Garden Home Park; part of Tualatin Hills Park and Recreation District; www.thprd.com

Community Publication: *Beaverton Valley Times*, www.beavertonvalleytimes.com

Public Transportation: TriMet, 503-238-RIDE, www.trimet.org; bus service to Portland, Beaverton, and Tigard, MAX service only from Sunset Transit Center in Beaverton

NORTH OF THE SUNSET HIGHWAY: WEST HAVEN, CEDAR MILL, OAK HILLS, BETHANY, AND ROCK CREEK

Boundaries: North: Unincorporated Washington County; **West**: Hillsboro; **South**: Sunset Highway (US 26); **East**: Portland; unincorporated Multnomah County; **Area**: approximately 10 square miles; **Population**: Approximately 40,000

The unincorporated neighborhoods west of the Multnomah County line and north of the Sunset Highway are generally residential and fairly affluent, with a highly educated population. These neighborhoods have become popular places for newcomers to settle, in large part because they offer relatively straightforward access to the major employment centers of Washington County and to downtown Portland (via the Sunset Highway or over the hills on Cornell Road or Barnes Road) and also because many new homes have been built here in recent years. Although it is densely developed, this area abuts the urban growth boundary, and rural landscapes are just a few minutes away.

Just west of Portland and the Multnomah County line, **West Haven** is basically an extension of the Sylvan area in Portland's West Hills. Most houses are tucked back into the woods, and while some are fairly ramshackle, others are grand, architect-designed structures. Barnes Road, however, is a busy commercial thoroughfare and alternate route between Beaverton and Portland; besides shopping plazas, office parks, and apartment complexes, the Barnes Road area is home to Providence St. Vincent Hospital, the exclusive Catlin Gabel School, and the Oregon College of Art & Craft. The Sunset Transit Center, an important stop on the Westside MAX line, is adjacent to the Sunset Highway on the neighborhood's southern boundary; the northern terminus of Highway 217, which runs south toward Tigard, is also here. Two bus lines serve the neighborhood, both of which connect to the Sunset Transit Center.

To the northwest, abutting both West Haven and Portland's Forest Heights neighborhood, **Cedar Mill** (not to be confused with Cedar Hills, a neighborhood south of the Sunset Highway) was named for a sawmill that operated here in the nineteenth century. Today, instead of forest, the neighborhood is an established area of culs-de-sac and generally quiet, sidewalk-less streets. Many residences here are older, nicely landscaped ranch-style or contemporary homes, mixed with some new housing developments and a few enormous custom homes on large lots. A commercial district along Cornell Road also includes some apartment complexes and a parade of merchants eager to meet all your everyday shopping needs. Cedar Mill also has a Saturday morning farmers' market (www.cmfmarket.org) from June through September, which takes place near the Sunset Swim Center on Cornell Road. There is bus service along Cornell Road, but much of the neighborhood has no regular transit service. (TriMet's Cedar Mill

Shuttle provides weekday rush hour service from Cedar Mill to Sunset Transit Center.)

A bit further west, **Bethany** is a sea of new housing developments. There are some high-density townhome and apartment developments, but the majority of the housing here consists of large, two-story homes in styles ranging from plain to "Craftsman-inspired." Most lots are quite small, but open space is abundant and most streets have sidewalks; main routes have bike lanes. The neighborhood around Claremont Country Club is made up of custom, mainly single-story homes; nearby Bethany Village (www.bethanyvillage.com) on Bethany Boulevard is a huge mixed-use development featuring housing, retail, and office space. The commercial center of the "Village" is a shopping complex with a supermarket, bank, and other essentials. The agricultural fields of North Bethany were recently brought into the urban growth boundary, and a wave of development that will bring thousands of new homes to the area is just beginning. Bethany might be a good place to start if you're looking for a brand-new home in Washington County.

The area of Bethany west of Northwest 143rd Avenue and south of West Union Road is known as **Oak Hills**. The homes here are generally older than those in the rest of Bethany, and consist mainly of contemporaries, ranches, and split-levels dating from the 1950s to the 1980s. Oak Hills also has a few Eichler-style modern homes built by the Rummer Company in the 1960s. Most streets have sidewalks, and some have bike lanes.

Portland Community College's Rock Creek Campus is in the northwest fringes of Bethany, on the edge of the eponymous **Rock Creek** neighborhood (sometimes spelled Rockcreek). The campus is also home to the Washington County Museum and Historical Society (www.washingtoncountymuseum.org). The community to the west is mainly residential, with winding streets and culs-de-sac centered on the Rock Creek Country Club. Most homes are two-story contemporary-style homes with cedar shake roofs; there are a few small-scale apartment buildings in a similar style. In the southeast part of the neighborhood, where it blends into Oak Hills, there are a few streets lined with older ranch homes and split levels; an occasional forlorn old farmhouse reminds residents that these neighborhoods were once agricultural landscapes. Thanks to the presence of the community college, both Bethany (including Oak Hills) and Rock Creek have decent bus service.

All these neighborhoods have excellent access to parks and open spaces, although these undeveloped parcels are not particularly large. Linear parks along stream or powerline corridors are especially common, and many homes back directly onto these greenspaces. Bethany in particular has a network of community trails. Homeowner associations maintain some parks; the remainder are part of the Tualatin Hills Park and Recreation District (www.thprd.com). These neighborhoods belong to the Beaverton School District (www.beavton.k12.or.us); the district's Sunset High School is located in Cedar Mill, and Westview High School is in the Rock Creek area. The elementary schools in this part of the district are generally highly regarded.

Web Site: www.co.washington.or.us

Zip Codes: 97006, 97225, 97229

Post Office: Cedar Mill Branch (contract post office), 12675 NW Cornell Rd, Suite B

Police Stations: Washington County Sheriff's Office, 215 SW Adams Ave, Hillsboro; East Precinct, 3700 SW Murray Blvd, Beaverton; 503-629-0111 (non-emergency), www.co.washington.or.us/sheriff/

Emergency Hospital: Providence St. Vincent Medical Center, 9205 SW Barnes Rd, 503-216-1234, www.providence.org/Oregon/

Libraries: Cedar Mill Community Library, 12505 NW Cornell Rd, 503-644-0043, cedarmill.org/library; Oregon College of Art & Craft Library, 8245 SW Barnes Rd, 503-297-5544

Parks: Dozens of small parks and open spaces; part of Tualatin Hills Park and Recreation District, www.thprd.com

Community Publication: *Beaverton Valley Times*, www.beavertonvalleytimes. com

Public Transportation: TriMet, 503-238-RIDE, www.trimet.org; MAX service from Sunset Transit Center; several bus lines along main roads and to Portland Community Center, plus rush-hour Cedar Mill Shuttle

ALOHA

Boundaries: North: Hillsboro; unincorporated Washington County; **West**: Hillsboro; unincorporated Washington County; **South**: Unincorporated Washington County; **East**: Beaverton; **Area**: 7.4 square miles; **Population**: 42,000

The most important thing to know about Aloha, the unincorporated area west of Beaverton, is that it has no connection to Hawaii. The name is pronounced "uh-LOW-uh," not "uh-low-HAH." According to *Oregon Geographic Names*, in 1912, the first postmaster "named the office Aloah after a small resort on Lake Winnebago in Wisconsin. During the application process the last two letters were transposed by the Post Office Department resulting in the shift from a midwest Indian name to a Hawaiian word." Ironically, Aloha has no particular resemblance to Wisconsin, either, and does not have any lakes, let alone lake resorts.

What Aloha does have is a sea—a sea of suburban housing. The area is not entirely residential—Metro has designated the center of Aloha as a regional "Town Center," and businesses and light industrial facilities of many kinds line busy Tualatin Valley Highway, including an Intel campus that was its first of many in Washington County—but the neighborhoods on either side of the highway are filled with postwar housing developments with plenty of culs-de-sac. The predominant housing style is the ranch in its various forms—standard ranch, daylight ranch, ranch with ill-advised second-story addition—along with some split-levels and contemporary-style homes. Lots are generally reasonably large without being gigantic. Some streets have sidewalks, although most do not. In short, Aloha should feel familiar to anyone who has spent much time in America's postwar suburbs.

Aloha has not yet experienced the surge of infill development that has transformed closer-in neighborhoods, and most homes are not especially new. Some new homes with views of the Tualatin Valley stand on the north slopes of Cooper Mountain, south of Farmington Road, however. (Farmington Road also has some supermarkets and other retail businesses.) Single-family homes make up the majority of housing options here, although there are some apartment complexes, especially in the eastern part of Aloha near the Beaverton border.

Aloha is rich in neighborhood parks and open spaces, including a swim center and the bucolic Jenkins Estate in the district's extreme southwestern corner. Aloha is convenient to both Beaverton and Hillsboro, although automobile travel to other parts of the metro area can be time-consuming and inconvenient. (The MAX line runs along Aloha's northern border.) It is reasonably likely that Beaverton (and possibly Hillsboro) will annex much of Aloha in the next decade or two, but the area should remain unincorporated for the near future. Most of Aloha is within the Beaverton School District (www.beavton.k12.or.us); the Hillsboro School District (www.hsd.k12.or.us) serves the western portion of Aloha.

Web Site: www.co.washington.or.us

Zip Codes: 97006, 97007

Post Office: Aloha Post Office, 3800 SW 185th Ave

Police Stations: Washington County Sheriff's Office, 215 SW Adams Ave, Hillsboro; East Precinct, 3700 SW Murray Blvd, Beaverton; 503-629-0111 (non-emergency), www.co.washington.or.us/sheriff/

Emergency Hospitals: Tuality Community Hospital, 225 SE 8th Ave, Hillsboro, 503-681-1111, www.tuality.org; Providence St. Vincent Medical Center, 9205 SW Barnes Rd, 503-216-1234, www.providence.org/Oregon/

Library: None; see Beaverton and Hillsboro

Parks: More than 20 parks and open spaces; part of Tualatin Hills Park and Recreation District, www.thprd.com

Community Publications: *Beaverton Valley Times*, www.beavertonvalleytimes.com; *Hillsboro Argus*, www.hillsboroargus.com

Public Transportation: TriMet, 503-238-RIDE, www.trimet.org; bus service along Tualatin Valley Highway and Farmington Road, with MAX light rail service along the neighborhood's northern edge

SOUTHEASTERN WASHINGTON COUNTY

The generally affluent southeastern chunk of Washington County is one of the fastest-growing areas in the state. Good schools, high-end shopping malls, access to parks and open space, and a concentration of nearby employers attract many new residents, as does housing that, while not cheap, is less expensive than in Lake Oswego, West Linn, or some other desirable suburban communities. On the downside, traffic congestion has increased markedly in recent years, both on Interstate 5 and on major city streets. If the suburban lifestyle appeals to you, and if you can handle the commute (or if you'll be working nearby), you may want to check out the cities and communities of this part of the metro area.

TIGARD

Boundaries: North: Beaverton; unincorporated Washington County; **West**: Beaverton; unincorporated Washington County; King City; **South**: Tualatin; Durham; **East**: Lake Oswego; Portland; **Area**: 10.9 square miles; **Population**: 48,000

Tigard (pronounced TY-gird, and not like the Winnie the Pooh character) was called Butte until the end of the nineteenth century, when the town became known as Tigardville, and eventually just Tigard, after early Pioneers Wilson and Polly Tigard. For many years, Tigard was little more than a farm community and minor center of trade. After the Second World War, however, Tigard began to develop into a bedroom community of Portland, only 9 miles to the northeast. The completion of Interstate 5 (which forms Tigard's eastern border) in the 1960s fueled a boom in commerce and population that continues to this day.

Tigard's small, original downtown lies just off Pacific Highway (Highway 99), the congested, strip mall–lined road that leads to Sherwood and Yamhill County. While the city hall, library, and a few shops are located in this area, the commercial center of gravity has moved to the areas along the city's two freeways, Interstate 5 and Highway 217. At Tigard's northern tip stands Washington Square, the metropolitan area's largest and most upscale traditional mall, surrounded by an honor guard of minor strip malls and commercial office buildings; at its southeastern corner is the region's premier "lifestyle" mall, Bridgeport Village. The zone between these two temples of commerce—essentially the eastern third of Tigard—is a mix of office parks, light industry, and big-box retailers, together with the occasional stray house or apartment building.

Behind this bulwark of economic vitality lie the city's residential neighborhoods. With the exception of the Pacific Highway strip, most of the western two-thirds of the city is residential. Homes in central Tigard, south of "downtown," run the gamut of mid-century styles. The southern part of the city is a landscape of culs-de-sac with newer, generally two-story homes, mixed with older ranches on older streets.

West of Pacific Highway, most housing developments are relatively new; some perch on slopes with impressive views of Mount Hood. Tigard also has a large stock of townhouses and apartment complexes, especially (but not exclusively) near Pacific Highway and in the Washington Square area. The average home price in Tigard in 2006 was about $330,000, but you can expect to pay substantially more for homes that are larger than average, relatively new, or that offer a view.

Tigard's inexorable growth, combined with the strong growth of nearby suburbs, has resulted in a high level of traffic congestion. The nine-mile commute to downtown Portland takes 15 minutes on a good day or during off-peak hours, but it can last 45 minutes or more if there is an accident or other mishap. Highway 217 is no better, and Pacific Highway is notoriously slow. Buses serve Pacific Highway and some other main streets, but are not often convenient except for commuters going to Portland, Tualatin, Washington Square, or Beaverton. There is no light-rail service, although the commuter train line between Beaverton and Wilsonville that is scheduled to open in 2008 will stop in downtown Tigard.

Despite its congestion, Tigard is considered a desirable place for families, and roughly one-third of the city's households are families with school-age children. Most of the city is part of the Tigard-Tualatin School District (www.ttsd.k12.or.us); a small area in the northern portion of the city is part of the Beaverton School District (www.beaverton.k12.or.us). Tigard High School offers an International Baccalaureate program. Tigard has some good city parks, including Cook Park on the north bank of the Tualatin River. The Tigard Farmers' Market (www.tigardfarmersmarket.com) is held in a parking lot near Washington Square on Sundays from June through October. The highlight of the municipal calendar is the Tigard Festival of Balloons—these are major hot-air affairs, not birthday party–grade helium balloons—held each June.

Web Site: www.ci.tigard.or.us

Zip Codes: 97223, 97224

Post Office: Tigard Post Office, 12210 SW Main St

Police Station: Tigard Police Department, 13125 SW Hall Blvd, 503-629-0111 (non-emergency)

Emergency Hospitals: Legacy Meridian Park Hospital, 19300 SW 65th Ave, Tualatin, 503-692-1212, www.legacyhealth.org; Providence St. Vincent Medical Center, 9205 SW Barnes Rd, 503-216-1234, www.providence.org/Oregon/

Library: Tigard Public Library, 13500 SW Hall Blvd, 503-684-6537, www.tigard-or.gov/library

Parks: Nine city parks, including Cook Park, Fanno Creek Park, and Summer Lake Park; www.ci.tigard.or.us/community/parks/

Community Publications: *The Times*, www.tigardtimes.com; *The Regal Courier*, www.theregalcourier.com

Public Transportation: TriMet, 503-238-RIDE, www.trimet.org; six bus lines along major routes to and from neighboring communities and downtown Portland. Commuter rail to Beaverton, Tualatin, and Wilsonville scheduled to begin in 2008

DURHAM

Durham is a tiny (265-acre) incorporated city of about 1,400 people wedged between Tigard and Tualatin along Upper Boones Ferry Road. The city is primarily residential, and although there are several office parks along Upper Boones Ferry, Durham has no retail establishments. (The city is, however, a short walk or drive to the Bridgeport Village shopping center just to the east.) Apart from a few small apartment complexes on Upper Boones Ferry, the city's housing is comprised of contemporary-style homes dating primarily from the 1960s to the 1980s. Most of these homes are on good-sized but not enormous lots on curving back streets and culs-de-sac, the names of which—Rivendell Drive, Woody End, Wilderland Court—suggest a developer with a Lord of the Rings fetish. Residents are justly proud of the city's canopy of mature conifers (a fact which is a bit ironic, as the city was named after a pioneer sawmill owner).

Durham is within the Tigard-Tualatin School District (www.ttsd.k12.or.us).

Web Site: www.durham-oregon.us

KING CITY

Turn off busy Pacific Highway at Southwest Royalty Parkway, behind Grocery Outlet, and you will find yourself in King City, a 1960s-era retirement community of just over 2,000 people. The streets, which generally have "royal" names—Imperial Avenue, King Richard Drive, Queen Victoria Place, etc.—wind around a semi-private golf course; watch for the "Golf Carts on Street" signs. Most homes are modest ranches and split-levels, and there are also some older condo complexes. Many King City residences (and the golf course) have Mount Hood views. If King City sounds like your kind of place, you may have to wait a while: Most properties have deed restrictions that require at least one owner to be over 55, and that bar anyone under 18 from living there. King City may annex nearby unincorporated areas in the next few years, however, and the deed restrictions probably won't apply in these new parts of the city. Look for the median age of King City residents (currently 75) to decline in the future.

Web Site: www.ci.king-city.or.us

TUALATIN

Boundaries: North: Tigard, Durham; **West**: Unincorporated Washington County; **South**: Unincorporated Washington County; **East**: Lake Oswego, unincorporated Clackamas County and Washington County; **Area**: 7.8 square miles; **Population**: 24,800

Tualatin (pronounced too-WALL-uh-tin), 12 miles south of downtown Portland, was once a sleepy small town on the south bank of the river for which it was named. Although it was incorporated in 1913, by 1970 the city still had fewer than 1,000 residents. Tualatin's population has since increased more than 25-fold, and the area continues to boom, with new residents drawn by the city's pleasant neighborhoods and greenspaces, strong public schools, and the growth of nearby high-tech businesses. These amenities don't come cheap, however: the average home price in 2006 was nearly $400,000.

While Tualatin has no real downtown, the city is centered on the area just south of the Tualatin River, between Southwest Boones Ferry Road and Martinazzi Avenue. This area contains Tualatin Commons; built on the former site of a pet food factory, the development now includes an artificial lake, offices, restaurants, apartments, and a hotel. The city hall and library are also located here. (The library proudly displays the skeleton of a mastodon that was excavated nearby in the 1940s.) A self-guided Artwalk wends through the city center area, past public art (including the mastodon) and a few historic structures, and even such oddball attractions as a garden of poisonous plants. A few old shopping plazas and apartment complexes blend into the new retail developments along Tualatin-Sherwood Road. The small part of the city that lies north of the Tualatin River contains most of Bridgeport Village, a popular upscale outdoor mall.

Outside this concentration of commercial and medium-density residential developments, single-family homes comprise the bulk of the city's built-up area. Tualatin's residential districts generally feature medium-to-large homes on quiet, curving residential streets and culs-de-sac. The predominant housing style is one- or two-story Northwest contemporary or "shed" design; some homes have rather interesting architecture, and most have pleasantly landscaped yards with trees. There are a few older neighborhoods of ranch homes and split-levels; some newer neighborhoods, especially in southwest Tualatin, veer towards the McMansion end of the spectrum, with plenty of three-car garages and "great rooms." There are also some townhomes and apartment complexes along Boones Ferry Road, near Interstate 5, and in East Tualatin near Legacy Meridian Park Hospital. The large planned development of Fox Hill perches above the Tualatin River in the easternmost part of the city. (East Tualatin is in Clackamas County.)

The city's main annual celebration is the Tualatin Crawfish Festival, which has survived for more than half a century despite the curse placed upon it by the Voodoo Queen of Acadiana in Louisiana, who felt perhaps overly protective of her region's claim to lifetime achievement in the field of crawfish. The city has a decent selection of community parks; Browns Ferry Park along the Tualatin River provides a launching point for canoes and kayaks.

The city's major streets and Interstate 5 are growing increasingly congested, and Tualatin-Sherwood Road is almost ridiculously slow at certain times of today. Strong population growth in Sherwood and Wilsonville will continue to affect the traffic situation in Tualatin. Although the city is very car-dependent, Tri-Met offers express bus service to Portland, and there is a park-and-ride near Interstate 5; the commuter rail line now under construction between Wilsonville and

Beaverton is scheduled to serve Tualatin beginning in 2008. SMART runs buses between Tualatin and Wilsonville.

Tualatin is part of the Tigard-Tualatin School District (www.ttsd.k12.or.us), and Tualatin High School offers an International Baccalaureate program.

Web Site: www.ci.tualatin.or.us
Zip Code: 97062
Post Office: Tualatin Post Office, 19190 SW 90th Ave
Police Station: Tualatin Police Department, 8650 SW Tualatin Rd, 503-629-0111 (non-emergency)
Emergency Hospital: Legacy Meridian Park Hospital, 19300 SW 65th Ave, Tualatin, 503-692-1212, www.legacyhealth.org
Library: Tualatin Public Library, 8380 SW Nyberg St, 503-691-3074
Parks: 11 parks, including Browns Ferry Park, Atfalati Park, and Ibach Park
Community Publication: *The Tualatin Times*, www.tualatintimes.com
Public Transportation: TriMet, 503-238-RIDE, www.trimet.org (bus service between Tualatin and Portland or Lake Oswego); SMART, 503-682-7790, www.ridesmart.com (bus service between Tualatin and Wilsonville). Commuter rail service to Wilsonville, Tigard, and Beaverton scheduled to begin in 2008.

BULL MOUNTAIN

The unincorporated area of Bull Mountain occupies the ridgeline and slopes of the mountain of the same name west of Tigard. Bull Mountain has more than 8,000 residents, but it recently narrowly rejected incorporation and has resisted annexation attempts by Tigard. Much of Bull Mountain consists of large, often custom-designed, homes with Mount Hood views, which may or may not be inside walled-in (although not necessarily gated) subdivisions. Newer homes here range from spacious to ostentatiously massive in size; many, if not most, are high up enough to have views of *something*, whether it be Mount Hood or the Tualatin Valley. There are also some neighborhoods of older ranches and split-levels, which are very nicely kept and landscaped with larger yards than many of the newer homes. The neighborhood is extremely quiet; there are no townhouses or apartments and no major through highways, and public transportation is not available. Bull Mountain school children attend Tigard-Tualatin schools (www.ttsd.k12.or.us). The area has no public parks.

SHERWOOD

Boundaries: North: Unincorporated Washington County; **West**: Unincorporated Washington County; **South**: Unincorporated Washington County; **East**: Unincorporated Washington County; **Area**: 4.1 square miles; **Population**: 16,200

The outlying community of Sherwood, about 16 miles southwest of downtown Portland, is on the fringe of the metropolitan area, surrounded on three sides by the farms and wooded hills of rural Washington and Yamhill Counties. (The city is far enough out to have its own urban growth boundary.) It is also one of the fastest growing cities in the state. This growth has brought traffic congestion and not-always-sensitive development; many outsiders experience Sherwood only along the two main through roads, Pacific Highway (Highway 99W) and Sherwood-Tualatin Road, which are lined by seemingly endless strip malls, punctuated only by occasional large apartment complexes and housing developments. This perception of the city is both unfortunate and inaccurate, as most of the city is a quiet, reasonably pleasant suburban community with a small-town feel.

The heart of this hidden city is Old Town Sherwood, a small, old-fashioned downtown where a beautiful new public library and a few new upscale businesses have started a minor revitalization. Old Town also hosts the Sherwood Saturday Market (www.sherwoodmarket.blogspot.com), held Saturday mornings from May through September. The adjacent Smockville neighborhood—Smockville was the original name of the town before its incorporation in 1892—is filled with bungalows and other older homes. Stella Olsen Park, at the neighborhood's western end, hosts concerts and outdoor movie screenings during the summer. Across the railroad tracks to the southeast stands a mix of generally modest single-family homes ranging in age from early twentieth-century cottages to ranches and contemporary-style homes. Newer tract homes dominate the southern and southwestern parts of the city. The newest developments tend to be large, self-contained and walled-off (although not actually gated) blocks of large single-family homes.

Despite Sherwood's substantial distance from the metropolitan center, real estate is not exactly cheap: the median home price is about $300,000. Traffic congestion can be a problem heading out of town toward Portland or Tualatin; there is frequent (but not necessarily lightning-fast) bus service to Tigard and Portland. Sherwood's biggest municipal festival is the annual Robin Hood Festival, complete with archery contest (robinhoodfestival.com). (The city was named, either directly or indirectly depending on which story you believe, for England's Sherwood Forest.) Most of Sherwood is within the city's own school district (www.sherwood.k12.or.us); a small part of the northern portion of the city is within the Hillsboro School District (www.hsd.k12.or.us).

Web Site: www.ci.sherwood.or.us
Zip Code: 97140
Post Office: Sherwood Post Office, 16300 SW Langer Dr
Police Station: Sherwood Police Department, 20495 SW Borchers Rd, 503-625-5523 (non-emergency)
Emergency Hospital: Legacy Meridian Park Hospital, 19300 SW 65th Ave, Tualatin, 503-692-1212, www.legacyhealth.org
Library: Sherwood Public Library, 22560 SW Pine St, 503-625-6688

Parks: Nine public parks, including Stella Olsen Park
Community Publication: *Sherwood Gazette*, www.sherwoodgazette.com
Public Transportation: TriMet, 503-238-RIDE, www.trimet.org; one bus line with frequent service and one express bus line to Tigard and downtown Portland

WESTERN WASHINGTON COUNTY

Western Washington County blends the wonders of the modern world with the splendors of the natural environment. The tech employers of booming Hillsboro attract skilled workers from around the world, while just a few miles away you'll find fog-shrouded forested hills and world-class wineries. It's not perfect—traffic can be a nightmare, and increasing immigration and other demographic changes have caused growing pains and general strife—but western Washington County remains one of the fastest-growing parts of the state and is a major economic engine for the Portland area.

HILLSBORO

Boundaries: North: Unincorporated Washington County; **West:** Unincorporated Washington County; **South:** Unincorporated Washington County; **East:** Aloha (unincorporated Washington County), Beaverton; **Area:** 21.6 square miles; **Population:** 84,600

Hillsboro is not named for the city's terrain—the landscape is best described as "rolling" at best—but rather for early pioneer David Hill, who arrived in Oregon in 1842 and settled in this region by 1845. It's safe to say that Hill would be astonished if he could see what has happened to his old homestead. Over the last three decades or so, Hillsboro has grown from a sleepy agricultural service center and county seat to become the pulsing heart of the so-called Silicon Forest and the fifth-largest city in Oregon. Computer-chip giant Intel has several facilities in the city (and is the largest private employer in the state); other technology companies with operations here include Epson, FEI, and Lattice Semiconductor. Most technology facilities are set in large industrial "campuses," which are heavily concentrated in the northeastern corner of the city, close to the Sunset Highway. (In addition to "Silicon Forest," this part of Washington County is sometimes referred to as the Sunset Corridor.) Hillsboro's economic transition has caused a demographic transition as well: The city's population is becoming increasingly diverse, with many new Hispanic, South Asian, and East Asian residents (some of whom have come on I-9 visas to work at the region's tech companies).

The northeastern part of Hillsboro, besides harboring many industrial campuses and office parks, also has abundant shopping and residential options. The Tanasbourne district offers several large retail developments, including the Streets of Tanasbourne (www.streetsoftanasbourne.com), an upscale "lifestyle" mall. The main streets nearby are lined with large residential developments, most commonly townhomes, with names usually following this formula: Name = [(cutesy or made-up noun) + (general location or geographical feature) + e,], e.g., "The Brookfordington at the Pointe."

This part of Hillsboro also includes the much-lauded Orenco Station development, named for the Oregon Nursery Company that used to operate farms on the site. Orenco Station is one of the country's first suburban New Urbanist developments—mixed-use, transit-oriented, and pedestrian-friendly planned communities—with a residential mix including apartments, neo-traditional single-family homes with big front porches, and brick townhomes with Brooklyn-style stoops (but without the Brooklyn-style interactions—you talkin' to me?). Housing surrounds a "town center" with shops and restaurants. The Orenco "station" is the adjacent stop on the Westside light rail; downtown Portland is 40 minutes away by train. Orenco Station also hosts one of Hillsboro's two weekly farmers' markets, on Sunday mornings during the summer months. Orenco Station has become so successful, in fact, that several other developments in the area have adopted the Orenco name to bask in the reflected glory of the original development; these other Orencos do not necessarily incorporate any elements of New Urbanist design.

West along Cornell Road, across from the Washington County Fairgrounds, Hillsboro Airport is home base for the local fleet of corporate jets, as well as less glamorous aircraft. Occasionally a plane crashes into a nearby home, but airplane noise is a bigger concern for most residents. The neighborhoods west of the airport, around Hillsboro High School, have a mix of ranch and contemporary homes. The Jones Farm area, near an Intel campus of the same name, features newer two-story houses on culs-de-sac and dead-end streets; the small park at the center of the neighborhood is reserved for the use of residents only. Other parts of Northwest Hillsboro offer mostly two-story contemporary homes from the 1980s and 1990s, as well as some new housing developments on the fringe of the built-up area.

Downtown Hillsboro is a mix of businesses, apartment complexes, and city and county government buildings, including a modern civic center and the historic county courthouse. This is the western terminus of the Westside MAX line; the trip from here to downtown Portland takes about 50 to 55 minutes. Main Street is lined with small shops and eateries, which stay open late for the Tuesday Market, held on Tuesday evenings from June through August. Downtown also hosts a farmers' market on Saturday mornings from May through October; see www.hillsboromarkets.org. The residential neighborhoods surrounding downtown include some bungalows and other older homes. The neighborhoods east of downtown feature ranches in varying states of repair and disrepair, mixed with some new apartment buildings; this area also contains small-scale cul-de-sac developments of newer homes, shoehorned into gaps in existing built-up areas. Hillsboro is experiencing rapid development on the city's southern fringe.

Hillsboro is a demographic grab-bag of singles, families, students, elderly long-time residents, new immigrants from other countries, affluent high-tech workers, and low-paid agricultural laborers. (Farms and wineries still exist just beyond the urban growth boundary.) Like Beaverton, it contains just about every kind of housing you could imagine (although it is not as dense, and a slightly higher percentage of the population own homes). The Hillsboro School District (www.hsd.k12.or.us) is a mixed bag, with both excellent and mediocre schools. The city operates an extensive network of parks, recreation centers, "linear parks," and open spaces, including aptly named Noble Woods Park; Shute Park, which includes an aquatic center and library; and Rood Bridge Park, which has a put-in for canoes and kayaks along the Tualatin River. Jackson Bottom Wetlands (www. jacksonbottom.org) is an extensive area of marshland and bird habitat just south of downtown.

Hillsboro has MAX light rail service to Beaverton and Portland, and a decent network of bus lines, but most residents get around by car, and the sprawling nature of development has resulted in significant congestion. The Sunset Highway commute to Portland can be a nightmare, while the slog along Tualatin Valley Highway to Beaverton is usually slow but manageable. People with jobs in or near Hillsboro are more likely to enjoy living here than people who work far away and intend to commute by car.

Web Site: www.ci.hillsboro.or.us

Zip Codes: 97006, 97123, 97124

Post Office: Hillsboro Post Office, 125 S 1st Ave

Police Station: Hillsboro Police Department, 250 SE 10th Ave, 503-681-6190 (non-emergency)

Emergency Hospital: Tuality Community Hospital, 225 SE 8th Ave, Hillsboro, 503-681-1111, www.tuality.org

Libraries: Hillsboro Main Library, 2850 NE Brookwood Pkwy; Shute Park Branch Library, 775 SE 10th Ave; 503-615-6500, hillsboro.plinkit.org

Parks: More than 25 developed parks and facilities, including Noble Woods Park, Shute Park (and Shute Park Aquatic and Recreation Center), and Rood Bridge Park; www.ci.hillsboro.or.us/ParksRec/

Community Publication: *Hillsboro Argus*, www.oregonlive.com/argus

Public Transportation: TriMet, 503-238-RIDE, www.trimet.org; bus service on many major thoroughfares and light rail service east to Beaverton and downtown Portland

CORNELIUS

Boundaries: North: Unincorporated Washington County; **West**: Forest Grove; **South**: Unincorporated Washington County; **East**: Unincorporated Washington County; **Area**: 1.9 square miles; **Population**: 10,820

Cornelius is perhaps the least-known of Portland's sizable suburbs; ask the average Portlander what they think about Cornelius, and the response is likely to be, "Who?" (The "who," by the way, is the colorfully named Colonel T.R. Cornelius, who sounds like a character in an animated 1960s Christmas special but was actually a settler in the area in the 1840s.) It's not too surprising that Cornelius is not better known; it lacks any major landmarks, shopping centers, significant employers, or indeed regional destinations of any kind, and the city officially proclaims itself "Oregon's family town," a motto which is unlikely to garner tons of press. Cornelius serves as both a farm and forest service center and as a dormitory community of commuters to other parts of the region; in sum, it's a pretty quiet place.

The average household income in Cornelius is lower than in many other Washington County communities, in part because many residents are recent immigrants, but the flip side of the income coin is that housing is less expensive here than elsewhere in the county. Moreover, the crime rate is lower than in many other parts of the metropolitan area, including more affluent Hillsboro and Beaverton.

State Highway 8 bisects the city in a couplet of one-way streets. The city has no real downtown, but the city hall and other public buildings are near the eastern end of the couplet, in the historic center of the community. Most of the city's older, prewar homes are in this area, while some new development is occurring in the northeastern corner of the city. The bulk of the city's housing stock is small, single-family homes (or mobile homes). Large numbers of houses painted unusual colors—magenta, chartreuse, purple, and pink, among others—enliven the rather conventional neighborhoods in the southwestern part of the city.

Part of Cornelius lies within both the Forest Grove School District (www.fgsd.k12.or.us), while the eastern portion is part of the Hillsboro School District (www.hsd.k12.or.us); the city is considering starting its own school district so that all children from the city can go to the same high school.

Web Site: www.ci.cornelius.or.us

Zip Code: 97113

Post Office: Cornelius Post Office, 1639 Baseline St

Police Station: Cornelius Police Department, 1311 N Barlow St, 503-359-1881 (non-emergency)

Emergency Hospital: Tuality Forest Grove Hospital, 1809 Maple St, Forest Grove, 503-357-2173, www.tuality.org

Library: Cornelius Public Library, 1355 N Barlow St, 503-357-4093

Parks: 12 city parks and open spaces; www.ci.cornelius.or.us

Community Publication: Forest Grove News-Times, www.forestgrovenewstimes.com

Public Transportation: TriMet, 503-238-RIDE, www.trimet.org; one bus line, with frequent service to Forest Grove, Hillsboro, and Beaverton

FOREST GROVE

Boundaries: North: Unincorporated Washington County; **West**: Unincorporated Washington County; **South**: Unincorporated Washington County; **East**: Cornelius; **Area**: 4.6 square miles; **Population**: 20,380

Forest Grove lies near the eastern foot of the Coast Range at the westernmost edge of the metropolitan area, 25 miles from Portland. While the city is not entirely unplugged from Washington County's high-tech economy—Merix, a circuit board manufacturer, is the city's largest employer, with 1,300 workers—Forest Grove remains an important agricultural service center. In addition to traditional farms and forestland—the city is named Forest Grove for a reason—the surrounding rural area includes several wineries, and even a sakery (SakeOne, www.sakeone.com). In many neighborhoods, farmland is literally just down the street, and the city feels much more like a small town than a suburb in an urban agglomeration of nearly two million people.

The city's cultural center is Pacific University, chartered in 1849 as Tualatin Academy, which occupies a bucolic (and rapidly expanding) campus in the center of town. The adjacent historic downtown includes several antique stores and restaurants as well as the Forest Theater (www.forest4movies.com), which shows second-run movies. A small farmers' market is held in a bowling alley parking lot on Wednesday evenings from June through mid-October; during market season, downtown merchants stay open late on the first Wednesday of each month.

South of downtown, the Clark Historic District is filled with old farmhouses, Queen Anne Victorians, Craftsman bungalows, and old cottages; some have been grandly restored, and while others have been neglected, the neighborhood feels a bit like it was lifted from a Norman Rockwell painting. North of downtown, small apartment complexes cluster around Pacific University. Further north, on the road to Banks, a few new multi-story duplexes and triplexes stand among modest ranches and smallish contemporary homes. The western end of town features winding streets and culs-de-sac with some new housing developments, while strip malls and commercial uses dominate the area along Pacific Avenue east of downtown. The most impressive establishment in this part of town is McMenamins Grand Lodge (www.thegrandlodge.com); this former Masonic & Eastern Star Lodge has been restored and converted to the standard McMenamins combo of guestrooms, multiple bars, a movie theater, and a soaking pool.

Forest Grove has several city parks and recreational facilities, including a popular aquatic facility, but the biggest recreational draws are Fernhill Wetlands, a prime bird-watching area in the city's southeast corner, and Henry Hagg Lake, a favorite swimming and boating destination in the foothills a few miles south of town. Many Forest Grove residents work in Hillsboro, a relatively manageable 20-minute drive away, but others face a long commute to workplaces elsewhere in the metro area. A single bus line runs from Forest Grove east to Hillsboro and

Beaverton. There has been some discussion of extending light rail from Hillsboro to Forest Grove, but no firm plans (or, more importantly, funding commitments) have been made. The city is part of the Forest Grove School District (www.fgsd. k12.or.us).

Web Site: www.ci.forest-grove.or.us
Zip Code: 97116
Post Office: Forest Grove Post Office, 1822 21st Ave
Police Station: Forest Grove Police Department, 2102 Pacific Ave, 503-992-3240 (non-emergency)
Emergency Hospital: Tuality Forest Grove Hospital, 1809 Maple St, Forest Grove, 503-357-2173, www.tuality.org
Library: Forest Grove City Library, 2114 Pacific Ave, 503-992-3247, www.ci.forest-grove.or.us/library/
Parks: Eight city parks, including Lincoln Park (with skate park), plus an aquatic center; www.ci.forest-grove.or.us/parks.html
Community Publication: *Forest Grove News-Times*, www.forestgrovenewstimes.com
Public Transportation: TriMet, 503-238-RIDE, www.trimet.org; one bus line, with frequent service to Cornelius, Hillsboro, and Beaverton

OUTLYING WASHINGTON COUNTY COMMUNITIES

Beyond the urban growth boundary, past the last office parks and townhouse developments, Washington County remains largely rural, with an economy based on agriculture and forestry rather than high-tech industry. Several small towns and cities dot the hinterlands; these communities are generally growing in population, in large part because of a minor influx of commuters, but they have so far been spared the indignity of turning into purely dormitory suburbs.

Hazelnut groves and rich farmland surround the city of **North Plains** (www.northplains.org), located just north of the Sunset Highway. The city has a diminutive downtown with civic buildings—a city hall, a police station, a fire station, and a new wood-and-stone public library with ceilings made from clear hemlock—along with a couple of taverns, a market, and a hardware store. (Other commercial establishments are in strip malls on Glencoe Road, just off the highway. Homes within city limits run the gamut from moss-covered, moldering shacks to developments of large new houses; a few multi-million-dollar estates lurk in the vicinity of world-class Pumpkin Ridge Golf Course just north of town. North Plains is part of the Hillsboro School District (www.hsd.k12.or.us).

A few miles further west, **Banks** (www.cityofbanks.org) lies near the eastern foot of the Coast Range, north of Forest Grove. Most businesses, schools and government buildings, and many houses, are located on or just off the city's main street (conveniently named Main Street). At the north end of town, huge piles of logs along the railroad track await milling. Most homes within city limits are bungalows or early twentieth-century styles, with the significant exception of a large new housing development in the southern half of the city. Several wineries are nearby, and Banks is also the terminus of the 21-mile Banks-Vernonia State Trail (www.oregonstateparks.org/park_145.php), a multi-use linear trail built on an old railway line, which leads into the foothills of the Coast Range. Despite its small size and tiny population (about 1,400 people), Banks has its own school district (www.banks.k12.or.us).

Other rural Washington County communities include **Gaston**, near Henry Hagg Lake in the foothills of the Coast Range; the logging town of **Gales Creek**, in a scenic valley northwest of Forest Grove; and **Roy**, known for its lavish holiday displays in December, when the entire town is tricked out with light bulbs and ostentatious holiday displays—look for clouds reflecting the glow on the western horizon. Public transportation is essentially nonexistent in the rural areas of Washington County.

CLACKAMAS COUNTY

Portland's self-appointed tastemakers used to consider most of Clackamas County (with the affluent exceptions of Lake Oswego and West Linn) a bit beyond the pale, a sort of semi-rural backwater, populated by slack-jawed yokels, that lacked both the urban amenities of Portland and the dynamic economic growth that justified Washington County's existence. (The widely publicized shenanigans of Clackamas County's Tonya Harding and Jeff Gillooly did not help to dispel this view.)

Anyone who still clings to this stereotype is woefully behind the times. While many of the outlying areas remain fairly rural, inner Clackamas County has experienced blistering population growth in recent years, and areas like Damascus are slated to accommodate much of the Portland area's population growth over the next 20 years. Parts of Clackamas County now boast some of the highest home prices in the region, and as for trendiness—well, for what it's worth, there are now more than 30 Starbucks locations in the county, and nary a yokel in sight. Newcomers who once would never have given Clackamas County serious consideration are now settling there in droves. More are coming. You might be one of them.

SOUTHWEST CLACKAMAS COUNTY

The suburbs of southwest Clackamas County—the area south of Portland and west of the Willamette—have some of Oregon's highest per capita incomes and most coveted real estate. A few areas, such as much of Wilsonville and the Kruse Way area of Lake Oswego, are regional commercial centers, but most of the land in this part of Clackamas County is devoted to residential (or outside the urban growth boundary, quasi-agricultural) uses.

DUNTHORPE AND RIVERDALE

These exclusive unincorporated neighborhoods lie mostly in Multnomah rather than Clackamas County, but demographically they are more akin to Lake Oswego, their affluent neighbor to the south, than to Portland. Genteel **Dunthorpe** (together with the neighboring enclave of **Riverdale**) is known for large homes on large lots with correspondingly large price tags: A Dunthorpe fixer might go for a million dollars. Home styles range from staid traditional to bold (but usually not too bold) contemporary. Because residents value privacy, properties are often fenced, walled, or hedged off, and many houses are not actually visible from the street. (This is not necessarily a bad thing—not everyone finds five-car garages attractive.) Many of the homes located along the Willamette River have boathouses or floating docks.

The area has its own excellent school district, Riverdale School District (www.riverdale.k12.or.us), which consistently produces some of the highest test scores and college matriculation rates in the metropolitan area. Riverdale Elementary School lies squarely in the middle of the neighborhood, off Riverside Drive, but Riverdale High School was built nearby in Southwest Portland (presumably to avoid the significant expense of condemning Dunthorpe real estate). Celebrities who have purchased homes here include various Portland Trail Blazers, actor Danny Glover, and Linus Torvalds, creator of the Linux open-source computer operating system.

LAKE OSWEGO

Boundaries: North: Portland; Dunthorpe; **West**: Tigard; **South**: West Linn; unincorporated Clackamas County; **East**: Willamette River; **Area**: 11.2 square miles; **Population**: 36,073

Lake Oswego is the Portland version of an East Coast old-money suburb: affluent, tidy, woodsy, and generally quiet. These features make it one of the most sought-after and prestigious places to live in the Portland area, and the same features also make it a subject of mockery in some quarters: "Lake Big Ego" is one of the more printable derisive nicknames you might hear. "Lake O" certainly has its share of million-dollar waterside homes and well-coifed Ferrari drivers, but it is actually more economically diverse than it appears to outsiders. While it's not a bargain-hunter's paradise—the average home price is now well over half a million dollars—Lake Oswego contains a fair number of reasonably affordable apartments and unassuming single-family houses, especially in the western neighborhoods. The city has 19 neighborhood associations, and every one of them is dedicated to preserving the quality of life in its own little slice of the city.

Lake Oswego centers on a three-and-a-half-mile artificial lake, fed by a canal from the Tualatin River; the lake is managed by the Lake Oswego Corporation (www.lakecorp.com), an association of lakeshore residents, and is closed to public use. The original settlement was a center for the iron industry—the ruins of the old iron foundry, the oldest on the West Coast, still stand in George Rogers Park on the Willamette River—but the area ultimately evolved into a community of summer cottages (a few of which still stand) on the shores of what was known until 1913 as Sucker Lake. Development for permanent housing began after the First World War, and accelerated during the suburban boom that followed the Second World War. Today the city is basically built out, with most development occurring as infill or in nearby unincorporated areas.

Lake Oswego's pleasant, small-scale downtown, at the northeast end of the lake, features a selection of upscale shops abutting Millennium Plaza Park, where a farmers market (www.ci.oswego.or.us/farmersmarket/) takes place on Saturdays from mid-May through mid-October. Nearby Lakewood Center for the Arts is home to a theater (and a theater company) and hosts the annual Lake Oswego Festival of the Arts, held in June. The nearby First Addition neighborhood, one of the city's first residential neighborhoods, features Craftsman bungalows, English Tudor–style cottages, and other quaint prewar-style homes on walkable streets. (With its old homes and grid layout, First Addition would be a good choice for people who love the feel of Portland's Eastside neighborhoods but want to live in the suburbs.) The neighborhood abuts the southern end of Tryon Creek State Natural Area.

Some apartments (and apartments that have been converted to condominiums) sprawl across the bluffs above the Willamette River or hover above the lake at its eastern end, but most waterfront (and water view) properties are single-family homes. Houses on or near the lakeshore sell at a substantial premium. A few charming old cottages and bungalows, and even some fairly nondescript ranches, remain here from a quieter era; however, many of these have been torn down to make way for enormous fenced-off mansions. Some of these homes are true architectural gems, while others are notable mainly for their size and obtrusiveness. Homes with views on the wooded bluffs above the lake are somewhat less expensive, but hardly cheap. The quiet neighborhoods in the rolling hills north and south of the lake tend to feature winding streets lined with 1960s- and 1970s-era homes.

The western end of Lake Oswego has evolved into a major regional commercial center; the Kruse Way area, full of new Class A office space, acts as a satellite of downtown Portland, and Boones Ferry Road is lined with smaller-scale commercial developments, including restaurants and markets. This part of the city has many new to new-ish townhouse and apartment communities. The hillside

Mountain Park neighborhood near Portland Community College's Sylvania campus features well-kept ranch-style homes, many with views over Washington County to the west, set on culs-de-sac and curving streets. The streets here seem to be in competition to see which has the most erudite name: Harvard Court and Princeton Court have nothing on Erasmus, Pericles, and Cervantes (which do not even deign to have designations as streets, or roads, or courts), while freedom-fighters gravitate to the heights of Nansen Summit, where Bolivar, Juarez, and Garibaldi frolic.

In addition to (or despite) the prestige factor, many people move to Lake Oswego for the excellent public amenities. The city runs a library, various community and senior centers, and many parks and natural areas, but a major draw is the excellent set of public schools. Lake Oswego School District (www.loswego.k12.or.us) operates nine elementary schools, two junior high schools, and two high schools (one recently rebuilt and the other remodeled). Although Lake Oswego has decent bus service, the area is quite car-dependent—outside the city center/First Addition area, many of the streets are completely unwalkable, let alone bikeable—and the drive to Portland via often pokey Highway 43 or congested Interstate 5, while not the worst commute in the world, can be slow. The same is true for the commute to Washington County via Highway 217. (Although not a viable option for commuters, the Willamette Shore Trolley [www.trainweb.org/oerhs/wst.htm], a vintage trolley operated by the Oregon Electric Railway Historical Society, runs along the Willamette River from downtown Lake Oswego to downtown Portland.)

Web Site: www.ci.oswego.or.us

Zip Codes: 97034, 97035

Post Offices: Lake Oswego Post Office, 501 4th St; Lake Grove Station, 15875 Boones Ferry Rd

Police Station: City Hall (2nd Floor), 380 A Ave, 503-635-0238 (non-emergency), www.ci.oswego.or.us/police/

Emergency Hospital: Legacy Meridian Park Hospital, 19300 SW 65th Ave, Tualatin, 503-692-1212, www.legacyhealth.org

Library: Lake Oswego Public Library, 706 4th St, 503-636-7628, www.lakeoswegolibrary.org

Parks: 22 developed and undeveloped parks and natural areas, including George Rogers Park, Foothill Park, Waluga Park, and Iron Mountain Park; www.ci.oswego.or.us/parksrec/

Community Publications: *Lake Oswego Review*, www.lakeoswegoreview.com

Public Transportation: TriMet, 503-238-RIDE, www.trimet.org; several bus lines with semi-frequent service within the city and to and from Portland, Oregon City, Tigard, and Beaverton

WEST LINN

Boundaries: North: Lake Oswego; **West**: Tualatin River, unincorporated rural area (Clackamas County); **South**: Willamette River, Tualatin River; **East**: Willamette River; **Area**: 7.9 square miles; **Population**: 24,075

West Linn is one of the most desirable, and certainly among the most expensive, communities in the Portland area. The primary draws are the city's excellent schools—the West Linn–Wilsonville School District (www.wlwv.k12.or.us) has one of the best reputations (and some of the highest test scores) in the state—combined with a relatively low crime rate and an abundance of parkland and natural areas. The city has more than 20 parks and open spaces; most are small, neighborhood parks, with playgrounds and tennis courts, although a few larger parks, such as Wilderness Park and Willamette Park, draw visitors from the whole city. The city also encompasses the large Mary S. Young State Park along the Willamette River and the Nature Conservancy's Camassia Natural Area, a unique plateau region that was sculpted during ice age floods.

The Willamette River makes a great bend around West Linn, and forms the city's eastern and southern boundary. West Linn's neighborhoods occupy the mile and a half or so between the river and the crest of the range of hills that parallels the river to the west. Because of the river's bend, the city is shaped something like a chubby arrowhead, with the point aimed at Willamette Falls and downtown Oregon City across the river. The northern half of this "arrowhead" extends southward from Lake Oswego and the attractive campus of Marylhurst University. Willamette Drive (State Highway 43) is the primary north-south artery here, but it is not a major commercial strip (although it is lined in places by a few nicely landscaped retail businesses, upscale supermarkets like Market of Choice, and small shopping centers). Uphill (west) of Willamette Drive, a few steep streets wind into the hills and lead to compact, rolling neighborhoods of loops and culs-de-sac lined with contemporary and custom multi-story homes. The hills (a southern spur of the Tualatin Mountains) top out at more than five hundred feet above the elevation of the river, so many of these homes have decks with dramatic views of the Cascade Mountains. While luxury homes abound on the heights, there are also a few townhome developments and small-scale condo complexes. Back on the lowlands between Willamette Drive and the river lie neighborhoods of split-levels and well-kept ranches, many with river views or even river access. South of Mary S. Young State Park, in the Bolton neighborhood, there are many older homes—cottages, bungalows, and even a few grand Victorians.

The south half of West Linn is also a mix of old and new. Interstate 205 bisects this part of town, then crosses the river into Oregon City (as does Willamette Drive, on a much less impressive bridge built in 1922). On the bluff above the river, a few old houses, many in disrepair, have views of Willamette Falls, as well as paper mills and other industrial facilities. The Sunset neighborhood, between Willamette Drive and the Interstate, features a range of newer and older homes (including some surprisingly shabby structures, and a few apartment buildings). To the west extend large developments of new, generally high-end—and, in some cases, truly enormous—homes. A new shopping center has sprung up to service these new developments, and the city hall relocated here in 1999.

South of the Interstate, where the Tualatin River flows into the Willamette, is the historic Willamette neighborhood; this formerly important river landing features many houses from the late nineteenth and early twentieth centuries and a general store built in 1915. Period-appropriate false front facades decorate the commercial buildings—even the new ones—along Willamette Falls Drive, but away from the riverfront, newer homes and apartments have cropped up opportunistically over the years, and the northern parts of the neighborhood offer a wide range of architectural styles.

Despite its popularity, West Linn is not for everyone. In addition to its increasingly unaffordable housing stock, the city is quite car-dependent, and it can be a long and tedious commute to some of the more distant employment centers, whether via Interstate 205 or up Highway 43 to downtown Portland. Some residents complain that there is no real downtown; although there are a few office parks and other businesses near I-205 and along some of the main streets, the city is overwhelmingly residential—82% of the city is zoned for that purpose. In case you're wondering, there is no Linn (or East Linn, for that matter); West Linn got its name in 1854 when its predecessor, Linn City, was renamed.

Web Site: www.ci.west-linn.or.us

Zip Code: 97068

Post Office: West Linn Post Office, 5665 Hood St

Police Station: West Linn Police Department, 22825 Willamette Dr, 503-655-6214 (non-emergency), www.westlinnpolice.com

Emergency Hospitals: Willamette Falls Hospital, 1500 Division St, Oregon City, 503-656-1631, www.willamettefallshospital.org; Legacy Meridian Park Hospital, 19300 SW 65th Ave, Tualatin, 503-692-1212, www.legacyhealth.org

Library: West Linn Public Library, 1595 Burns St, 503-656-7853, www.westlinn.lib.or.us

Parks: 22 parks and natural areas within city limits, including Willamette Park, Wilderness Park, and Mary S. Young State Park; www.westlinnparksandrec.com

Community Publications: *West Linn Tidings,* www.westlinntidings.com

Public Transportation: TriMet, 503-238-RIDE, www.trimet.org; two bus lines with semi-frequent service to Oregon City or Lake Oswego/downtown Portland

STAFFORD

The unincorporated zone between Lake Oswego, West Linn, Tualatin, and Wilsonville is one of the most scenic parts of the metropolitan area. This region of hills, woods, and fields, generally called Stafford, lies outside the metropolitan urban growth boundary, and so is lightly populated and nominally agricultural. The area's proximity to Portland—Interstate 205 runs right through Stafford—means that, in practice, most of the properties here are hobby farms. In particular, Stafford is horse country. Most properties are large, multi-acre spreads, and much of that acreage is devoted to horse barns, pastures, and other equestrian facilities. Many homes are situated on ridges, like Pete's Mountain, to take advantage of expansive views of the Cascades and the Willamette and Tualatin valleys.

While Stafford (www.staffordhamlet.org) is likely to remain predominately semi-rural—or more accurately, quasi-rural, since most residents actually make their living in white-collar professions—for the immediate future (barring major changes in land use laws), some small-scale developments are starting to crop up, such as the 30-odd luxury homes of The Quarry at Stafford (built on the former site of an actual quarry). Stafford is part of the West Linn–Wilsonville School District (www.wlwv.k12.or.us). Apart from a tiny commercial area at Wankers Corner (hold the snickers—it's pronounced "Wonkers"), at the intersection of Stafford Road and Borland Road, shopping and services are located primarily in surrounding communities. No public transportation serves the area.

WILSONVILLE

Boundaries: North: Unincorporated Washington County; **West:** Unincorporated Clackamas County; **South:** Willamette River (partial), unincorporated Clackamas County; **East:** Unincorporated Clackamas County; **Area:** 7.4 square miles; **Population:** 16,510

The fast-growing suburb of Wilsonville is 17 miles south of Portland via frequently congested Interstate 5, which neatly bisects the city. Wilsonville is unusual in having more jobs than residents: the city is home to technology companies like Mentor Graphics, InFocus, Xerox Office Group, and FLIR Systems, as well as to various corporate distribution centers that are located here to take advantage of good freeway access and proximity to Portland. These businesses cluster on either side of the Interstate, especially in the northern part of the city. Major retail developments like the massive Fry's Electronics complex also border the I-5, and people driving along the freeway can be forgiven for thinking that no one actually lives in Wilsonville at all.

In fact, not only do people live in Wilsonville, the city is one of the fastest-growing communities in Oregon, and the average home price has shot up past $400,000. Apartments comprise a relatively high percentage of the city's housing stock, with a concentration of complexes near Wilsonville Town Center, an agglomeration of decentralized shopping plazas, a park-and-ride lot, and Town Center Park on the east side of Interstate 5. On the edge of this quasi-downtown, Memorial Park slopes down to the banks of the Willamette River and features short climbing walls, an innovative playground, a tennis court, and a boat dock. The new developments to the north and northeast include some "apartment homes" and townhouses along with neighborhoods of very large single-family homes.

West of Interstate 5, beyond the office parks, light industrial facilities, distribution facilities, and the like, extend several quiet neighborhoods of townhomes and two-story, single-family contemporary-style homes, some of which overlook the Willamette. Some of these developments border shady alleys of hazelnut groves, which are almost certainly not long for this world. The big news in Wilsonville housing is the ongoing construction of Villebois (www.villebois.net). Billing itself as "drawing inspiration from a compact French urban village," this walkable, mixed-use development will contain a mix of shops, offices, and "green-built" residences in various traditional styles, arranged around a village center. Villebois is only partially built; it will ultimately include about 2,500 housing units upon its completion in 2013 or so.

Across the river, the Charbonneau District centers on a golf course, surrounded by one- and two-story contemporary houses, condos, and apartment complexes set amid fountains, lakes, and—of course—fairways. (Fore!) The district contains a small village center with basic services; a few pathways link the disparate parts of the neighborhood, but most people walk heedlessly in the middle of the streets, which lack sidewalks and fortunately have light traffic. Charbonneau's only link with the rest of Wilsonville is Interstate 5's Boone Bridge over the Willamette; the city has proposed building a new foot/bike bridge between Charbonneau and Memorial Park, but no firm plans are in place.

Wilsonville likes to think of itself as a family-friendly city, and one-quarter of the city's residents are under 18. The highly regarded West Linn–Wilsonville School District (www.wlwv.k12.or.us), which covers most of the city, is a major draw for many parents. Students from the Charbonneau area attend schools in the Canby School District (www.canby.k12.or.us). Despite the abundance of jobs within the city limits, most residents don't actually work in the city, so traffic can be heavy in either direction during rush hour. The Boone Bridge over the Willamette River at Wilsonville is the only road bridge on the river between Newberg and West Linn, and so it is a frequent traffic chokepoint. For some reason, Wilsonville is also the site of many accidents on Interstate 5. The city has its own public transit agency, **South Metro Area Rapid Transit** (SMART; 503-682-7790, www.ridesmart.com), which provides bus service within Wilsonville and between the city and Portland, Salem, Tualatin, and Canby. TriMet is creating commuter rail service from Wilsonville to Beaverton, via Tualatin and Tigard; SMART buses will connect with trains to carry commuters to and from the city's major employers. Service is scheduled to begin in 2008.

Web Site: www.ci.wilsonville.or.us
Zip Code: 97070
Post Office: Wilsonville Post Office, 29333 SW Town Center Loop East
Police Station: Wilsonville Station, Clackamas County Sheriff's Office, 8445 SW

Elligsen Rd, 503-655-8211 (non-emergency)

Emergency Hospital: Legacy Meridian Park Hospital, 19300 SW 65th Ave, Tualatin, 503-692-1212, www.legacyhealth.org

Library: Wilsonville Public Library, 8200 SW Wilsonville Rd, 503-682-2744, www.wilsonvillelibrary.org

Parks: Fifteen parks, trails, and natural areas, including Memorial Park, Town Center Park, and Graham Oaks Natural Area

Community Publications: *Wilsonville Spokesman*, www.wilsonvillenews.com

Public Transportation: South Metro Area Rapid Transit (SMART; 503-682-7790, www.ridesmart.com) runs several free bus lines within the city, and operates commuter buses to Portland, Tualatin, Canby, and Salem; TriMet commuter rail service to Tualatin, Tigard, and Beaverton is scheduled to begin in 2008.

CLACKAMAS COUNTY—SOUTHERN SUBURBS

North-central Clackamas County—the suburban expanse east of the Willamette River and south of the city of Portland—contains the county's oldest communities and much of its existing population. Portland's boom in housing prices initially passed this area by, and on the whole it is still one of the more affordable sections of the region, but these communities have played catch-up admirably in the last few years and now boast some of the highest appreciation rates (but not values) in the metropolitan area.

MILWAUKIE

Boundaries: North: Southeast Portland; **West:** Willamette River; **South:** Oak Grove, Oatfield (unincorporated Clackamas County); **East:** Clackamas (unincorporated Clackamas County); **Area:** 4.8 square miles; **Population:** 20,810

Founded in 1847, Milwaukie—home of the Bing cherry—was named after Milwaukee, Wisconsin (which later changed the spelling of its name, leaving its Oregon namesake with the original "ie" ending). For many years, Milwaukie was a fairly nondescript, under-the-radar suburb. Despite its proximity to Portland, Milwaukie did not experience the growth in population (and housing prices) that occurred in other area communities during the last two decades. Things have changed, however; thanks to its close-in location (and spillover from the adjoining red-hot Sellwood and Westmoreland neighborhoods in Portland), the city's real estate market has posted some of the largest gains in housing prices in the Portland area in the last few years.

A swath of railroad tracks and associated industrial facilities splits the city into two halves. (Noise from train whistles bothers some residents.) On the west side of the tracks, Milwaukee's small downtown is changing, as new shops and service businesses join the old-line establishments, and rowhouses spring up near the cute red brick city hall and Scott Park, where outdoor concerts are held in the summer. Downtown Milwaukie is something of a mecca for comic book fans, thanks to the presence of Dark Horse Comics (www.darkhorse.com) in an unassuming building on Main Street. A farmers' market takes place on Sundays during the summer (www.milwaukiefarmersmarket.com). Riverfront Park provides access to the Willamette, and hosts the Riverfest festival in July. The neighborhoods near downtown have a high concentration of older homes, with some apartment buildings and townhomes in the mix.

Busy McLoughlin Boulevard cuts off downtown Milwaukie from the Willamette, but two nearby neighborhoods do border the river. To the north, large traditional-style homes—in some cases, bona fide mansions—line the narrow, winding streets around the private Waverly Country Club. Just south of downtown, the compact Island Station neighborhood features smaller, generally older homes that overlook (or are a short walk from) the river. Undeveloped Elk Rock Island is usually accessible by foot except during high water in winter and spring.

Milwaukie's east side is largely given over to modest single-family homes, mostly ranches, Cape Cods, and older cottages, with a few newer two-story homes and nineteenth-century farmhouses to spice up the mix. There are a few small commercial areas, as well as some clusters of 1920s-era bungalows in neighborhoods where the old streetcar lines used to run. Some new infill development is occurring along the city's far eastern fringe. If you are considering property near Johnson Creek, be aware that the creek is subject to flooding.

Milwaukie is often overlooked as a relocation option, but it may be a good choice for some newcomers. Despite the recent price rise, the city still has many affordable houses, including a large stock of single-family homes with large lots, and it has good road and transit connections to downtown Portland and the city's entire East Side. Plans are afoot to extend the MAX light rail system from downtown Portland to Milwaukie in the next few years. In the meantime, bus service is decent to excellent throughout much of the city. A possible downside is that some areas have a relatively high crime rate. Milwaukie is part of the North Clackamas School District (www.nclack.k12.or.us), the sixth largest in the state; the city has several elementary schools and its own middle and high schools. Several private schools, including the Portland Waldorf School, are also located here.

Web Site: www.cityofmilwaukie.org

Zip Codes: 97222, 97267

Post Office: Milwaukie Post Office, 11222 SE Main St

Police Station: Milwaukie Police Department, 3200 SE Harrison St, 503-786-7400 (non-emergency)

Emergency Hospital: Providence Milwaukie Hospital, 10150 SE 32nd Ave, Milwaukie, 503-513-8300, www.providence.org/Oregon/

Library: Ledding Library, 10660 SE 21st St, 503-786-7580, www.milwaukie.lib.or.us

Parks: Riverfront Park, Scott Park, and several other small parks maintained by the city; North Clackamas Central Park, Spring Park, and a few others are part of the North Clackamas Parks & Recreation District, www.co.clackamas.or.us/ncprd

Community Publications: *Clackamas Review*, www.clackamasreview.com

Public Transportation: TriMet, 503-238-RIDE, www.trimet.org; multiple bus lines, with frequent service from Milwaukie Transit Center to Portland and Oregon City

OAK GROVE, JENNINGS LODGE, AND OATFIELD

Boundaries: North: Milwaukie; **West**: Willamette River; **South**: Gladstone; **East**: Clackamas (unincorporated Clackamas County); **Area**: 10 square miles; **Population**: Approximately 36,500

McLoughlin Boulevard (Highway 99E) achieves full strip mall glory in the expanse of unincorporated Clackamas County between Milwaukie and Gladstone. As you tool down the highway, past the B-17 hovering above the road in front of The Bomber Restaurant, it's easy to miss the quiet middle-class neighborhoods that extend to either side. To the west, between the highway and the Willamette River, lies the community of **Oak Grove**. Oak Grove developed along the trolley line that ran along what is now Arista Drive from 1893 until the 1950s, and the area contains a variety of homes of various ages, most on relatively large lots. (The old trolley right-of-way is being converted into a bike and pedestrian trail.) River Road parallels McLoughlin to the west; the former is a much quieter and more pleasant thoroughfare than the latter, and is lined by homes and a few apartment buildings.

The bulk of Oak Grove's housing stock consists of fairly modest postwar ranches and related architectural styles, but some prewar homes survive near the trolley line, and larger contemporary and custom homes crop up near the Willamette River. A few homes on the river itself are lavish affairs, with boathouses and private docks, but on the whole Oak Grove lacks the outright mansions that line parts of the Willamette's west bank. The neighborhood has lots of trees and several parks; there are few sidewalks, but there's not much traffic off the main roads. Away from McLoughlin, there are relatively few commercial establishments. (The old commercial center of the community, on Oak Grove Boulevard, is largely defunct.) To the south, **Jennings Lodge** has a similar mix of housing, but with a greater proportion of bungalows and old farmhouses. River Road and McLoughlin begin to converge in Jennings Lodge, and the neighborhoods between become increasingly less insulated as one proceeds south.

East of McLoughlin Boulevard, the **Oatfield** neighborhood is draped over a ridge that runs parallel to the highway. (Oatfield was not named for any former agricultural land use, but rather for the Oatfields, a prominent pioneer family.)

This area has generally newer and often larger homes than the neighborhoods west of McLoughlin; some homes have views of the Willamette or the Cascades. East of Oatfield Road, some subdivisions feature contemporary homes on winding culs-de-sac, a street feature not found in Oak Grove. Oatfield in general is somewhat more affluent than Oak Grove and Jennings Lodge, and housing prices are consequently slightly higher on average. The tiny enclave of **Johnson City** is an incorporated city composed entirely of a single mobile home park.

These neighborhoods have so far resisted periodic annexation attempts (we're looking at you, Milwaukie and Gladstone) and homegrown incorporation efforts. For now, the county provides the services that do exist—the area is part of the North Clackamas Parks and Recreation District, for example—but these three communities have their own water utility, the Oak Lodge Water District (www. oaklodgewater.org). (Get it? Oak Lodge serves *Oak* Grove and Jennings *Lodge*.) Oak Grove and the northern part of Oatfield are part of the North Clackamas School District (www.nclack.k12.or.us), while Jennings Lodge and the southern part of Oatfield belong to the Oregon City School District (www.orecity.k12. or.us). Considering its low density and absence of much in the way of regional destinations, the area has relatively good transit service: buses between Oregon City and Milwaukie run along River Road and Oatfield Road, and there is frequent bus service along McLoughlin Boulevard to downtown Portland.

Web Site: www.co.clackamas.or.us

Zip Codes: 97222, 97267

Post Office: Oak Grove Post Office, 3860 SE Naef St

Police Station: Oak Lodge Sub-Station, Clackamas County Sheriff's Office, 2930 SE Oak Grove Blvd, 503-655-8211 (non-emergency)

Emergency Hospital: Providence Milwaukie Hospital, 10150 SE 32nd Ave, Milwaukie, 503-513-8300, www.providence.org/Oregon/; Willamette Falls Hospital, 1500 Division St, Oregon City, 503-656-1631, www.willamettefalls hospital.org

Library: Oak Lodge Library, 16201 SE McLoughlin Blvd, 503-655-8543, www. clackamas.us/lib/

Parks: North Clackamas Parks & Recreation District, www.co.clackamas. or.us/ncprd

Community Publications: *Clackamas Review*, www.clackamasreview.com

Public Transportation: TriMet, 503-238-RIDE, www.trimet.org; three bus lines, with frequent service to Portland, Milwaukie, and Oregon City

GLADSTONE

Boundaries: North: Jennings Lodge, Oatfield (unincorporated Clackamas County); **West**: Willamette River; **South**: Clackamas River; **East**: Clackamas River; **Area**: 2.5 square miles; **Population**: 12,140

Gladstone is well-known for the parade of car dealerships along McLoughlin Boulevard, but once you get away from the guys in bad ties asking what it would take to get you into a vehicle today the city has a different feel. Gladstone was founded at the strategic confluence of the Willamette and Clackamas rivers; surrounded by water on three sides, it has a languid, small-town ambiance. This area was a gathering place of the original native inhabitants, and a large maple known as the Pow-Wow Tree, which still stands on Clackamas Boulevard, was ostensibly a meeting spot for local tribes. Today, the river banks are equally popular with local anglers; Meldrum Bar Park, on the Willamette just downstream from the mouth of the Clackamas, is an especially esteemed spot for fishing.

Gladstone's extremely modest downtown, which manages to support a few stores and eateries and the beautifully restored Flying A Gasoline Station (which no longer sells gas), is laid out in a strict grid north of the Clackamas River. Gladstone developed early, thanks to its proximity to Oregon City and the existence of a streetcar line from Portland, and for many years the city was the site of a popular Chautauqua, a sort of educational entertainment one-two punch that was popular in the late nineteenth and early twentieth centuries. (Gladstone's Chautauqua closed in 1927, but the city still holds a festival by that name each summer.) Older houses from the city's early days perch on a bluff above the Clackamas River and line the streets for several blocks inland. The riverfront area also has a few parks, including High Rocks Park (a favorite spot for swimming and notorious for occasional drownings).

Away from the river and north of downtown, a high ridge looms, and the city streets abandon the grid pattern as they wind uphill. Culs-de-sac lined with spacious split-levels and contemporaries occupy the slopes; near the top of the ridge, 1970s-era contemporary homes border the winding streets of Ridgegate and other woody, established neighborhoods. Some of these homes have expansive views of the Willamette and West Hills or of Mount Hood and the Cascades.

Gladstone has its own school district (www.gladstone.k12.or.us), with one elementary, one middle, and one high school. Gladstone is not particularly close to major centers of employment, but neither is it ridiculously far away; there are a range of transportation options for northbound commuters, but only two road bridges cross the Clackamas River to the south and none cross the Willamette between Oregon City and the Sellwood Bridge in Portland. (Westbound commuters headed for Washington County or Wilsonville generally take Interstate 205, which runs through the eastern end of the city.)

Web Site: www.ci.gladstone.or.us
Zip Code: 97027
Post Office: Gladstone Post Office, 605 Portland Ave
Police Station: Gladstone Police Department, 535 Portland Ave, 503-557-2760 (non-emergency)
Emergency Hospital: Willamette Falls Hospital, 1500 Division St, Oregon City, 503-656-1631, www.willamettefallshospital.org

Library: Gladstone Public Library, 135 E Dartmouth St, 503-656-2411, www.glad stone.lib.or.us

Parks: Eight parks, including Meldrum Bar Park, High Rocks Park, and Max Patterson Memorial Park

Community Publications: *Oregon City News*, www.oregoncitynewsonline.com

Public Transportation: TriMet, 503-238-RIDE, www.trimet.org; multiple bus lines, with service to Portland, Milwaukie, Oregon City, and Clackamas

OREGON CITY

Boundaries: North: Clackamas River; **West**: Willamette River; **South**: Unincorporated Clackamas County; **East**: Unincorporated Clackamas County; **Area**: 9.3 square miles; **Population**: 28,964

Historic Oregon City—the end of the Oregon Trail, first capital of the old Oregon Territory, and oldest incorporated city in the western United States—fell on hard times in recent years and is trying mightily to rise again. This fiscally troubled municipality still has trouble funding basic services like police and fire protection, but property values are rising and the city's old downtown is undergoing a slow renaissance. For people who are looking for an historic community and don't mind things being a bit rough around the edges, Oregon City might be a good choice. Don't expect any bargains, though: the median home price in the city has broken $300,000.

Oregon City's downtown occupies a narrow strip of level land on the Willamette River just downstream from Willamette Falls. The area near the Falls was an important fishing ground for Native Americans, and it became the site of the first European settlement in 1829. By the 1840s, Oregon City had become a bustling town, and it was incorporated in 1844. When the Oregon Territory was created four years later, Oregon City became the capital. (That honor was transferred to Salem in 1852.) Willamette Falls fueled the city's initial industrial growth—the falling water powered lumber mills and flour mills especially—and to this day Oregon City has a palpable industrial feel. The Blue Heron paper mill still operates at the south end, just below the falls, and the overall scene is reminiscent of an old New England mill town.

Most of the city's government offices (including the Clackamas County Courthouse), as well as a variety of businesses, are still located in Oregon City's historic downtown. The downtown area is slowly evolving into a less moribund place, as new businesses inject fresh life into the district. Downtown huddles at the foot of a near-vertical bluff, and one of the city's stranger sights is the Municipal Elevator, which resembles a flying saucer on a thick pillar. The elevator carries pedestrians up and down the face of the 90-foot bluff between the business district and literally named High Street at the clifftop.

The McLoughlin Historic District spreads for blocks across the relatively flat plateau at the top of the bluff. This area contains many lovingly restored houses from the late nineteenth and early twentieth centuries, an era when this neighborhood was Oregon City's most fashionable residential area. Some nondescript 1950s- and 1960s-era commercial buildings unfortunately occupy most of the view property at the brink of the bluff. Shops and restaurants border parts of Seventh Street, which runs through the heart of the district and is the commercial center for the neighborhood.

In the southeast section of the historic district, Seventh Street (and the landscape as a whole) rises steeply to another relatively flat terrace, which stretches away toward the Clackamas County hinterlands. Here Seventh Street becomes Molalla Avenue and heads southward, flanked by supermarkets and shopping plazas. A mix of newer subdivisions, old farmhouses, mobile home parks, apartments, and retirement communities sprawl across the high terrace. The outlying neighborhoods to the south and east feature predominantly newer homes, and new residential and commercial developments are rising on the fringes of the city. Clackamas Community College is in the city's southeastern corner.

Back along the river, the Canemah Historic District clings to the steep slopes overlooking the Willamette just upstream from the falls (and thus out of sight of the associated industrial facilities). The neighborhood is made up of some historic homes, some new townhomes and single-family homes (generally built in a neo-traditional style), and some small ranch houses. Some barely improved roads lead to the neighborhood, which includes a pioneer cemetery dating from the 1830s, and the area is easy to miss.

North of downtown Oregon City, some gigantic skeletonized (un)covered wagons mark the End of the Oregon Trail Interpretive Center (www.endoftheoregontrail.org), which is indeed located at the end of the Barlow Road segment of the Oregon Trail. Interstate 205 crosses the Willamette and cuts through this portion of the city; some industrial facilities border the freeway, and the low-density Park Place neighborhood lies to the east. A large mixed-use development is planned for the Clackamette area—which sounds like the noise a waterfowl would make, but denotes the confluence of the Clackamas and Willamette Rivers.

Despite Oregon City's woeful finances, the overall crime rate is not shockingly high. Still, some neighborhoods are plagued by drug dealing and property crime, so try to avoid choosing a residence sight-unseen. The Oregon City School District (www.orecity.k12.or.us) serves Oregon City and much of the outlying unincorporated area. Oregon City has decent transportation connections to the rest of the metropolitan area, both by car and by public transit. Amtrak's Cascades trains also stop here on their runs between Portland and Salem.

Web Site: www.orcity.org
Zip Code: 97045

Post Office: Oregon City Post Office, 19300 Molalla Ave

Police Station: Oregon City Police Department, 320 Warner Milne Rd, 503-657-4964 (non-emergency), www.ci.oregon-city.or.us/police/

Emergency Hospital: Willamette Falls Hospital, 1500 Division St, Oregon City, 503-656-1631, www.willamettefallshospital.org

Library: Oregon City Public Library, 362 Warner Milne Rd, 503-657-8269, www.oregoncity.lib.or.us

Parks: More than 20 parks and trails, including Clackamette Park, Singer Creek Park, and McLoughlin Promenade; www.oregoncityparks.org

Community Publications: *Oregon City News*, www.oregoncitynewsonline.com

Public Transportation: TriMet, 503-238-RIDE, www.trimet.org; multiple bus lines within city to Oregon City Transit Center, and service between Oregon City and West Linn, Portland, Milwaukie, Lake Oswego, and Clackamas; service to Canby via Canby Area Transit (503-266-4022), and service to Molalla via South Clackamas Transportation District (503-632-7000, www.southclackamastransportation.com).

CANBY

This center of the nursery industry—for plants, not babies—feels smaller and more isolated than it actually is. With a population approaching 15,000, Canby is no longer a small town, but the surrounding farmland helps the city maintain a countrified veneer. The lack of a direct road connection across the Willamette to the southern part of the metropolitan area increases the city's sense of isolation; the rustic Canby Ferry, just north of town, is one of the last public ferries across the Willamette. In truth, while it's not exactly centrally located, Canby is only about 15 minutes from the bona fide suburbia of Oregon City, West Linn, and Wilsonville, and busy Highway 99E cuts right through town.

The city attracts a diverse set of newcomers, including many professionals who work in the south metro but want to live in a small, quiet city in the sticks. The surprisingly extensive downtown, just north of the railroad tracks and the highway, has a few restaurants and shops, a public library, and a cute red brick city hall. The adjacent neighborhoods have some lovely older homes that date from an era when Canby really was a small town. The rest of the city has homes in a variety of postwar styles, including some new subdivisions; houses on acreage lurk just outside the city limits. If you're looking for a truly small town, the neighboring city of **Barlow**, incorporated in 1903, has fewer than 150 residents.

Canby has its own school district (www.canby.k12.or.us) as well as its own transit agency, Canby Area Transit (503-266-4022), which provides bus service between Canby and Oregon City, and Woodburn, as well as free bus service within Canby city limits.

Web Site: www.ci.canby.or.us

CLACKAMAS COUNTY—SOUTHEASTERN SUBURBS

The stretch of northern Clackamas County from Milwaukie east to Damascus was once a mostly rural landscape. By the 1980s, urban development had filled much of the area east to Interstate 205; development slowly began to spill into the areas beyond, and by the late 1990s areas like Sunnyside and Happy Valley were experiencing tremendous growth. This area, along with the new city of Damascus, is expected to continue to grow rapidly over the next two decades. Unfortunately, improvements in infrastructure have lagged behind population growth, and these areas are struggling to cope with crowded roads and classrooms. Much of the eastern part of this region is still semi-rural, however. Numerous newcomers select this part of Clackamas County because there are many new homes, and the area offers reasonably easy access both to Portland and to the Mount Hood region.

CLACKAMAS AND SUNNYSIDE

The unincorporated area known as **Clackamas** sits between Happy Valley and Milwaukie south of the Portland city limits. This area has no fixed boundaries that are popularly accepted (as opposed to census-designated), but "Clackamas" is generally understood to refer to the neighborhoods that extend to either side of Southeast 82nd Avenue in northern Clackamas County. The area is a mix of residential, commercial, and light industrial uses; 82nd Avenue itself is a long strip mall of questionable aesthetics.

Clackamas Town Center and neighboring Clackamas Promenade, at the intersection of 82nd Avenue and Sunnyside Road, is the retail and geographical heart of the area.

Residences in the Clackamas area run the gamut from squalid to luxurious. Low-rise apartment buildings and townhome complexes are abundant, and these often lie in close proximity to shopping plazas and other commercial facilities. Most single-family homes are solidly middle-class, although there are also some truly dilapidated affairs here; the neighborhoods west of 82nd Avenue are among the most affordable in the metropolitan area, but some pockets are plagued by crime problems.

The most expensive and desirable homes in the Clackamas area are located on Mount Scott, just east of Clackamas Town Center across Interstate 205. A warren of culs-de-sac and winding streets cover the lower slopes of this prominent hill; contemporary, custom, and neo-traditional homes, with a few stranded ranches and prewar homes, can all be found here. The neighborhood has lots of tiny wooded greenspaces, and many homes have good views west to downtown Portland. Homes that are higher up are generally newer and larger; some, or the largest houses, are actually visible from downtown Portland, especially in late afternoon when their picture windows reflect the westering sun. Near the summit, with its cluster of antennas, stand a few brand-new, high-end homes with panoramic views east to Mount Hood.

Sunnyside is the nearby unincorporated area; it extends along and to the south of Sunnyside Road, east of Clackamas Town Center and south of Happy Valley. Most housing here is quite new, in a range of styles and sizes from townhomes and apartment complexes to hulking three-story luxury homes with Mount Hood views. A few shopping plazas line Sunnyside Road. Forested Mount Talbert Nature Park, on a volcanic butte on the west side of the community, provides a large area of open space.

Although it is not centrally located, the entire Clackamas area is well-connected to the rest of the metropolitan area. Interstate 205 provides access to the southern suburbs and to Northeast Portland, while the Milwaukie Expressway (Highway 224) runs toward downtown Portland. TriMet buses run throughout most of the Clackamas area (although not up Mount Scott) and connect Clackamas to downtown Portland and to most destinations on the east side. A light rail line to Clackamas Town Center is scheduled to open in 2009.

Clackamas County agencies provide most public services in this area. The North Clackamas Park District manages local parks and public recreational facilities, including the popular North Clackamas Aquatic Park, which includes an indoor wave pool and diving well. North Clackamas School District (www.nclack. k12.or.us) provides public education.

Web Site: www.co.clackamas.or.us/

HAPPY VALLEY

If a high income can buy contentment, then Happy Valley is aptly named: the average household income is pushing six figures. At the same time, Happy Valley is one of the fastest-growing cities in Oregon, with new construction visible almost everywhere. In addition to growth through an influx of new residents, the city is expanding by annexing surrounding areas, and the city limits are weirdly discontinuous. (Happy Valley and Damascus recently reached an agreement about which unincorporated areas each city is entitled to gobble up.)

To the extent it has a center at all, Happy Valley is indeed centered in a valley along Mount Scott Creek, between Mount Scott on the west and Scouters Mountain on the east. The valley was once forestland and farmland, with a few houses on the valley bottom. The scene is very different today. Massive developments of large new homes sprawl up every hillside; styles range from "Northwest Lodge" to McMansions with giant entry arches and soaring great rooms, along with some basic, fairly nondescript (but still quite spacious) houses. A few dazed-looking bungalows and ranches, the survivors of the original rural community, remain standing near Mount Scott Creek. The average home price here exceeds $500,000.

Happy Valley has a fair number of parks and open spaces amid the sea of housing; there is not much commercial activity in the city itself, but the shopping plazas of Sunnyside Road and the Clackamas area are a short drive away. The city is part of the North Clackamas School District (www.nclack.k12.or.us). A TriMet bus provides service six days a week between Happy Valley and Clackamas Town Center.

Web Site: www.ci.happy-valley.or.us

DAMASCUS

Damascus is primed for radical change. (That's bucolic Damascus, Oregon, by the way, not its somewhat less bucolic namesake in Syria.) Metro's 2002 expansion of the urban growth boundary included Damascus, and a minor land rush is occurring in this semi-rural landscape of fields, berry farms, and modest country houses. Much of the region's growth in the next two decades is anticipated to occur here, and the area recently incorporated to help deal with the anticipated population explosion. Residential growth along existing thoroughfares is expected to begin as soon as water and sewer service is in place, although it will take many years to develop and finance infrastructure for the entire city. For now, development is basically limited to parcels of one-acre or more (i.e., parcels large enough for septic systems), although some denser development is already occurring in the Carver area along Highway 224 where water and sewer lines already exist.

As the area grows, transportation is likely to become a major issue; existing roads cannot handle projected traffic volumes. A Sunrise Corridor freeway (or perhaps a tollway) linking Damascus to Interstate 205 has been under review for years, but funding has not yet been committed. TriMet buses run to the neighboring communities of Happy Valley and Estacada; the only service in Damascus currently is to the Carver area. The city is part of the Gresham-Barlow School District (www.gresham.k12.or.us), and has its own elementary and middle schools.

Web Site: www.ci.damascus.or.us

OUTER CLACKAMAS COUNTY

The outlying communities of Clackamas County lie in lovely rolling countryside at the western foot of the Cascade Mountains. Some homes here stand atop rises with views of Mount Hood or the Willamette Valley, others are tucked down into mossy forested hollows, and still others are part of subdivisions that wouldn't look out of place in a close-in suburb, but which invariably are just a short distance from the farm fields and forest land that still dominate the landscape. Generally speaking, these communities are popular with people who are looking for a rural or small-town environment within striking range of a large city, and with easy access to the abundant recreational opportunities in the nearby mountains. Commuting can be a major chore or worse if you work in downtown Portland or Washington County, but is quite doable if your job is in the eastern fringes of the metro area (e.g., Gresham or Oregon City).

Boring, which was named for early settler W.H. Boring and not for its lack of diversions, is a small, rural community set amid plant nurseries southeast of Gresham. The small town center at the intersection of Southeast 282nd Avenue and Highway 212 includes the Boring-Damascus Grange, which dates from 1896. The Boring farmers' market, held on summer Saturdays, is possibly the only one in Oregon to bill itself as "equine-friendly." Boring children attend Oregon Trail School District schools (www.oregontrailschools.com). (The school district is unlikely to adopt that phrase as its slogan.) Boring has very limited commuter bus service to Gresham; it is, however, favorably situated for bike commuters at the end of the Springwater Trail Corridor that runs to the Willamette River in Southeast Portland.

A few miles to the southeast, **Sandy** (www.ci.sandy.or.us) is well known to Portlanders as a pit stop for cheap gas, ski rentals, and doughnuts on the way to Mount Hood. It is also a growing, bustling small city of about 7,000 people, with its own urban growth boundary, public transit system, and school district (Oregon Trail School District, www.oregontrailschools.com). Mount Hood Highway (US 26) is the main drag through town; the lower end is lined with supermarkets and shopping plazas, but the highway divides and traffic slows when the road reaches the city's pleasant downtown. Sandy offers a mix of housing, from 1950s-era ranches and brand-new luxury homes in Sandy proper to rural homes on acreage in the countryside nearby. The surrounding area is dominated by plant nurseries, berry farms, and even a winery; to the east, toward Mount Hood, the land quickly transitions to forest. Sandy is the closest city to Mount Hood, and many residents are avid snowsport devotees. Sandy Area Metro buses (503-668-5569) connect Sandy to Gresham, Estacada, and Rhododendron, further up the mountain.

About 10 miles to the southeast, **Estacada** (www.cityofestacada.org) stands on the bank of the Clackamas River. From Highway 224, which wends its way up the Clackamas River Valley into the Cascades, Estacada doesn't look terribly attractive—the strip of businesses along the highway is definitely not the city's best face—but the small, old-fashioned downtown behind is pleasant enough (with the exception of the Safari Club, roofed in fake green thatch, which is too ugly even to qualify as kitsch). Most of the city's houses stand on the hill behind downtown or are scattered in the forested areas nearby. Estacada's economy has traditionally been timber-dependent, and the city has not grown as quickly as some closer-in communities have, although a boom in large homes on big plots of land outside town has caused average home prices in the area to rise significantly. Estacada has its own school district (www.esd108.org), which serves a huge area of rural Clackamas County, including much of the Mount Hood National Forest. The Clackamas River offers abundant opportunities for fishing and boating, and Highway 224 leads deep into the heart of the Cascades. Although Estacada is decidedly outside the metropolitan area proper, a TriMet bus line runs between the city and Portland.

Over the river and through the woods, truly rural **Colton** is enveloped in the lush foothills along Highway 211 southwest of Estacada. This is working timber country, complete with clearcuts and log trucks, and the area has so far avoided an inrush of yuppies. Amenities are pretty much limited to a store and a restaurant at the crossroads. Colton has its own tiny school district (www.colton.k12.or.us), with an elementary school, a middle school, and a high school.

Heading back toward the lowlands, the much larger community of **Molalla** (www.molalla.net/~city) is also a lumber town, but its economy is slowly diversifying and the town is attracting more residents who commute to the Portland and Salem metro areas. Molalla has a very scenic setting on a rolling site where the Cascade foothills (and their supplies of timber) meet the Willamette Valley. The comparatively large, bustling downtown offers a bonanza of businesses: hardware stores, restaurants, banks, and more. The city's generally well-kept homes include dwellings in old, newer, and newest styles. The city is regionally known for the Molalla Buckeroo rodeo (www.molallabuckeroo.com), held each July at the rodeo grounds at the east end of town. Molalla has its own transit system, the South Clackamas Transit District (503-632-7000, www.southclackamastransportation.com), which connects the city to Canby, Mulino, and Oregon City by bus. **Mulino**, a few miles north of Molalla along the Cascade Highway (Highway 213), is not much larger than Colton—the community applied to the county for "hamlet" status in 2007—but it is certainly less remote. The Molalla River School District (www.molallariv.k12.or.us) serves both Molalla and Mulino.

Further north, a mile or two off Cascade Highway, just a few miles south of Oregon City, the hamlet of **Beavercreek** lacks much of a town center—there is a gas station, a fire station, a post office, and a couple of businesses, plus the Beavercreek Grange and historic Bryn Seion Welsh Church, the oldest Welsh church on the West Coast. Homes on large lots or small farms occupy the rolling hills. Some new developments are going up north of the community, especially near Cascade Highway, but Beavercreek as a whole remains decidedly rural. At the same time, it is only fifteen minutes from Oregon City, and lies within the Oregon City School District (www.orecity.k12.or.us).

Other small outlying communities in Clackamas County include Redland, Liberal, Eagle Creek, and Marquam. Some people commute to the metropolitan area from the mountain communities between Sandy and Mount Hood—Welches, Rhododendron, Zigzag, Wemme, and Brightwood—but distance, hazardous winter weather, and heavy through traffic on Highway 26 make this option less attractive than it might sound.

EAST MULTNOMAH COUNTY

Residents of eastern Multnomah County—the communities that extend east of Portland's city limits—often grumble about being neglected. The county's population (and hence representation on the board of commissioners) is Portland-centric, and many of the 130,000-plus people in the rest of the county feel, rightly or wrongly, that their corner of the world doesn't get its proper share of funding. There is periodic talk of secession, either to form a new county, or to join Clackamas County, but the law is unfavorable and it is unclear that being tacked on to another populous county would provide any advantages. For now, fast-growing East County simmers in political disgruntlement, cooled only by the bitter winds that issue from the Columbia River Gorge in winter.

GRESHAM

Boundaries: North: Fairview; Wood Village; Troutdale; **West**: Portland; unincorporated Multnomah County; **South**: Unincorporated Multnomah County; unincorporated Clackamas County; **East**: Unincorporated Multnomah County; **Area**: 23.2 square miles; **Population**: 97,914

Gresham (pronounced GRESH-um or, by true old-timers, GRAY-shum) is the fourth largest city in Oregon, but most Oregonians (or at least most Oregonians who live outside Gresham) seem blissfully unaware of this factoid. Ask the average Portlander what the fourth largest city in the state is, and you might hear Medford (no), Bend (not yet), or Beaverton (close but no cigar). In fact, many people in the Portland area largely ignore Gresham, except when they have to go through it to get to Mount Hood. It is the butt of tasteless jokes, and the scene of gory crimes on local television news reports, and that is all.

The region's collective diss of Gresham is a shame. While the city does have its share of problems, including a frighteningly high crime rate in some areas, it also has plenty of quiet, middle-class neighborhoods, some decent schools, an up-and-coming city center, a young, dynamic mayor, and a light rail line with a straight shot to Portland. It is close to recreational opportunities on Mount Hood and in the Columbia River Gorge, it has easy access to Portland International Airport, and parts of the city have awesome views of the mountains. Moreover, although home price growth has recently accelerated here—prices rose 20% between 2005 and 2006, one of the highest rates in the region—Gresham's late start means that real estate prices tend to be lower here than in much of Portland or the more fashionable western or southern close-in suburbs. In short, while Gresham is far from "hot," it might be worth a look.

Gresham's small downtown district (www.gresham.org) is surprisingly pleasant; the streets are lined with restaurants, shops, a few historic buildings, and even a couple of day spas, and some new townhomes and loft-style residential buildings have been built here. There is a farmers' market here on Saturdays from May to October (www.greshamfarmersmarket.com). Downtown Gresham is the eastern terminus of the MAX Blue Line, and many residents rely on light rail to commute to jobs in Portland. (The city has vague plans to further energize this area with new "transit-oriented" development.) The area around downtown is an odd mix of housing and commercial development. Apartments and town-home developments line many of the main roads (and some of the minor ones), while older subdivisions of single-family houses dot the landscape; even within walking distance of downtown, there are neighborhoods of 1960s-era homes on winding streets and culs-de-sac. The general impression is that opportunistic developers built haphazardly whenever old Mrs. Brown's farm (or its equivalent) went up for sale, without really giving any thought to how or whether their developments related to one another. (This is not to say that the neighborhoods are necessarily unpleasant; some of them just seem stranded.) The new Gresham Station commercial development west of downtown has brought a bevy of national retailers to the area.

Much of west-central Gresham consists of single-family homes mixed with high-density housing developments and apartments. Rents here are in many cases much lower than in close-in Portland neighborhoods, and the region has seen an influx of low-income workers who have been priced out of Portland by gentrification and rising rents. This area in general, and in particular the Rockwood neighborhood (which is being positioned as the "Gateway to Gresham"), has a reputation for gang activity and violent crime, although it's not exactly the South Bronx. Some urban renewal activity is taking place in this part of the city, especially along Burnside Street where the MAX line runs. Much of the city's northern area, especially the districts adjacent to Fairview and Wood Village and flanking Interstate 84, is devoted to light industry.

In southwest Gresham, developments of newer homes—in some cases, brand-new homes—abut hobby farms just over the city line in unincorporated Multnomah County. This area, set in a valley on the west side of Gresham Butte, features a hodgepodge of styles, with a mix of ranches, contemporary homes, split-levels, some low-rise apartment complexes and townhome developments, and a few brand-new subdivisions. The homes on Gresham Butte itself (much of which is now protected as open space) tend to be newer and correspondingly more expensive, with views of the Washington Cascades (or, for houses on the eastern side of the butte, of Mount Hood).

The neighborhoods of southeast Gresham, like those of southwest Gresham, feature a mix of styles, although the average home is relatively new. The Kelly Creek neighborhood, off Orient Road, has seen substantial new development right out to the city limits, where on Southeast 282nd Avenue you'll see dense developments right across the street from plant nurseries. This part of the city is well-positioned for quick trips to Mount Hood, and some homes have great views of the mountain looming to the southwest. Shopping plazas and light industrial facilities line the Mount Hood Highway (US 26) in this part of the city.

The Gresham-Barlow School District (www.gresham.k12.or.us) serves most of the city; students from the western fringe attend schools in the Centennial School District (www.centennial.k12.or.us), and the northern part of the city is part of the Reynolds School District (www.Reynolds.k12.or.us). Mount Hood Community College occupies a campus in the northeast corner of the city, and adds some cultural spice to the landscape. Gresham is reasonably well served by public transit; in addition to frequent MAX service, Tri-Met bus lines serve most of the main streets, and Sandy Area Metro buses run to Sandy. Interstate 84, which skirts Gresham to the north, is the main freeway route to Portland, but it can be very congested during rush hour, particularly between Interstate 205 and downtown Portland. Driving to Portland via the main east-west streets (Powell Boulevard, Division Street, Stark Street, Glisan Street, and Foster Road) can be slow and time-consuming, but it is a reasonable alternative if you are headed to Southeast Portland.

Web Site: www.ci.gresham.or.us
Zip Codes: 97030, 97080, 97230, 97233
Post Office: Gresham Post Office, 103 W Powell Blvd
Police Station: Gresham Police Department, 1333 NW Eastman Pkwy, 503-618-2318 (non-emergency)
Emergency Hospital: Legacy Mount Hood Medical Center, 24800 SE Stark St, Gresham, 503-674-1122, www.legacyhealth.org
Libraries: Gresham Library, 385 NW Miller Ave, 503-988-5387; Rockwood Library, 17917 SE Stark St, 503-988-5396; www.multcolib.org
Parks: More than 25 parks and natural areas, including Main City Park and Red Sunset Park, plus 5 miles of recreational trail; www.ci.gresham.or.us/departments/des/parksandrec/
Community Publications: *Gresham Outlook*, www.theoutlookonline.com
Public Transportation: TriMet, 503-238-RIDE, www.trimet.org; MAX light rail service to Portland and Washington County and bus service within Gresham and between Gresham and various points in Portland. Sandy Area Metro (503-668-5569, www.ci.sandy.or.us) runs buses from Gresham to Sandy.

FAIRVIEW, WOOD VILLAGE, AND TROUTDALE

Boundaries: North: Columbia River; **West**: Gresham; **South**: Gresham; **East**: Sandy River; **Area**: 3.5 square miles (Fairview); 0.9 square miles (Wood Village); 5.0 square miles (Troutdale); **Population**: 9,400 (Fairview); 2,900 (Wood Village); 15,000 (Troutdale)

The cities of Fairview, Wood Village, and Troutdale straddle Interstate 84 near the west end of the Columbia River Gorge, about 17 miles east of downtown Portland. These three "freeway-close" communities are sometimes lumped together—in this entry, for example—but all are separately incorporated and have different characteristics. Children from all three cities attend public schools in the Reynolds School District (www.Reynolds.k12.or.us).

The interstate runs right down the middle of **Fairview**, the closest of these three cities to Portland. The original heart of the city, just south of Intersate 84, is a relatively affordable neighborhood of Cape Cods and ranches; across Halsey Street to the south, Fairview Village (www.fairviewvillage.com) is a new mixed-use, pedestrian-friendly, master-planned development with townhomes, single-family homes, apartments, shops, and offices. The new Fairview City Hall is also located here. North of Interstate 84, the south shore of shallow Fairview Lake is lined with large, expensive new homes and a small park with a canoe dock. A short distance to the north is Blue Lake Regional Park, a Metro-run park with a popular swimming beach.

The city of **Wood Village** sprang into being as a company town for the Reynolds Aluminum plant during the Second World War. Today, the city is best-known as home of the now-closed Multnomah Greyhound Park (a.k.a. the "Dog Park") in the city's southeast corner; the site has been eyed for redevelopment as a massive entertainment complex and casino. The adjacent Wood Village Town Center features a mix of retailers and specialty stores together with a new housing development. The city government, aching for revenue, has proposed a local sales tax. If the plan is approved, Wood Village will be the first municipality in Oregon to have a sales tax.

Troutdale is the largest and most populous member of this civic trio. Troutdale's minuscule historic downtown (www.historictroutdale.com) borders the Historic Columbia River Highway, just up the hill and across the tracks from a very different shopping experience at the Columbia Gorge Factory Stores. Downtown Troutdale has several antique stores, restaurants and bars, and galleries, along with a couple of historic museums; a First Friday Art Walk takes place here, as does a farmers' and artists' market on Saturdays from April to mid-November. About a mile to the west on Halsey Street, the McMenamin brothers have converted the former Multnomah County Poor Farm into the 38-acre Edgefield complex, with a hotel, several restaurants and bars, a brewery, a winery, a golf course, a movie theater, and a glassblowing studio.

Troutdale's residential districts sprawl across the hills south of downtown. A few older houses still stand in the old grid above the historic downtown, and some farmhouses still dot the rolling highlands, but most homes date from the 1950s onward. As one proceeds south, the housing stock grows generally newer, and contemporary homes on culs-de-sac dominate much of the southern half of the city. Many of the houses on the ridges on either side of Beaver Creek offer views of Mount Hood and the Sandy River. The unincorporated zone between Troutdale and Gresham, in pretty countryside above the Sandy River, still has a definite rural feel.

These cities are literally at the doorstep of the Columbia River Gorge, and world-class hiking, windsurfing, and waterfall-gazing are only minutes away. At the same time, when the Gorge winds blow, Troutdale and vicinity take the brunt of the blast, and when they occur ice storms are more severe. (Trees with weak limbs do not fare well here.) Besides the Gorge winds, occasional nuisances include low-flying planes from Troutdale Airport and occasional whiffs of the paper and pulp mill across the Columbia River in Camas, Washington. These cities offer a reasonably quick commute to Portland International Airport, but traveling on Interstate 84 beyond Interstate 205 is fraught with peril at peak times. Decent bus service exists, but coverage is fairly limited.

Web Sites: www.ci.fairview.or.us; www.ci.wood-village.or.us; www.ci.troutdale. or.us

Zip Codes: 97024 (Fairview), 97060 (Wood Village and Troutdale)

Post Offices: Fairview Post Office, 1700 NE Market Dr; Troutdale Post Office, 647 SW Cherry Park Rd

Police Stations: Fairview Police Department, 1300 NE Village St, 503-823-3333 (non-emergency); Multnomah County Sheriff's Office, Wood Village City Hall, 2055 NE 238th Dr, 503-823-3333 (non-emergency); Troutdale Police Department, 141 SE Dora St, 503-665-6129 (non-emergency)

Emergency Hospital: Legacy Mount Hood Medical Center, 24800 SE Stark St, Gresham, 503-674-1122, www.legacyhealth.org

Library: Fairview-Columbia Library, 1520 NE Village St, Fairview, 503-988-5655, www.multcolib.org/agcy/frv.html

Parks: Fairview: four small city parks, plus Metro's Blue Lake Regional Park; Wood Village: City Park (www.ci.wood-village.or.us/dlrpark.htm); Troutdale: more than 20 parks and open spaces, including Glenn Otto Park on the Sandy River and Columbia Park (www.ci.troutdale.or.us/parks-facilities/); the Columbia River Gorge National Scenic Area and several state and regional parks on the Sandy River lie just east of Troutdale.

Community Publications: *Gresham Outlook,* www.theoutlookonline.com

Public Transportation: TriMet, 503-238-RIDE, www.trimet.org; four bus lines, with service to Portland and Gresham

CORBETT

The unincorporated community of Corbett lies on a rolling plateau between the Columbia and Sandy rivers near the western end of the Columbia Gorge, about 20 miles east of Portland. The area is largely a landscape of working farms, orchards, and wineries, with views of Mount Hood and the Columbia River from some places. Housing stock runs the gamut from old farmhouses and American vernacular homes to ranches and some new custom homes. The community's small commercial center lies on the Historic Columbia River Highway; Crown Point, the unofficial gateway to the Gorge, is just east of town. Although Corbett lacks big city amenities—or even small city amenities—it's a short drive from the eastern edge of the metropolitan area, and is close to recreational opportunities in the Gorge, on Mount Hood, and on nearby Larch Mountain. Corbett has its own small school district (www.corbett.k12.or.us) with one of the best high schools in the state.

Web Site: www.corbettoregon.com (unofficial)

VANCOUVER AND CLARK COUNTY

Once upon a time, back in the 1840s, Clark County included all of what is now the state of Washington. Although the county has diminished dramatically in size since then, it has grown just as dramatically in population. A steady flow of settlers and homesteaders arrived in the second half of the nineteenth century, and the county's towns and cities started to expand in the early decades of the twentieth, but the first big population boom occurred during the Second World War, when the Kaiser Shipyards in Vancouver employed nearly 40,000 people. During the war years, Vancouver's population exploded from 18,000 to 100,000; many of the new residents were housed in temporary facilities, and thousands of houses were thrown up in postwar years to accommodate the influx. More recently, Portland's growth, combined with lower average home prices and the lack of an urban growth boundary to constrain sprawl, have combined to attract tens of thousands of new residents, and Clark County's population now stands at about 400,000.

Unfortunately, job growth in Clark County has not kept pace with the area's explosive population growth, and many residents are forced to commute across the river to jobs in Portland. Rush-hour congestion along Interstate 5 between Vancouver and downtown Portland is, on average, the worst in the region, and the old Interstate Bridge is showing its age. A new bridge, together with associated access ramp changes, is expected to have a price tag in the billions. (See www.columbiarivercrossing.org for up-to-date information on plans for a new crossing.) The county's sprawling new developments have contributed to traffic congestion problems within the county as well, since road networks have not kept up with population growth.

Despite the congestion, Clark County remains a popular destination for newcomers. Home prices in some areas remain relatively affordable, although housing costs in places like Camas have zoomed past the metropolitan average and new growth management laws in Washington are putting the brakes on willy-nilly rural development. Washington is attractive to some because it has no personal income tax, although it has high sales and property taxes. (If you live in Washington but work in Oregon, you will be subject to Oregon income tax, however.) Clark County is also perceived (at least in Clark County) as having better schools on the whole than Oregon does, with lower student-teacher ratios and more stable funding, although this generalization definitely is not true across the board. Also, Clark County voters (especially North County voters) tend to be more politically conservative than their counterparts in Portland and its Oregon suburbs, although this generalization, too, does not paint a complete picture and is increasingly less true in Vancouver.

Vancouver and other large incorporated areas have their own neighborhood associations. (A map of Vancouver associations is available at www.cityofvancouver.us/nhoods.asp.) The unincorporated populated areas of Clark County also have neighborhood associations (see www.co.clark.wa.us/neigh borhoods/associations.html).

County Web Site: www.co.clark.wa.us

VANCOUVER

Boundaries: North: Hazel Dell, Felida, Orchards (unincorporated Clark County); **West**: Vancouver Lake; Columbia River; **South**: Columbia River; **East**: Camas; unincorporated Clark County; **Area**: 43 square miles; **Population**: 157,500

Poor Vancouver. Popularly relegated to the status of bland suburb of its much larger neighbor across the Columbia River, and dwarfed in public esteem by the more glamorous city of the same name in British Columbia, Vancouver USA (as the city has branded itself) has trouble getting noticed. Civic boosters point out that if Vancouver were in Oregon it would be the second-largest city in the state, and emphasize that the city predates Portland by a couple of decades: the British Hudson's Bay Company established Fort Vancouver as its western headquarters in 1825. But the 'Couv still gets treated like the quiet, homely sibling of its popular but wild sister south of the river.

Vancouver's stigma—if being thought of as completely unexciting is really a stigma—may be fading ever so slowly. Downtown redevelopment has given a breath of new life to the city's wheezing old commercial center, while annexations and a general influx of new residents have increased the city's population dramatically and have (at least theoretically) given it a bigger voice in the region. Moreover, it may be shedding some of its old provincial conservatism: the mayor, Royce Pollard, is a fan of light rail (which Clark County voters have so far refused to fund) and a newly declared enemy of global warming. (Pollard raised eyebrows in the community during his 2007 State of the City address; describing a trip to Alaska, he declared, "I even touched one of the glaciers and shared a moment with it—it spoke to me. It said, 'Mayor of America's Vancouver, help me. I'm melting.'")

Of course, many Vancouverites are happy with their city the way it is. Housing is more affordable here than in Portland, many neighborhoods have a great sense of community, the city is close to outdoor recreational opportunities, and there are plenty of amenities and mainstream shopping opportunities; at the same time, the cultural events and urban attractions of Portland lurk just across the river. The potential downsides of living in Vancouver include airplane noise (and, in some locations, train noise), high crime rates in some neighborhoods, sprawl and resulting car-dependency, and, for people who work in Oregon, Oregon income taxes and an increasingly congested commute. In short, Vancouver appeals to lots of people; whether you are one of those people depends on what you're looking for.

Downtown Vancouver, perched above the river just west of Interstate 5, manages the neat trick of being simultaneously down-at-heel and up-and-coming. Old pawn shops, check cashing joints, and seedy bars mix uneasily with new residential lofts, art galleries, and day spas, as well as a host of service businesses and office buildings. Once-seedy Esther Short Park has been transformed into a venue for outdoor music festivals, and also serves as the home of the city's year-round farmers' market (www.vancouverfarmersmarket.com); an underutilized new convention center is nearby. A railroad track cuts off downtown Vancouver from its waterfront, which the hulking Red Lion Hotel and its massive parking lot unfortunately dominate. It's too early to call downtown Vancouver trendy—or even to surmise that it will be trendy in the near future—but it has become a more attractive environment for residents and visitors than it was a few years ago.

Immediately to the north, the Uptown Village neighborhood (www.uptownvillage.com) offers a concentration of late nineteenth- and early twentieth-century homes, with some newer houses and apartments mixed in. Dozens of small shops, restaurants, and service businesses line Main Street; the Clark County Historical Museum (www.cchmuseum.org), housed in an old Carnegie library, is also here. Community spirit is strong, and Uptown Village events include a St. Patrick's Day parade, a street festival, outdoor summer movies, and Artwalk on the first Thursday of each month.

North of Fourth Plain Boulevard, ranches, Cape Cods, and other postwar styles predominate, and the businesses along Main Street become more utilitarian. Houses east of Main Street tend to get some freeway noise; across Main, train noise becomes a potential problem as you move west. Just beyond the train tracks, the Fruit Valley neighborhood has a few residences, and even some stranded orchards, but the area is primarily industrial.

East of Interstate 5, the reconstructed palisades of Fort Vancouver (www.nps.gov/fova) stand anachronistically next to historic Pearson Airpark, with its museum of antique airplanes. Nearby, the Vancouver Barracks, established in 1849 to guard the western end of the Oregon Trail, is still home to a Washington National Guard detachment; the grand Victorian houses of Officers Row, where General George Marshall and other military luminaries lived, have been converted to civic, nonprofit, and professional offices. While you cannot live in any of these places, you could live in the adjacent Hudson's Bay neighborhood, which includes many historic structures and (mostly) small houses, along with some new rowhouses.

The other neighborhoods that lie between interstates 5 and 205 contain a mix of single-family homes and small-scale apartments in a diverse range of styles and degrees of upkeep. Most homes here date from the 1940s to the

1970s, although some newer homes exist and infill development is occurring in certain areas. Homes along the Columbia have great views of the river, and in some cases of Mount Hood, as well as Portland International Airport just across the water. Unfortunately, these homes were built along a busy transportation corridor and suffer correspondingly from noise from trains, planes, and automobiles. Homes on the ridge that parallels the Columbia River north of Highway 14 also have views that extend to downtown Portland and the West Hills, but with somewhat less noise.

While much of this area features pleasant, middle-class housing, some neighborhoods have relatively high crime rates, particularly the neighborhoods near Fourth Plain Boulevard from Clark Community College to the Vancouver Mall. Given their age, many of the neighborhoods lack sidewalks, but there is a liberal sprinkling of public parks. Although much of the Columbia River shore is awaiting redevelopment, the Waterfront Renaissance Trail runs along the river for four miles from downtown Vancouver.

The neighborhoods east of Interstate 205 are generally newer than those west of the freeway, with a mix of commercial, retail, and residential development. Many of these neighborhoods were annexed by the city of Vancouver in recent years. Residential options include large single-family homes along with townhouses and some apartment complexes. Mill Plain Boulevard as it runs through the Cascade Park neighborhood is this area's commercial heart. Fishers Landing and the surrounding area, at the city's far eastern end near Camas, are among the newest and most popular neighborhoods in East Vancouver, but they are not to everyone's taste. Commuting into Oregon from East Vancouver can be a headache, although Portland International Airport and the surrounding industrial and commercial area is a short trip.

Two different school districts serve Vancouver. The Vancouver School District (www.vansd.org) covers the western half of the city; East Vancouver children attend Evergreen Public Schools (www.egreen.wednet.edu). Both districts are quite large, with more than 20,000 students apiece. Evergreen schools have a slightly better reputation overall, but both districts contain excellent and not-so-great schools.

Web Site: www.cityofvancouver.us

Zip Codes: 98660, 98661, 98662, 98663, 98664, 98682, 98683, 98684

Post Offices: Vancouver Post Office, 2700 Caples Ave, Vancouver; downtown Vancouver Post Office, 1211 Daniels St, Vancouver; Cascade Park Post Office, 304 SW Hearthwood Blvd, Vancouver

Police Stations: Vancouver Police Department, 605 E Evergreen Blvd, 360-487-7400 (non-emergency); Central Precinct, 2800 Stapleton Rd, 360-735-8800 (non-emergency); East Precinct, 520 SE 155th Ave, 360-487-7500 (non-emergency)

Emergency Hospitals: Southwest Washington Medical Center, 400 NE Mother

Joseph Pl, Vancouver, 360-256-2000, www.swmedicalcenter.com

Libraries: Vancouver Community Library, 1007 E Mill Plain Blvd, 360-695-1561; Cascade Pak Community Library, 301 SE Hearthwood Blvd, 360-256-7782; Vancouver Mall Community Library, 8700 NE Vancouver Mall Dr, Suite 285, 360-892-8256; www.fvrl.org

Parks: More than 60 city and county parks, trails, and recreational facilities, including Vancouver Lake Park, Marine Park, David Douglas Park, Haagen Park, the Burnt Bridge Creek Greenway, Columbia Springs Environmental Education Area, and Fort Vancouver National Historical Site; www.vanclark parks-rec.org

Community Publications: *The Columbian*, www.columbian.com

Public Transportation: C-TRAN, 360-695-0123, www.c-tran.com; extensive service near downtown Vancouver and in the western half of the city, with service to and from major destinations in East Vancouver and surrounding suburbs, and commuter bus service to downtown Portland and the Delta Park and Parkrose MAX stations

CAMAS

Boundaries: North: Unincorporated rural area (Clark County); **West:** Vancouver; **South:** Columbia River; **East:** Washougal; **Area:** 12.6 square miles; **Population:** 15,800

Founded in the 1880s as a paper mill town on the north shore of the Columbia River, Camas has evolved into a booming suburb and minor center for high-tech enterprise, with new facilities for such companies as WaferTech and Sharp Microelectronics. The city's population has roughly doubled in the last ten years, with new residents lured by relatively low taxes, access to open space (and buildable lots), and good public schools. The Georgia-Pacific paper mill is still the city's primary landmark and one of its major employers; recently installed pollution control equipment has largely eliminated its once legendary stench. Camas is a relatively easy 20-minute drive from Portland International Airport and the surrounding light-industrial area, but the commute to downtown Portland or Washington County can be grueling. Public transportation options from Camas are limited; some residents drive to transit centers in Vancouver or near the Portland Airport.

The city's old-school downtown (www.downtowncamas.com) includes the standard range of services, specialty shops, and restaurants; the 1920s-era Liberty Theater (www.libertytheater.com) shows first-run movies seven days a week. Many downtown businesses stay open late for an evening "art walk" on the first Friday of each month.

The neighborhoods near downtown Camas feature small bungalows and other traditional home styles, which blend into ranches and other postwar designs as one travels outward. A few lovely older homes stand on the banks of the

Washougal River. The majority of the city's housing stock is fairly new, and runs the gamut from small condos and apartments to massive custom homes with views of Mount Hood and the Columbia River. The new subdivisions on Prune Hill, an extinct volcanic cone in the western part of the city, offer particularly expansive views. Many otherwise attractive homes near the riverfront suffer from railroad noise and proximity to industrial uses. Housing prices have increased sharply here over the last few years, and Camas is no longer the real estate bargain it once was.

Camas has its own highly regarded school district (www.camas.wednet. edu). A full third of the city's population consists of children enrolled in public schools. Although the city has relatively few attractions of its own, it boasts a number of pleasant parks and offers easy access to the Columbia River Gorge and Gifford Pinchot National Forest. Lacamas Lake and its surrounding forested parklands and trails are especially popular.

Web Site: www.ci.camas.wa.us

Zip Code: 98607

Post Office: Camas Post Office, 440 NE 5th Ave

Police Station: Camas Police Department, 2100 NE 3rd Ave, 360-834-4151 (non-emergency)

Emergency Hospital: Southwest Washington Medical Center, 400 NE Mother Joseph Pl, Vancouver, 360-256-2000, www.swmedicalcenter.com

Library: Camas Public Library, 625 NE 4th Ave, 360-834-4692, www.ci.camas. wa.us/library/

Parks: 13 parks, including Lacamas Park, Crown Park, Forest Home Park; www. ci.camas.wa.us/parks/

Community Publications: *Camas-Washougal Post-Record*, www.camaspost record.com

Public Transportation: C-TRAN, 360-695-0123, www.c-tran.com; limited bus service to Vancouver, Washougal, and downtown Portland

WASHOUGAL

Boundaries: North: Unincorporated rural area (Clark County); **West**: Camas; **South**: Columbia River; **East**: Unincorporated rural area (Clark County); **Area**: 5 square miles; **Population**: 12,200

Washougal is the easternmost significant community in the metropolitan area, and like Camas it is one of the fastest-growing communities in southwest Washington. Although it is separately incorporated and has its own police department, library, and school district (www.washougal.k12.wa.us), Washougal can best be understood as an eastern extension of Camas. The city has a tiny old downtown on B Street, with a few other commercial establishments on E Street. The original center of Washougal lay between the Columbia and Washougal rivers, and the bulk of the city's older housing stock is here; many of the houses along the

Washougal River have very pleasant settings. Newer houses with river views occupy the bluffs north of the Washougal River. The area to the east of the city center—especially north of Evergreen Way and east of 32nd Street—has seen explosive residential growth in the last few years.

Washougal suffers from some of the same commuting headaches as Camas, but weekend recreational opportunities are abundant: Steigerwald National Wildlife Refuge and the Columbia River Gorge lie due east of the city. Much of the area along the Columbia is devoted to industrial uses, like the large port facility at the west end of town, but the three-mile Washougal Dike Trail leads east along the river from Steamboat Landing. Due to its proximity to the Gorge, Washougal is subject to occasional high winds and ice storms, and receives markedly more precipitation than Vancouver or Portland.

Web Site: www.cityofwashougal.org

Zip Code: 98671

Post Office: Washougal Post Office, 129 17th St

Police Station: Washougal Police Department, 1320 A St, 360-835-8701 (non-emergency)

Emergency Hospital: Southwest Washington Medical Center, 400 NE Mother Joseph Place, Vancouver, (360) 256-2000, www.swmedicalcenter.com

Library: Washougal Community Library, 1661 C St, 360-835-5393, www.fvrl.org/aboutus/washougal_main.htm

Parks: Eight parks, including Steamboat Landing and Hathaway Park; washougal.biz/cow/works/parks.htm

Community Publications: *Camas-Washougal Post-Record*, www.camaspostrecord.com

Public Transportation: C-TRAN, 360-695-0123, www.c-tran.com; two bus lines with limited service to Camas, Fishers Landing (East Vancouver), and downtown Portland

UNINCORPORATED CLARK COUNTY: HAZEL DELL, ORCHARDS, FELIDA, SALMON CREEK, AND BRUSH PRAIRIE

Along its northern fringe, the city of Vancouver transitions into several unincorporated communities, which in turn blend into one another in a band of urbanized area that extends perhaps seven miles from east to west.

Immediately north of Vancouver, the community of **Hazel Dell** straddles Interstate 5 and Highway 99, a frankly unattractive strip mall that parallels the freeway just to the east. The community was essentially rural into the 1940s, and a few large parcels, particularly east of Highway 99, still have a rustic feel. Houses here are a mix of ranches, split-levels, and contemporary homes; a ridge offers some views of Portland and Mount St. Helens. A few small developments of new homes and townhouses have cropped up in Hazel Dell, particularly in the northern half of the community. The communities to the east—**Walnut Grove, Five**

Corners, and **Orchards**—have similar or slightly newer housing stock. These communities have seen rapid development in recent years, and large subdivisions and chain stores have appeared in place of the fruit tree groves that gave Orchards its name. Home prices have leveled off recently as demand for new homes has slackened, and this inner ring of unincorporated suburbia is one of the most affordable parts of the Portland metropolitan area. Note that despite the abundance of new construction and shiny new commercial establishments, a few neighborhoods have a lingering crime problem.

Northwest of Hazel Dell and west of Interstate 5, the tidy **Felida** neighborhood—named for the original nineteenth-century postmaster's cat (family Felidae)—has an abundance of newer homes on culs-de-sac, as does the neighboring Lake Shore neighborhood. These communities have access to Vancouver Lake on the west and the Salmon Creek Greenway to the north; Lake Shore and Felida elementary schools have a good reputation, and many families are attracted to the area.

Just to the north and east, the **Salmon Creek** area groans under the weight of the massive homes that are rising in expensive new subdivisions. Nearly all the construction in Salmon Creek is relatively new—in some cases brand-new—and generally upscale. The culs-de-sac along the north side of Salmon Creek feature large contemporary homes and McMansions, some of which have grown up incongruously around mobile home parks. New commercial developments have opened to serve the area's burgeoning affluent population. In addition to the abundant single-family homes, there are some townhomes and apartment complexes. Washington State University's Vancouver campus is in Salmon Creek, and its academic presence adds some cultural spice to a community that would otherwise be a fairly standard, if pleasant, suburban community. Salmon Creek's schools are widely considered among the best in the Vancouver School District. Interstate 205 splits off from Interstate 5 here, so Salmon Creek residents have their choice of southbound commuting options.

East of Salmon Creek, **Brush Prairie** still has a low population density and fairly rural ambiance, but new housing is going up along Highway 503. Given the growth of nearby Salmon Creek, Orchards, and Battle Ground, it seems likely that Brush Prairie is fated to experience increasing development in the future.

Vancouver School District (www.vansd.org) covers the western half of this area (i.e., Hazel Dell, Felida, and Salmon Creek); Orchards is part of Evergreen Public Schools (www.egreen.wednet.edu), while Battle Ground Public Schools (www.bgsd.k12.wa.us) serve part of Brush Prairie; the remainder of Brush Prairie and some of the surrounding area is part of the Hockinson School District (www.hock.k12.wa.us). The city of Vancouver is widely suspected (or known) to covet this entire area, with the possible exception of Brush Prairie (which Battle Ground is slowly absorbing from the north). Most residents have been opposed to annexation in the past—the Clark County government already provides these

communities with many of the services that incorporated areas enjoy—but circumstances could easily change.

BATTLE GROUND

Boundaries: North: Unincorporated Clark County; **West**: Unincorporated Clark
County; **South**: Brush Prairie (unincorporated Clark County); **East**: Unincorporated Clark County; **Area**: 3.6 square miles; **Population**: 15,810

Battle Ground spreads across a scenic plain west of the Cascade foothills. A battle never took place here—apparently the founder just liked the name when he
platted the town in 1902—but today you will fight a battle just to get from the
city to anywhere else. Battle Ground is the fastest growing city in Clark County,
but it is not adjacent to any major highways, let alone mass transit options, so
it takes at least 15 minutes, and often longer, just to get to Interstate 5 or 205.
The city's population has quadrupled since 1990, expanding by more than 20%
in 1997 alone, and the road network simply has not kept up with the area's ex-
ploding growth. To exacerbate the situation, the city has only one job per two
households, so most workers have to commute to a job somewhere else.

As one would expect, most homes in Battle Ground are relatively new; some
are quite large, but there are also unostentatious developments of basic single-
family homes and townhomes. A few old landmark homes remain from the
town's early years, including the Henry Heisen House from the 1890s, Burdoin
House from 1903, and the Rieck House, a 1920s bungalow. Supermarkets and
other commercial services cluster along Main Street, especially near the intersection with Highway 503, but the majority of the city is residential. Battle Ground's
main disadvantage—its relative isolation—is also one of its chief attractions.
Fields and woodland surround the city, and recreational opportunities abound
in the Cascade foothills, in places such as Battle Ground Lake State Park and Lucia
Falls Park, Moulton Falls Park, and the Bells Mountain Trail on the East Fork of the
Lewis River. The city's Battle Ground Public Schools (www.bgsd.k12.wa.us) also
serve several surrounding rural communities. Battle Ground is expected to continue to grow rapidly, with a projected population of 50,000 by 2020.

Web Site: www.ci.battle-ground.wa.us
Zip Code: 98604
Post Office: Battle Ground Post Office, 418 W Main St
Police Station: Battle Ground Police Department, 507 SW 1st St, 360-342-5100
     (non-emergency)
Emergency Hospital: Legacy Salmon Creek Hospital, 2211 NE 139th St, Vancou-
     ver, 360-487-1000, www.legacyhealth.org
Library: Battle Ground Community Library, 12 W Main St, 360-687-2322, www.
     fvrl.org/aboutus/battleground_main.htm
Parks: Kiwanis Park and Fairgrounds Park, with a sports complex under construc-

tion; www.ci.battle-ground.wa.us/departments/public_parks.php

Community Publications: *The Reflector,* www.thereflector.com

Public Transportation: C-TRAN, 360-695-0123, www.c-tran.com; very limited bus service via North County Connector

RIDGEFIELD, LA CENTER, AND WOODLAND

These three small cities are (for the time being) separated from one another, and from the sprawl emanating from Vancouver, by miles of woods and fields. **Ridgefield** (www.ci.ridgefield.wa.us) is one of the fastest-growing cities in Washington; fittingly, it was the birthplace of U-Haul, and quite a few of that company's trucks can be seen today in the subdivisions that are sprouting up in the fields along Pioneer Street. Ridgefield's tiny Old Town by the river has a few shops and cafés; radiating east and southeast from the town center and on the slopes behind, you can see everything from modest ranch houses and mobile home parks to brand new "Northwest Craftsman-style" homes. Houses on higher ground have good views west to the low Tualatin Mountains in Oregon. Working farms, and even a winery, hem in the town on three sides, and it's possible to pick up rural acreage here; to the west, the small Lake River and the Ridgefield National Wildlife Refuge separate Ridgefield from the mainstream of the Columbia River. Ridgefield still has a small-town feel, especially near the old center, but it's hard to ignore the new residential and commercial development that is occurring here. Ridgefield has its own school district (www.ridge.k12.wa.us).

La Center (www.ci.lacenter.wa.us) huddles on a hillside above the East Fork of the Lewis River; seen from a distance, the compact city very faintly resembles a Northwest version of a Tuscan hill town. Unlike a Tuscan hill town, the town center has four card rooms offering poker and blackjack, but these establishments do not dominate the city. Houses are a variety of ages and styles, although there are few prewar homes left; some new construction is occurring around La Center, although noticeably less than in Ridgefield. The small La Center School District (www.lcsd.k12.wa.us) is well-funded and has an excellent reputation. The Cowlitz Tribe has proposed building a huge new casino complex near La Center, just off of Interstate 5.

The small city of **Woodland** (www.ci.woodland.wa.us) lies along Interstate 5 about 20 miles north of Vancouver, and thus at the approximate northern limit of what most sane people would consider possible commuting distance from Portland. (Most of the city actually lies within Cowlitz County.) Houses here range from modest ranches to large custom homes on the banks of the Lewis River. While Woodland doesn't have many attractions, barring the lovely Hulda Klager Lilac Gardens (www.lilacgardens.com), it is the gateway to the southern slopes of Mount St. Helens. Woodland has its own school district (www.woodland.wednet. edu).

Many newcomers choose these outlying areas because they are looking for small-town ambiance within striking distance of the amenities of a large city. Ironically, these attributes attract growth and sprawl, which in turn threaten to erode the small-town ambiance. (This dilemma is hardly unique to southwest Washington.) The continuing livability of these communities will likely depend on the way in which they manage (or attempt to manage) their growth.

As in other parts of Clark County, transportation is an issue of concern. If you don't have a job in these communities or nearby in Clark or Cowlitz Counties, be sure to test your anticipated commute before committing to buying a home here. C-TRAN's North County Connector offers very limited service from La Center and Ridgefield to Salmon Creek, where transfers to the regular bus system are available.

AMBOY AND YACOLT

These northern Clark County communities offer acreage, quiet, and long, long commutes. With an economy traditionally based on logging and agriculture, this area remains in large part a working rural landscape; mud-splattered pickup trucks outnumber passenger cars, there is no Starbucks for miles, and the local grange is still active. Many residents, even those who are not farmers, keep horses, llamas, or other large animals. Most homes here are relatively modest ranch homes or old farmhouses on farms or large lots; a few new, ostentatious homes are going up in choice spots in the region's verdant valleys or on forested hillsides. Some homes have views of Mount St. Helens.

Each July, unincorporated **Amboy** hosts Territorial Days, which features such events as logging demonstrations and lawn mower drag races. **Yacolt**, best known for the devastating Yacolt Burn of 1902, was incorporated six years later; it is the terminus of the Battle Ground, Yacolt, and Chelatchie Prairie Railroad, a scenic excursion train. Both communities offer a small range of essential services—groceries, auto repair, pizza, and the like—but most residents travel to Battle Ground or Vancouver for shopping. Yacolt has a primary school and Amboy has a middle school, both of which are part of the Battle Ground School District (www.bgsd.k12.wa.us). Public transportation is essentially nonexistent.

OTHER OUTLYING COMMUNITIES

COLUMBIA COUNTY AND SAUVIE ISLAND

Sauvie Island (often referred to colloquially as "Sauvie's Island") lies at the mouth of the Willamette River, between Multnomah Channel and the Columbia River. Sauvie is a classic delta island—flat, rich farmland dotted with shallow lakes and sloughs—and despite its proximity to Portland, the island is wholly rural. The forested Tualatin Mountains rise to the west, and on clear days a procession of

SURROUNDING COUNTIES

Cascade peaks appears in the east. The island is unincorporated, and has a single grade school—after sixth grade, island children go to school in Scappoose. The sole access to the mainland is an aging bridge over Multnomah Channel, and power outages are frequent during winter storms.

Sauvie Island is obviously a popular choice for people who like isolation and crave a rural lifestyle, but island living doesn't come cheap: The median price of a home here is about half a million dollars (although almost every dwelling comes with acreage). Moreover, isolation doesn't equal solitude; the island's beaches, wildlife refuges, U-pick farms, and fall pumpkin patches and corn mazes attract hordes of visitors (and bicyclists, who enjoy the flat, scenic roads), and it can take a long time to get on or off the island on summer and autumn weekends. A TriMet bus line with all-day service runs from the southern tip of the island to downtown Portland. (Note that a majority of Sauvie Island is actually within Multnomah County, but it has more affinities with predominantly rural Columbia County than with urbanized Multnomah County.)

The Columbia County line is a few miles north of the Sauvie Island Bridge. Columbia County has long been dependent on forest products and related industries for jobs; many long-time Portlanders don't think of it as part of the metropolitan area at all, even though Scappoose, the southernmost town in the county, is not much farther from downtown Portland than Wilsonville. The area is growing and evolving, however, with an influx of new residents who seek small-town living (and lower housing costs) within reach of jobs in the Portland area. Many of these new residents commute over the Tualatin Mountains to the tech centers of Washington County.

Scappoose (www.scappoose.or.us) stands opposite the northern end of Sauvie Island, about 20 miles north of downtown Portland. This small city's older neighborhoods and commercial establishments cluster along Highway 30 and the train tracks that run beside it; a farmers' market takes place in the city center (such as it is) on Saturdays in season. Newer houses perch in the hills just west of town, and some homes are tucked away in shady canyons. Scappoose itself lacks river frontage, although Scappoose Bay to the north has a marina and some of the best flatwater kayaking in the state. About eight miles north, **St. Helens** (www.ci.st-helens.or.us), the county seat, *is* on the Columbia River, and takes advantage of its setting. The city's "Olde Towne" historic district spreads out along the riverfront, which also features a marina with a few houseboats; the city is located far enough north that Mount St. Helens, not Mount Hood, dominates the eastern horizon. Newer homes spread out to the west, and as in Scappoose many homes outside of town are set in hollows in the hills. Just to the north of St. Helens, much smaller **Columbia City** (www.columbia-city.org) hugs the riverfront.

The Scappoose School District (www.scappoose.k12.or.us) serves Scappoose and Sauvie Island; the St. Helens School District (www.sthelens.k12.or.us) covers St. Helens and Columbia City. Commuting to Portland is via Highway 30, which is not a freeway for most of the way and carries a high volume of truck traffic. Although St. Helens is essentially just across the river from Ridgefield, Washington, there are no highway bridges between Longview and Vancouver, so commuting to Clark County is not a viable option unless you have a boat. The only transit service in Columbia County is the Columbia County Rider (www. co.columbia.or.us/transit/), which provides limited commuter service between St. Helens/Scappoose and downtown Portland and to Portland Community College's Rock Creek Campus; the trip from St. Helens to either destination takes an hour.

County Web Site: www.co.columbia.or.us

YAMHILL COUNTY

Yamhill County, southwest of Portland, is the heart of Oregon's wine country. Yamhill County is a less-moneyed, more laid-back version of California's Napa County, but don't let the dearth of Hollywood names fool you: winemakers here are serious about their product. The region is especially renowned for its Pinot Noir, which is among the very best in the world.

Of course, vineyards do not wholly, or even mostly, cover the county; the western half of the county encompasses a large, forested chunk of the Coast Range, while several small cities dot the landscape in the eastern half of the county. The closest of these cities to Portland is **Newberg** (www.ci.newberg. or.us), set picturesquely between the Willamette River and the Chehalem Mountains. This fast-growing city of more than 20,000 people has an old-fashioned downtown, with a nearby neighborhood of historic homes (including Herbert Hoover's boyhood home, which is now a museum). The city has an abundance of more recently built homes, as well as some brand-new developments and a large selection of apartment complexes. The presence of George Fox University ensures that Newberg has a more active cultural calendar than it otherwise would. A few miles down the highway, the much smaller (and somewhat quainter) city of **Dundee** (www.dundeecity.org) features a couple of respected bistros and even some wineries right on the main drag. If you crave your own *terroir*—and if you don't know what that means, you probably aren't interested—expensive homes on grape-planted acreage are available just outside either city. Homes on the Chehalem Mountains or the Dundee Hills are especially coveted for viticulture, and offer incredible views across the Willamette Valley to the Cascades. Newberg Public Schools (www.newberg.k12.or.us) serve both communities.

Still further down Highway 99W, **McMinnville** (www.ci.mcminnville.or.us) is the largest city in the county. Like Newberg, McMinnville is undergoing substantial growth, and many new developments have sprung up around town. The city's pleasant downtown was built up during the period from 1880 to 1920, and is filled with restaurants and cafés, interesting (and not-so-interesting) shops, the old Mack Theater, and the Hotel Oregon (another McMenamins restoration), with its popular rooftop bar. A farmers' market is held on Thursdays during the summer. The adjacent residential neighborhoods are filled with older homes, including some restored Victorians; more modern homes and low-rise apartment buildings dominate the rest of the city. Just south of downtown, Linfield College hosts an International Pinot Noir Celebration every summer. The giant Spruce Goose airplane spreads its comically long wings at the Evergreen Aviation Museum (www.sprucegoose.org), just outside town. McMinnville has its own school district (www.msd.k12.or.us). Although most areas of McMinnville are quite safe, a few neighborhoods are pretty dodgy, and the city has a surprisingly high rate of violent crime given its rural setting.

Although they are by no means remote, the communities of Yamhill County aren't really close to any major cities. Newberg and Dundee are reasonable possibilities for commuters to jobs in Portland's southwestern suburbs, such as Tigard, Tualatin, or Wilsonville; McMinnville is within striking distance of Salem. If you're seriously considering a move to Yamhill County, be aware that Highway 99W, the main artery that connects Yamhill County to Portland, has a chronic congestion problem. While it's not really a barrier to weekend sightseeing, traffic congestion hampers commuters and dampens the area's economic growth. The state is studying options for a new bypass highway (see www.newbergdundeebypass. org), including a toll highway proposal; as you drive through the area you'll see plenty of yard signs in opposition to the toll concept. There is effectively no public transportation for the general public in Yamhill County.

If you're looking for a small town in wine country, others worth checking out include Amity, Yamhill, Carlton, Lafayette, and Dayton.

County Web Site: www.co.yamhill.or.us

MARION COUNTY

The farmlands and rolling, wooded hills of Marion County lie smack-dab astride the mid-Willamette Valley, one of the nation's most productive agricultural regions. The region produces a range of crops, from iris bulbs to hazelnuts, and is perhaps best known as the home of the Marionberry, a tasty blackberry hybrid that was named after the county and has no relation to the former mayor of Washington, D.C. If you suffer from hay fever, beware: the central Willamette Valley has many grass farms, and in late spring high concentrations of grass pollen mean misery for allergy sufferers.

The town of **Aurora** (www.ci.aurora.or.us) began its existence in the 1850s as the Aurora Colony, a commune of German Christians—a Northwestern version of the Amana colonies. The commune eventually faded away, but left behind the nucleus of the city's historic district (www.auroracolony.com). Today, the historic district is packed with antique stores and small eateries; Aurora Mills Architectural Salvage (www.auroramills.com) and the Old Aurora Colony Museum are also located here. The neighborhood south of the historic center is a mix of century-old homes and postwar ranches. (A working train line runs nearby;

beware if you're sensitive to rumbling and train whistles.) Some new housing developments are beginning to crop up on the outskirts of the city, but for now Aurora remains surrounded by agricultural land and the city maintains a laid-back, small-town atmosphere.

A public bus line links Aurora with Canby and **Woodburn** (www.woodburn-or.gov), a major trade and service center for the northern Willamette Valley. Many Portlanders know Woodburn as the site of the Woodburn Company Stores outlet mall just off Interstate 5, but there's much more to the city. Highway 99E, which parallels I-5 to the east, is a strip mall lined with supermarkets, chain restaurants, and *taquerias*, but the adjacent neighborhoods contain plenty of modest single-family homes and apartments. A busy set of train tracks abuts Woodburn's tiny downtown; to the west lies a pleasant district of historic homes on tree-lined streets. Some new housing developments are rising in the fields that surround the town. Woodburn's official nickname is "City of Unity," which reflects the city's unusually diverse population, which includes large contingents of Hispanics and Russian Orthodox Old Believers. If you happen to have a highly polluting car—and shame on you if you do—you should know that Woodburn is at the northern frontier of the zone where emissions tests are not required; residents of all Oregon towns and cities further north have to take their vehicles to DEQ (Department of Environmental Quality) testing stations every two years.

Charming **Silverton** (www.silverton.us), set amid fields and orchards at the edge of the Cascade foothills, is an increasingly popular destination for a day trip or weekend getaway, but it also attracts newcomers who like the scenic location and small-town vibe. Neighborhoods of old bungalows and cottages surround a traditional downtown, filled with murals illustrating the city's history; outlying areas feature ranches and newer contemporary homes, and true farm living is just outside the city. Area attractions include the Oregon Garden and beautiful Silver Falls State Park. While too far from Portland for comfortable commuting, Silverton may be a reasonable choice for people who work in Salem or at the southern end of the Portland metropolitan area (e.g., Wilsonville).

Salem (www.cityofsalem.net), Oregon's state capital and second-largest city, is not the urban dynamo one might hope for. Except for a few bars, down-town Salem essentially shuts down after the state workers go home. That said, Salem can be a very pleasant place to live, and as it grows it is likely to become a more happening town. The city has redeveloped part of the Willamette River waterfront into a park, there is a new convention center, a brand-new Delta Airlines route serves the city's airport—for many years Salem residents had to go to Portland or Eugene to catch commercial flights—and downtown is getting its first upscale condos. Can high-end restaurants and posh boutiques be far behind?

Maybe not. For now, Salem remains the lowest-cost housing market on the West Coast, although prices are rising quickly, and its relative affordability is definitely part of the city's appeal. Several historic districts with attractive old homes border the State Capitol and the Willamette University campus; the neighborhood near Bush's Pasture Park is particularly lovely. Hilly South Salem offers pleasant neighborhoods of postwar ranches and newer contemporary homes (some with mountain or valley views); prices here tend to be relatively high (for Salem). West Salem has an abundance of newer homes, with many of the McMansion variety, and prices here are also quite high by Salem standards. Home prices are generally lower in North Salem and in the neighborhoods near Lancaster Drive, an extensive strip mall that parallels Interstate 5 on the city's east side.

Salem is a good bet for people who intend to work here or in a nearby community. The commute from Salem to Portland or Beaverton takes at least an hour—much longer if there's an accident—and traffic on Interstate 5 gets heavier every year. (The reverse commute from Portland to Salem is somewhat more manageable, but is still unpleasantly long.) Although many workers carpool or vanpool, there is currently no viable public transportation between the two cities; to get between the cities by bus, you would have to make multiple transfers and deal with two or three different transit agencies, and Amtrak trains run at times that are inconvenient for most commuters.

If you are looking for a small town in this area, you might also consider St. Paul, Mt. Angel, Hubbard, Gervais, Donald, or Scotts Mills.

County Web Site: www.co.marion.or.us

THERE WAS A TIME, YOU WILL BE ENDLESSLY REMINDED, WHEN Portland was considered one of the most affordable metropolitan areas in the country. No more. A steep and inexorable rise in home prices over the last few years has put the dream of home ownership beyond the reach of many (although renters have benefited in the short term from the downward pressure on rental rates as many renters became homeowners). Now, after several years of red-hot growth, the direction of real estate prices in the Portland area is anyone's guess. A noticeable slowdown in sales and in price appreciation and an increase in unsold inventory began in late 2006, but home prices have not actually dropped in most parts of the metro area.

Even so, Portland remains the least expensive large metropolitan area on the West Coast, and if you're moving here from the Northeast, California, or even Seattle, and your income is above the local median, you may think that home prices are entirely reasonable. (Much of the rise in Portland real estate values is arguably due to newcomers bringing their equity from more expensive markets rather than the robustness of the local economy. The median income has not kept up with the price of housing, so many local workers are completely priced out of the real estate market.) Although the process of finding a place to live can be frustrating and time-consuming, remember that Portland is not, say, Manhattan. Eventually, you *will* be able to find a dwelling that works for you.

GETTING TO KNOW THE NEIGHBORHOOD

You should be able to narrow down your initial neighborhood options by considering factors like the location of your new job, the availability of transit, your preferred housing type and style, the quality and location of schools, and the size of your housing budget. Once you come up with a short list of neighborhoods, how do you find out more detailed information about them? If you're looking for housing in the city of Portland, be sure to check out **www.PortlandMaps.com**, a free city-run web site. Simply type in an address or intersection, and you'll be able to see detailed information about the size and assessed value of neighborhood housing stock, potential natural hazards in the area, crime, airport noise, and a slew of other information; type in an actual address and you'll get details about the building (number of bedrooms, property taxes, roof type, and much more). Many of the larger suburban communities offer similar (but usually less comprehensive) online tools.

Of course, you would be unwise to base your decision solely on maps and statistics. The best thing to do when house or apartment hunting is to visit prospective neighborhoods in person. Have breakfast or lunch at a local eatery and walk around—don't just circle around in your car. Talk to people in the neighborhood to get some subjective opinions. Find out if the services and conveniences you are accustomed to are available nearby, and pay attention to your comfort level: If you don't like the "feel" of the neighborhood, or if it just doesn't seem like a great fit for you, you might want to explore other options.

Also consider the commute. If you plan to drive to work, test drive the route during both morning and evening rush hours to be sure of what you're getting into. If you have a job in Wilsonville, at the south end of the metro area, it might be unwise to settle in Woodland, Washington, unless you're a huge fan of books on tape. Many people are able to commute by bus or light rail, but the usefulness of transit depends on where you live, where you need to go, and what time you want to go there. If you plan to commute by bike, plan some potential bike routes and do a trial ride from your prospective neighborhood. See the **Transportation** chapter for more details.

For tips on researching schools, see the **Childcare and Education** chapter.

CRIME AND SAFETY

In addition to proximity to work and/or amenities, "feel" of the neighborhood, and other subjective or individualized factors in choosing a place to live, you may also be concerned about crime. Every major city in the United States has its "good" and "bad" sections, and Portland is no exception. The good news here is that the violent crime rate in Portland is relatively tame by big city standards—the murder rate is substantially lower than the national average, for example. (The rape rate in Portland is much higher than the national average, but this statistic may reflect a higher reporting rate by victims rather than a greater incidence of rape.) In general, while random violence is not unknown, it is not especially common either—despite the impression the evening news, with its "if it bleeds, it leads" ethos, might convey.

For most Portlanders, property crime is a bigger concern. In the city, high rates of burglary, auto theft, and larceny, fueled in part by the financial needs of methamphetamine addicts and other drug users, exceed the national average.

Property crime rates have dropped slightly over the last year or two, but certain neighborhoods remain plagued by frequent burglaries and car prowls. You can substantially reduce the likelihood that you will become a victim by taking some common-sense precautions, like locking your home and car—a shocking number of burglaries involve a burglar waltzing into a house through an unlocked door or open window.

The Portland Police Bureau's web site (www.portlandonline.com/police) offers a treasure trove of helpful information about crime and crime prevention. In particular, the online **CrimeMapper** tool (www.gis.ci.portland.or.us/maps/police/) is an excellent place to research crime rates in a given neighborhood; just type in an address, and you'll be shown the days, times, and locations of crimes reported in the previous 12 months in the immediate vicinity. Several surrounding communities have less robust versions of this tool, including Beaverton (beavertonpolice.org/crime/maps_stats.html) and Gresham (archie.ci.gresham.or.us/crimeout/default.htm). You can also call the local police or sheriff precinct or department that patrols your neighborhood of interest.

To find out if a registered sex offender lives in the neighborhood, visit the **Oregon Sex Offender Inquiry System** (www.sexoffenders.oregon.gov). In Washington, go to the web site of the **Washington State Sex Offender Information Center** (ml.waspc.org).

RENTING VS. BUYING

In the long run, buying may be cheaper than renting, and you end up with an asset to show for it—but then again, as British economist John Maynard Keynes helpfully pointed out, in the long run we are all dead. Many newcomers buy a house or condo too soon after moving to town, only to discover that the neighborhood, the commute, or the home itself is more than they bargained for or is simply not to their liking. Especially in light of the dramatic recent increase in home prices in Portland, it might be wise to rent to allow time to get to know the city before deciding where to put down permanent roots. If you have school-age kids, you might be in a hurry to get them settled into a school—but what do you do if you don't like the school? What if you come to hate the rain? What if your next-door neighbor keeps rusted-out cars on blocks in the yard? Buying a home is the biggest transaction most people ever make; it makes sense not to rush into a decision. And many newcomers simply don't have the financial resources to buy a home. Of course, if you know where you'll be working and you know where you want to live, it can be a smart decision to buy a home—especially if you're flush with equity from the house you just sold in California or the Northeast.

For number-crunching assistance in deciding whether to rent or buy, try out one of the many online **rent vs. buy calculators**, such as the comprehensive calculator available at www.dinkytown.net/java/MortgageRentvsBuy.html.

RENTING

After a long period of relatively stable rents—thanks in part to the low interest rates that lured many renters into the real estate market—rents in Portland are again starting to rise. Rents in the metropolitan area increased 6% in 2006 and are expected to continue to rise for several more years. As of early 2007, the vacancy rate was about 3%, which is essentially full occupancy. It will take persistence and possibly luck to find the ideal apartment or rental house, but it can be done.

FINDING A PLACE

Be prepared to pound some pavement. Start by scanning the online or print classifieds, but don't forget to go out and visit neighborhoods you're interested in and look for "For Rent" or "Vacancy" signs. Given the improving rental market, many landlords don't want or need to advertise; particularly in desirable, apartment-dense neighborhoods like Northwest Portland, it is often easy enough to find tenants simply by hanging a sign outside a building for a day or two. Also check for vacancy notices tacked on bulletin boards at neighborhood coffeehouses or grocery stores. In suburban areas, look for signs on main roads, or call a complex's rental office and ask about upcoming vacancies.

ONLINE AND NEWSPAPER RESOURCES

The Internet has changed the way people find real estate, and that goes for rental properties, too. There are plenty of web sites, such as **Move** (www.move.com), **Apartments.com** (www.apartments.com), and **Portland Rentals** (www.portlandrentals.com), that list Portland properties for rent. One of the most popular sites, especially for small landlords, is **Craigslist** (www.portland.craigslist.org). The "apts/housing" list gets hundreds of ads on a typical day; you can narrow your search based on number of bedrooms, rent amount, and whether cats or dogs are allowed, and you can search listings for specific terms (e.g., neighborhood names, fireplace, garage, etc.), but it still can be pretty overwhelming. The useful **HousingMaps** site (www.housingmaps.com) superimposes Craigslist ads (as long as the ad lists an address or intersection) on a Google map of Portland, which can be very useful if you are targeting specific neighborhoods or communities. In addition to the commercial sites, **HousingConnections.org** (www.housingconnections.org) lists thousands of affordable, accessible, and special needs housing units in the Portland metropolitan area.

The old-fashioned way of finding out about rentals is to pore over newspaper classified ads. Be aware that many landlords and rental property managers use both online and newspaper advertising, and by the time a property appears in print it may already be "stale." The following publications have the best selection of classified ads:

- **The Oregonian**; the Sunday edition of the biggest regional newspaper has the most comprehensive rental and real estate listings for Portland and the surrounding communities. Rentals are listed by location, i.e., by city quadrant or suburban locale. Classifieds are available online at www.oregonlive.com. New listings appear daily in both the print and online versions of the classifieds.
- The **Portland Tribune** has skimpier listings than the *Oregonian*, but its online classifieds (www.greenlightclassifieds.com) include listings from 17 community papers.
- **The Columbian** is the daily for Vancouver and Clark County, and is worth a gander if you're looking for rentals in southwest Washington; visit www.columbian.com for online classifieds.
- **Willamette Week**; this free arts and entertainment weekly is distributed each Wednesday. The paper often lists rental opportunities not included in the larger publications, but it is most valuable for those in search of short-term rentals, sublets, home share situations, or a roommate. To view ads online, visit www.wweek.com.
- The weekly **Portland Mercury** has similar listings; grab the hard copy on Thursdays or visit www.classifieds.portlandmercury.com.

OTHER RENTAL PUBLICATIONS

Several companies publish free rental guides. Most list newer apartment complexes or apartments that are maintained by large property management companies. You can pick up rental guides at most grocery or convenience stores, or in some sidewalk vending boxes.

- **Apartment Guide**, www.apartmentguide.com
- **For Rent**, www.forrent.com

RENTAL PROPERTY MANAGEMENT COMPANIES

Rental property management companies manage multiple properties. These companies often list available properties on their web sites, or you can call them to find out about upcoming vacancies. Here are a few of the larger management companies in the Portland area:

- **Aggressive Property Management**, 503-239-5555, www.aggressivepm.com
- **American Property Management**, 503-284-2147, www.apmportland.com
- **Bluestone & Hockley**, 503-222-3800, www.bluestonehockley.com
- **Guardian Management**, 503-802-3600, www.guardianmanagementllc.com
- **Performance Properties**, 503-635-0099, www.ppirentals.com

- **Rental Housing Association of Greater Portland**, 503-254-4723, www.rhagp.org
- **Residential Property Management**, 503-245-8022, www.rpmpdx.com
- **Portland Rental Service**, 503-292-4451, www.portlandrentalservice.com

PET-FRIENDLY RENTALS

Many landlords refuse to rent to tenants with pets, or at least with certain types of pets. (It's easier to find a landlord who will accept a cat or small dog than one who is willing to deal with your trio of Great Danes.) The **Oregon Humane Society** maintains a list of pet-friendly rentals online at www.oregonhumane.org/resources/rentals.asp. Also note that all properties managed by **Portland Rental Service** (www.portlandrentalservice.com) allow pets. If your landlord allows pets, you will probably have to pay an additional deposit and/or a non-refundable pet fee based on the kind, number, and size of your animals.

SUBLETS AND SHARING

If you're having trouble finding a long-term place to live, or if there will be a significant gap between your arrival date and the date you can move in to new digs, you may want to consider taking a short-term sublet. Sublets are most often available during the summer, but with luck you can find one at any time of year. Remember, however, that most leases say that a tenant can sublet only with the permission of the landlord. The original tenant generally remains responsible for unpaid rent and damage done to the apartment by the subtenant. If you're looking for a truly short-term situation, check out the **Temporary Lodgings** chapter.

If you're on your own, renting a room in an established group house can be a great way to get acquainted with the city without spending a whole lot on rent. Sometimes a group will get together and find a home, but more often one or two people will rent a house and then seek roommates through advertising or word-of-mouth referrals. The newspapers listed above (particularly *Willamette Week* and the *Portland Mercury*) list ads for both sublet and sharing situations, as does **Craigslist** (www.portland.craigslist.org). (Craigslist also has a "housing wanted" category, if you're feeling proactive and lucky.) **Ecumenical Ministries of Oregon** runs a (non-religious) shared housing matching service (503-225-9924, www.emoregon.org/shared_housing.php); there is a $10 application fee.

While perusing ads for house sharing situations, keep in mind that "420 friendly" (a popular term in Portland listings) means that members of the household indulge in recreational marijuana use (or at least don't mind those who do). If that's not your scene, you should probably avoid responding to such ads.

CHECKING IT OUT

You're on your way to the day's first rental appointment, you haven't had breakfast, the old college friends you're staying with keep quoting Ben Franklin ("Guests, like fish, begin to smell after three days"), your back is aching from a bad night's sleep on their sofa-bed, and twenty other people are waiting outside the prospective apartment when you drive up. You panic, take a quick glance around, like what you see, and grab an application. Three months later, you wonder how you landed in such a dump.

To avoid this scenario, tour each apartment with a clear idea of what you want. Consider making a checklist of specific things to look for; besides your personal musts and must-nots, here are a few specific questions you might want to answer ahead of time to avoid aggravation later:

- If you're looking at an apartment, is it on the first floor? If so, does it have burglar bars? Can you open the bars from the inside in an emergency?
- Are the appliances clean and in working order? Do the stove's burners work? How about the oven? Does the kitchen sink have one or two basins? Is there sufficient counter and shelf space?
- Do the windows open, close, and lock? Do the windows, particularly the bedroom windows, face a busy street or noisy area?
- Are there enough closets or other storage areas? Are the closets big enough to accommodate your belongings? In an apartment building, is there secure storage elsewhere in the building, and is it free? If you have a bike, is there a secure place to store it overnight?
- Do the faucets and shower heads have adequate water pressure?
- Are there enough outlets for all your plug-in electronics and appliances? (In older buildings it is common to have only one or two outlets per room.) Is there a working phone and/or cable jack in the room where you plan to put a modem? If you plan to sign up for cable television, are there cable jacks in the rooms where you would watch TV?
- Does the building have a washer and dryer? If not, is there a laundromat nearby?
- If you have a car, is there off-street parking? Does it cost extra? Is there enough? Where do guests park? If parking is on-street, is parking easy to find? It's best to check out on-street parking in the evening, when people are home from work.
- Is there convenient access to public transportation and grocery shopping? How late do buses run, and do they run on weekends?
- Do you feel comfortable outside? Will you feel safe here at night?
- If you are looking at a basement apartment, check to see if there are any water stains along the walls.
- Does it smell funny? Someone may have sprayed the apartment for bugs.
- If you are responsible for paying for utilities (see "Rental Agreements" below),

what is the heat source? Electric space heating can be much more expensive than gas heat. How well-insulated does the house or apartment seem to be? Are the windows single-pane or double-pane?

Finally, make sure you can afford the rent, along with the cost of any utilities you are responsible for. If everything passes muster, be prepared to stake your claim without delay!

STAKING A CLAIM

When you view a unit, come prepared. Bring your checkbook. If you are coming from out of state, or even if you aren't, you may be required to provide a cashier's check or money order instead of a check. Have cash on hand in case you cannot get to the bank and need to purchase a money order from a convenience store or check-cashing outlet. Often, the first person to come with a deposit is the person who gets the apartment. (Make sure you get a receipt for any money you pay.) Know your social security number, and have ready access to your references—both credit and personal—and your bank account information. Employment information is useful; if you have secured a job but haven't started work, ask your new employer to write a letter on company letterhead verifying your start date and salary.

In Portland's competitive rental market, it isn't just the early bird that gets the worm: it can also be the polite worm, the well-dressed worm, and the worm with the highest bid. It won't hurt to mention casually that you don't have a dog, cat, or monkey, and that you don't smoke or play the drums (assuming these things are true). Feel free to rave about the unit and how great it feels; after all, landlords have feelings too. If there is a garden, mention that you love gardening and have a very green thumb. If you do have a pet, get references from former landlords praising its good behavior. Keep in mind that landlords can request only non-smokers, they can prohibit pets other than service animals, and they can bar you from having overnight guests for more than a certain number of nights per year. (The number of nights should be reasonably high; the intent of the clause is to prevent unauthorized occupants from moving in. If you think you'll have lots of visitors, watch out for rental agreements containing such a clause, as it may not bode well for your landlord-tenant relationship.)

Almost all landlords or property managers will require a security deposit, usually equal to a month's rent, which will be refunded to you (less any damages) when you move out. Some landlords charge application or credit check fees of $10 to $40 as a way to discourage frivolous rental applications; the fee is sometimes credited toward your deposit if your application is approved. Consider that most landlords will want your net monthly earnings to be at least three times the monthly rent; if you have no earnings, you'll probably need to show that you have sufficient liquid assets to be able to pay the rent. Landlords who charge a screening fee must provide written information about what they screen for. Look at the information and decide whether you think you'll qualify *before* you pay the fee. If you're not sure, be honest up front, explain the situation, and ask the landlord or property manager if they think you'll qualify. If they say no, it might not be worth your money.

Once your rental application is approved, then it's time to sign a rental agreement.

TENANT/LANDLORD RELATIONS

RENTAL AGREEMENTS

In Oregon, a rental agreement does not have to be in writing unless it is a fixed-term lease, but you would be foolish not to get an agreement in writing. Review the rental agreement carefully before you sign it, and make sure that you understand key terms, such as:

- How much is the rent? To whom should it be paid? When is it due? If your rent is late, what are the penalties?
- When can the landlord increase the rent, and by how much? How much notice is required?
- Who pays for utilities such as electricity, gas, and water?
- Is the tenancy for a fixed period, such as six months or a year, or is the rental term indefinite? What is the move-in date?
- What repairs or cleaning has the landlord agreed to complete before you move in?
- What is the policy on subletting?
- Is a parking spot included? How many? Do they cost extra?
- What is the policy on repairs or maintenance?
- What is the policy on pets, smoking, or overnight guests?
- Is renter's insurance mandatory?
- If you are renting a house, who is responsible for mowing the lawn and maintaining the landscaping?
- What non-refundable fees are charged (cleaning fee, pet fee, etc.), and what is the policy for return of the security deposit?

Don't assume that the terms are completely nonnegotiable; many landlords are willing to make reasonable minor changes to their standard rental agreements. Make sure you get a copy of every document relating to your rental agreement, and keep them somewhere safe.

The type of tenancy you have is particularly important. If you have a **month-to-month tenancy**, either party can end the tenancy with 30 days' written notice, and a landlord can generally increase the rent at will (again, with 30 days' notice). If you have a tenancy for a fixed term, you have a **lease**. Most leases also provide that the rent is fixed for the lease term. If you have a lease, a landlord generally cannot evict you except for cause (such as your unexcused failure to pay rent); at the same time, you may not breach the lease without good cause (such as the landlord's breach of a material term of the rental agreement), even if you have what you think is a really good reason, like buying a house or moving to Tokyo.

If you must break a lease for reasons you can't blame on the landlord, you should expect to take a financial hit. You could try to sublet the unit for the remainder of the lease term, but keep in mind that the rental agreement may not allow sublets or your landlord may not approve the proposed subtenant. (Landlords must use the same criteria for sublessors as they do for other tenants.) Failing that, at a minimum you will lose your security deposit. Depending on the amount of rent at stake—the time remaining in the lease multiplied by the amount per month—and whether your lease specifies a fee for breaking the lease, your landlord might not bother to sue. Even if there is no specified fee for breaking a lease, you could, in theory, be sued for the full amount of rent you would pay through the remainder of the lease term (or until someone new moves in), but in practice, as long as it's a lively rental market, landlords seldom bother chasing down a leasebreaker for more than one or two months' rent. Keep in mind, though, that your next rental application will ask for contact information for your most recent landlord, so you'll be much better off if you negotiate an amicable deal. (One way to placate a jilted landlord is to recruit a new tenant yourself, to save the landlord the expense of advertising the vacancy.) If you need to leave before your lease expires, you should consult an attorney; the Oregon State Bar's Lawyer Referral Service (503-684-3763, 800-452-7636, www. osbar.org/public/ris/ris.html#referral) can provide referrals.

If possible, do a walk-through inspection of the property before you move in (or immediately after you take possession) to document the condition of the place. Get a copy for your records.

LANDLORD-TENANT RIGHTS AND RESPONSIBILITIES

In the landlord-tenant relationship, both sides have rights and responsibilities. Some are obvious—the tenant is generally obliged to pay rent and not trash the place, and the landlord has to keep the building up to code. Some are less universally known: For example, contrary to what some renters (and landlords) believe, a landlord may not enter your apartment whenever he or she wishes, but usually has to give you 24 hours' notice (except in case of emergency). The following organizations provide a wealth of useful information about landlord-tenant issues:

- The **Community Alliance of Tenants**, 2710 NE 14th Ave, 503-460-9702, www. oregoncat.org, maintains a comprehensive database of information for tenants, and renter's rights information and handouts are available online. If you have a problem with your landlord, visit the web site. If you can't find the information you're looking for, call the renter's rights hotline at 503-288-0130.

- **Legal Aid Services of Oregon's** legal information web site (www.oregon lawhelp.org) has a useful section on housing law.
- The **Oregon State Bar** runs the Tel-Law service (503-620-3000, 800-452-4776), which offers basic recorded messages about legal subjects (including landlord-tenant law); this information is also available online at www.osbar. org/public/legalinfo/tenant.html.

RENTER'S INSURANCE

Get it. The landlord's insurance generally covers damage to the building, not to your personal possessions. Renter's insurance provides relatively inexpensive protection against theft, water damage, fire, and in many cases, personal liability. Not only is it a good idea to have renter's insurance (unless perhaps the total value of your possessions is less than the deductible), but some landlords require it. Most insurance companies that sell homeowner's insurance also sell renter's insurance. The **Oregon Insurance Division** provides useful consumer information about renter's insurance on its web site (www.insurance.oregon. gov/consumer/homeowner-renter/home.html), or you can call 503-947-7984 or 888-877-4894 and ask for a free copy of the Division's *Consumer Guide to Homeowner and Tenant Insurance* (also available online at www.insurance.oregon. gov/publications/consumer/3253.pdf).

BUYING

For most people, buying a home is the biggest and most daunting transaction they will ever be involved in. Not only is a pile of money involved, but finding and buying a house, condo, or townhome is a complex and time-consuming process. Fortunately, the resources listed here—and a host of professionals in the area— can help you at every step: calculating your budget, choosing the right home in the right neighborhood, getting a mortgage, protecting your investment with adequate insurance, moving in, and making repairs and improvements. The **U.S. Department of Housing and Urban Development** has a useful online guide to buying a home at www.hud.gov/buying/index.cfm.

Many people move to Portland intending to buy real estate, but find that the cost of a home is just too high. Newcomers can avoid sticker shock by thoroughly researching home prices and neighborhoods before they arrive, and by keeping an open mind about the types of housing and the locations they are willing to consider. For instance, maybe you have your heart set on a big

Craftsman-style house in the Irvington neighborhood, but you could live with a mid-century ranch in Milwaukie that's in your price range. Or perhaps that condo in the Pearl is way too expensive, but there's a townhome in Hillsboro that you can afford (and hey, you'll be working out in Washington County anyway). It's important to determine your priorities ahead of time, but be flexible (and realistic) when possible.

Homes in Portland come in many forms, from traditional single-family detached houses, usually with a yard of some kind, to various multiple ownership situations, primarily condos and townhomes. To a surprising extent, Portland has traditionally been a city of **single-family houses**, at least outside of downtown and its immediate environs. While infill development and duplex-ization over the years has made the generalization less true than it was, it is still easy to find houses in close-in neighborhoods (although they are no longer cheap by any measure). **Condominiums** are relatively new to Portland, and first became popular in Washington County and other outlying areas. More recently, a boom in high-end condo tower and "loft" construction in places like the Pearl District, combined with the scramble to convert apartments to condos when real estate prices started to skyrocket, means that condos are much more common. When you buy a condominium, you are buying a unit within a larger complex; the complex is jointly owned and maintained, but the unit is yours to use, sell, or (usually) rent. (Keep in mind that monthly condo fees can be substantial.) In a **townhome**, another widespread form of multiple ownership, you own your unit and the land under it but you share one or more walls with adjacent attached units. Many townhomes have small back yards, while condos at most tend to offer decks or small patios.

Co-operative apartments are not common in Portland, but the area is home to an increasing number of **co-housing** projects. In these projects, which are sometimes called "intentional communities," each household owns its own unit but shares communal space such as a "common house." Co-housing residents often prepare and eat meals together and share gardening and other general maintenance responsibilities. Currently, there are five existing or developing co-housing projects in Portland. For more information about co-housing or for a list of locations, contact the Co-Housing Association of the United States (www.cohousing.org) or the Northwest Intentional Communities Association (www.ic.org/nica/).

POTENTIAL PITFALLS

When scouting for a home, be aware of the wide range of potential pitfalls. Not only will you have expenses for ongoing maintenance or necessary repairs (some of which a home inspection will uncover), but there may be issues specific to the property you're interested in. Some properties lie within conservation zones where regulations limit the owner's ability to build a deck or addition, for example. Other homes may have historic designations that affect remodeling options. Many homes in Southwest Portland and the outer Eastside neighborhoods are on unimproved streets, and the property owner is responsible for making (and paying for) repairs from the property line to the centerline of the public right-of-way. While a good real estate broker can help identify some of these issues, they should be on your personal radar screen before you get your heart set on a particular home.

Property taxes are another expense to consider. Oregon's unique property tax system makes it impossible to estimate property taxes based on market value; Washington's system is a bit more straightforward, but you should always check with your county assessor to find out the current property taxes on a specific property. (See **Money Matters** for information about property taxes.) Certain neighborhoods are **tax abatement areas** in which homebuyers, builders, or rehabbers pay reduced property taxes for a period of 10 years. Your real estate broker should be able to tell you which neighborhoods currently qualify. And speaking of taxes and other expenses…

GETTING YOUR FINANCIAL HOUSE IN ORDER

Assuming you aren't fortunate enough to be able to buy a house outright, you'll need to arrange a mortgage loan. It's a good idea to get pre-approved before looking for houses in earnest. Many sellers will not seriously consider an offer from a buyer who is not pre-approved, and the pre-approval process gives you a good idea of how much you can reasonably afford to spend on a house.

When you're ready to get pre-approved, go prepared with relevant financial documents and check your credit report in advance to make sure it is accurate. You can get one free copy of your credit report each year from each of the three major credit bureaus; visit www.annualcreditreport.com or call 877-322-8228. You are also entitled to a free credit report if you have been denied credit based on the contents of your credit report within the 30 days before your request. The national credit bureaus are:

- **Equifax**, 800-685-1111, www.equifax.com
- **Experian**, 888-397-3742, www.experian.com
- **TransUnion**, 800-916-8800, www.transunion.com

You might also want to check your FICO® score, the number that most lenders use to determine how creditworthy you are, and thus what interest rate you can get on your loan. The FICO score is available from Fair Isaac, the score's creators and overlords, at www.myfico.com. You may also be offered the chance to buy your score when you obtain a credit report. If the idea of having to pay to look at your own information—information that someone else is already profiting from—sticks in your craw, consider signing up for a credit monitoring service with a free 30-day trial period; you can usually get your credit score when you sign up. (Just remember to cancel before the free trial ends.)

It may be most convenient to get your pre-approval through a local bank, but shop around before you sign for your loan. While many banks offer competitive interest rates, mortgage brokers can often match or beat their best offers. Make sure you ask about closing costs, loan origination fees, and points when comparing interest rates. Of course, virtually no lender's loans are unique. Most lenders offer a variety of fixed-rate and adjustable-rate mortgage products and participate in government-insured VA and FHA loan programs, both of which require low down payments and have flexible qualifying guidelines.

If you need assistance with mortgage costs, several unique local resources are available. The **Portland Housing Center** (3233 NE Sandy Blvd, 503-282-7744, www.portlandhousingcenter.org) provides homebuyer education and offers financial assistance to eligible buyers (generally, first-time buyers with below-median incomes). Oregon Housing and Community Services offers the **Oregon Bond Loan** (877-ST8-BOND, www.oregonbond.us) for first-time homebuyers who meet income requirements. The **Portland Community Land Trust** (503-493-0293, www.pclt.org) helps people who are below the median income and who can't *quite* afford a house. The **Portland Development Commission** (www.pdc.us/housing, 503-823-1018) has a range of housing assistance programs, including purchase and renovation loans; some loans have income requirements or are available only to first-time buyers, and others only apply to the purchase of homes in certain targeted neighborhoods.

ONLINE RESOURCES—MORTGAGES

The following sites might be useful in researching interest rates and loan programs:

- **Bankrate**, www.bankrate.com, allows you to compare mortgage and home equity loan interest rates, and offers several online mortgage and housing calculators.
- **Freddie Mac**, www.freddiemac.com, offers information on current mortgage averages.
- **Interest.com**, www.interest.com, includes advice for first-time home buyers, suggestions for finding the lowest interest rate, and current interest rate comparisons.

HOUSE HUNTING

WORKING WITH A REAL ESTATE AGENT

When an agent who has listed a home shows it to you, he or she is representing the seller, not you. If you want an agent who will act on your behalf, you will need to hire a buyer's agent. There is no substitute for the advice of a knowledgeable local real estate agent, and there usually is no downside to working with one when you're buying a home. (The buyer's broker's commission almost always comes out of the selling broker's commission; the exception is if you buy a property that is for sale by owner and the owner refuses to pay a commission to your agent.)

Probably the best way to find an agent is through a referral from a friend or co-worker. Failing that, you might consider the agents who host open houses or seem to have a lot of listings in your neighborhood of choice. Most agencies claim to serve the entire Portland area, but often agents specialize (or claim to specialize) in certain neighborhoods or in certain kinds of homes, and are not shy about advertising their specialties in community newspapers and on bus benches. While neighborhood knowledge is important, it's also important that your agent be someone you trust, who knows the market, and who listens to you. A good agent will interview you in detail about your needs and interests—not just your preferred price range, but every detail of your lifestyle. Are you planning to have any (or more) children? Do you need space in a basement to set up your electric trains? Do you want to plant a garden, or would you prefer a small yard that requires little maintenance? Are you planning to commute by bike? The more information you can provide, the easier it will be for your agent to find a home that's a good match.

The companies listed below have multiple offices throughout the Portland area and account for most real estate listings. Don't be shy about exploring smaller, "off-brand" or alternative realtors, however, especially if you have a referral.

- **Coldwell Banker/Barbara Sue Seal Properties**, www.cbseal.com
- **Hasson Company Realtors**, www.hasson.com
- **John L. Scott Real Estate**, www.johnlscott.com
- **Prudential Northwest Properties**, www.prunw.com
- **Realty Trust Group**, www.realtytrust.com
- **RE/MAX Equity Group**, www.equitygroup.com
- **Windermere Real Estate**, www.windermere.com

HOUSEHUNTING RESOURCES

In addition to the standard places for classified advertising listed in the Renting section above—newspapers, Craigslist, and the like—a wide range of online resources target prospective homebuyers. Most agents will send lists of properties to you by email as soon as they come on the market. In addition, or even before you decide to use an agent, you might find the following web sites to be useful househunting resources:

- **Zillow**, www.zillow.com, seems like everyone's favorite real estate site these days. It purports to be able to give a market value for any house (based on recent sales in the neighborhood and the characteristics of the specific property) that is generally within 20% of the real market value. While the market values should be taken with a large grain of salt—a margin of error of 20% on a $300,000 house represents $60,000, after all—the data on comparable sales are invaluable.

- **RMLS**, www.rmls.com, is the multiple listing service for the Portland area. The site includes a searchable database of most homes for sale; you can search by price, ZIP code, number of bedrooms, etc., but many search options—such as the list of "green" and energy efficient features, introduced in February 2007— are only available to RMLS members (generally real estate brokers). Many real estate brokerages provide similar search functionality on their own web sites.

- If you prefer to buy a home without an agent—or at least to buy from an unrepresented seller—check out sites that specialize in for sale by owner listings, including **HomesbyOwner.com** (www.homesbyowner.com/portland_or/) or **Owners.com** (www.owners.com).

PURCHASE AGREEMENTS AND CLOSING

A purchase agreement is a legally binding contract between the buyer and seller that states the price and all terms of the sale. Although most Oregon brokers start with a standard form, the purchase agreement is the most negotiable and variable document produced in the homebuying process. The purchase agreement is also the place where you, the buyer, can attach contingencies that protect you from being legally bound by the purchase agreement if, for example, the house you are buying does not pass its mechanical and structural inspection, if the seller is unable to give you possession by a certain date, or you cannot obtain mortgage financing. Neither Oregon nor Washington regulates purchase agreements, but both states require sellers to provide certain property disclosures and a lead-paint disclosure.

Typically, once both parties have signed the purchase agreement, you will hire an independent home inspector or engineer to examine the foundation and overall structure, the HVAC and plumbing systems, and the roof. Also request that the inspector check for mold, particularly if the roof has been replaced recently or if there are signs of water damage in the basement. Your lender will appraise the house, but only to determine if its value will safely secure the loan.

If all goes well, eventually you'll close. Closings typically occur in the conference room of a title company, where you'll be asked to sign the tallest pile of papers you've ever seen. How do you avoid problems? First, schedule your closing at least six weeks from the date your purchase agreement was signed, then keep in contact with your lender to see if additional information is required. The week you close, your lender should send you a copy of the completed Settlement Statement, or HUD-1 form. (If the lender doesn't send it, ask for one. You have the legal right to see this form one business day before closing.) Compare the Settlement Statement to the good faith estimate of closing costs your loan officer gave you when you applied for the loan. The actual closing costs should not differ dramatically from the estimated costs. If they do, you may be getting scammed, although some costs, such as insurance premiums and the loan origination fee, can only be nailed down after your loan is approved because they are based on the amount of your loan and the final value of the property. Finally, make sure you bring the necessary papers—identification, proof of homeowner insurance, etc.—and a cashier's check to pay the balance of your down payment and unpaid closing costs.

INSURANCE

Your lender will require you to buy **homeowner insurance** to protect their investment (your home). Be sure the policy you choose adequately covers the house, its contents, and all outbuildings. A basic homeowner policy usually also includes liability insurance to protect you if someone is injured on your property, and living expense coverage that will pay for you to live elsewhere while the home is repaired or rebuilt. You may also want to purchase **earthquake coverage**, which most policies do not include. If your prospective home is in a floodplain, you'll need to purchase flood insurance from the **National Flood Insurance Program** (888-379-9531, www.floodsmart.gov).

You'll also need title insurance, which protects the lender in case your legal title to the property is faulty. (It doesn't protect you, though, so you may want to buy an owner's title policy. In Portland, it is usually customary for the seller to pay the premium on a buyer's title policy.) If you are putting down less than 20% as a down payment, you may also need mortgage insurance, which is required by many lenders as well as the FHA to cover them in case you default on the loan.

For advice on homeowner insurance from the **Oregon Insurance Division**, call 503-947-7984 or 888-877-4894 and ask for a free copy of the Division's *Consumer Guide to Homeowner and Tenant Insurance* (also available online at www. insurance.oregon.gov/publications/consumer/3253.pdf).

WORKING WITH CONTRACTORS

If you intend to remodel or significantly alter the home you buy, you might want to enlist the services of an architect or structural engineer, who can give you a general sense of what options might be available for a particular house before you commit to a purchase. Once you buy a house, you'll face the problems of finding a reputable contractor, getting the work done in a timely and competent fashion, and paying for the remodel.

Accomplishing all these tasks can be a daunting proposition. It is not un-heard-of for contractors to abscond with homeowners' money, and since the state currently only requires $15,000 in bond coverage, you could end up holding the bag—the empty bag that your money used to be in before you paid it to your contractor.

To help avoid this unpleasant scenario, the Oregon Attorney General and the **Oregon Construction Contractors Board** (CCB) suggest you take the following steps when dealing with any contractor:

- Check out the contractor in advance. It's always best to get recommendations from friends and family members who have had a good experience. Even a good recommendation, however, is no substitute for research. All contractors must be licensed, bonded, and insured. Check the contractor's license and history of complaints at the CCB's consumer web site, www.hirealicensedcontractor. com, or call 503-378-4621. (In Washington, contact the state **Department of Labor and Industries**, 800-547-8367, fortress.wa.gov/lni/bbip/.) The Oregon Attorney General warns, "A devious contractor may tell you that he or she is licensed or may give you a false or outdated CCB number, so make sure to check on your own." Also check with the Better Business Bureau and the state Department of Justice. (See "Consumer Protection" in **Helpful Services** for more suggestions.) If the contractor provides references, check them.
- Get multiple written estimates. The Attorney General suggests getting at least three estimates. Make sure the bids are in writing. Don't automatically choose the lowest bid; make sure you compare the materials specified and the scope of the work, and be suspicious of unrealistically low bids.
- Get a written contract. Once you've selected a contractor, put your agreement in writing. Make sure the contract states what work is to be done, when it is to be done, and how much it will cost, and that sufficient details are included: "build addition, $80,000" won't cut it. Try to limit how much you have to pay upfront; you may be able to negotiate payments over the course of a long project once the contractor has completed certain phases. Don't sign the contract unless you understand it completely, and make sure all changes are in writing.

Even if you follow these steps scrupulously, you might still get scammed—there are no guarantees—but you'll substantially reduce your vulnerability.

BUILDING YOUR OWN HOME

If you dream of building your own home, you'll face a scarcity of large buildable lots within the urban growth boundary. In Oregon, you cannot simply buy a 5-acre farm field in the exurbs and plunk down a house. The Portland area has a relative abundance of infill lots, although many of these lots are quite small and/or on steep slopes. Keep in mind that building a huge house on a small city lot may not endear you to your new neighbors. You might look into Portland's Living Smart program (www.livingsmartpdx.com), whose goal is to improve the design of new homes on "skinny" lots. You could also investigate doing a teardown of an existing, presumably dilapidated, house. If you must build a giant house on acreage, your best options are the rural exception zones outside the urban growth boundary in Oregon, or outer Clark County in Washington; in either case, be prepared for a *long* commute if you work in Portland.

B EFORE YOU START YOUR NEW LIFE IN PORTLAND, YOU AND YOUR worldly possessions have to get here. That task can be expensive and complicated, or cheap and simple, depending on how much stuff you've accumulated, where you're coming from, and how much of the heavy lifting you plan to do yourself.

TRUCK RENTAL

If you plan to move your own belongings, you can simply rent a vehicle and hit the road. Look in the Yellow Pages under "Truck Rental" and then call around for quotes. Even if you're dealing with a nationwide company, call the location nearest you to check pricing and availability. (Keep in mind that some of the national truck rental companies offer significant discounts for reserving a vehicle online, so it pays to check out their web sites as well.) If you just need a minivan or a small trailer, get quotes from a regular car rental company (listed in the **Transportation** chapter).

If you are comparing different moving options, factor in the cost of fuel—which can equal or exceed the cost of the basic truck rental—accommodation, and food. If you need to move a car, also consider whether you prefer to tow the car—most truck rental companies offer trailers or other car-towing options—or to have someone else drive it. (Companies such as **American Car Transport**, 866-322-3169, www.american-car-transport.com, will ship your car for you.)

If you need a truck during peak moving season (between May and September) be sure to reserve one at least a month in advance, especially for one-way rentals. If you can, consider timing your move for the middle, rather than the end, of the month, because demand is lower then.

The following four national truck rental companies have multiple locations in the Portland area:

- **Budget**, 800-462-8343, www.budgettruck.com
- **Penske**, 800-467-3675, www.penske.com
- **Ryder**, 800-297-9337, www.ryder.com
- **U-Haul**, 800-468-4285, www.uhaul.com

Once you're on the road, keep in mind that your rental truck may be a tempting target for thieves. If you must park it overnight, or for more than a couple of hours, try to find a well-lit place where you can keep an eye on it, and don't leave anything valuable in the cab.

COMMERCIAL FREIGHT CARRIERS AND CONTAINER-BASED MOVERS

If you don't want to drive a truck yourself, but you also don't want to hire a full-service mover, there's a third option: you can hire a commercial freight carrier to deliver a trailer or container to your home. You pack and load as much of it as you need, and the carrier delivers your trailer or container to your destination. In some cases, this option can be cheaper than renting and driving your own truck, especially when you consider the cost of fuel. **ABF U-Pack Moving** (800-355-1696, www.upack.com) uses commercial 28-foot freight trailers. ABF charges by the linear foot, and you only pay for the linear feet you use (subject to a minimum charge). When you've finished loading, you install a plywood bulkhead; ABF fills the remaining space with freight, which is unloaded before the trailer is delivered to your new home.

ABF, **PODS** (877-776-PODS, www.pods.com), **Door-to-Door Storage and Moving** (888-505-3667, www.doortodoor.com), and several other companies offer container-based moves. In this type of move, the carrier delivers plywood, metal, or fiberglass cubes or other containers to your home. You can generally take a few days to load the containers; when you're done loading, the company picks up the containers, transfers them to flatbed trucks, moves them to your destination city, and delivers them to your new home. You generally only pay to transport the containers you actually use, and, unlike a truck, the containers can be placed in storage at either end of the journey. However, a set of containers has a smaller storage capacity than a large truck, so this option may not work for people with large houses full of furniture. In addition, some large pieces of furniture—grandfather clocks, for example—may not fit inside the containers; if you have to move items that are very long or tall, ask the company for its containers' *interior* dimensions before you commit.

MOVERS

Probably the best way to find a mover is through a personal recommendation. Absent a reference from a trusted friend or relative, you can start with the Yellow Pages. For long-distance moves, the **American Moving and Storage**

Association (www.moving.org) keeps a list of certified movers that honor the organization's code of conduct.

Once you've identified potential movers, *do your homework.* The federal government eliminated the Interstate Commerce Commission in 1995. Currently, the Federal Motor Carrier Safety Administration (FMCSA), an agency of the Department of Transportation, is charged with regulating interstate moves, but it only has nine investigators and has no authority to step in on a consumer's behalf during a move. States do not have the authority to regulate interstate moving companies, and since the federal government basically won't, you're really pretty much on your own in your dealings with an interstate mover. Understandably, the interstate moving industry has degenerated into a largely unregulated free-for-all with thousands of unhappy, ripped-off customers. In fact, the Council of Better Business Bureaus reports that complaints against moving and storage companies rank near the top of all complaints received by their bureaus every year.

Watch out for shakedown schemes that begin with a lowball bid off the Internet and end with the mover holding your belongings hostage for a high cash ransom. Despite the fact that federal law says that movers cannot charge more than 10% over any written estimate, it is not unusual for unscrupulous movers to charge you several times their written estimates—and with your possessions in their possession, you may find yourself paying anyway, since companies that operate this way also won't tell you where they're holding your stuff.

For an informative—but terror-inducing—read, check out the **Moving-Scam** web site (www.movingscam.com). MovingScam.com provides sound, unbiased consumer education and is committed to bettering consumer protections in the moving industry. The site features a host of useful articles and recent moving news, and maintains a "Blacklist." Its message boards are tended by dedicated volunteers who respond promptly and knowledgeably to moving-related queries, free of charge. The FMCSA operates a similar web site (www.protectyourmove.gov). This web site provides one-click checking to make sure that an interstate mover is properly registered and insured. (You can also get this information by phone, at 888-368-7238 or 202-358-7028.) It also includes news of recent criminal investigations and convictions, and offers links to local Better Business Bureaus, consumer protection agencies, state attorneys general, and state moving associations. In general, consumer advocates and attorneys general around the country urge you to take precautions before hiring a mover by doing the following things:

- Make sure the mover is licensed and insured. If the companies you're interested in appear to be federally licensed, the next step is to contact the Better Business Bureau (www.bbb.org) and find out if the Bureau has a record of any complaints against them.

- Get several written estimates from companies that have actually sent a sales representative to your home to do a visual inspection of the goods to be moved. Don't worry about cost here; estimates should always be free. Don't do business with a company that charges for an estimate or wants to give you an estimate over the telephone. Do, however, make sure each company is giving you an estimate for approximately the same poundage of items to be moved, and for the same services. Finally, only accept estimates that are written on a document that contains the company's name, address, phone number, and signature of the salesperson. Note that estimates can be either binding or non-binding. A binding estimate guarantees the total cost of the move based upon the quantities and services shown on the estimate. A non-binding estimate is what your mover believes the cost will be, based upon the estimated weight of the shipment and the extra services requested. With a non-binding estimate the final charges will be based upon the services provided and the actual weight of your shipment. If you accept a mover's non-binding estimate, you must be prepared to pay up to 10% more than the estimated charges at delivery.
- Remember that price, while important, isn't everything, especially when you're entrusting all of your worldly possessions to strangers. Choose a mover you feel comfortable with.
- Ask for references—then check them.
- Be sure you understand the terms of the moving contract. Get everything in writing, including the mover's liability to you for breakage or loss. Consider whether to buy additional replacement insurance to cover loss or damage. Check your homeowner's or renter's insurance policy to see what, if any, coverage you may already have for your belongings while they are in transit. If the answer is "none," ask your insurer if you can add coverage for your move. You can purchase coverage through your mover. A mover's coverage, however, is normally based on the weight of the items being insured, not on their value. If you want to cover the actual value of your belongings, you will need to purchase "full value" or "full replacement" insurance. Though it's expensive, it's worth it—and you can lower the cost by increasing your deductible. Better yet, consider packing and moving irreplaceable, fragile or sentimental items, documents, and jewelry yourself. That way you can avoid the headache and heartache of possible loss or breakage of your most valuable possessions.
- Compile a detailed inventory of all items shipped and note their condition when they left your house. Take pictures of your important items, and be present for both the loading and unloading of your things. Since checking every item as it comes off the truck is probably impossible when you're moving the contents of an entire house, write "subject to further inspection for concealed loss or damage" on the moving contract to allow for damage you may discover

as you unpack.

- File a written claim with the mover immediately if any loss or damage occurs—and keep a copy of your claim, as well as all the other paperwork related to your move. If your claim is not resolved within a reasonable time, file complaints with the Better Business Bureau and appropriate authorities, as well. (See **Consumer Complaints—Movers,** below.)
- If you've followed the steps above and succeeded in hiring a reputable mover:
- Listen to what the movers say; they are professionals and can give you expert advice about packing and preparing. Also, be ready for the truck on both ends—don't make the movers wait. Understand, too, that there may be delays caused by factors—adverse weather, for example—that are beyond a carrier's control, and your belongings may not get to you at the time, or on the day, promised.
- Treat your movers well, especially the ones loading your stuff on and off the truck. Offer to buy them lunch, and tip them if they do a good job.
- Be prepared to pay the full moving bill upon delivery. The mover may require cash or a cashier's check. Some carriers will take VISA and MasterCard but it is a good idea to get written confirmation that you will be permitted to pay with a credit card; the delivering driver may not be aware of this arrangement and may demand cash.

INTRASTATE MOVES

If you are using a mover for a move that is wholly within Washington or Oregon, follow all the steps above for dealing with interstate movers: make sure they are licensed and insured, check with the Better Business Bureau, check estimates, check contracts, and check references. The regulatory entity for moves that start and end in Oregon is the **Oregon Department of Transportation, Motor Carrier Transportation Division** (MCTD) (503- 378-5849, egov.oregon. gov/ODOT/MCT/). The counterpart agency in Washington is the **Washington Utilities and Transportation Commission** (360-664-1160, 800-562-6150 for consumer complaints and information, www.wutc.wa.gov).

A complete list of state-authorized movers in Oregon is available from the MCTD at www.oregon.gov/ODOT/MCT/MOVERS.shtml. You can find out whether an Oregon moving company is licensed by calling 503-378-5985. The list of Washington-authorized moving companies is posted at www.wutc.wa.gov/consumer/movingtips; follow the "List of Registered Movers" link, or call the commission's toll-free consumer information line (800-562-6150) to ask if a specific company is registered.

PACKING AND ORGANIZING

Don't wait until the last minute to think about packing. You'll need plenty of boxes, tape, and packing material—probably more than you think. Moving and truck rental companies sell boxes, as do most office supply stores, but most grocery stores or liquor stores will let you scrounge some empty boxes. For foam "peanuts," bubble wrap, and other materials to protect fragile items, look in the Yellow Pages under "Packaging Materials"; if you have some especially fragile and valuable items, you might also want to look under "Packaging Service."

LOADING AND UNLOADING

If you are driving a rental truck or using a freight carrier, but you are disinclined to load and unload the truck yourself, many moving companies and independent businesses offer "pack and load" services. Companies that provide these services generally charge by the person/hour, with a minimum charge. (Call around, as hourly rates and minimums vary tremendously.) The same cautions that apply to hiring full-service movers apply equally to pack and loaders: try to get a recommendation from a trusted source, make sure the company is insured, and always check references. Beware of companies that use inexperienced temporary workers who may not be especially careful with either your belongings or your walls, and who may not pack your items securely in the truck—a fact which you may not discover until you unpack your crushed possessions at the end of your journey.

Because packing and loading do not involve the actual transport of goods, the businesses that provide these services are often unregulated. A 2003 Oregon law requires pack and loaders in the state to have insurance and to register with the Oregon Department of Transportation. A list of registered companies is available at www.oregon.gov/ODOT/MCT/MOVERS.shtml, under the heading "Registered Pack & Loaders." Washington does not currently require these companies to register with the state.

Whatever moving method you plan to use, make sure you'll have a spot at both ends of your move to park the truck or to place the trailer or containers. Some cities require a permit to park a truck or place containers on a public street; others don't require a permit, but will issue one so that you can reserve a parking place for your moving truck. (You can get such a permit from the city of Portland's Office of Transportation, 503-823-7002, www.portlandonline.com/transportation, for a nominal fee.) If you are moving to or from a large apartment building, check with the manager to see if you need to reserve a time to load or unload.

STORAGE

Most communities have commercial storage facilities where you can rent a secure, climate-controlled self-storage locker—your own little warehouse—to keep items that don't fit in your home or that you only use occasionally. These can also be convenient places to store your belongings temporarily while you find a new home or while you prepare to sell your old one, and many have moving vans for rent. Find a storage facility online by using a search engine or searching online yellow pages (such as www.qwestdex.com) under "Household and Commercial Storage." Alternatively, check the tangible Yellow Pages under "Storage—Household & Commercial." Keep in mind that demand for storage surges in the prime moving months of May through September, so try not to wait until the last minute to look for a storage unit.

If you plan to open your storage locker only twice—the day you fill it and the day you empty it—then consider a suburban location that will be cheaper than facilities closer to the heart of a city. If you need more frequent access to your locker, location will matter, and so will access fees. Also note that some storage facilities only allow daytime access. Others have gates that only open when a car or truck triggers a weight-sensitive lock, which can be a problem if you don't own a car. Ask about billing and security deposits, too, and don't be late with payments: if you fall behind, the storage company will not dump your stuff on your doorstep—they'll auction it off.

Mobile or modular storage is more convenient, and more expensive, than self-storage. The company delivers a large container to your door, you load it, and the company hauls it away until you call for it. This can save you a lot of time and effort—it's one less round of unpacking, re-packing, and transport—but it's not good for easy access.

Portland and its suburbs are awash in storage possibilities. Your best bet for finding storage is to focus on a geographic location and then explore options within that general area. The biggest storage company in the Portland area is **Public Storage**, with 27 locations in the city and suburbs. Call 800-447-8673 or visit www.publicstorage.com for locations and quotes. Here are a few other storage companies that you can contact to start your search:

- **Downtown Self Storage**, 1305 NW Davis St, 503-241-4700, and 1304 NW Johnson St, 503-241-6170, www.downtownselfstorage.com, has two locations in the Pearl District.
- **Northwest Self Storage,** www.nwselfstorage.com, is a network of independent storage companies; their web site provides links and contact information for dozens of storage facilities in Oregon and Washington.
- **Shurgard Self-Storage**, 800-748-7427, www.shurgard.com, has 17 locations in the metropolitan area.
- **U-Haul Self-Storage,** 800-468-4285, www.uhaul.com, has several storage fa-

cilities in the area; U-Haul sometimes offers free storage for one month with a one-way truck rental.

CONSUMER COMPLAINTS—MOVERS

To file a complaint about an Oregon mover, contact the **Motor Carrier Transportation Division** (550 Capitol St NE, Salem, 97301, 503-378-5849, egov.oregon.gov/ODOT/MCT). For a bad move within Washington, contact the consumer affairs staff of the **Washington Utilities and Transportation Commission**, P.O. Box 47250, 1300 S Evergreen Park Dr SW, Olympia, 98504, 800-562-6150, or visit www.wutc.wa.gov/fileacomplaint to use their online complaint form.

If yours was an interstate move, your options for government help are limited. The Federal Motor Carrier Safety Administration (FMCSA) recommends that you contact the Better Business Bureau in the state in which the moving company is licensed and that you register a complaint with that state's consumer protection office. You can also file a complaint directly with the FMCSA by telephone or online (888-DOT-SAFT [888-368-7238], www.1-888-dot-saft.com). Don't expect much from the agency, however; the complaint hotline is essentially just a database and you will only hear from the FMCSA if it looks at your complaint and determines that enforcement action is warranted.

If satisfaction still eludes you, start a letter-writing campaign: to the state attorney general, to your congressperson, to the newspaper, to the Internet—the sky's the limit. If the dispute is worth it, and the moving company has assets and hasn't vanished into the ether, you can always hire a lawyer and seek redress through the courts.

TAX DEDUCTIONS

If your move is work-related, and your employer is not reimbursing your moving costs, some or all of your moving expenses may be tax-deductible. Though eligibility and specific requirements vary—depending, for example, on whether you have a job or are self-employed—you can generally deduct the cost of moving yourself, your family, and your belongings, even if you don't itemize deductions. To take the deduction, your move must be employment-related; your new job must be at least 50 miles farther away from your former residence than your old job location; and you must work in the new location for at least 39 weeks of the first 12 months after your arrival.

In general, you can deduct:

- The cost of moving household goods from your old residence to your new one
- The cost of storing household goods in your new city for up to 30 consecutive days
- The cost of shipping your car

- The cost of moving your household pets
- The cost of your family's trip to your new residence (including transportation and lodging, but not meals)

Keep your receipts for these expenses.

If you take the deduction and then fail to meet the length-of-employment requirements, you will have to pay back the IRS (unless the failure is because your employer transferred you again or laid you off through no fault of your own). IRS publication 521 (available from the IRS web site at www.irs.gov or by phone at 800-829-3676) provides full details of the moving expenses deduction. It's a good idea to consult a tax expert if you are unsure whether, or to what extent, your move qualifies for the deduction.

CHILDREN

Moving can be hard on children. Kids that move to a new city are suddenly isolated from their friends and have to start over in an unfamiliar school and community. According to an American Medical Association study, children who move often are more likely to suffer from such problems as depression, aggression, and low self-esteem. Often their academic performance suffers as well. Besides avoiding unnecessary moves, there are a few things you can do to help your children cope with these stressful upheavals:

- *Talk about the move with your kids.* Be honest but positive. Listen to their concerns. Involve them in the process as fully as possible.
- *Make sure the children have their favorite possessions* with them on the trip; don't pack "blankey" or "bear" in the moving truck.
- *Plan some fun activities* on the other end. Your children may feel lonely in their new surroundings, and some ready-made activities can help them feel more comfortable.
- *Keep in touch with family and loved ones* as much as possible. Photos, phone calls, and e-mail are important ways to maintain links to the important people you have left behind.
- *If your children are of school age, take the time to involve yourself* in their new school and in their academic life. Don't let them get lost in the shuffle.

For younger children, there are dozens of good books designed to help explain, or at least help ease the transition of, moving. These books include *Max's Moving Adventure: A Coloring Book for Kids on the Move* by Danelle Till, illustrated by Joe Spooner; *Alexander, Who's Not (Do You Hear Me? I Mean It!) Going to Move* by Judith Viorst; *Goodbye/Hello* by Barbara Hazen; *The Leaving Morning* by Angela Johnson; *Little Monster's Moving Day* by Mercer Mayer; *Who Will Be My Friends?* (Easy I Can Read Series) by Syd Hoff; *I'm Not Moving, Mama* by Nancy White Carlstrom, illustrated by Thor Wickstrom; and *The Berenstain Bears' Moving Day* by Jan and Stan Berenstain.

For older children, try *The Moving Book: A Kid's Survival Guide* by Gabriel Davis; *Amber Brown is Not a Crayon* by Paula Danziger; *The Kid in the Red Jacket* by Barbara Park; *Hold Fast to Dreams* by Andrea Davis Pinkney; *Flip Flop Girl* by Katherine Paterson; and *My Fabulous New Life* by Sheila Greenwald.

PETS

Moving live animals across the country is stressful for everyone involved, whether animal or human. The **Pet-Moving Handbook** by Carrie Straub, available from First Books (www.firstbooks.com), provides practical answers for all your pet-moving questions and covers domestic and international moves via car, airplane, ferry, etc.

In general, driving your pets thousands of miles comes with its own set of challenges, including dealing with extreme weather (which could prevent you from leaving your pet in the car while you eat, for example) and finding pet-friendly overnight accommodation. If your pets fly, you'll have to navigate the maze of regulations, services, and prices that each airline has devised for animal transport; some airlines will not transport pets at all, others allow them only in the cabin as carry-on luggage, and still others will only transport animals when outdoor temperatures are moderate. A few airlines have special climate-controlled pet care facilities at their hub airports, and will place pets in a climate-controlled cargo bay on the plane. At a minimum, you'll need to get a health certificate from your veterinarian.

Given the complications of moving animals over long distances, you might want to leave the task to professionals. **WorldCare Pet Transport** will make all the arrangements with airports, airlines, and the licensing authorities at your destination—and, of course, they'll move your pet in accordance with the Animal Welfare Act and USDA specifications. Call 631-286-9104 or visit www.worldcarepet.com.

ONLINE RELOCATION RESOURCES

The following web sites feature moving tips and links to movers, real estate leads, and other relocation resources:

- **American Moving & Storage Association**, www.moving.org, offers referrals to interstate movers, local movers, storage companies, and packing and moving consultants.
- **Best Places**, www.bestplaces.net, compares quality-of-life and cost-of-living data for US cities.
- **Employee Relocation Council**, www.erc.org; if your employer is a member of this professional organization, you may have access to special services. Non-members can use the online database of real estate agents and related services.

- **First Books**, www.firstbooks.com, offers relocation resources and information on moving to Atlanta, Boston, Chicago, Los Angeles, New York, Portland, San Francisco, Seattle, Texas, Washington, D.C., and London, England. First Books also publishes the *Newcomer's Handbook for Moving to and Living in the USA*; *The Moving Book: A Kids' Survival Guide*; *Max's Moving Adventure: A Coloring Book for Kids on the Move*; and the *Pet-Moving Handbook*.
- **Move**, www.move.com, provides realty listings, moving tips, cost-of-living calculators, and more.
- **The Riley Guide**, www.rileyguide.com/relocate.html, is an online moving and relocation clearinghouse with links to dozens of useful relocation-related sites.
- To learn more about your rights and responsibilities with respect to interstate moving, check out the **United States Department of Transportation** (US-DOT) publication "Your Rights and Responsibilities When You Move," which is downloadable off the www.protectyourmove.gov web site. The **State of Oregon** has created a similar "Consumer Guide to Moving," available at egov. oregon.gov/ODOT/MCT/MOVING.shtml. The **Washington Utilities and Transportation Commission** has posted its useful tips for moving at www. wutc.wa.gov/consumer/movingtips.
- The **United States Postal Service** offers an online change of address form and general relocation information at moversguide.usps.com.

ONCE YOU FIND A HOME FOR YOURSELF AND YOUR STUFF, YOU'LL want to find a home for your money. Most financial institutions offer a variety of account options; fees (or their absence) are often dependent on the size of your balance. For major deposits, shop around for interest rates and perks, but for routine banking you'll be more interested in ATM fees and locations, online banking options, and direct deposit services (an increasingly common alternative to getting a paper paycheck). Small local banks may have lower fees than their colossal national competitors, while offering you a more navigable bureaucracy if you need help. If you do most of your banking at lunchtime or on the way to work, make sure the bank you're interested in has convenient branches or ATMs. If you currently have an account at a national bank with a Portland presence, check with a local branch; you may be able to keep your old account.

Once you decide on your new bank, it's usually a simple process to open a checking or savings account; generally you'll need photo identification, proof of address (if you haven't yet obtained an Oregon or Washington driver's license), your social security number, and money. Check with your prospective bank to find out what documents (and how much money) you'll need to bring with you.

Before you close your old bank accounts, keep in mind that many landlords and rental agencies will not accept a tenant who does not have a checking account, and some merchants will not accept the temporary checks most banks issue when you open an account, so it's probably wise to keep your old account current for at least a short time after you move.

BANK ACCOUNTS AND SERVICES

National, regional, and local banks all offer online and telephone banking, mortgages, and ATM, debit, and credit cards you can use practically anywhere in the world. Locally based banks, however, often specialize in (or at least advertise) personal service or special perks for customers; national banks generally offer the most comprehensive ATM networks and the widest array of services. In addition to the banks and credit unions listed below, many other local banks (some with only one or two branches) can be found in the Yellow Pages.

NATIONAL BANKS

These five large national banks have an extensive presence in the Portland area:

- **Bank of America,** 800-432-1000, www.bankofamerica.com, has dozens of branches and ATMs throughout the city and the surrounding suburbs.
- **Key Bank,** 800-539-2968, www.key.com, has more than 30 branches in the Portland area.
- **US Bank,** 800-872-2657, www.usbank.com; once based in Portland, this bank's corporate headquarters have moved to Minneapolis, but it still has one of the most extensive ATM and branch networks in Oregon.
- **WaMu,** 800-788-7000, www.wamu.com, formerly known as Washington Mutual, blankets the metropolitan area; some banking centers are located inside Fred Meyer supermarkets.
- **Wells Fargo,** 800-269-3557, www.wellsfargo.com; although it generated considerable ill will by closing branches across the region in the late 1990s, Wells Fargo has since re-established an extensive network of branches and ATMs in the Portland area.

LOCAL AND REGIONAL BANKS

- **Albina Community Bank,** 503-287-7537, 800-814-6088, www.albinabank. com, is a full-service community development bank with five branches; it invests its assets in lower- and middle-income communities in North and Northeast Portland.
- **Bank of Oswego,** 310 N State St, Suite 218, Lake Oswego; 3970 SW Mercantile Dr, Suite 105, Lake Oswego; 503-635-1699, www.bankofoswego.com; concentrates on offering personal service banking to the Lake Oswego area.
- **Bank of the West,** 800-488-2265, www.bankofthewest.com, which operates in 19 Western and Midwestern states, has branches throughout the metropolitan area.
- **Banner Bank,** 800-272-9933, www.bannerbank.com, based in Walla Walla, Washington, has five full-service branches in the Portland area.
- **Clackamas County Bank,** 503-668-5501, www.clackamascountybank.com, opened in 1911, serves Gresham, Sandy, and the communities of the Mount Hood foothills.
- **Pacific Continental Bank,** 877-231-BANK, www.therightbank.com, operates

branches in western Oregon and Washington, including Portland, Beaverton, and Tualatin.

- **Sterling Savings Bank,** 800-772-7791, www.sterlingsavingsbank.com, based in Spokane, Washington, has branches throughout the Northwest, including several in the Portland area.
- **Umpqua Bank,** 866-486-7782, www.umpquabank.com, headquartered in southern Oregon, has branches in Portland and each of the major suburbs.
- **Washington Federal Savings,** 206-624-7930, www.washingtonfederal.com, based in Seattle, has eight branches in the Portland area.
- **West Coast Bank,** 800-895-3345, www.wcb.com, has more than two dozen branches in the area, primarily in the suburbs.

CREDIT UNIONS

Credit unions are an alternative to consumer banking. These nonprofit, cooperative institutions offer most of the same the same services banks do, usually with lower fees, higher interest rates, and more personalized service. Membership is generally limited to employees of certain companies or government agencies or to residents of a certain area. To find a credit union in Oregon or Washington that you are eligible to join, use the Credit Union Match Up service (www.joinacu.org). Virtually any resident of the Portland metropolitan area is eligible to join at least one of the following three credit unions:

- **Columbia Credit Union,** 360-891-4000, 503-285-4521, 800-699-4009, www. columbiacu.org, has 12 branches in Clark County; anyone who lives or works in Washington State, or in Jantzen Beach/Hayden Island, Oregon (the northern fringe of North Portland), is eligible to join.
- **OnPoint Community Credit Union,** 503-228-7077, 800-527-3932, www. onpointcu.com, has nine branches in the Portland area; membership is open to anyone who lives or works in Benton, Clackamas, Columbia, Lane, Linn, Marion, Multnomah, Polk, Washington, or Yamhill county.
- **Unitus Community Credit Union,** 503-227-5571, 800-452-0900, www. unitusccu.com, has six branches; you are eligible for membership if you live or work in Multnomah, Washington, Clackamas, Marion, Polk, or Yamhill County.

CREDIT CARDS

Plastic is an increasingly common way to pay for goods and services—so much so that many Portland merchants will accept credit cards, but not personal checks. If you don't already have a credit card, you can compare credit card offerings—including interest rates, fees, special offers, and affinity features—at sites such as **CardWeb.com** (www.cardweb.com) or **Bankrate.com** (www.bankrate.com/brm/rate/cc_home.asp).

VISA (www.usa.visa.com) and **MasterCard** (www.mastercard.com/us/) cards are accepted by almost all merchants who take credit cards. **American Express** (www.americanexpress.com) and **Discover** (www.discovercard.com) cards are also widely accepted, though not universal. A smattering of businesses around town accept **Diner's Club** cards (www.dinersclub.com).

Most department stores and other major retail chains issue charge cards, sometimes with lines of credit. Usually these accounts are issued automatically and instantly if you already have a VISA or MasterCard account, often in combination with a discount on purchases made on the day you apply. Store accounts may have lower fees (or no fees) and lower interest rates than major credit cards, and perks may include advance notice of sales, access to special services, and cardholder discounts.

You can also buy **prepaid charge cards**. These work like debit cards, so you can give them to a teenager or use them for Internet shopping and know that you can't lose any more money than the amount already encoded on the card.

If you prefer to use a credit card that allows you to earn frequent flier miles, be aware that many airlines have only limited service from Portland—usually to their hub cities—and that as a result it can be very hard to redeem miles for a seat. The airlines that have the most flights from Portland are Alaska Airlines, United Airlines, and Southwest Airlines. For maximum flexibility, use a card that allows you to earn and redeem miles on one of those airlines or on a selection of carriers.

CONSUMER PROTECTION, IDENTITY THEFT, AND CREDIT REPORTS

Following a steady stream of disclosures of security breaches affecting major banks, credit card companies, government agencies, and businesses that collect and sell personal data, it seems nearly impossible to do anything to protect yourself from either credit card fraud or identity theft—and yet, if you're a victim, a fraud such as identity theft can nearly ruin your life. Victims spend an average of 600 hours trying to repair their credit; it's a daunting task. For more information, contact the **Identity Theft Resource Center** at 858-693-7935 or www.idtheftcenter.org, or check out the Federal Trade Commission's identity theft web site (www.ftc.gov/bcp/edu/microsites/idtheft).

That said, there is some good news: federal law generally limits your liability for unauthorized credit card charges to $50. Industry standards are even tougher and, in practice, consumers are often not held responsible for any unauthorized charges on their credit cards. The trick is to check your monthly statements carefully and notify your credit card company immediately when the charges are incorrect. So what else can you do to protect yourself? Security experts recommend several things. Don't print your full name and Social Security number on your checks, and don't carry your Social Security card in your wallet. Don't let your mail sit in your mailbox any longer than absolutely necessary, and shred personal documents before recycling them. Finally, think twice before you make a financial transaction over the Internet. Convenient though it may be, security failures have been identified even on web sites you might reasonably expect to be secure. Never send personal financial details through unencrypted email or submit them to an unsecured web site. Finally, check your credit rating periodically. You are entitled to one free credit report per year from each of the three major credit reporting companies, so if you request a report every four months from a different credit reporting company, you'll be able to keep tabs on your credit rating for free. You can visit **www.annualcreditreport.com** for online access to all three.

The national credit bureaus are:

- **Equifax**, 800-685-1111, www.equifax.com
- **Experian**, 888-397-3742, www.experian.com
- **TransUnion Corporation**, 800-916-8800, www.transunion.com

TAXES

The Portland metropolitan area includes two states with very different tax systems. Oregon has no sales tax, but collects a relatively high income tax; Washington has no state income tax, but collects a relatively high sales tax and has a wide range of other taxes and fees; and homeowners in both states pay property taxes. If you live, work, and shop in the same state, the tax situation is fairly straightforward. However, Washington residents who work or shop in Oregon face special rules.

FEDERAL INCOME TAX

Federal tax forms and publications are available online at www.irs.gov; they can also be ordered from the IRS by telephone by calling 800-829-3676. Preprinted paper forms are available during filing season (January–April 15) at some public libraries. Although you'll have to go through a metal detector to get them, paper forms are also available at the downtown Portland IRS office, 1220 SW 3rd Ave, 503-326-5441. You can get answers to your tax questions at this office, but some recent studies have found that the answer you get from an IRS representative often depends more upon the person giving it than on any clearly defined rule or regulation. (The same caution goes for advice provided on the IRS Tax Help Line, 800-829-1949.) The Service says it's working on standardizing responses.

Filing your tax return electronically can save you time and aggravation and can speed up your refund (if you're expecting one). Visit the IRS e-file site (www.

irs.gov/efile/index.html) for details, including a list of companies that offer tax software or online returns.

STATE INCOME TAX

Oregon's state income tax rate ranges from 5 to 9% of taxable income; most taxpayers fall into the 9% bracket, which kicks in at an extremely low level (taxable income of $6,850 for single filers and $13,700 for married filing jointly for the 2006 tax year). Tax forms and additional information are available from the **Oregon Department of Revenue**, 503-378-4988, www.oregon.gov/DOR.

Most (but not all) tax preparers and tax software publishers offer electronic filing for Oregon returns for a fee. Be aware that you will probably have to file an Oregon part-year resident tax return (Form 40P) for the year in which you move to Oregon; not all software publishers allow electronic filing for part-year returns, so check before committing to a program if electronic filing is important to you.

One unique aspect of the Oregon tax system is the "kicker." Whenever the state's two-year budget boasts a surplus of more than 2%, the entire surplus is refunded to taxpayers in odd-numbered years. The "kicker" kicks in more often than not, and many Oregonians look forward to receiving these tax refunds every two or four years. (The checks are conveniently timed to arrive just before the December holidays.) While understandably popular, the kicker system is controversial, and has been criticized for preventing the state from maintaining a reserve fund for years in which revenues fall below estimates.

Oregon currently has no local personal income taxes. A temporary Multnomah County income tax expired at the end of 2005.

Washington has no personal income tax. However, cross-border commuters cannot evade Oregon income tax: Washington residents who work in Oregon must pay Oregon income tax on their earnings from Oregon employment, and Oregon residents who have jobs in Washington must pay Oregon income taxes.

SALES TAX

Oregon does not have a sales tax.

Washington charges both a state sales tax (currently 6.5%) and an array of local sales taxes (which the consumer sees as a single, combined number at the cash register). In Clark County, the total sales tax ranges from 7.7% in unincorporated areas to 8.1% in Vancouver.

Washington also collects—or attempts to collect—use taxes from its residents who purchase items from other states for use in Washington. For most Clark County residents, the use tax will affect them if they purchase goods via mail-order or over the Internet from retailers who do not collect Washington sales tax, or if they shop in Oregon. A complete description of Washington's use tax can be found on the **Washington Department of Revenue** web site (http://dor. wa.gov/content/taxes/use/default.aspx). Although Washington has stepped up enforcement of the use tax, the large number of big box retailers that lurk conveniently on the Oregon side of both Columbia River bridges in Portland suggests that not all Washingtonians are diligent about reporting their purchases.

If you are an Oregon resident, you may not have to pay sales tax on items you buy at a store in Washington. Washington law allows (but doesn't require) retailers to exempt taxes on sales to Oregonians. (The exemption does not apply to meals, services, or lodging.) If the merchant agrees not to charge you sales tax, you'll be asked to show photo identification, and you may have to fill out a tax exemption certificate. Most retailers in Clark County welcome customers from Oregon, and are usually able to handle tax-free transactions. Merchants elsewhere in Washington, particularly small retailers, may not be set up to jump through the necessary tax exemption hoops, but it never hurts to ask.

PROPERTY TAXES

OREGON

In Oregon, county governments collect property taxes and distribute the funds to cities, school districts, and various special districts. The annual property tax is payable in thirds, with payments due on November 15, February 15, and May 15. A discount is available if you pay all or two-thirds of your annual tax by November 15. If you have a mortgage with an escrow account for taxes, your lender will pay the county directly.

Property taxes in Oregon generally increase at relatively low, predictable rates. Ballot Measure 5, passed in 1990, limited the overall property tax rate for education and general government purposes to $15 per $1,000 of assessed value. Voter-approved levies (for schools, libraries, or open space, for example) can (and do) raise property tax rates in some jurisdictions above the Measure 5 limit. Your property tax statement should have an itemized list of taxes, fees, and assessments from all the local taxing districts that provide services to your property. Some of these charges may not be based on assessed value.

In 1997, Ballot Measure 50 separated the taxable assessed value of a property from its real market value. Assessed value was initially set at 90% of a property's 1995 real market value, and subsequent increases in assessed value were limited to 3% per year. An exception to this rule is made for any improvements that raise the value of property by more than $10,000; if you buy a newly remodeled house, your property tax bill may be substantially higher than you expect. However, unlike in states such as California, a property's assessed value does not skyrocket to fair market value when the property is sold. If a taxpayer feels that the assessor incorrectly estimated the value of the property, he or she can file an appeal with their county's Board of Property Tax Assessment.

WASHINGTON

In Washington, property tax is collected by the counties. Property tax bills go out in February, and half of the total tax is due April 30; perhaps to increase Halloween's scare factor, the other half is due October 31. As in Oregon, there is a statewide limit on the property tax rate—1% of market value, exclusive of voter-approved levies. Unlike in Oregon, however, a property's assessed value is the same as its current fair market value, and there is no limit on how quickly a property's assessed value can rise. (In Clark County, property values are reassessed annually.) Washington law limits the rate of increase in local budgets to 1% per year unless voters approve a higher increase, so in practice property taxes do not increase at the same rate as real estate values (and would not necessarily decrease in case of a downturn in real estate values). Senior citizens and disabled persons may qualify for property tax exemptions or deferrals. Also note that homeowners generally qualify for a three-year exemption on the value of major remodels to single-family houses.

COUNTY OFFICES

For questions about assessments or property taxes for a specific property, check with your county's assessor:

- **Clackamas County Department of Assessment and Taxation**, 503-655-8671, www.co.clackamas.or.us/at/assessment/info.htm
- **Clark County (Washington) Department of Assessment and GIS**, 360-397-2391, www.co.clark.wa.us/assessor/index.html
- **Columbia County Assessor's Office**, 503-397-2240, www.co.columbia.or.us/assessorsoffice
- **Marion County Assessor's Office**, 503-588-5144, assessor.co.marion.or.us
- **Multnomah County Division of Assessment and Taxation**, 503-988-3326 (property tax information line), www.multcotax.org
- **Washington County Department of Assessment and Taxation**, 503-846-8741, http://www.co.washington.or.us/DEPTMTS/at/atmain.htm
- **Yamhill County Office of Assessment and Taxation**, 503-434-7521, www.co.yamhill.or.us/assessor

OTHER TAXES

If you are self-employed and you live within the TriMet transit district (which includes most of the Oregon portion of the metropolitan area), you will have to pay TriMet self-employment tax. This tax is collected by the Oregon Department of Revenue.

Although Washington has no income tax, the state levies a business and occupation tax (B & O) tax on gross business receipts. If you are self-employed, you will be subject to this tax. The B & O tax rate depends on the type of business activity you engage in. Full details are available at http://dor.wa.gov/content/taxes/busoccupation. Washington also levies a hefty state and local excise tax on the sale of real estate. This tax is generally paid by the seller, so it won't initially affect you if you are moving to Washington from another state.

STARTING A BUSINESS

The Oregon Secretary of State's **Corporation Division** publishes "How to Start a Business in Oregon," a helpful guide to opening a business in the state. The booklet is available online at www.filinginoregon.com/forms/pdf/business/1100.pdf, or by calling the Corporation Division at 503-986-2200. The **city of Portland's** online business portal (www.portlandonline.com/index.cfm?c=25781) has links to various sites that provide information and resources for starting and operating a business in the area, as does the Multnomah County Library's Small Business Incubator (www.multcolib.org/biz). Finally, the **Portland Development Commission** (503-823-3200, www.pdc.us) publishes a Business Resource Directory that is full of useful information for existing or prospective Portland businesses.

If you want to start a business in Washington, you must file an application for a Master Business License with the state. The Washington **Department of Licensing** web site (http://www.dol.wa.gov/business/startbusiness.html) contains useful information about the business startup and licensing process. You may also need a local business license. The **Clark County** web site (http://www.co.clark.wa.us/aboutcc/new_clarkcounty/startingbusiness.html) lists several resources for people thinking of starting a business in the area.

NOW THAT YOU'VE FOUND THE HOME OF YOUR DREAMS—OR AT least a place to hang your Gore-Tex jacket—you'll need to get the utilities turned on, get connected to the Internet or cable TV, and get rid of the pile of trash and recycling you've accumulated during your move. And you'll need to get a new driver's license and register your car (if you have one). And you'd better register to vote. You might want to subscribe to a newspaper. And you'll probably want a library card. And…well, moving in is just the first step to getting settled in Portland.

UTILITIES

A few large utilities (and several small ones) serve the two states and seven counties that make up the greater Portland metropolitan area. In most cases, you won't be able to choose which company provides your water, electric, cable, or gas service, so there's no need to compare prices. You can usually sign up for service directly with the utility, either by telephone or online. If you are unsure about which specific utility serves your new address, check with your new city or county government, your realtor, or your property manager.

To save a few steps, you can make online arrangements to start your new electric, phone, and cable service at **www.moveportlandor.com**. Just type in your address and the web site will automatically locate the providers that serve your new home. This service claims to provide the best deals available from each of the utility companies, but if you want to explore all available options you might prefer to deal directly with the utilities themselves.

Whichever utility company serves your new home, call the one-call utility locator service for your area before you start digging in your new yard. In Oregon, call the **Oregon Utility Notification Center** at 800-332-2344, or visit the center online at www.digsafelyoregon.com; in southwest Washington, contact the

Northwest Utility Notification Center, 800-424-5555, www.callbeforeyoudig. org.

ELECTRICITY

Two large investor-owned utilities and one public utility district (PUD) provide electricity to most of the Portland metropolitan area. The primary electric utility for most of the city of Portland and its suburbs in Oregon is **Portland General Electric** (PGE) (503-228-6322, 800-542-8818 for customer service, 503-464-7777 to report outages, www.portlandgeneral.com). Owned until recently by Enron, and thus one of that company's few real assets, PGE is now a stand-alone company. To start service, call customer service or visit www.cs.portlandgeneral.com.

Pacific Power (888-221-7070 for customer service and new accounts, 877-LITESOUT for outages, www.pacificpower.net), serves most of Northeast Portland and a portion of downtown Portland. Pacific Power is the local business name of PacifiCorp, a major power company that is owned by MidAmerican Energy Holdings Company.

In Clark County, Washington, electricity is delivered by **Clark Public Utilities** (360-992-3000 or 800-562-1736 for customer service, 360-992-8000 for outages, www.clarkpublicutilities.com), a customer-owned PUD.

A few PUDs, member-owned electric cooperatives, and municipal power companies provide electricity to outlying communities in Oregon:

- **Canby Utility**, 503-266-1156, is Canby's independent, city-owned utility.
- **Columbia River PUD**, 503-397-0590, www.crpud.net, provides electric service to much of Columbia County, including Scappoose and St. Helens, and a small part of northern Multnomah County.
- **Forest Grove Light and Power**, 503-992-3250, www.ci.forest-grove.or.us/ light1.html, is a department of the city of Forest Grove; it provides electricity to Forest Grove and part of the surrounding area.
- **McMinnville Water & Light**, 503-472-6158, www.mc-power.com, is the municipal utility company for the city of McMinnville.
- **Salem Electric**, 503-362-3601, www.salemelectric.com, serves portions of Keizer and Salem (primarily West Salem).
- **West Oregon Electric Cooperative**, 503-429-3021, 800-777-1276, www. westoregon.org, serves rural areas of Clatsop, Columbia, Tillamook, Washington, and Yamhill counties.

Most local utilities offer **green power** or renewable energy options to residential customers. PGE has three programs: **Green Source, Renewable Future,** and **Clean Wind.** Pacific Power's version is the **Blue Sky** program, which offers similar options. The Clark Public Utilities program is called **Green Lights**. Contact your utility or visit its web site for additional information and costs.

NATURAL GAS

Many houses and apartments in the Portland area do not use gas at all; some homes have electric heat and hot water heaters—a holdover from the days when the region's hydropower was ridiculously cheap—and a few older homes still have oil furnaces. If your home has a natural gas furnace or stove, **Northwest Natural Gas** is almost certainly your provider. To activate new service, call 503-226-4211 or 800- 422-4012 or visit www.nwnatural.com/services.

HEATING ASSISTANCE

In Oregon, the **Low Income Energy Assistance Program** (503-986-2094) and the **Oregon Energy Assistance Program** (503-986-6704) help low-income households pay their heating bills during the winter months; for details about heating assistance options, visit www.warmoregon.org. Washington has a similar program, the **Low Income Home Energy Assistance Program** (360-725-2866, www.liheapwa.org). Additional heating assistance programs, funded by the federal government or utility companies, may be available; in Oregon, visit www.warmoregon.org.

Washington has a disconnection moratorium rule that allows low-income households that have exhausted all other alternatives to keep their heat on from November 15 through March 15. To qualify, you must follow certain procedures, including contacting the utility and trying to work out a payment plan. Contact the **Washington Utilities and Transportation Commission** (800-562-6150, www.wutc.wa.gov/consumer) for details. Oregon does not have a similar moratorium rule; if you are unable to pay your utility bills during the winter, contact your utility directly to work out a payment plan to avoid disconnection.

TELEPHONE

AREA CODES

Portland and its Oregon suburbs have two area codes, **503** and **971**. The 971 area code was introduced in 2000 as an "overlay" area code for the Portland metropolitan area, and there is no geographic division between the two area codes. Telephone companies are required to exhaust their supply of 503 prefixes before assigning a 971 area code, and currently 971 numbers are mostly assigned to cell phones. As a result, the 503 area code is still by far the most common—so much so that many residents and businesses still only give out seven-digit numbers, with the "503" implied.

Because these two area codes overlap, you must dial the full ten-digit telephone number, including the area code (but not including an initial "1"), when you make a local call. To complicate matters, the 503 area code encompasses large parts of northwest Oregon outside the metro area, including Salem and the north coast; calls to these areas are toll calls, and you'll need to dial a "1" before the area code. There is unfortunately no way to tell from the area code alone whether a 503 number is a local or distance call.

The area code for the rest of the state is **541**; in the Willamette Valley, the 541 area code begins just south of Salem.

The area code for southwest Washington is **360**. Currently, it is not necessary to dial the area code first when making local calls.

LANDLINE PHONE SERVICE

Qwest has a virtual monopoly on local telephone service in Portland and much of the suburban area. You can order new residential service online at www.qwest.com/homeservice, or by calling 800-475-7526. **Verizon** is the incumbent carrier in Yamhill County, most of Washington County (except for North Plains, which is Qwest Territory), Gresham, Sandy, Happy Valley, Wilsonville, and Silverton. To set up local service, visit www22.verizon.com/pages/newconnect/ or call 800-483-4000. A few competitors offer alternatives to the main carriers for local phone service, although these newcomers primarily serve business rather than residential customers. In addition, **Comcast** offers cable-based phone service (see **Cable Television**, below), and if you have a broadband connection you can choose to use Internet-based phone service (see **VoIP**, below).

A few Clackamas County communities are served by independent telecom companies:

- **Beaver Creek Cooperative Telephone Company**, 503-632-3113, www.bctelco.com, provides telephone, wireless, cable television, and Internet service in Oregon City and Beavercreek.
- **Canby Telecom**, 503-266-8111, www.canbytel.com, provides telephone, Internet, and digital television (via DSL) service in Canby.
- **Colton Telephone & Cable TV**, 503-824-3211, www.colton.com, offers the services its name suggests, along with Internet service, in Colton.
- **Molalla Communications Company**, 503-829-1100, molalla.net, offers a similar range of services in Molalla.

In Washington, local telephone service is open to competition. While **Qwest** and **Verizon** are the dominant local carriers, consumers can use one of several other companies for residential phone service; check the listings in the front of the phone book or go to the **Washington Utilities and Transportation Commission** web site, www.wutc.wa.gov/telecom, to find authorized telecommunications companies.

LONG-DISTANCE AND INTERNATIONAL SERVICE AND PREPAID CALLING CARDS

You are under no obligation to use your local phone company for long-distance service. Many companies now offer unlimited long-distance calls for a flat fee, which can be a good deal if you make lots of long-distance calls. (Local phone companies often offer their customers "package" discounts on unlimited long-distance plans.) Otherwise, analyze your typical calling patterns and select a plan that offers the best deal based on the time of day and average duration of your calls. You can research and compare long-distance plans at web sites such as **www.saveonphone.com**, **www.phonedog.com**, and **www.tollchaser.com**.

Every convenience store and corner market sells **prepaid calling cards** in denominations of $5 and up. Some of these card companies advertise rates as low as 1.2 cents a minute. Those rates apply to actual talking time, though—with per-call charges and surcharges for using a pay phone, you'll deplete the card balance rapidly if you make lots of short calls. Still, prepaid cards can be cheaper than many long-distance plans if you tend to make only a few long calls.

Making international calls from your home phone can be shockingly expensive. Most long-distance companies offer general or country-specific international calling plans; there is often a monthly charge, so these plans work best for people who make frequent international calls. For occasional international calling, consider an international prepaid calling card. Alternatively, sign up for a service such as **Gorilla Mobile** (800-881-3004, www.gorillamobile.com), which offers low international rates for a $5 annual fee; you call a toll-free number to place your international calls, and the company bills your credit card for your usage each month.

VOIP

Voice over Internet Protocol, or VoIP, allows people with broadband connections to make voice telephone calls over the Internet, including international calls, for a flat monthly fee. Most major and some minor telephone, cable, and Internet providers now offer VoIP service, but the biggest players in this market are currently **Skype** (www.skype.com) and **Vonage** (www.vonage.com). VoIP may be a good value if you make many long-distance calls. However, VoIP has some downsides: it won't work during a power failure or if your broadband connection goes down, it can suffer from poor sound quality, and your location cannot always be identified if you call 911. For that last reason alone, it's advisable to keep a conventional landline or a cell phone for emergencies.

WIRELESS PHONE SERVICE

Portlanders, like urbanites around the world, increasingly view cell phones as a necessity. A growing number of residents have dropped their traditional long-distance service, or have even abandoned landlines entirely, preferring to rely instead on their cell phones (and their carriers' national rate plans) for all voice communication. This approach has potential pitfalls—for example, wireless reception in hilly neighborhoods can be spotty or nonexistent, and service can be inconsistent even in areas with otherwise adequate coverage—but it may be a good solution if you plan to get a mobile phone anyway. Keep in mind that vast swaths of the rural Northwest lack any coverage at all, and Oregon is one of the only states in the country where analog-compatible phones are still necessary in some remote areas. To be sure that you're not stuck with a cell phone that won't work where and when you need it, make sure your provider will allow you to test the phone within a specified time after you start service and to return the phone if reception is unacceptable.

Check the yellow pages for a complete list of cellular providers, and research the latest deals on service plans at a site like **www.point.com**. Be prepared to swallow a one-to-three year contract for the best monthly rates; if you don't need a free or subsidized phone, and you don't make lots of calls, a pay-as-you-go plan may be a better deal. The largest cellular carriers in the Portland area are:

- **AT&T/Cingular**, 888-333-6651, www.cingular.com; formerly AT&T, then Cingular, and now the "new" AT&T.
- **Cricket**, www.mycricket.com; a recent entrant to the Portland market, Cricket claims to have good wireless coverage in the Portland area and the Willamette Valley and offers unlimited calls and no contracts, but its coverage in the rest of Oregon is limited.
- **Sprint**, 800-SPRINT1, www.sprint.com
- **T-Mobile**, 800-TMOBILE, www.t-mobile.com; T-Mobile's web site includes a highly detailed mapping feature that depicts average signal strength for any specific address in its coverage area.
- **Verizon Wireless**, 800-922-0204, www.verizonwireless.com

Most of these carriers have stand-alone stores, and stores and kiosks at malls throughout the Portland area. Some electronics and office supply stores, and even online retailers like **Amazon.com**, sell phones and service plans on behalf of one or more carriers. In addition, Qwest and Verizon offer discounts for bundling cell and landline services; check with your prospective carrier for details.

INTERNET SERVICE

Your telephone or cable provider should be extremely eager to also provide you with Internet service. The bundled services they offer can often be good deals; however, it's worth shopping around for an Internet Service Provider (ISP) that will best support your particular needs (for web hosting, for example, or national dial-in access if you travel frequently). Be sure to check out local ISPs as well as the big national providers; local companies sometimes offer less-expensive (and more responsive) service than big players like MSN, AOL, or Earthlink.

If you're deciding between DSL and cable broadband service, be sure to compare the speeds of the services available in your specific neighborhood. Ask your neighbors about their experiences, and consider whether the room in which you plan to place your modem already has a phone or cable jack in place. (It can be expensive to add new jacks.)

WI-FI (WIRELESS INTERNET)

The good news is that a high-speed wireless cloud is slowly covering Portland: A company called MetroFi has a contract to provide Wi-Fi access across 95% of the city by mid-2008. (Portland's suburbs are not included.) Now for the bad news: If you want free Wi-Fi, you'll be subjected to banner ads. (The service is ad-supported.) Coverage is currently limited to downtown, Old Town and the Pearl District, the Lloyd District, and part of Southeast Portland, and service can be poor indoors or away from antennas. Moreover, for ad-free service, you'll have to cough up about $20 a month. Unless MetroFi service at your home or office is consistently strong and reliable, you may want to use a wired ISP as a primary or backup provider.

Many coffee shops, bars, libraries, and other establishments throughout the metropolitan area are Wi-Fi hotspots that provide free or paid wireless access to their patrons. Sites like **www.wifipdx.com** and **www.jiwire.com** provide extensive lists of Portland Wi-Fi hotspots. The **Personal Telco Project** (www.personaltelco.net) is an all-volunteer effort to create a public (as opposed to municipal) Wi-Fi network in Portland; check their web site for hotspot listings.

CABLE AND SATELLITE TELEVISION

CABLE TELEVISION

Comcast (888-824-8264, www.comcast.com) has a monopoly on cable television service in Portland and most suburban areas. In early 2008, however, **Verizon** plans to begin offering television programming over fiber-optic lines to many of its telephone subscribers in Washington County. (See **Landline Phone Service**, above, for contact and service area information.) Qwest reportedly also intends to seek regulatory approval to introduce a similar service at some distant date, likely several years from now. As they say in the TV business, stay tuned. In the meantime, the only area communities with non-Comcast cable options are Beavercreek, Colton, and Molalla, while Canby offers digital television over its municipal DSL lines.

SATELLITE TV

Satellite television is available throughout the region from **Direct TV** (888-777-2454, www.directv.com) and **Dish Network** (888-825-2557, www.dishnetwork.com).

WATER AND SEWER

Portland takes great pride in its drinking water system. The city boasts some of the highest-quality tap water in the country because its primary source is the protected Bull Run watershed near Mount Hood. (The city's backup source is drinkable but somewhat less tasty groundwater from a well field near the Columbia River.) Most Portlanders drink water directly from the tap; some people filter their water, which is a good practice if you live in an older home that may have lead in the water lines.

To set up water service in the city of Portland, contact the **Portland Water Bureau** (503-823-7770, www.portlandonline.com/water). Residential bills come every three months; the bill will include sewer and stormwater utility charges. The stormwater charge is based on the estimated volume of runoff from roofs and paved areas on your property. Through the Clean River Rewards program, homeowners and businesses can qualify for a discount on the stormwater charge if they take certain steps to prevent rainwater from flowing into streets or sewers. Visit www.cleanriverrewards.com for details.

Outside Portland, most incorporated cities provide municipal water and sewer service to their residents; to sign up or for more information, contact your city hall or visit your city's web site (See the **Useful Phone Numbers and Web Sites** chapter). Many unincorporated areas obtain water service from nearby municipal systems or from special water districts. The largest of the latter, **Tualatin Valley Water District** (503-642-1511, www.tvwd.org) serves nearly 200,000 residents in eastern Washington County, including parts of Beaverton, Hillsboro, and Tigard.

If you're concerned about the quality of your local tap water, or if you just want more information about it, you can contact your water utility and ask for a copy of their annual report (which is usually posted online); alternatively, contact the Environmental Protection Agency (call the safe drinking water hotline, 800-426-4791, or go to www.epa.gov/safewater).

CONSUMER PROTECTION–UTILITY COMPLAINTS

Try to resolve billing or other disputes with your phone, gas, or electric company on your own. If a problem persists, contact the Consumer Services Section of the **Oregon Public Utility Commission** (PO Box 2148, 550 Capitol St NE #215, Salem,

OR 97308-2148, 503-378-6600 [Salem], 800-522-2404 [Oregon outside Salem], www.puc.state.or.us/PUC/consume/comppro.shtml). OPUC's web site includes an explanation of the complaint procedure and a complaint form that you can submit online.

In Washington, contact the consumer affairs staff of the **Washington Utilities and Transportation Commission** (P.O. Box 47250, 1300 S Evergreen Park Dr SW, Olympia, WA 98504, 800-562-6150), or visit www.wutc.wa.gov/fileacomplaint to use their online complaint form. Note that these agencies only regulate investor-owned utilities, so if you have a dispute with a public utility district or municipal utility, you'll have to work out the problem with the utility.

TRASH AND RECYCLING

If you're renting, you can skip much of this section—Oregon law requires landlords to provide garbage and recycling collection—but if you're buying a home you'll need to arrange for trash pickup.

OREGON

TRASH

Metro, the Portland area's regional government, coordinates solid waste disposal and supports programs to increase recycling and reduce waste across the region. Local cities and counties franchise actual garbage pickup to a host of private companies. To find your garbage hauler, visit Metro's "Who's my garbage hauler?" page at www.metro-region.org/hauler or call 503-234-3000. Contact your hauler directly to set up garbage hauling service and to find out about available container sizes and monthly charges.

If you need to dispose of a large item—like that huge moldy sofa that the old owner of your new house "forgot" to take off the front porch—you can load it in your car, truck, or trailer, cover it with a tarp, and haul the thing to one of Metro's transfer stations:

- **Metro Central Station**, 6161 NW 61st Ave, Portland
- **Metro South Station**, 2001 Washington St, Oregon City

For directions and hours, call Metro Recycling Information at 503-234-3000 or visit www.metro-region.org/article.cfm?articleid=570. Alternatively, you can have a private company deliver (and take away) a large drop box; look in the Yellow Pages under "Garbage & Rubbish Collection."

If you live in Washington County, two other locations might be more convenient; Waste Management, a private company, operates both. The **Forest Grove Transfer Station** accepts the same kinds of materials for disposal and recycling as Metro's transfer stations. Call 503-992-1212 for hours and fee information. The **Hillsboro Landfill** accepts only "dry waste" (i.e., no kitchen waste or other materials that could decompose rapidly and cause odor or vector problems) and some recyclables. Call 503-640-9427 for hours, fees, and details about what kinds of waste the landfill will accept.

CAN IT BE REUSED OR RECYCLED?

If you don't want materials that are still potentially usable, you can call Metro Recycling Information at 503-234-3000 to talk with a recycling specialist who will help you find a convenient option for recycling, reusing, or disposing of the unwanted item. Alternatively, visit Metro's interactive "Find a Recycler" web page (www.metro-region.org/findrecycler), which features information about hundreds of reuse and recycling options across the region. (The call center maintains the database used for both the hotline and the Find a Recycler web tool, so you'll get the same information by phone or online.) The database is updated on almost a daily basis, so information is as current as possible.

RECYCLING

Franchised garbage haulers pick up **curbside recycling** and **yard debris.** Each local government regulates curbside recycling and determines what materials are accepted, although glass, paper, cans, and plastic bottles can be recycled at the curb throughout the region. Some jurisdictions offer more comprehensive recycling options; for example, in Clackamas County (except Estacada), you can recycle plastic tubs (e.g., yogurt containers) and lids at curbside.

In Portland, the **Office of Sustainable Development** (503-823-7202, www.PortlandOnline.com/OSD/recycle) administers the city's curbside recycling and yard debris pickup programs. For information about curbside recycling in other parts of the metro area, visit www.metro-region.org/article.cfm?ArticleID=527, call Metro at 503-234-3000, or contact your local government.

More ambitious recyclers can go beyond the limited range of materials recycled at the curb; to learn where to recycle packing peanuts, old batteries, antifreeze, and other hard-to-find-a-home-for items, visit www.metro-region.org/article.cfm?articleid=1383 or call Metro at—you guessed it—503-234-3000. Metro also accepts recyclables at its transfer stations.

If your new home will be in an outlying area beyond Metro's jurisdiction, contact your city or county government directly to find out how to set up garbage and recycling service. If you're going to live someplace *really* remote, you may have to haul your own garbage to the dump!

WASHINGTON

Waste Connections Inc. (360-892-5370, www.wcnorthwest.com) provides trash, recycling, and yard debris pickup in Clark County. Call them or visit their web site to set up service.

ELECTRONICS RECYCLING AND HAZARDOUS WASTE DISPOSAL

Electronic waste, such as television sets, computers, computer monitors, and the like, contains such heavy metals as lead, mercury and cadmium and should not be thrown out. If the item still works, consider donating it to a nonprofit such as **Free Geek** (1731 SE 10th Ave, 503-232-9350, www.freegeek.org), an organization that rebuilds used electronics and provides them to people and organizations in need.

To learn how to recycle electronic waste in the Portland area, visit Metro's electronics recycling web page at www.metro-region.org/findrecycler and select "electronics" from the list of recyclable items, or call 503-234-3000. If you live in Oregon outside Multnomah, Clackamas, and Washington counties, check the Oregon Department of Environmental Quality's online list of computer and electronics recyclers at www.deq.state.or.us/lq/electronics.htm. The Washington Department of Ecology posts a similar list at www.ecy.wa.gov/programs/swfa/eproductrecycle/. (A recent Washington law requires electronics manufacturers to make "consumer-convenient" recycling of electronic waste available by 2009; Oregon is considering similar legislation.)

Household hazardous waste such as paint, solvents, or chemicals is not safe to toss in the trash and should be disposed of properly. If you inherit such materials in the Portland area, you can take your household hazardous waste to Metro for free, safe disposal or recycling. Metro has two hazardous waste acceptance facilities, which are adjacent to the two transfer stations listed above and are open Monday through Saturday. For information and directions, call 503-234-3000 or visit www.metro-region.org/hhw. In Clark County, household hazardous waste can be taken to the **Central Transfer and Recycling Center** (11034 NE 117th Ave, Vancouver, 360-256-8482) on weekends from 8 a.m. to 4 p.m., or the **West Van Materials Recovery Center** (6601 NW Old Lower River Rd, Vancouver, 360-737-1727), on Friday or Saturday from 8 a.m. to 4 p.m. Both Metro and Clark County organize frequent community hazardous waste collection events from March through November.

Of course, you should properly dispose of your electronic and hazardous waste *before* you move to Portland; it's illegal and unsafe to transport hazardous waste, and getting rid of bulky electronics you no longer use will reduce the amount of stuff you have to move. Call 1-800-RECYCLE to find out where you can recycle electronics or dispose of hazardous waste in your area.

AUTOMOBILES

DRIVER'S LICENSES AND STATE IDs

OREGON

You must obtain an Oregon driver's license when you become an Oregon resident. (The law does not specify a time limit.) You must be at least 16 to obtain a driver's license. If you have a valid license from another U.S. state or territory, Canada, or Germany, and you're over 18, you will only need to pass a written test and an eye exam; a driving test is generally not necessary, although the DMV has the authority to require one. (Be aware, however, that the Oregon written exam has the reputation of being comparatively challenging.) Bring proof of identity (including your current out-of-state license); proof of current residence (such as mortgage documents, a credit card or utility bill, or a bank statement); and cash or check for the license fee (currently $54.50) to a regular or full-service **Oregon Driver and Motor Vehicles Services Division** (DMV) office.

To get a state identification card, bring proof of identity and residence and the $29 fee to a DMV office. You can obtain additional information about driver's licenses and state ID cards from the **DMV** (503-299-9999 [Portland area], www.oregon.gov/ODOT/DMV/). The helpful brochure "Doing Business with the DMV" is available in PDF format at www.odot.state.or.us/forms/dmv/6841.pdf.

You can get a new Oregon driver's license at any of the following DMV offices:

- 4250 SW Allen Blvd, Beaverton
- 10 82nd Dr, Gladstone
- 2222 E Powell Blvd, Gresham
- 1300 SW Oak, Ste H, Hillsboro
- 3 SW Monroe Pkwy, #V, Lake Oswego
- 1502 SW Sixth Ave, Portland (Downtown)
- 8260 N Interstate Ave, Portland (North)
- 1836 NE 82nd Ave, Portland (Northeast)
- 8710 SE Powell Blvd, Portland (Southeast)
- 37395 Hwy 26, Sandy
- 14240 SW Galbreath Dr, Sherwood
- 500 N Columbia River Hwy, Ste 400, St. Helens

A complete list of regular and express DMV offices in Oregon is available online at www.oregon.gov/ODOT/DMV/offices/index.shtml.

WASHINGTON

You must get a Washington driver's license within 30 days of the date you establish residency in the state. You'll need to go to a driver's licensing office with proof of identity (including your unexpired out-of-state license), your social security number (if you don't have it memorized), and a check or cash to pay the license and application fee (currently $45). If you already have a license from another state, you'll need to complete an application and pass a vision test, but you won't need to take a written or driving test unless your out-of-state license is expired. To get a state identification card, you'll need to go to a licensing office with proof of identity and $20. More information about driver's licenses and state ID cards is available from the **Washington Department of Licensing**, 360-902-3900, www. dol.wa.gov/driverslicense/. Two full-service licensing offices serve Clark County:

- 8000 NE 13th Ave, Hazel Dell, 360-576-6060
- 1301 NE 136th Ave, Vancouver, 360-260-6288

You can check current wait times at either office online at fortress.wa.gov/dol/ddl/lobbywaittime/.

OWNING A CAR

It is true that it is possible to live and move about happily in Portland without a car. It is also true that most Portland households own at least one car, and that trying to make your way through the suburbs without one can be a lonely, stressful, and time-consuming endeavor. Assuming you're in the car-owning majority, there are several steps you'll need to take to become a happy (or at least legal) Portland motorist.

AUTOMOBILE REGISTRATION

OREGON

You are required to register and title your car(s) in Oregon when you become an Oregon resident. You can register your vehicle at any of the state DMV offices listed above; to save time, try to combine errands and get a driver's license during the same visit. You'll need to bring the title and (for most vehicles) proof that your car has passed an emissions test (see below). You'll also need to have a VIN inspection; this brief procedure can be performed at any full-service DMV office or can be done during your emissions test. Oregon does not require a safety inspection, and registration is a fixed amount (currently $54 for passenger cars); fees are not based on a vehicle's weight or value. Registration is good for two years.

Be sure to bring a checkbook or enough cash to cover the registration, title, license plate, and VIN inspection fees; the DMV does not accept credit cards. If you have a passenger vehicle and you're not getting specialty or personalized plates, expect to pay a total of about $121. Full information on titling and registering a vehicle in Oregon is available on the **Oregon DMV** web site (www.oregon.gov/ODOT/DMV/vehicle/) or by calling 503-299-9999.

WASHINGTON

You must title and register your vehicle within 30 days of moving to Washington. You will need to submit your current title, a notarized Vehicle Certificate of Ownership Application, and possibly proof that the vehicle has passed a Washington emissions test (see below). You will also need to pay a host of fees and charges. These fees, which include a basic license fee and a weight-based fee, range between $40 and $60 for most vehicles. More details about vehicle registration, including specific fees, are available from the **Department of Licensing** (360-902-3770, www.dol.wa.gov/vehicleregistration/).

To register, mail your paperwork and fees to Department of Licensing, ATTN: Vehicle Licensing, Box 9909, Olympia, WA 98507-9909, or take them to any vehicle licensing office. (There are eight vehicle licensing offices in Clark County; a complete list is available online at fortress.wa.gov/dol/dolprod/vehoffices/. Note that Washington driver's licensing offices cannot process vehicle registrations.)

AUTOMOBILE INSURANCE

In **Oregon**, the legally required minimum liability insurance coverage is $25,000 per person/$50,000 per crash for bodily injury to others; $10,000 per crash for damage to the property of others; personal injury protection coverage of $15,000 per person; and uninsured motorist coverage of $25,000 per person/$50,000 per crash for bodily injury. You do not need to bring proof of insurance with you when you register your car (unless you are taking a driving test or have previously been convicted of driving without insurance), but you will need to certify that the vehicle has at least the legally required minimum insurance coverage.

Washington's mandatory insurance requirements for bodily injury or property damage to others are the same as Oregon's; personal injury protection and uninsured motorist coverage are not required. You must carry proof of insurance in your vehicle at all times.

EMISSIONS TESTING

In general, any vehicle brought into the Portland metropolitan area must pass an **emissions test** before it can be registered. Once your car is registered, you'll need to have it re-tested every two years.

OREGON

In Oregon, pre-1975 vehicles, motorcycles, and vehicles registered outside the Portland metropolitan area are exempt from testing. The testing fee is $21, payable by cash, credit card, or debit card only. Testing hours vary; generally, vehicle inspection stations are closed on Sundays and Mondays, and stay open late on Wednesday nights. There are six inspection stations, known as "clean air stations," in the Portland area:

- **Clackamas,** 9350 SE Clackamas Rd (off I-205 south of Clackamas Town Center)
- **Gresham,** 1200 SW Highland Dr (near 182nd Ave and Powell Blvd)
- **Northeast Portland,** 7701 NE 33rd Dr (between Columbia Blvd and Marine Dr)
- **Scappoose,** 52751 NE 1st (just off Hwy 30)
- **Sherwood,** 14962 SW Tualatin-Sherwood Rd (east of Sherwood off Pacific Hwy)
- **Sunset/Hillsboro,** 5130 NW Five Oaks Dr (off Cornelius Pass Rd, just north of the Sunset Hwy/US 26)

If you don't want to wait in line and can plan ahead, you can call 503-229-5066 to make reservations at the Clackamas, Gresham and Sunset/Hillsboro stations. Alternatively, you can check out the crowd on online "lane cams" before you go. Clean Air Stations are normally busiest on Tuesdays, so a visit on Wednesday evening, Thursday, or Friday will result in a shorter wait time. For complete details of Oregon's emissions testing program, including station hours and program requirements, visit the **Department of Environmental Quality Vehicle Inspection Program** web site (www.deq.state.or.us/aq/vip/) or call 971-673-1630 or 877-476-0583.

WASHINGTON

If you live in a non-rural part of Clark County, your car will probably have to pass an emissions test. Vehicles less than 5 or more than 25 years old are exempt from testing, as are hybrid vehicles with a city fuel economy rating of at least 50 miles per gallon. Note that Washington requires emissions tests every two years; the model year of your car determines whether your car gets tested in even or odd years. (1995 and older models get tested in even-numbered years for even model years and odd-numbered years for odd model years; confusingly, for 1996 and newer model years, the testing regime is reversed.) If you move to Washington with a car that would not otherwise have to be tested during the year you move, you can wait a year to get it tested (but you'll have to register the vehicle right away regardless).

The inspection fee is $15, payable by cash, check, or credit card. Complete information is available from the **Washington Department of Ecology** (800-453-4951 [in Clark County], www.ecy.wa.gov/programs/air/cars/automo tive_pages.htm).

Two emissions inspection stations serve Clark County:

- **West Vancouver,** 14110 NW 3rd Ct., Vancouver, 360-574-3731
- **East Vancouver,** 1121 NE 136th Ave, Vancouver, 360-254-2173

Inspection stations are open weekdays from 9 a.m. to 5 p.m., and Saturdays from 9 a.m. to 1 p.m.; they are closed Sundays, state holidays, and the day before Christmas, and during inclement weather (such as snowstorms). Reservations are not available, but wait times are generally shortest in the middle of each month.

PARKING

Several close-in Portland neighborhoods, including Nob Hill, Goose Hollow, the Central Eastside Industrial District, and the Homestead neighborhood near OHSU, are part of the city's **Area Parking Permit Program**. The proximity of these areas to downtown (and their lack of parking meters) would make them attractive places for commuters to park; at the same time, many people who live and work in these neighborhoods do not have off-street parking, so as a consequence on-street parking is already in short supply. The city introduced a permit program to address this potential problem. You generally cannot park in these zones for more than a specified length of time (typically two hours) during the day, but residents of each zone, and people who work there, can purchase zone parking permits that exempt their cars from the visitor parking time limit. (Street signs explain visitor parking restrictions, so don't worry too much about accidentally parking in a permit-only zone.) To find out whether your new address is in an Area Parking permit zone, or to learn how to apply for a permit, visit www. portlandonline.com/transportation/index.cfm?c=39277 or call the Portland **Office of Transportation** at 503-823-5185.

Some municipalities in the Portland area require you to obtain a permit to park overnight on a public street. Check with your county or city government to see if a permit is necessary in your neighborhood.

For information about parking garages, meters, towing, and park-and-ride lots, see the **Transportation** chapter.

OWNING A BICYCLE

Formalities for bicyclists are few. In Oregon, helmets are required for riders under 16. (Washington has no statewide helmet requirement, and Clark County has not mandated helmets for any age group.) Bicyclists must use lights between dusk and dawn and follow all applicable rules of the road. Bicycle registration is not required.

See the **Transportation** and **Green Living** chapters of this book for more details on being a Portland bicyclist.

VOTER REGISTRATION

Oregon is a vote-by-mail state. There are no polling places; the state mails a ballot to the address where you are registered, you complete the ballot, and you mail it back to the county elections office or drop it off at a designated ballot drop box. Clark County, Washington, also conducts elections by mail.

You can register to vote in either state when you get your driver's license. Alternatively, mail-in voter registration forms are available at libraries, community centers, and other public buildings, and are also available online (www.sos.state. or.us/elections/votreg/vreg.htm in Oregon; www.secstate.wa.gov/elections/reg ister.aspx in Washington). In **Oregon**, mail or drop off your voter registration form at your county elections office (see below). If you are a first-time Oregon voter, your registration must be postmarked at least 21 days before an election for you to be eligible to vote in that election.

In **Washington**, mail completed forms to the Office of the Secretary of State, Voter Registration by Mail, PO Box 40320, Olympia, WA 98504-0230. The deadline to register by mail is 30 days before an election. If you are not registered to vote in another Washington county, you can register in person at your county elections department up to 15 days before an election.

The following are the county elections offices in the Portland area:

- **Clackamas County Clerk, Elections Division,** 825 Portland Ave, Gladstone, 97027, 503- 655-8510, www.co.clackamas.or.us/elections/
- **Clark County Elections Office**, 1408 Franklin St, Vancouver, 360-397-2345, www.clark.wa.gov/elections/
- **Columbia County Clerk**, Columbia County Courthouse, 230 Strand St, St. Helens, 97051, 503-397-7214, www.co.columbia.or.us
- **Marion County Clerk, Elections Division**, 4263 Commercial St SE #300, Salem, 97302, 503-588-5041, 800-655-5388, clerk.co.marion.or.us
- **Multnomah County Elections Division**, 1040 SE Morrison St, Portland, 97214, 503-988-3720, www.mcelections.org
- **Washington County Elections Division,** 3700 SW Murray Blvd, Ste 101, Beaverton, 97005, 503-846-5800, www.co.washington.or.us/cgi/electhom/main. pl

- **Yamhill County Clerk**, 414 NE Evans St, McMinnville, 97128, 503-434-7518, www.co.yamhill.or.us/clerk/

Full information about voter registration, political parties, and election dates is available from the **Oregon Secretary of State, Elections Division** (503-986-1518, 877-ORE-VOTES, www.sos.state.or.us/elections/) or the **Washington Secretary of State** (360- 902-4180, 800- 448-4881, www.secstate. wa.gov/elections/).

POLITICAL CONTRIBUTIONS TAX CREDIT

Oregon taxpayers who make political contributions are eligible to claim a state tax credit for the amount of the contribution, subject to an annual maximum of $100 for a joint return or $50 for a single or separate return. Complete details are available from the **Oregon Department of Revenue** (503-378-4988, 800-356-4222; www.oregon.gov/DOR/PERTAX/docs/101-662.pdf).

Since Washington has no personal income tax, it does not offer a similar state tax credit.

PUBLIC LIBRARIES

Each county in the Portland area operates its own library system. The library systems are online, so you can scan for titles, place requests, check your borrowing records, and renew titles from home. (Phone renewals are also available.) Policies vary from library to library, but generally to get a library card you'll need to fill out an application form and present photo identification; applicants younger than 13 must get a parent's signature (but don't have to show photo ID). If you don't yet have an Oregon or Washington driver's license, you'll need to show a utility bill, credit card bill, or other quasi-official piece of mail that shows your local address. Check out the **Neighborhoods** chapter of this book or visit the appropriate system's web site to find the library nearest you.

Most of the library systems in the region belong to the Metropolitan Interlibrary Exchange, or MIX, which means that if you live anywhere in Multnomah, Washington, Clackamas, or Clark counties (as well as several other counties outside the metropolitan area), you can get a free library card from any library in the region. Note that MIX does not include community libraries in Columbia, Marion, or Yamhill counties (which do not have countywide systems), but does include much of southwest Washington. The following are the main library systems in the Portland area:

- **Multnomah County Library,** 503-988-5402, www.multcolib.org, serves the city of Portland and its eastern suburbs. It is the oldest public library system west of the Mississippi, and it is also, per capita, the nation's busiest: In 2005, library patrons checked out 19.5 million items, an average of 28 books for each resident of the county.

- **Washington County Cooperative Library Services,** 503-846-3222, www.wilinet.wccls.lib.or.us, is a cooperative network of 14 city, community, and specialty libraries in Washington County.
- The **Library Information Network of Clackamas County,** 503-723-4888, www.lincc.org, is an organization of several county and city libraries in Clackamas County.
- **Fort Vancouver Regional Library District**, 360-695-1561, www.fvrl.org, covers a large swath of Southwest Washington, including nearly all of Clark County (with the exception of the city of Camas, which operates its own public library).

Some academic libraries at Portland-area colleges and universities are open to the public and may allow borrowing privileges. For a list of colleges in the region, see the **Higher Education** chapter.

PASSPORTS

Getting a passport can take upward of six weeks, so be sure to give yourself plenty of time. If you're leaving the country imminently, you can pay an extra fee and receive two-week expedited service; if you need even faster service, search the Internet for passport expediting services.

If you don't currently have a valid passport, apply in person at any passport acceptance facility (a designation that includes many post offices and other government offices). To find the facility nearest you, check the government pages of the phone book or search by zip code at the State Department's Passport Acceptance Facility page (iafdb.travel.state.gov). You must submit two identical full-face passport photos of yourself, proof of U.S. citizenship (such as an original or certified birth certificate, an expired passport, or a naturalization certificate), a completed passport application and proper payment, and a driver's license or other valid form of photo identification.

Many Portlanders travel to **Canada**—Vancouver and Victoria in British Columbia are only about 6 hours away (traffic permitting) and are popular weekend destinations. Currently, U.S. citizens traveling by land must show either a U.S. passport or other proof of U.S. citizenship, such as an original or certified birth certificate together with photo identification. (U.S. citizens traveling by air must present a U.S. passport.) As of January 1, 2008, all U.S. citizens traveling to Canada, including those traveling by land, must carry a U.S. passport or other authorized document.

A single parent traveling with children, or grandparents or other guardians traveling with children, should carry proof of custody or letters from the non-accompanying parent(s) authorizing travel out of the country. (These documents are in addition to proof of the child's citizenship.) Hunters may take ordinary rifles and shotguns into Canada (provided they are declared), but fully automatic and assault-type weapons are prohibited. A complete list of restricted and prohibited firearms can be found at the **Canada Firearms Centre** web site (www.cfc-cafc.gc.ca). In addition, anyone with a criminal record (including a drunk driving conviction) should contact the Canadian embassy or nearest consulate before going to Canada. For complete information about traveling to Canada, peruse the **Consular Services** web page of the U.S. mission to Canada (www.amcits.com).

PRINT AND BROADCAST MEDIA

TELEVISION

For old-fashioned broadcast (i.e., free) television, the Portland market features the major national networks plus a few independents. Of course, if you've ordered cable or satellite TV, the channels will differ from those given here. The main local television stations are:

- Channel 2: **KATU** (pronounced K-2) (ABC), www.katu.com
- Channel 6: **KOIN** (CBS), www.koin.com
- Channel 8: **KGW** (NBC), www.kgw.com
- Channel 10: **KOPB** (Oregon Public Broadcasting, PBS affiliate), www.opb.org; OPB broadcasts digital versions of its programs on channel 27
- Channel 12: **KPTV** (Fox), www.kptv.com
- Channel 24: **KNMT** (TBN), www.tbn.org
- Channel 32: **KRCW** (CW), portlandscw.trb.com
- Channel 49: **KPDX** (MyNetworkTV), www.kpdx.com

RADIO

From jazz to punk, country to classical (and classic rock), NPR's "All Things Considered" to Rush Limbaugh, Portland's radio menu offers something for almost every taste (or absence thereof). In addition to the usual fungible selection of Clear Channel stations and other nationally programmed radio fodder, Portland boasts several excellent independent, locally owned stations. Here's a brief guide to what's available on the Rose City's radio airwaves; remember that most radio stations now stream programming over the Internet, so you can try out local stations even before you move to Portland.

NEWS AND TALK

- **KBNP**, 1410 AM, www.kbnp.com (business and finance)
- **KEX**, 1190 AM, www.1190kex.com (news and syndicated talk)
- **KFXX**, 1080 AM, www.1080thefan.com (sports and sports talk)

- **KPAM**, 860 AM, www.kpam.com (local and syndicated talk)
- **KPOJ**, 620 AM, www.620kpoj.com (progressive talk)
- **KUIK**, 1360 AM, www.kuik.com (local and syndicated talk)
- **KTRO**, 93.1 FM, 910 AM, www.931fmktro.com (syndicated talk, Portland State University sports)
- **KXL**, 750 AM, www.kxl.com (news, talk, Portland Trail Blazers basketball)

MUSIC (COMMERCIAL)

- **KGON**, 92.3 FM, www.kgon.com (classic rock)
- **KIJZ**, 105.9 FM, www.kijz.com (smooth jazz)
- **KINK**, 101.9 FM, www.kink.fm (album-oriented rock)
- **KKCW**, 103.3 FM, www.k103.com (soft rock)
- **KKAD**, 1550 AM, www.1550kkad.com (big-band, classic American standards, Portland Beavers baseball)
- **KKRZ**, 100.3 FM, www.z100portland.com (top 40)
- **KLTH**, 106.7 FM, www.khits1067.com (60s and 70s)
- **KNRK**, 94.7 FM, 947.fm (alternative)
- **KRSK**, 105.1 FM, www.1051thebuzz.com (adult contemporary, top 40)
- **KUFO**, 101.1 FM, www.kufo.com (heavy metal)
- **KUPL**, 98.7 FM, www.kupl.com (country)
- **KVMX**, 107.5 FM, www.mix1075portland.com (80s)
- **KWJJ**, 99.5 FM, www.kwjj.com (country)
- **KXJM**, 95.5 FM, www.jamminfm.com (hip-hop, rhythmic top 40)
- **KYCH**, 97.1 FM, www.charliefm.com (miscellaneous pop)

PUBLIC AND MEMBER-SUPPORTED RADIO

- **KBOO**, 90.7 FM, www.kboo.org (progressive/alternative community radio)
- **KBPS**, 89.9 FM, www.allclassical.org (classical)
- **KMHD**, 89.1 FM, www.kmhd.org (jazz)
- **KOPB**, 91.5 FM, www.opb.org (Oregon Public Broadcasting: NPR, PRI, news, talk, and public affairs)
- **KPSU**, 1450 AM, www.kpsu.org (college radio from Portland State University)

CHRISTIAN

- **KBVM**, 88.3 FM, www.kbvm.com (Catholic broadcasting)
- **KFIS**, 104.1 FM, www.1041thefish.com (contemporary Christian music)
- **KKSL**, 1290 AM
- **KKPZ**, 1330 AM, www.kkpz.com
- **KLVP**, 88.7 FM, 1040 AM, www.klove.com (adult contemporary Christian)
- **KPDQ**, 93.9 FM, 800 AM, www.kpdq.com

SPANISH LANGUAGE

- **KGDD**, 520 AM
- **KMUZ**, 1230 AM (Spanish-language oldies)
- **KSZN**, 1010 AM
- **KWIP**, 880 AM, www.kwip.com

CHILDREN'S PROGRAMMING

- **KDZR**, 1640 AM, radio.disney.go.com/mystation/portland/index.html (Radio Disney)

NEWSPAPERS AND MAGAZINES

Whether your interest is restaurants, parenting, or New Age living, there is a local (and probably free) newspaper or magazine for you. In addition to the publications listed below, the freebie racks at local libraries and natural foods stores groan under the weight of dozens of niche magazines and newspapers.

The *Oregonian* (www.oregonlive.com/oregonian) is Portland's long-established "serious" news daily. Like many metropolitan dailies nowadays, its quality is wildly inconsistent, but the *Oregonian* occasionally wins Pulitzer prizes. It is the only Oregon newspaper with a statewide circulation. Upstart competitor the **Portland Tribune** (www.portlandtribune.com), part of the local Pamplin Media Group empire, is published on Tuesdays and Fridays; the *Tribune* focuses primarily on local and regional news, and is available for free at many locations around the metropolitan area. Pamplin Media also publishes community weeklies that serve most of the major suburbs; the combined efforts of the conglomerate's news staff are posted on a rolling basis at www.localnewsdaily.com.

Business news junkies may enjoy perusing the **Portland Business Journal** (portland.bizjournals.com/portland/) and the **Daily Journal of Commerce** (www.djc-or.com). Across the Columbia River, the Vancouver **Columbian** (www.columbian.com) covers communities in Clark County seven days a week. If the local papers are insufficiently urbane for your taste, the **New York Times** (www.nytimes.com) offers home delivery of its Northwest regional edition.

Willamette Week (www.wweek.com) is a free weekly that covers the local arts and entertainment scene and dabbles (often successfully) in serious journalism; its coverage of local politics is in some cases superior to that of mainstream newspapers. Copies are available at supermarkets, record stores, stand-alone kiosks, and restaurants and cafes throughout Portland and in some of the suburbs. The *Willy Week*'s edgier-than-thou weekly competitor, the **Mercury** (www.portlandmercury.com), is likely to annoy most readers over the age of 30, but its coverage of the local music scene is excellent. **Just Out** (www.justout.com), an arts and entertainment paper that covers events of interest to Portland's gay and lesbian community, comes out every two weeks.

Several local glossy monthlies beckon from newsstands and supermarket checkout aisles. **Portland Monthly** (www.portlandmonthlymag.com) covers shopping, dining, personalities, getaways, and current events in the metro area for a readership with apparently substantial disposable income; despite the preponderance of ads, the writing can be entertaining and informative. **PDX Magazine** (www.pdxmagazine.com), available for free at many area stores, offers slighter but marginally hipper coverage of Portland places and happenings. The bimonthly **Oregon Home** (www.mediamerica.net/oregon_home_magazine.php) caters to the nesting and home-remodeling crowd. If you're interested in the movers and shakers of the local economy, **Oregon Business** (www.oregonbusiness.com) will keep you in the loop, while **NW Women's Journal** (www.nwwomensjournal.com) focuses specifically on the concerns of professional women.

Monthly community papers like the **Southwest Community Connection** (www.swcommconnection.com) and the **Southeast Examiner** (www.inseport land.com) cover items of local interest to the various quadrants of the city; these publications are typically delivered to area residents for free, and are also available at libraries and local shops.

Several papers report on events of interest to specific ethnic communities, including the **Asian Reporter** (www.asianreporter.com), the **Jewish Review** (www.jewishreview.org), and **El Hispanic News** (www.elhispanicnews.com); the **Portland Observer** (www.portlandobserver.com) and the **Skanner** (www.theskanner.com) emphasize coverage of events of interest to the city's African-American community.

Portland is awash in a sea of regional special-interest publications, including activity-centric 'zines like **Oregon Cycling**, New Age and alternative health magazines like **New Connexion** (www.newconnexion.net), and such parenting publications as **Portland Family Magazine** (www.portlandfamily.com) and **Metro Parent** (www.metro-parent.com). If your only dependent is a dog, then **Spot** (www.spotmagazine.net) is your newspaper. The **Portland Alliance** (www.port landalliance.org) and the **Peaceworker** (www.oregonpeaceworks.org) preach leftist politics to the converted. Scores of other niche publications await your discovery and/or avoidance at public places around the city.

KNOWING WHERE TO GO FOR A PARTICULAR SERVICE IS PARTICULARLY important when you move to a new place. The following information, which includes information about various services, including renting furniture, hiring a housekeeper, pest control, shipping services, and consumer protection, might make your life a bit easier. This chapter also includes sections about services for the disabled, seniors, new residents from abroad, and gays and lesbians.

RENTAL SERVICES

If you need to furnish a home right away and you don't have time to shop for the perfect furniture and appliances, of if you won't be in town for more than a couple months, you can rent practically anything you need. Be careful, though: If you rent household items for more than a few months, you will almost always end up paying more than if you had bought new furniture. Even credit purchases are usually cheaper in the long run than "rent-to-own" plans. Use these services sparingly.

Most rental stores now rent all kinds of household items, including furniture, electronics, and appliances. The following are a few established rental outfits:

- **Aaron's Sales & Lease Ownership**, 800-950-7368, www.shopaarons.com, has eight locations in the Portland area.
- **Cort Furniture Rental**, 9495 SW Cascade Ave, Beaverton, 503-520-8800, 800-568-8010, www.cort.com
- **People's Furniture Rental**, 10855 SW Cascade Ave, Tigard, 503-684-0118, 360-253-8638, www.peoples1.com
- **Rent-A-Center**, 800-665-5510, www.rentacenter.com, has eight stores in the Portland area

DOMESTIC SERVICES

As with any service, satisfied friends and trusted colleagues are the best sources of recommendations for domestic service providers. Failing that, **Angie's List** (503-220-4100, 866-854-0631, www.angieslist.com) advertises itself as a list of plumbers, auto mechanics, painters, and the like recommended by members, but you should still check references as you would (or should) with any contractor or service provider. There is a fee to join. Because Angie's List is relatively new to Portland, local coverage is growing but is not as comprehensive as in some other cities.

For other goods and services, take a look at the **Shopping for the Home** chapter.

HOUSE CLEANING

You might decide to use a house-cleaning service on a one-off basis (before you move into a new house, for example) or on an ongoing basis. Before you employ any cleaner or cleaning service, be sure to check references and only use cleaners who are insured. (Agencies that employ bonded and insured cleaners usually say so in their advertisements.) Personal recommendations are your best source for finding cleaners, but of course cleaning services are also listed in the Yellow Pages (under "House Cleaning").

If you're trying to minimize the use of chemicals in your home, both **Domestica** (503-222-2334, www.domesticaclean.com) and **Sister Suds Cleaning Company** (503-975-4047, www.sistersuds.com) use only nontoxic, environmentally safe products to clean your home.

PEST CONTROL

While typical Oregon pests lack the horrifying cachet of, say, hissing cockroaches, they can nonetheless be troublesome to have around the house. In the insect department, dampwood termites and carpenter ants, if left unchecked, can cause structural damage, and other insects can be nuisances. Mammals that sometimes pose problems include possums, raccoons, skunks, bats, squirrels, moles, or even nutria, huge, non-native rodents from Argentina that resemble giant beavers with orange teeth. (This is true.) Rats often infest areas where invasive English ivy has established itself.

If these critters have invaded your home or yard and setting traps yourself has not worked or is not an option, consider calling an exterminator, or visit www.pestweb.com for comprehensive information about dealing with your unwelcome houseguests. If your problem requires a professional solution, consult one of the many services listed under "Pest Control Services" in the Yellow Pages.

If your problem is with furry creatures, many services offer live trapping. You're unlikely to want that solution for insects, but the following services claim to use less-toxic (although not necessarily nontoxic) chemicals:

- **All Natural Pest Elimination**, 503-635-0822, 877-662-8449, www.nobuggy. com
- **Alpha Ecological**, 503-972-8733, www.alphaecological.com
- **Bugaboo Pest Control**, 503-289-0576, www.getbugs.com
- **EcoCare**, 503-742-8998 (eastside), 503-222-5566 (westside), www.ecocare.biz

POSTAL AND SHIPPING SERVICES

Portland's main post office is located just north of downtown, near Union Station, at 715 Northwest Hoyt Street (the main entrance is on Glisan). Hours of operation are Monday through Friday, 7 a.m. to 6:30 p.m., and Saturdays from 8 a.m. to 5 p.m. The Airport Mail Facility at 7640 Northeast Airport Way (503-335-7920) is open seven days a week from 8:30 a.m. until midnight. To find your local post office (including contract post offices housed in local businesses), or to look up ZIP codes or postal rates, call 800-ASK-USPS (800-275-8777) or visit www.usps.com.

If you're between addresses and need a place to receive mail, you can rent a box at a local post office or choose a private mail receiving service. Many of the private services allow call-in mail checks and mail forwarding, but they are often more expensive than the post office.

MAIL RECEIVING SERVICES

Look in the Yellow Pages under "Mail Boxes-Rental" to find the most conveniently located private mail receiving services. The following services have multiple locations in the Portland area:

- **Postal Annex**, 800-456-1525, www.postalannex.com
- **The UPS Store**, 800-742-5877, www.theupsstore.com

SHIPPING SERVICES

In addition to parcel shipment and next-day or second-day delivery, most of the familiar national shipping services offer freight service for large items.

- **DHL**, 800-225-5345, www.dhl-usa.com
- **FedEx**, 800-463-3339, www.fedex.com
- **United Parcel Service (UPS)**, 800-742-5877, www.ups.com
- **United States Postal Service**, 800-275-8777, www.usps.com

JUNK MAIL AND TELEMARKETING

A deluge of junk mail will almost certainly follow you after you move, and everyone from the phone company to your mortgage lender will be anxious to sell your name to marketers. To curtail the onslaught, write to the **Direct Marketing Association** (Mail Preference Service, P.O. Box 282, Carmel, NY 10512) or submit an online form at www.dmaconsumers.org. (Either way, they'll charge you $1 for the privilege of removing your name from mailing lists.) Most—but not all—businesses and charities that send junk mail will exclude addresses registered with this service, but it may take 30 to 90 days for junk mail to slow. Registration with the DMA will not deter marketers that do not buy the organization's preference lists.

The major credit bureaus share an opt-out line that allows you to reduce the volume of prescreened offers for credit and insurance that you receive. Call 1-888-5-OPTOUT (888-567-8688) or visit www.optoutprescreen.com to have your name removed from mailing lists that the credit bureaus sell to direct-mail marketers.

You can stop those annoying dinnertime calls from commercial telemarketers (but not charities or political organizations) by adding your number to the Federal Trade Commission's **National Do Not Call Registry**. Call 800-382-1222 or visit www.donotcall.gov.

AUTOMOBILE REPAIR AND MAINTENANCE

Finding a trustworthy mechanic is often difficult, to say the least. The best way to find a good shop is to ask coworkers, neighbors, and friends, particularly those with the same make of car, for recommendations. Shop around for a mechanic before you need one; if you wait until your car is virtually immobile, you're likely to be tempted to take it to the nearest chop shop. Auto dealerships are generally reliable, if pricier than independent mechanics; at least they have the parts, equipment, and (one hopes) expertise to service the cars they sell.

If you're considering an independent shop, you may want to check with the Better Business Bureau to see if any complaints have been filed against it. (See "Consumer Protection" below.) If it's just advice you need, consider tuning in to Tom and Ray Magliozzi (better known as Click & Clack), the guys on National Public Radio's *Car Talk* program. Locally, the program is broadcast on KOPB (91.5 FM) on Saturdays at 10 a.m. and Sundays at 11 a.m., or visit www.cartalk.com for podcasts and contact information. The "Mechanics Files" page of their web site (www.cartalk.com/content/mechx/) is a database of recommended (and reviled) mechanics, as reviewed by Car Talk listeners.

If the question isn't who will repair your car, but rather who to call to have it towed, you'll find lots of options listed in the Yellow Pages under "Towing-Auto." To avoid a frantic search for towing companies after you've broken down, consider joining an automobile club. The **American Automobile Association (AAA)** (contact AAA of Oregon/Idaho, 503-222-6900, www.aaaorid.com) is the best-known club; it offers towing services, travel guides and maps, and lists of approved mechanics, among other services. The lesser-known (and locally based) **Better World Club** (503-546-1137, 866-238-1137, www.betterworld.com) offers similar services, and doesn't spend members' money lobbying for highway construction. Many national service station chains and insurance companies also offer road service plans.

HEALTH CARE

HEALTH INSURANCE

Employer-sponsored plans cover most Oregonians (and Washingtonians) who have health insurance. If your employer doesn't provide coverage, or if you're self-employed (or unemployed), you'll need to shop around for health insurance. Be sure to get quotes from multiple companies, and compare deductibles and co-pays, the percentage covered for various procedures, restrictions on which doctors you can use, the extent of prescription drug coverage, and exemptions for pre-existing conditions. Insurance premiums can vary dramatically from one company to another.

The **Insurance Division** of the Oregon Department of Consumer and Business Services (350 Winter St NE, Salem, 503-947-7980, www.insurance.oregon. gov) regulates health insurance in Oregon. The Division's web site includes an informative consumer's guide to health insurance; visit www.insurance.oregon. gov/consumer/health-insurance/health.html. A range of consumer publications, including health insurance buyer's guides and complaint statistics for various insurers, is available for download at the Insurance Division web site, or you can call 503-947-7984 or 888-877-4894 to request publications by mail. In Washington, the **Office of the Insurance Commissioner** (5000 Capitol Blvd, Tumwater, Washington, 360-725-7080, 800-562-6900, www.insurance.wa.gov) provides similar services; health insurance information for consumers is available at www. insurance.wa.gov/consumers/health/healthinsurance.asp.

HEALTH CARE PLANS

According to the Oregon Insurance Division, the following eight companies provide the vast majority of private health insurance coverage in the state. In 2005 (the most recent year for which statistics are available), all other health insurers combined had an Oregon market share of only 9% (measured as a percent of total premium dollars). Many of these companies also operate in southwest Washington.

- **Health Net,** 888-802-7001, www.healthnet.com.
- **Kaiser Permanente,** 877-313-3424, www.kaiserpermanente.org
- **LifeWise Health Plan of Oregon,** 800-596-3440, www.lifewiseor.com
- **ODS,** 503-243-3962, 877-605-3229, www.odscompanies.com
- **PacifiCare,** 800-624-8822, www.pacificare.com
- **PacificSource Health Plans,** 541-686-1242, 800-624-6052, www.pacificsource.com
- **Providence Health Plans,** 503-574-7500, 800-878-4445, www.providence.org/health_plans/
- **Regence BlueCross Blue Shield of Oregon,** 503-225-5336, 800-452-7390, www.or.regence.com

HEALTH CARE ASSISTANCE PROGRAMS

- Oregon's **Family Health Insurance Assistance Program** subsidizes monthly insurance premiums for uninsured individuals and families, including people who have access to workplace insurance plans but cannot afford the premiums. Call 800-542-3104 or visit www.oregon.gov/OPHP/FHIAP/index.shtml for details.
- **Medicare** is the federal government's health insurance program for people age 65 and older and qualified disabled individuals of any age. For information about Medicare eligibility or to apply for Medicare benefits, call the **Social Security Administration** at 800-877-1213. In Oregon, volunteers at the **Senior Health Insurance Benefits Assistance Program** (SHIBA) provide free, individualized counseling about Medicare and related programs, including Medicare-supplement insurance and long-term care insurance. Their helpful booklet *Free Help with Medicare and Other Health Insurance*, which lists contact information for SHIBA sites around the state, is available online at www.oregon.gov/DCBS/SHIBA/docs/2371.pdf, or you can request a free copy by calling 800-722-4134. **Washington's** similar SHIBA program (see below) is not limited to Medicare advice.
- The **Oregon Health Plan** is the state's version of the federal government's Medicaid program. Administered by the Oregon Department of Human Services, the Oregon Health Plan provides health coverage for working people with very low incomes, as well as people with disabilities. Call 800-359-9517 or visit www.oregongov./DHS/healthplan for information about coverage and eligibility requirements.
- If you're an Oregon resident who has been denied health insurance because of a chronic illness or other medical condition, you may be able to obtain coverage through the **Oregon Medical Insurance Pool** (800-848-7280, www.omip.state.or.us). There's a surcharge of 25% over regular insurance premiums, and if you haven't been insured in the 63 days before you enter the pool you may have to wait up to six months for coverage of pre-existing conditions.

Washington offers a similar **Washington State Health Insurance Pool** (800-877-5187, www.wship.org).

- Washington's **Statewide Health Insurance Benefits Advisors** (SHIBA) network dispenses advice and distributes information on a range of health insurance matters, including private insurance as well as government programs such as Medicare and Medicaid. Information is available from the SHIBA web site (www.insurance.wa.gov/consumers/Shiba_HelpLine/dirdefault.asp) or by calling the HelpLine at 800-562-6900.

- **Washington Basic Health** (800-660-9840, www.basichealth.hca.wa.gov) is a state-sponsored plan for low-income Washington residents who are not eligible for Medicare.

COMPLAINTS

For insurance-related complaints, contact the Oregon Insurance Division's **Consumer Advocacy Unit** (503-947-7984, 888-877-4894, www.insurance.oregon.gov), which can help with resolving complaints. Their web site includes an online complaint form. In Washington, contact the Insurance Commissioner's **Consumer Protection Division** (800-562-6900, fortress.wa.gov/oic/complaints/).

FINDING A DOCTOR

If your job includes health benefits, your insurance plan or HMO may require you to use a participating doctor or facility (or may pay a reduced benefit if you use a medical care provider who is "out-of-plan"). If you have a choice of physicians, there's no substitute for word-of-mouth; if you can, ask for a referral from a friend or trusted coworker. If that option is unavailable, such web sites as www.drscore.com, www.healthgrades.com, and www.physicianreports.com purport to rate physicians, but the ratings should probably be taken with a grain of salt (and an aspirin, then call them in the morning). The **Oregon Board of Medical Examiners** (971-673-2700, www.oregon.gov/BME/) regulates physicians in Oregon; contact them to check on a doctor's credentials and history of lawsuits or professional sanctions, or to make a formal complaint about a doctor or other medical professional. In Washington, the state's **Medical Quality Assurance Commission** (360-236-4700, https://fortress.wa.gov/doh/hpqa1/HPS5/Medical/default.htm) provides a somewhat equivalent service.

Portland is a national center for alternative and naturopathic medicine. As always, a personal recommendation is the best way to find a health care provider. Failing that, the **Natural Health Center** at the National College of Naturopathic Medicine (2220 SW 1st Ave, 503-552-1551, www.ncnm.edu/clinics/natural_health_center.php) is a good place to start.

HOSPITALS

- **Adventist Medical Center**, 10123 SE Market St, 503-257-2500, www.adventistmedicalcenter.com
- **Kaiser Sunnyside Medical Center**, 10180 SE Sunnyside Rd, Clackamas, 503-652-2880
- **Legacy Emanuel Hospital & Health Center (and Children's Hospital)**, 2801 N Gantenbein Ave, 503-413-2200, www.legacyhealth.org
- **Legacy Good Samaritan Hospital and Medical Center**, 1015 NW 22nd Ave, 503-413-7711, www.legacyhealth.org
- **Legacy Meridian Park Hospital**, 19300 SW 65th Ave, Tualatin, 503-692-1212, www.legacyhealth.org
- **Legacy Mount Hood Medical Center**, 24800 SE Stark St, Gresham, 503-674-1122, www.legacyhealth.org
- **Legacy Salmon Creek Hospital**, 2211 NE 139th St, Vancouver, 360-487-1000, www.legacyhealth.org
- **Oregon Health & Science University (OHSU) Hospital and Clinics**, 3181 SW Sam Jackson Park Rd, 503-494-8311, www.ohsu.org/health/clinics-and-services/
- **Providence Milwaukie Hospital**, 10150 SE 32nd Ave, Milwaukie, 503-513-8300, www.providence.org/Oregon/
- **Providence Portland Medical Center**, 4805 NE Glisan St, 503-215-1111, www.providence.org/Oregon/
- **Providence St. Vincent Medical Center**, 9205 SW Barnes Rd, 503-216-1234, www.providence.org/Oregon/
- **Southwest Washington Medical Center**, 400 NE Mother Joseph Pl, Vancouver, 360-256-2000, 503-972-3000, www.swmedicalcenter.com
- **Tuality Community Hospital**, 225 SE 8th Ave, Hillsboro, 503-681-1111, www.tuality.org
- **Tuality Forest Grove Hospital**, 1809 Maple St, Forest Grove, 503-357-2173, www.tuality.org
- **Willamette Falls Hospital**, 1500 Division St, Oregon City, 503-656-1631, www.willamettefallshospital.org

AFFORDABLE HEALTH CARE

COMMUNITY AND PUBLIC CLINICS

Community clinics and some public health clinics offer free or low-cost treatment to low-income individuals and families; some clinics use sliding fee scales based on income.

- **The Coalition of Community Health Clinics** (503-546-4991, www.coalitionclinics.org) is a coalition of community clinics located throughout the city of

Portland. Their comprehensive web site includes links to non-member clinics, including clinics that provide low-cost dental and chiropractic services.

- **Free Clinic of SW Washington**, 4100 Plomondon St, Vancouver, 360-313-1390, www.freeclinics.org
- **The Multnomah County Health Department** (www.mchealth.org) operates several safety-net clinics in Portland and Gresham; for clinic appointments call 503-988-3333.

PHARMACIES

Most hospitals and large clinics have their own pharmacies. So do most major supermarkets and discount stores, including **Fred Meyer** (888-247-4439, www.fredmeyer.com/pharmacy.htm), **Safeway** (877-723-3929, www.safeway.com), **Albertsons** (877-932-7948, www.albertsons.com), **Bi-Mart** (800-456-0681, www.bimart.com), and **Target** (800-440-0680, www.target.com). In addition to such national drugstore chains as **Rite Aid** (800-748-3243, www.riteaid.com) and **Walgreens** (800-925-4733, www.walgreens.com), Portland still has a fair number of friendly, independently owned pharmacies; walk around your neighborhood, or look in the Yellow Pages under "Pharmacies" for locations.

The following pharmacies are open **24 hours**. Many emergency hospitals also have 24-hour pharmacies on-site.

- **Rite Aid**: 2021 NW 185th Ave, Hillsboro, 503-645-7704; 10860 SE Oak St, Milwaukie, 503-652-8058
- **Walgreens**: 940 SE 39th Ave, 503-238-6053; 2829 N Lombard St, 503-737-0317; 12405 SE 82nd Ave, 503-653-1526; 14600 SW Murray Scholls Dr, Beaverton, 503-579-1878; 13939 SW Pacific Hwy, Tigard, 503-670-9812; 10903 SE Oak St, Milwaukie, 971-233-1002; 1950 NE Burnside Rd, Gresham, 503-674-8482; 1905 SE 164the Ave, Vancouver, 360-885-2938

ADVANCE DIRECTIVES

An advance directive allows you to state your wishes for medical care in the event that you are unable to make decisions for yourself; it also allows you to designate a person who will make health care decisions on your behalf. If you already have an advance directive in another state, it is a good idea to complete the form in your new state to ensure your wishes are honored. **Oregon** advance directives are available online at egov.oregon.gov/DCBS/SHIBA/advanced-directives.shtml; hard copies are available from Oregon Health Decisions (503-241-0744, 800-422-4805, www.oregonhealthdecisions.org), or from most hospitals. You can download a **Washington** health care directive at a number of web sites, including that of the Washington State Medical Association (www.wsma.org/patients/who_decide.html); hard copies are available from hospitals or physicians.

HEALTH LAW—PROTECTING PRIVATE INFORMATION

A variety of federal and state laws, most notably the federal Health Insurance Portability and Accountability Act of 1996 (HIPAA), restrict health care providers' ability to use and disseminate personal health information. The general rule is that a provider cannot share your health information with a third party unless you have given your written consent or there is a law that authorizes the provider to share your information. If you believe your right to privacy of medical records has been violated, you can file a complaint with the United States Department of Health and Human Services at their **Region X Office for Civil Rights** in Seattle. You can send a complaint by email to OCRComplaint@hhs.gov, by mail to 2201 Sixth Ave, Suite 900, Seattle WA 98121-1831, or by fax to 206-615-2297.

CONSUMER PROTECTION

The best way to prevent fraud and consumer victimization is to avoid it in the first place. Read all contracts down to the smallest print, save all receipts and cancelled checks, get the names of telephone sales and service people with whom you deal, date every paper you sign, make sure contractors are properly licensed and bonded, and check with the Attorney General's office or the Better Business Bureau for complaints before you do business with a company.

Sometimes, despite your best efforts and suspicious nature, you'll get ripped off. You negotiate, calmly but firmly and with documents in hand, but to no avail. What can you do? First, contact the local **Better Business Bureau** at 503-212-3022 or online at www.thebbb.org. This organization will keep a permanent record of unresolved complaints, but its first priority is to encourage its affiliated businesses to address all reasonable complaints promptly and thoroughly. The BBB will not get involved until you have exhausted the usual channels of complaint—contacting the supervisor, manager, or owner, for example. You can also file a complaint—or threaten to file a complaint—with the **Federal Trade Commission** (877-382-4357, www.ftc.gov) or with the agency responsible for consumer protection in the state where the offending business is located:

- **Oregon Department of Justice, Office of the Attorney General**, 503-229-5576 (Portland area), 503-378-4320 (Salem area), 877-877-9392 (toll-free in Oregon), www.doj.state.or.us/finfraud/
- **Washington State Office of the Attorney General,** 800-551-4636 (to request that a complaint form be mailed to you), www.atg.wa.gov/FileAComplaint.aspx

If all else fails, you can go to court—unless your contract provides for mandatory arbitration. (You did notice that arbitration clause in paragraph 37 when you read the contract in full, right?) You can file a small claims action without an attorney in cases where the amount at issue is $5,000 or less ($4,000 or less in Washington). Contact the clerk of court in your county for details. The **Oregon State Bar** has useful information about consumer protection and small claims court on its web site (www.osbar.org), and also operates a lawyer referral service; call 503-684-3763 or 800-452-7636, or visit the web site for details. In Clark County, Washington, contact the **Southwest Washington Lawyer Referral Service** at 360-695-0599.

SERVICES FOR PEOPLE WITH DISABILITIES

GETTING AROUND

CARS

To obtain a disabled person parking permit, contact the Oregon **DMV** (503-299-9999, TTY 503-945-5001, www.oregon.gov/ODOT/DMV/driverid/disparking.shtml). (In Washington, apply to the state **Department of Licensing**, 360-902-3900, www.dol.wa.gov/vehicleregistration/parking.html.)

The car rental companies listed in the **Transportation** chapter can usually accommodate special needs with 48 to 72 hours' notice.

PUBLIC TRANSPORTATION

Given at least 24 hours' notice, most local and national passenger carriers will make any needed accommodations for passengers with special needs.

TriMet is fully accessible; buses have ramps or power lifts, and light rail (MAX) cars and the Portland Streetcar have extending ramps. Stations have Braille signage, and bus operators announce stops in advance; computerized recordings announce stops on MAX and the Portland Streetcar. Service animals are allowed on all public transit. People with disabilities travel at reduced fares. For more information, visit TriMet's accessibility page (www.trimet.org/access/) or call 503-962-2455 (TTY 503-238-5811). TriMet's **LIFT** paratransit program offers shared-ride transportation for people whose disabilities prevent them from using fixed-route public transportation. Call 503-802-8200 (TTY 503-802-8058) for details or visit www.trimet.org/lift/. Portland's aerial tram is also fully accessible.

Ride Connection (503-528-1720, www.rideconnection.org) helps older adults and people with disabilities with transportation to jobs, medical appointments, shopping, or local transport hubs. Their **RideWise** program helps people with disabilities travel independently on public transportation.

In Clark County, **C-TRAN** (360-695-0123, TTY 360-695-2760, www.c-tran. com) operates lift-equipped buses. C-TRAN also operates the C-VAN paratransit service; call 360-695-8918 (TTY 360-695-9715) for details.

AIR TRAVEL

The **U.S. Department of Transportation** publishes a free booklet entitled *New Horizons: Information for the Air Traveler with a Disability*, also available online at airconsumer.ost.dot.gov (click on "Travel Tips & Publications"). For more informa-tion, call the DOT **Disability Hotline** at 800-778-4838 or TDD 800-455-9880.

TRAVEL RESOURCES

- **Adventures Without Limits**, 1341 Pacific Ave, Forest Grove, 503-359-2568, www.awloutdoors.com, designs outdoor adventure activities for people of all abilities.
- **The Boulevard** (www.blvd.com) is a web portal for disability resources that includes a section on accessible travel and recreation.
- Eugene-based **Mobility International USA** (541-343-1284, www.miusa.org) publishes several guides to international travel, exchange, and development for people with disabilities.
- **Society for Accessible Travel & Hospitality**, 212-447-7284, www.sath.org

COMMUNICATION

Telecommunications Relay Service allows deaf and hard-of-hearing individu-als to communicate with hearing people through a trained operator using a text telephone (TTY). The relay operator translates both parties' words verbatim and is required by law to keep all conversations strictly confidential. The service is free. To use the service, dial **711** from any phone or call 800-735-1232 (from Or-egon) or 800-833-6388 (from Washington).

Access Services Northwest, 503-289-0570, www.accessservicesnw. com, and **Northwest American Sign Language Associates**, www.idwiz.com/ nwasla/, provide sign language interpreters and other communication facilita-tion services for deaf, hard-of-hearing, and hearing individuals in Oregon and southwest Washington.

INDEPENDENT LIVING

The following local organizations offer up-to-date information about, and advo-cacy for, accessible housing, transportation, employment, and other community resources.

- **Disability Resources of Southwest Washington,** 360-694-6790, www.darsw. com
- **Independent Living Resources,** 2410 SE 11th Ave, 503-232-7411, www.ilr. org

ADDITIONAL RESOURCES

The most comprehensive sources of information for people with special needs are **www.disAbility.gov**, a portal to hundreds of federal government sites and related links, and the **International Center for Disability Resources on the Internet**, www.icdri.org. A few local resources include:

- **The Arc of Multnomah-Clackamas,** 503-223-7279, www.thearcmult.org) provides information and referrals for people with physical or mental disabilities. **The Arc of Clark County** (360-254-1562, www.arcofclarkcounty.org) performs the same role in southwest Washington.
- Multnomah County Aging and Disability Services Division's **Network of Care** web site (multnomah.or.networkofcare.org) includes a comprehensive database of services and resources for people with disabilities.
- **The Oregon Advocacy Center** (503-243-2081, www.oradvocacy.org) provides legal advocacy and protection for Oregon residents with disabilities. This organization provides information and advice about issues including civil rights, special education, rights to services, health care, and guardianship. **The Alliance of People with Disabilities** (206-545-7055, www.disabilitypride.org) offers similar services to Washington residents.
- The Oregon Department of Human Services' **Seniors and People with Disabilities** division (503-945-5811, 800-282-8092, www.oregon.gov/DHS/spd) has a wealth of useful information and helpful links. In Washington, the state's **Aging and Disability Services Administration**, www.aasa.dshs.wa.gov, provides a similar function.

SERVICES FOR SENIORS

The federal government's **Senior Citizens' Resources** web page (www.usa.gov/ Topics/Seniors.shtml) is a useful starting place for general information for seniors, including tips on consumer protection, health, housing, and finances. In Oregon, contact the state Department of Human Services' **Seniors and People with Disabilities** division (503-945-5811, 800-282-8092, www.oregon.gov/DHS/spd) for information about services for Oregon seniors. In southwest Washington, the Southwest Washington Agency on Aging (7414 NE Hazel Dell Ave, 360-694-6577, www.helpingelders.org) is a helpful resource.

Seniors with mobility difficulties or disabilities should peruse the "Getting Around" section of Services for People with Disabilities, above. Note that TriMet and other public transit agencies charge a reduced fare for "honored citizens." The following are a few more local resources for older adults.

- **Adult Placement Network**, 503-659-2029, www.adultplacementnetwork. com, is a referral agency for retirement homes, assisted living facilities, and other housing options for older adults who cannot or choose not to live alone.
- **Loaves and Fishes**, 503-736-6325, www.loavesandfishesonline.org, provides nutritious hot lunches to people over the age of 60 at 30 meal sites in Multnomah, Washington, and Clark counties. The organization also runs **Meals-on-Wheels**, 503-736-6325 (Multnomah and Washington counties), 360-699-6325 (Clark County), www.loavesandfishesonline.org/content/services/meals-on-wheels.asp, which delivers hot lunches to seniors who are unable to come to a Loaves and Fishes site.
- **Metropolitan Family Services**, 1808 SE Belmont St, 503-232-0007, www. metfamily.org, reaches out to older adults through programs that encourage and assist with independent living and provide volunteer opportunities for seniors.
- Multnomah County Aging and Disability Services Division's **Network of Care** web site, multnomah.or.networkofcare.org, includes a comprehensive database of services and resources for older adults.
- Portland State University's **Senior Adult Learning Center**, 503-725-4739, web. pdx.edu/~psu01435/salc.html, provides continuing education for seniors and allows people over 65 to audit regular PSU classes for free.

SERVICES FOR INTERNATIONAL NEWCOMERS

The U.S. Census Bureau estimated in 2002 that Oregon has more than 300,000 residents who were born in other countries. The Portland area is home to tens of thousands of immigrants, including substantial communities from Mexico, Southeast Asia, Russia, Ukraine, West and East Africa, and the Indian subcontinent.

If you are one of these international newcomers, or if you want to be, a variety of helpful information is available online at the **U.S. Citizen and Immigration Services** web site (uscis.gov). If you have specific questions, you can also contact the USCIS national customer service center (800-375-5283, TTY 800-767-1833). (Once you know what you need to do, you'll inevitably have to fill out paperwork.)

If you need legal aid in immigration matters, you can contact one of the following organizations:

- **Catholic Charities Immigration Legal Services**, 901 SE Oak St, Suite 105, 503-542-2855, www.catholiccharitiesoregon.org
- **Immigration Counseling Service**, 510 SW Park, Suite 610, 503-221-1689, www.immigrationcounseling.org

- **Sponsors Organized to Assist Refugees (SOAR)**, 2906 NE Glisan St, 503-284-3002, www.emoregon.org/soar.php

International newcomers who are experiencing culture shock can get a quick overview of American culture, etiquette, expectations, and quirks in the *Newcomer's Handbook for Moving to and Living in the USA* by Mike Livingston, published by **First Books**. Call 503-968-6777 or visit www.firstbooks.com to order a copy.

CONSULATES

Most foreign consulates on the West Coast are located in San Francisco, Los Angeles, and/or Seattle. The following countries have honorary consuls in Portland, who may or may not be able to assist citizens of the nations they nominally represent: Austria, Barbados, Belgium, Canada, Cyprus, Czech Republic, Denmark, Fiji, Finland, France, Germany, Guatemala, Iceland, Italy, Ivory Coast, Japan, Korea, Lithuania, Luxembourg, Malaysia, the Netherlands, Norway, Poland, Romania, Sweden, Thailand, and the United Kingdom. Addresses and telephone numbers for most of these honorary consulates are listed in the Yellow Pages under "Consulates & Foreign Governments"; unlisted consuls are unlikely to be of much use to foreign nationals.

The only full consulate in Portland is the **Consulate of Mexico**, 1234 SW Morrison St, 97205, 503-274-1442, www.sre.gob.mx/portland/.

GAY AND LESBIAN LIFE

According to a 2006 study by UCLA's Williams Institute, 8.8% of Portland's population identify themselves as gay, lesbian, or bisexual, and a 2007 article in *The Advocate* named Portland as one of the top 10 best cities in the U.S. for gays and lesbians to live. While this may be news to some, it comes as no surprise to Portland's thriving and well-established gay, lesbian, bisexual and transgender (GLBT) community. Rainbow flags and "Queer Nation" bumper stickers are common in neighborhoods in much of the city (and to a lesser extent, in some of the suburbs), and many private employers recognize domestic partnership for insurance purposes. Many business leaders are openly gay, and City Commissioner Sam Adams is the first openly gay member of the Portland City Council.

While Portland is on the whole a tolerant and friendly home for gay singles, couples, and families, homophobia and discrimination certainly exist. A 2004 ballot measure amending the state constitution to ban gay marriage passed with nearly 57% of voters in favor (although majorities in two counties, including Multnomah County, voted against the measure). While this ban still stands, in 2007 Oregon passed legislation outlawing discrimination based on sexual orientation or gender identity in housing, employment, public education, and public accommodations, with some exemptions for religious organizations. (Washington passed a similar law in 2006.) Also in 2007, both Oregon and Washington passed laws providing for state recognition of domestic partnerships.

GLBT RESOURCES

The biweekly arts, entertainment, and news magazine *Just Out* (www.justout. com) is an indispensable source of information about Portland's GLBT community. *Portland's Gay and Lesbian Yellow Pages* (www.PDXGayYellowPages.com), available for free at many area libraries, bookstores, and business, lists gay-owned or gay-friendly businesses, and includes listings for local GLBT clubs and organizations. (Otherwise, beyond being smaller than the phone company's Yellow Pages and having generally more interesting ads, it's really just a phone directory.) There are too many organizations that address the concerns and interests of GLBT community in Portland to list them all here, but the following organizations are a good starting point:

- **Basic Rights Oregon**, 503-222-6151, www.basicrights.org, works for equal rights for gays and lesbians.
- **It's Time, Oregon**, www.geocities.com/itstimeoregon/, works for the rights of transgendered persons; the web site includes links to helpful resources.
- **Love Makes a Family**, 503-228-3892, www.lmfamily.org, advocates in support of sexual minority families and youth.
- **PFLAG (Parents and Friends of Lesbians and Gays)** sponsors monthly meetings and discussions; visit www.pflagpdx.org for information.
- **Portland Area Business Association (PABA)** (503-280-7222, www.paba.com) works to build business and career opportunities in the GLBT community.
- **Pride Northwest** (503-295-9788, www.pridenw.org) organizes and promotes Portland's annual Pride festival, held in downtown Portland each June.
- **The Q Center** (69 SE Taylor St, 503-234-7837, www.pdxqcenter.org) is a community center for GBLT and Questioning individuals.
- **Sexual Minority Youth Resource Center** (2100 SE Belmont St, 503-872-9664, www.smyrc.org) provides counseling and a free drop-in center for GLBT and questioning youth under age 24.

A MOVE TO A NEW CITY ALMOST ALWAYS INCLUDES RUNNING LOTS of errands—from buying new curtains to replacing mops and brooms that didn't make it into the moving truck. Portland offers plenty of shopping choices, from major national department stores and big-box behemoths to hole-in-the-wall thrift shops. If you've moved from somewhere other than Alaska, Montana, New Hampshire, or Delaware, you'll be delighted to find that Oregon does not (yet) have a state sales tax. (If you've moved to Washington, you're out of luck; see **Money Matters** for more details.)

SHOPPING DISTRICTS AND MALLS

NEIGHBORHOOD SHOPPING DISTRICTS

Portlanders are rightly proud of the variety and distinctiveness of their city's neighborhood shopping districts. While almost every city neighborhood has its own commercial node, some of these districts are larger and more diverse than others. The following are the main shopping districts that draw visitors from beyond the surrounding neighborhoods. Most of these districts have formal business organizations with web sites.

- **Alberta Arts District**, NE Alberta St between Martin Luther King Jr. Blvd and 33rd Ave, www.albertaartsdistrict.com; the last decade has seen this area blossom from a somewhat sketchy neighborhood into a thriving strip of cafés, boutiques, and art galleries. This mile-long strip offers a funky mix of businesses—there's even a rain barrel store (Rainbarrelman, 5024¾ NE 30th Ave, 503-978-1668, www.rainbarrelman.com)—and it hosts an evening art fair on the last Thursday of each month.
- **Downtown Portland**, www.downtownportland.org; downtown Portland has

about every kind of good and service you might need, in almost every price range. Unfortunately, the stores are scattered all over the place, not in a nice little row, although the traditional center of gravity for downtown shopping is the area surrounding Pioneer Courthouse Square. Downtown shopping options include independently owned establishments and national chains, including some upscale chains such as Tiffany & Co. and such department stores as Nordstrom and Saks Fifth Avenue. Most downtown stores are an easy stroll from transit; if you're driving, many downtown merchants will validate parking at certain garages, including Smart Park garages.

- **Hawthorne District**, SE Hawthorne Blvd between 12th and 58th avenues (greatest concentration of businesses between 32nd and 39th avenues), www. hawthorneblvd.com, www.thinkhawthorne.com; the Hawthorne District has long had a reputation as Portland's hippie shopping district, but the area actually offers a quite diverse shopping experience (the occasional bong store and tie-dye establishment notwithstanding). For several blocks, restaurants, bars, cafés, and many gift and specialty shops line the street. The district is on the whole quite laid-back and unpretentious (especially compared to, say, the Pearl), although some chains are moving in and even a few new lofts have been built. A smaller but similar shopping district extends along **Belmont Avenue** (www.belmontbusiness.org), which runs parallel to Hawthorne Boulevard a few blocks to the north.

- **Multnomah Village**, centered on the intersection of SW Capitol Hwy and 35th Ave, www.multnomahvillage.org; the "Village in the heart of Portland" harbors an eclectic range of specialty shops, antique stores, and restaurants, cafés, and pubs. Its Southwest Portland location means it tends to be less hipster-focused and more family-oriented than some Eastside shopping districts.

- **North Mississippi**, North Mississippi Ave between Mason St and Fremont St; like the Alberta Arts District, North Mississippi Avenue was a down-and-out neighborhood not many years ago. Its subsequent transformation into a vibrant commercial district is, depending on your point of view, either an urban success story or an example of relentless gentrification. Either way, the result from the visitor's perspective is a small collection of restaurants and interesting shops, including a comic book store, a gourmet salt shop, a small nursery, and a sunlamp vendor.

- **Northeast Broadway**, NE Broadway between Grand Ave and 28th Ave; Northeast Broadway businesses cater both to residents of the adjacent (and generally affluent) Irvington neighborhood and to people from other parts of the city who come to shop and dine here. This district runs eastward from the Lloyd Center shopping mall area towards Hollywood, and includes a mix of old-line businesses such as Helen Bernhard Bakery (since 1924; 1717 NE Broadway, 503-287-1251, www.helenbernhardbakery.com), a variety of dining establishments, and some brand-spanking-new boutiques.

- **Northwest Portland (Nob Hill)**, NW 21st and 23rd avenues, from Burnside St north to Vaughn St, www.nobhillbiz.com; Northwest Twenty-Third (sometimes derisively called Trendy-Third) Avenue (and, to a lesser extent, Northwest Twenty-First Avenue, which runs parallel two blocks east) is one of the brightest stars in Portland's shopping firmament. The street is lined with a dazzling range of stores, with an emphasis on clothing, household goods, antiques, and knickknacks of all kinds, as well as restaurants and cafés that cater to all tastes and budgets. Chains such as Pottery Barn and Restoration Hardware have made inroads here in recent years, but many stores remain locally owned (or at least small-scale). Parking can be hard to find on weekends, but the area is eminently walkable and easily accessible by bus and streetcar.

- **Pearl District**, north of West Burnside St, between 8th Ave and Interstate 405, 503-227-8519, www.shopthepearl.com. Call it frou-frou, call it trendy, call it spendy—and you'd be right. The Pearl is not the neighborhood to look for bargains. Barring a few businesses such as Powell's Books that predated the neighborhood's transformation into a playground for the affluent, options range from upscale independent stores to upscale chain stores. That said, the Pearl offers lots of unique merchandise that cannot be found anywhere else in Portland. Shops and restaurants are sprinkled liberally throughout this large neighborhood, which makes the Pearl a great destination for a walking/shopping/gourmet food sampling expedition.
- **Sellwood/Westmoreland**, centered in SE Thirteenth Ave and Tacoma (Sellwood) and SE Milwaukie Ave at Bybee (Westmoreland); Sellwood and Westmoreland are two separate districts only half a mile apart, and both offer a mix of interesting boutiques, popular restaurants (including nationally known Caprial's Bistro, 7015 SE Milwaukie Ave, 503-236-6457, www.caprial andjohnskitchen.com), art galleries, and plenty of antique stores. Although it is not particularly far away from the city center, the area remains off the radar screen for many Portlanders, and so is (on the whole) less self-consciously trendy than some close-in shopping zones.

Shopping districts in most communities outside Portland tend to be of the strip mall variety, but some of the older, more established suburbs such as Lake Oswego, Forest Grove, and Gresham (www.gresham.org) have walkable downtown shopping districts; Vancouver's Uptown Village district (www.up townvillage.com) is also worth a visit.

While not a shopping district per se, the Portland Saturday Market (503-222-6072, www.saturdaymarket.org) functions as an outdoor weekend bazaar from April through Christmas. It is located under the west end of the Burnside Bridge.

MALLS

Although Portland's neighborhood shopping districts are fantastic, that doesn't mean the vast seas of pavement surrounding the area's malls are empty. Indeed, it can be hard to find a parking space at all on weekends and during the holiday shopping season. If nothing else, malls are a great place to stretch your legs (and your credit limit) if you fear going out in the winter drizzle.

In addition to its ongoing love affair with traditional indoor malls, Portland is getting plugged into the one of the country's newest shopping trends, the "lifestyle mall," which features upscale retailers in faux-Main Street settings. The **Streets of Tanasbourne** mall in Hillsboro (NW Cornell Rd at Stucki Ave, 503-533-0561, www.streetsoftanasbourne.com), which opened in 2004, was the first local avatar of this trend, but perhaps the area's prime example is **Bridgeport Village** (503-968-8940, www.bridgeport-village.com), which opened in 2005 at Lower Boones Ferry/Bridgeport Rd and Interstate 5 (exit 290), straddling the Tigard-Tualatin border and across the freeway from Lake Oswego. In addition to national retailers such as Anthropologie and Design Within Reach, Bridgeport Village has also attracted several local retailers, including Mario's (clothing) and Carl Greve (jewelry). The complex also includes spas and salons, several restaurants and cafés, and no fewer than two natural foods supermarkets (Whole Foods and Wild Oats, although Wild Oats may ultimately close following its FTC-contested purchase by Whole Foods). Bridgeport Village is popular enough to cause traffic backups on I-5. The success of these initial developments is likely to spawn imitators, and indeed, older indoor malls such as Washington Square and Cedar Hills Crossing have revamped their exteriors to make them more open and accessible from the outside and less forbiddingly featureless, and Clackamas Town Center is expanding to include what the management describes as "a dynamic street of shops and a pedestrian-friendly shopping environment."

Here's a list of the other major (and more traditional) shopping malls in the Portland area:

- **Cedar Hills Crossing**, 3205 SW Cedar Hills Blvd, Beaverton, 503-643-7117, www.cedarhillscrossing.com; once upon a time this was the nearly moribund Beaverton Mall. Following a major redesign several years ago, it is now Cedar Hills Crossing, and boasts such indicators of relevance as a new Powell's bookstore, an Apple Store, and a New Seasons supermarket.
- **Clackamas Town Center**, 12000 SE 82nd Ave, Clackamas, 503-653-6913, www.clackamastowncenter.com; Clackamas Town Center is one of the area's primary suburban shopping centers. Anchored by a Macy's, Sears, Nordstrom, and JC Penney, Clackamas Town Center offers few surprises. The mall proper is expanding by some 250,000 square feet in 2007, and several satellite shopping centers have sprung up around it, including Clackamas Promenade just across the street.
- **Jantzen Beach Supercenter**, off Interstate 5, exit 308, Jantzen Beach, Portland, 503-286-9103, www.jantzenbeachsupercenter.com; judging from the license plates in the parking lot, this complex caters in large part to Washington residents who scoot across the Columbia River for some surreptitious tax-free shopping. The food court includes a restored, working 1921 carousel.

- **Lloyd Center Mall**, NE Multnomah St at 11th Ave, 503-528-8515, www.lloyd centermall.com; one of the first enclosed malls in the country, Lloyd Center, in close-in Northeast Portland, is Portland's primary "urban" mall. In addition to the usual mall shops, department stores (Nordstrom, Macy's, Sears), discount stores (Marshall's, Ross Dress for Less), a food court, and a multi-screen cinema, Lloyd Center houses an ice skating rink smack-dab in the middle of the mall.
- **Pioneer Place**, 700 SW 5th Ave, 503-228-5800, www.pioneerplace.com; this downtown Portland mall is fairly unobtrusive (partly because it lacks an adjacent surface parking lot, and partly because much of it is underground). As a result, Pioneer Place manages to function reasonably well as part of the downtown shopping scene. Most of the stores are relatively upscale, and the only department store anchor is Saks Fifth Avenue. The underground food court gets ridiculously crowded during weekday lunch hours.
- **Washington Square**, 9585 SW Washington Square Rd, Tigard, 503-639-8860, www.shopwashingtonsquare.com; along with Clackamas Town Center, Washington Square is one of the two main suburban malls in the Portland area. Both malls have the same four anchor department stores (although Washington Square's Nordstrom is the largest in the state). Washington Square's overall retail mix is somewhat more upscale than most other area malls, reflecting the relative affluence of its Washington County surroundings.
- **Westfield Shoppingtown Vancouver**, 8700 NE Vancouver Mall Dr, Vancouver, 360-892-6255, westfield.com/Vancouver/; the name is corporate gobbledygook for the Vancouver Mall, which is what everyone calls this mall near the intersection of Interstate 205 and State Route 500.

OUTLET MALLS AND FACTORY STORES

Factory discount stores often stock overruns and imperfect goods. While they can offer great bargains, shoppers should pay special attention to merchandise quality. There are two major outlet malls within an hour's drive of Portland. **Columbia Gorge Premium Outlets** (450 NW 257th Ave, Troutdale, 503-669-8060, www.premiumoutlets.com/columbiagorge), with 45 stores, is just south of Interstate 84 at exit 17. **Woodburn Company Stores** (1001 Arney Rd, Woodburn, 503-981-1900, 888-664-7467, www.woodburncompanystores.com), a 100-store complex of "craftsman-inspired" storefronts, sometimes backs up traffic on Interstate 5 at exit 271.

In addition to the outlet malls, several local companies operate stand-alone factory outlet stores:

- **Columbia Sportswear Outlet Stores,** 1323 SE Tacoma St, 503-238-0118; 3 Monroe Pkwy, Lake Oswego, 503-636-6593

- **Hanna Andersson Outlet Store**, 7 Monroe Pkwy, Lake Oswego, 503-697-1953
- **Nike Factory Store**, 2650 NE Martin Luther King Jr Blvd, 503-281-5901
- **Norm Thompson Outlet Store**, 9 Monroe Pkway, Lake Oswego, 503-697-2931
- **Pendleton Woolen Mills Outlet Store**, 2 17th St, Washougal, 360-835-1118

DEPARTMENT STORES

Most Portland-area department stores are attached to malls, although there are a few stand-alone establishments.

- **JC Penney**, Clackamas Town Center, 503-653-8830; Washington Square, 503-620-0750; Vancouver Mall, 360-254-6594; www.jcpenney.com; JC Penney sells everything from washing machines and dishwashers to jewelry and cosmetics.
- **Kohl's**, 11055 SW Canyon Rd, Beaverton, 503-350-0407; 7360 NE Butler St, Hillsboro, 503-640-5083; 22257 NE Park Ln, Wood Village, 503-665-1327; 17001 SE Mill Plain Rd, Vancouver, 360-254-6594; www.kohls.com; Kohl's competes with Sears and JC Penney, and runs sales almost continuously on everything from clothing to coffee makers.
- **Macy's**, six Portland-area locations (including downtown Portland, store closed for renovation until 2008), 800-289-6229, www.macys.com. In 2006, Macy's, which had never had a Portland presence, bought long-time Portland department store chain Meier & Frank. To some local consternation, it changed the names of all Meier & Frank stores to Macy's (as it had done with other acquisitions, such as Marshall Field's in Chicago) and "Macified" the stores and their product lines. Many Portlanders still refer to Macy's stores as Meier & Frank.
- **Nordstrom**, 701 SW Broadway, 503-224-6666; Lloyd Center, 503-287-2444; Washington Square, 503-620-0555; Clackamas Town Center, 503-652-1810; Vancouver Mall, 360-256-8666, www.nordstrom.com; thanks to its reputation for superb customer service, Nordstrom dominates the local market for high-end clothing and shoes.
- **Saks Fifth Avenue**, 850 SW 5th Ave, 503-226-3200, www.saksfifthavenue.com; fortuitously located on Fifth Avenue, this is the only Northwest outpost of Saks, a retailer of top-of-the-line clothing. The men's department is in a separate building across Fourth Avenue.
- **Sears**, Lloyd Center, 503-528-3200; Clackamas Town Center, 503-786-5200; Washington Square, 503-620-1510; Vancouver Mall, 360-260-4200; www.sears.com; known for Craftsman power tools, Sears no longer sells the craftsman bungalows and other kit homes that helped many of Portland's eastside neighborhoods grow in the early twentieth century. The store is a mainstay for family clothing, appliances, and home electronics.

DISCOUNT DEPARTMENT STORES

Some upscale departments stores (such as Nordstrom—see Nordstrom Rack, below) have their own outlets where they sell discontinued, overstocked, or slightly irregular merchandise at reduced prices. Such goods are also sold through discount outlets such as Marshall's, Ross Dress for Less, and T.J. Maxx. Other discount chains—Target, Kmart, and Wal-Mart—carry name-brand goods, but generally not the designer labels available at upscale department stores.

- **Fred Meyer**; most Fred Meyer supermarkets have an attached department store for non-grocery items. See "Supermarkets" below for details.
- **Kmart**, seven Portland-area stores, 866-562-7848. www.kmart.com
- **Marshall's**, Lloyd Center, 503-287-6441; 3849 SW 117th Ave, Beaverton, 503-646-2554; 16200 SW Pacific Hwy, Tigard, 503-620-7230; 861 NE 25th Ave, Hillsboro, 503-547-2841; www.marshallsonline.com
- **Nordstrom Rack**, 245 SW Morrison St, 503-299-1815; 18100 NW Evergreen Pkwy, Beaverton, 503-439-0900; 8930 SE Sunnyside Rd, Clackamas, 503-654-5415; www.nordstrom.com
- **Ross Dress for Less**, 11 Portland-area stores, 800-945-7677, www.rossstores.com
- **Target**, 14 Portland-area locations, 800-440-0680, www.target.com
- **T.J. Maxx**, 11370 SE 82nd Ave, 503-653-7913; 3805 SW 117th Ave, Beaverton, 503-641-1828; 8635 SW Tualatin-Sherwood Rd, Tualatin, 503-612-0000; 8101 NE Parkway Dr, Vancouver, 360-256-9606; www.tjmaxx.com
- **Wal-Mart**, six Portland-area stores, www.walmart.com

And don't forget membership warehouse stores such as **Costco** and **Bi-Mart**. They offer low prices on food, electronics, cameras, small appliances, housewares, and automotive supplies. Membership fees apply, and you don't get—or pay for—the level of service you expect from a regular department store. See the "Food" section below for more details.

HOUSEHOLD SHOPPING

In addition to the businesses listed below, most department stores (and many discount department stores) carry a wide range of household goods, from mattresses and sheets to home electronics and appliances. One new category-defying option for furniture, accessories, and Swedish ginger cookies is **IKEA** (www.ikea.com), which opened just off I-205 at the Portland International Airport exit in July 2007. (Budget-conscious Euro-design junkies previously had to make the three-hour haul up Interstate 5 to the Renton, Washington, store, just south of Seattle, to get their fix.)

APPLIANCES, COMPUTERS, AND ELECTRONICS

Portland is well supplied with the usual range of big-box electronics and household appliance stores, including **Best Buy** (six Portland-area stores, 888-BEST-BUY, www.bestbuy.com), **Circuit City** (four Portland-area stores, 800-843-2489, www.circuitcity.com), and **CompUSA** (stores in Portland and Tigard, 800-CompUSA, www.compusa.com). For appliances, you might also consider home improvement retailers such as **Home Depot** and **Lowe's** (see "Hardware and Paint" below). For computers, also check prices and offerings at office supply chains such as **Office Depot** (ten Portland-area stores, 800-GO-DEPOT, www.officedepot.com), **Staples** (four Portland-area stores, 800-3STAPLE, www.staples.com), and **OfficeMax** (eight Portland-area stores, 800-283-7674); all three of these companies place advertising inserts in the Sunday *Oregonian*.

For specialist or smaller-scale computer dealers, check the Yellow Pages under "computers"; look for other home electronics and appliance retailers under "Appliances," "Stereo & Hi Fi-Dealers," and "Television-Dealers," or try one of these stores:

- **Apple Store**, Pioneer Place, 503-222-3002; Bridgeport Village, Tigard, 503-670-8400; Washington Square, Tigard, 503-603-9800; www.apple.com
- **Bang & Olufsen**, Pioneer Place, 503-221-0123, www.bang-olufsen.com
- **Basco Builders Appliance Supply Company**, 1411 NW Davis St, 503-226-9235, www.bascoappliances.com
- **Belmont Computers**, 4505 SE Belmont St, 503-236-5364, www.belmontcomputers.com, specializes in custom-built computers and computer parts.
- **Bose Showcase Store**, Pioneer Place, 503-224-5772
- **Division Maytag Home Appliance Center**, 4035 SE Division St, 503-234-0873, www.divisionmaytag.com
- **Echo Audio**, 425 SW 10th Ave, 503-223-2292, 888-248-3246, www.echohifi.com
- **Fred's Sound of Music Audio/Video**, 3760 SE Hawthorne Blvd, 503-234-5341, www.fredssoundofmusic.com
- **Fry's Electronics**, 29400 SW Town Center Loop, Wilsonville, 503-570-6000, www.frys.com
- **George Smith Appliance Warehouse**, 5010 NE Oregon St, 503-281-2100; 10487A SW Cascade Blvd, Tigard, 503-624-7443; carries new appliances, but is best known for its close-out merchandise and used appliances.
- **The Mac Store**, 700 NE Multnomah St, 503-238-1200; Cedar Hills Crossing, Beaverton, 503-620-3550; www.thecomputerstore.com; this Pacific Northwest chain is one of several Mac specialists in the Portland area.
- **NW Natural Appliance Center**, 2610 SE 8th Ave, 503-220-2362, www.nwnaturalappliances.com; this is the gas company's appliance showroom, so don't come looking for electric cooktops here.

- **Pearl Audio Video**, 1022 NW Johnson St, 503-222-2599, www.pearlaudiovideo. com
- **Radio Shack**, 800-843-7422, www.radioshack.com, has stores all over town.
- **Spencer's Appliances**, 7115 NE Glisan St, 503-254-7977
- **Standard TV & Appliance**, 5240 SW 82nd Ave, 503-777-3377; 3600 SW Hall Blvd, Beaverton, 503-619-0500; 11674 SW Highway 99W, Tigard, 503-620-0123; www.standardtvandappliance.com; Standard has one of the area's best selections of major appliances.
- **Stereotypes Audio**, 1401 SE Morrison St, 503-280-0910, www.stereotypes audio.com
- **Vern L. Wenger Company Video/Audio**, 5904 SW Beaverton-Hillsdale Hwy, 503-292-9211
- **Video Only**, 1900 N Hayden Island Dr, 503-283-3400; 8200 SE Sunnyside Rd, Clackamas, 503-653-8200; 12000 SW Canyon Rd, Beaverton, 503-520-0520; www.videoonly.com

CARPETS, RUGS & TILE

Portland has scores, if not hundreds, of carpet and tile retailers, ranging from discount warehouses to small stores that specialize in antique Persian rugs. For a complete list, look in the Yellow Pages under "Carpet & Rug Dealers" or "Tile-Ceramic-Contractors & Dealers." If you're in the market for gorgeous, high-end designer tile, be sure to check out the showrooms of two Portland-based companies: **Ann Sacks Tile & Stone** (1210 SE Grand Ave, 503-233-0611, www.annsacks. com) and **Pratt & Larson Tile and Stone** (1201 SE 3rd Ave, 503-231-9464, www. prattandlarson.com).

FURNITURE

A home furnishings showroom may be one of the first places you visit as you try to fill the empty spaces of your new home or apartment. There are plenty of furniture stores waiting for you, both in the city and in the strip malls and shopping centers of almost every suburban community. Check the Yellow Pages under "Furniture-Retail" for a complete listing. Many department stores also offer good selections of traditional home furnishings. If you're looking for something beyond standard pieces in traditional styles, Portland has a plethora of options, with a heavy concentration in the Pearl District and on the Inner East Side. Here's a partial list of stores to try:

- **Design Within Reach**, 1200 NW Everett St, 503-725-3057; Bridgeport Village, Tigard, 503-684-2048; www.dwr.com; offers a wide selection of modern furniture, including authorized reproductions of classic designs such as the Eames lounge and ottoman.

- **Eco PDX**, 2289 N Interstate Ave, 503-287-8181, www.ecopdx.com; hand-crafted furniture from salvaged tropical lumber.
- **Gingko Home Furnishings**, 610 SW 12th Ave, 503-224-5993, www.gingko furniture.com, creates Asian-inspired modern designs.
- **Hip,** 1829 NW 25th Ave, 503-225-5017, www.ubhip.com, specializes in the kind of clean-lined Euro-style furniture that's perfect for your new condo in the Pearl.
- **Hive**, 820 NW Glisan St, 503-242-1967, www.hivemodern.com, carries a wide selection of modern furniture, lighting, and accessories.
- **J.D. Madison**, 1307 NW Glisan St, 503-827-6037, www.jdmadison.com, sells modern, pricey furniture.
- **The Joinery**, 4804 SE Woodstock Blvd, 503-788-8547, www.thejoinery.com, builds dressers, tables, and other pieces from certified sustainably harvested wood.
- **Natural Furniture**, 800 NE Broadway, 503-284-0655; 11606 SW Pacific Hwy, Tigard, 503-684-4099; www.naturalunfinishedfurniture.com; Natural Furniture sells ready-to-finish tables, chairs, bookcases, and other wood furniture.
- **Portland Furniture,** 1971 W Burnside St, 503-546-5468, www.portlandfurni tureonline.com, has a wide selection of living room, dining room, and bedroom furniture in styles ranging from respectably traditional to uber-modern.
- **Sorel's,** 3713 SE Hawthorne Blvd, 503-232-8482, sells a range of furniture styles, including mid-century modern and Asian-inspired designs.
- **P.H. Reed,** 1101-1115 NW Glisan St, 503-274-7080, www.phreed.com; still more modern furniture, stylishly occupying a 10,000-square-foot showroom in the Pearl.

HARDWARE AND PAINT

As they do nearly everywhere in America, **Home Depot** (www.homedepot.com) and **Lowe's** (www.lowes.com) dominate Portland's home improvement market. These stores offer everything from paint and wallpaper to lumber, lighting, flooring, countertops, appliances, and plumbing fixtures under one very expansive roof. But the big boys haven't yet put neighborhood hardware stores and specialty retailers out of business; Portland and the surrounding communities still have quite a few traditional hardware stores, many of them affiliated with **Ace** (www.acehardware.com) or **True Value** (www.truevalue.com). Look in the Yellow Pages under "Hardware-Retail" or "Building Materials-Retail" or go for a walk in your neighborhood to find more options. Most hardware stores (as well as Home Depot and Lowe's) now carry paint and can match colors, but for the best quality and a wider (or at least different) selection you may want to try a specialty paint store (listed in the Yellow Pages under "Paint-Retail"). Here are a few paint and hardware options:

- **A-Boy Plumbing & Electrical**, www.aboysupply.com, is a locally owned chain with six locations in the Portland area.
- **Chown Hardware**, 333 NW 16th Ave, 503-243-6500, www.chown.com, has knowledgeable staff members and a vast selection of hardware and fixtures.
- **George Morlan Plumbing Supply,** 2222 NW Raleigh St, 503-224-7000, 5529 SE Foster Rd, 503-771-1145, 12585 SW Pacific Hwy, Tigard, 503-624-7381, www. georgemorlan.com; this is a veritable supermarket of plumbing fixtures, supplies, and related items.
- **Miller Paint Co.**, www.millerpaint.com, is a local company with more than a dozen stores in the Portland area. Among the featured paint lines is Devine Color, a unique "color from the Northwest" high-end specialty interior paint designed by Gretchen Schauffler, a nationally recognized Portland-area artist, color consultant, and entrepreneur.
- **Mr. Plywood**, 7609 SE Stark St, 503-254-7387, www.mrplywoodinc.com, is a basic, close-in lumber yard and building supply store.
- **Parr Lumber**, www.parr.com, is a local hardware company with 10 Portland-area retail yards plus two cabinet outlet stores.
- **Rodda Paint**, www.roddapaint.com, is another local paint manufacturer with multiple stores in the Portland area.

HOUSEWARES, KITCHENWARE, AND LINENS

If the department stores don't have just what you're looking for, one of these specialty stores might:

- **Bed, Bath & Beyond**, eight Portland-area stores, 800-462-3966, www.bed bathandbeyond.com
- **Compleat Bed & Breakfast**, 615 NW 23rd Ave, 503-221-0193, www.compleat bed.com; not a bed & breakfast at all, but rather a retailer of linens.
- **Crate & Barrel**, Bridgeport Village, Tigard, 503-598-9005, www.crateandbarrel. com
- **French Quarter Linens**, 1313 NW Glisan St, 503-282-8200; Bridgeport Village, Tigard, 503-639-3800; www.frenchquarterlinens.com; luxuriate in high thread counts and the silkiness of fine Egyptian cotton at this purveyor of European bedding and towels.
- **In Good Taste**, 231 NW 11th Ave, 503-248-2015, www.ingoodtastestore.com; part cookware store, part specialty grocer and wine shop, this shop stocks the latest and greatest tools and supplies for foodies.
- **Kitchen Kaboodle.** www.kitchenkaboodle.com; this local kitchenware chain has six stores in the area, and also sells furniture.

- **Linens-N-Things**, four Portland-area stores, 888-568-7378, www.lnt.com
- **Mirador**, 2106 SE Division St, 503-231-5175, www.mirador-pdx.com, sells an eclectic collection of natural (e.g., made from organic fibers) linens, kitchenware, and other items for the home.
- **Natural Spaces**, 6401 SW Macadam Ave, 503-892-2373, www.naturalspaces.com, offers natural linens and products made from recycled glass.
- **Please Be Seated**, 8309 SE 13th Ave, 503-595-1736, has a little bit of everything for the table: linens, china, glassware, and more.
- **Sur la Table**, 1102 NW Couch St, 503-295-9679; 390 N State St, Lake Oswego, 503-636-2181; Bridgeport Village, Tigard, 503-670-9562; www.surlatable.com
- **Williams-Sonoma**, 638 SW 5th Ave, 503-827-8383; Washington Square, Tigard, 503-684-2784; www.williams-sonoma.com

LAMPS AND LIGHTING

Many building supply stores, hardware stores, and furniture stores sell light fixtures. In addition, lighting "superstores" such as **Lamps Plus** (9369 SE 82nd Ave, 503-788-7772; 8748 SW Hall Blvd, Beaverton, 503-641-7546; www.lampsplus.com) and **Globe Lighting** (six Portland-area stores, www.globelighting.com) carry thousands of different light fixtures. For something a bit out-of-the-mainstream, or for historical reproduction lighting, try one of the following stores:

- **Light Design Center**, 800 SW Washington St, 503-52-LIGHT, www.lightdesigncenter.com, carries a (literally) dazzling range of specialty lights, with an emphasis on modern designs.
- **Lumen Essence Lighting**, 418 NW 8th Ave, 503-721-0939, www.lumenessencelighting.com, sells antique and period reproduction fixtures.
- **Lux**, 1333 NW Glisan, 503-227-2364, has a large selection of unique lighting.
- **Rejuvenation**, 1100 SE Grand Ave, 503-238-1900, www.rejuvenation.com; this Portland-based company manufactures reproduction light fixtures from periods ranging from the early electric era to the "atomic age" of the mid-twentieth century.
- **Schoolhouse Electric**, 330 SE MLK Jr Blvd, 503-230-7113, www.schoolhouselectric.com; another period lighting maker, Schoolhouse Electric casts many of its shades from the original early–twentieth century molds.

MATTRESSES AND FUTONS

For a standard, mass-produced mattress, your cheapest options are generally department stores or such chains as **BedMart** (www.bedmart.info), **Mattress World** (www.mattressworldsuperstores.com), and **SleepCountry USA** (www.sleepcountry.com), all of which have multiple Portland-area locations. At any of these establishments, you'd be very unlucky to drop in on a day without a mattress sale in progress. For a futon or custom-made mattress, try one of the following stores:

- **Cotton Cloud Futons and Mattresses**, 701 NE Broadway, 503-335-0758, www. cottoncloudfutons.com
- **Mulligan Mattress Co.**, 1200 SE 7th Ave, 503-222-3723, ww.mulliganmattresses. com, offers custom-built mattresses made with natural latex and organic cotton.
- **Rock Soft Futon**, 3200 SE Hawthorne Blvd, 503-236-0921; 2751 NE Broadway, 503-249-7195; 1606 NW 23rd Ave, 503-222-1329; www.rocksoftfuton.com

GARDEN CENTERS AND NURSERIES

Thanks to Portland's mild, maritime climate, many kinds of plants thrive here. A single small urban yard might contain a rose bush, a windmill palm tree, an alpine rock garden, a dwarf Japanese maple, and an ancient rhododendron. As you might imagine, gardening is a popular pastime here, and there are plenty of in-town garden centers, both large and small, that cater to the horticulturally inclined. Beyond the urban fringe, horticulture is a major part of Oregon's agriculture industry, and Portland's hinterlands are dotted with tree and plant nurseries. Some of these nurseries are highly specialized, and many sell directly to the public.

Here are a few of the more popular local garden centers and nurseries:

- **Cistus Nursery**, 22711 NW Gillihan Rd, Sauvie Island, 503-621-2233, www. cistus.com; billing itself as "the home of zonal denial," Cistus sells hardy subtropicals and southern hemisphere plants that can (and do) grow in Portland.
- **Cornell Farms**, 8212 SW Barnes Rd, 503-292-9895, www.cornellfarms.com, has a vast selection of shrubs and annual and perennial garden plants.
- **Dennis' Seven Dees** and **Drake's Seven Dees**, four Portland-area garden centers, www.sevendees.com. (The "seven dees" stand for the first initials of the founders' children, not the era of disco and bell bottoms.)
- **Garden Fever**, 3433 NE 24th Ave., 503-287-3200, sells specialty plants, seeds, and garden accouterments.
- **Joy Creek Nursery**, 20200 NW Watson Rd, Scappoose, 503-543-7474, www. joycreek.com; this nursery 18 miles north of Portland is worth the trip to buy unusual cultivars and hard-to-find plant species.
- **Pistils**, 3811 N Mississippi Ave, 503-288-4889, www.pistilsnursery.com; this small neighborhood nursery focuses on locally and sustainably grown plants.
- **Portland Nursery,** 5050 SE Stark St, 503-231-5050, 9000 SE Division St, 503-788-9000, www.portlandnursery.com; Portland Nursery has huge selections of both garden-variety and unusual plants, and is one of the best close-in sources for trees and large shrubs.

SECOND-HAND SHOPPING

Shopping for second-hand stuff is a thrifty, sometimes quirky, and generally environmentally sound activity, and consequently is a favorite pastime of many Portland residents. What better way to spend a drizzly afternoon than searching for treasures that (usually) cost so little?

ANTIQUE DEALERS

Portland is chock-full of stores that sell original and reproduction antiques (and that generally identify which is which, so you don't need to fear embarrassment when you show up with your treasure on *Antiques Roadshow*). The city's largest concentration of such stores is on Antique Row, an extended parade of stores and antique malls that stretches along Southeast 13th Avenue in Sellwood, but dozens of antique dealers are scattered throughout the city, with additional notable clusters in Multnomah Village, the Hawthorne District, the Pearl District, and Northwest/Nob Hill. Many suburban communities, especially historic communities such as Aurora or affluent suburbs such as Lake Oswego, also have antique stores.

One unusual store outside the urban area that might justify a pilgrimage is **RD Steeves Imports,** 140 W Main St, Yamhill, 503-662-3999, www.rdsteeves imports.com, which imports 40-foot shipping containers full of English antiques and vintage furnishings.

ARCHITECTURAL SALVAGE

You never know what you might find at Portland's architectural salvage stores; a single establishment could have everything from Victorian oak mantels to rows of 1950s movie theater seats. Inventories change often, so you may need to check in frequently if there's something in particular you're looking for.

- **Aurora Mills Architectural Salvage**, 14971 1st St NE, Aurora, 503-678-6083, www.auroramills.com
- **Hippo Hardware**, 1040 E Burnside St, 503-231-1444, www.hippohardware. com
- **Northwest Salvage and Second Hand House**, 7402 NE St Johns Rd, Vancouver, 360-694-0662
- **Rejuvenation**, 1100 SE Grand Ave, 503-238-1900, www.rejuvenation.com; best known for its reproduction light fixtures (see **Lamps and Lighting**, above), Rejuvenation also sells original salvaged hardware and house parts.
- **The Rebuilding Center**, 3625 N Mississippi Ave, 503-331-1877, www.rebuild ingcenter.org, markets high-quality salvaged, surplus, and green building

materials and provides jobs for residents of North Portland. Because they are often called in to dismantle and salvage reusable building materials from homes, you have a good shot at finding a match for your own old doors here.

GARAGE SALES AND FLEA MARKETS

If your idea of the perfect Saturday afternoon is spending a few hours poking through tubs of other people's flotsam, you're in luck. Most Portland garage and yard sales take place from May through September, but there are always at least a few sales on any given weekend. In addition to the widely used sign-on-the-utility-pole method, garage sales are advertised in the *Oregonian* classifieds (available online at www.oregonlive.com/classifieds/garagesales/) and on Craigslist (portland.craigslist.org/gms/).

Portland's **flea markets** come and go, and some of the more fleeting flea markets seem suspiciously like clearinghouses for stolen goods, but the legitimate versions can offer good deals. Keep an eye on the classifieds for large semi-regular events at such places as the Memorial Coliseum. Two established weekend indoor markets to try are **M & M Swap Meet**, 346 SW Walnut St, Hillsboro, 503-846-0691, which is largely geared to Hispanic shoppers, and the diverse **Fantastic Flea Market**, 19340 SE Stark St, 503-618-9119, www.fantastic-flea-market.com.

VINTAGE AND SECOND-HAND STORES

There is a fine line between "antique" and "vintage." There is an equally fine line between "vintage" and "junk." Portland has an abundant selection of places to try your hand at distinguishing between the two qualities, as well as plenty of ordinary second-hand stores. If you poke around any Portland neighborhood, you're bound to find at least one or two vintage or second-hand stores where you can try your shopping luck. Be aware that the stock at most vintage and thrift stores turns over frequently, so be ready to buy if you find something you want. (Conversely, if you like the store but didn't find what you were looking for, try again in a few days.) Here are a few suggestions to get you started:

- **Bombshell Vintage**, 811 E Burnside St, 503-239-1073, is a great place to look for vintage dresses and World War II–era fashions.
- **City Liquidators**, 8233 SE 3rd Ave, 503-238-4477, www.cityliquidators.com, carries everything from a rotating stock of used and new commercial furniture (very useful if you need to furnish an office) to boxes of artificial flowers. Several other unrelated businesses in the immediate area also sell used office furniture.

- **Decades Vintage Company**, 328 SW Stark St, 503-223-1177, www.decades vintage.com, sells everything from original 1950s eyeglass frames to vintage men's Hawaiian shirts.
- **Goodwill**, 1943 SE 6th Ave, 503-238-6165, plus more than 20 other Portland-area locations, www.meetgoodwill.com; you're unlikely to find a cheap Matisse now that Goodwill has started selling its most valuable donated goods on eBay, but you can still find some good used stuff here. Goodwill's four outlet stores, a.k.a. "The Bins," which overflow with jumbled masses of cheap, unsorted goods, are infamous for their treasure hunting possibilities.
- **Xtabay Vintage**, 3515 SE Clinton St, 503-230-2899, sells mid-century clothing and accessories.

FOOD

MAJOR SUPERMARKET CHAINS AND WAREHOUSE STORES

Almost every neighborhood in the Portland metropolitan area is only a short distance from one or more major chain supermarkets. **Fred Meyer** (888-247-4439, www.fredmeyer.com) probably has the most pervasive presence; known to three generations of Portlanders as "Freddy's," the chain was indeed founded by a man named Fred G. Meyer in downtown Portland in 1922. Most Fred Meyer stores offer one-stop shopping for food, hardware, toys, sporting goods, small appliances, low-end household furniture, and the like. The chain is now owned by Ohio-based Kroger, as is the more upscale and less ubiquitous **QFC** (Quality Food Centers) supermarket chain (800-201-6261, www.qfconline.com). **Safeway** (877-723-3929, www.safeway.com) runs neck-and-neck with Fred Meyer for local market dominance. Both **Albertsons** (www.albertsons.com) and **Thriftway** (www.thriftwaystores.com) also have numerous stores in the area. (Thriftway stores are individually owned, and their names often bear identifiers, as in Bales Thriftway or Lamb's Thriftway.) Bellingham, Washington–based **Haggen** (www.haggen.com) has expanded into the Portland area in recent years, with stores in Beaverton, Hillsboro (Tanasbourne), Oregon City, and Tualatin.

A few discount supermarkets such as **WinCo Foods** (www.wincofoods.com) can be found in outlying neighborhoods and in surrounding communities.

Two warehouse store chains in the Portland area, **Costco** (seven Portland-area locations, www.costco.com) and **Bi-Mart** (nearly 20 Portland-area stores, www.bimart.com) offer good deals on bulk foods and other household items. (Sam's Club does not have any local stores.) Both stores have membership requirements. Call ahead or check out their web sites for details.

SMALL AND SPECIALTY SUPERMARKET CHAINS

Low prices and convenience are consumers' most-cited reasons for shopping at large chains. However, don't miss out on the unique offerings of Portland's smaller supermarket chains, most of which boast larger selections of natural and locally produced foods, organic and specialty produce, and esoteric wines and cheeses than the big chain stores do—for a modest price premium, of course.

Zupan's Markets (3401 SE Belmont St, 503-239-3720; 2340 W Burnside St, 503-497-1088; 7221 SW Macadam Ave, 503-244-5666; 8235 SW Apple Way, Raleigh Hills, 503-203-5962; www.zupans.com) and Eugene-based **Market of Choice** (8502 SW Terwilliger Blvd, 503-892-7331; 5639 Hood St, West Linn, 503-594-2901; www.marketofchoice.com) both focus on relatively affluent shoppers. Market of Choice has one of the best supermarket cheese selections around.

Portland is an ideal breeding ground for natural foods supermarkets. Locally owned **New Seasons Market** (www.newseasonsmarket.com) has eight supermarkets in the Portland area, with two more on the way. New Seasons focuses on natural foods, but still stocks staples such as Hershey's chocolate syrup. New Seasons has higher prices than the major chain stores, but its customer service is outstanding and the wheels on the shopping carts actually revolve freely. National natural foods supermarket chain **Whole Foods** (1210 NW Couch St, 503-525-4343; 7830 SW Bridgeport Rd, Tigard, 503-639-6500; www.whole foodsmarket.com) is in the process of digesting its erstwhile competitor **Wild Oats** (www.wildoats.com), which has seven Portland-area stores (including one at Bridgeport Village in Tigard, directly across the street from a Whole Foods). The Wild Oats experience illustrates the evolution and consolidation of natural foods supermarkets. Colorado-based Wild Oats bought Nature's Fresh Northwest, a local chain. Refugees from Nature's in turn started the New Seasons chain in 1999. Now Whole Foods, based in Texas, is buying Wild Oats, although the purchase is subject to FTC approval, which may not be forthcoming. If the deal goes through, Wild Oats stores in the Portland area will either be closed or remodeled (and possibly re-branded) as Whole Foods markets. The situation is in flux.

While it's not really a full-service supermarket, California-based **Trader Joe's** (seven Portland-area stores, www.traderjoes.com) is an indispensable stop for many shoppers. Famous for its cheap wine, Trader Joe's offers a giant selection of packaged and frozen foods and specialty items, many branded under its own private label. It offers a wide selection of bread and dairy products, but its fresh produce selection is quite limited.

FOOD CO-OPS

Besides offering unsprayed produce and the gamut of "free" foods—wheat-free, free-range, etc.—co-ops sell many foods in bulk, allowing you to buy the exact one tablespoon of celery seed that you need to make your favorite tempeh marinade. Co-ops sell shares to members, and some allow you to volunteer at the store for a discount on groceries, but non-members are welcome as well. There are three co-ops in Portland:

- **Alberta Cooperative Grocery**, 1500 NE Alberta St, 503-287-4333, www.alberta grocery.coop, is a sparkling new store with a diverse selection of foods.
- **Food Front Cooperative,** 2375 NW Thurman St, 503-222-5658, www.food front.coop, has some of the city's best and freshest produce.
- **People's Food Co-Op**, 3029 SE 21st Ave, 503-674-2642, www.peoples.coop, is probably the kind of place you think of when you think of a co-op. Besides its vast bulk foods section and selection of organic foods, this venerable co-op (which has expanded into a "green" remodeled space) hosts a year-round farmers' market on Wednesdays.

SPECIALTY FOODS

Here are some of the best-known specialty foods stores in Portland:

- **Big City Produce**, 722 N Sumner St, 503-460-3830, has some of the best (and least expensive) produce in town.
- **Bob's Red Mill**, 5209 SE International Way, Milwaukie, 503-654-3215, www. bobsredmill.com/wholegrainstore.htm; this is basically the factory store for this nationally known miller of whole and stone-ground grain and seed products. And yes, Bob is a real person.
- **City Market,** 735 NW 21st Ave, 503-221-3012, offers an outstanding (but expensive) selection of imported cheeses, fresh fish, fresh pasta, and sausages and pâtés.
- **Curds & Whey**, 8036 SE 13th Ave, 503-231-2877, www.pdxcheese.com, has a scrupulously winnowed selection of artisanal cheeses. Do not come here expecting Velveeta and cans of Cheez Whiz.
- **Daily Grind**, 4026 SE Hawthorne Blvd, 503-233-5521, is an all-vegetarian natural foods market. It has an extensive bulk foods section, a vegan bakery, and a vegetarian/vegan deli.
- **Food Fight**, 4179 SE Division St, 503-233-3910, www.foodfightgrocery.com, is an only-in-Portland (OK, maybe it would work in a few other places, but not many) phenomenon: a vegan convenience store.
- **Foster & Dobbs**, 2518 NE 15th Ave, 503-284-1157, www.fosteranddobbs.com, sells artisanal food products, with an emphasis on cheese, wine, and cured meats.
- **Gartner's Meats**, 7450 NE Killingsworth St, 503-252-7801, www.gartnersmeats. com, is one of the city's most popular non-nightclub meat markets. Gartner's not only sells meat but will also butcher your dead moose, elk, or deer.

- **Lamb's at Stroheckers**, 2855 SW Patton Rd, 503-223-7391, www.lambs markets.com/stroheckers.html; while it sounds like a vendor of young sheep, Stroheckers is actually an upscale grocery store perched high up in Portland's West Hills, with a specialty foods selection (including an in-store crepery) that reflects its affluent surroundings.
- **Limbo**, 4707 SE 39th Ave, 503-774-8008, conveniently located next door to a largely produce-less Trader Joe's, Limbo has some of the best produce around, as well as an impressive bulk herb section. The majority of their fruits and vegetables are locally produced and organic.
- **Pastaworks**, 3735 SE Hawthorne Blvd., 503-232-1010, www.pastaworks.com; best known for its fresh pasta, Pastaworks also sells meats, cheeses, and various local and imported grocery items.
- **Penzey's**, 11322 SE 82nd Ave, 503-653-7779, www.penzeys.com; the only Northwest outpost of this Wisconsin-based spice chain is in an unassuming strip mall on Southeast 82nd Avenue.
- **Proper Eats Market and Café**, 8638 N Lombard St, 503-445-2007, www.proper eats.org, sells local organic produce; its kitchen serves prepared vegan and vegetarian food.
- **Sheridan Fruit Co.**, 408 SE 3rd Ave, 503-236-2114, www.sheridanfruit.com; this Portland institution dates back more than 90 years. Besides fruit (and vegetables), Sheridan's stocks meats, bulk and specialty food items.
- **Steve's Cheese**, 2321 NW Thurman St, 503-222-6014, www.stevescheese.biz; Steve focuses on domestic artisanal cheeses.

MAKE-AND-TAKE MEAL ASSEMBLY

An option that might be more of a bargain than you'd expect is **make-and-take meal assembly**, where the store does the prep and all you do is the assembly. The now popular national concept actually originated in the Pacific Northwest in 2002. A few of the more popular companies, all with multiple Portland-area locations, follow. You can also go to the Easy Meal Prep Association's web site, www. easymealprep.com, for updated lists and locations.

- **Dinners Done Right**, www.dinnersdoneright.com
- **Dinners Ready**, 425-776-2636, www.dinnersready.com
- **Dream Dinners**, 425-876-8987, www.dreamdinners.com

FARMERS' MARKETS AND COMMUNITY-SUPPORTED AGRICULTURE

If you're searching for the freshest fruits and vegetables, your best bet is to buy directly from the growers. Portlanders enthusiastically support local farmers' markets, which are generally open one day a week in season (usually Wednesday, Thursday, Saturday, or Sunday). Except for the year-round Hillsdale, People's, and Vancouver markets, and the Portland Farmers' Market at PSU (which remains open through mid-December), local farmers' markets are generally open from May through September or October. In addition to fresh produce from local farmers, offerings typically include locally produced cheese and cured meat, fresh bread, and fresh meat or seafood. Arts and crafts vendors are common at some markets, banned at others. For a complete statewide list of farmers' markets, visit www.oregonfarmersmarkets.org.

The following farmers' markets are located in the city of Portland:

- **Alberta Farmers' Market**, NE 15th Ave at Alberta St, 503-287-4333; open May–September, Saturdays, 10 am–2 pm
- **Hillsdale Farmers' Market**, Wilson High School–Rieke Elementary School parking lot, SW Capitol Highway at Sunset Blvd, 503-475-6555, www.hillsdalefarmersmarket.com; open May–October, Sundays, 10 am–2 pm, and November–April, two Sundays per month, 10 am–2 pm
- **Hollywood Farmers' Market**, NE Hancock St between 44th and 45th, 503-709-7403, www.hollywoodfarmersmarket.org; open May–October, Saturdays, 8 am–1 pm, and early November, Saturdays, 9 am–1 pm
- **Interstate Farmers Market**, Overlook Park, N Fremont St at Interstate Ave, 503-832-3453, www.interstatefarmersmarket.com; open mid-May–September, Wednesdays, 3 pm–7 pm
- **Lents International Farmers Market**, Crossroads Plaza at SE 92nd Ave and Foster Rd, 503-621-7655; open June–mid-October, Sundays, 9 am–2 pm
- **Moreland Farmers Market**, SE Bybee Blvd at 14th Ave, 503-341-9350, www.morelandfarmersmarket.org; open mid-May–September, Wednesdays, 3:30 pm–7:30 pm
- **OHSU Farmers Market**, MacKenzie Hall Courtyard, OHSU, 503-494-8792; open mid-May–early October, Tuesdays, 3 pm–7 pm
- **People's Farmers Market**, People's Food Co-Op, 3029 SE 21st Ave, 503-232-9051, www.peoples.coop; open year-round, Wednesdays, 2 pm–7 pm
- **Portland Farmers Market – Downtown**, South Park Blocks at SW Salmon St, 503-241-0032, www.portlandfarmersmarket.com; open May–October, Wednesdays, 10 am–2 pm
- **Portland Farmers Market – Eastbank**, SE Salmon St at 20th Ave, 503-241-0032, www.portlandfarmersmarket.com; open June–September, Thursdays, 3:30 pm–7:30 pm
- **Portland Farmers Market at EcoTrust**, NW 10th Ave between Irving and Johnson, 503-241-0032, www.portlandfarmersmarket.com; open June–September, Thursdays, 3:30 pm–7:30 pm
- **Portland Farmers Market – PSU**, South Park Blocks between SW Montgomery St and SW Harrison St, 503-241-0032, www.portlandfarmersmarket.com;

open April–October, Saturdays, 8:30 am–2 pm, and November–mid-December, Saturdays, 9:30 am–2 pm

In addition to the markets in Portland proper, there are farmers' markets in the following surrounding communities: **Beaverton** (503-643-5345, www.beavertonfarmersmarket.com), **Canby** (503-263-5151), **Cedar Mill** (503-913-7733, www.cmfmarket.org), **Estacada** (503-630-4490, www.estacadafarmersmarket.4t.com), **Fairview** (503-408-5209, www.windancefarmsandart.com/market.html), **Forest Grove** (503-992-0078), **Gresham** (503-727-9828, www.greshamfarmersmarket.com), **Hillsboro** (503-844-6685, www.hillsboromarkets.org), **Lake Oswego** (503-697-6590, www.ci.oswego.or.us/farmersmarket/), **Milwaukie** (503-407-0956, www.milwaukiefarmersmarket.com), **Oregon City** (503-557-1622, www.orcityfarmersmarket.com), **Scappoose** (503-543-3469, www.scappoosefarmermarket.com), **Sherwood** (503-682-1604, sherwoodmarket.blogspot.com), **Tigard** (503-244-2479, www.tigardfarmersmarket.com); **Troutdale** (503-408-5209, www.windancefarmsandart.com/market.html), **Vancouver** (360-737-8298, www.vancouverfarmersmarket.com, Indoor Market open year-round); and **West Linn** (503-875-5483).

As a supplement or alternative to your nearest farmers' market, you might consider community-supported agriculture (CSA). In CSA, you buy "harvest shares" from a local farm, and in return you receive a proportionate amount of the farm's production, usually on a weekly basis during the growing season. For information about CSA and a list of local farms that participate in CSA programs, visit the web site for the **Portland Area CSA Coalition** (www.pacsac.org).

HOME DELIVERY

If you're after supermarket goods but don't want to fight supermarket crowds, **Albertson's** (www.albertsons.com), **New Seasons** (www.newseasonsmarket.com) and **Safeway** (www.safeway.com) all offer home delivery. For bins of fresh organic produce and natural groceries delivered to your door, try **Organics to You**, 503-236-6496, www.organicstoyou.org, or **Pioneer Organics**, 877-632-3424, www.pioneerorganics.com.

ETHNIC MARKETS

The small grocery stores full of delicacies from other parts of the world that are scattered around Portland and its surrounding communities reflect the region's growing ethnic diversity. Interestingly, the majority of ethnic food stores of all kinds are located in suburban communities, a fact that mirrors the current pattern of immigrant settlement in Oregon (as well as the generally high housing prices and rents in close-in neighborhoods). Although many local supermarkets offer a selection of foods for ethnic cooking, try some of the stores below for a more authentic experience (and remember, this is a very incomplete list):

- **Anzen,** 736 NE MLK Jr Blvd, 503-233-5111, is a long-established Japanese food store.
- **Barbur World Foods,** 9845 SW Barbur Blvd, 503-244-0670, www.barburworld foods.com; it initially seems like an ordinary supermarket, stocked with a standard range of groceries and produce, but a few minutes spent perusing shelves filled with such Middle Eastern products as carob molasses and candied mulberries will cure you of your delusion.
- **Caribbean Spice,** 4516 NE 42nd Ave, 503-493-2737, sells groceries produced throughout the tropical world, from West African fufu flour to Caribbean hot sauces.
- **Dashen International Groceries,** 3022 NE Glisan St, 503-234-7785; formerly Becerra's, this store sells Mexican and other Latin American groceries.
- **Fiji Emporium,** 7814 N Interstate Ave, 503-240-2768, www.fijiemporium.com, sells East Indian and Australian(!) foods.
- **Fubonn,** 2850 SE 82nd Ave, 503-517-8877 www.fubonn.com; this complex of shops, restaurants, and a supermarket bills itself as the largest Asian mall in Oregon.
- **India 4-U,** 3341 SE Hawthorne Blvd, 503-239-8000; most Portland-area Indian and Pakistani food markets seem to be housed in strip malls in Washington County, but India 4-U is centrally located in the Hawthorne District.
- **International Food Supply,** 8005 SE Stark St, 503-256-9576, www.yahala restaurant.com/ifs.htm, concentrates on Middle Eastern foods.
- **Pacific Supermarket,** 6750 NE Broadway. 503-251-0524, is chock-full of Vietnamese products.
- **Roman Russian Food Store,** 6911 SE Foster Rd, 503-777-2614; although prices aren't listed in rubles, this place feels plenty authentic—most of the signs are in the Cyrillic alphabet.
- **Taste of Europe,** 1739 SE Hawthorne Blvd, 503-238-3693, www.tasteofeurope. net, has a large selection of European imports, including foods from Eastern Europe.
- **Uwajimaya,** 10500 SW Beaverton-Hillsdale Hwy, Beaverton, 503-643-4512, www.uwajimaya.com; the sole Oregon outlet of a Seattle-based chain, Uwajimaya offers a vast selection of Asian groceries and goods, as well as some of the area's best fresh seafood.

WINE, BEER, AND LIQUOR

In both Oregon and Washington, wine and beer are sold at convenience stores and supermarkets, but hard liquor is only available at bars and state-licensed liquor stores. Most markets of any size carry a good range of domestic beer (including microbrews) and the most popular import brands; for one of the city's best selections of imported beers, try **Belmont Station**, 4500 SW Stark St, 503-232-8538, www.belmont-station.com. While some supermarkets also have surprisingly good wine selections, the area's wine shops are great for more esoteric offerings, and usually offer personalized recommendations and in-store wine tastings. Here's a partial list of Portland wine shops:

- **Carpe Vinum**, 4831 SE Division St, 503-232-1550, www.carpevinumpdx.com
- **Cork**, 2901 NE Alberta St, 503-281-CORK, www.corkwineshop.com
- **E & R Wine Shop**, 6141 SW Macadam Ave, 503-246-6101
- **Great Wine Buys,** 1515 NE Broadway, 503-287-2897, www.greatwinebuys. com
- **Liner & Elsen**, 2222 NW Quimby St, 503-241-WINE, 800-903-WINE, www. linerandelsen.com
- **Mt. Tabor Fine Wines**, 4316 SE Hawthorne Blvd, 503-235-4444, www.mttabor finewines.com
- **Oregon Wines on Broadway**, 515 SW Broadway, 503-228-4655, 800-943-8858, www.oregonwinesonbroadway.com
- **The Pearl Wine Shop**, 1314 NW Glisan St, 503-226-2976, 877-732-7555, www. pearlwineshop.com
- **Portland Wine Merchants,** 1439 SE 35th St, 503-234-4399, www.portland winemerchants.com
- **Sip D'Vine**, 7829 SW Capitol Hwy, 503-977-WINE, www.sipdvine.com
- **Square Deal Wine Company**, 2321 NW Thurman St, 503-226-9463, www. wineaccess.com/store/squaredeal/
- **Terra Sol Wine**, 908 SE Hawthorne Blvd, 503-232-5605, www.terrasolwine. com
- **Vinideus**, 1019 NW 11th Ave, 8317 SE 13th Ave, 503-235-8002 (both locations), www.vinideus.net
- **Vino**, 1226 SE Lexington St, 503-235-8545, 888-922-8545, www.vinobuys.com
- **Vinopolis Wine Shop**, 1025 SW Washington St, 503-223-6002, www.vinopo liswineshop.com
- **Woodstock Wine & Deli**, 4030 SE Woodstock Blvd, 503-777-2208, www.wood stockwineanddeli.com

Perhaps you prefer to cut out the middleman and go directly to the source—i.e., wineries and brewpubs. For a list of wineries in the region check out the online directories of **Willamette Valley Wineries** (www.willamette wines.com) or the **Oregon Wine Board** (www.oregonwine.org); for Portland-area craft breweries, go to the **Oregon Brewers Guild's** Portland brewery map (www.oregonbeer.org/mapport.html). If your taste runs more to hard cider, there are several cideries in the region; try **Ford Farms Cyderworks** (www.cyderworks. com) or **Wandering Aengus Ciderworks** (www.wanderingaengus.com). There is even a sakery in the western suburb of Forest Grove: **Saké One**, 820 Elm St, Forest Grove, 503-357-7056, www.sakeone.com. Portland is also one of the centers of a burgeoning microdistillery movement. The granddaddy of local distillers, **Clear Creek Distillery** (2389 NW Wilson St, 503-234-3790, www.clearcreek distillery.com; tours and tastings by appointment), produces some of the best brandy and eau-de-vie in the world.

EATING OUT

A comprehensive listing of Portland restaurants would double the size of this book. Since you're interested in a guide, not a paperweight, suffice it to say that Portland has restaurants for every type of palate and pocketbook, with more opening all the time. For current restaurant reviews and recommendations, try **Willamette Week's Restaurant Guide**, published each fall in print form, or check out their online Food Finder (foodfinder.wweek.com). The **Oregonian** online restaurant guide is available at www.oregonlive.com/dining/; the paper's Friday A&E section always includes full and capsule restaurant reviews. **Citysearch** (portland.citysearch.com) is another popular, if not always reliable, site for restaurant listings; for happy hour listings, check out **Unthirsty**, www.unthirsty.com.

OTHER SHOPPING

ART SUPPLIES

- **Art Media**, 902 SW Yamhill St, 503-223-3724; 2710 SW Cedar Hills Blvd, Beaverton, 503-646-9347; 10317 SE 82nd Ave, Clackamas, 503-777-3860; www.artmediaonline.com
- **Columbia Art & Drafting Supply**, 1515 SE Burnside St, 503-232-2216, www.columbiaart.com
- **Muse Art + Design**, 4224 SE Hawthorne Blvd, 503-231-8704, museartanddesign.com
- **Oblation Papers and Press**, 516 NW 12th Ave., 503-223-1093, www.oblationpapers.com
- **The Paper Garden**, 1713 NE 15th Ave, 503-249-0337
- **Utrecht Art Supplies**, 1122 NW Everett St, 503-417-1569, www.utrecht.com

BOOKS

For a list of local bookstores, see the **Cultural Life** chapter.

CIGARS

If you must indulge, **Rich's Cigar Store** (820 SW Alder, 503-228-1700, 800-669-1527, www.richscigar.com) is your source for fine tobaccos. Established in 1894, Rich's has a walk-in humidor and, for nonsmokers, stocks more than 2,500 periodicals from around the world.

FOR CHILDREN

Children's clothing, furniture, and toys are available at most department stores and discount stores. Such spelling-challenged national retailers as **Babies "R" Us**, **Toys "R" Us** (both at www.toysrus.com), and **Gymboree** (www.gymboree.com) all have multiple stores in and around Portland. Portland also has many independent stores that specialize in children's stuff. Here are a few:

- **Black Wagon,** 3964 N Mississippi Ave, Portland, 866-916-0004, www.blackwagon.com, serves up large helpings of hip designer clothes for the 0–6 crowd.
- **Child's Play**, 907 NW 23rd Ave, 503-224-5586, www.toysinportland.com, has a wide selection of toys.
- **Goodnight Room**, 1517 NE Broadway, 503-281-5516, Bridgeport Village, 7823 SW Bridgeport Rd, Tigard, 503-684-9510, www.goodnightroom.com, has high-end children's furniture, toys, and accessories.
- **Grasshopper**, 1816 NE Alberta St, 503-335-3131, www.grasshopperstore.com, sells an eclectic assortment of children's books, clothes, and toys.
- **Haggis McBaggis**, 6802 SE Milwaukie Ave, 503-234-0849, www.haggismcbaggis.com, specializes in children's footwear, including many hard-to-find brands.
- **Henny Penny,** 405 NW 10th Ave, 503-222-7676, stocks several lines of European children's clothing and accessories.
- **Kids at Heart**, 3445 SE Hawthorne Blvd, 503-231-2954, www.kidsathearttoys.com, sells high-quality children's toys and books.
- **OMSI Science Store**, Oregon Museum of Science and Industry, 1945 SE Water Ave, 503-797-4626, www.omsi.edu; not exactly a children's store, the gift shop at OMSI nonetheless carries a huge selection of science-related toys, kits, and assorted gadgets for kids of all ages.
- **Polliwog**, 2900 SE Belmont St, 503-236-3903, www.polliwogportland.com, offers clothing and accessories for newborns to first-graders.
- **Segal's for Children**, 14755 SW Teal Blvd, Beaverton, 503-579-1477, www.segalsforchildren.com, sells car seats, strollers, and children's furniture, including hard-to-find brands and models.
- **Thinker Toys**, 7784 SW Capitol Hwy, 503-245-3936, www.thinkertoysoregon.

com, in Multnomah Village, sells a large selection of toys, games, and kits for preschoolers to high schoolers.
- **Toys in Style,** 7283 SW Garden Home Rd, 503-977-1555, www.toysinstyleus. com, sells only German toys (primarily wooden toys).

MUSIC

The quality and range of music sellers in Portland is truly astounding. In addition to the standard assortment of mall chain stores, big-box retailers, and book/record/DVD purveyors such as Borders, there are more than 25 independent record and CD shops in the city of Portland alone. Southeast Hawthorne Boulevard boasts the largest concentration of these shops, but every Eastside neighborhood seems to have at least one claustrophobic but much-loved used record store. Many of Portland's indie record shops specialize in specific genres—punk is a particular favorite—while others practically define the word eclectic; virtually any music store in the city is worth a browse.

PARTY SUPPLIES

Got balloons for that housewarming party? If not, check the Yellow Pages, or better yet, pay a visit to **Lippman Company**, 50 SE Yamhill St, 503-239-7007, www. lippmancompany.com. This festive establishment offers 12,000 square feet of pirate gear, balloons, and other party supplies in the Eastside Industrial District. Come for the helium tanks, stay for the practical joke selection.

PHOTO SUPPLIES AND PROCESSING

When your photo processing needs go beyond 35mm prints, **Blue Moon Camera and Machine**, 8417 N Lombard St, Portland, 503-978-0333, www.bluemoon camera.com, processes all kinds of arcane and rare film types. As a further gesture to iconoclasm, Blue Moon also sells refurbished manual typewriters.

RAINWEAR

At some point, you'll need good rainwear. You should be able to find something appropriate at any discount or full-service department store, at sporting goods stores (see **Sports and Recreation** for a list), or from mail order suppliers such as Land's End (www.landsend.com) or L.L. Bean (www.llbean.com). Or you might try one of the following sportswear retailers:

- **Columbia Sportswear**, 911 SW Broadway, 503-226-6800, www.columbia.com, is the company's downtown flagship store; also consider checking out Columbia Sportswear's outlet stores in Sellwood, Lake Oswego, and Woodburn Company Stores. (See "Outlet Malls" above.)
- **The North Face**, 1202 NW Davis St, 503-227-0200, www.thenorthface.com, has lots of high-end mountaineering gear, as well as a selection of jackets made from expensive waterproof/breathable fabrics.
- **Patagonia**, 907 NW Irving St, 503-525-2552, www.patagonia.com, has pricey, nicely made activewear, including rainwear.

ODD AND HARD-TO-FIND GOODS AND SERVICES

Angie's List (see discussion under Domestic Services in the **Helpful Services** chapter) is always a useful resource.

DIAPER SERVICE

Unless you want to wash 'em youself, **Tidee Didee** (503-777-3856 [Portland], 360-694-9456 [Vancouver], www.tideedidee.com) is the only game in town for handling non-disposable diapers.

FURNITURE RESTORATION AND REPAIR

Did you unpack the moving truck only to find that it was a bad idea to pack your unpadded "claw" sculpture next to that Stickley dresser? Portland has many furniture hospitals, most of which are listed in the Yellow Pages under "Furniture-Repair and Refinish."

E VEN IN FAMILIAR SURROUNDINGS, FINDING QUALITY CHILDCARE and good schools is one of the most challenging and overwhelming tasks parents face, and a move to a new area compounds the difficulty. With time and effort, however, it is usually possible to find a good situation for your child, whether it is in-home or on-site daycare, a nanny, an after-school program, or a good public or private school. The keys, of course, are research and persistence, and perhaps a bit of luck. Keep in mind that even institutions with the best reputations may not be suited to your child's individual needs. Get comfy with the phone book and the web, and prepare to talk with other parents.

CHILDCARE

Probably the best way to find a good childcare provider is by referral from someone you know and trust. As a newcomer, however, you may not have such resources at your disposal. A good place to start your research is the **Oregon Child Care Resource and Referral Network** (www.OregonChildCare.org), a network of local referral agencies that can help you find and select childcare providers. You can search online for providers in your area, or contact your local referral agency directly for assistance. (Call 503-548-4400 in Multnomah County, 971-223-6100 in Washington County, or 503-675-4100 in Clackamas County.) The Network's web site also offers a helpful checklist for choosing quality care. In Clark County, **Child Care Resource and Referral of Southwest Washington** (360-750-9735, www.esd112.org/ccrr/) offers similar services.

In Oregon, the **Oregon Employment Department, Child Care Division** (www.oregon.gov/EMPLOY/CCD/) regulates childcare providers. There are several options for care, and each is subject to different regulations. A **child care center** is a facility other than a private home that provides care for more than 13 children; such centers must be state-certified, are subject to mandated adult-child ratios, and must offer a program of age-appropriate activities. A **certified family child care home**, which is subject to similar requirements, is a facility in the provider's family residence that provides care for a maximum of 12 children (including the provider's children). Family child care homes that care for no more than 10 children (including the provider's children) need only be licensed with the state; certification is not required.

A wide range of small-scale child care providers are exempt from licensing requirements, including providers who care for no more than three children (in addition to the provider's own children), nannies and others who provide care in a child's home, and caregivers who provide care on an occasional basis only or who are related to the child. Programs run by government agencies are also exempt, as are preschools (i.e., facilities that offer an educational curriculum for children from three years old through kindergarten-age) that provide care for less than four hours per day. To check on the licensing status of a childcare provider or find out about complaints, call the Child Care Division's hotline at 800-556-6616.

Washington requires virtually anyone who is paid to care for children on a regular basis to be licensed (unless the children are related to the caregiver). The **Washington Department of Early Learning** (www.del.wa.gov) regulates child-care providers in that state. To check the license status and complaint history of a childcare provider, visit the department's web site or call 866-482-4325.

In addition to the required state certifications, you may want to look for childcare centers that are accredited by third-party organizations like the **National Academy of Early Childhood Programs** (NAEYC), www.naeyc.org.

WHAT TO LOOK FOR IN CHILDCARE

When searching for the best place for your child, be sure to visit prospective providers—and make an appointment. A security-conscious caregiver should not let a random stranger on the premises unannounced; a staff member should accompany you at all times. In general, look for a safe and clean environment and a caring attitude. Are areas that children use child-proofed? Are the kitchen, toys, and furniture clean and safe? Are outdoor play areas fenced and free of hazards? Observe other kids at the facility. Do they seem happy? Are they well behaved? Is the adult-child ratio acceptable? Ask for the telephone numbers of parents who use the service and talk to them. It's a good idea to request a daily schedule—look for both active and quiet time, and age-appropriate activities. Keep in mind that wet Portland winters don't allow for daily outdoor play. Is there an adequate covered space for active play in winter? Does the facility have adequate insurance? Finally, keep in mind that a license does not necessarily guarantee quality childcare. It is your responsibility as a parent to make sure that the caregiver delivers the standard of care you expect.

NANNIES AND AU PAIRS

NANNIES

Hiring a nanny is generally the most expensive childcare option, but under the right circumstances it can be a very rewarding arrangement for everyone involved. In the Portland area you can expect to pay at least $400 a week for a full-time nanny—more (and sometimes much more) for a nanny with more experience or who will be expected to care for multiple children or do housework.

Several agencies help match nannies with families. While these services tend to charge significant placement fees, many agencies perform background checks or psychological testing (for the nanny, not you) during the applicant screening process. Nannies are not state-licensed, and screening processes vary, so you may want to ask each agency about its specific screening criteria. Most agencies can also help with temporary childcare needs. Local nanny placement agencies include:

- **A Brilliant Nanny**, 7409 SW Capitol Hwy, 503-459-4055, www.abnanny.com
- **Auntie Fay Agency**, 10725 SW Barbur Blvd, Suite 60, 503-293-6252
- **Care Givers**, 503-244-6370, www.cgpa.com
- **Karoline's Nannies**, Hillsboro, 503-649-1908, www.karolinesnannies.com
- **Northwest Nannies**, 11830 SW Kerr Pkwy, Suite 330, Lake Oswego, 503-245-5288, www.nwnanny.com

If you are contracting directly with your nanny for his or her services, rather than going through an agency, you'll have to get an employer identification number from the IRS and pay certain taxes, including social security, Medicare, and possibly unemployment insurance tax, and you'll have to withhold income tax—unless of course you're planning on being nominated for a high-profile federal job and would like a good scandal to torpedo your nomination, in which case by all means neglect to pay taxes for your nanny. You'll also need to carry workers' compensation, which you may be able to purchase through your homeowner's or automobile insurance provider. For assistance with taxes for childcare providers, contact **HomeWork Solutions** (800-626-4829, www.nanitax.com) or **GTM Associates** (888-432-7972, www.4easypay.com).

Be sure to check references before hiring a nanny. Although most agencies run background checks, if you're not using an agency or if you simply want a second opinion, several companies can perform pre-employment screening. Look in the Yellow Pages under "Employment Screening" or "Background Screening," or type "employment screening" into your search engine for links.

AU PAIRS

Au pairs are young adults, usually college-age women, visiting the United States with a special visa status that allows them to provide childcare and light housekeeping in exchange for room and board, international airfare, and a weekly stipend. The host family benefits from cultural exchange as well as relatively in-expensive childcare, but the placement usually only lasts one year and an au pair might not offer the same level of maturity and experience as a career nanny. Keep in mind that the au pair will be in a foreign country and will be interested in traveling and meeting people her age, but may not have fully considered how restricted her free time will be. At the same time, many parents have unre-alistic expectations of their au pair, and assume that she will be a combination nanny, babysitter, and full-time housekeeper, with few outside interests or social engagements. That said, the au pair arrangement can be a great experience for those families and au pairs who understand the trade-offs of the system and have the same expectations for their year together.

The US State Department's **Bureau of Educational and Cultural Affairs** (202-203-5096, www.exchanges.state.gov/education) regulates au pair place-ment agencies. The following national au pair agencies will connect you with a local placement coordinator:

- **Au Pair in America**, 800-928-7247, www.aupairinamerica.com
- **AuPairCare**, 800-428-7247, www.aupaircare.com
- **Au Pair USA/InterExchange**, 800-287-2477, www.aupairusa.org
- **Cultural Care Au Pair**, 800-333-6056, www.efaupair.org
- **EurAuPair**, 800-713-2002, www.euraupair.com

SCHOOL-AGE PROGRAMS

Many organizations offer care to school-aged children before and/or after school hours and during school vacations. In many cases, care is provided on-site at an elementary school, or at a nearby location to which children are transported by bus after school. Check with your child's school for convenient options. Note that school-age programs that are operated by a public school or other government agency are exempt from state certification requirements (but the programs may choose to be certified anyway).

SCHOOLS

There are hundreds of public and private schools in the Portland area, and choosing the right one for your child can be a complicated and time-consuming task. While the public school systems in Portland and in many of the surrounding communities rely primarily on neighborhood-based schools (i.e., schools that draw from a set attendance area), they also offer a growing number of magnet programs and specialty schools; add transfer options, private schools, and charter schools into the mix and the range of options is dizzying. Fortunately, there are some sources that can help with your initial search.

The **Oregon Department of Education** is responsible for statewide curriculum, instructional, and assessment testing programs. The department issues an annual statewide report card that covers every public school in the state. The annual report cards are available from the Department's web site (www.ode. state.or.us), which also offers a tremendous amount of additional information about public education in Oregon. In Washington, the office of the **Washington Superintendent of Public Instruction** (www.k12.wa.us) plays a similar role and issues report cards for schools in that state.

The **Chalkboard Project** (www.chalkboardproject.org) is another good source of information about Oregon public schools. This organization is involved in a side project, the **Open Books Project** (www.openbooksproject.org), which allows parents—and others—to track how educational funding dollars are spent in Oregon; the web site provides information about statewide educational spending and spending by district, and allows for district-by-district comparisons.

Other sources for gathering specific information about schools include **Great Schools** (www.greatschools.net), a nonprofit organization dedicated to providing clear and objective information about local schools; the **National Center for Educational Statistics** (www.nces.gov), a federal center that collects and analyzes information from states; and **SchoolMatters** (www.schoolmatters. com), a service of the Standard & Poor's company. Information on private schools is notoriously hard to come by; they are not subject to state curriculum requirements, and do not have to release certain information (such as standardized test scores or teacher credentials) that public schools are required to disclose.

When researching schools, bear in mind that statistics and summary progress assessments paint a picture that is at best incomplete. While objective measures may help support or guide your decision, there is really only one way to choose a school, public or private, that is right for your child: visit.

When visiting a school, pay attention to your gut reaction. Ask yourself these questions:

- Am I comfortable here? Will my child be comfortable here?
- Does the school feel safe? Are the bathrooms clean and free of graffiti?
- Do the students seem to be engaged? Is student work on display?
- Are classrooms crowded? (Class sizes can vary enormously from school to school.) Do teachers appear to be overworked?
- Are adults present throughout the building and grounds?
- Are desks, instructional materials, and computers plentiful and up-to-date?
- Does the school offer academic and extracurricular opportunities for students to explore their own special interests, such as art, music, sports, or science?
- In an elementary school, pay attention to the way the children are moving around—are they interacting naturally, but staying on task? In a middle school

or high school, notice how students interact with each other and with teachers at the beginning and end of class, and in the halls.

- Ask elementary teachers about reading and math groups and find out if children move up as they build skills.
- Are parents encouraged to volunteer? To paraphrase JFK, ask not only what your school can do for your child, but what you can do for your child's school. The level of parent and community involvement in a school is one key to that school's success.

PUBLIC SCHOOLS

Public schools in the Northwest face many challenges, including rapid growth in districts on the urban fringe, declining enrollments in inner cities, and an increasingly diverse student population. In Oregon, a roller-coaster ride of inconsistent (and often inadequate) funding over the last decade or so has exacerbated these problems. As the *Oregon Blue Book*, the state's official government directory, succinctly puts it, "Oregon public school finance is unique and very complicated for several reasons." In a nutshell, mandatory property tax limits reduced local governments' ability to fund schools, and today about two-thirds of the money for public schools comes directly from the state. While state funding has helped reduce the disparity in resources between districts, it leaves school funding vulnerable to economic cycles and competing demands for limited revenue (despite a state constitutional amendment, passed in 2000, which requires the legislature to appropriate sufficient funds to allow schools to meet legally established quality goals). State funding also means that communities that place a high value on their schools have only a limited ability to increase support for those schools using local tax revenues.

The most recent funding crunch, during the recession of the early 2000s, led some districts to cut electives, increase class sizes, and (most infamously) lop several days off the school year to reduce costs. In response to this deterioration in school services, some parents placed their children in private schools or simply moved to more affluent school districts. Since those dark days, an improved economy—and in many districts, voter-approved property tax levies—have helped stabilize school funding. (Washington has not experienced a similar school funding crisis, although money is not exactly gushing into the state's public education coffers.)

Unlike in many states, school district boundaries in Oregon and Washington do not necessarily correspond to city or county boundaries. (Five different school districts serve the city of Portland, for example, and the Portland Public Schools district draws from both Multnomah County and a small portion of Washington County.)

Both Oregon and Washington have educational service districts (ESDs), which generally encompass multiple districts and which provide certain programs and services that are too costly or specialized for districts to provide on their own. Most parents don't deal directly with ESDs.

PORTLAND PUBLIC SCHOOLS

The Portland Public Schools district—the largest of five districts that encompass parts of the city of Portland, and the most populous school district in the state—serves 46,000 students. Although enrollment is declining, Portland is one of the few large cities in America in which the middle class has not largely abandoned the public schools, and close to 85% of Portland children attend public school. To be sure, some schools are far stronger than others, with state report card ratings running the gamut from "low" to "exceptional," but some Portland schools are among the best in the state, and overall test scores are improving.

Portland Public Schools is emerging from a time of great uncertainty—not merely financial turmoil, but controversy over the direction of the city's public schools. Former Superintendent Vicki Phillips, who left in mid-2007 to join the Gates Foundation, tackled thorny issues, stirring up controversy and vocal opposition along with community support. She attempted to reform and streamline the district's operations and to place the district on sounder financial footing. Because of changing demographics and dropping enrollments district-wide, she closed a half-dozen schools (and tried to close several more), including several small, high-performing elementary schools in affluent neighborhoods. She pushed for a new core curriculum, bringing new textbooks and classroom materials to teachers and students, but also bringing accusations of top-down standardization. At the same time, some parents with children in lower-achieving schools worry about the district's plans, or lack thereof, for improving those schools. On the plus side, the wave of school closures is complete for the time being, and in 2006 voters overwhelmingly (with a majority of 63%) supported a local property tax measure that promises stable school budgets for five years. However, guiding a large urban school district inevitably involves controversy, and the next superintendent (who has not yet been selected as of press time) will not have an easy ride.

The school district web site (www.pps.k12.or.us) includes a great deal of information about individual schools (click on "schools" in the left column) and about school choices, with a handy look-up function to find the neighborhood school for a specific address. (Your child is guaranteed a spot at your neighborhood school.) The Enrollment and Transfer Center is also a great resource; send an email to enrollment-office@pps.k12.or.us or call 503-916-3205.

REGISTRATION

To register your child, go to your assigned neighborhood school. (Keep in mind that the school that is closest or most convenient to your residence may not necessarily be your neighborhood school.) Call first to make sure the staff member you need to see will be available, and bring the following documents:

- A completed Student Registration form, available in hard copy from the school or online at www.pps.k12.or.us/news-c/student_registration_form.php.
- Proof of the student's age (e.g., a birth certificate or passport). Children who are five years or older by September 1 may enroll in kindergarten.
- Records of immunization for diphtheria, tetanus, hepatitis B, chicken pox, polio, hemophilus influenza type B (HiB), mumps, measles, and rubella, unless you are seeking an exemption for religious or medical reasons.
- Proof of residence: You must provide two or more recent documents showing your name and current home address, such as utility bills, credit card bills, a rental agreement, or the deed to your home.
- The name and contact information for any previous school your child attended outside the Portland Public Schools district.

You can register at any time, but it is better for everyone (including your child) if you register as early as possible. Most schools hold informational meetings and provide tours for prospective parents during the winter months.

TRANSFERS

If you would prefer that your child attend a school other than your neighborhood school, you can apply for a transfer. Transfer applications are due in late winter. Popular schools generally have more transfer applications than open slots, and applicants are selected by lottery in the spring; in 2007, more than three-quarters of applicants got into one of their top choices. A few schools, particularly those with new and expanding programs, including language immersion programs, may have spaces available in select grades until late August. (Be aware that, as a newcomer and given the timetable for transfer requests, your child will likely have to attend your neighborhood school initially unless he or she is not yet school age.) For details about the transfer process, visit www.schoolchoice.pps.k12.or.us or call the Enrollment and Transfer Center at 503-916-3205.

MAGNET SCHOOLS AND LANGUAGE IMMERSION PROGRAMS

Portland has several magnet schools that concentrate on arts, math and science, or other disciplines; contact the school district for specifics. In addition, language immersion programs are available in Spanish, Russian, Japanese, and Mandarin

Chinese. (The Mandarin kindergarten-to-college immersion program, which begins at Woodstock Elementary School and continues at Hosford Middle School and Cleveland High School, is the only one of its kind in the United States.) For more information, contact the Portland Public Schools Immersion Coordinator at 503-916-5404 x 1044.

SUBURBAN DISTRICT SCHOOLS

The suburban districts in the Portland area defy generalization. Some are huge, with thousands of students, and others are tiny; some have sparkling new facilities and adequate budgets, others have frankly decrepit buildings and are struggling financially; some have some of the highest test scores and graduation rates in the state or country, and others—well, not so much. In fact, school conditions and academic performance can vary dramatically not only between but within districts, so research is in order.

Registration procedures are fairly uniform throughout the Portland area—go to the appropriate school and present an enrollment form, proof of residence, immunization records, proof of the child's age, and prior school contact information. Contact your school district for specific enrollment requirements and information.

The following are the main school districts in the four-county metropolitan area:

OREGON

Beaverton School District
16650 SW Merlo Rd
Beaverton, OR 97006
503-591-8000
www.beaverton.k12.or.us

The Beaverton School District, the third-largest in the state, educates nearly 38,000 students from the city of Beaverton, part of Tigard, and many of the surrounding unincorporated areas of Washington County (and a tiny portion of Multnomah County). The district as a whole has a very good reputation—its overall academic performance is among the best of the state's large school districts—although some schools are much better than others. The district has a wide range of "option" schools, including the International School (currently limited to grades 6–10, but expanding to 6–12 by fall 2009), a candidate school for the International Baccalaureate program; the Arts & Communication Magnet Academy for grades 6 through 12, which claims to be the only stand-alone arts magnet school in Oregon; and a new Health & Science High School, which opened in Fall 2007 for ninth graders only—it will add a grade each year until the school includes grades 9 through 12—and which follows the "Expeditionary Learning" model.

Canby School District
1130 S Ivy St
Canby, OR 97013
503-266-7861
www.canby.k12.or.us

The Canby School District has 5,300 students in Canby and in much of the surrounding (primarily rural) area, including the Charbonneau District of Wilsonville.

Centennial School District
18135 SE Brooklyn St
Portland, OR 97236
503-760-7990
www.centennial.k12.or.us

This jurisdiction-busting district containing about ten schools serves outer Southeast Portland, western Gresham, and portions of unincorporated Multnomah and Clackamas counties.

Corbett School District
35800 E Historic Columbia River Hwy
Corbett, OR 97019
503-695-3600
www.corbett.k12.or.us

This tiny, three-school district—one elementary, one middle, and one high school—in eastern Multnomah County has one of the best high schools in the state, with a literally unbeatable 100% graduation rate.

David Douglas School District
1500 SE 130th Ave
Portland, OR 97233
503-252-2900
www.ddouglas.k12.or.us

The David Douglas School District serves nearly 10,000 students in a large swath of East Portland (east of Interstate 205 and west of the Centennial School District). Much of this part of the city is experiencing significant immigration from Mexico, Eastern Europe, and Southeast Asia, and district enrollment is growing at a rapid rate. More than one-quarter of students are English language learners.

Forest Grove School District

1728 Main St
Forest Grove, OR 97116
503-357-6171
www.fgsd.k12.or.us

Forest Grove School District covers the city of Forest Grove, part of the adjacent city of Cornelius, and nearby unincorporated areas.

Gladstone School District

17789 Webster Rd
Gladstone, OR 97027
503-655-2777
www.gladstone.k12.or.us

The Gladstone School District largely (but not entirely) corresponds with the boundaries of the city of Gladstone. With one elementary, one middle, and one high school (which has only 800 students), this is one of the smallest suburban districts.

Gresham-Barlow School District

1331 NW Eastman Pkwy
Gresham, OR 97030
503-618-2450
www.gresham.k12.or.us

The Gresham-Barlow school district serves a socioeconomically and ethnically diverse student population in much (but not all) of Gresham and the new city of Damascus. The district has more than 12,000 students in 20 schools (including one charter school); performance varies from school to school.

Hillsboro School District

3083 NE 49th Pl
Hillsboro, OR 97124
503-844-1500
www.hsd.k12.or.us

The fourth-largest district in Oregon, Hillsboro School District educates nearly 20,000 students in much of western Washington County; in addition to the city of Hillsboro, the district includes all or part of North Plains, Cornelius, and unincorporated areas from Aloha south to the edge of Sherwood. There are 23 elementary schools, four middle schools, and four high schools (as well as two alternative schools). As one might expect, school performance and offerings vary substantially within the district. Hillsboro High has an International Baccalaureate program.

Lake Oswego School District
2455 Country Club Rd, PO Box 70
Lake Oswego, OR 97034
503-534-2000
www.loswego.k12.or.us

This well-funded, sought-after district includes nine elementary schools, two junior high schools, and two high schools. The district boasts some of the highest test scores and high school graduation rates in the state.

North Clackamas School District
4444 SE Lake Rd
Milwaukie, OR 97222
503-353-6000
www.nclack.k12.or.us

North Clackamas School District extends from Milwaukie and Oak Grove in the west to Happy Valley and Sunnyside in the east. Schools within the district vary in quality, from excellent to mediocre at best.

Oregon City School District
1417 12th St
Oregon City, OR 97045
503-785-8000
www.orecity.k12.or.us

This sprawling district encompasses Oregon City and large sections of unincorporated Clackamas County, including Jennings Lodge, Beavercreek, and Redland. Oregon City High School, with more than 2,000 students, is one of the largest high schools in the state.

Parkrose School District
10636 NE Prescott St
Portland, OR 97220
503-408-2100
www.parkrose.k12.or.us

The Parkrose School District can trace its origins to the 1880s. Today, it serves a smallish area of Northeast Portland, primarily east of Interstate 205, with four elementary schools, a middle school, and a high school.

Reynolds School District
1204 NE 201st Ave
Fairview, OR 97024
503-661-7200
www.reynolds.k12.or.us

Reynolds School District serves the east Multnomah County cities of Fairview, Troutdale, and Wood Village, as well as portions of outer Northeast Portland and northern Gresham.

Riverdale School District
11733 SW Breyman Ave
Portland, OR 97219
503-636-8611
www.riverdale.k12.or.us

Riverdale School District serves perhaps the most affluent area in Oregon, and test scores, graduation rates, and college attendance prospects are correspondingly high. Riverdale Grade School serves students in kindergarten through eighth grade; older students attend Riverdale High School, located near Lewis and Clark College in Portland.

Sherwood School District
23295 SW Main St
Sherwood, OR 97140
503-625-8100
www.sherwood.k12.or.us

This generally well-regarded school district in southwestern Washington County has three elementary schools (and a charter school), one middle school, and one high school.

Tigard-Tualatin School District
6960 SW Sandburg St
Tigard, OR 97223
503-431-4000
www.ttsd.k12.or.us

Tigard-Tualatin School District, which covers most of the cities of Tigard and Tualatin, as well as the surrounding communities of Durham, Bull Mountain, and Metzger, is one of the most sought-after districts in the state. Average student performance, school ratings, and test scores are generally high throughout the district. Both of the district's high schools—Tigard High School and Tualatin High School—offer International Baccalaureate courses.

West Linn–Wilsonville School District
22210 SW Stafford Rd, PO Box 35
West Linn, OR 97068
503-673-7000
www.wlwv.k12.us

The West Linn–Wilsonville School District covers the two non-adjacent cities of West Linn and (most of) Wilsonville, as well as the unincorporated areas that lie between them. This well-regarded district has seven elementary schools, three middle schools (two in West Linn and one in Wilsonville), and a high school in each city, along with a grades 4–8 charter school and the Arts & Technology Charter High School.

WASHINGTON

Battle Ground Public Schools
PO Box 200
Battle Ground, WA 98604
360-885-5300
www.bgsd.k12.wa.us

Battle Ground Public Schools has 11,000 students in Battle Ground and the surrounding unincorporated areas of Clark County, including parts of Brush Prairie, Amboy, and Yacolt.

Camas School District
1919 NE Ione St
Camas, WA 98607
360-833-5400
www.camas.wednet.edu

The growing Camas School District, one of the most sought-after districts in Southwest Washington, serves the city of Camas and part of unincorporated Clark County. The district has five elementary schools, one middle school, and a new high-tech high school; another middle school is being developed on the site of the old high school.

Evergreen Public Schools
13501 NE 28th St
Vancouver, WA 98668
360-604-4000
www.egreen.wednet.edu

The generally well-regarded Evergreen Public Schools system serves the eastern half of Vancouver and much of nearby unincorporated Clark County. Mountain View High and Evergreen High each offer more than 20 Advanced Placement classes (one of the highest totals in the metropolitan area).

Hockinson School District
17912 NE 159th Ave
Brush Prairie, WA 98606
360-448-6400
www.hockk12.wa.us

This largely rural district includes most of Brush Prairie and parts of the surrounding areas of unincorporated Clark County.

Vancouver School District
2901 Falk Rd
Vancouver, WA 98661
360-313-1000
www.vansd.org

The Vancouver School District educates more than 22,000 children in the western half of the city of Vancouver and a large chunk of unincorporated Clark County. The district has several magnet schools, including the Vancouver School of Arts & Academics, which boasts a 99% graduation rate.

PRIVATE AND PAROCHIAL SCHOOLS

The Portland area is home to many excellent private and parochial schools. The following are some of the better known (but by no means the only) private schools in the region.

- **Catlin Gabel School** (P–12), 8825 SW Barnes Rd, 503-297-1894, www.catlin.edu
- **Central Catholic High School** (9–12), 2401 SE Stark St, 503-235-3138, www.centralcatholichigh.org
- **French American International School** (P–8), 8500 NW Johnson St, 503-292-7776, www.faispdx.org
- **German American School of Portland** (P–5), 3900 SW Murray Blvd, Beaverton, 503-626-9089, www.gspdx.com
- **The International School** (P–5), 025 SW Sherman St, 503-226-2496, www.intlschool.org
- **Jesuit High School** (9–12), 9000 SW Beaverton-Hillsdale Hwy, 503-292-2663, www.jesuitportland.com
- **Northwest Academy** (6–12), 1130 SW Main St, 503-223-3367, www.nwacademy.org
- **Oregon Episcopal School** (P–12), 6300 SW Nicol Rd, 503-768-3115, www.oes.edu
- **Portland French School** (P–5), 6318 SW Corbett Ave, 503-452-4160, www.portlandfrenchschool.org
- **Portland Jewish Academy** (P–8), 6651 SW Capitol Hwy, 503-244-0126, www.portlandjewishacademy.org
- **Portland Waldorf School** (P–12), 2300 Harrison St, Milwaukie, 503-654-2200, www.portlandwaldorfschool.org
- **St. Mary's Academy** (9–12), 1615 SW 5th Ave, 503-228-8306, www.stmaryspdx.org

A complete list of nonpublic schools in Oregon is available from the **Oregon Department of Education** (www.ode.state.or.us), and in Washington from the Washington Superintendent of Public Instruction's **Office of Private Education** (www.k12.wa.us/PrivateEd/).

HOMESCHOOLING

Parents who have misgivings about public schools have the right to take their children's education into their own hands. Many parents believe that they are best qualified to design an educational program that will engage and challenge their children, responding to each child's unique psychological and intellectual traits. Homeschooling is especially popular among strongly religious parents who object to the secular nature of public schools, and among liberal parents who object to, among other things, public schools' increasing reliance on corporate sponsorship.

Teaching is not easy—you will need a lot of time and energy to plan and execute a study program that will enable your children to earn a high school diploma at home—but there are plenty of organizations and resources to help you. The **Oregon Home Education Network** (503-321-5166, www.ohen.org) and the **Washington Home Education Network** (www.homestead.com/wa homeednet/index.html) are good places to start.

CHARTER SCHOOLS

Many school districts in Oregon, including Portland, offer public charter schools—schools run autonomously, but with the approval of the local school board. Unlike most public schools, charter schools, which are bound by their own charter agreements, are free from some traditional school regulations. For more information about charter schools in Oregon, including a current list of charter schools, visit the **Oregon Department of Education** charter school page at www.ode.state.or.us/search/results/?id=124, or the Oregon School Boards Association's **Charter Resource Center** (www.osba.org/hotopics/charters/index.html).

Washington does not currently have a charter school law.

T HE PORTLAND METROPOLITAN AREA IS HOME TO MORE THAN A dozen colleges and universities, five community college systems, and a dazzling number of specialized degree-granting (and non–degree granting) institutions.

Oregon's 16 accredited, not-for-profit private colleges and universities belong to the **Oregon Independent Colleges Association**; the association's web site (www.oicanet.org) includes school profiles and general information about attending a private college. Of the seven institutions that constitute the public **Oregon University System** (www.ous.edu), only one—Portland State University—is based in Portland. (Oregon Health & Science University [OHSU], also in Portland, is an OUS affiliate.) The system's flagship campuses, University of Oregon (in Eugene) and Oregon State University (in Corvallis), while not within reasonable commuting distance of Portland, have tens of thousands of alumni in the area and offer lectures, professional courses, and extension courses through local satellite centers (503-725-8598, pdx.uoregon.edu, and 541-737-1000, oregonstate.edu/dept/pdx/, respectively). **Washington State University** has a campus in Vancouver. Addresses below are in Oregon unless otherwise noted.

REDUCED OUT-OF-STATE TUITION OPTIONS

Unlike some states, Oregon and Washington do not have a full reciprocity agreement that allows residents of one state to attend public colleges or universities in the other state at a reduced tuition rate. However, residents of certain "border" counties in Oregon (including Multnomah, Washington, Clackamas, and Columbia counties) are eligible to pay resident tuition rates at Washington State University–Vancouver for course loads of eight credits or less. Similarly, residents of "border" counties in Washington (including Clark County) are eligible to pay resident tuition at Portland State University (for course loads of eight credits or less) and at OHSU's undergraduate program in nursing. Residents of either state qualify for resident tuition status at the other state's community colleges.

The **Western Interstate Commission for Higher Education** (WICHE) manages student exchange programs for 15 western states, including Washington and Oregon. Washington and Oregon residents may qualify for resident or reduced nonresident tuition at certain programs in certain institutions in other WICHE states. A complete description of the various exchange programs and their (fairly complex) rules is available on the WICHE web site (www.wiche.edu/sep).

SAVING FOR COLLEGE

Oregon taxpayers who have pre–college-age children may be interested in Oregon's 529 college savings plans. These plans allow individuals to open special accounts to invest for college; earnings are exempt from state and federal tax, as are withdrawals for qualified educational purposes (tuition, room and board, supplies, etc.). Money in a 529 plan can be used at practically any college or university in the country, not just at Oregon institutions. In addition, Oregon taxpayers may deduct up to $2,000 per year on their state income tax return for contributions to an Oregon 529 plan. (Note that this deduction is also available to Washington residents who work in Oregon and pay Oregon income taxes.) Further information is available from the **Oregon 529 College Savings Network** (www.oregon529network.com).

Washington does not have a college savings plan, but it does have a **Guaranteed Education Tuition** program (www.get.wa.gov), which is essentially a tax-advantaged prepaid tuition plan. Washington residents (and Oregon residents) are generally eligible to contribute to 529 plans run by other states. For more information on other states' 529 plans, visit www.savingforcollege.com or www.collegesavings.org.

PORTLAND-AREA UNIVERSITIES AND COLLEGES

- **Concordia University**, 2811 NE Holman St, Portland, 97211, 503-288-9371, 800-321-9371, www.cu-portland.edu; a private Lutheran college, Concordia University, part of the national Concordia University System, offers degrees in arts and sciences, education, management, and theology. Enrollment: about 1,500.
- **George Fox University**, 414 N Meridian St, Newberg, 97132, 503-538-8383, www.georgefox.edu; founded by Quakers in 1891, this private Christian university offers more than 50 undergraduate, graduate, and seminary degree programs at its residential campus in Newberg (southwest of Portland) and at satellite campuses in Portland, Salem, Redmond (Central Oregon), and Boise, Idaho. Enrollment: about 3,000.

- **Lewis and Clark College**, 0615 SW Palatine Hill Rd, Portland, 97219, 503-768-7000, www.lclark.edu; this private liberal arts college with an excellent national reputation occupies a rolling, wooded campus in the hills of Southwest Portland. In addition to its College of Arts and Sciences, Lewis and Clark is home to a Graduate School of Education and Counseling and to one of Oregon's three law schools. Enrollment: about 3,400.
- **Linfield College**, 900 SE Baker St, McMinnville, 97128, 503-883-2200, www.linfield.edu; a Baptist liberal arts college, Linfield is located in the small city of McMinnville, about 45 minutes southwest of Portland. Enrollment: about 1,750.
- **Marylhurst University**, 17600 Pacific Hwy (Hwy 43), Marylhurst, 97036, 503-636-8141, 800-634-9982, www.marylhurst.edu; this coeducational Catholic university in Portland's southern suburbs (between Lake Oswego and West Linn) serves working adults who want to earn an undergraduate or graduate degree or professional certification but require a flexible timetable. Marylhurst is known for its small class sizes, generous credits for life experience, and distance learning options. Enrollment: about 1,250.
- **Oregon Health & Science University**, 3181 SW Sam Jackson Park Rd, Portland, 97239, 503-494-8311, www.ohsu.edu; this gleaming complex of hospitals, research laboratories, clinics, and classrooms perches atop Marquam Hill south of downtown Portland, and is one of the city's most recognizable landmarks (especially at night, when it blazes with light). OHSU comprises medical, dental, and nursing schools, as well as the Oregon Graduate Institute, a science and engineering graduate school located on a separate campus in Beaverton. Enrollment: about 2,400.
- **Pacific Northwest College of Art**, 1241 NW Johnson St, Portland, 97209, 503-226-4391, www.pnca.edu; located in the heart of the trendy Pearl District, PNCA offers B.F.A. degrees in several art-related majors, including painting, photography, and communication design; an M.F.A. program is scheduled to begin in fall 2007. Enrollment: about 300.
- **Pacific University**, 2043 College Way, Forest Grove, 97116, 503-352-6151, 877-PAC-UNIV, www.pacificu.edu; Pacific University, one of the state's oldest post-secondary institutions, has an extensive campus in the western suburb of Forest Grove. The school offers degrees in more than 50 undergraduate majors, as well as graduate degrees in education, optometry, pharmacy, and several other disciplines. Enrollment: about 2,500.
- **Portland State University**, P.O. Box 751, Portland, 97201, 503-725-3000, 800-547-8887, www.pdx.edu; PSU, which anchors the southern end of downtown Portland's Park Blocks, boasts the largest overall college or university enrollment in Oregon. Largely a commuter school, PSU offers well over 100 undergraduate and graduate programs at several different schools and colleges, ranging from the College of Liberal Arts and Sciences to the nationally known College of Urban and Public Affairs. PSU also offers extension and continuing

education classes to the community at large. Enrollment: about 24,000.

- **Reed College,** 3203 SE Woodstock Blvd, Portland, 97202, 503-771-1112, www. reed.edu; Reed, regarded as one of the top liberal arts colleges in the country, has a reputation for both academic rigor and social permissiveness. (Some locals refer to Reed, perhaps enviously, as a 4.0 party school.) The school occupies a lovely residential campus, complete with canyon and ivy-clad brick buildings, in Southeast Portland. Enrollment: about 1,300.

- **University of Portland,** 5000 N Willamette Blvd, Portland, 97203, 503-943-7911, www.up.edu; this large Catholic institution, which sits atop a bluff overlooking the Willamette River in North Portland, is consistently ranked among the top regional universities in the West. In addition to its College of Arts & Sciences, which offers dozens of possible undergraduate and graduate degrees, the university has schools of nursing, education, engineering, and business administration. Enrollment: about 3,200.

- **Warner Pacific College,** 2219 SE 68th Ave, Portland, 97215, 503-517-1000, 800-804-1510, www.warnerpacific.edu; this small Christian liberal arts college is located on the south slope of Mount Tabor in Southeast Portland; Warner Pacific also offers a master's program in management and organizational leadership. Enrollment: about 660.

- **Washington State University–Vancouver,** 14204 NE Salmon Creek Ave, Vancouver, WA 98686, 360-546-WSUV, www.vancouver.wsu.edu; this young, relatively small branch of the state's land grant university offers 14 different undergraduate degrees and 10 graduate degrees; it occupies a sprawling new campus in outer northeast Vancouver. Enrollment: about 2,300.

- **Willamette University,** 900 State St, Salem, 97301, 503-370-6300, www.willamette.edu; founded in 1842 (and thus the oldest college in the western United States), Willamette is located in Salem, about an hour south of Portland; although primarily a liberal arts college, it has graduate schools of management and education and is home to one of Oregon's three law schools. Enrollment: about 2,600.

AREA COMMUNITY COLLEGES

These community colleges offer two-year degrees and collectively serve tens of thousands of students in the Portland region. They also offer a wide range of adult education and special-interest courses to local residents.

- **Chemeketa Community College,** Salem, 503-399-5000, www.chemeketa. edu, is the community college for Salem and the mid-Willamette Valley (including Marion County and much of Yamhill County).

- **Clackamas Community College,** Oregon City, 503-657-6958, www.clackamas. cc.or.us, serves most of the populated portions of Clackamas County (except Lake Oswego, Boring, Damascus, and Sandy); there are satellite campuses in Harmony (Clackamas Town Center) and Wilsonville, and extension classes are offered in Canby, Estacada and Molalla.

- **Clark College,** Vancouver, 360-699-NEXT, www.clark.edu, serves Vancouver and Clark County, Washington; the main campus is near downtown Vancouver, and some classes are held at WSU-Vancouver.
- **Mt. Hood Community College,** Gresham, 503-491-6422, www.mhcc.edu, has a vast district that covers eastern Multnomah County (including outer Northeast Portland) and parts of Clackamas County from Damascus and Boring to the summit of Mount Hood; the main campus in Gresham has a satellite in Northeast Portland.
- **Portland Community College,** Portland, 503-244-6111, www.pcc.edu, serves Lake Oswego, most of the city of Portland, all of Washington County, and parts of Columbia and Yamhill counties; the three main campuses are Cascade (in North Portland), Rock Creek (off the Sunset Highway in the western suburbs near Hillsboro), and Sylvania (in outer Southwest Portland), and additional centers are located in Southeast Portland, Northeast Portland, Aloha, and Hillsboro. Community education classes take place at dozens of sites around the area.

OTHER DEGREE-GRANTING INSTITUTIONS

The Portland area supports dozens of other institutions of higher or continuing education. Some of these institutions, like Western Culinary Institute (www.wci.edu) and the National College of Natural Medicine (www.ncnm.edu), offer specialized instruction in specific disciplines; others are run by national for-profit corporations and focus on career or business education. You can find a complete list of approved degree-granting programs in Oregon on the web site of the state Student Assistance Commission's **Office of Degree Authorization** (www.ossc.state.or.us/oda). A similar list for Washington is available from that state's **Higher Education Coordinating Board** (www.hecb.wa.gov/autheval).

THE OCTOBER 2006 ISSUE OF *DOG FANCY* RANKED PORTLAND AS THE best all-around city for dogs in the United States. With Portland's human-to-dog ratio reportedly approaching four to one, there is a corresponding boom in dog-friendly events and businesses. A **Doggie Dash** run (www.dog giedashportland.com) is held each May, canine day care centers seem to be springing up on every other block, and the three **Lucky Labrador Brewing Company** pubs (www.luckylab.com) welcome dogs at their outdoor tables. (Cats are at least as popular as dogs in Portland, but being more self-sufficient and less gregarious, they require fewer public amenities.) In short, Portland's a great city for pet-lovers, but you'll have to find another home for your gorilla, lion, bear, anaconda, etc.—dangerous or exotic pets are illegal in Portland and Multnomah County.

PET LICENSES

In Multnomah County (which includes the city of Portland), both dogs and cats must be licensed within 30 days of becoming "resident" in the county. To license your pet, you'll need to pay a fee, which varies depending on the duration of the license, the type of animal, and whether it has been spayed or neutered; one-year licenses range from $4 to $30. You'll also need to provide proof that your pet has a current rabies vaccination. Licenses are available from veterinary clinics or directly from **Multnomah County Animal Services** (MCAS; 503-988-7387, www.co.multnomah.or.us/dbcs/pets/Licensing.shtml). Newcomers to the county can get a free 60-day "starter" license online at the MCAS web site.

Pet licensing requirements across the Columbia River are similar. Licenses are required for dogs, cats, and wild animals that are kept in Vancouver, Yacolt, or unincorporated Clark County. License information and applications are available from **Clark County Animal Protection and Control** (1300 Franklin St, Third Floor, Vancouver, WA, 360-397-2488, www.clark.wa.gov/animal/licensing/index.

html). Most other incorporated areas in Clark County, including Camas, require municipal licenses for dogs; check with your city hall for specific requirements.

In Clackamas, Columbia, Marion, Yamhill, and Washington counties, in Oregon, licenses are required for dogs only. Generally, as in Multnomah and Clark counties, fees vary depending on whether the pet is sterile or fertile, and you must provide evidence of rabies vaccination.

- **Clackamas County Dog Services**, 2104 Kaen Rd, Oregon City, 503-655-8628, www.co.clackamas.or.us/dc/contact/license.htm
- **Columbia County Clerk, Dog License Division**, 230 Strand St, St. Helens, 503-397-3796, www.co.columbia.or.us/clerk/clerk.m.asp
- **Marion County Dog Control**, 3550 Aumsville Hwy SE, Salem, 503-566-6966, www.mcdogs.net
- **Washington County Animal Services**, 1901 SE 24th Ave, Hillsboro, 503-846-7041, www.co.washington.or.us/deptmts/at/dog/services/licensing.htm
- **Yamhill County Dog Control**, Yamhill County Fairgrounds, 2070 Lafayette Ave, McMinnville, 503-434-7538, www.co.yamhill.or.us/sheriff/index.asp?sel=dog_control

VETERINARY CARE

Satisfied friends and neighbors are the best sources of veterinarian referrals. If you can't get a personal recommendation, look in the Yellow Pages, do an Internet search, or contact the **Oregon Veterinary Medical Association** (503-399-0311, 800-235-3502, www.oregonvma.org), which offers a "find a vet" service. (In Washington, contact the **Washington State Veterinary Medical Association**, 425-454-8381, www.wsvma.org.) **Banfield, The Pet Hospital** (800-838-6738, www.banfield.net) is a national chain that started in Portland and is still headquartered here; they have eight locations in the metro area.

Dove Lewis (www.dovelewis.org) operates two emergency animal hospitals in Portland:

- **Northwest Hospital**, 1945 NW Pettygrove St, 503-228-7281
- **Eastside Hospital**, Plaza 205, 10564 SE Washington St, 503-262-7194

The Dove Lewis emergency hotline is 503-228-7281. Other area emergency veterinary clinics include:

- **Clark County Emergency Veterinary Service**, 6818 NE Fourth Plain Blvd, Vancouver, 360-694-3007
- **Emergency Veterinary Clinic of Tualatin**, 19314 SW Mohave Ct, Tualatin, 503-691-7922
- **Northwest Veterinary Specialists**, 16756 SE 82nd Ave, Clackamas, 503-656-3999, www.northwestvetspecialists.com
- **Salem Veterinary Emergency Center**, 3215 Market St NE, Salem, 503-588-8082

PET ADOPTION

If you want to adopt a pet, a local animal shelter is a good place to begin. Kittens and dogs will come with their first vaccinations and a discount coupon to have them spayed or neutered. Area shelters include:

- **Animal Aid,** 5335 SW 42nd Ave, 503-292-6628, www.animalaidpdx.org/adopt. htm
- **Bonnie L. Hays Small Animal Shelter,** 1901 SE 24th Ave, Hillsboro, 503-846-7041, www.co.washington.or.us/deptmts/at/dog/dog.htm
- **Cat Adoption Team**, 14175 SW Galbreath Dr, Sherwood, 503-925-8903, www.catadoptionteam.org
- **Clackamas County Dog Services**, 2104 Kaen Rd, Oregon City, 503-655-8628, www.co.clackamas.or.us/dc/adoption/adopt.htm
- **Columbia Humane Society,** 2084 Oregon St., St. Helens, 503-397-4353, www.columbiahumane.org
- **Homeward Bound Pets**, 10605 SE Loop Rd, Dayton, 503-472-0341, sites.on linemac.com/evergreen%2Ddoe/adoptioncenter.htm
- **Humane Society for Southwest Washington**, 2121 St Francis Ln, Vancouver, 360-693-4746, southwesthumane.org
- **Marion County Animal Shelter**, 3550 Aumsville Hwy SE, Salem, 503-566-6966, www.mcdogs.net
- **Multnomah County Animal Shelter**, 1700 W Columbia River Hwy, Troutdale, 503-988-7387, www.co.multnomah.or.us/dbcs/pets/AdoptionInfo.shtml
- **Oregon Humane Society**, 1067 NE Columbia Blvd, 503-285-7722, www.oregonhumane.com
- **PAWS Animal Shelter**, 1741 Willamette Falls Dr, West Linn, 503-60-0855, www.pawsanimalshelter.org
- **Willamette Humane Society**, 4246 Turner Rd SE, Salem, 503-585-5900, www.willamettehumane.org

OTHER RESOURCES FOR PET OWNERS

Several publications and web sites focus on pet-related service providers, upcoming events, and news of interest to Portland-area pet owners. Check out **www.portlandpooch.com**, the **Oregon Humane Society's** Community Resources directory (www.oregonhumane.org/resources/community.asp), and the *Oregonian's* **Dog Blog** (www.oregonlive.com/dogs/weblog/), or pick up a copy of *Spot* (www.spotmagazine.net) at your local library or pet supply store. You might just learn about some new indispensable service. (Pet psychics? Who knew?)

PET SITTERS, DOGGIE DAY CARE, AND KENNELS

Not counting in-home doggie day care centers, the city of Portland harbors well over twenty doggie day care and canine "social clubs," most of which have punbased names. (Example: **Virginia Woof Dog Daycare Center**, 1520 E Burnside St, 503-224-5455, www.virginiawoof.com.) The suburbs have at least a dozen more, and new facilities open every month. As with most services, it's best to get a personal recommendation for a pet sitter, doggie day care provider, or kennel. Failing that, contact the **Oregon Humane Society** (503-285-7722) for a referral. One local business publishes a useful list of "Questions to Ask When Considering a Dog Day Care," available at www.happygoluckydog.com/images/links/Daycare_s.pdf.

For up-to-date listings of doggie day care centers and pet sitters, check out the online resources listed above; the Oregon Humane Society's list of pet care providers is at www.oregonhumane.org/resources/daycare.asp. The **Oregon Pet Sitters Association** (www.oregonpetsitters.com) and **Pet Sitters International** (www.petsit.com/locate_us.asp) both offer online listings of pet sitters. Ads for in-home or private doggie day care are sometimes posted in the community/pets forum of craigslist.com. For kennels (including cat-only boarding facilities) look in the Yellow Pages under "Pet Boarding" or "Dog and Cat Kennels." If you need to board your pet because you're leaving the city by air, the unique **Airpet Hotel** (6212 NE 78th Ct, Suite B, 503-255-1388) allows you to "park, board your pet, and board your plane."

DOG PARKS

Portland has more public off-leash areas per capita than any other city in the country—31 as of early 2007, up from only 4 in 2000. (Sadly, the explosive growth of off-leash areas in Portland was partly the result of increasing conflict between dog-owning and non-dog-owning park users; this conflict culminated most visibly and tragically with the fatal poisonings of more than a dozen dogs in Laurelhurst Park in 2003.) Five of these areas are fully fenced, dedicated off-leash areas, eight are unfenced areas that are open during most park hours, and the remaining 18 are open for off-leash use during specific hours only. The **Portland Parks & Recreation** off-leash program web site (www.portlandonline.com/parks/index.cfm?c=38287) lists off-leash areas, hours, and regulations, and provides links to maps of each specific park—and off-leash area within each park.

Outside Portland, off-leash areas have been established in Beaverton, Happy Valley, Milwaukie, Tigard, Lake Oswego, Wilsonville, and Vancouver, and in several area state parks; dog parks are in the planning stages in several other suburbs. **PortlandPooch.com** has created an up-to-date, comprehensive online map of dog parks in the Portland region; visit www.portlandpooch.com/dogparks/map.htm, and click on any location marker to find the name and location of the dog park, with a description of the off-leash area. A companion comparison chart, which includes user ratings for each park, is located at www.portlandpooch.com/dogparks/comparison.htm.

THE AVERAGE TRANSPLANT TO PORTLAND IS UNLIKELY TO NAME "cultural life" as his or her primary motivation. But Portland has an incredibly vibrant arts and entertainment scene—in some respects, arguably the best in the country for a city of its size—and it's filled with big and small arts venues that offer high-caliber and occasionally world-class performances in practically any artistic genre you could name. It also tends to attract enough young artists of all kinds to give the local arts scene a surprisingly avant-garde flavor.

This chapter also covers **Museums**, **Literary Life**, and **Culture for Kids.**

WHAT'S GOING ON?

The *Willamette Week* (www.wweek.com) and the **a&e** insert in the Friday *Oregonian* offer the most complete listings of upcoming performing arts events, exhibit openings and closings, film screenings, dance clubs, and the like, with the weekly *Portland Mercury* (www.portlandmercury.com) a runner-up. The Friday issue of the biweekly *Portland Tribune* (www.portlandtribune.com) has basic listings of major events and movie times.

TICKETS

As in most US cities, tickets to the majority of cultural events in Portland can (or must) be bought through **Ticketmaster** (503-224-4400, online at www.ticketmaster.com, or at retail outlets, including many area Fred Meyer stores). For especially popular events, such as major rock concerts, you may have no choice but to buy from Ticketmaster. However, for many events and performances you can avoid paying the extra Ticketmaster service fee by purchasing tickets directly at the box office of the event venue.

Several local venues use the ticket service **TicketsWest** (800-992-8499, www.ticketswest.com), which has retail outlets at most Safeway supermarkets.

Events at the Rose Garden Arena and Memorial Coliseum are sold through **ComcastTix** (www.ComcastTIX.com). You may occasionally encounter one of several other online ticket services, including **TicketWeb** (www.ticketweb.com) and the "fair trade" ticket service **Brown Paper Tickets** (800-838-3006, www.brownpapertickets.com).

If you have your heart set on going to a sold-out performance, a ticket broker can usually accommodate you, but expect to pay a significant premium for the privilege. Look in the Yellow Pages under "Ticket Sales—Entertainment & Sports," or check out online sites like craigslist.org, eBay (www.ebay.com), www.ticketsnow.com, or www.stubhub.com.

CONCERT HALLS

Most of Portland's "high" cultural events—major theatrical productions, dance and classical music performances, and the like—take place at the venues listed below. Portland also has an impressive range of high-quality alternative performance spaces, and many events are held in the city's churches and synagogues, in high school and college campus theaters and auditoriums, at neighborhood community or cultural centers, or in cafés and rock clubs. Some smaller theater companies have their own dedicated performance spaces.

- **Arlene Schnitzer Concert Hall**, 1037 SW Broadway, 503-248-4335, www.pcpa.org/events/asch.php; the "Schnitz" is part of the downtown Portland Center for the Performing Arts complex on Broadway. This ornate, formal concert hall hosts Oregon Symphony performances, lectures, various classical, dance, and theatrical productions, and the occasional rock concert.
- **Brunish Hall**, 1111 SW Broadway, 503-248-4335, www.pcpa.com/events/brunish.php; this small, flexible space in the downtown Portland Center for the Performing Arts complex sees a diverse set of small-scale performances.
- **Dolores Winningstad Theatre**, 1111 SW Broadway, 503-248-4335, www.pcpa.com/events/winny.php; another star in the Portland Center for the Performing Arts constellation, this small Elizabethan-style theatre hosts a variety of theatrical productions, and is an especially popular venue for Shakespeare plays.
- **Gerding Theater**, 128 NW 11th Ave, www.pcs.org/armoryTheater.html; housed in Portland's old Armory (which was renovated as a certified green building), the Gerding includes the Main Stage Theater and a smaller, more flexible Studio Theater.
- **Keller Auditorium**, 222 SW Clay St, 503-248-4335, www.pcpa.org/events/keller.php; formerly the Civic Auditorium, the Keller Auditorium provides a

home for the Portland Opera, the Oregon Ballet Theatre, and most touring Broadway shows that come through Portland.

- **Newmark Theatre**, 1111 SW Broadway, 503-248-4335, www.pcpa.com/events/newmark.php; this intimate, Edwardian-style theater is yet another Portland Center for the Performing Arts venue.

PERFORMING ARTS

While the lists below include almost all the city's professional performing arts companies, and many of its major nonprofessional organizations, they are by no means exhaustive.

DANCE

- **BodyVox**, 1300 NW Northrup St, 503-229-0627, www.bodyvox.com, is a dynamic, innovative modern dance company that is based in Portland but frequently tours around the country.
- **Oregon Ballet Theatre**, 503-222-5538, www.obt.org; this nationally recognized professional ballet company performs a series of shows every two to three months. The OBT's Christmastime *Nutcracker* performances are wildly popular. The OBT also operates a ballet school.
- **Solo Flamenco/Flamenco Arts Academy**, www.flamencodance.com, promotes flamenco dance performance in Portland. Their efforts culminate most visibly in the Northwest International Flamenco Festival (503-972-1178, www.nwiff.com), held in late July and early August, which features dancers from Jerez de la Frontera, Spain.
- **White Bird Dance**, 503-245-1600, www.whitebird.org, brings regional, national, and international contemporary dance companies to Portland.

MUSIC—SYMPHONIC, OPERA, CHAMBER MUSIC

Portland's classical music resources are surprisingly good, and some of its professional performers are of national or international caliber. Moreover, Portland attracts more musicians and singers than it can support professionally, so even nonprofessional groups put on performances of surprisingly high quality.

- **Beaverton Chamber Symphony**, 503-525-5960, www.bcsym.org; this amateur orchestra focuses on the "great works" of classical music.
- **Chamber Music Northwest**, 503-294-6400, www.cmnw.org; CMNW is not a performance group, but rather an organization devoted to bringing high-caliber chamber music artists to Portland to perform. It arranges events

throughout the year, but the culmination of its efforts is a summer chamber music festival held at Reed College and the Catlin Gabel School.

- **Friends of Chamber Music**, 503-224-9842, www.focm.org, brings several world-class chamber ensembles to Portland each year.
- **Oregon Symphony**, 503-228-1353, www.orsymphony.org; the Oregon Symphony, now more than a century old, is one of the largest and most highly regarded orchestras in the country. In addition to its performances of classical standards and the occasional contemporary piece, the Symphony presents a yearly pops series with guest non-classical performers. Most performances take place at the Arlene Schnitzer Concert Hall.
- **Portland Baroque Orchestra**, 503-222-6000, 800-494-8497, www.pbo.org; one of the best orchestras of its kind in the world, the Portland Baroque Orchestra indeed plays Baroque music, including some obscure pieces. PBO uses only original period instruments or reproductions.
- **Portland Chamber Orchestra**, 503-771-3250, www.portlandchamber orchestra.org, is the oldest professional-amateur chamber orchestra in the United States.
- **Portland Columbia Symphony Orchestra**, 503-234-4077, www.columbia symphony.org, composed of both professional and semiprofessional musicians, performs several concerts from autumn through spring of each year.
- **Portland Opera**, 503-241-1802, www.portlandopera.org; based in the Keller Auditorium, the Portland Opera is regarded as one of the top opera companies in the United States. While most of its productions are time-tested works, it also stages some innovative and contemporary productions, such as *Nixon in China*.
- **Sinfonia Concertante Orchestra**, www.sinfoniapdx.org, is a professional chamber orchestra that presents many rarely performed works.
- **Vancouver Symphony Orchestra**, 360-735-7278, www.vancouversymphony. org; billing itself as "America's Vancouver Symphony" (to avoid confusion with the organization of the same in Vancouver, British Columbia), the Vancouver Symphony is the leading orchestral group in the suburbs north of the Columbia River.

MUSIC—CHORAL

Portland is rich in vocal music groups of all ages and abilities. The following list provides a glimpse of some of the city's choral groups that offer public performances.

- **Cappella Romana**, 503-236-8202, www.cappellaromana.org, performs works of Byzantine complexity—literally. The group's focus is music of the Byzantine and Eastern Orthodox traditions, and most of their singing is in Greek or Russian.

- **Choral Arts Ensemble of Portland**, 503-488-3824, www.caeportland.com, performs a diverse range of choral music.
- **David York Ensemble**, www.feedyourears.org, is a chamber choir that performs new and original works.
- **Novum Chamber Singers**, 503-642-9368, www.novumchambersingers.org; this 24-member choir presents at least four concerts per year.
- **Oregon Repertory Singers**, 503-230-0652, www.orsingers.org; both the quality and the sheer volume of this 60-voice choir will knock your socks off.
- **Portland Gay Men's Chorus**, 503-226-2588, www.pdxgmc.org, gives an eclectic series of performances each year.
- **Portland's Singing Christmas Tree**, 503-557-TREE, www.singingchristmas tree.org; a seasonal phenomenon, Portland's Singing Christmas Tree is actually a group of human singers and not a caroling evergreen.
- **Portland Symphonic Choir**, 503-223-1217, www.pschoir.org; this accomplished and well-respected choir offers a full program of choral performances each year. (The group's annual Wintersong! celebration is a particular highlight.)

MUSIC—CONTEMPORARY

For all the diversity of the city's arts community as a whole, Portland's contemporary music scene gets the most national press. Portland is currently an indie music hotbed—locally based bands like the Shins, the Decemberists, and the now-disbanded Sleater-Kinney have achieved international success—and the city's alternative music pedigree stretches from proto-garage band The Kingsmen (immortalized by their one hit, "Louie Louie") to Elliott Smith and Everclear. However, Portland is also one of the jazz, blues, and acoustic music hotspots of western North America, and the area boasts accomplished contemporary musicians working in almost every genre.

Given the range of the local music scene, it's not surprising that the majority of Portland's live music venues are at least moderately cross-genre, and some venues, such as the Crystal Ballroom and Mississippi Studios, take pride in presenting a diverse slate of acts. The venues listed below generally offer live music at least four or five nights a week. Many bars, restaurants, pubs, and nightclubs offer live music on a less-frequent basis, especially on weekends.

ARENAS

Rock and pop superstars tend to play in the city's sports arenas, both located in the Rose Quarter/Lloyd District area of Northeast Portland:

- **Memorial Coliseum**, 300 Winning Way, 503-235-8771, www.rosequarter.com
- **Rose Garden Arena**, One Center Court, 503-235-8771, www.rosequarter.com.

(The Rose Garden arena should *not* be confused with the International Rose Test Garden in Washington Park. More than one newcomer has made the mistake, and the potential for confusion is exacerbated on the occasions where the Washington Park rose garden hosts outdoor summer concerts.)

CABARET

While many of Portland's bars, restaurants, nightclubs, and performance spaces offer an occasional cabaret performance, the city's only dedicated cabaret is **Darcelle XV** (208 NW 3rd Avenue, 503-222-5338, www.darcellexv.com), which has staged female impersonator cabaret shows since the late 1960s.

FOLK, ACOUSTIC, BLUEGRASS, CELTIC

- **Aladdin Theater**, 3017 SE Milwaukie Ave, 503-233-1994, www.aladdin-theater.com; the Aladdin is one of the city's most comfortable concert venues—it actually is a theater, with full seating, plus tasty food and good beer—and gets its fair share of big-name touring folk, rock, and country acts. The seating arrangement is ideal for enjoying folk acts and singer-songwriters, but renders crowd surfing and mosh pit formation impractical.
- **Alberta Street Pub**, 1036 NE Alberta St, 503-284-7665, myspace.com/albertastreetpub, has acoustic, Celtic, and bluegrass performances most nights.
- **Biddy McGraws**, 6000 NE Glisan St, 503-233-1178, www.biddymcgraws.com; despite the name, Biddy's features more than just Irish music (although there is plenty of that).
- **Kells**, 112 SW 2nd Ave, 503-227-4057, www.kellsirish.com, has live Irish music every night of the week.
- **Produce Row Café**, 204 SE Oak St, 503-232-8355, www.producerowcafe.com; this friendly pub/restaurant has an outstanding beer selection and is a great place to see a mellow acoustic show.

JAZZ & BLUES

For complete information on local events and gigs, check out the web sites of **Portland Jazz** (www.portlandjazz.com), the **Jazz Society of Oregon** (www.jsojazzscene.org), and the **Cascade Blues Association** (www.cascadeblues.org).

- **Andina**, 1314 NW Glisan St, 503-223-5058, www.andinarestaurant.com; this upscale and deservedly popular Peruvian restaurant in the Pearl District has live jazz and Latin music almost every night.
- **The Blue Monk**, 3341 SE Belmont St, 503-595-0575, www.thebluemonk.com, literally an underground club, has great live jazz, an excellent beer selection,

and a full restaurant. The Blue Monk must be one of the few jazz clubs in the world with an extensive selection of vegetarian entrees.

- **Candlelight Café & Bar**, 2032 SW 5th Ave, 503-222-3378, www.candlelight cafébar.com, in the south end of downtown near Portland State, is primarily a blues and soul venue.
- **Jax Bar**, 826 SW 2nd Ave, 503-228-9128, www.jaxbar.com; a popular hangout for the happy hour crowd downtown, Jax has frequent live jazz performances.
- **Jimmie Mak's,** 221 NW 10th Ave, 503-295-6542, www.jimmiemaks.com, is widely regarded as Portland's foremost live jazz venue, and is graced by occasional performances by living legends of jazz.
- **LV's Uptown Jazz & Eats**, 310 SW Lincoln, 503-221-0140, www.lvuptown.com; like the name says, jazz and eats, near Portland State University.
- **Tillicum Club**, 8585 SW Beaverton-Hillsdale Hwy, 503-292-1835, www.tillicum club.com; this unpretentious restaurant/bar on the fringe of the suburbs hosts regular live performances, with an emphasis on blues.
- **Trail's End Saloon**, 1320 Main St, Oregon City, 503-656-3031, in a nineteenth-century building in Oregon City, provides a venue for some of the best blues performers in Oregon.
- **Tony Starlight's**, 3728 NE Sandy Blvd, 503-517-8584, www.tonystarlight.com; if you can ignore the cheesy name, Tony Starlight's offers a good selection of jazz performances, including traditional jazz and swing.
- **Wilf's**, Union Station, 800 NW 6th Ave, 503-223-0070, www.wilfsrestaurant. com; who would have guessed that a restaurant in an Amtrak station would have such great live music?

ROCK, POP, ALTERNATIVE

This category is a catch-all for all the diverse styles spawned from rock-and-roll or R&B—punk, pop, surf, rockabilly, hip hop, alternative, indie, metal, speed metal, death metal, and so on. As noted above, most "rock" clubs also host shows by other types of performers.

- **Ash Street Saloon**, 225 SW Ash St, 503-226-0430, www.ashstreetsaloon.com; live music seven nights a week in a non-trendy, saloon atmosphere.
- **Berbati's Pan**, 231 SW Ankeny St, 503-248-4579, www.berbatis.com, is one of the city's first live venues to go non-smoking. Berbati's has an active schedule of local performers and some national acts.
- **Buffalo Gap Saloon & Eatery**, 6835 SW Macadam Ave, 503-244-7111, www. thebuffalogap.com; this Johns Landing establishment books an eclectic selection of local and touring rock, jazz, and country acts.
- **Crystal Ballroom**, 1332 SW Burnside St, 503-249-7474, www.danceonair.com; the Crystal Ballroom (a bona fide, actual ballroom) is locally famous for its sprung floor and psychedelic wall murals. Many local, national, and international acts headline here. The cool kids hang out in Lola's Bar, one floor down.

- **Dante's**, 1 SW 3rd Ave, 503-226-6630, www.danteslive.com; one of Portland's most eclectic clubs, Dante's hosts everything from cabaret to punk in a dark space with lots of red décor. (Get it?)
- **Doug Fir Lounge**, 830 E Burnside St, 503-231-9663, www.dougfirlounge.com; worth visiting for the underlit floor alone, this hip Eastside bar hosts an impressive roster of shows, including performances by artists of national renown.
- **Duff's Garage**, 1635 SE 7th Ave, 503-234-2337, www.duffsgarage.com; this Southeast Portland venue presents bands running the stylistic gamut from roots rock and rockabilly to country, jazz, and blues.
- **The Goodfoot**, 2845 SE Stark St, 503-239-9292, www.thegoodfoot.com; this Southeast pub hosts frequent live performances, including more funk and soul acts than most Portland venues.
- **Hawthorne Theatre**, 1507 SE 39th Ave, 503-233-7100, www.hawthorne theatre.com, an all-ages venue in the Hawthorne District, has (almost) nightly live shows.
- The **Laurelthirst Public House**, 2958 NE Glisan St, 503-232-1504, www. laurelthirst.com; this comfy pub/restaurant on the edge of the Laurelhurst neighborhood is more than just a clever name: local and some touring bands play here almost every night.
- **Mississippi Studios,** 3939 N Mississippi Ave, 503-288-3895, www.mississippi studios.com; this intimate club on North Mississippi Avenue hosts everything from vintage jazz to alternative bands like Franz Ferdinand.
- **Roseland Theater**, 10 NW 6th Ave, 503-224-2038, www.doubletee.com; the Roseland pulls in some big-name national and international acts. Depending on the evening bill, you could mix with punks, hipsters, teeny-boppers, Rasta-farians, aging hippies, or all of the above.
- **Towne Lounge**, 714 SW 20th Pl, 503-241-8696, www.townelounge.com; this relatively new entrant to the live music scene hosts a diverse assortment of local and touring acts.
- **Wonder Ballroom**, 128 NE Russell St, 503-284-8686, www.wonderballroom. com; the historic Wonder Ballroom is yet another venue with a remarkably diverse slate of performers, including some national acts.

THEATER

Portland has many, many theater companies and ensembles; some go a year or more between productions. For a (relatively) complete list of area theater groups, as well as notices of upcoming events, visit the web site of the **Portland Area Theater Alliance** (www.patagreenroom.org).

Here are some companies that produce plays on a more or less regular basis:

- **Artists Repertory Theatre**, 1516 SW Alder St, 503-241-1278, www.artistsrep.

org; this accomplished professional nonprofit company stages a regular program of serious and comedic plays in its intimate downtown theater.

- **The Broadway Rose Theatre Company**, 503-620-5262, www.bwayrose.com; the Broadway Rose, a professional theatre company based in Tigard, focuses on Broadway musicals.
- **CoHo Productions**, 2257 NW Raleigh St, 503-220-CoHo, www.cohoproductions.org; this award-winning company puts on an always-intriguing slate of plays at its intimate performance space in Northwest Portland (which it shares on occasion with other local and touring theatrical organizations).
- **defunkt theatre**, Back Door Theater, 4319 SE Hawthorne Blvd, 503-481-2960, www.defunktheatre.com, produces innovative, intriguing, and sometimes edgy plays.
- **Do Jump! Extremely Physical Theater**, The Echo Theatre, 1515 SE 37th Ave, 503-231-1232, www.dojump.org; when this genre- and gravity-defying troupe of "actorbats" performs, the result is part theater, part dance, and part circus. (DoJump! also offers lessons in theater and what can best be described as creative movement.)
- **Hand2Mouth Theatre**, 6551 N Maryland Ave, 503-235-5284, www.hand2mouth; this lively company produces somewhat barebones but well-executed original productions.
- **Hillsboro Artists Regional Theatre**, 503-693-7815, www.hart-theatre.org; this community theater puts on several productions each year in western Washington County.
- **Imago Theatre**, 17 SE 8th Ave, 503-231-9581, www.imagotheatre.com; known best for its imaginative, long-running production *Frogz*, Imago focuses on physical theatre and oddball costumes and sets. Most of their original productions delight both children and adults.
- **Lakewood Theatre Company**, 368 S State St, Lake Oswego, 503-635-3901, www.lakewood-center.org; Lakewood Theatre Company has an active calendar of generally noncontroversial productions.
- **Miracle Theatre Group**, 425 SE 6th Ave, 503-236-7253, www.milagro.org, is a group of three Latino arts and culture organizations—Miracle Mainstage, Teatro Milagro, and Bellas Artes—that present English-language, Spanish-language, and bilingual productions.
- **Northwest Classical Theatre Company**, The Shoebox Theater, 2110 SE 10th Ave, 503-262-5503, www.nwctc.org; the Northwest Classical Theatre Company focuses on the plays of Shakespeare and other established playwrights.
- **Portland Actors Ensemble**, 503-467-6573, www.portlandactors.com; this troupe is best known for its free summer Shakespeare-in-the-Park performances in Portland public parks.
- **Portland Center Stage**, Gerding Theater at the Armory, 128 NE 11th Ave, 503-445-3700, 877-PCS-TKTS, www.pcs.org, is one of the Northwest's largest and most respected theater companies; its productions range from classic dramas to contemporary comedies (and vice versa).

- **Profile Theatre**, Theater! Theatre!, 3420 SW Belmont St, 503-242-0080, www. profiletheatre.org; each season, Profile Theatre produces a series of plays from a single playwright. (The 2006-07 season honored Pulitzer-winner Wendy Wasserstein.)
- **Theatre Vertigo**, Theater! Theatre!, 3420 SW Belmont St, 503-306-0870, www. theatrevertigo.org; one of several companies that perform in its Belmont-area space, Theatre Vertigo takes on a diverse mix of old and new works.
- **Third Rail Repertory**, 503-235-1101, www.thirdrailrep.org, is a permanent ensemble that stages serious (and tragicomic) plays with a high level of professionalism.

COMEDY AND IMPROV

Why did the chicken cross the road? Perhaps to get to one of Portland's improv shows or comedy clubs. (Of course, being a chicken, it didn't get any of the jokes.)

COMEDY CLUBS

- **Comedy Club Westside**, 8775 SW Canyon Ln, Beaverton, 503-296-0586
- **Harvey's Comedy Club**, 436 NW 6th Ave, 503-241-0338, www.harveyscomedy club.com, is the place to see actual and would-be stand-up comics, including some touring headliners.

IMPROV AND SKETCH COMEDY

A combination of stand-up comedy and acting, improvisational theater uses audience suggestions to create a scene, which is then played for laughs. Sketch comedy is generally scripted, but often has a similar freewheeling feel. Most improv and sketch comedy groups perform on weekends only; call ahead or check web sites as times and locations change frequently.

- **The 3rd Floor**, www.the3rdfloor.com
- **Brainwaves**, 503-796-9550, www.brainwavesimprov.com
- **The Brody Theater**, 1904 NW 27th Ave, 503-224-0688, www.brodytheater. com
- **ComedySportz**, 1963 NW Kearney St, 503-236-8888, 866-512-5233, www. portlandcomedy.com
- **Funny Business,** 503-703-3026, www.funnybusinesspdx.com
- **Kick the Squirrel**, www.kickthesquirrel.com
- **The Liberators**, www.theliberators.net

FILM

Portland offers a variety of cinematic experiences, from first-run Hollywood blockbusters to art house and foreign films. Look in the daily or weekly newspapers (or on their web sites) for movie listings and show times, or peruse www.portlandmovietimes.com.

Portland and its suburbs have an abundance of multiplexes that show mainstream releases: The main chain is **Regal Cinemas** (www.regmovies.com), which has more than a dozen multiplexes in the metropolitan area, but several other multi-screen cinemas are owned by different companies. A few independent or neighborhood theatres also screen first-run movies, including **Cinetopia** (11700 SE 7th St, Vancouver, 360-213-2800, www.cinetopiatheaters.com), which has several comfy auditoriums (some with leather seats or pillow pits); tapas from its restaurant are available before some films. In addition to movies in traditional formats, there is a giant-screen **Omnimax** theater at the Oregon Museum of Science and Industry (OMSI; 1945 SE Water Ave, 503-797-4640, www.omsi.edu).

Portland is also blessed with a wealth of second-run movie houses. While these are especially common on Portland's East Side, they also exist in such suburbs as Milwaukie, Gresham, and Vancouver. A true Portland experience is watching a movie in one of the **McMenamins** "theater pubs" (movie line 503-249-7474, www.mcmenamins.com), which serve pizza and beer in the restored buildings—the ornate Bagdad Theater on Southeast Hawthorne was once a true 1920s movie palace (and is rumored to be haunted), while the theater at the Kennedy School on Northeast 33rd Avenue, once an elementary school auditorium, is filled with sofas and armchairs.

The cinemas listed below screen independent, foreign, classic, documentary, and other non-mainstream films. If nothing at the theaters catches your fancy, Portland is also home to one of the country's best video rental stores, **Movie Madness** (4320 SW Belmont St, 503-234-4363, www.moviemadnessvideo.com).

- **Cinema 21 Theatre**, 616 NW 21st Ave, 503-223-4515, www.cinema21.com
- **Clinton Street Theater and Brewpub**, 2522 SE Clinton St, 503-238-8899, www.clintonsttheater.com
- **Hollywood Theatre**, 4122 NE Sandy Blvd, 503-493-1128, www.hollywoodtheatre.org
- **Living Room Theaters**, 341 SW 10th Ave, 971-222-2010, www.livingroomtheaters.com
- **Northwest Film Center**, Whitsell Auditorium, 1219 SW Park Ave, 503-221-1156, www.nwfilm.org
- **Regal Fox Tower Stadium 10**, 822 SW Park Ave, 800-326-3264 x327, www.fandango.com/TheaterPage.aspx?radius=30&tid=AAOZW
- **World Cavalcade Travel Films**, Scottish Rite Center, 1512 SW Morrison St, 503-241-2575, www.worldtravelfilms.com

FILM FESTIVALS

- **Cascade Festival of African Films**, 503-244-6111 x3630, www.africanfilm festival.org
- **Faux Film Festival**, Hollywood Theatre, 4122 NE Sandy Blvd, 503-493-1128, www.fauxfilm.com
- **Jewish Film Festival**, 503-221-1156, www.nwfilm.org
- **Longbaugh Film Festival**. www.longbaugh.com
- **Northwest Film and Video Film Festival**, 503-221-1156, www.nwfilm.org
- **PDX Film Festival**, 503-282-6082, www.peripheralproduce.com/pdx_film_ fest/
- **Platform International Animation Festival**, 818-508-9186, www.platform festival.com
- **Portland International Film Festival**, 503-221-1156, www.nwfilm.org
- **Portland Lesbian and Gay Film Festival**, Cinema 21, 616 NW 21st Ave, 503-223-4515, www.plgff.org
- **Portland Underground Film Festival**, Clinton Street Theater, 2522 SE Clinton St, 503-238-8899, www.clintonsttheater.com/puff
- **Reel Music Festival**, 503-221-1156, www.nwfilm.org
- **Young People's Film and Video Festival**, 503-221-1156, www.nwfilm.org

NIGHTCLUBS & DISCOS

Many of Portland's nightclubs have live music on some nights. Others are simply bars with a DJ, and still others are full-fledged dance clubs. The Portland club scene changes almost weekly: Once-hot spots fall out of favor, new clubs draw the city's bright young things, owners get indicted or mysteriously disappear. Here's a current sampling of Portland nightclubs:

- **Acme**, 1305 SE 8th Ave, 503-230-9020, www.acme-pdx.com
- **Andrea's Cha-Cha Club**, 832 SE Grand Ave, 503-230-1166
- **Barracuda**, 9 NW 2nd Ave, 503-228-6900, www.bar71.com/venues_barra cudas.html
- **Bettie Ford Lounge**, 1135 SW Washington St, 503-445-8331, www.bettieford lounge.com
- **Crush**, 1400 SE Morrison St, 503-235-8150, www.crushbar.com
- **Fez Ballroom**, 316 SW 11th Ave, 503-221-7262, www.fezballroom.com
- **Greek Cusina**, 404 SW Washington St, 503-224-2288, www.greekcusina.com
- **H2O**, 204 SW Yamhill St, 503-241-8132
- **Holocene**, 1001 SE Morrison St, 503-239-7639, www.holocene.org
- **Ohm**, 31 NW 1st Ave, 503-224-5562, www.ohmnightclubpdx.com
- **Pala**, 105 NW 3rd Ave, 503-242-0700, www.palalounge.com
- **Pi-Rem**, 433 NW 4th Ave, 503-227-5494, www.pi-rem.com

- **Rotture**, 315 SE 3rd Ave, 503-234-5684, www.rotture.com
- **Someday Lounge**, 125 NW 5th Ave, 503-248-1030, www.somedaylounge.com
- **Voodoo Lounge**, 53 NW 1st Ave, 503-241-3840, www.voodoopdx.com

TEEN/ALL AGES CLUBS

- **Rock N Roll Pizza**, 11140 SE Powell Blvd, 503-260-7646, www.rocknrollpizza.com
- **Satyricon**, 125 NW 6th Ave, 503-243-2380, www.satyriconpdx.com
- **The Zone**, 126 SW 2nd Ave, 503-497-9113, www.bar71.com/venues_quest.html

VISUAL ARTS

ART GALLERIES AND MUSEUMS

Given the vibrancy of Portland's arts scene, it's a bit surprising that the city has only a handful of art museums with permanent exhibits:

- **3D Center of Art & Photography**, 1928 NW Lovejoy St, 503-227-6667, www.3dcenter.us, celebrates 3-D imagery in art, film, and commerce.
- The **Museum of Contemporary Craft,** 134 NW 8th Ave, 503-223-2654, www.contemporarycrafts.org, opened in July 2007 in its new space in the Pearl District, following years located in Lair Hill.
- **Portland Art Museum**, 1219 SW Park Ave, 503-226-2811, www.portlandartmuseum.org; when Portlanders speak of "*the* art museum," this is what they mean. The Portland Art Museum is the oldest art museum in the Northwest, and holds significant collections of European, American, and East Asian painting and sculpture, Native American art, and silver; it unveiled the Jubitz Center for Modern and Contemporary Art in 2005. In addition to its permanent exhibits, the museum holds frequent temporary exhibits and hosts traveling international exhibitions.

Many area colleges have gallery spaces that host rotating exhibits; the best known of these are **Cooley Art Gallery** at Reed College (3203 SE Woodstock Blvd, 503-777-7829, web.reed.edu/gallery) and the **Art Gym** at Marylhurst University (17600 Pacific Hwy [Hwy 43], Marylhurst [between Lake Oswego and West Linn], 503-699-6243, www.marylhurst.edu/theartgym/). In addition, the **Portland Institute for Contemporary Art (PICA)** (224 NW 13th Ave, Suite 305, 503-242-1418, www.pica.org) sponsors frequent exhibits of contemporary art—broadly defined to include film, dance, drama, and other art forms.

Portland's art scene really thrives in its galleries, some of which have received national acclaim. The city has scores of art galleries showcasing everything from traditional to cutting edge art; they reach critical mass in the Pearl District and Northwest Portland. A fairly complete list of galleries is available at the **Portland Art Dealers Association** web site (www.padaoregon.org), and the local arts & entertainment papers include listings of galleries and their current exhibits.

ART WALKS

Several neighborhoods with a high concentration of galleries host evening art walks, when galleries stay open late and various forms of live entertainment usually take place. On **First Thursday** (the first Thursday of each month), Pearl District galleries welcome the art-loving throngs, although the focus of this neighborhood tradition has shifted somewhat from art to bar-and-restaurant hopping. See www.firstthursday.org for details. (To cast a wider First Thursday net, take the free Russell Shuttle/Groove Bomb Bus (www.markwoolley.com), which operates on a continuous loop from the Pearl to select bars and galleries of Northeast Portland.) The Alberta Arts District hosts a similar **Last Thursday**, which is just as much a "scene" as First Thursday, but of a very different and more bohemian kind.

Other neighborhood art walks include the Central Eastside's **First Friday** (www.firstfridayart.com) a competing **First Friday** in Sellwood and Westmoreland, and Mississippi Avenue's **Second Thursday**. Far less frequent is the annual two-day **Southeast Area Art Walk** (www.seportlandartwalk.com), which includes the Hawthorne and Division/Clinton Street districts. Several suburban communities also sponsor semi-regular art walks.

For a different kind of art walk, the Regional Arts and Culture Council and the Portland Visitors Association produce a self-guided **walking tour** of Portland's outdoor public art; visit racc.org/publicart/docs/WalkingTour.pdf to download a copy or call 503-823-5111 to have a copy mailed to you.

MUSEUMS

For art museums and galleries, see the preceding section.

CULTURE AND HISTORY

In addition to the museums listed below, many of the older communities in the Portland area maintain small museums of pioneer life or have historic houses that are open to the public.

• **Clark County Historical Museum**, 1511 Main St, Vancouver, 360-993-5679, www.cchmuseum.org; nearly a century old, this museum houses exhibits of Clark County's rich history, ranging from thirteenth-century Native American artifacts to the coming of European traders and pioneers through the development of modern Vancouver.

- **End of the Oregon Trail Interpretive Center**, 1726 Washington St, Oregon City, 503-657-9336, www.endoftheoregontrail.org; housed in what resembles a train of giant skeletal prairie schooners—the storm-damaged coverings to the "covered" wagons have been removed on a semi-permanent basis—the EOTIC illustrates the history of the overland migration to Oregon in the mid-nineteenth century.
- **Fort Vancouver**, 1501 E Evergreen Blvd, Vancouver, 360-696-7655, www.nps. gov/fova; years before Portland was a gleam in its coin-tossing founders' eyes, Fort Vancouver served as the administrative center of the British Hudson Bay Company's fur-trading empire, which stretched from Alaska to California.
- **Museum of the Oregon Territory**, 211 Tumwater Dr, Oregon City, 503-655-5574, www.orcity.com/museum; Oregon City was the original capital of the Oregon Territory, and this museum's high points are the exhibits that reveal everyday life during Oregon's territorial and early statehood periods.
- **Oregon Historical Society**, 1200 SW Park Ave, 503-222-1741, www.ohs.org; this vast repository of artifacts and documents also presents permanent and temporary exhibits about Oregon history, including the large and elaborate "Oregon My Oregon" exhibit.
- The **Oregon Jewish Museum**, 310 NW Davis St, 503-226-3600, www.ojm.org, focuses on the history and experience of the Jewish community in the Pacific Northwest from pioneer days to the present.
- **Oregon Maritime Museum**, Waterfront Park at Pine St, 503-224-7724, www.oregonmaritimemuseum.org; housed on a retired sternwheeler floating on the Willamette River downtown, the Oregon Maritime Museum highlights Portland's rich past (and present) as a major port and maritime center.
- **Oregon Military Museum**, Camp Withycombe, 10101 SE Clackamas Rd, Clackamas, 503-557-5359, www.swiftview.com/~ormilmuseum/; while Oregon has been the site of relatively few battles, Oregonians have fought in military conflicts around the world. This museum focuses on artifacts—uniforms, weapons, vehicles, and the like—that relate to the military service of Oregonians during the twentieth century.
- The **Oregon Sports Hall of Fame & Museum**, 321 SW Salmon St, 503-227-7466, www.oregonsportshall.org, presents facts and memorabilia about the history of sports in Oregon.
- **Pittock Mansion**, 3229 NW Pittock Dr, 503-823-3623, www.pittockmansion. com; this chateauesque mansion near the summit of the West Hills was built in the early twentieth century for an Oregon pioneer-cum-newspaper baron.
- **Portland Police Museum**, 1111 SW 2nd Ave, Suite 1682, 503-823-0019, www.portlandpolicemuseum.com; housed on the 16th floor of the city's justice

center (i.e., jail building and police headquarters), this museum showcases the history of the Portland Police Bureau and the experiences of individual officers.

- **Washington County Museum**, 17677 NW Springville Rd, 503-645-5353, www. washingtoncountymuseum.org; this museum of Washington County history is located on the Rock Creek Campus of Portland Community College.

SCIENCE AND TECHNOLOGY

- **Evergreen Aviation Museum**, 500 NE Captain Michael King Smith Way, McMinnville, 503-434-4180, www.sprucegoose.org; this museum's big attraction—and it is truly a *big* attraction—is Howard Hughes's Spruce Goose, by some measures the largest airplane ever built.
- **Oregon Museum of Science and Industry (OMSI)**, 1945 SE Water Ave, 503-797-4000, 800-955-6674, www.omsi.edu; housed in a large facility on the east bank of the Willamette River, OMSI has several galleries devoted to science and technology. Most of the exhibits are interactive, and many are tailored to children. OMSI also gives tours of the USS *Blueback* submarine, which is permanently docked outside the museum, and hosts frequent visiting exhibits.
- **Pearson Air Museum**, 1115 E 5th St, Vancouver, 360-694-7026, www.pearson airmuseum.org; located at the country's oldest operating airfield, Pearson Air Museum includes a collection of antique airplanes, the oldest of which is from 1913.
- **Rice NW Museum of Rocks & Minerals**, 26385 NW Groveland Ave, Hillsboro, 503-647-2418, www.ricenwmuseum.org; modestly housed in the founders' former home in an out-of-the-way corner of Hillsboro, this is nonetheless one of the nation's finest museums of rocks and minerals.
- **World Forestry Center Discovery Museum,** Washington Park, 4033 SW Canyon Rd, 503-228-1367, www.worldforestry.org; this mostly hands-on museum focuses on forestry and the ecology of forests around the world generally and in the Pacific Northwest in particular. The canopy lift and the "raft ride" are particularly popular with children.

OFFBEAT MUSEUMS

With the demise of the 24-Hour Church of Elvis, Portland lost its most beloved, or at least most famous, oddball attraction. Fortunately, the city continues to host a few offbeat museums.

- **The Hat Museum**, 1928 SE Ladd Ave, 503-232-0433, www.thehatmuseum. com (by reservation); the name of this museum speaks for itself.

- **Stark's Vacuum Museum**, 107 NE Grand Ave, 503-232-4101, www.starks.com; tucked away inside the headquarters store of Stark's Vacuums is a museum of vacuums. The staff are used to visitors who joke that the museum's exhibits suck.
- **Velveteria**, 518 NE 28th Ave, 503-233-5100, www.velveteria.com; yes, it's a museum of velvet paintings; no, they're not all Elvises. Check out the black light room.

ARCHITECTURE AND WALKING TOURS

Portland has traditionally been pretty conservative when it comes to architecture (the Michael Graves–designed Portland Building, an early exemplar of Postmodernism, notwithstanding). That conservatism is rapidly evaporating, and some remarkable new structures have risen over the last decade or so. (The federal courthouse downtown, capped by a soaring "wing," is one example of this.) Moreover, much of the city's historic architecture is both well-preserved and noteworthy. The Architecture Foundation of Oregon has produced a *Look Around Guide* to 41 different notable architectural sites in Portland; the guide is available for download at www.af-oregon.org. The **Architectural Heritage Center** (701 SE Grand Ave, 503-231-7264, www.architecturalheritagecenter.org) focuses on historical preservation; in addition to providing information about Portland's historic structures and hosting architectural history exhibits in its gallery space, the Center is a great resource if you've bought a vintage home.

Portland is a great city for strolling, but if you're looking for something a bit more organized and informative, contact **Portland Walking Tours** (503-774-4522, www.portlandwalkingtours.com); their tours focus on downtown and the surrounding neighborhoods, but they also offer tours of outlying neighborhoods on request. For a journey through the infamous **Shanghai tunnels** of Old Town, where drunken bar patrons were unknowingly "crimped" to crew for free on trans-Pacific sea voyages, contact the Cascade Geographical Society at 503-622-4798 or visit www.shanghaitunnels.info.

LITERARY LIFE

With its gunmetal gray winter skies and frequent drizzle, Portland is a great bookstore town. Area residents flock to book groups, book signings, and fiction, non-fiction, and poetry readings (often given by well-known local authors). In addition to bookstore- and library-hosted events, **Literary Arts** (224 NW 13th Ave, Ste 306, 503-227-2583, www.literary-arts.org) sponsors lectures and readings by local, national, and international authors and poets; its Portland Arts & Lectures series usually brings several Pulitzer prize winners to the city.

BOOKSTORES

While the city has chain bookstores like Barnes & Noble and Borders, many residents are fiercely loyal to Portland's independent booksellers. The largest of these is **Powell's City of Books** (1005 W Burnside St, 503-228-4651, 800-878-7323, www.powells.com), which is the largest bookstore in North America and occupies an entire city block in the Pearl District. (Powell's also has two satellite stores, at 3723 SE Hawthorne Blvd, and at Beaverton's Cedar Hills Crossing mall, 3415 SW Cedar Hills Blvd). Most best-selling authors who come to Portland on book tours make an appearance at Powell's, although smaller independent bookstores sometimes snag big-name writers for in-store readings and book signings.

The following is a selection of general-interest and specialty booksellers in Portland proper:

GENERAL-INTEREST BOOKSTORES

- **Annie Bloom's Books**, 7834 SW Capitol Hwy, 503-246-0053, www.annie blooms.com
- **Barnes & Noble Booksellers**, Lloyd Center, 503-249-0800, www.bn.com
- **Borders Books**, 708 SW 3rd Ave, 503-220-5911, www.bordersstores.com
- **Broadway Books**, 1714 NE Broadway, 503-284-1726
- **Looking Glass Bookstore**, 7983 SE 13th, 503-227-4760, www.lookingglass bookstore.com
- **Powell's** (see above)
- **St. Johns Booksellers**, 8622 N Lombard St, 503-283-0032
- **Twenty-Third Avenue Books**, 1015 NW 23rd Ave, 503-224-6203, www.23rdavebooks.com
- **Wallace Books**, 7241 SE Milwaukie Ave, 503-235-7350

SPECIAL-INTEREST BOOKSTORES

- **A Children's Place**, 4807 NE Fremont St, 503-284-8294, www.achildrensplace bookstore.com
- **In Other Words,** 8 NE Killingsworth St, 503-232-6003, www.inotherwords.org (women's and feminist)
- **Laughing Horse Books**, 3652 SE Division St, 503-236-2893, www.geocities.com/laughinghorsebooks/ (progressive politics)
- **Murder by the Book**, 3210 SE Hawthorne Blvd, 503-232-9995, www.mbtb.com
- **New Renaissance Bookshop**, 1338 NW 23rd Ave, 503-224-4929, www.new renbooks.com (New Age)
- **Reading Frenzy**, 921 SW Oak St, 503-274-1449, www.readingfrenzy.com (independent presses)

USED BOOKSTORES

- **Cameron's Books & Magazines**, 336 SW 3rd Ave, 503-228-2391, www.cameronsbooks.com
- **Daedalus Books**, 2074 NW Flanders St, 503-274-7742, www.abebooks.com/home/daedalus/
- **Dragon's Head Books**, 6016 NE Glisan St, 503-235-5995, www.dragonshead books.com
- **Great Northwest Bookstore**, 3314 SW 1st Ave, 503-223-8098, www.great northwestbooks.com
- **Hawthorne Boulevard Books**, 3129 SE Hawthorne Blvd, 503-236-3211
- **Longfellow's Books**, 1401 SE Division St, 503-239-5222
- **Paper Moon Books**, 4707 SE Belmont St, 503-239-8848
- **Second Glance Books**, 4500 NE Sandy Blvd, 503-249-0344
- **Title Wave**, 216 NE Knott St, 503-988-5021, www.multcolib.org/titlewave/ (Multnomah County Library surplus)

LIBRARIES

Portland-area public libraries host frequent literary events and exhibitions. See the **Getting Settled** chapter for a list of library systems in the region.

CULTURE FOR CHILDREN

Portland has so many cultural opportunities for kids they may become surly, disinterested teenagers long before they can take advantage of them all. The *Oregonian's* weekly a&e supplement includes a "Get Out" section (which is apparently not ironically named, and which is available online at www.oregonlive.com/AandE/getout) that lists events and activities of interest to families.

The following listing of child-oriented organizations and places represents only a small part of what Portland has to offer its young residents. In addition to organizations that are geared specifically to children, many of the "grownup" groups in town offer special performances for children. The Oregon Symphony, for example, puts on a Kids Concert series every year. Several museums that are not specifically "children's" museums offer a wide range of child-friendly exhibits; OMSI and the World Forestry Center Discovery Museum have particularly extensive kid-oriented displays. For more ideas on ways to entertain the young'uns, including family and holiday festivals, see **A Portland Year**.

MUSIC

- **Metropolitan Youth Symphony**, 503-239-4566, www.playmys.org; the Metropolitan Youth Symphony comprises several hundred young musicians (in several different groups) from throughout the metropolitan area, with an age range of six years through college.

- The **Oregon Children's Choir & Youth Chorale**, 503-697-1596, www.occyc. org, consists of three choirs divided by grade level; membership is by audition only, and the two older groups embark on summer tours to national or international destinations.
- **Portland Boychoir**, 503-697-3872, www.portlandboychoir.org, does not require musical training for boys 6 to 10 years old; boys over 10 with choral or other musical training must audition.
- **Portland Symphonic Girlchoir**, 503-226-6162, www.girlchoir.com, comprises multiple ensembles for girls 6 to 18 years old.
- **Portland Youth Philharmonic**, 1037 SW Broadway, 503-223-5939, www.port landyouthphil.org; the country's oldest youth orchestra has come a long way from its roots as the "Sagebrush Symphony." The organization now encompasses two full orchestras as well as a string orchestra and a wind ensemble. Membership is by open audition, and the musicians occasionally embark on national and international tours.

MUSEUMS AND OUTDOOR ATTRACTIONS

- **Kidd's Toy Museum**, 1300 SE Grand Ave, 503-233-7807; no, it's not misspelled—this museum houses more than 10,000 toys from the collection of Frank Kidd.
- **Oregon Zoo**, Washington Park, 4001 SW Canyon Rd, 503-226-1561, www. oregonzoo.org; the Oregon Zoo continues to expand its offerings. Besides the usual collection of animals from around the world—including a renowned herd of Asian elephants and an associated elephant museum—the zoo has several exhibits devoted to the fauna of the Pacific Northwest. The zoo also hosts frequent festivals and concerts.
- **Portland Children's Museum**, Washington Park, 4015 SW Canyon Rd, 503-223-6500, www.portlandchildrensmuseum.org; this is the city's largest kid-centric museum, and it has a correspondingly large array of theme play areas/exhibits, including a dig pit, "market," water play area, clay studio, etc.
- **Safety Learning Center and Fire Museum and the Historic Belmont Firehouse**, 900 SE 35th Ave, 503-823-3615 (open by advance arrangement and on the second Saturday of each month); the city's oldest working firehouse focuses on life safety education, but also includes the requisite fire pole, fire engine, and other hands-on firehouse accouterments.
- **Bonneville Fish Hatchery** off I-84, exit 40, west of Cascade Locks, 541-374-8393, www.nwp.usace.army.mil/op/b/dir_hatch.asp; the fish hatchery adjacent to Bonneville Dam (which can be an interesting destination for older kids in its own right) includes a sturgeon viewing pond with underwater view-

ing windows that allow visitors to peer at a variety of impressive fish, including Herman the Sturgeon, a 12-footer.

THEATER AND DANCE

- **Krayon Kids Musical Theater Company**, 503-656-6099, www.krayonkids.org, based in Oregon City, organizes musical productions cast entirely with kids.
- **New Blue Parrot Children's Theater**, 360-696-1155, www.newblueparrot. com, is an amateur children's theater based in Washougal.
- **Northwest Children's Theater and School**, 1819 NW Everett St, 503-222-4480, www.nwcts.org; based in the Northwest Neighborhood Cultural Center, Northwest Children's Theater stages several youth-oriented productions each year and offers acting, theater, and film and video classes for children.
- **Oregon Children's Theater**, 503-228-9571, www.octc.org; the Oregon Children's Theater is Oregon's largest nonprofit professional children's theater company, and puts on several productions each year, generally in one of the large downtown theaters. The OCT offers acting and production classes and workshops for children ages 4 and older.
- **Tears of Joy Puppet Theatre**, 503-248-0557 (Portland), 360-695-3050 (Vancouver), www.tojt.com; most Tears of Joy productions are designed (or at least suitable) for children, but a few of its performances are definitely adults-only.

PORTLAND IS A GREAT SPORTS AND RECREATION TOWN, PARTICU-larly for weekend warriors who like playing games as much as (or more than) they like watching them. Portland doesn't have many major profes-sional teams—the city government has called Portland the most under-served professional sports market in the country—but the area's abundant recreation-al opportunities more than make up for the lack of big-league luster. Besides taking advantage of a great environment for year-round outdoor recreation, Portlanders also engage in some quirky quasi-sports, like geocaching (which was invented here). Unless you're into something really esoteric like ice kiting, you're bound to find congenial surroundings for whatever pastime literally or figuratively floats your boat.

Health clubs and sporting goods stores are listed at the end of this chapter.

PROFESSIONAL AND SEMIPROFESSIONAL SPORTS

Portland has only one major professional sports team—the Trail Blazers National Basketball Association franchise—but the city nonetheless offers a decent range of opportunities to watch talented athletes play various games. If you need a major league baseball or NFL fix, you'll need to make the trek north to Seattle to see the Mariners or the Seahawks in action.

BASEBALL

Portland is the largest metropolitan area in the United States without a major league baseball team. Various civic boosters periodically launch efforts to lure an existing or expansion team to Portland, and came reasonably close to get-ting the relocating Montreal Expos (a team that Washington, D.C., ultimately bagged; they're now the Nationals). For now, Portland has to be content with Triple-A baseball, which has the advantage of being less expensive and arguably more fun to watch than major league baseball. The **Portland Beavers** (www. portlandbeavers.com), a farm team for the San Diego Padres, play at PGE Park (1844 SW Morrison St, 503-553-5400, www.pgepark.com), located on the MAX line just west of downtown. Tickets are available through Ticketmaster or at the box office before each home game.

BASKETBALL

The **Portland Trail Blazers** (www.blazers.com) won their only NBA championship in 1977. Since then, the Trail Blazers have fielded some strong teams that have vied for and won the NBA Western Conference title, as well as mediocre rosters that included players who had run-ins with the law. (The latter circumstance begat the "Jail Blazers" nickname.) Still, the Blazers are the only major sports franchise in town, and they enjoy strong (if not necessarily broad-based) community support even when their record is abysmal. The Blazers play in the Rose Garden (the arena in Northeast Portland, not the rose garden in Washington Park—more than one newcomer has made that mistake). Tickets are available through the team web site or by calling the Blazer Ticket Line (503-797-9600).

The Portland area is also home to not one but two teams in the minor-league International Basketball League (IBL). The **Portland Chinooks** represent Portland, while their presumably hated rivals, the **Vancouver Volcanoes**, lurk across the Columbia. Information about both teams is available on the IBL web site, www.iblhoopsonline.com. While IBL basketball is purportedly fast-paced and high-scoring, you'll be hard-pressed to find many people other than diehard sports fans who have heard of either of these teams.

HOCKEY

The "major-junior" **Portland Winter Hawks** (www.winterhawks.com) compete in the Calgary-based Western Hockey League, which mainly comprises teams based in western Canadian cities. The Winter Hawks enjoy a fiercely loyal fan base, and games can be rowdy (although actual fights are generally confined to the players). Half-time activities, which sometimes involve hapless fans slipping around on the ice in a quest for some prize, can be surprisingly entertaining in a low-key way. During their fall and winter season, the Winter Hawks play most home games in the Memorial Coliseum, which is near the Rose Garden arena in the Rose Quarter of Northeast Portland. Tickets are available from Ticketmaster or at the Memorial Coliseum and Rose Quarter box offices.

Portland is frequently named as a contender for an NHL franchise when and if the league expands, but don't hold your breath.

LACROSSE

The **Portland LumberJax** (www.portlandjax.com) play professional indoor lacrosse in the Rose Garden. The team began playing in 2006 as part of the National Lacrosse League. The season runs from December to April. Tickets are available online through the team's web site or by telephone at 866-983-5656.

SOCCER

The **Portland Timbers** (www.portlandtimbers.com) play professional soccer as part of the United Soccer Leagues First Division (one tier below Major League Soccer). The season runs from April to September. The Timbers play home games at PGE Park. Tickets are available through Ticketmaster or from the PGE Park box office.

In early 2007, a group of investors announced their intention to bring a Major League Soccer team to Portland by 2010. Will they be more successful than the baseball boosters? Only time will tell.

COLLEGIATE AND HIGH SCHOOL SPORTS

Portland lacks the sort of college sports powerhouses that vie for national championships in football and basketball. The nearest Pac 10 schools are Oregon State University in Corvallis (about 90 minutes away), and the University of Oregon in Eugene (two hours south), and those schools' athletic programs suck up most of the state's college sports money and attention. That said, most nearby colleges and universities field intercollegiate teams in at least one sport. Probably the most watchable teams, at least for non-alumni, are the **University of Portland Pilots** women's and men's soccer teams. (The women's squad won the 2005 NCAA championship.) For more information, visit www.portlandpilots.com.

High school sports can be exciting, and not just for players and their friends and parents. In addition to football, baseball, basketball, and soccer, some schools offer lacrosse, water polo, and other less mainstream sports. Most high school athletic activities in Oregon are coordinated through the Oregon School Activities Association (www.osaa.org). (In Washington, the equivalent organization is the Washington Interscholastic Activities Association, www.wiaa.com.) For news coverage of Portland high school athletics, check out the sports section of the *Oregonian* or visit www.oregonlive.com/highschool/.

PARTICIPANT SPORTS AND OUTDOOR RECREATION

If you ask residents what they love about Portland, you're liable to get an earful about the great selection of outdoor recreational opportunities. From watching the sunset over the city from Mount Tabor Park to climbing Mount Hood, and from walking around the block to running the Portland Marathon, hundreds of activities are available for every level of athletic ability.

For general information about local parks, pools, community centers, tennis courts, or community athletic programs, start with your local parks department. In the city of Portland, contact **Portland Parks & Recreation** (503-823-PLAY, www.portlandparks.org). Contact information for other communities' parks departments is listed in the **Useful Phone Numbers and Web Sites** chapter.

BICYCLING

In Portland, bicycling is wildly popular, both as a recreational activity and as a means of transportation. (For information about bike routes, bike commuting, and getting around by bicycle generally, see the **Transportation** chapter.) Portland has an abundance of bike lanes and "bike boulevards"—streets with low traffic volume and, often, obstacles to through car traffic—and a developing system of paved off-street trails allows bicyclists to ride fairly long distances without having to dodge motorized vehicles. The longest of these urban trails is the 17-mile Springwater Corridor, which runs from the east bank of the Willamette River to Boring as part of the still incomplete 40-Mile Loop (see www.40mileloop.org for details); other off-street trails include the new Eastbank Esplanade and the Willamette Greenway; a long trail paralleling Marine Drive on the south shore of the Columbia River; and some not especially peaceful trails that parallel Interstate 205 and part of the Sunset Highway. Just west of the metro area, the **Banks-Vernonia State Trail** is a 21-mile rails-to-trails project that has been converted into a linear state park; see www.oregonstateparks.org/park_145.php for more information. Serious riders can practice, or race, on the scarily banked **velodrome** at Alpenrose Dairy in Southwest Portland (6149 SW Shattuck Rd, www.obra.org/track/information/index.html).

The bike touring possibilities outside Portland are legion. Thanks to the region's urban growth boundary, densely populated areas rather quickly give way to farmland and forest, laced with paved roads that, in many cases, have relatively low traffic volume. Your route could lead through flat farmlands, shady valleys in the Cascade foothills, and rolling vineyard country—all in one day. Pancake-flat Sauvie Island is an especially popular nearby destination; the fact that the island is reachable by public transportation (bikes allowed) adds to the appeal.

Road biking gets much of the press in Portland, but the region has outstanding mountain biking opportunities, too. Forest Park is a justly popular destination, with options for riders of various abilities. (Bikes are restricted to designated trails.) **Fat Tire Farm** (2714 NW Thurman St, 503-222-3276, www.fat tirefarm.com), is conveniently located virtually next door to the park; the store rents mountain bikes and can point out appropriate routes. Besides the miles of trails in Forest Park, there are plenty of lesser-known routes, including singletrack and doubletrack trails, outside the city; take a look at a mountain biking guidebook for suggestions, or contact Portland United Mountain Pedalers (see contact information below).

RESOURCES

The city of Portland's **Office of Transportation** posts extensive information its web site (www.portlandonline.com/transportation/) about bicycling in Portland, including bike maps and routes, a list of bicycle-related organizations and shops, and suggested bike touring itineraries; click on the "Getting Around Portland" tab, then select "Transportation Options," then "Bicycles." Several bike-related nonprofits, including the **Bicycle Transportation Alliance** (503-226-0676, www. bta4bikes.org), **Portland Cycling** (www.portlandcycling.net), the **Community Cycling Center** (1700 NE Alberta St, 503-288-8864, www.communitycycling center.org), and **Shift** (503-542-6900, www.shift2bikes.org), are very helpful sources of information for Portland bicyclists. **Oregon Cycling** magazine, available on freebie 'zine racks around town, publishes news and information for the cycling community and lists upcoming bike events.

EVENTS

If you like to bike in a group, or at least to follow an organized (and supported) itinerary, consider signing up for one of the many organized recreational rides that take place around the area. The biggest of these are **Cycle Oregon** (503-287-0405, www.cycleoregon.com), a week-long tour through a scenic part of the state—the itinerary changes each year—and the **Seattle to Portland Bicycle Classic** (206-522-3222, www.seattletoportland.com), a one- or two-day pedal between the two cities. Some of the many shorter bike tours that attract more casual riders include the **Worst Day of the Year Ride** (503-459-4508, www. worstdayride.com), held in typically rainy and chilly February; the **Night Ride** (503-459-4508, www.thenightride.com), which offers an after-dark tour of Portland that culminates in a midnight donut feed; and **Providence Bridge Pedal** (503-281-9198, www.providence.org/oregon/events/bridge_pedal), which wends its way across all ten of Portland's Willamette River road bridges. **ORbike** (www.orbike.com) maintains the most complete and up-to-date online list of bicycling events in the area.

BICYCLE CLUBS

The following organizations organize rides and events around the area.

- **Oregon Bicycle Racing Association**, www.obra.org
- **Portland United Mountain Pedalers (PUMP)**, www.pumpclub,org
- **Portland Velo**, www.portlandvelo.net
- **Portland Wheelmen Touring Club**, www.pwtc.com
- **Vancouver Bicycle Club**, www.vancouverbicyclingclub.com

BIRDING

Whether you're an experienced birder who's new to Portland or someone investigating the activity for the first time, the **Audubon Society of Portland** (5151 NW Cornell Rd, 503-29-6855, www.audubonportland.org) is a great place to start. The Society has its own 180-acre sanctuary adjacent to Forest Park in the West Hills, which includes an interpretive center, a care center for injured birds, and a store that sells field guides and other birding essentials. The Society's rare bird alert hotline is 503-292-6855.

BOATING

The **Oregon State Marine Board** (503-378-8587, www.boatoregon.com) provides a wealth of information about boating in the state, including current boating regulations, navigational hazards, and water access points. Its web site is useful for both motorized and non-motorized boaters. (Washington does not have a centralized source for boating information.)

CANOEING AND KAYAKING

Sea kayaking, whitewater kayaking, and canoeing are very popular throughout the Northwest. Non-motorized watercraft are generally permitted on any navigable body of water, but accessible public launch points may be hard to find. Popular nearby places for paddling include the Columbia Slough in North and Northeast Portland; coastal rivers and bays, such as Tillamook Bay; lakes and reservoirs, such as Blue Lake in Fairview (a good spot for fledgling canoeists); and the Clackamas, Tualatin, Sandy, Columbia, and Willamette rivers.

It is possible to make some epic river trips to or from Portland; if you have the time, you can float downstream on the mostly flat water of the Willamette for well over a hundred miles from Eugene to Portland, with a single portage at Willamette Falls in Oregon City. On the Columbia, the 146-mile Lower Columbia Water Trail (www.columbiawatertrail.org) leads from Bonneville Dam to Astoria.

(Be aware that paddling the Columbia can force you to contend with strong winds, surprisingly large waves, treacherous currents, and oceangoing ship traffic.) Some skilled ocean kayakers seeking saltwater brave the open Pacific, but others regularly head north to the protected waters of Puget Sound or southern British Columbia. For more specific information and suggested routes, check out one of the guidebooks listed in **A Portland Reading List** or contact one of the following local clubs:

- **DragonSports USA**, www.dragonsports.org (dragon boat paddling)
- **Lower Columbia Canoe Club**, www.l-ccc.org
- **Oregon Kayak and Canoe Club**, www.okcc.org
- **Oregon Ocean Paddling Society (OOPS)**, www.oopskayak.org
- **Portland, Oregon, Lesbian and Gay Kayaking Club**, www.outkayaking.org
- **Willamette Rowing Club**, www.willametterowing.com

RENTALS

If you'd like to dabble in paddling and don't want the hassle of transporting a boat, you can rent a watercraft from one of the following locations, all of which are located within easy carrying distance of a launch point:

- **Alder Creek Kayak & Canoe** (www.aldercreek.com) has three Portland-area locations: near OMSI on the east bank of the Willamette River (49 SE Clay St, 503-285-1819,), at Jantzen Beach on the Columbia (250 NE Tomahawk Island Dr, 503-285-0464), and at Brown's Ferry Park in Tualatin, on the Tualatin River (5855 SW Nyberg Ln, 503-691-2405, open Memorial Day–Labor Day only).
- **Portland River Company** (www.portlandrivercompany.com) has two locations on the west bank of the Willamette: RiverPlace Marina in downtown Portland (0315 SW Montgomery St, Suite 300, 503-229-0551), and at Willamette Park in South Portland (6342 SW Macadam Ave, 503-459-4050).

MOTORBOATS

Many Northwesterners own motorboats; small boats with outboard motors that can be transported by trailer and used for fishing are particular popular and versatile, although you'll also see folks with ski boats, jetskis, and motor yachts. Major rivers and larger lakes and reservoirs generally have convenient boat ramps or other access points; the **Oregon State Marine Board** provides a list of access points on its web site (www.boatoregon.com/Access/index.html). For Washington water access points, check the web site of the **Office of the Interagency Committee** (www.iac.wa.gov/maps/boat.htm).

Several marinas for larger boats are located along the Columbia River or on Multnomah Channel; the **RiverPlace Marina** (503-241-8283) is on the Willamette, right downtown. Most marinas offer motorboat rentals to qualified boaters.

If you're bringing in a boat from out-of-state, you'll need to register it. In Oregon, the **Oregon State Marine Board** coordinates boat registration; in Washington, you'll need to go through the **Washington Department of Licensing** (360-902-3900, www.dol.wa.gov/vehicleregistration/registerboat.html).

SAILING

Sailing on Portland-area rivers and lakes is enjoyable and can be challenging, but it is also constricting. The open North Pacific is often stormy, and the only access from Portland to the ocean is over the treacherous Columbia Bar. (Serious sailors who can afford it keep boats moored in Puget Sound, two to three hours north of Portland, which gives them access to hundreds of miles of protected sailing grounds.) For local sailing opportunities, including classes and races, contact the **Island Sailing Club** (515 NE Tomahawk Island Dr, 503-285-7765, www. islandsailing club.com) or the **Willamette Sailing Club** (6336 SW Beaver Ave, 503-246-5345, www.willamettesailingclub.com).

WHITEWATER RAFTING

Oregon is full of classic whitewater trips: the Deschutes River in central Oregon; the Snake River in Hells Canyon, on the Oregon-Idaho border; the McKenzie River, east of Eugene; the Owyhee River in remote southeastern Oregon; and the Rogue and Umpqua rivers in southern Oregon. Exciting whitewater is available closer to Portland on the Clackamas River, only an hour away; the North Santiam River, east of Salem; and the Wind, White Salmon, and Klickitat rivers on the Washington side of the Columbia River Gorge. Commercial rafting companies operate on all of these streams; check the yellow pages under "Rafts & Raft Trips" for company listings. For more specific information on whitewater rafting in Oregon, contact the **Northwest Rafters Association** (www.nwrafters.org) or the **Oregon Whitewater Association** (www.oregonwhitewater.org).

FISHING AND HUNTING

FISHING

The fishing and shellfishing opportunities available in Oregon are nothing short of amazing. In the Portland area, you can find salmon, trout, and other game fish in nearly every river and reservoir, including the Willamette River as it flows through downtown Portland. (You wouldn't be wise to eat bottom feeders from the lower Willamette unless your idea of a delicious meal includes not-so-delectable PCBs.)

The **Oregon Department of Fish and Wildlife** (ODFW) (3406 Cherry Ave NE, Salem, 503-947-6000, www.dfw.state.or.us) regulates fishing and hunting activity in Oregon, and is the best place to go for general information about license requirements and current regulations and restrictions. (In Washington, the equivalent agency is the **Washington State Department of Fish and Wildlife**, 360-902-2200, wdfw.wa.gov.) In Oregon, everyone 14 or older needs a license to fish; angling license fees range from $6.50 (for residents under 18) to $61.50 (for an annual nonresident license). One-day to seven-day licenses are available at reduced prices. Shellfish collection requires a separate license; fees range from $6.50 to $16.50. (Washington requirements and prices are similar.) Licenses are available at most sporting goods stores and many grocery stores.

OFDW also publishes useful pamphlets (most of which are available online) on a variety of fish and wildlife topics; they're not going to reveal anyone's secret fishing hole, but they can point you in the right direction. For specialized flyfishing information and equipment (including rentals), stop by **Countrysport Limited** (126 SW 1st Ave, 503-221-4545, www.csport.com).

HUNTING

Inner-city Portland isn't really a pickup-and-gun-rack kind of place (although there are certainly residents who enjoy hunting), but hunting, including bowhunting, is a popular activity in some surrounding areas, particularly in the Cascade foothills and the Coast Range. Targets range from such big game as deer, elk, or bear to waterfowl, rabbits, and quail. Check with **ODFW** for current regulations and license or tag requirements.

GEOCACHING AND ORIENTEERING

Geocaching is a relatively new activity that has only been around since 2000, and that actually originated just outside Portland in the town of Boring. It is essentially a high-tech game of hide-and-seek, in which a collection of objects is "cached" at specific coordinates and the seeker uses a global positioning system to find the cache. (Geocaching etiquette requires that if you take something from the cache, you leave something else in its place.) For information about geocaching in the area, check out **Portland Geocaching**, www.pdxgeocaching.com or **Oregon Geocaching**, www.oregongeoaching.org.

Orienteering is decidedly less high-tech, and involves point-to-point route-finding, sometimes over difficult or brushy terrain, using only a map and (usually) a compass. The **Columbia River Orienteering Club** (www.croc.org) organizes orienteering events in the Portland area.

GOLF

It's admittedly no Florida or Phoenix, but Portland harbors some surprisingly good golf courses. Even the weather helps the reasonably hardy golfer here: Mild temperatures and incessant precipitation keep the fairways green, and if you don't mind the rain, you can pretty much golf all winter. Also, you usually don't need to schedule summer tee times to avoid the midday heat, and given the infrequency of thunderstorms in western Oregon you are unlikely to be struck by lightning while hoisting your putter into the air in triumph after your impressive birdie on the eighth hole. If you're serious about your golf game, consider joining the **Oregon Golf Association** (www.oga.org), which also covers southwest Washington.

Below is a list of the public or semi-private golf courses within Portland, as well as some of the most popular courses in surrounding communities. Because one person's putt-putt is another's Pebble Beach, we've made no attempt to rank the courses, and there is a challenge here for every skill level. For a complete list of area courses check the yellow pages or visit the Oregon Golf Association web site (www.oga.org). For detailed information and course descriptions, visit **Oregon Golf** (www.oregongolf.com).

- **Broadmoor Golf Course**, 3509 NE Columbia Blvd, 503-281-1337, www.broad moor-1931.com
- **Camas Meadows Golf Club**, 4105 NW Camas Meadows Dr, Camas, 360-833-2000, 800-750-6511, www.camasmeadows.com
- **Charbonneau Golf Club**, 32020 SW Charbonneau Dr, Wilsonville, 503-694-1246, www.charbonneaugolf.com
- **Colwood National Golf Club**, 7313 NE Columbia Blvd, 503-254-5515, www.colwoodgolfclub.com
- **Eastmoreland Golf Course**, 2425 SE Bybee Blvd, 503-775-2900, www.eastmorelandgolfcourse.com
- **Forest Hills Golf Course**, 36260 SW Tongue Ln, Cornelius, 503-357-3347, www.golfforesthills.com
- **Glendoveer Golf Course**, 14015 NE Glisan St, 503-823-4653, www.metro-region.org/article.cfm?articleid=158
- **Heron Lakes Golf Course**, 3500 N Victory Blvd, 503-289-1818, www.heron lakesgolf.com
- **Langdon Farms Golf Club**, 24377 NE Airport Rd, Aurora, 503-678-3262, www.langdonfarms.com
- **Meriwether National Golf Club**, 5200 SW Rood Bridge Rd, Hillsboro, 503-648-4143, www.meriwethergolfclub.com
- **Mountain View Golf Course**, 27195 SE Kelso Rd, Boring, 503-663-4869
- **Pumpkin Ridge Golf Club**, 12930 Old Pumpkin Ridge Rd, North Plains, 503-647-9977, 888-594-4653, www.pumpkinridge.com

- **Quail Valley Golf Course**, 12565 NE Aerts Rd, Banks, 503-324-4444, www.quailvalleygolf.com
- **Redtail Golf Center**, 8200 SW Scholls Ferry Rd, 503-646-5166, www.golfredtail.com
- **The Reserve Vineyards & Golf Club**, 4805 SW 229th Ave, Aloha, 503-649-8191, www.reservegolf.com
- **Rose City Golf Course**, 2200 NE 71st Ave, 503-253-4744
- **Stone Creek Golf Club**, 14603 Stoneridge Dr, Oregon City, 503-518-4653, www.stonecreekgolfclub.net
- **Tri Mountain Golf Course**, 1701 NW 299th St, Ridgefield, 360-887-3004, 888-874-6686, www.trimountaingolf.com
- **Wildwood Golf Course**, 21881 NW St Helens Rd, 503-621-3402

Farther afield, the region around Bend in **Central Oregon** is a major golf destination, as is, to a lesser extent, the **Oregon Coast**.

HIKING AND WALKING

The amount of green you see on an Oregon state map speaks for itself. The majority of the state is public land, much of it national forest, and thousands of miles of hiking trails lace the region. It's not necessary to venture very far to get a hiking fix, however; almost every neighborhood in Portland is within hailing distance of a walking path or hiking trail. The longest and "wildest" trails are in the West Hills, especially in Washington Park and Forest Park. (The Wildwood Trail runs for 28 miles along the spine of the West Hills, from near the Oregon Zoo to the northern reaches of Forest Park, crossing paved roads only a few times along the way.) Many of the trails in the region are interconnected, and given world enough and time you could walk all the way across the state.

Portland is also a great city for urban rambles, especially near downtown and on the East Side, where sidewalks are abundant. If you like some direction to your walks, buy, beg, or borrow one of the walking or hiking guides described in **A Portland Reading List**, or visit peripatetic guidebook writer William L. Sullivan's web site (www.oregonhiking.com). For something more structured and informative, try one of tours offered by **Portland Walking Tours** (503-774-4522, www.portlandwalkingtours.com). (Note that their "Epicurean Excursion" through the Pearl District is unlikely to promote weight loss.)

Walking Toward Fitness (www.walkaboutmag.com), a free publication available at many natural food supermarkets and sporting goods stores, lists events of interest to Northwest walkers. If you prefer to walk with a partner or group, look into the following organizations:

- **Columbia River Volkssport Club** (www.crvcwalking.org) organizes recreational walks, usually about 6 miles in length, in scenic locations around the Portland area.

- Although best known as a mountaineering club, the **Mazamas** (527 SE 43rd Ave, 503-257-2345, www.mazamas.org) sponsor frequent hikes, including some for beginning hikers.
- Portland-based **Racewalkers Northwest**, www.rwnw.org, organizes local training walks and racewalk competitions.
- **Wonders of Walking**, www.wondersofwalking.com, sponsors various recreational and competitive walking events in the Northwest.

Portland Parks and Recreation (www.portlandparks.org) also organizes walks and hikes, as do many environmental organizations, including the **Sierra Club's** local Columbia Group (www.oregon.sierraclub.org/groups/columbia/).

HORSEBACK RIDING AND EQUESTRIAN SPORTS

Most equestrian activities necessarily take place outside of Portland, although there are some trails in the larger parks, such as Forest Park, that allow horses. If you're interested in trail rides, try **Flying "M" Ranch** (23029 NW Flying M Rd, Yamhill, 503-662-3222, www.flying-m-ranch.com) or **Cow Creek Ranch** (41670 Lodge Rd, Banks, 503-324-5983, www.cowcreekranch.net). For more serious trail riding, the nonprofit **Oregon Equestrian Trails** (www.oregonequestriantrails. org) is an excellent resource. If you're looking for riding lessons, or if you actually own or want to own a horse, check out the listings at **Oregon Horse** (www. oregonhorse.net) or the **Oregon Equestrian Network** (541-846-0327, www. oregonequest.com).

HOT AIR BALLOONING

Several area companies will carry you into the sky in a hot air balloon (and bring you back down again). Try **Morning Star Hot Air Balloon Company** (Ridgefield, Washington, 360-887-2388, www.nwplace.com/mornstar.html), **Portland Rose Hot Air Balloon Adventures** (18965 SW Olson Ct, Lake Oswego, 503-638-1301, 877-934-6359, www.portlandroseballoons.com), or **Vista Balloon Adventures** (23324 SW Sherk Pl, Sherwood, 503-625-7385, 800-622-2309, www.vistaballoon. com). Flights generally occur over outlying areas.

ICE SKATING

Portland lacks the convenient frozen ponds of, say, Minneapolis, so ice skating necessarily takes place in indoor rinks. All of the rinks below offer public skating, skate rentals, and lessons; most sponsor hockey, speedskating, and other ice-related activities. Please be tactful and bear in mind that Tonya Harding jokes wore out their welcome long ago.

- **Lloyd Center Ice Rink**, Lloyd Center Mall (lower level), 503-288-6073, www. lloydcenterice.com
- **Mountain View Ice Arena**, 14313 SE Mill Plain Blvd, Vancouver, 360-896-8700, 503-235-8176, www.mtviewice.com
- **Sherwood Ice Arena**, 20407 SW Borchers Dr, Sherwood, 503-625-5757, www. sherwoodicearena.com
- **Valley Ice Arena**, 9250 SW Beaverton-Hillsdale Hwy, 503-297-2521, www. valleyicearena.com

Amateur figure skaters may be interested in the **Portland Ice Skating Club** (www.pisc.org). If ice skating is too strenuous for your taste, try **curling**. The Evergreen Curling Club (www.evergreencurling.org) is ready and willing to help you out.

MUSHROOM HUNTING

If you know the difference between a morel and a false morel—or if you'd like to—consider joining the **Oregon Mycological Society** (503-659-1668, www. wildmushrooms.org). OMS organizes frequent mushroom hunts and educates its members about mushroom identification and other mycological issues. OMS puts the "fun" in fungi!

PAINTBALL & LASER TAG

If shooting at people is your hobby, and you want to keep it legal, paintball and laser tag are among your few available non-military options. Here are a few establishments that will facilitate your murderous predilections:

- **Action Acres**, 10381 S Mulino Rd, Canby, 503-266-5733, www.actionacrespb. com
- **LaserPort**, 6540 SW Fallbrook Pl, Beaverton, 503-526-9501, www.laserportof beaverton.com
- **Paintball Island**, 6255 Arndt Rd, Canby, 503-309-9900, www.paintballisland. net
- **Portland Paintball**, 631 NE Grand Ave, 503-233-1105, www.portlandpaintball. us
- **Ultrazone Laser Tag**, 16074 SE McLoughlin Blvd, Milwaukie, 503-652-1122, www.ultrazoneportland.com
- **Xtremez**, 1212 W Fourth Plain Blvd, Vancouver, 360-567-2520, www.xtremez. com

For something a bit more cloak-and-dagger, try **PDX Assassin** (www.pdxas sassin.net). This group periodically organizes city-wide, um, assassination games, in which water-pistols and water-balloons are the weapons, and each player is both target and assassin. The fun and paranoia can go on for weeks!

RACQUET SPORTS

Many city and suburban public parks have outdoor tennis courts, the majority of which are lighted. Given the inevitable heartbreak and soggy tennis balls that result from playing on a court full of puddles, Portland thankfully also has its share of indoor courts. The following indoor courts are public facilities:

- **Lake Oswego Indoor Tennis Center**, 2900 Diane Dr, Lake Oswego, 503-635-5550, www.ci.oswego.or.us/parksrec/tennis.htm
- **Portland Tennis Center**, 324 NE 12th Ave, 503-823-3189, www.pdx10s.com
- **St. Johns Racquet Center**, 7519 N Burlington Ave, 503-823-3629, www.pdx10s.com

There are several private racquet clubs in the area, too; check the Yellow Pages under "Tennis Courts-Private" for listings. In addition, some of the larger health clubs feature racquetball and squash courts.

ROCK CLIMBING AND MOUNTAINEERING

ROCK CLIMBING

The area around Portland is blessed with many good rock climbing and bouldering options, ranging from climbs in abandoned quarries to ascents of towering natural cliffs; a few decent outdoor sites are within city limits, notably Rocky Butte quarry in Northeast Portland. (An online climbing map of Rocky Butte is available at ors.alpineclub.org/AAC/rocky1.html.) Smith Rock State Park in Central Oregon (www.oregonstateparks.org/park_51.php or www.smithrock.com) is one of the premier climb destinations in the country.

If you want to learn to climb, or just need to keep your skills up, try one of the following rock gyms. (Rock gyms are also good sources of information on local climbing options and routes.)

- **The Circuit Bouldering Gym**, 6050 SW Macadam Ave, 503-246-5111, www.thecircuitgym.com
- **Portland Rock Gym**, 21 NE 12th Ave, 503-232-8310, www.portlandrockgym.com
- **Stoneworks Climbing Gym**, 6775 SW 111th Ave, Beaverton, 503-644-3517, www.belay.com

In addition, some area health clubs have climbing walls.

MOUNTAINEERING

The Northwest offers abundant possibilities for serious mountaineers. The most obvious local destination is glacier-covered Mount Hood, reputedly one of the world's most-climbed peaks. At 11,240 feet, Mount Hood is not especially high, but it is a challenging and potentially treacherous climb that should not be attempted lightly: People die on the mountain every year. Other tempting (and potentially deadly) glaciated Cascade volcanoes include Mount Jefferson, Mount Adams, Mount Baker, and Mount Rainier.

The **Mazamas** (527 SE 43rd Ave, 503-227-2345, www.mazamas.org) is the area's largest mountaineering club; the group has a large new clubhouse in Southeast Portland and it offers excellent classes on mountaineering basics. The Oregon Section of the **American Alpine Club** (ors.alpineclub.org) is also active locally.

RUNNING AND JOGGING

The surprising numbers of lycra-clad bodies sloshing down the street in the damp winter pre-dawn attest to the local popularity of recreational running. (Unlike in some higher-crime cities, the people you see dashing down the street usually aren't running away from anything, except perhaps their inner demons.)

RESOURCES

Portland Runner (www.portlandrunner.com) is an online running magazine that includes event listings and an interesting (to runners) blog. Although it's in the business of selling running shoes and apparel, the **Portland Running Company** (11355 SW Scholls Ferry Rd, Beaverton, 503-524-7570, www.port landrunningcompany.com) also offers training tips, lists suggested routes, and provides links to area running organizations and events. Most Northwest races and running events are listed on **www.racecenter.com**, which also offers online registration.

EVENTS

Recreational and competitive running (and walking) events take place all year. They run the gamut from seasonal activities like **First Run** (held at midnight on New Year's) or the **Red-Nosed Rundeer** (www.rednosedrun.com) to such themed events as the **Hippie Chick Half-Marathon** (for women only) (www.all womenshalf.com). The two biggest running events on the local calendar are the **Hood to Coast** relay (503-292-4626, www.hoodtocoast.com in July, which wends its weary way from Timberline Lodge on Mount Hood to the Oregon Coast, and the **Portland Marathon** (503-226-1111, www.portlandmarathon.org), held in October.

RUNNING CLUBS

- **Oregon Road Runners Club**, www.orrc.net
- **Portland Frontrunners**, www.portlandfrontrunners.org (gay/bi/lesbian running club)
- **Team Red Lizard Running Club**, www.redlizardrunning.com

SKATING AND SKATEBOARDING

In Portland, skates and skateboards are a recognized form of transportation, and the city has actually designated a few "preferred skating routes" downtown. The web site for the city's **Office of Transportation** lists rules and safety suggestions for skaters who use public streets. Visit www.portlandonline.com/transportation/index.cfm?c=34780 for more information.

ROLLER SKATING/IN-LINE SKATING

In-line skating remains a popular activity on Portland's paved paths, particularly along the downtown waterfront and on the East Blank Esplanade, and it looks like old-school roller skates may be making a comeback, too. Visit www.portlandskate.com for event listings and information about recreational in-line skating in Portland. If you prefer to skate indoors, the **Oaks Skating Rink** at Oaks Amusement Park in Sellwood (7100 Oaks Park Way, 503-236-5722, www.oakspark.com/skating.html) boasts a 20,000 square foot wooden floor. **Indoor Goals** (16340 NW Bethany Ct, Beaverton, 503-629-9500, www.indoorgoals.com) hosts inline hockey leagues.

SKATEBOARDING

Portland's a totally sick place to get your ollie on, bro. (Note: to a skateboarder, this is a good thing.) Not only is skateboarding legal on public streets (see above), but skateparks are increasingly common, even in suburban communities. The city of Portland has approved a master plan for the development of a network of 19 skateparks; visit the web site of **Skaters for Portland Skateparks** (www.skateportland.org) for details. The granddaddy of all Portland skateparks is the legendary and semi-official **Burnside Skatepark** (burnsideskatepark.blogspot.com), which lurks under the east side of the Burnside Bridge like a gnarly concrete troll. The private **Department of Skateboarding** (15 NE Hancock St, 503-493-9480, www.departmentofskateboarding.com) is an indoor wooden skatepark—very appealing on those cold, damp winter days—but you'll have to sign a waiver and pay a fee to use the facility.

SkateOregon (www.skateoregon.com) offers comprehensive information about skate parks throughout the state and beyond.

SKYDIVING

If you're the sort of person who gets a rush out of jumping out of planes, try **Skydive Oregon**, 12150 S Hwy 211, Molalla, 503-829-3483, 800-934-5867, www.skydiveoregon.com.

TEAM SPORTS

BASKETBALL

Many gyms, community centers, and even city parks have indoor (or at least covered) basketball courts, and pick-up games are easy to find. If you're after a more structured experience, **PortlandBasketball.com** (www.portlandbasketball.com) claims to be the world's largest adult basketball league, with 190 teams (including co-ed teams) for every age and skill level. The less grandiose **RecBasketball.com** (503-249-1986, www.recbasketball.com) also organizes adult basketball leagues.

HOCKEY

Most area ice rinks can point you in the right direction for ice hockey leagues. (See "Ice Skating" above.) For information about organized roller hockey, contact **Indoor Goals** (16340 NW Bethany Ct, Beaverton, 503-629-9500, www.indoorgoals.com).

SOCCER

Soccer is undoubtedly the most popular team sport in Portland. The **Oregon Youth Soccer Association** (503-626-4625, 800-275-7533, www.oregonyouthsoccer.org) oversees the vast majority of youth soccer leagues and games in the state; adult footballers bow to the mighty **Oregon Adult Soccer Association** (503-292-1814, www.oregonadultsoccer.com), which coordinates various soccer leagues. **Northwest United Womens Soccer** (www.oregonwomenssoccer.com) organizes women-only leagues.

Several indoor soccer facilities organize league play on astro-turfed, hockey-rink-like fields. Portland-area indoor soccer arenas include **Portland Indoor Soccer** (418 SE Main St, 503-231-6368, www.pdxindoorsoccer.com); the **Mittleman Jewish Community Center** (6651 SW Capitol Hwy. 503-452-3427, www.oregonjcc.org/indoorsoccer); **Soccerplex** (8785 SW Beaverton-Hillsdale Hwy, 503-297-4145, www.soccerplex.com); **Indoor Goals** (16340 NW Bethany Ct, Beaverton, 503-629-9500, www.indoorgoals.com); and **Tualatin Indoor Soccer** (11883 SW Itel St, Tualatin, 503-885-9300, www.tualatinindoor.com).

A new option for indoor soccer is **Portland Futsal** (3401 SE 17th Ave, 503-2FUTSAL, www.portlandfutsal.com). Futsal is a Brazilian variant of indoor soccer that dispenses with walls.

SOFTBALL

The **Portland Metro Softball Association** (PMSA) (www.portlandsoftball.com) offers one-stop shopping for all your organized softball needs. PMSA coordinates play for 10,000 players; the 700 member teams include men's, women's, and co-ed teams.

OTHER TEAM SPORTS

Underdog Portland (503-756-4176, www.underdogportland.com) sponsors coed kickball and flag football leagues. **Portlandfootball.com** (www.portlandfootball.com) is another flag football organization. **Lacrosse Northwest** (www.laxnw.com) and **Oregon Lacrosse** (www.oregonlax.com) are your go-to organizations for both youth and adult lacrosse. **Recesstime Sports Leagues** (503-381-5056, www.recesstimesports.com) organizes leagues in dodgeball, kickball, ping pong, and bowling. The **Oregon Sports Union Rugby Club** (www.orsu.org) tackles men's and women's rugby, while if you prefer a sport with more tea breaks and fewer cracked ribs, check out the **Multnomah Cricket Club** (www.multnomahcc.com).

ULTIMATE AND DISC GOLF

Many Portland parks have adequate space for a casual game of Frisbee. If ultimate Frisbee is your game of choice, the **Portland Ultimate Frisbee Federation** (www.portlandultimate.org) coordinates league play and designates times and places for pick-up games.

Disc golf is played at a growing number of Portland-area parks. The **Oregon Disc Sports Alliance** (www.odsa.com) maintains an up-to-date list of Pacific

Northwest disc golf courses on its web site, and provides detailed descriptions of each course as well as links to regional disc golf events, leagues, and clubs.

WATER SPORTS

SCUBA DIVING

While there are no real recreational dive sites in Portland proper—you wouldn't really want to encounter the sorts of things you might find in the murky lower Willamette—the area nonetheless nurtures an active dive community. Hood Canal in Washington State (an arm of Puget Sound) is a popular dive destination that's not too far away, and there are plenty of challenging dives off the Oregon Coast. If you'd like to get certified in advance of a trip to someplace like Belize, check with one of the clubs listed below for recommendations, or look in the Yellow Pages under "Scuba Diving Instruction" for a list of scuba schools.

The following are a few local dive clubs. (If you're looking for a different kind of dive club, perhaps one with dim lights and lots of secondhand smoke, try looking under "Nightclubs and Discos" in the **Cultural Life** chapter.)

- **Innerspace Dive Club**, www.innerspacedive.com
- **Northwest Dive Buddies**, www.nwdivebuddies.com
- **Oregon Scuba Divers**, www.oregonscuba.com

SURFING/WINDSURFING/KITEBOARDING

Surfing at the Oregon Coast is at best a full wetsuit proposition. Much of the coastline is viable surfing territory for the suitably skilled and equipped, but many Oregon surfers are reluctant to divulge the locations of their favorite breaks. (Be aware that surfers in certain towns are notorious for a "locals only" attitude, especially when they encounter vehicles with out-of-state plates.) For basic information about surfing in Oregon, visit **www.oregonsurf.com**. One professional surfing event, the Nelscott Reef Tow (www.nelscottreef.com), in which jetskis tow surfers into position, takes place off Lincoln City.

Some of the world's best **windsurfing** is found in the nearby Columbia River Gorge; the sheer-sided gorge serves as a wind tunnel for air moving between the Columbia Basin and the Willamette Valley, which means that afternoon winds are generally strong and reliable. The Oregon windsurfing capital is Hood River, about an hour east of Portland. The town is filled with windsurf-related businesses—even the local Full Sail brewery is named in honor of the sport. Hood River is also a major destination for **kiteboarding**, a sport in which a rider on a small kiteboard or surfboard is pulled along by a large kite or sail; sustained gusts or large waves can give the rider serious air-time.

Any boardsport store can help with rental equipment or lessons. If you're a first timer, it's probably most efficient to start in Hood River. In Portland, try **All Surf Industry** (532 SE Clay St, 503-239-8973, www.allsurfindustry.com) or **Gorge Performance** (7400 SW Macadam Ave, 503-246-6646, www.gorgeperformance. com).

SWIMMING

SWIMMING BEACHES

When the first wave of hot weather strikes Portland, many people head for nearby streams like the Sandy River and Clackamas River. Because the rivers are usually still frigid and full of snowmelt, however, drownings and deaths by hypothermia (often exacerbated by excessive alcohol consumption) make the news every year. That said, water temperatures usually warm up nicely by July in most area lakes and rivers. The Pacific is a different story; only the very hardy (or foolhardy) can stand to remain in the ocean in Oregon for very long without a wetsuit.

Public **swimming beaches** in the Portland region include:

- **Blue Lake Regional Park**, 20500 NE Marine Dr, Fairview, 503-797-1850, www. metro-region.org/article.cfm?articleid=149, has a very popular swimming beach.
- **Henry Hagg Lake**, 503-846-8715, www.co.washington.or.us/deptmts/sup_ serv/fac_mgt/parks/hagglake.htm, at Scoggins Valley Park in Gaston, south of Forest Grove, nestles in the foothills of the Coast Range; the water here warms up into the mid-70s in high summer.
- **Rooster Rock State Park**, 503-695-2261, www.oregonstateparks.org/park_ 175.php, hugs the shore of the Columbia River east of Troutdale (at Exit 25 off Interstate 84). The park offers two swimming beaches, one of which is a designated nude beach.
- **Sauvie Island** has a couple of beaches on the Columbia River (basically at the end of the island's road). The beaches, which can be steep when water levels are low, offer interesting views of passing barges and oceangoing cargo ships; nearby Collins Beach (an officially designated nude beach) offers views of a different kind.
- **Vancouver Lake**, 6801 NW Lower River Rd, Vancouver, 360-619-1111, www. co.clark.wa.us/parks/vancouverlake.html; the lake has a designated swimming area, and water quality is regularly monitored for excessive amounts of *E. coli* bacteria and blooms of toxic blue-green algae. (That is supposed to make you feel safe, by the way.)

SWIMMING POOLS

Portland Parks and Recreation operates six indoor pools (open year-round) and seven outdoor pools (open mid-June through early September). Pools have scheduled times for lap swimming, open play, family play, and water exercise classes; the indoor pools at Mt. Scott Community Center and Southwest Community Center have separate children's water play areas with spraying water toys and 115-foot waterslides. For information call 503-823-SWIM or visit www.port landonline.com/parks/index.cfm?c=38284.

If you live outside Portland, check with your local parks and recreation department (listed in the **Useful Phone Numbers and Web Sites** chapter) for aquatic centers and outdoor pools in your area. Note that many area health clubs also have swimming facilities.

WINTER SPORTS

Sometime in November, as raindrops keep falling on their heads and white flakes start to pile up in the Cascades, the thoughts of many Portlanders turn to winter sports. Transplants from outside the Northwest will notice four distinctive features of snow in this region. First, it tends to be heavy and wet: Particularly at lower elevations on the west side of the Cascades, Oregon's climate is not cold and dry enough to reliably produce the kind of powder that falls in the Rockies, and the result is sometimes referred to derisively as "Cascade concrete." Second, there's usually lots of the stuff: Even in an average year snowfall totals exceed 40 feet in places like Crater Lake, while in exceptional years truly monumental levels can accumulate. (In February 1999, the Mount Baker ski area in Washington state had to close for several days because 70 feet of snow had buried the chair lifts.) Third, it sticks around: several ski areas regularly stay open into June, and Timberline's Palmer Snowfield, high on Mount Hood, is open almost year-round. (Timberline is a popular summer training center for Olympic skiers and snowboarders.) And last, it doesn't fall much at low elevations: To get your snow fix, you'll have to head east and uphill.

SNO-PARK PERMITS

If plan to ski, snowboard, snowshoe, or just play in the snow, you'll need to get a **Sno-Park permit**. If you park in a designated Winter Recreation Area—and most places you'll park for winter sports and snow play will be so designated—between November 15 and April 30, you must display a permit inside your windshield. (The fees from the permit program pay for snow removal in the parking areas.) You can buy a permit at some government offices and most ski areas and sporting goods stores. One-day permits for Oregon cost $3, three-day permits cost $7, and season permits cost $15; in Washington, one-day permits cost $8 and seasonal and special groomed trail permits cost $20. Vendors generally charge an additional convenience fee. Oregon honors Sno-Park permits issued by Washington, California, and Idaho (and vice-versa). If you have Washington plates, you must purchase a Washington permit to park in a Washington Sno-Park.

For more information, or for a map of winter parking areas where permits are required, visit www.oregon.gov/ODOT/DMV/vehicle/sno_park_permits. shtml (for Oregon) or www.parks.wa.gov/winter/permits.asp (for Washington).

For information about chain and traction tire requirements for winter driving, see the **Transportation** chapter.

DOWNHILL SKIING AND SNOWBOARDING

The most popular and developed ski areas in the state are on Mount Hood and elsewhere in the northern Oregon Cascades, one to four hours from Portland. The closest ski areas to Portland are:

- **Cooper Spur Mountain Resort**, 541-352-6692, www.cooperspur.com; this old-school, family-friendly ski area on the east side of Mount Hood has one chair lift, a rope tow, and an inner tube tow.
- **Hoodoo**, 541-822-3799, www.hoodoo.com; closer to Salem and Eugene than to Portland, Hoodoo offers 7 lifts and 800 skiable acres, with a good mix of beginner, intermediate, and advanced runs.
- **Mt. Bachelor**, 541-382-2442, 800-829-2442, www.mtbachelor.com; not really a day trip, Mt. Bachelor is 20 miles west of Bend, in Central Oregon. Despite the distance from Portland, Mt. Bachelor's weather (sunnier than Mount Hood) and generally good snow conditions, combined with more than 3,500 acres of skiable terrain, make it a popular destination.
- **Mt. Hood Meadows**, 800-SKI-HOOD, www.skihood.com; with 11 lifts, including five high-speed quads, Meadows is the largest ski area on Mount Hood. Including a snowcat skiing option, Meadows has almost a 4,000-foot vertical, and its location on the mountain's east side gives it noticeably more sun. On the downside, it's a longer drive than Timberline or Skibowl.
- **Mt. Hood Skibowl**, 503-222-2695, 800-SKI-BOWL, www.skibowl.com; this large ski area has a large number of black diamond runs and is the closest ski area to Portland; because of its relatively low base elevation, snow conditions can be iffy during winter warm spells. In summer, Skibowl turnss into an adrenaline sports park.
- **Summit Ski Area**, 503-272-0256, www.summitskiarea.com; perched above the rest area at Government Camp, near Mount Hood, this small ski, snowboard, and tubing area opened in 1927 and is the oldest ski area in the Northwest.
- **Timberline**, 503-272-3311, www.timberlinelodge.com; with an annual average snowfall of more than 400 inches, Timberline usually has the deepest

snow base of any Oregon ski area, and has a stunning setting high on the south slope of Mount Hood. Fans of *The Shining* will recognize Timberline's Depression-era lodge.

Most of Oregon's large ski areas, and some of the small ones, offer night skiing. Mt. Hood Skibowl claims to have the largest night ski area in the country. If you don't own your own equipment, rentals are available at outdoor stores in the Portland area; in Sandy, Welches, and other communities along Highway 26 on the way to Mount Hood; and at the ski areas themselves.

Farther afield, several ski areas in eastern and southern Oregon have small or nonexistent crowds. **Ski Anthony Lakes** (www.anthonylakes.com), in the Blue Mountains near Baker City, usually has the best powder and some of the most challenging terrain in the state. Many diehard Portland skiers and boarders make the seven-plus hour trek north to British Columbia's **Whistler Blackcomb** resort (www.whistlerblackcomb.com), where the 2010 Winter Olympics will be held.

Several Portland-area ski and snowboard clubs sponsor outings, races, lessons, and social events. For a fairly complete list of local clubs, visit the **Northwest Ski Club Council** web site, www.nwskiers.org.

NORDIC AND TELEMARK SKIING

The mid-to-high elevations of Oregon's national forests are laced with Nordic (cross-country) ski trails for all abilities. Extensive trail networks radiate out from Government Camp on Mount Hood, Santiam Pass east of Salem, and in the Mount Bachelor area near Bend. There are several good guidebooks to cross-country ski routes in Oregon and Washington (see **A Portland Reading List** for suggestions). Telemark skiers have abundant opportunities as well; for a memorable experience, do a spring ascent of Mount St. Helens on a clear day, and ski most of the way down (permit required).

Novice snowshoers (and occasionally large dogs) sometimes obliterate ski tracks on some cross-country routes. To guarantee a clear trail, try one of the following groomed trail networks:

- **Cooper Spur Nordic Center** (541-352-6692, www.cooperspur.com/Adven tures/crosscountry.aspx), near Cooper Spur Ski Area on the east side of Mount Hood, has 6.5 kilometers of groomed trails.
- **Mount Hood Meadows Nordic Center** (503-337-2222, 800-SKI-HOOD, www. skihood.com/mountain/nordiccenter/), off Highway 35 on the southeast side of Mount Hood, maintains 15 kilometers of groomed trails.
- **Mount Bachelor Nordic Center** (800-829-2442, www.mtbachelor.com/ winter/crosscountry), near Bend in central Oregon, offers 56 kilometers of groomed trails, and includes a Nordic freestyle terrain park.
- The **Teacup Lake Nordic Club** (www.teacupnordic.org) maintains a 20-kilo-

meter network of groomed trails off Highway 35 on the east side of Mount Hood.

If you'd like to hobnob with likeminded skiers, contact the Portland chapter of the **Oregon Nordic Club** (www.onc.org/pdx.html) or the **Bergfreunde Club** (503-245-8453, www.bergfreunde.org).

SNOWSHOEING

Snowshoeing has exploded in popularity in the last five years, The sport has several attractions: it's free (apart from the cost of renting or buying the snowshoes), it requires no special skills or training, and it can be done pretty much anywhere there is a snowed-over road or trail. If you're following a ski trail, please be courteous and keep to one side to avoid obliterating ski tracks.

If you'd like to try snowshoeing, but don't want to set out on your own, **Portland Parks and Recreation** (503-823-PLAY, www.portlandparks.org) offers several snowshoe excursions each winter.

SNOWMOBILING

Snowmobiling is allowed on many national forest roads and trails; access is generally from sno-parks or from private resorts. For more information, contact the **Oregon State Snowmobiling Association**, www.oregonsnow.org.

OTHER RECREATIONAL ACTIVITIES

AUTOMOBILE RACING

Portland International Raceway (West Delta Park, 1940 N Victory Blvd, 503-823-7223, www.portlandraceway.com) hosts a variety of auto races and other motorsport events. It recently announced its intention to be the first carbon-neutral motorsports park in the country. The **Woodburn Dragstrip** (7730 Highway 219, Woodburn, 503-982-4461, www.woodburndragstrip.com), located in the Willamette Valley between Portland and Salem, generally limits its offerings to drag races.

BILLIARDS AND POOL

Many bars around Portland have pool tables, but for a dedicated pool hall ambiance try one of the following establishments:

- **Hot Shots Westside Family Billiards**, 4900 SW Western Ave, Beaverton, 503-644-8869, www.hotshotspool.com
- **Rialto Poolroom Bar & Café**, 529 SW 4th Ave, 503-228-7605, www.rialtopoolroom.com
- **Sam's Hollywood Billiards**, 1845 NE 41st Ave, 503-282-8266
- **Uptown Billiards Club**, 120 NW 23rd Ave, 503-226-8980, www.uptownbilliards.com

BOWLING

Some might argue that it's more a sport (or a way of life) than a pastime, but however you classify it bowling is a popular activity. Most bowling alleys host at least one, and usually several, bowling leagues; check with the alley for signup information. Alleys are sometimes completely reserved for tournaments, league play, or birthday parties, so call first to find out when open bowling is available. If ordinary bowling is too tame for your taste, most area lanes offer glow-in-the-dark bowling and other jazzed-up versions of the game.

The Portland metropolitan area has more than two dozen bowling alleys; the lanes listed below are the most centrally located. For more options, peruse the Yellow Pages listings for "Bowling."

- **AMF Pro 300 Lanes,** 3031 SE Powell Blvd, 503-234-0237, www.amf.com/pro300lanes/
- **Hollywood Bowl**, 4030 NE Halsey St, 503-288-9237, www.hollywood-bowl.net
- **Interstate Lanes**, 6049 N Interstate Ave, 503-285-9881
- **Valley Lanes**, 9300 SW Beaverton-Hillsdale Hwy, 503-292-3523, www.valleylanes.com

The late, lamented Grand Central Bowl at Southeast Eighth and Belmont, famed for its kitschy 1960s-era exterior "Let's Go Bowling!" mural, is ostensibly being renovated as part of a larger redevelopment project.

If you prefer your bowling outdoors, the **Portland Lawn Bowling Club** (www.portlandlawnbowling.org) has a clubhouse and green in Westmoreland Park, at Southeast 22nd Ave and Bybee Blvd. (If your tastes lean to the even more esoteric, note that this green is also used by the **Portland Pétanque Club**, www.portlandpetanque.org.)

CASINOS

The Oregon Lottery (www.oregonlottery.org) promotes scratchoffs, Powerball tickets, and the video poker machines that infest every smoky tavern in town (while halfheartedly reminding Oregonians that lottery games should not be played for investment purposes). For real casino games like blackjack and dollar slots you'll have to visit a tribal casino. Indian casinos are among the state's biggest attractions, and although there are no casinos in the metropolitan area, the following establishments are within a two-hour drive:

- **Chinook Winds Casino Resort**, 1777 NW 44th St, Lincoln City (Oregon Coast), 541-996-8735, 888-CHINOOK, www.chinookwindscasino.com
- **Kah-Nee-Ta High Desert Resort and Casino**, Highway 8, Warm Springs (Warm Springs Reservation), 503-984-9830, 888-220-9830, www.kahneeta. com; this casino may move to Cascade Locks in the Columbia River Gorge, but fierce opposition from many locals (and from other tribes) has delayed the project.
- **Spirit Mountain Casino**, Highway 18 at Grande Ronde (west of Salem), 503-879-3705, 866-861-6606, www.spiritmountain.com

CHESS

The **Portland Chess Club** (503-246-2978, www.pdxchess.com) organizes tournaments and casual play for all ages. Local organizations that focus on younger players include the **Oregon Scholastic Chess Federation** (www.oscf.org) and **Chess for Success** (www.chessforsuccess.org). **Northwest Chess** (www. nwchess.com) is an excellent source of information about chess in the region, including chess news, tournaments, activities, and club listings.

DANCING

If you're interested in pursuing dance moves that go beyond random night-club gyrations, you'll have plenty of company. Portland harbors a wide range of dance-oriented clubs that offer lessons, organize competitions, and host dances. **Portland Dancing** (www.portlanddancing.com) is a clearinghouse of information on clubs and events, and covers styles ranging from Lindy Hop to country line dancing and from salsa and tango to Israeli folk dancing. You can also check *Willamette Week* or the A&E section of the Friday *Oregonian* for dance events and get-togethers. For formal dance instruction, look in the Yellow Pages under "Dance Instruction."

HORSE RACING

The horses are on the track from October through May at **Portland Meadows** (1001 N Schmeer Rd, 503-285-9144, www.portlandmeadows.com) at Delta Park in North Portland.

MODEL RAILROADING

The **Columbia Gorge Model Railroad Club**, 2505 N Vancouver Ave, 503-28-TRAIN, www.cgmrc.com, owns its own building, which contains a truly amazing 500+ square foot scale model of train lines in the Columbia River Gorge.

YOGA

In addition to the private studios listed below, **Portland Parks & Recreation** (503-823-PLAY, www.portlandparks.org) offers yoga classes at many of its facilities; check its web site or its seasonal printed catalogs for details. Some health clubs also offer yoga classes to members, as do many spas and wellness centers. The following establishments are solely yoga studios:

- **Amrita**, 0110 SW Bancroft St, 503-552-YOGA, www.amritasanctuary.com
- **Bikram's Yoga College of India**, 4831 NE Fremont St, 503-284-0555, www.bikramportland.com
- **Core Power**, 2277 NW Quimby St, 503-226-9642, www.corepoweryoga.com
- **Gudmestad Yoga Studio**, 3903 SW Kelly, Suite 210, 593-223-8157, www.gudmestadyoga.com
- **The Movement Center**, 1025 NE 33rd Ave, 503-231-0994. www.mcyoga.com
- **Portland Yoga Arts**, 4400 NE Glisan St, www.portlandyogaarts.com
- **Prinanda Yoga and Arts Center**, 1920 N Kilpatrick St, 503-249-9303, www.prananda.com
- **Sacred Onion**, 6937 SW 55th Ave, 503-452-8154, www.sacredonion.org
- **Yoga Bhoga**, 1401 SE Morrison St #B, 503-241-5058, www.yogabhoga.com
- **Yoga Pearl**, 925 NW Davis St, 503-525-9642, www.yogapearl.com
- **The Yoga Project**, 1229 SE Nehalem St, 503-235-1155, www.theyogaproject.com
- **Yoga Shala**, 3249 SE Division St, 503-281-4552; 3808 N Williams St, 503-963-YOGA; www.yogashalapdx.com

HEALTH CLUBS

Portland is full of health clubs and gyms. Most have workout equipment, conditioning classes, and personal training programs, and some offer swimming pools, yoga, specialized workouts, and child care. Call or visit the club you're interested in to get details on their programs.

If you work for a reasonably large organization, ask human resources about membership discounts for fitness clubs. Note that the health club business is generally one without fixed prices; the dripping person on the adjacent treadmill may have paid twice as much or half as much as you did. Also, it pays to read the fine print on any agreement; the terms "annual membership" and "no fees" may not mean what you think they do. Be aware that many clubs offer frequent promotions—membership fee discounts or waivers, the first month at half price, free seven-day passes, and the like—so if you're in no hurry to join a club it might be worth waiting to see if a better deal comes up.

The following list of Portland health clubs should help you start your search. For a complete list, check the Yellow Pages under "Health Clubs." In addition to private clubs, many municipal community centers have exercise facilities; check with your local parks and recreation department for details.

- **Alameda Fitness Center**, 4016 NE Fremont St, 503-548-4011, www.alameda fitness.com
- **Bally Total Fitness**, 800-515-2582, www.ballyfitness.com, has 11 locations in the region.
- **Cascade Athletic Club**, 9260 SE Stark St, 503-257-4142; 2456 SE Powell Blvd, Gresham, 503-618-4142; 19201 SE Division St, Gresham, 503-665-4142; www. cascadeathleticclubs.com; a FitLife network member (see below)
- **Curves**, 800-848-1096, www.curves.com; this worldwide network of franchised women-only fitness clubs has more than 40 locations around the metropolitan area.
- The **FitLife Club Network** includes dozens of independent fitness clubs in Oregon, Washington, and Montana, including 12 clubs in the Portland metro area. Members of each club get reciprocal use of other member clubs. Visit www.fitlifeclubs.com or call 503-445-6235 for a list of network clubs.
- **Giant's Gym**, 5223 NE Sandy Blvd, 503-281-4776, www.giantsgym.com
- **Gold's Gym**, 2025 NW Overton St, 503-228-2626; 23500 SE Stark St, Gresham, 503-667-2290; www.goldsgym.com
- **Lloyd Athletic Club**, 815 NE Halsey St, 503-287-4594, www.lloydac.com; a FitLife network club
- **Loprinzi's Gym**, 2414 SE 41st Ave, 503-232-8311; this unpretentious, old-school-style neighborhood gym offers affordable, pay-as-you go memberships.
- **Metro Family YMCA**, 2831 SW Barbur Blvd, 503-294-3366, www.metro-family. org; in addition to this bright, well-equipped facility near downtown Portland, the YMCA has fitness facilities in Beaverton, Sherwood, and Vancouver. (See www.ymca-portland.org for details.)
- **Mittleman Jewish Community Center**, 6551 SW Capitol Hwy, 503-244-0111, www.oregonjcc.org
- The venerable **Multnomah Athletic Club**, 1849 SW Salmon St, 503-223-6251, www.themac.com, has long been a place where Portland's movers and shakers could, well, move and shake, as well as hobnob. The eight-story clubhouse and 600-car parking garage remind you that you are not in Kansas anymore. Sadly for would-be Gatsbys, the MAC is currently not accepting new members.
- **Nelson's Nautilus Plus**, 8333 NE Russell St, 503-254-7710; 10466 SE Main St,

Milwaukie, 503-659-4111; 1715 S Beavercreek Rd, Oregon City, 503-657-7717; www.nelsonsnautilus.com
- **Northwest Personal Training**, 2714 NE Broadway, 503-287-0655; 1011 Broadway, Vancouver, 360-574-7292; www.nwpersonaltraining.com
- **RiverPlace Athletic Club**, 0150 SW Montgomery St, 503-221-1212, www.therac. com, is a full-service health club, with a long list of amenities that include two pools, saunas and steam rooms, squash courts, oodles of classes, and on-site childcare. Plus, the RAC is a FitLife network club.
- **10th Avenue Athletic Club**, 1111 SW 10th Ave, 503-294-7420, www.10thac. com
- **24 Hour Fitness**, 800-224-0240, www.24hourfitness.com, has 13 locations in the Portland area.
- **West Coast Health & Fitness**, 2640 NE Alberta St, 503-288-94500; 7522 N Lombard St, 503-283-5404, www.westcoasthealthandfitness.com; a FitLife network club
- **West Side Athletic Club**, 555 SW Oak St, 503-222-7800, www.westsideathletic club.com

SPORTING GOODS STORES

Whether you're heading out of town for a two-week backpack on the Pacific Crest Trail or spending an hour at the park with a Frisbee, you may need to go shopping first. Portlanders take their sports and recreational activities seriously, so there's no shortage of places to find just the right equipment. The following list should get you started. If you're not sure whether you want or need to buy an expensive item, inquire about testing or renting.

- **Andy and Bax**, 324 SE Grand Ave, 503-234-7538, www.andyandbax.com, sells military surplus goods as well as more mainstream camping and outdoor equipment.
- **Big 5 Sporting Goods**, 800-898-2994, www.big5sportinggoods.com, has nine stores in the Portland-Vancouver area.
- **ClimbMax Mountaineering**, 928 NE 28th Ave, 503-797-1991, www.climbmax mountaineering.com, is one of the best mountaineering equipment stores in the United States.
- **Joe's**, www.joessports.com, has 10 stores in the Portland area; this local chain, known for 55 years (until early 2007) as "G.I. Joe's," sells a huge selection of sporting goods and auto supplies.
- **Mountain Shop**, 628 NE Broadway, 503-288-6768, www.mountainshop.net
- **Next Adventure**, 426 SE Grand Ave, 503-233-0706, nextadventure.net, sells both new and used equipment.
- **Oregon Mountain Community**, 2975 NE Sandy Blvd, 503-227-1038, www. e-omc.com
- **Play It Again Sports**, 10355 NE Halsey St, 503-254-4993; 9244 SW Beaver-

ton-Hillsdale Hwy, 503-292-4552; 8101 NE Parkway Dr, Ste A1, Vancouver, 360-260-9440; www.playitagainsports; these stores focus on used (and thus generally affordable) sports equipment, but they also stock some new sporting goods.

- **REI**, 1405 NW Johnson St, 503-221-1938; 7410 SW Bridgeport Rd, Tualatin, 503-624-8600; 2235 NW Allie Ave, Hillsboro, 503-617-6072; www.rei.com; Seattle-based REI (short for Recreational Equipment Incorporated) is the country's largest consumer cooperative. Members receive an annual dividend based on their total purchases over the previous year.
- **Sports Authority**, www.sportsauthority.com, is the country's largest sporting goods retailer; there are three stores in the metro area.
- **US Outdoor Store**, 219 SW Broadway, 503-223-5937, www.usoutdoor.com

PORTLAND'S LANDSCAPE IS A VISIBLE MANIFESTATION OF VARIOUS geological forces: volcanic eruptions, grand shifts and collisions of the earth's crustal plates, tremendous ice age floods, enormous landslides, and the ceaseless flow of two major rivers and dozens of tributary streams. Add to this mix a lush canopy of native forest and it's easy to get distracted by the grandeur of the city's surroundings, and to think of the region as one enormous park.

Hundreds of city, regional, state, and national parks and forests and other greenspaces provide abundant opportunities for enjoying the area's natural beauty. Some of these parks are little more than expanses of grass, maybe with a swing set or a softball diamond thrown in; others, like Mount Hood National Forest, include vast tracts of roadless wilderness. Metro, the regional government, has an online "Find a Park" tool at www.metro-region.org/article.cfm?ArticleID=3885, which searches a database of more than 1,000 parks in the region; simply type in a street address or intersection and click boxes to indicate what amenities you are looking for, and you'll get a list of parks with the desired attributes, sorted by distance from the address you typed in. For suggested guidebooks to parks and hiking trails in the region, see **A Portland Reading List**.

PARKS

CITY PARKS—PORTLAND

Portland is richly endowed with parks of all sizes and descriptions. The city maintains more than 250 park and recreation facilities that cover in total about 10,000 acres. The city's original park plan, drawn up by John Olmsted in 1904, called for a series of parkways, city squares, and many types of parks. While the plan was never fully realized—Southwest Terwilliger Boulevard is the only parkway in Olmsted's plan that was actually built, for example—the city did take his advice and buy up large chunks of land for use as parkland. Today, nearly every neighborhood has at least one neighborhood park, and hardly any point in the city is more than a few blocks from a park or open space of some kind. For a complete list of city parks, visit the **Portland Parks & Recreation** web site at www.port landparks.org, or call the bureau at 503-823-PLAY (503-823-7529)

Downtown Portland is laid out with greater attention to commerce than to outdoor recreation, but it has a few locally important parks. **Tom McCall Waterfront Park** occupies the west bank of the Willamette River from RiverPlace north to the Steel Bridge. A highway used to run along the riverfront until the 1970s; today, lunch hour joggers do. On sunny days the park is crowded with runners, walkers, rollerbladers, idlers, and, in the northern reaches, unabashed drug dealers. The park hosts frequent music and food festivals during the summer months. Although the park borders the river, the downtown seawall makes access to the water difficult. A few blocks inland, the shady **South Park Blocks**, chock-a-block with heroic statues and other public art pieces, extend through the southern half of downtown from Portland State University to Salmon Street; after a few blocks' interruption by parking lots and office buildings, the arrangement continues in the **North Park Blocks**, which run from Ankeny Street to Glisan Street in the Pearl District. A few other small parks, such as **Keller Fountain Park** at 3rd and Clay and **Lownsdale** and **Chapman** squares near the county and federal courthouses—not to mention Pioneer Courthouse Square, the city's "living room"—make convenient lunch spots for downtown office workers. To the north, in the Pearl District, **Tanner Springs Park** and **Jamison Square** give the neighborhood's condo dwellers some breathing space.

In the forested hills just west of downtown, **Washington Park** encompasses a variety of attractions: hiking trails, the International Rose Test Garden, the Oregon Zoo (503-220-2781, www.oregonzoo.org), two museums, a Vietnam Veterans Memorial, the Oregon Holocaust Memorial, tennis courts, soccer fields, one of the city's best playgrounds, and the Japanese Garden (see "Gardens" below). To the north, a series of smaller parks—Hoyt Arboretum (see "Gardens"), the grounds of city-owned Pittock Mansion, and **Macleay Park**, which includes the popular Balch Creek Trail—connect Washington Park with **Forest Park**, the city's largest and wildest park. This 5,000-acre gem extends along the spine and eastern slopes of the low Tualatin Mountains, which run northwest from downtown Portland. The park is a favorite haunt of hikers, mountain bikers, and the occasional elk. The 30-mile Wildwood Trail runs from Washington Park into the northern reaches of Forest Park; it's part of the 40-mile loop (see "Regional Trails" below).

Besides the green gem of Tryon Creek State Natural Area (see below), Southwest Portland has several parks that contain wooded areas in the West Hills, including **Marquam Nature Park**, **Marshall Park**, **George Himes Park**, and

Keller Woodland, adjacent to an especially scenic portion of Terwilliger Boulevard. **Council Crest Park** perches atop the highest hill in Portland, and offers expansive views in almost every direction; in the early twentieth century, Council Crest was the site of a popular amusement park, complete with roller coasters, and was linked to downtown Portland by trolley. **Willamette Park**, in the Johns Landing neighborhood, is one of the few parks in Portland with direct access to the Willamette River; it's a popular location for boat launching. In the more suburban precincts of Vermont Hills, 90-acre **Gabriel Park** has a host of recreational facilities, including the popular Southwest Community Center.

The eastside grid features dozens of parks of various sizes. Almost every neighborhood has its own park; indeed, several neighborhoods are known by the name of the local park. Such is the case with one of the loveliest parks in Portland, **Laurelhurst Park**. Designed in 1912, the park is planted with now-mature specimen trees, such as giant sequoias, coast redwoods, and native Douglas firs, which border broad "meadows" and recreation areas; the grounds center on a shallow lake that is popular with ducks. Further east, **Mount Tabor Park** includes an extinct volcano—look for evidence of the old crater near the carved-out basketball courts—as well as acres of second-growth forest, miles of jogging paths, hiking trails, and winding roads cut into the side of the hill, a playground, tennis courts, an amphitheater, and three old city reservoirs. Mount Tabor offers excellent views, and the lawn just west of the summit is a popular place to watch the sunset over the West Hills, with the bright lights of Hawthorne Boulevard stretching away below. Other major parks in Southeast Portland include **Sellwood Park**, **Clinton Park**, **Westmoreland Park**, **Woodstock Park**, **Lents Park**, and the extensive **Powell Butte Natural Area**.

North and Northeast Portland lack the wooded hill parks of other parts of the city, but they have an abundance of popular neighborhood parks. **Grant Park**, **Irving Park**, **Wilshire Park**, **Alberta Park**, and **Normandale Park** are major parks in Northeast Portland; **Peninsula Park**, **Overlook Park**, **Columbia Park**, and **Pier Park** are some of the prime parks in North Portland. **Cathedral Park**, under the east end of the St. Johns Bridge, hosts a popular jazz festival each July; the park also has boat launching facilities. **Kelley Point Park** occupies the tip of the North Portland peninsula at the confluence of the Willamette and Columbia rivers. **Delta Park**, which is full of sports fields, sits on the former site of Vanport, a large community that was washed away in a 1948 flood. Several miles to the east, just off Interstate 205 in Northeast Portland, **Rocky Butte** has some of the best rock climbing in Portland and offers a panoramic view from the summit.

REGIONAL TRAILS

The Portland area has a reasonably extensive trail network that links various parts of the metropolis. The primary component of the regional trail system is the **40-Mile Loop** (www.40mileloop.org) of walking and biking trails, which, although incomplete, is now substantially longer than 40 miles. The largest links in this chain are the Eastbank Esplanade and other trails along both sides of the Willamette from downtown Portland south to the Sellwood Bridge; the Springwater Corridor from Southeast Portland east to Gresham and Boring; the Wildwood Trail through Washington Park and Forest Park (hikers only); and a path along the Columbia River, off Marine Drive in Northeast Portland. Other major regional trails include the bikeway that parallels Interstate 205, the Fanno Creek Trail in Washington County, and the trails along the north side of the Columbia River in Vancouver and Washougal.

CITY, COUNTY, AND REGIONAL PARKS— SURROUNDING COMMUNITIES

Most incorporated communities in the Portland area have a parks department that deals with city parks and natural areas; these suburban parks are primarily of interest to the residents of nearby neighborhoods. In addition to the municipal departments, there are several multi-community park districts and county park departments in the region. The **Tualatin Hills Park and Recreation District** (503-645-6433, www.thprd.org) manages more than 200 parks and 35 miles of trails in Beaverton and the surrounding areas. The crown jewel of this network is **Tualatin Hills Nature Park** (503-629-6350), a natural area of more than 220 acres, with five miles of trails, essentially in the middle of Beaverton. **Washington County Parks** (503-846-8715) operates three facilities, of which the only one of any size is the expansive **Scoggins Valley Park/Henry Hagg Lake** in the foothills of the Coast Range; the lake is a popular swimming destination in summer.

    North Clackamas Parks & Recreation District (503-794-8002, www.co.clackamas.or.us/ncprd/) covers a large swath of northern Clackamas County from Milwaukie to Happy Valley and south to Gladstone. The **Clackamas County Parks Department** (503-353-4400, www.co.clackamas.or.us/dtd/parks/) operates several county parks, including popular **Barton Park** on the Clackamas River.

    Across the Columbia, **Vancouver-Clark Parks** (360-696-8171, www.vanclarkparksrec.org) administers dozens of neighborhood, community, and regional parks and trails in Clark County. Major regional parks include **Lacamas Park** and the adjacent Lacamas Lake Greenway and Lacamas Heritage Trail, near Camas; **Moulton Falls Park** and **Lucia Falls Park**, together with the 7.5-mile Bells Mountain Trail, on the East Fork of the Lewis River outside Battle Ground; and **Vancouver Lake**, a large lake on the west side of Vancouver that is popular for swimming, windsurfing, and kayaking.

    Metro manages many greenspaces and natural areas, including undeveloped sites, in the Portland area; for a fairly complete list, visit www.metro-region.org and click the Quicklink for "Parks, trails and greenspaces." In North Portland,

Smith and Bybee Wetlands Natural Area (503-797-1850) is a major surprise; this 2,000-acre expanse of lakes, sloughs, and surrounding wetlands is just a few minutes from downtown Portland, and is essentially surrounded by commercial and industrial facilities, but is rich in wildlife, including bald eagles. You can explore the park on a paved trail or by non-motorized boat. One of the most popular developed sites is **Blue Lake Regional Park** (503-665-4995), which encompasses a large, swimmable lake near the Columbia River. **Oxbow Regional Park** (503-663-4708), on the lower Sandy River about 20 miles east of downtown Portland, includes a stand of old-growth forest; you can watch Chinook salmon spawn here in the fall.

There are no Multnomah County parks; Metro took over management and ownership of the county's parks in the 1990s.

GARDENS

Portland's temperate, maritime climate is ideal for gardening. Both visitors and locals alike delight in the region's public gardens, botanical gardens and arboreta.

- **The Berry Botanic Garden**, 11505 SW Summerville Ave, 503-636-4112, www. berrybot.org, displays both native and exotic plant species in a lush landscape. Specialty gardens include a garden of endangered plants and the largest public rock garden on the West Coast.
- **Crystal Springs Rhododendron Gardens**, SE 28th Ave at Woodstock Blvd, 503-771-8386, www.portlandonline.com; this picturesque, nearly 10-acre garden of rhododendrons, azaleas, and related woody plants surrounds a small lake in Southeast Portland. You'll have plenty of company here in May.
- **Elk Rock Garden of the Bishop's Close**, 11800 SW Military Ln, 503-636-5613, 800-452-2562, www.diocese-oregon.org/theclose/; this beautiful 13-acre garden, originally a private estate and now the office of the bishop of the Episcopal Diocese of Oregon, overlooks the Willamette River in Dunthorpe.
- **The Grotto**, NE 85th Ave at Sandy Blvd, 503-254-7371, www.thegrotto.org; a combination garden and religious shrine, the National Sanctuary of Our Sorrowful Mother is a peaceful retreat in Northeast Portland.
- **Hoyt Arboretum**, Washington Park, 4000 SW Fairview Blvd, 503-865-8733, www.hoytarboretum.org; laced by 12 miles of trails, Hoyt Arboretum displays more than 1,000 different species of trees and shrubs from around the temperate world. Hunt for unusual specimens, like the collection of southern beech (*Nothofagus*) trees from South America and Tasmania.
- **Hulda Klager Lilac Gardens**, 115 Pekin Rd, Woodland, WA, 360-225-8996, www.lilacgardens.com, is filled with lilac blooms, and those who admire lilac blooms, in late April and early May.
- **International Rose Test Garden**, Washington Park, 400 SW Kingston Ave, 503-823-3635, www.portlandparks.org; photographers usually take the iconic picture-postcard image of Portland, showing Mount Hood looming behind

downtown skyscrapers, from the International Rose Test Garden in Washington Park. But the garden offers more than just a pretty panorama; it displays more than 500 varieties of roses in several sub-gardens, including a Shakespeare Garden and a collection of miniature roses.

- **The Japanese Garden**, Washington Park, 611 SW Kingston Ave, 503-223-1321, www.japanesegarden.com; one of the finest and most authentic Japanese gardens in North America occupies the hillside just above the International Rose Test Garden. This is an especially appealing spot to wander in spring, when the cherries are in bloom, or in autumn, when the leaves of Japanese maples turn orange and crimson.
- **Leach Botanical Garden**, 6704 SE 122nd Ave, 503-761-9503, www.leach garden.org; located a bit off the beaten path in outer Southeast Portland, Leach Botanical Garden is nonetheless one of the finest public gardens in the state with more than 2,000 species of North American, and particularly Northwestern, native plants on display in an informal, naturalized setting.
- **Portland Classical Chinese Garden**, NW 3rd Ave at Everett St, 503-228-8131, www.portlandchinesegarden.org, occupies a city block in Chinatown. Based on traditional Chinese garden design, this garden features a series of courtyards and pavilions, lined by bridges and winding pathways, set around an artificial lake.

NATIONAL AND STATE FORESTS

NATIONAL FORESTS

The mountain ranges of the Pacific Northwest are blanketed in forests, and more than a dozen national forests contain much of the timberland (or clear-cut former timberland, as the case may be) in western Oregon and Washington. Four of these national forests are reasonably close to the Portland area.

- **Mount Hood National Forest** (503-668-1700, www.fs.fed.us/r6/mthood/) covers more than a million acres of the northern Oregon Cascades east of Portland, including Mount Hood and most of the surrounding mountain region. Hikers, bikers, climbers, campers, loggers, anglers, mushroom hunters, and participants in winter sports of all kinds are all heavy users of the Mount Hood National Forest, but nearly a fifth of the forest is designated wilderness area where crowds are greatly diminished.
- To the south, **Willamette National Forest** (541-225-6300, www.fs.fed.us/r6/ willamette/) encompasses the central Oregon Cascades west of the Cascade Crest, including the Mount Jefferson Wilderness, Detroit Lake, and other popular recreational areas within a two-hour drive of Portland.
- **Siuslaw National Forest** (541-750-7000, www.fs.fed.us/r6/siuslaw/) occupies

a discontinuous stretch of the northern and central Coast Range, including some sites along the coast itself.

- **Gifford Pinchot National Forest** (360-891-5000, www.fs.fed.us/gpnf/), in the southern Washington Cascades, includes some remote, little-visited regions, as well as the blockbuster attraction of **Mount St. Helens National Volcanic Monument** (360-449-7800, www.fs.fed.us/gpnf/mshnvm/). The monument includes the volcanic crater itself, the blast zone that was devastated by the 1980 eruption, and much of the relatively untouched south side of the mountain. Three visitor centers provide interpretive context for this still-active volcano.

Most recreational activities in the national forests now require users to purchase a daily or annual **Northwest Forest Pass**. You must display this pass in your car when you park at a trailhead or other area where the pass is required. Passes are available from Forest Service offices and some retail stores; you can also order the pass online or by telephone from Nature of the Northwest (800-270-7504, www.naturennw.org). Daily passes are $5 and annual passes cost $30.

STATE FORESTS

The **Oregon Department of Forestry** manages nearly 800,000 acres of forestland around the state. The closest state forest to Portland is **Tillamook State Forest** (503-357-2191, egove.oregon.gov/ODF/TSF/tsf.shtml) in the Coast Range about an hour west of the city. Beginning in 1933, this area was the site of a series of periodic fires that ultimately devastated 355,000 acres of timberland. The forest today is almost entirely hand-planted second-growth; recreational opportunities include hiking, mountain biking, fishing, camping, and horseback riding. The new Tillamook Forest Center (866-930-4646, www.tillamookforestcenter.org) provides interpretation of the forest and its history. To the north, less-developed **Clatsop State Forest** (503-325-5451, egov.oregon.gov/ODF/FIELD/ASTORIA/aboutastoria.shtml) has a few hiking trails and campgrounds.

In Washington, the **State Department of Natural Resources** manages several state forests. The only state forest in Southwest Washington is **Yacolt Burn State Forest** (360-577-2025, www.dnr.wa.gov/htdocs/lm/recreation/yacoltburn/index.html), which, like Oregon's Tillamook State Forest, was once consumed by a massive, devastating fire. Yacolt Burn State Forest has trails for hiking and mountain biking, but it is especially popular with off-road vehicle enthusiasts.

COLUMBIA RIVER GORGE NATIONAL SCENIC AREA

The **Columbia River Gorge National Scenic Area** (541-308-1700, www.fs.fed.us/r6/columbia/forest/) is one of Portland's favorite playgrounds, featuring outstanding scenery and unique geology. Recreational opportunities abound; as the National Scenic Area's web site declares in dry, bureaucratic prose: "Hiking, mountain biking, windsurfing, camping, fishing, boating, wildlife watching, birding, wildflower viewing, photography, picnicking, rock climbing. You can do all this and more in the Columbia River Gorge National Scenic Area." While the description is accurate, please do not try to do all these activities simultaneously.

The National Scenic Area is a patchwork of federal, state, municipal, and private land; some 20 Oregon and Washington state parks within the NSA protect some of the Gorge's most scenic and popular destinations. (See "State Parks" below for contact information.) A Northwest Forest Pass is required at many trailheads and parking areas in the Gorge.

STATE AND NATIONAL PARKS

STATE PARKS

OREGON

Oregon has 234 state parks and recreation areas, including several in the Portland area. A full list and map is available online from the **Oregon State Parks** web site, www.oregonstateparks.org, or call the State Parks Information Center at 800-551-6949. The following are the most popular state parks near Portland:

- **Banks-Vernonia State Trail**, in the Coast Range west of Portland, is a 21-mile "linear park" based on a former railroad line that has since been turned into a multi-use trail.
- **Government Island State Recreation Area**, in the Columbia River near the Interstate 205 bridge, is accessible by boat only; the island's small sandy beaches make tempting destinations on a hot summer day.
- **Mary S. Young State Park**, on the west bank of the Willamette River in West Linn, is a pleasant park full of forests, fields, and riverside, linked by eight miles of trails.
- **Milo McIver State Park**, on the Clackamas River near Estacada, offers excellent boating, hiking, fishing, and camping opportunities.
- **Molalla River State Park** (www.oregonstateparks.org/park_111.php), near Canby, protects 566 acres of riparian wetlands where the Molalla River flows into the Willamette. The Park is a popular site for boating, birdwatching, and other wildlife viewing, and hiking.
- **Tryon Creek State Natural Area** (503-636-9886, SW Terwilliger Blvd, www.oregonstateparks.org/park_144.php or www.tryonfriends.org); this 650-acre, hilly, wooded park in Southwest Portland protects the watershed of Tryon Creek. Several miles of shady trail lace the park, and a nature center provides interpretive materials and trail maps.

WASHINGTON

Washington maintains 120 state parks and recreation areas; visit www.parks.wa.gov or call 360-902-8844 for details. Apart from the parks in the Columbia River Gorge (see above), only two state parks are close to the Portland area:

- **Battle Ground Lake State Park,** just east of Battle Ground, centers on a small lake of volcanic origin (a sort of miniature Crater Lake) that is a popular spot for swimming and camping.
- **Paradise Point State Park** is a water-centered park on the Lewis River; the proximity of Interstate 5 makes the park less inviting than it might otherwise be.

NATIONAL PARKS

Several national parks and monuments lie within a day's drive of Portland, including **Crater Lake National Park** in the southern Oregon Cascades, **Mount Rainier National Park** southeast of Seattle, **Olympic National Park** on the Olympic Peninsula west of Seattle, and **North Cascades National Park** on the Canadian border. (See **Quick Getaways** for more information.)

WILDLIFE REFUGES

Oaks Bottom Wildlife Refuge, on the east shore of the Willamette River near Sellwood and Westmoreland, is an urban wildlife refuge managed by the city of Portland. It is an excellent site for birdwatching—look for great blue herons, the official city bird. Less than a mile from downtown Hillsboro, **Jackson Bottom Wetlands Preserve** (503-681-6206, www.jacksonbottom.org) encompasses some 750 acres of wildlife-rich wetlands with more than four miles of hiking trails.

The U.S. Fish and Wildlife Service manages the **Tualatin River National Wildlife Refuge** in Sherwood (503-590-5811, fws.gov/tualatinriver), which hosts almost 200 bird species, although it protects less than 1% of the river's watershed. In Washington, the **Ridgefield National Wildlife Refuge Complex** (360-887-4106, www.fws.gov/ridgefieldrefuges/) includes four refuges along the Columbia River in Southwest Washington; only Ridgefield National Wildlife Refuge is open to the public.

OTHER GREENSPACES

- The **Audubon Society of Portland** (503-292-6855, www.audubonportland.org) owns a 143-acre preserve along Balch Creek, below Cornell Road in Northwest Portland.

- The federal **Bureau of Land Management** (Oregon state office: 503-808-6002, www.blm.gov/or/) manages about two million acres of land in Western Oregon. Most BLM land is timberland, often mixed with Forest Service land in a checkerboard pattern of ownership. The most popular BLM facility near Portland is Wildwood Recreation Site (503-622-3969) on the Salmon River near Welches on the western slopes of Mount Hood.
- **The Nature Conservancy** owns or manages 48 sites in Oregon, including three in the Portland area; visit www.nature.org/Oregon for a complete list, directions, and access restrictions.
- Several schools and colleges maintain public open space; scholastic natural areas include **Reed College's** small but surprisingly wild canyon and the wetlands on the **Oregon Episcopal School** campus.
- **Sauvie Island**, while it is not a park but rather a working agricultural landscape, is nonetheless a popular destination for biking, beachgoing, and wildlife viewing.
- The region's navigable **rivers**—the Willamette, the Columbia, the Tualatin, the Sandy, and the Clackamas—provide exciting water-based recreational opportunities, including canoeing and kayaking, powerboating and jetskiing, whitewater rafting, and sailing.

Y OU'VE FOUND A PLACE TO LIVE, UNPACKED, AND GOTTEN SETTLED
into your new home. Now it's time to get involved in the community.
This chapter lists a variety of options for community involvement, from
volunteering, to social clubs, to places of worship.

COMMUNITY INVOLVEMENT

Volunteering for an organization is a satisfying way to make a difference in
your new community while at the same time meeting people who share similar
interests.

VOLUNTEER MATCHING AND PLACEMENT

The following organizations coordinate many volunteer activities in the Portland
area. Contact them and they will help you find an organization in need of your
time and talents.

- **Hands on Greater Portland**, 503-413-7787, www.handsonportland.org,
  matches volunteers with 200 nonprofits and other community organizations
  around the region.
- **Clackamas County Volunteer Connection**, www.co.clackamas.or.us/
  socialservices/involved/volun/vc.htm, matches volunteers with volunteer opportunities from more than 150 community partners in Clackamas County.
- **Earth Share of Oregon**, a federation of environmental nonprofit organizations, lists current volunteer opportunities on its web site; call 503-223-9015 or
  visit www.earthshare-oregon.org/volunteer/ for more information.
- **Volunteer Match**, www.volunteermatch.org, and **ServeNet**, servenet.org, allow you to search for volunteer opportunities by distance from any zip code.

In addition, the Living section of the Thursday *Oregonian* lists organizations that need volunteers for specific projects.

AREA CAUSES

Portland has hundreds, if not thousands, of nonprofit organizations that provide a range of services, and many of them are in constant need of volunteer help. The following list is just a sample of the organizations that use volunteers; some have structured volunteer programs with training sessions and schedules, while others are grateful when you walk in off the street and help sort donated clothing for an hour. In addition to the organizations listed in this chapter, keep in mind that many of the community institutions listed elsewhere in this book rely on volunteers.

Note that you may be greeted with caution when you offer your services to an agency that deals directly with children. Don't take it personally; since you care enough about children to volunteer in an after-school program or summer camp, you understand the agency's duty to check your references and perhaps run a criminal background check.

If you have special skills (legal or medical training; experience with web design, desktop publishing, writing and editing, or accounting; a license to drive large trucks and buses; or a background in catering and the know-how to prepare meals for 400 people), be sure to mention them. Don't be shy. Any nonprofit organization will be happy to hear from you.

AIDS AND HIV

- **Cascade AIDS Project**, 620 SW 5th Ave, Suite 300, 503-223-5907, www.cascadeaids.org
- **Ecumenical Ministries of Oregon HIV Services**, 2941 NE Ainsworth St, 503-460-3822, www.emoregon.org/HIV-day_center.php
- **Our House**, 2727 SE Alder St, 503-234-0175, www.ourhouseofportland.org

ALCOHOL AND DRUG DEPENDENCY

- **Oregon Partnership**, 503-244-5211, 800-282-7035, www.orpartnership.org

ANIMALS

- **Audubon Society of Portland**, 5151 NW Cornell Rd, 503-292-6855, www.audubonportland.org
- **Cat Adoption Team**, 14175 SW Galbreath Dr, Sherwood, 503-925-8903, www.catadoptionteam.org
- **Feral Cat Coalition of Oregon**, 503-797-2606, www.feralcats.org
- **Oregon Humane Society**, 1067 NE Columbia Blvd, 285-7722, www.oregonhumane.com

CHILDREN AND YOUTH

Besides the organizations listed below (and other nonprofits focused on children and youth), almost any public school will have volunteer opportunities.

- **Big Brothers Big Sisters Northwest**, 1827 NE 44th Ave, 503-249-4859, www. bbbsnorthwest.org
- **Boys and Girls Aid Society**, 018 SW Boundary Ct, 503-222-9661, 877-932-2734, www.boysandgirlsaid.org
- **Boys and Girls Clubs of Portland Metropolitan Area**, 7119 SE Milwaukie Ave, 503-232-0387, www.bgcportland.org
- **Children's Home Society of Washington**, 360-695-1325, www.chs-wa.org
- **Janus Youth Programs**, 707 NE Couch St, 503-233-6090, www.janusyouth. org
- **Kids on the Block—Powerful Puppetry**, 824 SE 12th Ave, 503-736-3200, 360-433-5697, www.powerfulpuppetry.org
- **R.E.A.P. (Reaching and Empowering All People)**, 503-341-6161, www.reap usa.org
- **Schoolhouse Supplies**, 2735 NE 82nd Ave, 503-249-9933, www.school housesupplies.org

CULTURE AND THE ARTS

Practically every institution listed in the "Cultural Life" chapter relies to some extent on volunteers. The **Regional Arts & Culture Council** (503-823-5111, www. racc.org) lists volunteer opportunities on its web site.

DISABILITY

- **Independent Living Resources**, 2410 SE 11th Ave, 503-232-7411, www.ilr. org
- **Oregon Advocacy Center**, 620 SW 5th Ave, 5th Floor, 503-243-2081, www. oradvocacy.org
- **Special Olympics Oregon**, 5901 SW Macadam Ave, Suite 100, 503-248-0600, www.soor.org

ENVIRONMENT

- **The City Repair Project**, 2122 SE Division St, 503-235-8946, www.cityrepair. org
- **Community Energy Project**, 422 NE Alberta St, 503-284-6827, www.commu nityenergyproject.org
- **Friends of Trees**, 3117 NE Martin Luther King Jr. Blvd, 503-284-8733, www. friendsoftrees.org

- **No Ivy League**, 503-823-3681, www.noivyleague.com
- **Northwest Environmental Advocates**, 133 SW 2nd Ave, 503-295-0490, www. northwestenvironmentaladvocates.org
- **Oregon Trout**, 503-222-9091, www.oregontrout.com
- **Sierra Club (Oregon Chapter)**, 2950 SE Stark St, Suite 110, 503-238-0442, www.oregon.sierraclub.org
- **Stop Oregon Litter and Vandalism (SOLV)**, 800-333-SOLV, www.solv.org
- **Tualatin Riverkeepers**, 12360 SW Main St, Suite 100, Tigard, 503-620-7507, www.tualatinriverkeepers.org

GAY & LESBIAN

- **Basic Rights Oregon**, 503-222-6151, www.basicrights.org
- **Love Makes a Family**, 503-228-3892, ww.lmfamily.org
- **Q Center**, 69 SE Taylor St, 503-234-7837, www.pdxqcenter.org

HEALTH AND HOSPITALS

Most hospitals welcome volunteers; just give the nearest institution a call, or contact one of the following organizations:

- **African American Health Coalition**, 2800 N Vancouver Ave, Suite 100, 503-413-1850, www.aahc-portland.org
- **American Red Cross, Oregon Trail Chapter**, 3131 N Vancouver Ave, 503-284-1234, www.redcross-pdx.org

HUNGER, HOMELESSNESS, AND POVERTY

- **Central City Concern**, 232 NW 6th Ave, 503-294-1681, www.centralcity concern.org
- **Community Warehouse**, 2267 N Interstate Ave, 503-235-8786, www.oregon communitywarehouse.org
- **Food Not Bombs**, www.foodnotbombs.net/oregon.html
- **Goose Hollow Family Shelter**, 1838 SW Jefferson St, 503-228-3195, www. fumcpdx.or/GooseHollowFamilyShelter/
- **Growing Gardens**, 2003 NE 42nd Ave #3, 503-284-8420, www.growing-gardens.org
- **Habitat for Humanity**, 503-287-9529, www.pdxhabitat.org
- **JOIN**, 3338 SE 17th Ave, 503-232-2031, www.joinpdx.com
- **Metropolitan Family Services**, 1808 SE Belmont St, 503-232-0007, www.met family.org

- **Northeast Emergency Food Program**, 1912 NE Killingsworth St, 503-284-5470, www.emoregon.org/NE_food_program.php
- **Oregon Food Bank**, 7900 NE 33rd Ave, 503-282-0555, www.oregonfoodbank.org
- **Outside In**, 1132 SW 13th Ave, 503-535-3800, www.outsidein.org
- **Portland Rescue Mission**, 111 W Burnside St, 503-227-0421, www.portland rescuemission.org
- **REACH Community Development**, 1135 SE Salmon St, 503-231-0682, www.reachcdc.org
- **Sisters of the Road**, 133 NW 6th Ave, 503-222-5694, www.sistersoftheroad cafe.org
- **Transition Projects**, 475 NW Glisan St, 503-823-4930, www.tprojects.org

INTERNATIONAL RELIEF AND DEVELOPMENT

- **Medical Teams International**, 14150 SW Milton Ct, Tigard, 503-624-1000, 800-959-4325, www.medicalteams.org
- **Mercy Corps**, 3015 SW 1st Ave, 800-292-3355, www.mercycorps.org

LITERACY

- **Financial Beginnings**, 7327 SW Barnes Rd, #213, 503-201-9717, www.financial beginnings.org
- **Start Making a Reader Today (SMART)**, 219 NW 12th Ave, Suite 203, 503-230-2944 ext 22, 877-598-4633, www.getsmartoregon.org

MENTORING AND CAREER DEVELOPMENT

- **Dress for Success Oregon**, 503-249-7300, www.dressforsuccessoregon.org
- **Oregon Tradeswomen**, 1714 NE Alberta St, 503-335-8200, www.trades women.net
- **Service Corps of Retired Executives (SCORE)**; Portland: 601 SW 2nd Ave, Suite 950, 503-326-3441, www.scorepdx.org; Vancouver: 1704½ Main St, Vancouver, 360-699-1079, www.scorevancouver.org

POLITICS

In addition to the various large and small political parties that are active in the area, Portland has many nominally nonpartisan political organizations, most of which are focused on one or more particular issues (the environment, gay rights, homelessness, etc.) and are thus listed in the appropriate section. **CascadeLink** has a useful, if basic, online guide to political parties and organizations in the area; it's available at www.cascadelink.org/elect/. The **City Club of Portland** (901 SW Washington St, 503-228-7231, www.pdxcityclub.org) is a nonpartisan—but well-connected—group that focuses on public affairs.

REFUGEES AND IMMIGRANTS

- **Immigrant and Refugee Community Organization**, 503-234-1541, www. irco.org
- **Sponsors Organized to Assist Refugees** (SOAR), 2906 NE Glisan St, 503-284-3002, www.emoregon.org/soar.php

SENIORS

- **Loaves and Fishes/Meals-on-Wheels**, 503-736-6325, www.loavesandfishes online.org
- **Metropolitan Family Services**, 1808 SE Belmont St, 503-232-0007, www.met family.org
- **Neighborhood House**, 7780 SW Capitol Hwy, 503-246-1683, www.nhweb. org
- **Northwest Pilot Project**, 1430 SW Broadway, Suite 200, 503-227-5605, www. nwpilotproject.org
- **Ride Connection**, 503-528-1720, www.rideconnection.org

WOMEN'S SERVICES

- **Bradley-Angle House**, 503-282-9940, www.bradleyangle.org
- **Lola Green Baldwin Foundation**, 503-236-7244, www.prostitutionrecovery. org
- **Portland Women's Crisis Line**, 503-235-5333, www.pwcl.org
- **Sexual Assault Resource Center**, 9450 SW Barnes Rd, Suite 240, 503-384-0480, www.sarcoregon.org

CHARITABLE GIVING

Not everyone can give time or talent to a good cause. Another way to help is to donate something that virtually every charity needs: money. Before donating, consider checking out the charity's fiscal responsibility and its ratio of overhead to program spending; if the charity spends 95% of its money on fundraising efforts and overhead and 5% on program delivery, you might want to pass. Third-party watchdog sites like **Charity Navigator** (www.charitynavigator.org), **Guidestar** (www.guidestar.org), or the Better Business Bureau's **Wise Giving Alliance** (www.give.org) can help you assess a charity's performance.

MEETING PEOPLE

As a rule, Portlanders are friendly and not particularly reticent; you can usually start a conversation with a stranger without being immediately suspected of having an ulterior motive, and people you meet in social settings are more likely than not to be chatty (sometimes unnervingly so). That said, as a newcomer, it's not always easy to meet people with similar interests. Volunteer organizations (see

"Community Involvement" above), cultural events (see **Cultural Life**), recreational sports clubs (see **Sports and Recreation**), and, for the spiritually inclined, religious groups (see "Places of Worship" below) are all excellent places to meet new friends. The arts and entertainment papers (see "What's Going On?" in **Cultural Life**) are full of event listings. Dating and matchmaking services, let alone online social networking sites like MySpace, are beyond the scope of this book, but here are some suggestions for making friends and meeting people in your new home.

ALUMNI GROUPS

Most local, regional, and large national colleges and universities have alumni groups in Portland. If there's no organized alumni group, you should be able to find other graduates of your school living in the area. Check with your alma mater's alumni or development office.

BUSINESS GROUPS

If you have a particular professional focus, there is probably a business group for you. Most of these groups exist in whole or in part for networking purposes, so social events are usually frequent.

POLITICAL GROUPS

Whether you're a government-out-of-my-hemisphere Libertarian or a fist-pounding Trotskyite, or even if your political leanings fall somewhere in between those extremes, you're bound to find a *simpatico* political group in town. If you hate politics, consider founding a Portland Apathy Association—assuming you can be bothered.

OUTDOOR ADVENTURES

Several organizations, including Portland Parks and Recreation, organize outdoor adventures—hikes, snowshoe treks, rafting trips, and more. You can often find out about trips by checking out the bulletin boards of sporting goods stores. **Adventurous Young Mazamas** (www.mazamas.org/your/adventure/starts-here/C74/) and the **Trails Club of Oregon** (503-233-2740, www.trailsclub.org) maintain very active calendars of outdoor events.

SPECIAL INTERESTS

It seems like every niche interest has a club, from the **Portland Skyliners Tall Club** (503-222-7373, www.tall.org/clubs/or/portland/) for women over 5'10" and men over 6'2" to the **Society for Creative Anachronism's** Kingdom of Antir (www.antir.sca.org) for medieval re-creationists (and recreationists). (Would-be knights or damsels of above-average height can go wild and join both clubs!) Just do a web search for your favorite interest or characteristic, or even your favorite celebrity, and you're bound to come up with something.

For a calendar of upcoming meetings from clubs and groups of all kinds, check out the listings at **www.meetup.com**; just type in your ZIP code, select a subject from the resulting list, and you'll likely have dozens of options to choose from.

PLACES OF WORSHIP

The Pacific Northwest is, by some measures, the most unchurched region in the United States. A low rate of weekly church attendance, however, does not translate to a lack of spirituality or an absence of places of worship. The Portland area has hundreds of houses of worship representing every major faith and denomination (and a host of minor ones, too). If you are at all religiously inclined, you'll almost certainly be able to find a spiritual home.

If you belong to a congregation in your old hometown, your religious leader might be able to refer you to a kindred congregation in Portland. On Saturdays, the Living section of the *Oregonian* includes a page of classified ads that list places of worship and their weekly and daily services. In addition, the Yellow Pages has extensive listings under "Churches," "Synagogues," and "Mosques"; the church listings are organized by denomination and include sections for nondenominational, interdenominational, and independent churches as well as metaphysical centers.

The following interfaith agencies, representing congregations working together to address hunger, homelessness, and other urban problems, also might be able to refer you to a congregation that fulfills your spiritual needs:

- **Ecumenical Ministries of Oregon**, 0245 SW Bancroft St, Suite B, 503-221-1054, www.emoregon.org
- **Interfaith Council of Greater Portland**, 3956 NE Couch St, 503-239-1155, www.ifcgp.org

The list of resources below is by no means complete, and it is not a substitute for the Yellow Pages or newspaper listings, but it includes local and regional societies or associations for a range of religious groups.

ALTERNATIVE WORSHIP

GAY & LESBIAN SPIRITUAL GROUPS

The **Community of Welcoming Congregations** (503-665-8711, www.welcoming congregations.org) is an association of more than 80 congregations in Oregon and southwest Washington that welcome worshipers of all sexual orientations and gender identities.

NEW AGE SPIRITUALITY, PAGANISM, AND MORE

For a comprehensive guide to New Age spiritual centers, Ayurveda, meditation, mysticism, and other spiritual resources, visit the web site for *New ConneXion* magazine (www.newconnexion.net). Wiccans, pagans, and other adherents of *really* old-time religion can visit the web site of *Open Ways* magazine (www.9houses. org/OpenWays/intro.html), which features listings of Northwest pagan organizations and activities. Alternatively, pick up free copies of these magazines at area libraries, bookstores, or natural food stores.

BAHA'I

* **Portland Baha'i Center**, 8720 N Ivanhoe St, 503-289-6331, www.pdx-bahai. org

BUDDHIST

The **Portland Buddhist Hub** (www.portlandbuddhisthub.org) provides links to local temples and groups practicing in a variety of traditions, and lists local events and resources. The Seattle-based **Northwest Dharma Association** (206-441-6811, www.nwdharma.org) also covers Portland-area groups and events.

CHRISTIAN

The following major denominations have an organized local or regional presence. Independent and nondenominational churches are, by definition, not part of a denomination, and so have no collective regional organization; the same is true for many small denominations with relatively few adherents in the area, as well as some larger groups, such as Christian Scientists and Jehovah's Witnesses, which are governed from a national headquarters.

APOSTOLIC

The worldwide **Apostolic Faith Church** (503-777-1741, www.apostolicfaith.org) is headquartered in the Woodstock neighborhood of Southeast Portland.

ASSEMBLIES OF GOD

• **Oregon Ministry Network of the Assemblies of God**, www.oregonag.org

BAPTIST

• **American Baptist Churches of Oregon**, 503-228-8394, www.vibrant-life.net
• **CB Northwest**, 503-669-1515, www.cbnw.org (Conservative Baptist)
• **Northwest Baptist Convention**, www.nwbaptist.org (Southern Baptist)

CATHOLIC

• **Archdiocese of Portland**, 503-234-5334, www.archpdx.org

CHURCH OF GOD

• **Association of the Churches of God**, 503-393-3510, 800-873-7729, www.orwacog.org

CHURCH OF JESUS CHRIST OF LATTER-DAY SAINTS (MORMONS)

The Mormons are one of the largest denominations in Oregon. There are many local churches scattered around the area. The regional Temple (13600 SW Kruse Oaks Blvd, Lake Oswego, www.lds.org) is hard to miss: its giant marble spires loom just west of Interstate 5 near the Highway 217 interchange.

EMERGING CHURCHES

So-called "emerging churches" are nondenominational, often loosely organized, and definitely non-hierarchical. Services take place in schools, community centers, or even pubs. Here are a few local examples.

• **Evergreen Community**, Portland, 971-506-9429, evergreenlife.org
• **Imago Dei**, Portland, 503-231-5096, www.imagodeicommunity.com
• **The Pearl Church**, Portland, 503-784-0584, www.pearlchurch.org
• **Southgate Chapel**, Canby, 503-651-4040, www.southgatechapel.com

EPISCOPAL

• **Episcopal Diocese of Oregon**, 503-636-5613, www.diocese-oregon.org

FRIENDS (QUAKERS)

Several Society of Friends groups meet in the local area. The **Multnomah Monthly Meeting** (www.multnomahfriends.org) encompasses some (but not all) local worship groups.

LUTHERAN

- **Evangelical Lutheran Church in America** (ELCA), Oregon Synod, 503-413-4191, www.oregonsynod.org
- **Northwest District of the Lutheran Church–Missouri Synod**, 503-288-8383, 888-693-5267, www.nowlcms.org

MENNONITE

- **Pacific Northwest Mennonite Conference**, 503-492-4216, www.pnmc.org.

METHODIST

- **Oregon-Idaho Conference of the United Methodist Church**, 503-226-7931, 800-593-7539, www.umoi.net

NAZARENE

- **Oregon Pacific District of the Church of the Nazarene**, 503-581-3950, www.orpac.org

ORTHODOX

- **Pacific Northwest Deanery**, Diocese of the West, The Orthodox Church in America, 253-537-4883, www.ocadow.org/pacific_nw.htm

PRESBYTERIAN

- **Synod of the Pacific**, Presbyterian Church USA, 800-754-0669, www.synodpacific.org

SEVENTH-DAY ADVENTIST

- **Oregon Conference of Seventh-Day Adventists**, 503-850-3500, www.oregonconference.org

UNITARIAN UNIVERSALIST

- **Pacific Northwest District of the Unitarian Universalist Association**, 800-313-7693, www.pnwd.org

UNITED CHURCH OF CHRIST

- **Central Pacific Conference of the United Church of Christ**, 503-228-3178, www.cpcucc.org

WESLEYAN

- **Northwest District of the Wesleyan Church**, 360-693-1677, www.nw wesleyan.org

HINDU

There is no centralized source of information on Hinduism in Portland. Two good places to look into are the **Vedanta Society of Portland** (1157 SE 55th Ave, 503-235-3919, www.vedanta-portland.org), which is a branch of the Ramakrishna Order of India, and the **Portland Hindu Temple** (Brahma Premananda Ashram), 11515 SW Hall Blvd, Tigard, www.portlandhindutemple.org.

ISLAMIC

The **Islamic Society of Greater Portland** (www.isgponline.com) sponsors social and community events for members of the local Muslim community; its web site includes links to local mosques and Islamic schools.

JAIN

- **Jain Society of Oregon**, 503-292-1965, www.jainworld.com/society/Oregon. htm

JEWISH

The **Jewish Federation of Greater Portland** (6680 SW Capitol Hwy, 503-245-6219, www.jewishportland.org) is a great resource for the Jewish community. The organization's comprehensive web site lists local events and contains links to Jewish resources, agencies, camps, schools, and congregations, including Conservative, Reform, Orthodox, Reconstructionist, Sephardic, and unaffiliated congregations in the metropolitan area and elsewhere in the Northwest.

B Y NOW, YOU'VE PROBABLY HEARD A FEW NOT ESPECIALLY FUNNY jokes about Oregon rain. One old saw holds that Oregonians don't tan—they rust. Another states that Portland's rainy season only runs from September 1 to August 31. Yet another asks, "What do you call two consecutive days of rain in Portland?" (Answer: the weekend.) Then there's the story about the hapless fellow waiting to be admitted into hell. He watches anxiously as Satan throws almost every soul in line ahead of him into the fiery pit, but notices that every so often the devil chucks someone off to the side instead. Intrigued, he summons up the courage to peep, "Excuse me, Prince of Darkness, but I notice that you seem to be throwing some people off to the side instead of into the inferno." "Oh, them," the devil replies ruefully. "They're from Portland. They're too wet to burn." Har har har. Endless rain. How very droll.

It *does* rain a lot in Oregon. Rumors of a nine-month deluge, however, are greatly exaggerated. The sun comes out *sometimes*, even in winter, and summers are typically glorious. And even if the weather's often wet and gray, it's somewhat comforting that the region's best known climatic feature is its drizzle rather than, say, category 5 hurricanes, killer tornadoes, or paralyzing blizzards.

Which is not to say that Portland is not at risk from natural disasters. All that rain sometimes begets mudslides and floods, and the area is subject to earthquakes, volcanic eruptions, forest fires, and the occasional ironic drought. It's all part of the price you pay for living in a paradise—a soggy, geologically unstable paradise.

WEATHER AND CLIMATE

According to the Portland office of the **National Weather Service** (www.wrh. noaa.gov/pqr/), Portland enjoys or suffers through (depending on your point of view), on average, about 36 inches of precipitation per year. Portland's total annual rainfall is less than that of most cities in the Northeast and Southeast—

Miami's average rainfall is more than 50% higher. The difference, of course, lies in the number of rainy days. Portland's precipitation rarely comes in the form of brief cloudbursts; rather, like the quality of mercy in *The Merchant of Venice*, it droppeth as the gentle rain from heaven upon the place beneath. Stated more bluntly, it falls over long, gray weeks of intermittent drizzle and light rain, resulting in an average of more than 150 days per year with measurable precipitation. Here's the bad news in statistical form, courtesy of the National Weather Service:

Month	Normal Precipitation (in Inches)	Mean Number of Days with Precipitation (.01 inch or more)
January	5.35	18
February	3.85	15.6
March	3.56	16.9
April	2.39	14.4
May	2.06	11.8
June	1.48	9.2
July	0.63	3.9
August	1.09	4.9
September	1.75	7.5
October	2.7	12.3
November	5.34	18
December	6.13	18.7
Yearly Total	36.3	150.9

You'll notice that more than 90% of the city's total rainfall falls from September to May. While the uneven distribution of rainfall during the year does mean the winter months are that much soggier, it also means that summers tend to be dry—newcomers who arrive during July and August are often shocked to find the city a patchwork of brown lawns. So when the pitter-patter of rain on your windows for the umpteenth day in a row threatens to drive you to suicide (or to the sunny environs of Las Vegas, which for some people amounts to the same thing), think hopefully of the blue skies and warm days of July.

While you may struggle to believe it in December, Portland is actually one of the drier locations in northwest Oregon. Frequent moisture-laden storms off the Pacific Ocean drop 60 to 80 inches of rain each year on most coastal communities, and when the storm clouds hit the Coast Range and begin to rise and condense, the rain really begins to pour down. Some locations high in the Coast Range average nearly 180 inches of rain each year—that's five times as much as Portland gets! By the time the storm reaches the Willamette Valley and the Portland area, much of the moisture has already been wrung out of the storm. (This "rain-shadow" effect is why Portland tends to get gray skies and drizzle rather than constant downpours.) Then, when the storm hits the Cascade foot-hills and the clouds once again begin to rise, cool, and condense, precipitation amounts rise correspondingly. (The high Cascades get more than 100 inches of "rain-equivalent" precipitation, but due to the high elevation it mostly falls as hundreds of inches of snow.) By the time the storm passes to the east side of the Cascades, there is usually very little moisture left, which is why much of central and eastern Oregon is high desert.

Despite its proximity to the Cascade Mountains and its northerly lati-tude—more than 45 degrees north latitude, about the same as Minneapolis and Montreal—Portland is not a snowy city. The Portland Airport averages only 6.6 inches of snow per year, and in some winters there's no snow at all on the valley floor. Elevations over 500 feet, including much of the West Hills, often get more snow than downtown Portland or the East Side (or get snow when those places do not), but even at higher elevations a heavy snowfall is rare in the metropolitan area. Near the Gorge and in the Cascade foothills, however, snow is much more common.

You may notice that extended forecasts seem to call for snow far more often than snow actually falls. According to local weatherman Matt Zaffino, "It comes down to basic climatology and geography, and Portland snow storms have to buck both to really have a chance." Moisture usually comes from the west, out of the relatively warm North Pacific, while cold Arctic air from the North American interior has to get past the natural barriers of the Rockies and the Cascades. Of-ten, during the winter, a computer model will predict that everything is coming together just right to produce several inches of snow, but ultimately either the moisture or the cold air fails to arrive. Explains Zaffino, "everything has to fall into place just right, and against the natural tendency of our weather patterns, to produce a big Willamette Valley snow storm." The relative scarcity of snow means that anything more than a dusting of snow results in school closures and mas-sive traffic disruptions. If you're from a snowy part of the world, you'll probably find this behavior amusing, frustrating, or both.

Although snow is rare, ice storms do occur with some frequency, particular-ly in East Portland, Gresham, Troutdale, Camas, and other communities near the western end of the Columbia River Gorge. Cold air rushing through the Gorge from eastern Oregon sets the stage for ice storms by creating a layer of sub-freez-ing air at ground level, with warmer air at altitude. When a storm moves in from the west, precipitation begins to fall as rain, but the rain turns to ice while falling (or freezes on contact with the ground). While ice storms can be treacherous, the effects are usually short-lived (although every few years heavy ice accumula-tions bring down branches all around eastern Multnomah County).

The same maritime influence that brings frequent precipitation to Port-land also gives the city relatively mild temperatures. Here are the average high and low temperatures for each month, courtesy of your friends at the National Weather Service:

Month	Normal High	Normal Low
January	45.4	33.7
February	51	36.1
March	56	38.6
April	60.6	41.3
May	67.1	47
June	74	52.9
July	79.9	56.5
August	80.3	56.9
September	74.6	52
October	64	44.9
November	52.6	39.5
December	45.6	34.8

The hottest temperature ever recorded in Portland was 107; the lowest was -3. In an average year, however, the mercury may hit 100 on one or two days in summer, and fall to the mid-teens on the coldest winter nights. In general, summer days are not terribly muggy; a 95-degree day in Portland may be more comfortable than an 85-degree day in Atlanta.

As a result of its complex topography, the Portland metropolitan area has many microclimates. The West Hills receive more rain than the surrounding lowlands (and create a miniature rain shadow for downtown Portland), while Cascade foothill towns like Sandy and Estacada average more than 55 inches of rain each year. Downtown Portland and the densely populated East Side demonstrate a heat island effect; forested areas outside the heart of the city are noticeably cooler on hot days and cool down more rapidly on clear nights. Areas near the Columbia River tend to be breezy, and therefore cooler in the summer; the eastern part of the metropolitan area, near the mouth of the Columbia River Gorge, is subject to fierce winds whipping down the Gorge from the interior. The lesson here is to choose your location carefully if you have strong preferences about weather. For detailed information about Oregon weather and climate, including fun facts about record-shattering events, visit the web site of the **Oregon Climate Service**, www.ocs.oregonstate.edu.

AIR POLLUTION

Portland is not an especially smoggy city, and most of the region's air quality problems are seasonal. On hot, still summer days, emissions from cars and industry, together with emissions from other sources (such as boat and lawnmower engines, and even paint fumes), react with oxygen to create ground-level ozone or smog. To help combat the problem, vehicle emission tests are required in the Portland metropolitan region, including Clark County, Washington. (See the **Get-**

ting Settled chapter for testing requirements and locations.) For the most part, however, Portland meets national standards for clean air.

Air toxics are a more insidious problem. In winter, particles associated with smoke from wood stoves and fireplaces can build up in the air and cause health problems, and particulate pollution from burning diesel fuel can be a problem at any time of year. Moreover, gasoline sold in the Pacific Northwest (and thus car exhaust) contains high levels of benzene, a toxic chemical that presents an increased cancer risk. The new cleaner-burning diesel fuel and more-efficient diesel engines required by the EPA should decrease particulate pollution in the next few years, and new EPA standards for benzene in gasoline are set to take effect between 2009 and 2011.

The Oregon Department of Environmental Quality's **Air Quality Division** (503-229-5359, www.oregon.gov/DEQ/AQ/) is charged with enforcing federal, state, and local air quality laws. The DEQ provides current air quality reports for Portland on its web site (www.deq.state.or.us/aqi/aqiStationsPortland.aspx). The department offers the following tips for improving air quality:

- Drive less.
- If you use a woodstove, use an efficient, EPA-certified model, and dry firewood at least six to twelve months before using it.
- During hot weather, refuel your vehicle during cooler evening hours, and make sure your gas cap seals properly.
- Wait until temperatures decrease and breezes pick up before you mow the lawn or use gasoline-powered garden equipment.
- Consider using non-gasoline powered equipment, like a manual push mower instead of a gasoline-powered lawn mower.

NATURAL DISASTERS

Natural disasters happen. The City of Portland has put together cheerful online maps showing your relative danger of being swept away in a landslide, scorched by wildfire, or pulverized in an earthquake; just visit **Portland Maps** (www.port-landmaps.com), type in any address or intersection, click on "Maps," then click "Hazard." A similar mapping feature is available for most of the Oregon portion of the metropolitan area at www.metro-region.org/article.cfm?ArticleID=15113.

MUDSLIDES

Mudslides are one of the most common (if not necessarily the most life-threatening) natural disasters in northwest Oregon. The same steep hills that offer residents spectacular views also render their homes and roads vulnerable to mudslides during extended periods of heavy rain. While they are certainly not an everyday occurrence, mudslides happen often enough to warrant concern if you live (or are considering living) on or near a steep slope. (According to the Oregon Department of Geology and Mineral Industries, 9,500 landslides occurred in the state during the exceptionally soggy period from February 1996 through January 1997.)

Geologists warn that steep bluffs and hillsides where earth movement has occurred in the past or where geology favors such movement are most at risk. Such conditions exist in large swaths of the West Hills and other hilly parts of the metropolitan area. If you are considering buying a home in a potentially slide-prone area, you might want to consult with a geologist or geotechnical engineer to analyze the property in question.

WILDFIRES

Western Oregon occasionally experiences drought conditions, which in turn set the stage for dangerous wildfires. While large fires are more prevalent in the drier eastern half of the state, forested neighborhoods in the Portland area, including close-in neighborhoods in the West Hills, are theoretically at risk from wildfires. The National Fire Association offers tips on protecting your home from wildfire on its web site, www.firewise.org.

EARTHQUAKES AND TSUNAMIS

Oregonians live in a geologically unstable region. Earthquakes measuring at least 5 on the Richter scale hit northwest Oregon in 1962, 1964, and 1993—the last of these, centered near Salem, damaged the state Capitol building—and the Nisqually Earthquake that struck the Puget Sound region in 2001, which had a magnitude of 6.8 and caused an estimated $2 billion in damage, reminded Portland that bigger quakes are by no means impossible. Several faults run right through the metropolitan area, including one that runs directly under downtown Portland, and a large temblor on any of those faults could potentially cause significant damage and loss of life. More troubling, geologists advise us that it is only a matter of when, not if, the "Big One"—a quake of a magnitude of 9 or more—occurs along the Cascadia subduction zone 90 miles or so off the Oregon coast. The last time that happened, in about the year 1700, a tsunami hit the coast and a massive landslide temporarily dammed the Columbia River.

For more light bedtime reading about earthquake hazards in the region, visit the web site of the **Pacific Northwest Seismic Network** (www.pnsn.org), which includes data about the location and magnitude of recent (generally very small) area quakes. Also remember that earthquake coverage is not usually part of a standard homeowner's insurance policy; be sure to look into purchasing earthquake insurance if you own, or plan to own, a home here.

While it isn't really an issue in Portland proper, the entire Northwest coast is a potential **tsunami** danger zone. Signs in Oregon coastal communities point the way to evacuation routes; if you're at the coast and you feel an earthquake, head inland to higher ground immediately. The threat is not merely theoretical; the 1964 Good Friday Earthquake in Alaska generated a tsunami that struck the Oregon coast and drowned four campers on the beach at Newport.

VOLCANIC ERUPTIONS

Four major, non-extinct volcanoes—Mounts Hood, St. Helens, Adams, and Rainier—are visible from downtown Portland. While three of those volcanoes are inactive (although not extinct), Mt. St. Helens, only 50 miles away, erupted spectacularly on May 18, 1980. The blast blew the top 1,300 feet off the mountain and sent a plume of ash as far east as Oklahoma. The United States Geological Survey's **Cascades Volcano Observatory** in Vancouver, Washington, provides abundant information about the region's volcanoes on its web site (vulcan. wr.usgs.gov).

While Portland is far enough from all of these volcanoes that an eruption is unlikely to cause destruction in the city itself, significant disruption is certainly possible. In particular, if Mount Hood were to erupt, Portland's source of municipal water (the Bull Run reservoirs on the west side of the mountain) could become unusable.

EMERGENCY PREPAREDNESS

The Oregon Trail Chapter of the **American Red Cross** publishes a useful booklet about emergency preparedness called *Together We Prepare Oregon*. You can download a copy from the "Disaster Services" section of the chapter's web site (www.redcross-pdx.org/services/Disaster_services_home.htm), or you can call 503-528-5665 to request a free copy by mail. The Red Cross recommends taking the following steps.

MAKE A PLAN

- Research the kinds of disasters that could happen in the Northwest, and talk with your family about them.
- Learn how to use emergency equipment, such as fire extinguishers, and know how to shut off utility service to your home. Pick two places to meet in case of an emergency, one right outside your home and one outside your neighborhood.
- Put together a disaster kit and a stockpile of emergency supplies.

- Make a list of emergency contact numbers and tell everyone in your house-hold where the list is kept.
- Practice your plan and maintain your supplies in a state of readiness.

BUILD A KIT

Put together a disaster supply kit with water (one gallon per person, per day) and a three-day supply of non-perishable food. The kit should include:

- A complete first-aid kit and first-aid reference guide
- Portable battery-operated radio and spare batteries
- Flashlights and spare batteries
- Blankets and extra clothing, including rain gear and sturdy shoes
- A three-day supply of critical medication and a spare pair of eyeglasses
- Comfort items for children, such as toys, games, stuffed animals
- Food, water, and carrying cages and other supplies for pets
- Plastic sheeting, duct tape, a pocket knife, matches, rope, a whistle, and other survival gear
- A crescent wrench, screwdrivers, a hammer, an axe, and other essential tools
- Sanitation supplies, such as toilet paper, soap, detergent, bleach (for water purification), diapers, feminine sanitary supplies, trash bags, and pre-moistened towelettes
- Copies of important documents and a stash of emergency cash

It may seem like a hassle to prepare so thoroughly for a disaster, given the seemingly low risk of catastrophe. However, as the Red Cross's booklet points out, "The greatest risk here in Oregon could be complacency, as many people are not aware of the potential for natural and manmade disasters in our communities. By taking these simple steps, you can help prepare your family, community, neighborhood school and workplace."

Portland enjoys a national reputation as a leader in progressive transportation policy, and rightly so, but that doesn't mean you'll find a utopia of limitless transit options and constantly free-flowing freeways. If you need to drive on major highways at peak hours, you will certainly encounter traffic congestion. If you have moved here from, say, Los Angeles, you may dismiss Portlanders as lightweights, but the perception that traffic conditions are getting worse has prompted cries of woe-is-me from commuters and truckers alike. In fact, traffic congestion is getting measurably worse. The good news is that congestion is not getting worse as fast as it is in other cities: the Texas Transportation Institute, which keeps track of such things, estimates that the average car traveler in the Portland area lost 39 hours to congestion in 2003, versus 33 hours in 1993. Many other cities got much worse, much faster. Those facts may not soothe you as you sit motionless on Interstate 5 at 5 p.m., but you can take consolation in the thought that traffic will be speeding along again in an hour or two.

Lots of hand wringing about transportation is going on in the area, particularly about transportation in growing suburban communities, with the transit boosters facing off against the road builders (and with most people seemingly in the middle). The perceived problem is in part a deliberate regional choice to preserve existing neighborhoods and expand transit options rather than building big new freeways. The proposed Mount Hood Freeway, which would have obliterated many neighborhoods in Southeast Portland (along with 1% of the city's housing stock), was killed off in the 1970s. The money that would have gone toward freeway construction was diverted to other projects instead, most notably the Eastside MAX project. The anti-freeway ethos also prevented massive expansion of existing highways; since most highway engineers will tell you that freeway capacity fills up shortly after it is created, the result is that Portland's rush hour features congested four- and six-lane freeways instead of congested ten- or twelve-lane freeways. Instead of drastically expanding freeway capacity, Portland's transportation planners have tinkered with the system, for example adding metered on-ramps to smooth the flow of merging traffic.

The regional government, Metro, is taking a "New Look" at the region's transportation plan to figure out how to accommodate the one million newcomers expected to arrive in the next 25 years. The New Look will help determine what the future mix of transportation options should be, whether and where to expand highways, and how to deal with aging transportation infrastructure. While you may not be in a position to determine the region's transportation future, as a newcomer you at least have the chance to influence your personal transportation future: If you don't want to spend a lot of time in traffic, consider living close to your workplace or someplace where you're likely to have access to convenient public transportation. If you choose to commute across the metropolitan area, or to live in an outlying area and work in Portland, accept that traffic congestion is not likely to improve much in the future. Good luck with those gas prices, too.

BY CAR

The U.S. Census Bureau estimates that, in 2005, 73% of workers in the Portland area commuted to work by car, alone. That percentage seems to be declining slightly, and it's lower than in some other metropolitan areas, but the fact remains that most people in the Portland area get around primarily by car.

MAJOR FREEWAYS

As you get to know Portland, you'll find alternatives to the freeways, highways, and major thoroughfares (unless you have to cross a bridge, in which case your options are limited). Until then, here are some of the major traffic arteries.

- **Interstate 5** is the main north-south highway artery, not just for the Portland area, but for the entire West Coast. It travels through the southern suburbs and Southwest Portland, crosses the Willamette at the south end of downtown, and runs along the east bank of the river and due north through North Portland and across the Columbia River into Vancouver. The northbound stretch of I-5 north of downtown during the evening commute is the most congested section of highway in the metro area.
- **Interstate 84** (the Banfield Freeway), the main east-west artery on the east side, runs from Interstate 5 just across the river from downtown Portland to outer Northeast Portland, through the Columbia River Gorge, and ultimately to Idaho. The I-5/I-84 interchange is often extremely congested.
- The **Sunset Highway** is the name for US Highway 26 west of downtown Portland. It runs over the West Hills to skirt Beaverton and Hillsboro to the north

before losing its freeway characteristics and continuing on to the coast. According to the Oregon Department of Transportation, traffic on the Sunset is the most inconsistent in the area: one day, the commute is relatively free-flowing, and the next day it's an ever-living-nightmare. During peak hours, the latter condition is more common than the former. (Be aware that east of I-405, US 26 is not a freeway; it crosses the Ross Island Bridge to Southeast Portland and becomes Powell Boulevard. At the east end of Gresham, it again becomes a limited-access highway—the Mount Hood Highway—and runs to Sandy and eventually (as a regular highway) over the shoulder of Mount Hood to Central Oregon.

- **Interstate 405** (the Stadium Freeway) loops around the west side of downtown Portland. In its short existence it branches off of Interstate 5, connects with the Sunset Highway, skirts downtown and the Northwest Industrial District, crosses over the Willamette on the Fremont Bridge, and reconnects with I-5.

- **Interstate 205** is the closest thing Portland has to a beltway (albeit only a half beltway). This 37-mile eastern alternate to I-5 branches off that highway in Tualatin, loops through West Linn and Oregon City, and travels north through Clackamas and East Portland before passing near the airport and crossing over the Columbia into eastern Vancouver. It eventually rejoins I-5 in Salmon Creek, Washington. I-205 is a useful bypass if you're traveling north or south through the metro area and you want to avoid downtown, although the I-5 through route is shorter. I-205 is officially named the Veterans Memorial Freeway, but almost no one ever calls it that.

- **Highway 217** connects the Sunset Highway north of Beaverton with Interstate 5 in Tigard. Traffic is often stop-and-go here, even on weekends, and the short distances between on- and off-ramps tend to exacerbate congestion.

- **Washington State Highway 14** runs from downtown Vancouver east along the Columbia River to Camas, and continues into the Gorge as a two-lane highway.

MAJOR BRIDGES

If you need to cross either the Willamette River or the Columbia River, the bridges can be a major chokepoint.

COLUMBIA RIVER

Only two bridges cross the Columbia in the Portland area. The **Interstate Bridge** carries I-5 over the Columbia between Portland and Vancouver. It has no shoulders, its drawbridge is occasionally raised to allow ship traffic to pass, and it is likely to be replaced in the next decade or so, at an estimated cost of up to $2 billion. Interstate 205 crosses the river at the **Glen Jackson Bridge** east of the airport.

WILLAMETTE RIVER

Several bridges span the river in or near downtown Portland. From north to south, the **Broadway**, **Steel**, **Burnside**, **Morrison**, **Hawthorne**, and **Ross Island** bridges carry local traffic between the east side neighborhoods and downtown. With the exception of the Ross Island, all of these bridges are drawbridges of one kind or another, and passing barge or other boat traffic can cause auto traffic backups; the Hawthorne Bridge tends to get raised more often than the others. Two double-decker freeway bridges also bracket the downtown waterfront. At the south end, Interstate 5 crosses the river on the hulking, unlovely **Marquam Bridge**, which has the redeeming quality of offering an excellent view of downtown. The much more elegant **Fremont Bridge** carries I-405 over the river at the north end of downtown.

The only road bridge over the Willamette downstream (north) of the Fremont Bridge is the **St. Johns Bridge**, a beautiful suspension bridge opened in 1931 that connects the St. Johns neighborhood of North Portland with the Linnton neighborhood on the west bank.

South of downtown, the narrow, aging **Sellwood Bridge** links Sellwood on the east bank with Macadam Avenue (Highway 43) south of the Johns Landing area. Upstream of the city of Portland, three other bridges cross the river in the metro area—the **Boone Bridge** for I-5 at Wilsonville and the **I-205 (George Abernethy)** and **Highway 43** bridges between West Linn and Oregon City. The **Canby Ferry** (toll required) shuttles passenger vehicles (and passengers) across the river north of Canby.

TRAFFIC REPORTS

Most Portland radio and television stations provide frequent traffic updates during morning and evening rush hours, but you'll need to know the nicknames of area highways to make heads or tails of the information. (See "Major Freeways" and "Major Bridges" above.) Frequent bottlenecks with non-obvious meanings include "Delta Park," the area in North Portland where Interstate 5 goes from three lanes to two (which is also referred to as the "lane drop"); the "Tunnel," where Highway 26 (a.k.a the Sunset Highway) passes through the Vista Ridge Tunnel just west of downtown; and the "Terwilliger curves" (or often just "the curves"), the stretch of Interstate 5 south of downtown where the highway goes around a series of relatively sharp curves near the Terwilliger Boulevard exit. (The latter location is reputed to have the highest traffic accident rate of any spot on Interstate 5 between Canada and Mexico.)

The Oregon Department of Transportation's **tripcheck.org** web site has a map showing current freeway speeds, construction, and expected delays; you can also check out the view from one of ODOT's many strategically placed highway cameras. Across the Columbia River, the Washington State Department of Transportation posts traffic information at www.wsdot.wa.gov/traffic. A new Google Maps service shows real-time traffic conditions. Go to maps.google.com, type in the location you're interested in (e.g., Beaverton), and click on the "Traffic" button in the upper right corner of the map. Various color codes indicate current speeds: green means more than 50 mph, orange 25–50 mph, red means pretty darn slow, and gray denotes a lack of data. In general, the evening commute is slightly worse than the morning commute, but freeways are typically free-flowing by 6:30 p.m.

PARKING

Parking is free in most suburban communities, except in a few older commercial districts that still have street meters. In Portland, you'll have to pay to park downtown and in the Pearl District, Old Town/Chinatown, the South Waterfront neighborhood, and in parts of the Inner East Side, like the Lloyd District/Rose Quarter neighborhood. Some neighborhoods require parking permits; if you don't live or work in the neighborhood, you'll be limited to two hours or so of free parking. (See **Getting Settled** for details.)

Most street meters in downtown Portland and other close-in neighborhoods have been replaced by high-tech, solar-powered SmartMeters. Look for a SmartMeter at the center of the block instead of next to your parking space; to pay, you select the amount of time you plan to park (up to the maximum time allowed) and insert cash or a credit or debit card. (There is a $1 minimum charge for credit and debit cards.) The machine spits out a two-part receipt; stick the larger half of the receipt to the inside of the window on the sidewalk side of your car. The receipt shows the expiration time; if you return to your car with time remaining, you can park in another spot until time is up. (Just be sure the receipt is still on the sidewalk side of the car.)

Parking garages are abundant downtown and in the Pearl District. Around the periphery of downtown and in Old Town/Chinatown, surface parking lots predominate. Many lots cater to commuters and charge relatively high rates for short-term parking on weekdays, but the city-owned **Smart Park** garages (www. portlandonline.com/smartpark/) charge low hourly rates for four hours or less, and many downtown merchants will validate parking for two hours with a minimum purchase. You can find Smart Park garages in the following locations:

- **SW 1st Ave at Jefferson St**
- **SW 3rd Ave at Alder St**
- **SW 4th Ave at Alder St**
- **SW 10th Ave at Yamhill St**

- **O'Bryant Square, SW Stark St at 9th Ave**
- **NW Davis St at Naito Pkwy**
- **Station Place, NW Station Way at Marshall St**

TOWED VEHICLES

Hope that your car is never towed against your will. The City of Portland imposes some minor regulations on towing companies—the so-called "temper fee," imposed on people who manifest anything more than mild bemusement when they see their car being towed away, is not allowed, for example—but beyond those limited protections you're stuck with the whims of what Portland City Commissioner Randy Leonard has called "a cowboy industry with few rules."

DRIVING RULES AND HABITS

Oregon and Washington don't have many unusual traffic rules. Northwesterners are generally pretty good about following rules of the road—crazy drivers are invariably dismissed as California transplants—and you may be pleasantly surprised at the ease with which you can merge onto highways. In fact, in 2007, an automobile club named Portland motorists the most courteous drivers in the country, based on a survey assessing the frequency of road-rage behaviors in major U.S. cities. At the same time, you may be infuriated by cars that travel in the fast (passing) lane at or just above the speed limit, even when there is nothing in front of the car and nothing preventing the car from moving into the slow lane. It's a regional habit you'll have to learn to live with.

Be aware of one-way streets, especially in downtown Portland. Red-light and speed cameras are used in Portland and some surrounding jurisdictions, so keep your speed down and don't try to run yellow lights. Don't attempt to pump your own gas in Oregon, where self-help of that kind is illegal. (Oregon and New Jersey are the only states without self-service.) In winter, you are required to carry chains or traction tires—generally studded tires that tear up roads and make a distinctive clacking sound on dry pavement—when you travel through snow zones. (Snow zones include most of the state's mountainous regions, but even some urban roads, like West Burnside Street as it crosses the West Hills, meet the definition.) During ice or snow storms, chains or traction tires may be required (although four-wheel-drive and all-wheel-drive vehicles are usually exempt from this requirement except when conditions are unusually severe).

CAR SHARING

If you want the freedom of driving a car without the trouble and expense of owning one, consider joining **Flexcar**. This car-sharing service places vehicles in strategic locations throughout Portland and in some suburban communities. Flexcar members determine their monthly driving needs, and choose an hourly or monthly rate plan; costs range from a straight $9 per hour (with 10 free miles) to $700 per month for 100 hours and 1000 miles. The company pays for gas, insurance, parking, and maintenance. For more information, call 877-353-9227 or visit www.flexcar.com.

CARPOOLING

Local governments offer significant incentives to employers to arrange carpools or vanpools. If you're interested in carpooling but your employer doesn't sponsor carpools, and you don't already know someone you can share a ride in with, visit www.carpoolmatchnw.com or call 503-CARPOOL (503-227-7665). Carpools qualify for reduced parking rates in designated spots in downtown Portland, the Lloyd District, and the Pearl District. The only HOV (High-Occupancy Vehicle) or carpool lane in the Portland area is on I-5 northbound north of downtown.

CAR RENTAL

The following car rental companies have multiple locations in the metropolitan area. For smaller companies and airport-only options, look in the Yellow Pages under "Auto Renting."

- **Avis**, 800-831-2847, www.avis.com
- **Budget**, 800-527-0700, www.budget.com
- **Dollar**, 800-800-4000, www.dollar.com
- **Enterprise**, 800-736-8222, www.enterprise.com
- **Hertz**, 800-654-3131, www.hertz.com
- **Thrifty**, 503-254-2277, www.portland.thrifty.com

BY BIKE

Despite its hilly terrain and the wet, chilly fall and winter weather, Portland is perhaps the most bike-centric city in America. *Bicycling* magazine has repeatedly named Portland the best overall cycling city in the country, and although it's no Amsterdam, Portland is a reasonably easy place to get around by bike. On an average day, more than 12,000 bicycles cross Portland's bridges (the vast majority of them downtown), and the city has 167 miles of striped bike lanes, 69 miles of bike paths, and 30 miles of "bike boulevards"—city streets with low auto traffic volume and (sometimes) obstacles to through car traffic. At press time, nearly 11 more miles of bikeways have been funded, but the exciting news is that an additional 339.7 miles of bike lands, bike paths, and bike boulevards have been recommended—more than double the existing length of the bikeway network. (The bad news is that as yet no funds have been allocated to create these hundreds of additional miles.)

If you're interested in commuting or otherwise getting around by bicycle, even on a part-time basis, a host of organizations stand ready to help. The Portland **Office of Transportation** (503-823-CYCL, www.gettingaroundportland. org) provides extensive bicycling information, both online and in hard copy. The following nonprofits are also excellent resources for actual and prospective bicyclists:

- **Bicycle Transportation Alliance**, 1979 SW 5th Ave, 503-226-0676, www. bta4bikes.com
- **Portland Cycling**, www.portlandcycling.net
- **Community Cycling Center**, 1700 NE Alberta St, 503-288-8864, www. communitycyclingcenter.org
- **Shift**, 503-542-6900, www.shift2bikes.org

The Portland Office of Transportation publishes several neighborhood bike maps, as well as the fairly comprehensive (and free) *Portland by Bicycle* map and guide. Multnomah (503-988-5050), Washington (800-537-3149), and Clackamas (503-353-4524) counties all publish county-level bike maps, but the best region-wide map is *Bike There*, available for $6 at most bike shops, bookstores, and some natural foods supermarkets and co-ops. A free map of Vancouver bike routes is available from the city of Vancouver's Transportation Services office; call 360-696-8290 to request one. For something higher-tech, try the Google Maps "mashup" bicycle trip planner for Portland at tripplanner.bycycle.org.

Many businesses have bicycle parking for patrons and/or employees, and some downtown parking garages have free covered bike parking. For information about bike locker rentals downtown, call 503-823-6841. In addition, bike storage lockers are available at some transit centers and MAX stations; call 503-226-0676 for details.

Bicycles are allowed on all public buses and light rail trains in the Portland area, as well as the Portland Streetcar and the Aerial Tram: Buses have a fold-down front rack with space for two bikes, and trains have designated areas for bicycles. For details on how to take your bike on public transit, call 503-962-7644 or visit www.trimet.org, or call 503-823-CYCLE to request a *Bikes on TriMet* guide.

BICYCLE SAFETY

The Oregon Department of Transportation produces the **Oregon Bicyclist Manual**. While at times overly basic—the first of the "Four Basic Principles" presented in the manual is "Maintain Control of Your Bicycle," and the list of "Practices to Avoid" includes the helpful hint, "Don't dart out suddenly into the roadway"— the booklet does contain a useful rundown of rules of the road for bicyclists. The manual is available for download online (visit www.oregon.gov/ODOT/HWY/ BIKEPED and click on the "Publications" link) or you can order a copy by calling 503-986-3556. The Portland Office of Transportation publishes the less patronizing *A Guide to Your Ride* and *Safe Biking: A City Cycling Handbook*.

Although helmets are not required for bicyclists 16 years and older in Oregon (and not at all in Clark County), you would be very unwise not to wear one. (Some young hipsters seem to think that helmets look uncool, but permanent brain damage is even less cool.) For more information about helmets, visit the **Bicycle Helmet Safety Institute** web site (www.helmets.org).

ROADSIDE ASSISTANCE

Roadside assistance for bicyclists? You bet! Contact **Better World Club** (503-546-1137, 866-238-1137, www.betterworldclub.com); bicycle plans start at about $40 per year.

WALKING AND SKATEBOARDING

Much of Portland is ideal walking territory, with plentiful sidewalks and short blocks. If your own two feet aren't good enough for you, it is legal to skate, skateboard, or ride a (non-motorized) scooter on any street or sidewalk in Portland, except downtown, where you'll have to stick to streets. (Certain downtown streets have been designated as skate routes.) Visit www.portlandonline.com/ transportation/index.cfm?c=34780 for more information.

PUBLIC TRANSPORTATION

TriMet (503-238-RIDE, www.trimet.org) is by far the largest transit agency in Oregon. TriMet operates bus and light rail (MAX) networks in most of the Portland metropolitan area. The system averages more than 300,000 weekday boardings. Whether and how well the system will serve you depends on where you live, where you need to go, and when you need to get there.

TriMet's service area is divided into three zones. Zone 1 covers downtown Portland and close-in neighborhoods; Zone 2 extends approximately to the borders of Washington and Clackamas counties on the west and south, the Columbia

River to the north, and Interstate 205 to the east. Everywhere else (including the airport) is in Zone 3. Tickets and passes are sold on a two-zone or all-zone basis. At press time, a single two-zone ticket costs $1.70 and an all-zone ticket costs $2 (transfers are free); youths under 18 (or in high school) pay $1.35, honored citizens (i.e., the elderly and disabled) pay $.85, and children under 7 ride free. Fares generally increase by a nickel or so each September.

You can pay a single cash fare or buy an all-day ticket when you board a bus; bills are accepted, but exact change is required. Tickets are also available from the self-service vending machines at MAX stations; some of these machines accept credit cards. You can buy books of tickets and monthly passes at the **TriMet Ticket Office** at Pioneer Courthouse Square downtown (701 SW 6th Ave) or at many area supermarkets. You can also order tickets and passes online at www. trimet.org.

Public transportation is free within an area known as **Fareless Square**. Fareless Square covers a 330-square-block area that includes most of downtown Portland between the Interstate 405 loop and the Willamette River, with Northwest Irving Street as its northern limit, and a portion of the Lloyd District and the vicinity of the Convention Center on the east side. (See www.trimet.org/fares/farelessmap.htm for a map of Fareless Square.)

Ride Connection (503-528-1720, www.rideconnection.org) facilitates travel for older adults and people with disabilities, both by helping with independent travel on public transit and by providing public transit alternatives.

Other regional transit agencies serve southwest Washington and outlying areas in Clackamas County. These agencies currently operate buses only; see "Bus" below for specifics.

LIGHT RAIL

The **Metropolitan Area Express (MAX)** light rail system currently has three lines with a total of 44 miles of track. MAX is the backbone of the transit system in that, although light rail accounts for only about a third of all trips on TriMet, most bus lines connect with MAX. (Some riders have complained that what was formerly a single bus trip now requires a transfer to MAX.) See p. 444-445 for a system map.

The 33-mile **Blue Line** runs from Hillsboro in the west to Gresham in the east, via Beaverton, downtown Portland, and Northeast Portland. The eastern portion of this line, from Portland to Gresham, was the region's first light rail line when it opened in 1986. The Westside MAX opened in 1998. If, for some reason, you wanted to ride the line from end to end, it would take about an hour and a half.

The **Red Line** serves Portland International Airport. This line, opened in 2001, shares tracks with the Blue Line from Beaverton Transit Center to Gateway Transit Center in Northeast Portland, then runs the 5.5 miles to the airport on a spur line. It takes about 40 minutes to get to the airport terminal from downtown Portland.

The **Yellow Line** runs from downtown Portland to the Rose Quarter Transit Center on Blue Line/Red Line tracks, then heads north along Interstate Avenue to the Expo Center in North Portland, just south of the Columbia River. It takes about half an hour to travel the 5.8-mile length of the line. (If you're hopping on MAX downtown, note that Blue, Red, and Yellow Line trains all travel on the same tracks; pay attention to the train's final destination or you could end up somewhere you did not intend to go.)

The I-205/Portland Mall Light Rail project will add 6.5 miles of track to the MAX system. When it opens in September 2009, the line will run from Gateway Transit Center to Clackamas Town Center along Interstate 205; it will share track with Blue Line and Red Line trains between Gateway and downtown Portland, and will travel through downtown on a new north-south alignment between Union Station and Portland State University. A new MAX line through Southeast Portland to Milwaukie is under consideration, as is an extension to Vancouver, Washington. A few other potential lines—a line along Barbur Boulevard and a Blue Line extension to Forest Grove, among others—have been proposed informally.

BUS

TriMet runs 91 bus lines, including 16 "frequent service" lines, through the metro area. Almost all buses run to or from either downtown Portland or one of 18 regional transit centers. Bus service runs the gamut from frequent and excellent to nonexistent: lines with heavy ridership, or that serve major corridors, run at least every 15 minutes (and more often during rush hour), while other lines provide commuter service only, sometimes in only one direction. Most bus lines fall somewhere in between these service extremes.

Most bus stops on "frequent service" lines have printed time point information at the stop, and most major bus stops on other lines have schedules posted for the lines that stop there. Every official stop has a stop identification number. In theory, you can obtain up-to-the-minute arrival information by calling 503-238-RIDE (503-238-7433) and entering the Stop ID number. If your bus is stalled or broken down somewhere, however, it can be "arriving in three minutes" for half an hour or more.

In downtown Portland, most bus lines run down the bus mall (5th and 6th avenues). However, these streets are currently torn up to allow for the installation of light rail tracks and reconstruction of the bus mall. (The official take on the new transit mall is online at www.portlandmall.org.) While construction lasts, most bus routes that formerly ran along the mall run two blocks east, along Third and Fourth avenues; a few lines have been diverted to Jefferson and Columbia streets.

In addition to TriMet, the following transit agencies provide bus service in the Portland metropolitan area:

- **C-TRAN**, 360-695-0123, www.c-tran.com, provides bus service in Clark County, including commuter service between Vancouver and downtown Portland as well as to the Expo Center and Parkrose MAX stations.
- **Canby Area Transit**, 503-266-4022, www.ci.canby.or.us/transportation/CAThomepage.htm, provides free service within Canby and between Canby and Oregon City and Canby and Woodburn (via Aurora).
- **Columbia County Rider**, 888-462-6526, www.co.columbia.or.us/transit/, provides limited commuter service between downtown Portland and St. Helens and Scappoose. Buses also run between St. Helens/Scappoose and Portland Community College's Rock Creek Campus.
- **Sandy Area Metro (SAM)**, 503-668-5569, www.ci.sandy.or.us, runs buses within Sandy and between Sandy and Gresham, Estacada, and Rhododendron.
- The **South Clackamas Transportation District**, 503-632-7000, www.south clackamastransportation.com, serves Molalla and runs between Molalla and Canby, Mulino, and Clackamas Community College.
- **South Metro Area Rapid Transit (SMART)**, 503-682-7790, www.ridesmart. com, serves Wilsonville. In addition to routes within the city, SMART runs buses that connect Wilsonville with Portland, Tualatin, Salem, and Canby.

PORTLAND STREETCAR

The Portland Streetcar (www.portlandstreetcar.org) runs desultorily between Northwest Portland and the South Waterfront district, via the Pearl District, downtown Portland, and Portland State University. The modern, Czech-made trains are the pokey little puppies of the transit system: they get you there, but at a leisurely speed. In fact, you could probably walk (and could certainly jog) faster than the streetcar trundles along. It takes half an hour (more or less) to ride the line from one end to another. TriMet tickets and passes are valid on the streetcar; a streetcar ticket is good for an entire day on the streetcar, and for two hours on TriMet. An annual streetcar pass is $100. (Keep in mind that much of the streetcar's route is within Fareless Square.)

An Eastside Streetcar that will run down Grand Avenue and Martin Luther King Jr. Boulevard is in the planning stages and is fairly likely to be built; streetcar lines have also been proposed for Burnside and Couch streets and for Hawthorne Boulevard.

PORTLAND AERIAL TRAM

Portland's sleek, expensive aerial tram opened in early 2007 to fanfare and criticism. Two futuristic, Swiss-made silver pods travel the 3,000 linear (and 500 vertical) feet between the Oregon Health and Science University (OHSU) campus high on "Pill Hill" and the rapidly developing (but still semi-industrial) South Waterfront district. Critics include many neighborhood residents, who do not appreciate tram cars passing back and forth high overhead (thus giving passengers birds'-eye views of back yards), and fiscal watchdogs, who note that the tram cost $57 million, more than triple the original estimated cost. (OHSU picked up the bulk of the cost, with the city of Portland kicking in several million dollars.) The tram is not really a convenient transit option unless you're headed to or from OHSU, but on a clear day it offers a heck of a view.

Tram tickets currently cost $4 round-trip; OHSU staff, patients with appointments, and children six and under ride free. Tickets are only sold at the lower station. (For the moment, it's an open secret that this system results in a useful loophole: If you board at the top and ride down one-way, as a practical matter you won't need to pay, although technically you are required to have a valid ticket.) Although the tram is nominally part of Portland's public transit system, regular TriMet tickets and transfers are not valid (although monthly TriMet and C-TRAN passes and annual Portland Streetcar passes are accepted). The tram runs weekdays from 6 a.m. to 10 p.m. and Saturdays from 9 a.m. to 5 p.m.; there is as yet no permanent Sunday service, although the tram will run Sunday afternoons in summer 2007 as a test of potential demand. As one would expect from a mode of transport that serves a hospital, the Aerial Tram is fully accessible. For more information, visit www.portlandtram.org.

COMMUTER RAIL

A new 14.7-mile commuter rail line from Wilsonville to Beaverton is expected to open in September 2008. This suburb-to-suburb line, one of the few such lines in the country, will make intermediate stops in Tualatin and Tigard. For more information visit www.trimet.org/commuterrail/. There is already talk of extending the line to Salem or adding spurs to other suburbs, but none of this discussion yet goes beyond the wishing-and-hoping stage.

PARK & RIDES

There are more than 50 park & ride lots in TriMet service territory. You can park at these lots for free (usually for up to 24 hours) and take a bus or MAX train to your destination. Note that some of the more popular park & ride lots fill up early, and you have no guarantee of finding a parking space. Also, many of these lots are provided by churches or other private entities and are intended for weekday use only. For a list of park & ride locations, visit www.trimet.org/parkandride/index. htm, or call 503-238-RIDE. C-TRAN has five park & rides in Clark County; visit www. c-tran.com or call 360-695-0123 for locations.

TAXIS

Unless you're downtown or at the airport, you'll probably need to telephone for a cab rather than hail one on the street. The following are the major (but not the only) Portland taxi companies:

- **Broadway Cab**, 503-227-1234, www.broadwaycab.com
- **Green Cab and Green Shuttle**, 503-234-1414, www.greentrans.com
- **Radio Cab**, 503-227-1212, www.radiocab.net

REGIONAL/NATIONAL TRAVEL

AIR TRAVEL

Portland International Airport (503-460-4040, 877-739-4636, www.flypdx. com) is one of the country's more pleasant major airports; its airport code, PDX, is often used as shorthand for the entire Portland metropolitan area. The airport is located in northeast Portland, just south of the Columbia River. Although there are several concourses for passenger flights, there is only one terminal.

The check-in and security screening process is usually not the nightmare it can be at some airports, but the official advice is to arrive at least two hours before your flight is scheduled to depart. In most cases, you won't need nearly that much time unless you're traveling at peak hours, but at least the airport shops and restaurants are above average, and in many cases are outposts of local businesses like Powell's Books and Beaverton Bakery. You'll often encounter live entertainment at PDX—pianists, guitarists, singers, a harpist, and even a roaming concertina performer. You can also hook up to free wireless Internet service in most parts of the airport, or let the kids work off pre-flight energy at one of the two play areas in the terminal.

Members of certain airline mileage plans, travelers with special needs, and travelers going from Portland to Seattle can go through an "express lane" at the security checkpoint. Security requirements are constantly in flux, so check with the airport or your airline for the latest information on check-in procedures, availability of curbside check-in, identification requirements, and handling of liquids, electronics, shoes, and other potentially dangerous objects.

Because Portland is not a national hub, no one airline dominates the market; however, PDX serves as a regional hub for Alaska/Horizon and United/United Express, and those airlines, together with Southwest, carry about two-thirds of all passengers who come through the airport. There are nonstop flights from Portland to most major cities in the United States and to most mid-size cities (and some small cities) in the West; in addition, there are nonstop international flights to Frankfurt, Tokyo, Vancouver, Mexico City, and several other cities in Mexico.

The following airlines serve Portland:

- **Air Canada Jazz**, 888-247-2262, www.flyjazz.ca
- **Alaska Airlines**, 800-252-7522, www.alaskaair.com
- **American Airlines**, 800-433-7300, www.aa.com
- **Big Sky Airlines**, 800-237-7788, www.bigskyair.com
- **Continental Airlines**, 800-523-3273, www.continental.com
- **Delta Air Lines**, 800-221-1212, www.delta.com
- **Frontier Airlines**, 800-432-1359, www.frontierairlines.com
- **Hawaiian Airlines**, 800-367-5320, www.hawaiianair.com
- **Horizon Air**, 800-547-9308, www.alaskaair.com
- **JetBlue Airways**, 800-538-2583, www.jetblue.com
- **Lufthansa**, 800-645-3880, www.lufthansa.com
- **Mexicana**, 800-531-7921, www.mexicana.com
- **Northwest Airlines**, 800-225-2525, www.nwa.com
- **Southwest Airlines**, 800-435-9792, www.southwest.com
- **United Airlines and United Express**, 800-864-8331, www.united.com
- **US Airways**, 800-428-4322, www.usairways.com

Travelers who live in the southern suburbs might find **Salem's** McNary Field more convenient, but currently the only commercial flights from Salem (SLE) are on Delta Air Lines to Salt Lake City; visit www.flysalem.org for details.

GETTING TO AND FROM THE AIRPORT

TriMet's Red Line **MAX** (light rail) trains run directly to the terminal; the airport station is just east of baggage claim. At press time, a one-way ticket to or from downtown Portland is $2.00 for adults, and the trip takes about 35 to 40 minutes.

If you're driving, make your way to Interstate 205 and take the exit for Airport Way West, then follow Airport Way to the terminal. Sandy Boulevard makes a good alternative route during the evening rush hour; take Sandy to Northeast 82nd Avenue, and go north to Airport Way. When it reaches the terminal, the airport roadway splits into two levels: the upper roadway is for departures, and the lower roadway is for arrivals. Stopping is allowed only for active pick-up or drop-off of passengers and loading or unloading luggage. If you need to park, see "Airport Parking" below.

Taxis, door-to-door shuttles, charter buses, long-haul shuttles, and courtesy shuttles for airport hotels, off-airport parking and car rental facilities, and long-term parking lots depart from the lower roadway outside baggage claim. Many downtown hotels offer shuttle service to or from the airport; call ahead for times, costs, and companies. (Transport may be free or at a reduced rate if you are a hotel guest.) For a list of door-to-door shuttle services and other airport transportation options, visit www.flypdx.com/Grnd_Trans.aspx or call the airport's ground transportation office at 503-460-4686.

AIRPORT PARKING

The airport **parking garage** is connected to the terminal by tunnels and skyways, so it's convenient for parking when curbside drop-off or pick-up won't do. Parking is $3 per hour; people on expense accounts with no time to lose can park here for $24 per day. Motorcycle and bicycle parking is free. The uncovered **long-term parking** lot is in front of the garage; it's a long walk from the terminal, but shuttles run frequently; parking is $3 per hour with a $14 daily maximum. The red and blue **economy lots** are not really walking distance from the terminal; you'll have to rely on the shuttle bus, but parking is only $8 per day. (If you park for a week, the seventh day is free).

Various **off-airport lots** also serve PDX travelers. You can browse off-airport lots and make parking reservations at www.airportparkingreservations. com; they charge a $5 booking fee. In many cases, unless you have a coupon or other discount, the off-airport lots are only marginally cheaper than the official economy lots. If you have a very early departure or very late arrival, many airport hotels offer hotel and parking packages that often are no more expensive than the cost of a room; you can usually leave your car at the hotel for a week or more. Some (but not all) of these deals are available from www.parksleepfly.com; alternatively, just call an airport hotel directly or visit its web site. (See **Temporary Lodgings** for some suggested airport hotels.)

TRAIN

Amtrak passenger trains stop at historic Union Station, just north of downtown at the northern end of Portland's Transit Mall. The popular **Cascades** service (www.amtrakcasacades.com) runs from Eugene to Vancouver, British Columbia, via Seattle. Currently there are four trains a day in each direction from Portland to Seattle, and two trains in each direction between Portland and Eugene. Scheduled travel time to Seattle is about three-and-a-half hours, which is slightly longer than the driving time between the cities if there's no traffic; since the Amtrak train shares tracks with freight trains, the train is subject to delays. Given the likelihood of traffic congestion, however, especially north of Olympia, and the certainty of aggravation, the train is a great alternative to driving (or for that matter, to flying) if you're headed from one downtown to the other. Locally, the Cascades service also stops in Oregon City and in Vancouver, Washington. Current plans call for significantly increasing the number of trains between Portland and Seattle and cutting travel time by an hour.

The **Coast Starlight** from Seattle to Los Angeles via Oakland passes through Portland once per day in each direction. It's not uncommon for the Coast Starlight to arrive 10 hours or more behind schedule, and the train's chronic tardiness has given it the nickname "Starlate." The **Empire Builder** runs once daily to and from Chicago via Spokane, the Idaho panhandle, the southern border of Glacier National Park, various exciting cities in eastern Montana and North Dakota, Saint Paul, and Milwaukee. The trip takes a minimum of 46 hours, and sleeping compartments and a dining car are available.

For schedules, fare information, and reservations on Amtrak trains, visit www.amtrak.com or call 800-USA-RAIL (800-872-7245). Be sure to ask about promotions and discounts.

INTERCITY BUS

Portland's **Greyhound** terminal (503-243-2361) is located at 550 Northwest Sixth Avenue, just south of Union Station. Greyhound buses can take you from Portland to any major city along the Interstate 5 corridor between Canada and Mexico. Greyhound buses also run east to Spokane via Washington's Tri-Cities, and southeast to Boise, Idaho, via Pendleton. For schedules and reservations visit www.greyhound.com or call the national reservation number, 800-231-2222.

There are two other options for regional intercity bus transport. **Oregon Coachways** (541-265-2253) operates Amtrak Thruway buses between Portland and Eugene and Portland and Cannon Beach, Seaside, and Astoria, while **Valley Retriever Buslines** (541-265-2253, www.kokkola-bus.com/ValleyRetrieverBuslines.html) runs one bus per day in each direction from Portland to Newport via McMinnville, Salem, Albany, and Corvallis.

MOST PORTLANDERS ARE PROUD OF THEIR CITY'S REPUTATION for environmental leadership, and with good reason. Portland regularly garners accolades for its green policies, the state government is trying hard to establish Oregon as a leader in green business and renewable energy, and in 2006 the SustainLane media company ranked Portland number one out of 50 cities surveyed for sustainability. Of course, not everyone in the area is on board with the whole sustainability thing—we're looking at you, guy in the Hummer with the "I Am the Scourge of Bicycles" bumper sticker—but if you're reading this chapter, you're probably interested in reducing your environmental impact. There are plenty of local resources and lots of like-minded people to help you out.

GREENING YOUR HOME

The quickest and easiest way to have a green home is to buy one that is no bigger than you need—smaller homes consume fewer resources—and that is already well-insulated and energy-efficient, that incorporates nontoxic and sustainably produced materials, or that has features like solar-assisted hot water heating. Since early 2007, the local real estate Multiple Listing Service, **RMLS** (www.rmls.com), has allowed prospective home buyers to include green home features in their searches. (This search option is currently only available to licensed real estate agents and other RMLS members.) Assuming you're not lucky enough to move into an existing eco-dwelling, there's plenty you can do to make your home more environmentally friendly.

GREEN REMODELING

Portland's **Office of Sustainable Development** (721 NW 9th Ave, Suite 350, 503-823-7222, www.portlandonline.com/osd) publishes a *Green Home Remodeling*

Guide, available for download at its web site or for purchase at The ReBuilding Center or Environmental Building Supplies (see below). Other green building materials are also available from the office.

In many cases, the greenest building materials are those that someone else has already used. The **ReBuilding Center** (3625 N Mississippi Ave, 503-331-1877, www.rebuildingcenter.org) stocks used building materials that have been donated or salvaged from "deconstructed" buildings. **Habitat ReStore** (66 SE Morrison St, 503-283-6247, www.pdxrestore.org) also sells donated used and new construction materials, and proceeds go to Habitat for Humanity. You might consider poking around the region's architectural salvage stores (see **Shopping for the Home** for listings).

If it's new materials you're after, **Environmental Building Supplies** (819 SE Taylor St, 503-222-3881, www.ecohaus.com) carries everything from cork and marmoleum flooring to recycled glass tiles, cotton batt insulation, and photovoltaic cells. The **Northwest Green Directory** (www.nwgreendirectory.com) lists regionally available green building products and services. If you're doing structural work, consider using green-certified wood products; the **Forest Stewardship Council** (www.fscus.org) is a widely known certification program. Also use nontoxic or least-toxic glues and finishes whenever possible; local paint companies **YOLO Colorhouse** (503-493-8275, www.yolocolorhouse.com), **Miller Paint** (multiple area stores, www.millerpaint.com), and **Rodda Paint** (multiple area stores, www.roddapaint.com) produce quality zero-VOC (volatile organic compounds) and low-VOC paint.

ENERGY EFFICIENCY

Reducing your home's energy consumption, particularly its consumption of energy produced by fossil fuels or other non-renewables, is probably the single most effective way to create a greener home. In most homes, furnaces and air conditioners, appliances, and lighting are the biggest energy hogs, and you'll get the most bang for your buck by weatherizing your home and making these systems work more efficiently. The following steps are typically recommended for boosting your home's energy efficiency:

- **Insulate and weatherize your home**. Poorly insulated walls, ceilings, and floors allow heated or cooled air to escape from your house, needlessly raising your energy use (and energy bill). Also seal ductwork, insulate hot water pipes in non-conditioned spaces, and seal or caulk leaks around doors, windows, pipes, vents, attics, and crawlspaces. Replace or repair leaky old windows. These steps will also reduce drafts and increase comfort levels in your home.
- **Upgrade your heating and cooling systems**. Old furnaces and air conditioning units are usually much less efficient than new models. Once you've insulated and weatherized your home, consider replacing old units with new, efficient units, and make sure that they are properly sized for your home. A

programmable thermostat can also help reduce energy consumption by adjusting the inside temperature automatically when you're at work or asleep.

- **Upgrade inefficient appliances.** Replacing old, inefficient washing machines, dishwashers, water heaters, and especially refrigerators with more efficient models can have a major effect on your energy consumption (and, in the case of washing machines and dishwashers, on your water consumption, too).
- **Install efficient lighting.** Compact fluorescent light bulbs use 75% less energy and last up to ten times longer than standard incandescent bulbs. They also generate less heat. For an assurance of quality, choose ENERGY STAR® bulbs.

Fortunately, you don't have to figure out how to accomplish these things on your own. **Energy Trust of Oregon** (866-368-7878, www.energytrust.org) can help make your home more energy-efficient. They offer cash incentives to help you pay for energy-saving improvements, and their web site includes a free online home energy use analyzer tool. You can also schedule a free on-site home energy review (complete with installation of complimentary compact fluorescent light bulbs and low-flow showerheads). For a comprehensive whole-house energy assessment and energy recommendations, consider hiring an Energy Trust–certified contractor to do a Home Performance with ENERGY STAR analysis.

Energy Trust provides energy efficiency services and cash incentives for Oregon customers of Portland General Electric, Pacific Power, NW Natural, and Cascade Natural Gas. Many other utilities offer similar services and incentives. When you're ready to start investing in energy efficiency, low-cost loans and utility or manufacturer rebates are available for some projects, and in many cases the **Oregon Department of Energy** (800-221-8035, www.oregon.gov/energy) offers state tax credits as well. Federal tax credits are also available; visit the federal government's **Energy Star** web site (www.energystar.gov) or talk to your accountant for details.

In Washington state, contact your local utility for help with energy audits and information about financial incentives for making your home more efficient. (Because Washington has no state income tax, it does not offer tax credits to homeowners.)

RENEWABLE ENERGY

Consider buying green power from your local utility; look in the "Utilities" section of the **Getting Settled** chapter for details. If you are interested in going further in your support of renewables, not only can you make your home more energy-efficient, but you can make energy in your home. Despite the cloudy climate, **solar energy**, including solar water heating and photovoltaic electricity, is actually quite viable in Portland; depending on your home's location, wind power or geothermal heating systems may also be potential options. **SolarOregon** (www.solaroregon.org), a local nonprofit, offers a monthly workshop on how to go solar, and its web site provides useful information about solar power. Significant federal and state tax credits and other incentives are available for purchasing renewable energy systems; contact **Energy Trust** for specific information.

WATER CONSERVATION

Although you've supposedly moved to a rainy city, water conservation is still important: July and August can be virtually rainless, and even in years with abundant precipitation a reduction in water use means that we can get by with fewer storage facilities, pipes, sewer treatment facilities, and new water sources. Plus, because Portland's household sewer charge (which is higher than the water charge) is tied to your water consumption, you'll save money, too. For water conservation tips, visit the web site of the **Regional Water Providers Consortium** (www.conserveh2o.org) or click on the "Conservation" tab on the **Portland Water Bureau's** web site (www.portlandonline.com/water). The Portland Water Bureau will also send its customers free water conservation devices; use their online order form or call 503-823-7439.

LANDSCAPING

Don't forget to make your home green on the outside, too (and we're not talking about paint color). Reduce or eliminate pesticides and chemical fertilizers, and use as little supplemental water as possible. (The resources listed in "Water Conservation" above also have handy tips for water-smart irrigation.) The regional government entity **Metro**, which is responsible for, among other things, managing waste in the metropolitan area, provides useful information about natural gardening techniques, including composting. Visit Metro's "Natural Gardening" page at www.metro-region.org/pssp.cfm?ProgServID=4, or call 503-234-3000 to request brochures.

Landscaping with native plants is a great way to reduce your yard's environmental impact. Because native plants are adapted to the local climate and soils, they often practically take care of themselves; at the very least, they don't require constant watering and fertilization. **PlantNative** (503-248-0104, www.plantnative.com) and the Portland chapter of the **Native Plant Society of Oregon** (www.portland.npsoregon.org) are good resources for learning how to use native plants in your yard. And for goodness' sake, don't plant English ivy or other highly invasive species in your yard; contact the **No Ivy League** (503-823-3681, www.noivyleague.com) for details on why doing so is very naughty.

ENVIRONMENTALLY FRIENDLY PRODUCTS AND SERVICES

Your pocketbook is one of your most powerful weapons in the environmental fight. Your decision to support environmentally friendly businesses not only helps those businesses, but indirectly creates additional consumer demand for environmentally benign choices (a demand that could ultimately change the behavior of less environmentally focused businesses). Here are a few resources for finding green products and services.

- The **Chinook Book** (www.chinookbook.net) is full of coupons for sustainable products and services from businesses in Portland and Eugene. The publisher uses several screening criteria to weed out inappropriate businesses. The book is available at many stores and restaurants (especially businesses with coupons inside), and local schools and nonprofits also sell Chinook Books during fundraisers.
- The Consumers Union guide to environmental labeling is online at **www.eco-labels.org**; the site includes a report card for various environmental claims and labels and assesses whether the claim is meaningful and/or verified.
- *Consumer Reports* maintains a web site that assesses the environmental soundness of various products; visit **www.greenerchoices.org**.
- The **Re-Direct Guide** (www.redirectguide.com), available for free at many libraries and businesses, is a directory of local businesses that are (or purport to be) sustainable or otherwise environmentally friendly.

FOOD

Most environmentally aware consumers know about the benefits of organic farming, but it is also important to buy locally produced food when possible. Not only does supporting local farmers keep money circulating in the region, but it reduces the amount of greenhouse gases and other pollution associated with transporting the food from faraway fields. Most local co-ops and natural food stores, and some supermarkets, identify the geographic origin of their produce. Farmers markets generally sell locally grown produce; check the **Shopping for the Home** chapter for more information. *Edible Portland* (503-223-1200, www.edibleportland.com) is a bi-monthly publication covering local food issues.

When buying food in the store, in addition to organic labels look for certifications from **Salmon Safe** (www.salmonsafe.org), certifying that the source farm or vineyard uses watershed-friendly practices; the **Marine Stewardship Council** (www.msc.org), which certifies seafood as being from sustainable fisheries; and **Food Alliance** (www.foodalliance.org), which certifies farms and ranches for sustainable and humane practices.

Finally, consider reducing the amount of meat in your diet. (Livestock production is an extremely resource-intensive activity.) For information and moral support, contact **Northwest VEG** (503-224-7380, www.nwveg.org).

GREEN MONEY

You can use environmental criteria to decide not only where to spend your money but where to keep it. Some banks, including large national banks, are making efforts to become "greener" in their operations and lending practices. One bank that has gone further than most is **ShoreBank Pacific** (888-326-2265, www.eco-bank.com), which was founded with the mission of fostering environmentally sustainable community development; although the bank's headquarters are in coastal Washington, it maintains a loan office in Portland (721 NW 9th Ave, Suite 195, 503-916-1552). Be on the lookout for banks that offer incentives for specific eco-friendly transactions. For example, a few banks and credit unions, including **Unitus Community Credit Union** (www.unitusccu.com), offer reduced loan rates for the purchase of hybrid vehicles. Other banks and mortgage lenders may let you qualify for a larger home loan if you are buying a home with energy-efficient features that reduce your monthly outlay for utility costs.

Green investing is also taking off, and many mutual funds now claim to invest only in environmentally and/or socially responsible companies. One of these funds, Portland-based **Portfolio 21** (877-351-5115 x21, www.portfolio21. com), uses environmental sustainability as one of its primary investing criteria. For more information about green investing, visit **GreenMoneyJournal** (www. greenmoneyjournal.com) or **The Progressive Investor** (www.sustainablebusiness.com/progressiveinvestor/).

GREENER TRANSPORTATION

Probably the single best transportation choice you can make is to live close to your place of work, or in a place where you have a public transit option to get to work. The **Transportation** chapter lists alternatives to travel by automobile; when using a car is necessary or desirable, combine errands, carpool when possible, and ask your employer about telecommuting options. The **Drive Less/Save More** web site (www.drivelesssavemore.com) offers more ideas for reducing the amount you drive, explains why driving less is good for your pocketbook, and offers a handy driving cost calculator to hammer the point home.

If you need or want to drive, consider driving a more fuel-efficient vehicle. You can even get (or convert to) a fully electric car, if you have the money or skills. The most efficient mass production cars are gas-electric hybrids like the Toyota Prius or the Honda Civic hybrid. A hybrid car consumes less fuel, and you may be entitled to federal and Oregon state tax credits if you buy one. (In Washington, certain alternative-fuel vehicles and hybrid cars are exempt from emissions testing; starting in 2009 most small hybrids and some alternative-fuel vehicles will be exempt from state sales and use taxes.) You'll have company, too: the Portland metropolitan area boasts the country's highest hybrid ownership rate.

Whatever kind of car you drive, make sure the car gets routine maintenance to ensure that the engine runs as efficiently as possible. The **Eco-Logical Busi-**

ness Program, sponsored by several local governments, certifies automobile repair shops that take steps to minimize pollution; visit www.ecobiz.org for details or call 503-823-7807.

Finally, if you want to join an automobile club for roadside assistance and travel advice, consider **Better World Club** (503-546-1137, 866-238-1137, www. betterworld.com). Better World Club bills itself as the nation's only environmentally friendly auto club; they offer the usual menu of auto club services, along with discounts on hybrid rentals, bicycle roadside assistance, and a frequently hilarious electronic newsletter, *Kicking Asphalt*.

ALTERNATIVE FUELS

You can buy or modify cars to run on alternative fuels like pure ethanol or even natural gas, but by far the most popular alternative fuel in Portland is **Biodiesel**. Biodiesel is essentially diesel fuel made from vegetable oil, and is usually sold blended with petroleum diesel fuel. The blend name designates the percentage of biodiesel: B100 is pure biodiesel, while B20 is 20% biodiesel and 80% petroleum diesel. You'll see "Powered by Biodiesel" stickers on everything from city trucks to TriMet buses to old Volvo station wagons, and as of July 2007, all diesel fuel sold within Portland city limits had to contain a minimum blend of 5% biodiesel.

You can find current lists of stations that sell biodiesel or other alternative fuels at **www.pdxbiodiesel.org** or the **Columbia-Willamette Clean Cities Coalition** web site (www.cwcleancities.org/locator.php). The **GoBiodiesel Cooperative** (www.gobiodiesel.org) converts waste vegetable oil into B100 (i.e., zero-petroleum) biodiesel. They also sell fuel to non-members. The FAQ (frequently asked questions) section of their web site provides a wealth of information about using biodiesel.

Bear in mind that the use of biodiesel—particularly biodiesel blended with petro-diesel—is not without potential particulate pollution problems. If you already own a diesel-powered vehicle, biodiesel is a great choice that reduces dependence on oil. However, unless you plan to run your car on B100 exclusively, you might think twice about buying a car just so you can fuel it with biodiesel. (New passenger car models with cleaner-burning diesel engines may become available in the next few years, which could change the calculus.)

Also remember that, although biodiesel is made from vegetable oil, it is *not* the same as straight vegetable oil (SVO) fuel (a.k.a. "French fry car fuel"); most diesel engines can run on pure biodiesel or biodiesel blends—at most, you'll have to replace a hose or two—but SVO fuel requires substantial modifications to your car (including in most cases a second fuel tank).

If your home has oil heat, note that B20 biodiesel also works in most oil-fired home furnaces.

GREEN RESOURCES

The following are just a fraction of the resources on sustainability and environmental protection that are available in the region:

- **Ecotrust**, 721 NW 9th Ave, Suite 200, 503-227-6225, www.ecotrust.org; headquartered in the spiffy, eco-friendly Jean Vollum Natural Capital Center in the Pearl District, Ecotrust describes its mission as building "Salmon Nation." Its web site offers lots of helpful information about the coastal eco-region from Alaska to California, along with links to pages about regional conservation issues.
- Almost everyone uses fossil fuels, whether indirectly or directly. Consider offsetting the resulting greenhouse gas emissions with **carbon offsets**. Carbon offsets fund projects that store carbon or reduce carbon emissions from other sources, such as tree planting projects, energy efficiency projects, and alternative energy investments. In theory, you can thus offset the carbon dioxide you generate. Offsets are available from sources like **Green Tags** (503-248-1905, www.greentagsUSA.org) and **My Climate** (www.myclimate.org).
- The city of Portland's **Office of Sustainable Development**, 721 NW 9th Ave, Suite 350, 503-823-7222, www.portlandonline.com/osd, provides information and assistance on topics ranging from green building and recycling to solar energy development. OSD's resources are useful for people who live outside the city of Portland, too.
- The **Oregon Environmental Council**, 503-222-1963, www.oeconline.org, conducts outreach on a wide range of environmental topics that affect Oregonians.
- The **Regional Environmental Information Network** (REIN), www.rein.org, an online clearinghouse of environmental information, is part of the Metro regional government's Nature in Neighborhoods program.
- The United States Department of Energy's **Energy Efficiency and Renewable Energy** web site (www.eere.energy.gov) has some useful links and detailed (if not especially cutting-edge) information about renewable energy.
- The **Center for Earth Leadership**, 503-227-2807, www.earthleadershipcenter.org, offers classes and workshops, on such topics as "Assessing Your Ecological Footprint," for citizens who seek to play an effective role in creating a sustainable future.
- The **Northwest Earth Institute**, 503-227-2807, www.nwei.org, offers discussion courses, home eco-parties, and other programs dealing with environmental issues.
- **1000 Friends of Oregon**, 503-497-1000, www.friends.org, works on forest and land conservation and urban planning issues.

C HANCES ARE YOU'LL NEED TEMPORARY LODGINGS FOR AT LEAST A few nights at some point during your move to Portland, either during a house-hunting trip or while you're waiting for your lease to start or your home purchase to close. As a regional hub for business and tourism, Portland has a large selection of hotels and motels offering various levels of service, convenience, amenities, and cleanliness. If you need temporary lodgings for more than a week or so, an extended-stay hotel, sublet, or short-term lease might suit you better than a standard hotel or motel. (See **Extended-Stay Options,** below, for some suggestions.)

Note that the listings in this chapter are by no means comprehensive. For painfully complete listings, check the Yellow Pages under "Hotels and Other Accommodations." The **Portland Oregon Visitors Association (POVA)** (877-678-5263, www.travelportland.com) can provide a lengthy list of non-skanky hotels in the area.

RESERVATIONS AND DISCOUNTS

Lodging rates in Portland tend to be at their highest during the summer months and when big conventions hit town; at these peak times, you can usually find lower rates in outlying areas or at smaller downtown hotels.

If you plan to stay in a traditional hotel, there are several ways to save money off the "rack" or official rate. First, while last-minute bargains are not unknown, especially during winter, you'll generally get the best rates if you book well in advance of your visit. Second, always ask about discount offers—many aren't advertised and may change from day to day—and discounts for seniors, veterans, military personnel, and AAA members are common. Third, it's a good idea to check the hotel's web site (if it has one), because some establishments offer Internet-only rates or special offers that might beat other available discounts.

Finally, check with an online reservation service; some have relationships with hotels and can offer lower rates than the hotels themselves. In addition to national companies like **Expedia.com**, **Orbitz.com**, **Hotels.com** (800-246-8357), **Travelocity.com**, and **Quikbook** (800-789-9887, www.quikbook.com), the local tourism office, **POVA** (877-678-5263, www.travelportland.com), can book rooms by telephone or online, and sometimes offers discounts or packages at participating local hotels. If you know when you're coming but don't have any particular hotel in mind, **kayak.com** crawls various travel web sites (including hotel chain web sites) and shows the lowest available rates for more than 200 Portland-area hotels.

Note that some reservation services charge cancellation fees or require payment in advance, and their discounts usually cannot be combined with promotions offered by hotels or membership organizations.

LODGINGS

LUXURY AND BOUTIQUE HOTELS

For a splurge, consider staying in one of Portland's downtown luxury or boutique hotels. Prices are high by Portland standards—rack rates typically start at $175 or so and climb skyward from there—but you get a lot more for your money than you would at a hotel in, say, Manhattan.

- **Avalon Hotel & Spa,** 0455 SW Hamilton Ct, 503-802-5800, www.avalon hotelandspa.com; located just south of downtown, on the west bank of the Willamette River, the Avalon offers stylish, modern accommodation and luxury spa treatments.
- **The Benson Hotel**, 309 SW Broadway, 503-228-2000, 888-523-6766, www. bensonhotel.com; the Benson is the kind of grand, traditional hotel that has dark paneled wood, marble floors, and giant crystal chandeliers in the lobby, with all the opulent comfort that implies. Guests enjoy wine tasting in the evenings and live jazz at night.
- **Hotel Monaco Portland,** 506 SW Washington St, 503-222-0001, 866-861-9514, www.monaco-portland.com; formerly the elegant Fifth Avenue Suites, in early 2007 the hotel became the *luxe* Hotel Monaco Portland. Every room contains a stellar set of amenities, including a 32" plasma television. All this, plus guests who arrive in hybrid vehicles get a 50% discount on hotel parking.
- **The Governor Hotel**, 614 SW 11th Ave, 503-224-3400, 800-554-3456, www. govhotel.com; nearly a century old, this *grande dame* was recently renovated and offers plush, traditional luxury. It stands on the streetcar line on the western fringe of downtown, not far from the Pearl District, so it makes a good base for car-free exploration.

- **Heathman Hotel**, 1001 SW Broadway, 503-241-4100, 800-551-0011, www. heathmanhotel.com; this elegant and venerable luxury hotel is favored by authors on book tours and the occasional aging rock star, as well as less il-lustrious classes of well-heeled travelers. The hotel is adjacent to Portland's main performing arts complex, and offers, among other unusual amenities, a complimentary library of more than 400 films. Some of the rooms are surpris-ingly small.
- **Heathman Lodge**, 7801 NE Greenwood Dr, Vancouver, 360-254-3100, 888-475-3100, www.heathmanlodge.com; the Heathman's suburban sister hotel, just outside Vancouver, Washington, offers log-cabin luxury in a Northwest lodge-style building.
- **Hotel deLuxe**, 729 SW 15th Ave, 503-219-2094, 800-228-8657, www.hotel deluxeportland.com; the decor has a "Golden Age of Hollywood" theme—to heighten the experience, you can stay in the top-of-the-line Marlene Dietrich Suite—but the amenities, including flat-screen televisions and iPod docks, are thoroughly modern. The hotel is on the periphery of downtown, convenient to the Pearl District. Some rooms are quite small.
- **Hotel Lucia**, 400 SW Broadway, 503-225-1717, 877-225-1717, www.hotellucia. com; this luxury boutique hotel manages to seamlessly combine a modern de-sign aesthetic and hip vibe with traditional standards of comfort. Perhaps for this reason, the Lucia tied for fourth place (with the substantially more staid Four Seasons in Chicago) in the 2006 Condé Nast Traveler's Readers' Choice poll for North American hotels. Among the many nice touches is a pillow menu that allows you to order the kind and number of pillows you'd like for the night.
- **Hotel Vintage Plaza,** 422 SW Broadway, 503-228-1212, 800-243-0555, www. vintageplaza.com; you might surmise from its name that the Vintage Plaza has some kind of wine thing going on, and if you did you'd be right. The hotel hosts a wine hour each evening, and every room is dedicated to a local winery or vineyard.
- **Inn @ Northrup Station**, 2025 NW Northrup St, 503-224-0543, 800-224-1180, www.northrupstation.com; this small boutique hotel sits alongside the Port-land Streetcar line in Northwest Portland. Filled with retro furnishings and bright colors, the Inn @ Northrup Station caters to a hip and evidently email-literate crowd. (This hotel also has among the lowest boutique hotel rates in the city.)
- **Paramount Hotel**, 808 SW Taylor St, 503-228-3233, 800-227-1333, www. portlandparamount.com; this relatively new boutique hotel is the Benson's hipper, younger cousin. Guestrooms are generally spacious, with luxury baths.
- **RiverPlace Hotel**, 1510 SW Harbor Way, 503-228-3233, 800-227-1333, www. riverplacehotel.com; downtown's only truly riverfront hotel—a marina lies at its doorstep—the RiverPlace offers understated comfort and relative quiet.
- **Westin Portland**, 750 SW Alder St, 503-294-9000, 888-627-8401, www.westin.

com/Portland; this centrally located hotel, while tailored to business travelers, offers more comforts and amenities than most chain hotels.

LARGE HOTELS

Most large hotels in Portland belong to big chains, and if they lack character they are at least predictable and generally clean. The available amenities are fairly standard—restaurants, room service, business centers, and often fitness centers. These hotels tend to focus on business travelers and conventioneers, and so the heaviest concentrations are in downtown Portland, in the Lloyd Center/Convention Center neighborhood, and near the airport. Rates are generally at least $100 a night, and sometimes much more.

- **Courtyard by Marriott Beaverton/Portland**, 8500 SW Nimbus Dr, Beaverton, 503-641-3200, 800-321-2211, www.marriott.com/pdxcy
- **Courtyard by Marriott Lloyd Center**, 435 NE Wasco St, 503-234-3200, 800-321-2211, www.marriott.com/pdxcl
- **Courtyard by Marriott Portland Airport**, 11550 NE Airport Way, 503-252-3200, 800-321-2211, www.courtyard.com/pdxca
- **Courtyard by Marriott Portland North Harbour**, 1231 N Anchor Way, 503-735-1818, www.marriott.com/pdxnh
- **Courtyard by Marriott Portland Southeast**, 9300 SE Sunnybrook Blvd, 503-652-2900, 800-321-2211, www.courtyard.com/pdxck
- **Crowne Plaza Portland Lake Oswego**, 14811 Kruse Oaks Blvd, Lake Oswego, 503-624-8400, 800-227-6963, www.crowneplaza.com/lakeoswegoor
- **DoubleTree Hotel Lloyd Center**, 1000 NE Multnomah St, 503-281-6111, 800-996-0510, www.portlandlloydcenter.doubletree.com
- **Embassy Suites Portland Downtown**, 319 SW Pine St, 503-279-9000, 800-362-2779, www.embassyportland.com
- **Embassy Suites Hotel Portland Airport**, 7900 NE 82nd Ave, 503-460-3000, 800-362-2779, www.portlandairport.embassysuites.com
- **Embassy Suites Portland – Washington Square**, 9000 SW Washington Square Rd, Tigard, 503-644-4000, 800-586-5455, www.embassysuitestigard.com
- **Four Points by Sheraton Portland Downtown,** 50 SW Morrison St, 503-221-0711, 888-627-8263, www.fourpoints.com/portlanddowntown
- **Hilton Portland & Executive Tower**, 921 SW 6th Ave, 503-226-1611, 800-445-8667, www.hilton.com
- **Holiday Inn Express Hotel & Suites – Northwest Portland**, 2333 NW Vaughn St, 503-484-1100, 866-492-1100, www.hiexpress.com
- **Holiday Inn – Portland Downtown/Convention Center**, 1441 NE 2nd Ave, 503-233-2401, www.holiday-inn.com/hiprtldwtn
- **Holiday Inn Portland Airport**, 8439 NE Columbia Blvd, 503-256-5000, 800-

465-4329, www.holidayinnpdx.com
- **Marriott City Center**, 520 SW Broadway, 503-226-6300, 800-228-9290, www. marriott.com/pdxct
- **Marriott Residence Inn at Lloyd Center**, 1710 NE Multnomah St, 503-288-1400, 800-331-3131, www.marriott.com/pdxlc
- **Marriott Residence Inn – Portland Downtown at Riverplace**, 2115 SW River Pkwy, 503-552-9500, 800-331-3131, www.marriott.com/pdxri
- **Marriott Residence Inn – Portland North Harbour**, 1250 N Anchor Way, 503-285-9888, 800-331-3131, www.marriott.com/pdxph
- **Monarch Hotel & Conference Center**, 12566 SE 93rd Ave, 503-652-1515, 800-492-8700, www.monarchhotel.cc
- **Portland Marriott Downtown Waterfront**, 1401 SW Naito Pkwy, 503-226-7600, 800-228-9290, www.marriott.com/pdxor
- **Radisson Hotel Portland Airport**, 6233 NE 78th Ct, 503-251-2000, 800-994-7878, www.radisson.com/portlandor_airport
- **Red Lion Hotel Portland – Convention Center**, 1021 NE Grand Ave, 503-235-2100, 800-343-1822, www.redlion.com
- **Red Lion Hotel on the River**, 909 N Hayden Island Dr, 503-283-4466, 800-733-5466, www.redlion.com
- **Red Lion Hotel on the Quay**, 100 Columbia St, Vancouver, 360-694-8341, 800-733-5466, www.redlion.com
- **Sheraton Portland Airport Hotel**, 8235 NE Airport Way, 503-281-2500, 800-325-3535, www.sheratonportland.com
- **University Place – Portland State University**, 310 SW Lincoln St, 503-221-0140, 866-845-4647, www.uplace.pdx.edu

SMALL HOTELS

Portland has several small hotels that tend to attract tourists and couples rather than the business travelers who stay in the big chain hotels. If you book ahead and ask about promotions, you might get into one of these establishments for as little as $70 a night, and even the premium rooms are less expensive than those at luxury hotels, although the service and atmosphere can be just as charming.

- **Ace Hotel**, 1022 SW Stark St, 503-228-2277, www.acehotel.com/Portland/; this new Portland outpost of the small Ace hotel chain is another entrant into the hip-yet-elegant field.
- **Jupiter Hotel**, 800 E Burnside St, 503-230-9200, 877-800-0004, www.jupiter hotel.com; hip, retro, and often bustling, the Jupiter Hotel is not the place to come for a quiet weekend. Look for their edgy ads in local weeklies.
- **Mark Spencer Hotel**, 409 SW 11th Ave, 503-224-3293, 800-548-3934, www. markspencer.com; favored by small tour groups and foreign visitors.
- **Park Lane Suites**, 809 SW King Ave, 503-226-6288, 800-532-9543, www. parklanesuites.com; this hotel is close to Washington Park and Northwest

Portland. All of its functional but comfortable studios and one- or two-bedroom suites have kitchens, making it a good choice for longer stays.

BUDGET HOTELS AND MOTELS

The Portland area has plenty of small hotels and motels. At these no-frills establishments, you can almost always get a room for less than $100, and sometimes for as little as $30 or $40. Many of the area's budget hotels represent such national chains as **Best Western** (800-780-7234, www.bestwestern.com), **Days Inn** (800-329-7466, www.daysinn.com**),** **La Quinta** (800-642-4271, www.lq.com), **Motel 6** (800-4-MOTEL6, www.motel6.com), **Travelodge** (800-578-7878, www.travelodge.com), **Shilo Inn** (800-222-2244, www.shiloinns.com), and several others. Several chains, including Comfort Inn, Econo Lodge, and Quality Inn, are under the umbrella of **Choice Hotels International** (877-424-6423, www.choicehotels.com).

Although the chains predominate, Portland still has dozens of independent motels, both in the city itself and in many of the suburbs. Look in the Yellow Pages under "Motels & Other Accommodation" and "Hotels & Other Accommodation" for complete listings. The greatest concentration of budget motels is found along Northeast and Southeast 82nd Avenue, especially at the northern end near the Airport. Other clusters of budget lodging exist along Southeast Powell Boulevard, Southwest Barbur Boulevard, and Highway 99 north of Vancouver, and at the southern end of downtown Portland, near Portland State University. Note that some of the cheapest motels, particularly those along parts of 82nd Avenue, are in high-crime areas and/or are frequently used for various illicit purposes. If one hotel or motel makes you uneasy, try another. You'll almost always be able to find an acceptable option in a decent neighborhood.

BED & BREAKFASTS AND GUESTHOUSES

If you're in the mood for quaint, consider a bed and breakfast ("B&B") or guesthouse. In Portland, most of these establishments are in residential areas outside the downtown core, so staying in one can be a good way to check out neighborhoods you're interested in. Keep in mind, however, that there's good quaint and bad quaint, and then there's just awful. Properties affiliated with an organization like the **Oregon Bed and Breakfast Guild** are usually good bets; call 800-944-6196 or visit www.obbg.org for information and reservations. Portland-area B&Bs and guesthouses include:

- **Bluebird Guesthouse**, 3517 SE Division St, 503-238-4333, 866-717-4333, www.bluebirdguesthouse.com
- **Blue Plum Inn**, 2026 NE 15th Ave, 503-288-3848, 877-288-3844, www.bluepluminn.com

- **The Broetje House**, 3101 SE Courtney Rd, Milwaukie, 503-659-8860, www.the broetjehouse.com
- **Georgian House Bed & Breakfast**, 1828 NE Siskiyou St, 503-281-2250, 888-282-2250, www.thegeorgianhouse.com
- **Heron Haus**, 2545 NW Westover Rd, 503-274-1846, www.heronhaus.com
- **Lion and the Rose Victorian Bed & Breakfast Inn**, 1810 NE 15th Ave, 503-287-9245, 800-955-1647, www.lionrose.com
- **MacMaster House,** 1041 SW Vista Ave, 503-223-7362, 800-774-9523, www.macmaster.com
- The **McMenamins** brewpub empire (www.mcmenamins.com) includes several complexes that offer unique bed & breakfast accommodation. The **Kennedy School** (5736 NE 33rd Ave, 503-249-3983, 888-249-3983) in Northeast Portland was once an actual elementary school (some of the rooms still have chalkboards, and the hallway drinking fountains are at kid height); the **Edgefield** (2126 SW Halsey St, Troutdale, 503-669-8610, 800-669-8610) was the county poor farm; and the **Grand Lodge**, 3505 Pacific Ave, Forest Grove, 503-992-9533, 877-992-9533) used to be a Masonic lodge.
- **Portland Guest House**, 1720 NE 15th Ave, 503-282-1402, home.teleport.com/~pgh/
- **Portland International Guesthouse**, 2185 NW Flanders St, 503-224-0500, www.pdxguesthouse.com
- **Portland's White House**, 1914 NE 22nd Ave, 503-287-7131, 800-272-7131, www.portlandswhitehouse.com
- **Rebecca House & Bungalow**, 8 N Bridgeton Rd, 503-970-6988, www.rebeccahousebungalow.com
- **Terwilliger Vista Bed & Breakfast**, 515 SW Westwood Dr, 503-244-0602, 888-244-0602, www.terwilligervista.com
- **Vintage Inn**, 310 W 11th St, Vancouver, 360-693-6635, 888-693-6635, www.vintage-inn.com

HOSTELS

Portland has two official **Hostelling International** youth hostels, both of which are well-located for the car-less.

- **Northwest Portland International Hostel and Guesthouse,** 425 NW 18th Ave, 503-241-2783, 888-777-0067, www.nwportlandhostel.com; close to the bustle of Northwest Portland and the Pearl District, this hostel is close in without actually being downtown.
- **Portland Hawthorne Hostel (Hostelling International)**, 3031 SE Hawthorne Blvd, 503-236-3380, 866-447-3031, www.portlandhostel.org; a converted house with an eco-roof and a huge front porch, this popular hostel is close to the shops, restaurants, and bars of the Hawthorne district.

Several cheap downtown hotels offer ostensible "hostel" rooms, but those establishments are best avoided by all but the truly desperate. If you don't mind being out of town and not having access to a kitchen, **McMenamin's Edgefield**, in Troutdale, has some hostel-style dorm rooms. (See "Bed & Breakfasts and Guesthouses" above.)

EXTENDED-STAY OPTIONS

It could take you a few weeks or months to find a perfect (or at any rate a permanent) home. If you anticipate spending more than a week or two on your home search, one of the most convenient arrangements is an extended-stay hotel. These facilities, sometimes called corporate apartments, offer furnished suites with kitchens by the day, week, or month. Some extended-stay options in Portland include:

- **BridgeStreet Worldwide**, 800-278-7338, www.bridgestreet.com, operates two locations in the Pearl District and two locations in Washington County.
- **Extended Stay Hotels**, 800-804-3724, www.extendedstayhotels.com, has seven locations under various monikers in the metro area.
- **Larkspur Landing Hillsboro**, 3133 NE Shute Rd, Hillsboro, 503-681-2121, www.larkspurlanding.com/hotels/hillsboro/
- **Oakwood Worldwide**, 877-902-0832, www.oakwood.com, has more than three dozen locations in and around Portland.
- **Park Lane Suites**, 809 SW King Ave, 503-226-6288, 800-532-9543, www.parklanesuites.com, offers an extended-stay discount.
- **Residence Inn by Marriott**, 888-236-2427, www.residenceinn.com, has seven locations in the greater Portland area.
- **U.S. Suites**, 503-443-2033, 800-US-SUITE, www.ussuites.com, has multiple locations in and around Portland.

A potentially less expensive option is a sublet or short-term lease. In this type of arrangement, you rent or sublease all or part of a house, condo, or apartment for several weeks to several months while the owner or renter is away. Sublets aren't always furnished, and you would be very lucky to find one where the sublease term perfectly matches the dates for which you need lodgings, but when they work out subleases can be a great choice. To find sublets, look on **Craigslist** (portland.craigslist.org/sub/) or check out the classifieds in *Willamette Week*. Some rental property management companies and apartment complexes may offer short-term rentals, although such rentals are typically unfurnished.

ONCE YOU'VE SETTLED IN TO PORTLAND, YOU'LL INEVITABLY WANT to explore your surroundings. After all, you didn't move to one of the most beautiful regions in the world just so you could spend all your time in the city, did you? Within a few hours' drive (or in some cases, a bus, train, and/ or ferry ride) you'll find volcanic peaks, raging rivers, dense forests, high desert plateaus, an atmospheric coastline, cosmopolitan cities, and some of the richest farmland in America. It really doesn't matter which direction you go (although if you head too far west your hat will begin to float). Anywhere in the region, you're bound to encounter interesting destinations and some beautiful scenery.

For general Oregon travel information, suggested destinations, an accommodation guide, and much, much more, call **Travel Oregon** at 800-547-7842 or visit their comprehensive web site at www.traveloregon.com. The **Washington State Tourism Office** (360-725-5052, www.experiencewa.com) is equally helpful; thankfully, it shelved its terrifying "Say WA" tourism campaign in 2006. For information on some of Oregon's natural areas, scan the **Greenspace** chapter of this book.

MOUNT HOOD AND THE NORTHERN OREGON CASCADES

Mount Hood, Portland's most visible natural landmark (at least on a clear day), is the city's favorite year-round destination for outdoor recreation. While thousands of people summit the 11,240-foot glaciated peak every year—a feat that requires technical mountaineering skills and a fair amount of fortitude—the vast majority of visitors come to ski or snowboard, to hike, to mountain bike, or just to sightsee and enjoy the mountain air. The mountain's southwest slopes are only an hour from Portland.

The most direct route to the mountain is US Highway 26 from Gresham. (Unless you're coming from the southeast part of the metro area, it's fastest to take Interstate 84 east to Exit 16, then head south on NE 238th/242nd to Burnside, and take Burnside southeast to US 26. Otherwise, you'll be making a long slog on Powell Boulevard through Portland and Gresham.) Highway 26 climbs gently past ornamental plant nurseries, Christmas tree farms, and stands of dense forest, and through the towns of Sandy, Brightwood, Welches, Zigzag, and Rhododendron, until it reaches the outpost of **Government Camp** at 3500 feet. Government Camp is the main commercial center on the mountain, and offers ski rentals, grocery stores, a gas station, restaurants, a brew pub, and various overnight accommodation options. Government Camp is a good base for hiking and skiing—Mount Hood Skibowl is directly across the highway—but it's more of a convenient way station than a destination in itself.

From Government Camp, a six-mile road winds tortuously uphill to **Timberline Lodge** (800-547-1406, www.timberlinelodge.com) and its ski area (which is open almost all year). If the 1930s-vintage lodge looks familiar, you may have already seen it in the 1980 horror film *The Shining*. (Sweet dreams, kids.) The lodge's name is derived from its location at timberline on Mount Hood, at 6,600 feet above sea level; the slopes above are virtually devoid of trees, except for a few gnarled old specimens. On a clear day, it feels as if you could reach out and touch the summit of the mountain, although it's actually nearly a mile higher.

Back at Government Camp, US 26 continues east and south over two 4,000-foot passes toward dry Central Oregon (see below). A few miles east of Government Camp, State Highway 35 branches off and leads around the east side of Mount Hood and down the Hood River Valley (see below). A network of forest roads (many of them unpaved) lead to other destinations around Mount Hood, including picture-postcard-pretty **Lost Lake** (541-386-6366, www.lostlakeresort.org) on the mountain's north side; **Cooper Spur** on the east side, from where it is possible to hike to an elevation of 8,700 feet in late summer (complete with an overlook of Eliot Glacier); and the Salmon River, upstream from Welches, which flows out of the **Salmon-Huckleberry Wilderness**. An extensive zone surrounding Mount Hood's summit is also a designated wilderness area, as is the **Badger Creek Wilderness** east of the mountain.

Many of the forest trails around Mount Hood (including mountain bike trails and Nordic ski routes) depart directly from US 26 or Highway 35, but the ease of access from Portland ensures that these trails are crowded on sunny weekends. The farther you get from the main highways, however, the fewer people you are likely to encounter; if you actually get out and hike more than a few miles it's possible to find solitude even in mid-summer. If you'd like to spend a bit more time on the mountain, there are plenty of inexpensive forest service campgrounds for tent or trailer camping; backpackers will find an abundance of backcountry campsites, especially in designated wilderness areas. For shelter under a roof, you can stay in one of several hotels, or rent a cabin in Government Camp or in one of the communities on the mountain's west side.

South of Mount Hood, the Cascade Mountains are a rolling patchwork of clear cuts, stands of second-growth timber, and a few roadless and wilderness areas. State Highway 224 winds from Estacada up the scenic valley of the Clacka-mas River; the river drainage harbors destinations like Bagby Hot Springs (which unfortunately has been plagued by frequent parking-lot break-ins) and the **Bull of the Woods Wilderness**. The adjacent **Opal Creek** area, east of Salem, harbors one of the finest remaining stands of old-growth forest in the state. The other main road to penetrate this region, State Highway 22, runs east from Salem past Detroit Lake, a reservoir that is a popular destination for boaters. Various byways and forest roads connect the two main roads and lead to out-of-the-way spots like **Breitenbush Hot Springs** (503-854-3320, www.breitenbush.com) and **Olal-lie Lake** (541-504-1010, www.olallielake.com). At the crest of the range looms Oregon's second-highest peak, Mount Jefferson; the surrounding area, including such beauty spots as Jefferson Park (a lake-dotted meadow basin near timber-line) and the curiously shaped peak of Three Fingered Jack, is part of the **Mount Jefferson Wilderness**, where motorized vehicles are prohibited.

Much of the Mount Hood region lies within Clackamas County; for trip ideas, contact the county tourism department, **Oregon's Mt. Hood Territory** (503-655-8490, 888-622-4822, www.mthoodterritory.com).

THE COLUMBIA RIVER GORGE AND THE HOOD RIVER VALLEY

Traffic permitting, you can drive east from downtown Portland on Interstate 84 and, within half an hour, find yourself amid the splendor of the **Columbia River Gorge**. Here, the Columbia River forces a passage westward through the Cascades, through a palisade of basalt cliffs that tower hundreds or thousands of feet above the river. The Gorge isn't wilderness—multiple dams shackle the Columbia, major highways and railroad tracks run along the river's northern and southern shores, and several towns and small cities perch on the banks—but it is nonetheless a spectacular place.

Interstates run the length of the Gorge on the south side of the river, but by far the best sightseeing route is the Historic Columbia River Highway, which branches off from the interstate at Exit 17 in Troutdale and climbs through the town of Corbett to historic **Vista House** (www.vistahouse.com) at Crown Point, a promontory high above the river that offers a spectacular view upriver. From Crown Point, the highway descends through mossy forest, past several spectacu-lar waterfalls, including two-stage, 620-foot **Multnomah Falls**, the state's biggest natural tourist draw. The area at the base of the falls can get very crowded on summer weekends, when tour buses disgorge their passengers to gawk at the spectacle, but the parking lot off the historic highway is often nearly deserted on winter weekdays. (A separate parking area, accessible from Interstate 84, attracts passing motorists all year.) A word of warning about parking near the waterfalls: These parking lots are notorious sites for car prowls, so be sure to lock your car and keep all "attractive" possessions out of sight. Nearby **Oneonta Gorge** is a narrow, rock-bound chasm that leads to yet another waterfall. Many more waterfalls are accessible by trail only, as are the most spectacular views, which are available from Angel's Rest (a 4-mile roundtrip hike from the historic highway) and other clifftop perches on both sides of the Gorge.

Take a break from natural splendor at **Bonneville Dam** (541-374-8820, www.nwp.usace.army.mil/op/b/home.asp) and admire the engineering feats that inspired Woody Guthrie. The dam's visitor center and fish ladder (with viewing window) are generally open daily from 9 a.m. to 5 p.m., and tours of the powerplant are sometimes offered, but heightened security can cause closures on short notice; call or visit the web site before scheduling a visit. Upstream of the dam, at the town of **Cascade Locks** (541-374-8820, www.cascadelocks.net), the Bridge of the Gods leads to the Washington side of the Gorge. (The Pacific Crest Trail also crosses the river on this bridge.) Washington State Highway 14 runs along the north bank of the river for the length of the Gorge, and makes a good alternate or return route. The Washington side includes such attractions as **Beacon Rock State Park**, several hot springs resorts, and **Skamania Lodge** (www.skamania.com), a resort outside Stevenson.

Continuing eastward on the Oregon side, as you approach **Hood River** (www.hoodriver.org) the climate quickly becomes noticeably drier, with oaks and ponderosa pines replacing the Douglas firs that cling to the mountainsides further west. Hood River, long a small regional commercial center and windsurfing town, has recently boomed, and housing appreciation rates are among the highest in the state. It's easy to see why—with Mount Hood to the south and the Columbia River and Mount Adams to the north, with abundant outdoor recreational opportunities, and with substantially less rain than Portland, it would be surprising if the place *didn't* boom. While not all locals are happy about Hood River's changing demographics, the change has led to the opening of several excellent (albeit spendy) restaurants in the historic, hilly downtown. At just over an hour from Portland, Hood River is a wonderful destination for a weekend getaway; try one of the many bed and breakfasts, or stay at the historic (and reputedly haunted) **Columbia Gorge Hotel** (541-386-5566, 800-345-1921, www.columbiagorgehotel.com).

From Hood River, you have a range of options for continuing your tour. You can turn south through the scenic **Hood River Valley**, a major fruit-growing region. The valley is especially beautiful in spring, when the apple, pear, and cherry orchards are in bloom (with a snow-covered Mount Hood looming picturesquely behind), and during the late summer and fall harvest, when fruit stands and pumpkin patches open for visitors. You can follow the so-called Fruit Loop (www.hoodriverfruitloop.com), and so start and end at Hood River, or continue up the valley on Highway 35, pass over the shoulder of Mount Hood, and return to Portland via US Highway 26.

If you chose to continue upstream along the Columbia from Hood River, you will pass scenic wonders like the Nature Conservancy's **Tom McCall Preserve**, which puts on a colorful show of wildflowers in April and May. At **The Dalles** (www.thedalleschamber.com), once a major stopover on the Oregon Trail, visit the **Columbia Gorge Discovery Center** (541-296-8600, www.gorgediscovery. org). About 24 miles east of The Dalles, on the Washington side, stands the peculiar, castle-like **Maryhill Museum of Art** (509-773-3733, www.maryhillmuseum. org). Built in the nineteen-teens by Quaker entrepreneur Sam Hill (who was *not* the basis for the expression, "What in the sam hill?"), the museum now houses an eclectic collection of European, America, and Native American art, including a major assemblage of Auguste Rodin sculptures and watercolors.

Much of the Gorge is protected within the **Columbia River Gorge National Scenic Area** (www.fs.fed.us/r6/columbia/). For general tourism information, contact the **Columbia River Gorge Visitors Association** (800-98-GORGE, www. crgva.org).

THE OREGON COAST

Just over an hour to the west (as always, traffic permitting), the often fog-bound beaches and rugged headlands of Oregon's Pacific Ocean coastline beckon. The drive west on US 26 climbs over the low crest of the Coast Range—**Saddle Mountain State Natural Area** (www.oregonstateparks.org/park_197.php) encompasses the highest point in the northern Coast Range and makes a good detour on a rare clear day—and then leads through damp mossy valleys toward the sea. Eventually, Highway 26 dead-ends at US Highway 101, which runs the length of the Oregon Coast (and almost the entire length of the West Coast of the United States, in case you feel like heading to L.A.). Be aware that lumbering recreational vehicle traffic on 101 can be a nightmare during the summer if you are actually trying to get somewhere eventually.

Seaside (www.seasideor.com), the first town to the north, has a bit of a carnival atmosphere, with a busy waterside promenade, several factory outlet stores, and plenty of saltwater taffy vendors. To the south, artsier **Cannon Beach** (www.cannonbeach.org) offers a long stretch of sand, with locally iconic Haystack Rock accessible at low tide. Between these two towns, scenic **Ecola State Park** (www.oregonstateparks.org/park_188.php) beckons visitors with isolated beaches, tidepools, and the rocky cliffs of Tillamook Head.

The short stretch of Highway 101 north of Seaside leads through the quiet, affluent resort town of Gearhart to **Fort Stevens State Park** (www.oregonstateparks.org/park_179.php) and its excellent beach (complete with a small shipwreck) just south of the mouth of the Columbia River. Nearby **Fort Clatsop** (www.nps.gov/lewi/planyourvisit/fortclatsop.htm) marks the spot where Lewis and Clark passed the winter of 1805-06 (moaning all the while in their journals about the incessant rainfall). The city of **Astoria** (503-325-6311, 800-875-6807, www.oldoregon.com) lies just inland from the mouth of the Columbia. This historic, quirky, and slightly gritty (yet generally attractive) town has a strong

Scandinavian heritage—there are still Finnish saunas in Astoria—and a strong maritime flavor, as the exhibits in the **Columbia River Maritime Museum** attest. Victorian homes on steep hillsides are reminiscent of San Francisco homes (but with bigger lots), and on (infrequent) clear days there is a magnificent view from the Astoria Column, perched on the city's highest hill. The city has seen a recent boom in good restaurants and boutique hotels.

From Astoria, you can loop back to Portland via Highway 30 along the Columbia River, or continue north over the Astoria-Megler Bridge to the beaches of the southern Washington coast. The community of **Long Beach** (360-642-2400, 800-451-2542, www.funbeach.com) is reputed to have the longest drivable beach in the world; this claim leaves unanswered the question of why you would want to drive 17 miles down a beach, avoiding volleyball players and giant chunks of driftwood, and hoping you don't get stuck in the sand with the tide advancing.

If, instead of heading north from Seaside, you choose to drive south from Cannon Beach, you'll pass through the small vacation communities of Arch Cape and Manzanita on your way to **Tillamook**, the state's cheese capital. The Tillamook Creamery (www.tillamookcheese.com), although not the experience it once was, is still one of the most popular destinations on the coast, and the gift shop sells cheddar cheese curds. From Tillamook, take the **Three Capes Scenic Route** past Capes Meares, Lookout, and Kiwanda as an alternative to busy Highway 101.

Heading south, some consider bustling **Lincoln City** to be a great base for exploration, while others view it as an overbuilt tourist trap. The attractions in slightly more laid back **Newport** (www.discovernewport.com) include the **Oregon Coast Aquarium** (541-867-3474, www.aquarium.org), one of the country's finest aquaria and famous as a halfway house of sorts for the orca Keiko, a.k.a. Free Willy. South of Newport, the coast gets fewer visitors. You'll pass through rugged coastal scenery and often fog-bound towns like Waldport and Yachats on your way to Florence and the **Oregon Dunes National Recreation Area**, a 40-mile strip of sand dunes that in some places are more than 500 feet high; the dunes area also contains several swimmable freshwater lakes. Beyond **Coos Bay** and its large working harbor, the south coast includes towns such as Bandon (famous for its cheese, cranberries, and lightning-fast broadband network), Port Orford, Brookings (the so-called banana belt of Oregon, which often has the state's warmest winter temperatures), and **Gold Beach** (800-525-2334, www. goldbeach.org), a good base for jet boat excursions up the Rogue River.

For more information on visiting the Oregon Coast, contact the **Oregon Coast Visitors Association** (888-628-2101, www.visittheoregoncoast.com). Dozens of the most scenic areas along the coast are part of the **Oregon State Parks** system (800-551-6949, www.oregonstateparks.org); while some state parks are little more than waysides open for day use only, others are fairly large and substantial parks with camping facilities, and sometimes yurts or cabins.

THE WILLAMETTE VALLEY AND OREGON'S WINE COUNTRY

The Willamette Valley stretches south from Portland for more than 100 miles. This broad valley is home to some of the nation's richest agricultural land, as well as the cities of Salem, Albany, **Corvallis** (541-757-1544, 800-334-8118, www.visit corvallis.com), and **Eugene**. The latter two cities, home to Oregon State University and the University of Oregon, respectively, are both worthy stopovers, but the Willamette Valley generally lacks major tourist attractions. Its appeal lies primarily in its small towns and farm fields, some of which are full of unusual crops like peppermint and lavender, and its slower pace of life. To see the valley at its best, get off the main highways (Interstate 5 and highways 99E and 99W) and putter around the back roads; better still, tour the valley by bicycle.

For wine lovers, the most compelling destinations in the Willamette Valley lie along its margins, on the low ranges of hills that rise from the flat valley floor. Here, on slopes that shed cold winter air and collect summer sunshine, grow the vineyards that support the dozens of **wineries** in the six AVAs—American Viticultural Areas—in the Willamette Valley region. Oregon is globally famous for its pinot noirs, but it produces many other kinds of wines as well. The greatest concentration of wineries is in Yamhill County, especially around **Dundee**, less than an hour southeast of Portland. For more information about wineries, as well as non-wine tourism options, call 503-646-2985 or visit www.willamettevalley wines.com.

One don't-miss destination, especially for waterfall lovers, is **Silver Falls State Park** (www.oregonstateparks.org/park_211.php) east of Salem. The park contains a canyon with no fewer than ten waterfalls, some of which are short walks from parking areas on the canyon rim; an 8.7-mile trail links the falls and actually passes through small rock amphitheaters behind four of them. Nearby, just south of Silverton, the **Oregon Garden** (503-874-8100, 877-674-2733, www. oregongarden.org) presents a wide range of specialty gardens, as well as the only Frank Lloyd Wright–designed house in Oregon.

For more ideas about Willamette Valley tour routes, contact the **Willamette Valley Visitors Association** (866-548-5018, www.oregonwinecountry.org).

CENTRAL OREGON

Fast-growing **Bend** (541-382-8048, 877-245-8484, www.visitbend.com) sprawls on the banks of the Deschutes River as it flows from forested highlands into the high desert. The hub of scenic central Oregon, Bend is a minimum three-hour drive from Portland via Mount Hood and Madras or Salem and Santiam Pass. Bend offers an ever-increasing number of high-end restaurants and hotels, as well as the acclaimed **High Desert Museum** (541-382-4754, www.highdesert museum.org), but the real attraction of central Oregon is the stunning landscape and the consequent recreational opportunities. The region immediately surrounding Bend is a semi-arid plateau of sagebrush, juniper, and ponderosa pine, but the volcanic peaks of the central Cascades rise just to the west, and scenic beauty can be found in every direction.

Mount Bachelor (541-382-2442, 800-829-2442, www.mtbachelor.com), only 20 miles away from Bend, is a major winter-sports destination, while one of the largest designated wilderness areas in the state, with more than 240 miles of hiking trails, surrounds the nearby **Three Sisters**. (South Sister, at 10,358 feet, is the third-highest mountain in the state; you don't need technical climbing skills to reach the top in summer.) The McKenzie Pass Highway runs west from Sisters, a small, touristy town northwest of Bend, over a bleak, lava-strewn pass between Mount Washington and the Three Sisters, while the Cascade Lakes Highway, a National Scenic Byway, runs south from Mount Bachelor past a series of high mountain reservoirs (and abundant campsites).

North of Bend, past lower and drier (but also fast-growing) Redmond is **Smith Rock State Park** (www.oregonstateparks.org/park_51.php), one of the premier rock climbing destinations in the country. Much of the land nearby is part of the **Crooked River National Grassland**. To the east, the relatively low, forested Ochoco Mountains are much less visited than the Cascades, and the range includes three small wilderness areas. South of Bend, the **Newberry National Volcanic Monument** (541-383-5300, www.fs.fed.us/r6/centraloregon/newberry nvm/) includes lava tubes, cinder cones, and two beautiful, crystal-clear crater lakes set in a geologically active caldera. Practically anyplace in the region makes a great jumping-off point for backcountry trips.

For obvious reasons, central Oregon is a major outdoor sports center. Downhill and cross-country skiing and other winter sports bring crowds in the winter, while hiking and backpacking, mountain and road biking, rafting and other forms of boating, and golf are all popular pursuits during the summer and fall. Central Oregon has also become something of a hub for destination resorts; the two most venerable and best-known of these resorts are **Sunriver** (800-801-8765, www.sunriver-resort.com), about 15 miles south of Bend, and **Black Butte Ranch** (866-901-2961, www.blackbutteranch.com), off Highway 20 between Sisters and Santiam Pass. Closer to Portland, **Kah-Nee-Ta High Desert Resort and Casino** (800-554-4SUN, www.kah-nee-taresort.com) is located on the Warm Springs Indian Reservation. For more information on destinations in the region, contact the **Central Oregon Visitors Association** (541-389-8799, 800-800-8334, www.visitcentraloregon.com).

SOUTHERN OREGON

The Willamette Valley peters out south of Eugene, and the terrain becomes a fairly rugged jumble of forested mountains cleft by the valleys of the Umpqua and Rogue rivers and their various tributaries. Most southern Oregon cities, including

Roseburg, Grants Pass, and Medford, huddle in the river valleys. **Roseburg** (541-672-9731, 800-444-9584, www.visitroseburg.com), although not particularly exciting, makes a good base for exploring the Umpqua Valley wine region (541-673-5323, ww.umpquavalleywineries.org) and **Wildlife Safari** (541-679-6761, www.wildlifesafari.org), a drive-through wild animal park.

The Rogue River Valley in far southern Oregon, the site of Medford and Grants Pass, is a region of orchards, loggers, retirees, more wineries, and, surprisingly, smog. **Jacksonville** (www.jacksonvilleoregon.org), just west of Medford, is a well-preserved nineteenth-century gold-mining town, but the most popular "urban" destination in southern Oregon is **Ashland**. Home to the **Oregon Shakespeare Festival** (541-482-0446, www.orshakes.org), a nearly nine-month-long annual theatre series (and the attendant nice restaurants and hotels), as well as to large communities of environmentalists and California retirees, Ashland is an intriguing place to visit at any time of year. In winter, when the Shakespeare Festival is not going on, the **Mount Ashland Ski Area** (541-482-2897, www.mtashland.com) is a half-hour drive away.

Still more wineries nestle in the Applegate Valley, which runs through the botanically and geologically unique **Siskiyou Mountains**. Few roads pierce this rugged range (and none enter the large Kalmiopsis Wilderness), but US Highway 199 runs from Grants Pass toward the redwood country of northern California through the hippie-meets-logger community of Cave Junction (where there are still *more* wineries). A spur road leads to **Oregon Caves National Monument** (541-592-2100, www.nps.gov/orca), which features a marble cave system high in the Siskiyous.

The iconic natural attraction of southern Oregon, and arguably of the state as a whole, is **Crater Lake National Park** (541-594-3000, www.nps.gov/crla/). More than 1,900 feet deep and almost impossibly blue, Crater Lake fills the crater of ancient Mount Mazama, which erupted 7,700 years ago in a fashion that makes the 1980 Mt. St. Helens eruption look like a hiccup. Much of the park is inaccessible during the winter—the area averages some 44 *feet* of snow each year—but during the summer it's possible to drive around the lake, climb to the top of several neighboring peaks, or hike down to the water and take a boat to the mini-volcano of Wizard Island. Other regions of the Cascade spine north and south of the park are included within several wilderness areas, which receive far fewer visitors than the wilderness areas in the central and northern parts of the state. On the east side of the mountains, the city of **Klamath Falls** (www.travelklamath.com) lies near broad, shallow Upper Klamath Lake, a major stopover point for migratory birds.

Information about southern Oregon destinations and accommodation options is available from the **Southern Oregon Visitors Association** (541-779-4691, 800-448-4856, www.sova.org).

EASTERN OREGON

Away from the Interstate 84 corridor (which follows the old route of the Oregon Trail), high, dry eastern Oregon receives comparatively few visitors. While it may not have many urban attractions—**Pendleton** (www.pendletoncham ber.com), home of the annual Pendleton Round-up (www.pendletonroundup. com), being the main exception—this part of the state offers incredible scenery and wide-open spaces. Major mountain ranges—the Blue Mountains, the Strawberry Mountains, and the jagged, granitic Wallowas—thrust upward from the sagebrush and grassland, and offer outstanding and generally uncrowded recreational opportunities. The Wallowas in particular make an excellent hiking and backpacking destination; most of the range is protected within the vast **Eagle Cap Wilderness**, and more than 500 miles of trails link beautiful alpine lake basins. Non-hikers can enjoy the towns of Joseph and Enterprise, just north of glacial Wallowa Lake. Not far to the east, on the Oregon-Idaho border, is difficult-to-reach **Hells Canyon**, where the Snake River runs through North America's deepest river gorge.

The mountain-and-valley country of east-central Oregon includes the **John Day Fossil Beds National Monument** (www.nps.gov/joda); the monument has three separate units which protect not only abundant fossils but also the colorful Painted Hills. Remote southeastern Oregon has a host of adventurous destinations, including the canyons of the Owyhee River, Malheur and Harney lakes, and Hart Mountain Antelope Refuge, but the region's crown jewel is probably **Steens Mountain**. This fault-block mountain range rises fairly gradually from west to east; then, from the highest point at nearly 10,000 feet, the east side plunges precipitously to the Alvord Desert, Oregon's driest place, thousands of feet below. The mountain features aspen forests, cirque lakes, and bighorn sheep. A rough dirt road runs from Frenchglen most of the way up the west side of the mountain (road open summer only).

WASHINGTON STATE

Washington, like Oregon, is a topographically diverse state that encompasses coast, mountains, and semi-arid plateau, and has a correspondingly impressive range of getaway options.

One of the main attractions of southwestern Washington is clearly visible from Portland on a clear day. Mount St. Helens, which famously blew its top in May 1980, is now part of the **Mount St. Helens National Volcanic Monument** (360-449-7800, www.fs.fed.us/gpnf/mshnvm/). You can visit one of the two observatories that offer views of the crater (which contains a growing new lava dome), hike into the recovering blast zone, or make a long, ashy (or snowy) slog to the new summit at the crater rim (permit required). Ape Cave, on the south side of the mountain, is the longest lava tube in the Western Hemisphere; it's a great place to take kids. The next volcano to the east, **Mount Adams** (also visible from Portland), tops out at 12,276 feet and is thus more than 1,000 feet taller than Mount Hood. The area between the peaks is part of the **Gifford Pinchot National Forest** (360-891-5000, www.fs.fed.us/gpnf/), which contains many wonderful (and, considering the proximity to Portland, surprisingly uncrowded) hiking and backpacking options, including three wilderness areas; the lake-dotted Indian Heaven Wilderness is a particularly appealing destination. The small community of **Trout Lake** makes a good base for exploring the Mount Adams region.

Moving north along the Cascades, **Mount Rainier National Park** (360-569-2211, www.nps.gov/mora) surrounds the mountain of the same name, which at an elevation of 14,410 feet is the highest peak in the Pacific Northwest. In addition to the mountain itself and its many glaciers, the park offers alpine meadows, old-growth forest, and the 93-mile Wonderland Trail. Moving north along the spine of the Cascades, you can visit the Alpine Lakes Wilderness, Mount Baker and its adjacent wilderness and National Recreation Areas, and the rugged, glacier-clad peaks and steep-sided valleys of **North Cascades National Park** (360-856-5700, www.nps.gov/noca) on the Canadian border.

The bulk of Washington's population lives in the lowlands west of the Cascades along Puget Sound. Although cities like Olympia (the state capital), pleasant Bellingham, and gritty Tacoma are all worth a stop, the Big Kahuna of Washington cities is **Seattle**. Portlanders carry on a love-hate relationship with Seattle, 170 miles to the north. Despite legitimate gripes about Seattle's sprawl, traffic congestion, and high prices, Portlanders still flock to the city for its cultural attractions (which are arguably better and certainly more numerous than Portland's), its professional sports teams, and its matchless setting on the water between two mountain ranges (when you can see them). You can make a great weekend out of visiting Seattle's museums, sampling its cafés and restaurants, dodging fish carcasses at Pike Place Market, and maybe even going to a Mariners or Seahawks game. Best of all, you can relax and go by train. For the official line on tourism in Seattle, contact the **Seattle Convention and Visitors Bureau** (206-461-5840, www.visitseattle.or/visitors/).

The mountains visible across Puget Sound from Seattle are the Olympics, largely protected within **Olympic National Park** (360-565-3130, www.nps.gov/olym/). The park is incredibly diverse; besides the mountains, which are impressive enough, the park includes such attractions as the Hoh Rain Forest, the alpine meadows near Hurricane Ridge, and the longest stretch of wilderness coastline in the contiguous United States. Since 95% of the park is designated wilderness, the best way to explore its charms is on foot (with lots of time). Outside the park boundaries, the tourism potential of the Olympic Peninsula has obviously suffered from overzealous forestry practices, but the region also includes interesting towns such as Port Angeles, Poulsbo, and charming, historic **Port Townsend** (www.ptguide.com).

Puget Sound's islands offer fun maritime getaways, although they tend to be crowded with visitors from the Seattle area on summer and holiday weekends. Although largely rural, **Vashon Island** (206-463-6217, www.vashonchamber. com), southwest of Seattle, is home to many commuters to the city, who travel back and forth by ferry. Further north, the state's largest island, **Whidbey Island**, can be reached by ferry from either side of the Sound or by the bridge over Deception Pass; nearby **Camano Island** has bridge access only. Information about both destinations is available at www.whidbeycamanoisland.com.

At the northern end of the sound, the atmospheric **San Juan Islands** are accessible only by ferry (or air). It's best to give yourself at least a long weekend here; the wait for the ferry can take several hours, especially on weekends. Once you arrive, you'll find secluded beaches, charming towns, cozy coffee shops, and an abundance of quaint bed and breakfasts. Each of the three main islands—Lopez, Orcas, and San Juan—is worth a visit; you can stay on all three islands over the course of a visit, or you could plan to use one as a base and take ferry rides to the others. If possible, bring or rent a bicycle or kayak and tour the islands that way. For more information, contact the **San Juan Islands Visitors Bureau** (888-468-3701, www.guidetosanjuans.com). For details about ferry routes and schedules throughout the Puget Sound region, visit the **Washington State Ferries** web site at www.ws.dot.wa.gov/ferries/, or call their helpline at 888-808-7977 (206-464-6540 from outside Washington).

Eastern Washington, like eastern Oregon, is much drier than the western half of the state. The most popular draws are actually in the eastern Cascades or its fringes: Lake Chelan, the "Bavarian" village of **Leavenworth** (509-548-5807, www.leavenworth.org), and the cross-country skier's paradise of **Methow Valley**. Semi-arid eastern Washington contains some thriving cities, including Yakima, the Tri-Cities (Richland, Pasco, and Kennewick), and Spokane, along with vast fields of wheat; the major draws, however, are the reservoirs along the Columbia River (including Lake Roosevelt, behind Grand Coulee Dam) and the mountain ranges of northeast Washington. In southeastern Washington, the area around **Walla Walla** (www.wallawalla.org) is a highly regarded wine-producing region; contact the **Walla Walla Valley Wine Alliance** (509-526-3117, www.walla wallawine.com) for details.

BRITISH COLUMBIA

Both cosmopolitan Vancouver and self-consciously anglophilic Victoria are popular getaways. **Vancouver**, which is accessible from Portland by train as well as car or bus, is a cosmopolitan port city with a spectacular setting, great shopping, and some of the best Asian restaurants on the West Coast. Thousand-acre Stanley Park, jutting out into Burrard Inlet not far from the central business district, is widely considered one of the most beautiful public parks in the world. For more information, contact **Tourism Vancouver** (www.tourismvancouver.com).

Victoria (www.tourismvictoria.com), near the southern tip of Vancouver Island, is a smaller and more laid-back destination that is sometimes called the most English city outside England. Apart from the double-decker buses and high tea at the Empress Hotel, Victoria has some beautiful gardens, the most famous of which is **Butchart Gardens** (866-652-4422, www.butchartgardens.com), which were created out of a former quarry. Ships cruise directly to Victoria's Inner Harbour from downtown Seattle, Bellingham, and Port Angeles, while ferries from Anacortes, Washington and the British Columbia mainland port of Tsawwassen go into Sidney or Swartz Bay, a few kilometers north of the city.

Beyond the province's big cities, major destinations include **Pacific Rim National Park** on the west coast of Vancouver Island, the **Gulf Islands** (the Canadian continuation of Washington's San Juan Islands, between Vancouver Island and the B.C. mainland), the world-class **Whistler Blackcomb** ski resort (www. whistlerblackcomb.com), and the semi-arid, fruit-and-wine-producing **Okanogan Valley**.

FARTHER AFIELD

There are more than enough diversions in the Pacific Northwest to keep anyone busy for a lifetime. If you have a bad case of wanderlust (or sunshine lust), however, it's easy to venture farther afield. For one thing, driving is less stressful (or at least less crowded) here than in more heavily populated regions. In the Northeast, a drive from Boston to Washington, D.C., on Interstate 95 would pass through Providence, New York City, Newark, Philadelphia, Wilmington, and Baltimore (not to mention innumerable toll plazas); a drive of the same distance south from Portland on Interstate 5 wouldn't even get you to Sacramento.

A day's drive or less south from Portland could take you to the redwood forests of the northern California coast; 14,180-foot Mount Shasta or its nearby houseboat-infested reservoir, Lake Shasta; Lassen Volcanic National Park; the Trinity Alps; Napa Valley or Sonoma; San Francisco; Lake Tahoe (or Reno, Nevada); or the California gold country. Heading east, you have access to most of Idaho (the scenic panhandle, rugged central Idaho, or Boise), as well as western Montana (including Glacier National Park and Missoula), the southern Canadian Rockies, and, if you have a really high tolerance for long-distance driving, Yellowstone National Park.

If you have the cash, and don't mind extravagantly spewing carbon into the atmosphere, Portland has nonstop flights to most major cities in the western United States. Even with now-permanently heightened airport security, you can easily get away for a winter weekend in Palm Springs, Las Vegas, San Diego, Tucson, or even Cabo San Lucas.

ORTLAND'S EVENTS CALENDAR STARTS OFF SLOWLY IN THE DAMP, gray depths of winter, then builds to a crescendo in July, when the weather is reliably warm and dry. During the cooler, wetter months, most big events take place under cover; Portland is just not cold or snowy enough to support winter carnivals, and there is no ChillyDrizzleFest (yet). In contrast, summer celebrations tend to be outdoor affairs in parks and other open spaces. A sampling of Portland's more distinctive annual events is listed below.

Most Portland neighborhoods and suburban communities have one or more community festivals—street fairs, art festivals, intentionally cheesy historical celebrations, and the like—that are popular with local residents and make for fun, inexpensive outings.

JANUARY

- **Portland International Auto Show**, 877-559-6828, www.paragonexpo. com/201.html; a celebration of all things automotive, the Portland International Auto Show fills the Oregon Convention Center with current-year car models and accessories, sneak peeks of forthcoming models, and a few concept cars that may never see production.
- **Reel Music**, 503-221-1156, www.nwfilm.org/festivals/reel_fest.php; in January, the NW Film Center presents the first of many film festivals held each year in Portland. The Reel Music festival focuses on music on film, but it is not just a theatrical clone of MTV.
- **RiverCity Bluegrass**, 503-282-0877, www.rivercitybluegrass.com; acoustic bluegrass rocks—well, reels, anyway—the Oregon Convention Center for three days in early January.

FEBRUARY

- **Chinese New Year Cultural Fair**, 503-819-9702, www.portlandchinesetimes. us, celebrates Chinese culture (and food) at the Oregon Convention Center.
- **Oregon Seafood & Wine Festival**, 360-210-5275, www.eventsnw.net/ENW/ Sea&Wine.html; held at the Oregon Convention Center in the middle of the Dungeness crab season, this festival indeed focuses on Oregon seafood and wine, which go together like a horse and carriage.
- **Portland Home & Garden Show**, 503-246-8291, www.otshows.com, is one of many home and garden–related trade shows held every year in Portland. The Home & Garden Show fills the Expo Center in North Portland with display gardens, art, and the booths of eager contractors. This event is usually held concurrently with the **Yard, Garden & Patio Show**, 503-682-5089, www.ygp show.com, sponsored by the Oregon Association of Nurseries, at the Oregon Convention Center.
- **Portland International Film Festival**, 503-221-1156, www.nwfilm.org/ festivals/portland_international.php; this two-week filmstravaganza is Oregon's biggest film festival. Now more than 30 years old, PIFF usually screens around 100 films from more than two dozen countries, including some fresh-from-Sundance offerings.
- **Portland Jazz Festival,** 503-228-5299, www.pdxjazz.com; this multi-day festival, held at multiple venues in and around downtown Portland, features appearances by jazz artists of international renown, as well as dozens of free performances and educational events.

MARCH

- **St. Patrick's Day**. Although it's no Boston, Portland celebrates St. Patrick's Day in style with a host of events scattered around the city. Fitness buffs can tackle the Shamrock Run (www.ontherunevents.com/shamrock/). The All-Ireland Society hosts an annual family celebration at the Holy Rosary Church Hall (376 NE Clackamas St, 503- 235-3163). As in other cities, bars and brewpubs all over town bedeck themselves in green and serve copious amounts of Harp and Guinness. Two downtown Irish-themed pubs throw the biggest bashes: **Paddy's** (65 SW Yamhill, 503-224-5626) sponsors a St. Paddy's Blues & Brews, while **Kells Irish Restaurant & Pub** (112 SW 2nd Ave, 503-227-4057) throws a massive three-day block party in heated tents (see www.kellsirish.com/port-land/festival.html).

APRIL

- The **Trillium Festival**, sponsored by Friends of Tryon Creek, 503-636-4398, www.tryonfriends.org, celebrates the emergence of spring in general, and the blooming of the native trillium in particular, at Tryon Creek State Natural Area in Southwest Portland. Festivities include a native plant sale.

- **Wooden Shoe Tulip Festival**, 800-711-2006, www.woodenshoe.com; flower-lovers and Dutch-o-philes from all over Northwest Oregon converge on 40 acres of tulips near Woodburn from late March to late April.

MAY

- **Cinco de Mayo**, 503-222-9807, www.cincodemayo.org; Waterfront Park in downtown Portland hosts this annual celebration of Mexican food, entertainment, and *artesanía*.
- **Mother's Day Rhododendron Show**, Crystal Springs Rhododendron Garden, SE 28th Ave at Woodstock Blvd, 503-771-8386; Portland has an ideal climate for rhododendrons, and their blooms are usually at their most spectacular during this annual show.
- **Portland Indie Wine Festival**, 503-595-0891, www.indiewinefestival.com; described as "Sundance meets wine tasting," this oenophilic extravaganza in the Pearl District showcases Oregon's best limited-production wineries.

JUNE

- **Lake Oswego Festival of the Arts**, Lakewood Center for the Arts, 368 S State St, Lake Oswego, 503-636-1060, www.lakewood-center.org, is one of the largest art fairs in the region. In addition to an extensive art exhibition, a craft fair, and live entertainment, the festival usually highlights a specific art form or individual artist.
- **Portland Rose Festival**, 503- 227-2681, www.rosefestival.org, is the biggest event on the Portland calendar. Seriously, some people in Portland live for this. The festival includes such diverse diversions as the Grand Floral Parade, the more lighthearted Starlight Parade, a raucous waterfront carnival, dragon boat races, fireworks, a children's parade, a rose show and competition, auto races, an arts festival, the crowning of the Rose Queen and her court, and the arrival of ships from the U.S. Coast Guard and the U.S. and Canadian navies. The Rose Festival is so big, so all-encompassing, and so long-lasting, that virtually no one dares to schedule any other events in Portland in June, except for the…
- **Portland Pride Festival & Parade**, 503-295-9788, www.pridenw.org; the Portland Pride march, festival, and parade are boisterous events held at Waterfront Park in mid-June, after the Rose Festival detritus has been removed. The parade route winds through downtown and ends in the Pearl District; participants range from local politicians to "dykes on bikes."
- **Tigard Festival of Balloons**, 503-612-8213, www.tigardballoon.org; if the Rose Festival has not exhausted your appetite for fun, skedaddle to the southwest suburb of Tigard for this festival of balloons—the big, hot air kind, not the kind that clowns twist into animal shapes.

JULY

- **Chamber Music Northwest Summer Festival**, 503-294-6400, www.cmnw. org, held on the Reed College and Catlin Gabel School campuses, is one of the largest chamber music festivals in the country; the festival program includes concerts, open rehearsals, and free lectures.
- **Concours d'Elegance Car Show**, 800-359-2313, www.forestgroveconcours,org, held on the Pacific University campus in Forest Grove, is the largest classic car show in the Pacific Northwest.
- **da Vinci Days**, 541-757-6363, www.davinci-days.org; science, technology, and weirdness intersect wonderfully in this annual celebration of creativity in Corvallis, about 1½ hours south of Portland. The kinetic sculpture race is a particular highlight.
- **Fourth of July Fireworks**. Fireworks shows take place in many locations around the metropolitan area, including over the Willamette River in downtown Portland. (You may also find that neighborhood teenagers set off bottle rockets on an unofficial, and illegal, basis.) The big pyrotechnics, however, happen at Fort Vancouver, which puts on what boosters claim is the largest fireworks display west of the Mississippi.
- **Oregon Brewers Festival**, 503-778-5917, www.oregonbrewfest.com; a tradition among Portland beer aficionados, the Oregon Brewers Festival at Waterfront Park is one of the country's premier showcases of craft and micro brews. Admission is free, but tasting will cost you.
- **Oregon Country Fair**, 541-343-4298, www.oregoncountryfair.org; love it or hate it, Oregon Country Fair is unlike anything else anywhere in the world. Part Renaissance fair, part hippie revival, and part art-and-entertainment extravaganza, the Country Fair is more an experience than an event. It takes place over three days in Veneta, just outside Eugene, about two hours south of Portland. Look for cars around town that proudly display parking stickers from multiple years of the event.
- **Portland Scottish Highland Games**, 503-293-8501, www.phga.org, are a celebration of Scottish music, dancing, and such uniquely Celtic athletic contests as the Caber toss and the Scottish hammer throw. (Stay behind the safety nets.) Events usually take place at Mt. Hood Community College in Gresham.
- **Seattle to Portland Bicycle Classic**, 206-522-3222, www.seattletoportland. com; the Cascade Bicycle Club annual ride is one of the most anticipated long-distance cycling events in the country. Up to 9,000 participants from around the world cover the 200-odd miles between Seattle and Portland in one or two days.
- **Waterfront Blues Festival**, 503-973-FEST, www.waterfrontbluesfest.com, held at Waterfront Park in downtown Portland in early July, bills itself as the largest blues festival west of the Mississippi. The event benefits the Oregon Food Bank and features multiple stages and big-name blues artists from around the country.

AUGUST

- **Bite of Oregon**, 800-452-6079, www.biteoforegon.com; no, it's not a mouthful of soil. The Bite of Oregon features food from dozens of local restaurants, Oregon wine and beer, an Iron Chef Oregon competition, and musical and comedy events on four different stages at Waterfront Park downtown.
- **Festa Italiana**, www.festa-italiana.org; the latter half of this week-long celebration of local Italian heritage and culture transforms Pioneer Courthouse Square into an Italian piazza, complete with food court, wine garden, strolling musicians, and a variety of entertainment and activities for the whole family.
- **Hood to Coast Relay**, 503-292-4626, www.hoodtocoast.com; thousands of runners take part every year in this event, which is exactly what its name implies: a relay race from Mount Hood to the Oregon Coast.
- **Mount Hood Jazz Festival**, 503-491-5950, www.mthoodjazz.com; the area's most venerable jazz festival features world-renowned headliners and lesser-known talents. Now more than a quarter-century old, the festival takes place in Gresham. Posters from past festivals are local collectibles.
- **Portland Festival Symphony**, 503-245-7878, www.portlandfestivalsymphony. org; for more than 25 years, the Portland Festival Symphony has presented free classical music concerts in Portland's city parks.
- **Portland Indy Animation Festival**, www.pdxanimation.com, held at the Hollywood Theatre on Northeast Sandy Boulevard, is one of several animation festivals to hit Portland every year.
- **Providence Bridge Pedal**, www.providence.org/oregon/events/bridge_pedal, is your chance to ride your bike over all 10 of the city's Willamette River road bridges, including the Marquam (Interstate 5) and Fremont (Interstate 405) bridges. (The freeway bridges are closed to traffic in one direction, so you won't be dodging speeding semis.)
- **Street of Dreams**, 503-684-1880, www.streetofdreamspdx.com; every year, the Home Builders Association of Metropolitan Portland creates a showcase of luxury (i.e., ridiculously expensive) homes. More than 100,000 people tour the homes to gawk at new innovations in high-end building trends.
- **Tualatin Crawfish Festival**, www.tualatincrawfish.com; this family-friendly festival honors the crustaceans that lurk in the Tualatin River. The festival features live entertainment, food and craft vendors, and of course copious crawfish consumption.

SEPTEMBER

- **Art in the Pearl**, 503-722-9017, www.artinthepearl.com, takes place in the North Park Blocks over Labor Day weekend. In addition to art, the festivities include musical and theatrical performances, plenty of food, and hands-on activities for children and adults.

- **Cycle Oregon**, 503-287-0405, www.cycleoregon.com, is the highlight of the Oregon bicycle touring calendar. Each year, this week-long bike trek takes in a different scenic, rural, and (alas) hilly portion of the state; participants camp in small towns, which usually offer a hearty welcome.
- **Oktoberfest**. Most Portland area Oktoberfests actually take place in September, when the weather is more likely to be dry. The biggest such event is the family-oriented Mt. Angel Oktoberfest (503-845-9440, www.oktoberfest.org), held in the town of Mt. Angel, about 45 minutes south of Portland. Other Oktoberfest celebrations occur at Oaks Park in Southeast Portland, in St. Helens, and at brewpubs and German restaurants throughout the region.
- **Oregon State Fair**, 800-833-0011, www.oregonstatefair.org; while it's not really a match for the state fairs of the Midwest, Oregon's version, held at the state fairgrounds in Salem, features the same winning combination of agricultural displays, carnival rides, live entertainment, and deep-fried foods.
- **Susan G. Komen Race for the Cure**, 503-552-9160, www.komenoregon.org/Race_for_the_Cure/; tens of thousands of people walk or run through downtown Portland each year in Portland Race for the Cure, an event that raises funds for breast cancer research.

OCTOBER

- The **Salmon Festival**, 503-797-1850, www.metro-region.org/salmonfestival, marks the return of Chinook salmon to the Sandy River. Held at Oxbow Regional Park, near Troutdale, the event includes storytelling, nature walks, arts and crafts displays, and a hands-on "school of fish" where children (and adults) can learn more about salmon and their lifecycle.
- **Greek Festival**, Holy Trinity Greek Orthodox Church, 3131 NE Glisan, 503-234-0468, goholytrinity.org/festival.php; a church in the Laurelhurst neighborhood throws this popular fundraiser every year. Look for very homemade Greek food, including scrumptious baklava and other pastries.
- **Howloween**, 503-226-1561, www.oregonzoo.org/Events/Howloween/index.htm; the Oregon Zoo gets spooky in late October. Activities include mildly scary storytelling and a kids' scavenger hunt, but the highlight is the opening event, where the zoo's elephants smash a giant pumpkin.
- **Pumpkin Patches and Corn Mazes**. Many Portland families make it an annual tradition to troop out to one of the many pumpkin patches outside Portland, pick a pumpkin or two from the fields, and wander through a corn maze. Two of the most popular and well-established pumpkin patches are on Sauvie Island: The Pumpkin Patch, 503-621-7110, www.portlandmaze.com, and Sauvie Island Farms, 503-621-3988, www.sauvieislandfarms.com.
- **Portland Marathon**, 503-226-1111, www.portlandmarathon.org; the highlight of the Portland running calendar, the Portland Marathon's course takes in both sides of the Willamette River. Weather can be crisp and dry or completely

sodden. The related festivities include a wheelchair competition, a 2-mile run for children, and a 10-kilometer fitness walk.

- **Portland Open Studios**, 503-285-3131, www.portlandopenstudios.com; during the second and third weekends of October many Portland artists—painters, sculptors, glassblowers, metalsmiths, potters, and more—open their studios to visitors.

NOVEMBER

- **Civil War**. No, not a re-enactment of the War Between the States, but the annual game between the University of Oregon and Oregon State University football teams (and associated tailgate parties), which takes place alternately in Eugene and Corvallis. Either way, if you're not going to the game, stay off Interstate 5 south of Portland on game day.
- **Wordstock**, 503-546-1012, www.wordstockfestival.com, is an annual literary event at the Oregon Convention Center that features renowned and up-and-coming authors, writing workshops, and a children's festival.
- **Macy's Holiday Parade**. For years, the Meier & Frank Holiday Parade sent a meandering line of floats, marching bands, and costumed figures (including Santa) through downtown Portland on the day after Thanksgiving. Following Macy's purchase of the Meier & Frank chain in 2006, the parade continues under a new name.
- **Columbia Gorge Model Railroad Show**, 2505 N Vancouver Ave, 503-28TRAIN, www.cgmrc.com; every November, the Columbia Gorge Model Railroad Club opens its clubhouse for public viewing of its enormous and incredibly detailed scale model of railroad operations in the Columbia Gorge.
- **Wine Country Thanksgiving**, 503-646-2985, www.willamettewines.com; more than 100 wineries and tasting rooms, many otherwise closed to visitors, open to the public over Thanksgiving weekend for tastings, tours, and special events. (A similar event takes place during Memorial Day weekend.)

DECEMBER

- **Festival of Lights at the Grotto**, NE 85th Ave at Sandy Blvd, 503-261-2400, www.thegrotto.org/events/lights.htm; the Grotto (formally the National Sanctuary of Our Sorrowful Mother) decorates its peaceful grounds in Northeast Portland with a walk-through display of more than 500,000 lights. Other attractions include nativity scenes, choral events, and a petting zoo.
- **Parade of Christmas Ships**, www.christmasships.org; two brightly lit flotillas ply the Willamette and Columbia rivers every night for two weeks in December. Riverside restaurants are frequently booked months in advance.
- **Peacock Lane,** one block east of SE 39th Ave between Stark St and Belmont St, www.peacocklane.net. In mid-December, this street of modest English-style

homes becomes a wonderland of dazzling holiday decorations, many of which are quite elaborate and have been trotted out every holiday season for many years. It's best to walk down the street, both to avoid traffic snarls and to be better able to buy hot chocolate and other refreshments.

- The **Holiday Ale Festival**, 503-252-9899, www.holidayale.com, features winter ales and other holiday-themed brews. The event is held outdoors, at Pioneer Courthouse Square downtown (albeit under the shelter of a huge tent).
- **ZooLights**, 503-226-1561, www.oregonzoo.org//Events/ZooLights/index.htm; another bulb-related spectacle, the month-long ZooLights event sees the Oregon Zoo festooned with nearly a million lights. Light-peeping visitors are also treated to live performances and train rides.

THE VOLUME OF WRITING ABOUT THE PACIFIC NORTHWEST IN general, and Portland in particular, can be overwhelming, particularly if you walk into a place like the Pacific Northwest Room at Powell's Books, or even a branch library. This chapter lists only a few of the most useful and distinctive books about Portland and the region.

ARCHITECTURE AND URBAN PLANNING

Portland cries out for a comprehensive book about its historic and modern architecture. The following books are the best currently available choices.

- *An Architectural Guidebook to Portland* by Bart King
- *A Century of Portland Architecture* by Thomas Vaughn and George McMath, published in 1967, is out of print but worth seeking out for its detailed descriptions of the city's older buildings (many of which are still standing 40 years later).
- *Classic Houses of Portland, Oregon, 1850-1950* by William J. Hawkins III and William Willingham
- *The Portland Bridge Book* by Sharon Wood Wortman and Ed Wortman is an engaging guide to—surprise!—Portland's bridges.

Urban planning may not be the sexiest topic around, but a grounding in the subject is essential to understanding Portland's development. Here are a few tomes to get you started:

- *City Limits: Walking Portland's Boundary* by David Oates describes the author's stroll along the entire urban growth boundary of the Portland metropolitan area.
- Portland State University professor of urban studies Carl Abbott has written several books about Portland urban life, history, and urban planning. Although an academic rather than a popular title, *Greater Portland: Urban Life and Land-*

scape in the Pacific Northwest ties together Portland's natural setting, culture, and urban planning. Abbott's history of the city's planning and growth, *Portland: Planning, Politics, and Growth in a Twentieth-Century City*, is out of print but is available at most public libraries.

- *The Portland Edge: Challenges and Successes in Growing Communities*, edited by Connie P. Ozawa, is a compendium of essays about planning and its discontents.

FICTION

Lots of authors make their home in Portland—Ursula K. Le Guin, Chuck Palahniuk, Jean Auel, Phillip Margolin, and Katherine Dunn are a few of the city's best known fiction writers—but not all of them use Portland as the setting for their stories. The majority of novels set in Portland seem to be mysteries and thrillers; the city's weather makes for great noirish, Raymond Chandleresque atmosphere. Novels and stories that are set in whole or in part in Portland include:

- Several of Beverly Cleary's children's stories, notably the *Ramona* books, which are set in Portland; Ramona Quimby (named after Portland's Quimby Street, just like Mayor Quimby of Springfield in *The Simpsons*) lives on Klickitat Street (an actual Northeast Portland thoroughfare).
- *Geek Love* by Katherine Dunn; narrated by an, um, hunchbacked albino dwarf, this truly disturbing novel is set partly in Portland.
- *The Lathe of Heaven* by Ursula K. Le Guin; this 1971 novel takes place in a post-apocalyptic (and yet not so—it's hard to explain) future Portland.
- *Paranoid Park* by Blake Nelson is a new teen skate thriller (and soon-to-be major motion picture).

A new anthology, *Reading Portland: The City in Prose*, edited by John Trombold and Peter Donahue, includes several short story selections about the Rose City. The many novels set elsewhere in Oregon include several Ken Kesey titles (such as *Sometimes a Great Notion* and *One Flew Over the Cuckoo's Nest*) and *Honey in the Horn* by H.L. Davis, a novel about homesteaders in Oregon in the first decade of the twentieth century, which won the Pulitzer Prize for fiction in 1936.

GUIDEBOOKS

GENERAL

There are probably dozens of regional or city-specific tourist guidebooks that include Portland, from mainstream series like Fodor's and Frommer's to "backpacker" guides from Lonely Planet and Rough Guide. You probably won't need any of them. You're not a tourist; you live here now, and the sort of shallow coverage and narrow advice that most guidebooks and travel articles provide—stay downtown, eat in the Pearl District, then fly home!—is just not going to be useful. Here are a few guidebooks that may interest residents as well as visitors.

- The *Best Places* series of guidebooks (*Best Places Portland, Best Places Northwest*, etc.) is geared towards visitors, but the restaurant and leisure listings could be useful to newcomers.
- *Don't Jump! The Northwest Winter Blues Survival Guide*, by Seattle writers Traci Voget and Novella Carpenter, is a tongue-in-cheek guide to living with gray, rainy weather.
- For a unique and very alternative view of the city, try *Fugitives and Refugees: A Walk in Portland, Oregon* by Portland novelist Chuck Palahniuk (author of *Fight Club*, among other things).
- *Living With Earthquakes in the Pacific Northwest* by Robert S. Yeats
- *The Zinester's Guide to Portland: A Low/No Budget Guide to Visiting and Living in Portland, Oregon*, by Shawn Granton and Nate Beaty, will be useful for certain demographics and not useful (but still amusing) to certain others.

OUTDOOR GUIDES

Visit your local bookstore and you'll find more hiking guides and other outdoor guidebooks to Oregon than you can shake a lightweight trekking pole at, not to mention field guides for everything from newts and ferns to whales and trees. Here are a few suggestions to get you started:

- **The Mountaineers Books** (www.mountaineersbooks.org), based in Seattle, publishes a slew of outdoor guides for Oregon and Southwest Washington, including guides to hiking, snowshoeing, cross-country skiing, bicycling, climbing, and boating. If you have a specialized interest, you'll want to check out their publications on the topic. The guidebooks with the broadest appeal include *The Waterfall Lover's Guide to the Pacific Northwest* by Gregory Plumb; *Best Short Hikes in Northwest Oregon* by Rhonda and George Ostertag; *100 Classic Hikes in Oregon* by Douglas Lorain; and *Best Hikes with Kids: Oregon* by Bonnie Henderson.
- *Portland Hill Walks: Twenty Explorations in Parks and Neighborhoods*, by Laura O. Foster, and *Walking Portland*, by Sybilla Cook, outline interesting walking tours around the city.
- Eugene-based explorer and prolific writer William L. Sullivan has authored many guidebooks about the state, including the popular "100 Hikes" series; the Portland-area entry, *100 Hikes in Northwest Oregon and Southwest Washington*, now in its third edition, is possibly the best local hiking guide available. Other useful books include *Exploring Oregon's Wild Areas* (another Mountain-

eers Books title) and *Hiking Oregon's History: The Stories Behind Historic Places You Can Walk To.*

- *Wild in the City: A Guide to Portland's Natural Areas*, edited by Mike Houck, the Audubon Society of Portland's urban naturalist, and travel writer M.J. Cody, exhaustively catalogues greenspaces in and near the metropolitan area; dozens of local writers and naturalists describe the landscape and natural history of these areas, and suggest walking, paddling, biking, and birdwatching tours.

REGIONAL HISTORY

- *Fire at Eden's Gate: Tom McCall and the Oregon Story* by Brent Walth tells the story of Oregon's dynamic governor Tom McCall, who was largely responsible for many of the state's environmental innovations—the bottle bill, public ownership of the entire coastline, and statewide land use planning, among others—in the 1960s and 1970s. Read this and come away with the realization that they don't make 'em like they used to.
- *The Great Extravaganza: Portland and the Lewis Exposition* by Carl Abbott; that's "exposition," not "expedition"—the 1905 fair that marked the centennial of Lewis and Clark's expedition was a turning point in Portland's development.
- *Naked Against the Rain: The People of the Lower Columbia River 1770-1830* by Rick Rubin (out of print) tells the story of the native peoples of Northwest Oregon at the dawn of European settlement in the region.
- *Oregon: This Storied Land* by William G. Robbins
- *The Oregon Story: 1850-2000*, put together by the *Oregonian* newspaper, is a concise, accessible history of the state.
- *Portland: People, Politics and Power 1851-2001*, by Jewel Lansing, provides surprisingly juicy historical details about Portland's politics, personalities, and general development over the last 150 years.
- *Portland Then and Now* by Linda Dodds and Carolyn Buan is interesting mainly as a visual record of the city's evolution; the book juxtaposes old and new photos of various locations around Portland.
- *Sweet Cakes, Long Journey: The Chinatowns of Portland, Oregon* by Marie Rose Wang
- *Timberline and a Century of Skiing on Mount Hood* by Jean Arthur
- *Willamette Landings: Ghost Towns of the River* by Howard M. Coming describes the many riverboat landings along the river, and how every town vied to become the state's big metropolis.

REFERENCE BOOKS

- The *Atlas of Oregon*, issued by the University of Oregon Press, features nearly 300 pages of beautifully rendered, highly detailed maps dealing with virtually every aspect of the state's history, natural environment, and demographics, ranging from Native American language groups (circa 1850) to soil types, urban development patterns, and county-by-county voting results in every presidential election since 1928. If you get just one reference book about Oregon, this should be the one.

- Each year, the Oregon Secretary of State publishes the *Oregon Blue Book*, a compendium that's chock full o' facts and figures about state government. *The Oregon Almanac* by Andrea Jarvela is an unofficial compendium of interesting facts about the state.

- *Oregon Geographic Names* by Lewis McArthur describes the origins of thousands of Oregon place names, from Aaron Mercer Reservoir to Zwagg Island.

F OR HELP ON FINDING 800 NUMBERS, AND ESPECIALLY for tips on how to reach an actual human being at hundreds of companies, go to **www.gethuman.com**.

211, Referral to Community Health and Social Services
411, Telephone Directory Assistance (charge may apply)
511, Road Conditions
711, Telecommunications Relay Service
911, Police, Fire, or Medical Emergencies

ANIMALS

See also "Veterinarians, Emergency Clinics" below.

- **Clackamas County Dog Services**, 503-655-8628, www.clackamas.us/dogs/
- **Clark County Animal Protection and Control**, 360-397-2488, www.clark.wa.gov/animal/
- **Humane Society for Southwest Washington**, 360-693-4746, www.southwesthumane.org
- **Multnomah County Animal Services**, 503-988-7381, www.co.multnomah.or.us/dbcs/pets/
- **Oregon Humane Society**, 503-285-7722, www.oregonhumane.com
- **Washington County Animal Services and Bonnie L. Hays Small Animal Shelter**, 503-846-7041, www.co.washington.or.us/deptmts/at/dog/dog.htm

AUTOMOBILES

- **Oregon Department of Environmental Quality Vehicle Inspection Pro-

gram (emissions testing), 971-673-1630, 877-476-0583, www.deq.state.
or.us/aq/vip/
- **Oregon Driver and Motor Services Division**, 503-299-9999, www.oregon.
gov/ODOT/DMV/
- **Washington Department of Ecology** (emissions testing), 800-453-4951,
www.ecy.wa.gov/programs/air/cars/automotive_pages.htm
- **Washington Department of Licensing**, 360-902-3900, www.dol.
wa.gov/driverslicense/

BIRTH AND DEATH CERTIFICATES

- **Oregon Center for Health Statistics**, 971-673-1190, www.oregon.
gov/DHS/ph/chs/
- **Washington Center for Health Statistics**, 360-236-4300, www.doh.
wa.gov/EHSPHL/CHS/

CONSUMER PROTECTION AND SERVICES

- **Better Business Bureau**, 503-212-3022, www.thebbb.org
- **Federal Trade Commission**, 877-382-4357, www.ftc.gov
- **Identity Theft Resource Center**, 858-693-7935, www.idtheftcenter.org
- **Oregon Department of Justice, Office of the Attorney General**, 503-229-
5576 (Portland area), 503-378-4320 (Salem area), 877-877-9392, www.doj.
state.or.us/finfraud/
- **Oregon Insurance Division**, 503-947-7984, 888-877-4894, www.insurance.
oregon.gov
- **Oregon Public Utility Commission**, 503-378-6600, 800-522-2404, www.puc.
state.or.us
- **Oregon Construction Contractors Board**, 503-378-4621, www.hirealicensed
contractor.com
- **Washington Department of Labor and Industries**, 800-547-8367, fortress.
wa.gov/lni/bbip/
- **Washington State Office of the Attorney General**, 800-551-4636, www.atg.
wa.gov
- **Washington Utilities and Transportation Commission**, 800-562-6150, www.
wutc.wa.gov

CREDIT BUREAUS

- **Equifax**, 800-685-1111, www.equifax.com
- **Experian**, 888-397-3742, www.experian.com
- **TransUnion**, 800-916-8800, www.transunion.com

CRISIS HOTLINES AND EMERGENCY SOCIAL SERVICES

It is always appropriate to call 911 and request police and/or emergency medical services if any person is in immediate danger of physical harm. In a non-emergency situation, dial **211** to be connected to community social services.

- **Aging & Disability Services 24-Hour Help Line**, 503-988-3646
- **Alcohol and Drug Abuse HelpLine**, 800-923-HELP
- **Child Abuse Hotline**, 503-731-3100, 800-509-5439
- **HopeLine** (suicide hotline), 800-SUICIDE
- **Mental Health Crisis Hotline**, 503-988-4888
- **National Domestic Violence Hotline**, 800-799-SAFE, www.ndvh.org
- **National Suicide Prevention Lifeline**, 800-273-TALK
- **Portland Women's Crisis Line**, 503-235-5333, www.pwcl.org
- **Teen Crisis and Counseling Line**, 877-553-TEEN
- **Sexual Assault Resource Center**, 503-384-0480, www.sarcoregon.org

DISABLED, SERVICES FOR

711, Telecommunications Relay Service

- **Alliance of People with Disabilities** (Washington), 206-545-7055, www.disabilitypride.org
- **The Arc of Multnomah-Clackamas** (advocacy and support for the developmentally disabled), 503-223-7279, www.thearcmult.org
- **The Arc of Clark County** (advocacy and support for the developmentally disabled), 360-254-1562, www.arcofclarkcounty.org
- **Disability Resources of Southwest Washington**, 360-694-6790, www.darsw.com
- **Independent Living Resources**, 503-232-7411, www.ilr.org
- **Network of Care** (database of services and resources), multnomah.or.networkofcare.org
- **Oregon Advocacy Center**, 503-243-2081, www.oradvocacy.org
- **Oregon Department of Human Services, Seniors and People with Disabilities Division**, 503-945-5811, 800-282-8092, www.oregon.gov/DHS/spd
- **Ride Connection** (transportation services), 503-528-1720, www.rideconnection.org
- **Washington Aging and Disability Services Administration**, www.aasa.dshs.wa.gov

EMERGENCY

- **Fire, Police, Medical**, 911
- **Poison Control Center**, 800-222-1222

GARBAGE

See "Trash and Recycling" below

GOVERNMENT

PORTLAND

- **City Hall**, general information, 503-823-4000, www.portlandonline.com
- **City Ombudsman**, 503-823-0144
- **Mayor's Comment Line**, 503-823-4127
- **Office of Neighborhood Involvement**, 503-823-4519, www.portlandonline.com/oni
- **Portland Maps**, www.portlandmaps.com

OTHER AREA CITIES

- **Banks**, 503-324-5112, www.cityofbanks.org
- **Battle Ground**, 360-342-5000, www.ci.battle-ground.wa.us
- **Beaverton**, 503-526-2260, www.beavertonoregon.gov
- **Camas**, 360-834-6864, www.ci.camas.wa.us
- **Canby**, 503-266-4021, www.ci.canby.or.us
- **Cornelius**, 503-357-9112, www.ci.cornelius.or.us
- **Damascus**, 503-658-8545, www.ci.damascus.or.us
- **Durham**, 503-639-6851, www.durham-oregon.us
- **Estacada**, 503-630-8270, www.cityofestacada.org
- **Fairview**, 503-665-7929, www.ci.fairview.or.us
- **Forest Grove**, 503-992-3207, www.ci.forest-grove.or.us
- **Gaston**, 503-985-3340
- **Gladstone**, 503-656-5225, www.ci.gladstone.or.us
- **Gresham**, 503-661-3000, www.ci.gresham.or.us
- **Happy Valley**, 503-760-3325, www.ci.happy-valley.or.us
- **Hillsboro**, 503-681-6100, www.ci.hillsboro.or.us
- **King City**, 503-639-4082, www.ci.king-city.or.us
- **La Center**, 360-263-2782, www.ci.lacenter.wa.us
- **Lake Oswego**, 503-635-0270, www.ci.oswego.or.us
- **Maywood Park**, 503-255-9805
- **Milwaukie**, 503-786-7555, www.cityofmilwaukie.org
- **Molalla**, 503-829-6855, www.molalla.net/~city
- **North Plains**, 503-647-5555, www.northplains.org
- **Oregon City**, 503-657-0891, www.orcity.org

- **Ridgefield**, 360-887-3557, www.ci.ridgefield.wa.us
- **Sandy**, 503-668-5533, www.ci.sandy.or.us
- **Sherwood**, 503-625-5522, www.ci.sherwood.or.us
- **Tigard**, 503-639-4171, www.ci.tigard.or.us
- **Troutdale**, 503-665-5175, www.ci.troutdale.or.us
- **Tualatin**, 503-692-2000, www.ci.tualatin.or.us
- **Vancouver**, 360-696-8200, www.cityofvancouver.us
- **Washougal**, 360-835-8501, www.cityofwashougal.org
- **West Linn**, 503-657-0331, www.ci-west-linn.or.us
- **Wilsonville**, 503-682-1011, www.ci.wilsonville.or.us
- **Wood Village**, 503-667-6211, www.ci.wood-village.or.us

COUNTY AND REGIONAL GOVERNMENTS

- **Clackamas County**, 503-655-8656, www.clackamas.us
- **Clark County**, 360-397-2000, www.co.clark.wa.us
- **Marion County,** 503-566-3916, www.co.marion.or.us
- **Multnomah County**, 503-823-4000, www.co.multnomah.or.us
- **Metro** (Regional Government), 503-797-1700, www.metro-region.org
- **Washington County**, 503-846-8685, www.co.washington.or.us
- **Yamhill County,** 503-472-9371, www.co.yamhill.or.us

STATE GOVERNMENT

- **State of Oregon**, www.oregon.gov
- **State of Washington**, www.washington.gov

HOSPITALS

See **Health Care** chapter.

HOUSING AND REAL ESTATE

- **Community Alliance of Tenants**, 503-460-9702, www.oregoncat.org
- **Craigslist**, www.portland.craigslist.org
- **Portland Development Commission**, 503-823-1018, www.pdc.us
- **Portland Housing Center**, 503-282-7744, www.portlandhousingcenter.org
- **RMLS** (multiple listing service), www.rmls.com
- **U.S. Department of Housing and Urban Development**, www.hud.gov

LEGAL REFERRALS

- **Legal Aid Services of Oregon**, www.oregonlawhelp.org
- **Oregon State Bar**, 503-684-3763, 800-452-7636, www.osbar.org
- **Southwest Washington Legal Referral Service**, 360-695-0599

LIBRARIES

- **Library Information Network of Clackamas County**, 503-723-4888, www.lincc.org
- **Fort Vancouver Regional District Library**, 360-695-1561, www.fvrl.org
- **Multnomah County Library**, 503-988-5402, www.multcolib.org
- **Washington County Cooperative Library Services**, 503-846-3222, www.wilinet.wccls.lib.or.us

NEWSPAPERS AND MAGAZINES

See **Getting Settled** chapter.

NUISANCES AND DISPUTES

- **Abandoned Auto Hotline** (City of Portland), 503-823-7309
- **Graffiti Abatement Hotline** (City of Portland), 503-823-4TAG
- **Liquor License Issues** (City of Portland), 503-823-3092
- **Neighborhood Mediation Center** (City of Portland), 503-823-3152
- **Noise Control Office** (City of Portland), 503-823-7350
- **Nuisance, Housing Code Violations** (City of Portland), 503-823-7306
- **Resolutions Northwest** (mediation), 503-595-4890, www.resolutionsnorthwest.org

PARKS AND RECREATION

LOCAL AND REGIONAL

- **Camas Parks and Recreation**, 360-834-5307, www.ci.camas.wa.us/parks/
- **Canby Parks & Recreation**, 503-266-9404
- **Clackamas County Parks Department**, 503-353-4400
- **Cornelius Parks & Recreation**, 503-357-3011
- **Forest Grove Parks & Recreation**, 503-992-3237, www.ci.forest-grove.or.us/parks.html

- **Gresham Parks & Recreation**, 503-618-2626, www.ci.gresham.or.us/departments/des/parksandrec/
- **Hillsboro Parks & Recreation**, 503-681-6120, www.ci.hillsboro.or.us/ParksRec/
- **Lake Oswego Parks & Recreation**, 503-675-2549, www.ci.oswego.or.us/parksrec/
- **Metro Regional Parks and Greenspaces Department**, 503-797-1850 , www.metro-region.org
- **North Clackamas Parks & Recreation District**, 503-794-8002, www.clackamas.us/ncprd/
- **Oregon City Parks and Recreation**, 503-657-8299, www.oregoncityparks.org
- **Portland Parks & Recreation**, 503-823-PLAY, www.portlandparks.org
- **Tigard Parks**, 503-639-4171, www.ci.tigard.or.us/community/parks/
- **Troutdale Parks & Facilities**. 503-666-8303, www.ci.troutdale.or.us/parks-facilities/
- **Tualatin Parks and Recreation Division**, 503-639-4171, www.ci.tualatin.or.us/departments/communityservices/parks/
- **Tualatin Hills Park and Recreation District**, 503-645-6433, www.thprd.org
- **Vancouver-Clark Parks**, 360-696-8171, www.vanclarkparksrec.org
- **Washington County Parks**, 503-846-8715
- **West Linn Parks & Recreation**, 503-557-4700, www.westlinnparksandrec.com

STATE

- **Oregon State Parks**, 800-551-6949, www.oregonstateparks.org
- **Washington State Parks**, 360-902-8844, www.parks.wa.gov

POLICE

- **Emergency**, 911

PORTLAND

- **Portland Police Bureau**, non-emergency police assistance, 503-823-3333
- **Portland Police Bureau**, information and referral, 503-823-4636, www.portlandonline.com/police

SURROUNDING AREAS

- **Banks Police Department**, 503-324-3270
- **Battle Ground Police Department**, 360-342-5100
- **Beaverton Police Department**, 503-629-0111, www.beavertonpolice.org

- **Camas Police Department**, 360-834-4151
- **Canby Police Department**, 503-266-1104, www.canbypolice.com
- **Clackamas County Sheriff**, 503-655-8211, www.clackamas.us/sheriff/
- **Clark County Sheriff**, 360-397-2211, www.co.clark.wa.us/sheriff/
- **Cornelius Police Department**, 503-359-1881
- **Fairview Police Department**, 503-823-3333
- **Forest Grove Police Department**, 503-992-3240
- **Gladstone Police Department**, 503-557-2760
- **Gresham Police Department**, 503-618-2318
- **Hillsboro Police Department**, 503-681-6190
- **King City Police Department**, 503-629-0111
- **La Center Police Department**, 360-263-2745
- **Lake Oswego Police Department**, 503-635-0238
- **Milwaukie Police Department**, 503-786-7400
- **Multnomah County Sheriff**, 503-823-3333, www.co.multnomah.or.us/sheriff/
- **North Plains Police Department**, 503-647-2604
- **Oregon City Police Department**, 503-657-4964, www.ci.oregon-city.or.us/police/
- **Oregon State Police**, 503-731-3030, www.egov.oregon.gov/OSP/
- **Ridgefield Police Department**, 360-887-3556
- **Sandy Police Department**, 503-668-5566
- **Sherwood Police Department**, 503-625-5523
- **Tigard Police Department**, 503-629-0111
- **Troutdale Police Department**, 503-665-6129
- **Tualatin Police Department**, 503-629-0111
- **Vancouver Police Department**, 360-487-7400, www.cityofvancouver.us/police.asp
- **Washington County Sheriff's Office**, 503-629-0111, www.co.washington.or.us/sheriff/
- **Washougal Police Department**, 360-835-8701
- **West Linn Police Department**, 503-655-6214, www.westlinnpolice.com

RADIO/TV STATIONS

See **Getting Settled** chapter.

RECYCLING

See "Trash and Recycling" below.

RELOCATION

- **American Moving and Storage Association**, www.moving.org
- **Federal Motor Carrier Safety Administration**, 202-358-7028, 888-368-7238, www.protectyourmove.gov
- **MovingScam**, www.movingscam.com
- **Oregon Department of Transportation, Motor Carrier Transportation Division**, 503-378-5849, egov.oregon.gov/ODOT/MCT/
- **Washington Utilities and Transportation Commission**, 360-664-1160, 800-562-6150, www.wutc.wa.gov

POST OFFICES

- **USPS**, 800-275-8777, www.usps.com

SCHOOLS

See **Childcare and Education** chapter.

SENIOR CITIZENS, SERVICES FOR

- **Network of Care** (database of services and resources), multnomah. or.networkofcare.org
- **Loaves and Fishes/Meals-on-Wheels**, 503-736-6325, 360-699-6325, www. loavesandfishesonline.org
- **Metropolitan Family Services**, 503-232-0007, www.metfamily.org
- **Oregon Department of Human Services, Seniors and People with Disabilities Division**, 503-945-5811, 800-282-8092, www.oregon.gov/DHS/spd
- **Southwest Washington Agency on Aging**, 360-694-8144, 888-637-6060, www.helpingelders.org

TAXES

FEDERAL

- **Internal Revenue Service**, 800-829-3676, tax help line 800-829-1949, www. irs.gov

STATE

- **Oregon Department of Revenue**, 503-378-4988, 800-356-4222, www.oregon.gov/DOR/
- **Washington Department of Revenue**, 800-647-7706, www.dor.wa.gov

COUNTY

- **Clackamas County Department of Assessment and Taxation**, 503-655-8671, www.co.clackamas.or.us/assessor/index.html
- **Clark County Department of Assessment and GIS**, 360-397-2391, www.co.clark.wa.us/assessor/index.html
- **Multnomah County Division of Assessment and Taxation**, 503-988-3326, www.multcotax.org
- **Washington County Department of Assessment and Taxation**, 503-846-8741, www.co.washington.or.us/DEPTMTS/at/atmain.htm

TAXIS

- **Broadway Cab**, 503-227-1234, www.broadwaycab.com
- **Green Cab and Green Shuttle**, 503-234-1414, www.greentrans.com
- **Radio Cab**, 503-227-1212, www.radiocab.net

TOURISM

- **Central Oregon Visitors Association**, 541-389-8799, 800-800-8334, www.visitcentraloregon.com
- **Columbia River Gorge Visitors Association**, 800-98-GORGE, www.crgva.org
- **Eastern Oregon Visitors Association**, 541-523-9200, www.eova.com
- **Oregon Coast Visitors Association**, 888-628-2101, www.visittheoregoncoast.com
- **Oregon's Mt. Hood Territory** (Clackamas County Tourism), 503-665-8490, 888-622-4822, www.mthoodterritory.com
- **Portland Oregon Visitors Association**, 877-678-5263, www.travelportland.com
- **Southern Oregon Visitors Association**, 541-779-4691, 800-448-4856, www.sova.org
- **Travel Oregon**, 800-547-7842, www.traveloregon.com
- **Washington State Tourism Office**, 360-725-5052, www.experiencewa.com
- **Willamette Valley Visitors Association**, 866-548-5018, www.oregonwinecountry.org

TRANSPORTATION

- **Oregon Department of Transportation**, 888-275-6368, www.oregon.gov/ODOT/
- **Portland International Airport**, 503-460-4040, 877-739-4636, www.flypdx.com
- **Portland Office of Transportation**, 503-823-5185, www.portlandonline.com/transportation/
- **Washington Department of Transportation**, 360-705-7000, www.wsdot.wa.gov

ROAD CONDITIONS

- **Oregon Road Conditions**, 511 or 800-977-6368 (503-588-2941 outside Oregon), www.TripCheck.com
- **Washington Road Conditions**, 511, www.wsdot.wa.gov/traffic/

BICYCLING

- **Bicycle Transportation Alliance**, 503-226-0676, www.bta4bikes.org
- **Shift**, 503-542-6900, www.shift2bikes.org

PUBLIC TRANSPORTATION

- **C-TRAN**, 360-695-0123, www.c-tran.com
- **Canby Area Transit**, 503-266-4022
- **Sandy Area Metro**, 503-668-5569
- **South Clackamas Transportation District**, 503-632-7000, www.southclackamastransportation.com
- **South Metro Area Rapid Transit (SMART)**, 503-682-7790, www.ridesmart.com
- **TriMet**, 503-238-RIDE, www.trimet.org

NATIONAL TRAIN AND BUS SERVICE

- **Amtrak**, 800-872-7245, www.amtrak.com
- **Greyhound**. 800-231-2222, www.greyhound.com

TRASH AND RECYCLING

- **Metro** (Oregon), 503-234-3000, www.metro-region.org
- **Portland Office of Sustainable Development**, 503-823-7202, www.portlandonline.com/OSD/recycle
- **Waste Connections Inc.** (Clark County), 360-892-5370, www.wcnorthwest.com

UTILITIES

- **Northwest Utility Notification Center** (buried utility locations in Washington), 800-424-5555, www.callbeforeyoudig.org
- **Oregon Utility Notification Center** (buried utility locations in Oregon), 800-332-2344, www.digsafelyoregon.com

ELECTRICITY

- **Clark Public Utilities**, 360-992-3000, 800-562-1736, outages 360-992-8000, www.clarkpublicutilities.com
- **Pacific Power**, 888-221-7070, outages 877-LITESOUT, www.pacificpower.net
- **Portland General Electric**, 503-228-6322, 800-542-8818, outages 503-464-7777, www.portlandgeneral.com

NATURAL GAS

- **Northwest Natural**, 503-226-4211, 800-442-4012, gas leaks 800-882-3377, www.nwnatural.com

TELEPHONE

- **Do Not Call List**, 888-382-1222, TTY 866-290-4236, www.donotcall.gov
- **Qwest**, 800-475-7526, www.qwest.com
- **Verizon**, 800-483-4000, www.verizon.com

CABLE AND SATELLITE TELEVISION

- **Comcast**, 888-824-8264, www.comcast.com
- **Direct TV**, 888-777-2454, www.directv.com
- **Dish Network**, 888-825-2557, www.dishnetwork.com

WATER

- **Portland Water Bureau**, 503-823-7770, www.portlandonline.com/water
- **Tualatin Valley Water District**, 503-642-1511, www.tvwd.org

VETERINARIANS, EMERGENCY CLINICS

- **Banfield, The Pet Hospital**, 800-838-6738, www.banfield.net
- **Clark County Emergency Veterinary Service**, 360-694-3007
- **Dove Lewis** (emergency animal hospitals), 503-228-7281, www.dovelewis.org
- **Emergency Veterinary Clinic of Tualatin**, 503-691-7922
- **Northwest Veterinary Specialists**, 503-656-3999, www.northwestvetspecialists.com

VOTING

- **Oregon Secretary of State, Elections Division**, 503-986-1518, 877-ORE-VOTES, www.sos.state.or.us/elections/
- **Washington Secretary of State**, 360-902-4180, 800-448-4881, www.secstate.wa.gov/elections

COUNTY ELECTIONS OFFICES

- **Clackamas County Clerk, Elections Division**, 503-655-8510, www.co.clackamas.or.us/elections
- **Clark County Elections Office**, 360-397-2345, www.clark.wa.gov/elections/
- **Multnomah County Elections Division**, 503-988-3720, www.mcelections.org
- **Washington County Elections Division**, 503-846-5800, www.co.washington.or.us/cgi/electhom/main.pl

WEATHER

- **National Weather Service**, Portland office, www.wrh.noaa.gov/pqr/
- **Oregon Department of Environmental Quality** (air pollution reports), www.deq.state.or.us/aqi/aqiStationsPortland.aspx

ZIP CODE INFORMATION

- **USPS**, 800-275-8777, www.usps.com

INDEX

BRYAN GEON moved to Portland for the first time in 1993 as a fresh-faced college grad. He left the area for law school and work, but Portland has always drawn him back, and has spent over a decade relentlessly exploring and enjoying the city and its surroundings. He has lived in four of the city's five sections and in three different Oregon counties (although not simultaneously). As both a long-time resident and a serial newcomer, Bryan is well qualified to guide other newcomers to the region. He has traveled to all 50 states and more than 50 foreign countries, and he is happy to click his heels together and repeat at least three times that there is no place like Portland. When not practicing law or writing, he enjoys traipsing around the Northwest and spending time with his wife and two sons.

TRI◉MET
MAX Light Rail

Legend

- **Blue Line**—Hillsboro/City Center/Gresham
- **Red Line**—Airport/City Center/Beaverton TC
- **Yellow Line**—Expo Center/City Center
- ○ MAX Light Rail Station
- ⓣ Transit Center
- ⓟ Park & Ride
- Fareless Square

Portland

PGE Park
15T 18 51

Galleria/SW 10th Ave

SW
City
SW

Library/SW 9th Ave

Hillsboro

Blue Line

Hatfield Government Center
Hillsboro Central/SE 3rd Ave
46 47 48 57
Tuality Hospital/SE 8th Ave
Washington/SE 12th Ave
Fair Complex/Hillsboro Airport
46
Hawthorn Farm
47
Orenco/NW 231st Ave
Quatama/NW 205th Ave
47 48 52 59 88
Willow Creek/SW 185th Ave
Elmonica/SW 170th Ave
Merlo/SW 158th Ave
67
Beaverton Creek

Beaverton

Millikan Way
62
Beaverton Central
20 52 53 54 57 58 61 67 76 78 88
Beaverton
20 59 60 62 89
Sunset

No stops in Zone 2

Washington Park
6 58 63 68
Goose Hollow/SW Jefferson
63
Kings Hill/SW Salmon

PGE Park
15T 18 51

| Zone 3 | Zone 2 | Zone 1 |

Travel Time

| 8 Min. | 9 Min. | 11 Min. | 10 Min. | 12 Min. |

Yellow Line

- Ⓟ Expo Center
  16
- Ⓟ Delta Park/Vanport
- ◯ Kenton/N Denver Ave
  6
- Ⓣ N Lombard
  4F 6 75
- ◯ N Portland Blvd
  44M
- ◯ N Killingsworth St
  72
- ◯ N Prescott St
- ◯ Overlook Park
- ◯ Albina/Mississippi
  33F 35G 85
- ◯ Interstate/Rose Quarter 33F 35G

✈ **Red Line**
- ◯ Portland International Airport
- ◯ Mt Hood Ave
- ◯ Cascades
- Ⓣ Parkrose/Sumner
- Ⓟ 12S 15B 71 86 87 C-TRAN

6 Min.

14 Min.

Zone 1 Zone 2

Travel Time

14 Min.

Gresham

Blue Line

SW 1st Ave

Oak Street/SW 1st Ave
Skidmore Fountain
Old Town/Chinatown
70 74 77 85 95 C-TRAN
Rose Quarter
4F 8F 10T 44M
6 Convention Center
NE 7th Ave
8F 10T 70 74 95
Lloyd Center/NE 11th Ave
66 75 77
Hollywood/NE 42nd Ave
71 NE 60th Ave
72 77 NE 82nd Ave
19G 22 23 25 27 33F
Gateway/NE 99th Ave
15B 20
E 102nd Ave
71 E 122nd Ave
E 148th Ave
E 162nd Ave
E 172nd Ave
E 181st Ave
20 25 27 82 87
Rockwood/E 188th Ave
Ruby Junction/E 197th Ave
4D 12S 82
Gresham City Hall
4D 9P 12S 20 80 81 82 84
Gresham Central
Cleveland Ave

Zone 1 Zone 2 Zone 3

0 Min.   14 Min.   17 Min.   Travel Time 6 Min.

RELOCATION TITLES

MOVING WITH KIDS?

Look into *The Moving Book: A Kids' Survival Guide*.

Divided into three sections (before, during, and after the move), it's a handbook, a journal, and a scrapbook all in one. Includes address book, colorful change-of-address cards, and a useful section for parents.

Children's Book of the Month Club "Featured Selection"; American Bookseller's "Pick of the List"; Winner of the Family Channel's "Seal of Quality" Award

And for your younger children, ease their transition with our brand-new title just for them, *Max's Moving Adventure: A Coloring Book for Kids on the Move*. A complete story book featuring activities as well as pictures that children can color; designed to help children cope with the stresses of small or large moves.

GOT PETS?

The Pet Moving Handbook: Maximize Your Pet's Well-Being and Maintain Your Sanity by Carrie Straub answers all your pet-moving questions and directs you to additional resources that can help smooth the move for both you and your pets.

"Floats to the top, cream of the crop. Awesome book; I'm going to keep one on the special shelf here." – Hal Abrams, Animal Radio

NEWCOMER'S HANDBOOKS®

Regularly revised and updated, these popular guides are now available for Atlanta, Boston, Chicago, London, Los Angeles, Minneapolis–St. Paul, New York City, Portland, San Francisco Bay Area, Seattle, and Washington DC.

"Invaluable ...highly recommended" – Library Journal

If you're coming from another country, don't miss the *Newcomer's Handbook® for Moving to and Living in the USA* by Mike Livingston, termed "a fascinating book for newcomers and residents alike" by the *Chicago Tribune*.

Introducing NEWCOMER'S HANDBOOKS® NEIGHBORHOOD GUIDES!

This new series provides detailed information about city neighborhoods and suburban communities, helping you find just the right place to live. The first volume is for Dallas-Fort Worth, Houston, and Austin. More locations to come!

6750 SW Franklin Street
Portland, Oregon 97223-2542
Phone 503.968.6777 • Fax 503.968.6779
www.firstbooks.com

FIRST BOOKS

READER RESPONSE

W e would appreciate your comments regarding this third edition of the *Newcomer's Handbook® for Moving to and Living in Portland: Including Vancouver, Gresham, Hillsboro, Beaverton, and Wilsonville.* If you've found any mistakes or omissions or if you would just like to express your opinion about the guide, please let us know. We will consider any suggestions for possible inclusion in our next edition, and if we use your comments, we'll send you a free copy of our next edition. Please e-mail us at readerresponse@firstbooks.com, or mail or fax this response form to:

Reader Response Department
First Books
6750 SW Franklin, Suite A
Portland, OR 97223-2542
Fax: 503.968.6779

Comments: _____

_____

_____

_____

_____

_____

_____

_____

Name: _____

Address: _____

_____

_____

Telephone: (   ) _____

Email: _____

6750 SW Franklin, Suite A
Portland, OR 97223-2542
USA
P: 503.968.6777
FIRST BOOKS   **www.firstbooks.com**

FIRST BOOKS

Visit our web site at
www.firstbooks.com
for information about
all our books.